PEARSON
BACCALAUREA

STANDARD

Che y

DEVELOPED S

CATRIN BROWN • MIKE FORD

Pearson Education Limited is a company incorporated in England and Wales, having its registered office at Edinburgh Gate, Harlow, Essex, CM20 2JE. Registered company number: 872828

www.pearsonbaccalaureate.com

Text © Pearson Education Limited 2008

First published 2008

20 19 18 17 16 15 14 13
IMP 13 12 11 10 9 8 7 6

ISBN 978 0 435994 46 4

Edited by Marilyn Grant with thanks to Lesley Montford and Penelope Lyons

Designed by Tony Richardson

Typeset by Tech-Set Limited

Original illustrations © Pearson Education Ltd 2008

Illustrated by Tech-Set Limited

Cover design by Tony Richardson

Cover photo © Getty Images

Indexed by Catherine Harkness

Printed in Malaysia, KHL-CTP

Acknowledgements

The publisher would like to thank Mike Scamell for his professional guidance. The authors and publisher would also like to thank Maria Muñīz Valcárel for her valuable contribution to the book, and the following individuals and organisations for permission to reproduce photographs:

Bananastock p.24; Getty Images/Photo Disc p.1; Getty Images/Photo Disc p.436; Photolibrary/Phototake Inc. p.130 (iodine); Science Photo Library pp.20, 33 (Dalton's symbols), 50 (PT from 1869), 96 (James Prescott Joule), 203 (bag), 205 (fabric), 357 (Hodgkin), 448 (tomatoes), 461, 525 (Robert Boyle); Science Photo Library/Adam Hart-Davis pp.33 (water molecule), 163; Science Photo Library/ A. Dex, Publiphoto Diffusion p.344; Science Photo Library/Adrienne Hart-Davis p.307 (polystyrene); Science Photo Library/AJ Photo/Hop American p.179 (hair removal); Science Photo Library/Alex Bartel p.179 (cans); Science Photo Library/Alexis Rosenfeld p.429 (algae); Science Photo Library/Alfred Pasieka pp.290 (molecular tube), 378 (leaf) , 467; Science Photo Library/Andrew Lambert Photography pp.4, 15, 59 (potassium), 60 (Cl_2, Br_2 and I_2), 61 (chlorine water into potassium bromide solution), 61 (solutions of chlorine, bromine and iodine in water and cyclohexane), 61 (silver halides precipitates), 68 (ions of iron), 68 (Fehlings test), 124 (effect of concentration on rate), 130 (bromine), 135, 149, 151 (litmus solution), 158, 166, 170, 171 (chlorine + NaBr), 173, 174, 196 (secondary alcohol), 196 (tertiary alcohol), 203 (alkane vs alkene), 205 (alcohol lamp), 207 (alcohol oxidation), 207 (distillation), 207 (reflux), 215 (alcohol thermometer), 216, 387 (spray cans), 404 (recycling symbol), 431, 434, 448 (ethene), 449, 459 (24 DNP reaction), 459 (melting point determination), 460, 475, 523 (diffraction grating pattern); Science Photo Library/Astrid & Hanns-Frieder Michler pp.125, 294, 306; Science Photo Library/Bill Barksdale/AGStockUSA p.438 (cotton plants); Science Photo Library/ Bio Photo Associates p.282; Science Photo Library/Bjorn Svennson pp.352, 354, 366 (traffic), 382; Science Photo Library/Bob Edwards p.451; Science Photo Library/Brian Bell p.259; Science Photo Library/BSIP Barrelle p.99 (woman); Science Photo Library/BSIP Chassenet pp.415, 419; Science Photo Library/BSIP VEM p.273 (atherosclerosis); Science Photo Library/Carlos Dominguez p.252; Science Photo Library/CDC p.328; Science Photo Library/Charles Bach p.355 (Alka seltzer); Science Photo Library/Charles D Winters pp.7, 58 (sodium), 59 (potassium), 60 (sodium reacting), 97, 136, 146, 151 (Mg + HCL), 162, 246 (sample testing), 246 (sample testing after), 308, 309 (brooms); Science Photo Library/Chemical Design Ltd p.303; Science Photo Library/ Chris Knapton p.214; Science Photo Library/Christian Darkin p.529; Science Photo Library/Christina Pedrrazini pp.215 (cylinder), 377 (erosion); Science Photo Library/Clive Freeman, The Royal Institute pp.315, 463; Science Photo Library/Cordelia Molloy pp.101, 154, 272 (trans fats foods), 276, 426 (green tea), 440 (meringue), 527; Science Photo Library/D Phillips p.129; Science Photo Library/D. Phillips/The Population Council p.272 (lipid drops); Science Photo Library/Daniel Sambraus p.435; Science Photo Library/David A Hardy p.43 (continuous spectrum); Science Photo Library/David Campione p.390; Science Photo Library/David Grossman p.485; Science Photo Library/ David Hay Jones p.384 (ozone research); Science Photo Library/David Parker p.324 (carbon monotube); Science Photo Library/David R. Frazier p.369; Science Photo Library/David Scharf p.83 (silicon chip); Science Photo Library/David Taylor p.42 (flame tests on copper); Science Photo Library/ Dept. of Physics/Imperial College p.43 (visible emission spectrum of hydrogen); Science Photo Library/Dirk Weirsma pp.292, 403 (car bodies); Science Photo Library/Dr David Wexler, Coloured by Dr Jeremy Burgess pp.183, 271, 523 (diffraction pattern); Science Photo Library/Dr Jurgen Scriba p.227; Science Photo Library/Dr Mark J. Winter pp.261, 347, 453; Science Photo Library/Dr Tim Evans pp.263 (albumen), 360 (amantadine); Science Photo Library/Dr. Keith Wheeler p.399; Science Photo Library/Emilio Segre Visual Archives/American Institute of Physics p.138 (Fritz Haber); Science Photo Library/Equinox Graphics pp.360 (AIDS), 518; Science Photo Library/Eye of Science p.83 (quartz); Science Photo Library/Franz Himpsel/University of Wisconsin pp.323, 324 (nanowires); Science Photo Library/Freidrich Saurer pp.355 (caffeine), 522 (methane molecule), 522 (methane molecule no.2); Science Photo Library/Geoff Lane/CSIRO p.232; Science Photo Library/Geoff Thompkinson pp.114, 237, 243, 466; Science Photo Library/George D Lepp p.98; Science Photo Library/George Steinmetz p.370; Science Photo Library/Gianni Tortoli p.39 (shroud); Science Photo Library/Graham J Mills p.32 (atomic lattice of gold); Science Photo Library/Gustoimages pp.67, 254; Science Photo Library/Hank Morgan pp.172, 404 (recycled card); Science Photo Library/Health Protection Agency p.318; Science Photo Library/Helen McArdle p.12; Science Photo Library/Hewlett-Packard Laboratories p.324 (C60 structure); Science Photo Library/ Hybrid Medical Animation p.273 (HDL and LDL); Science Photo Library/J.C Revy p.267; Science Photo Library/James Bell p.320 (DNA crystal); Science Photo Library/James King-Holmes p.312; Science Photo Library/James Prince p.215 (analytical balance); Science Photo Library/Jean-Claude Revy, ISM p.296 (bauxite); Science Photo Library/Jean-Loup Charmet p.524 (Zosimus page); Science Photo Library/Jeremy Walker p.300; Science Photo Library/Jerry Mason p.42 (flame tests on sodium), 42 (flame tests on potassium); Science Photo Library/Jesse p.179 (electroplating); Science Photo Library/Jim Dowdalls p.339; Science Photo Library/ Jim Varney p.348; Science Photo Library/John Bavosi p.338; Science Photo Library/John McLean p.199; Science Photo Library/John Paul Kay, Peter Arnold INC. p.280; Science Photo Library/Juergen Berger p.330; Science Photo Library/Kari Greer p.96 (conifer trees); Science Photo Library/Kenneth Edward/Biografx pp.109,197; Science Photo Library/Kenneth Libbrecht p.87 (snowflake), Science Photo Library/Kevin Curtis p.524 (soft drinks); Science Photo Library/Laguna Design pp.65, 71, 325, 351, 454, 466, 473, 474; Science Photo Library/Lawrence Berkeley National Laboratory p.73; Science Photo Library/Lawrence Lawry p.81(diamond); Science Photo Library/Manfred Kage p.296 (brass); Science Photo Library/Martin Bond pp.102, 153 (acid rain response), 378 (Lake Gardsjon); Science Photo Library/ Martin Dohrn p.39 (Cobalt-60 gamma rays); Science Photo Library/Martyn F. Chillmaid pp.58 (cut lithium), 119, 124 (milk powder fire), 171 (Mg + CuO) , 176, 298, 304, 366 (carbon monoxide detector), 374, 440 (emulsion), 440 (emulsion separating), 528; Science Photo Library/Massimo Brega/Eurelios p.286; Science Photo Library/Matt Meadows p.11; Science Photo Library/Mauro Fermariello pp.242 (MRI), 245, 346, 437 (particle gun), 484, 525 (pills); Science Photo Library/Maximilian Stock Ltd pp.27, 32 (high purity gold), 161, 169, 248, 408, 410, 411, 416; Science Photo Library/Mehau Kulyk p.242 (normal brain); Science Photo Library/Mere Words p.405; Science Photo Library/M.H. Sharp p.321; Science Photo Library/Michael Marten p.391; Science

The publisher would like to thank the International Baccalaureate Organization for permission to reproduce its intellectual property.

This material has been developed independently by the publisher and the content is in no way connected with nor endorsed by the International Baccalaureate Organization.

Chapters 1, 2, 3, 5, 11, 12, 14, 16, 17 by Mike Ford
Chapters 4, 6, 7, 8, 9, 10, 13, 15, 18 by Catrin Brown

Websites
There are links to relevant websites in this book. In order to ensure that the links are up to date, that the links work, and that the sites are not inadvertently linked to sites that could be considered offensive, we have made the links available on our website at www.heinemann.co.uk/hotlinks. When you access the site, the express code is 4259P.

Contents

Contents

Introduction

Welcome to your new course! This book is designed to act as a comprehensive course book, covering both the core material and all the options you might take while studying for the IB Diploma in Chemistry at Standard Level. It will also help you to prepare for your examinations in a thorough and methodical way.

Content

As you will see when you look at the table of contents, there is a chapter for each of the core topics, and for each of the options you might choose to take. Within each chapter, there are numbered exercises for you to practise and apply the knowledge that you have gained. They will also help you to assess your progress. Sometimes, there are worked examples that show you how to tackle a particularly tricky or awkward question.

Worked example

Calculate how many hydrogen atoms are present in 3.0 moles of ethanol, C_2H_5OH.

Solution

There are 6 H atoms in 1 molecule of ethanol.

In 1 mole of ethanol molecules there are 6 moles of H atoms.

In 3 moles of ethanol there are 18 moles of H atoms.

Number of H atoms $= 18L = 6.01 \times 10^{23} \times 18 = 1.08 \times 10^{25}$

At the end of each chapter, there are practice questions taken from past exam papers. Towards the end of the book, just before the index, you will find pages with answers to all the exercises and practice questions that have been included. The answers are grouped into Exercises and Practice questions for each chapter.

After the options chapters, you will find a Theory of Knowledge chapter, which should stimulate wider research and the consideration of critical thinking in the field of chemistry.

Finally, there are two short chapters offering advice on internal assessment and on writing extended essays.

Information boxes

Throughout the book you will see a number of coloured boxes interspersed through each chapter. Each of these boxes provides different information and stimulus as follows.

> Assessment statements
> 1.1 The mole concept and Avogadro's constant
> 1.1.1   Apply the mole concept to substances.

You will find a box like this at the start of each chapter. They are the numbered objectives from the IB Chemistry guide for the topic that you are about to read and they set out what content and aspects of learning are covered in the chapter.

The Celsius scale gives an artificial description of temperature and the Kelvin scale a natural description. Do the units we use help or hinder our understanding of the natural world?

In addition to the Theory of Knowledge chapter, there are TOK boxes throughout the book. These boxes are there to stimulate thought and consideration of any TOK issues as they arise and in context. Often they will just contain a question to stimulate your own thoughts and discussion.

A billion of your atoms once made up Shakespeare, another billion made up Beethoven, another billion St. Peter and another billion the Buddha.

These boxes contain interesting information which will add to your wider knowledge and help you see how chemistry connects with other subjects.

A mole is the amount of a substance which contains the same number of chemical species as there are atoms in exactly 12 g of the isotope carbon-12.

These key facts are drawn out of the main text and **are highlighted**. This makes them useful for quick reference. They also enable you to identify the core learning points within a section.

Scientists have developed the SI system – from the French *Système International*, to allow the scientific community to communicate effectively both across disciplines and across borders.

These boxes indicate examples of internationalism within the area of chemistry. The information covers environmental and political issues raised by the topic, as well as moral and ethical considerations, and helps you to gain a global perspective.

● **Examiner's hint:** Pay attention to significant figures. When multiplying or dividing, the number of significant figures in the result should be the same as the least precise value in the data.

These boxes can be found alongside questions, exercises and worked examples and they provide insight into how to answer a question in order to achieve the highest marks in an examination. They also identify common pitfalls when answering such questions and suggest approaches that examiners like to see.

Carry out your own carbon hydrogen analysis.
Now go to heinemann.co.uk/ hotlinks, insert the express code 4259P and click on this activity.

These boxes direct you to the Heinemann website, which in turn will take you to the relevant website(s). On the web pages you will find background information to support the topic, video simulations and other related features of interest.

Worked solutions

Full worked solutions to all exercises and practice questions can be found online at www.pearsonbacc.com/solutions.

Now you are ready to start. Good luck with your studies!

1 Quantitative chemistry

Chemistry was a late developer as a physical science. Newton was working on the laws of physics more than a century before the work of the French chemist Antoine Lavoisier (1743–1794) brought chemistry into the modern age. Chemical reactions involve changes in smell, colour and texture and these are difficult to quantify. Lavoisier appreciated the importance of attaching numbers to properties and recognized the need for precise measurement. His use of the balance allowed changes in mass to be used to analyse chemical reactions. There are practical problems with this approach as powders scatter, liquids splash and gases disperse. It is essential to keep track of all products and it is perhaps significant that Lavoisier was a tax collector by profession. A quantitative approach to the subject helped chemistry to develop beyond the pseudoscience of alchemy.

This chapter is central to the practice of chemistry as it builds a foundation for most of the numerical work in the course. The two threads to this chapter, a description of the states of the matter and its measurement, are both based on a particulate model of matter. The unit of amount, the mole, and the universal language of chemistry, chemical equations, are introduced.

◀ Mole calculations are used to work out the relative amounts of hydrogen and oxygen needed to launch the space shuttle.

Assessment statements

1.1 The mole concept and Avogadro's constant

1.1.1 Apply the mole concept to substances.

1.1.2 Determine the number of particles and the amount of substance (in moles).

1.2 Formulas

1.2.1 Define the terms *relative atomic mass* (A_r) and *relative molecular mass* (M_r).

1.2.2 Calculate the mass of one mole of a species from its formula.

1.2.3 Solve problems involving the relationship between the amount of substance in moles, mass and molar mass.

1.2.4 Distinguish between the terms *empirical formula* and *molecular formula*.

1.2.5 Determine the empirical formula from the percentage composition or from other experimental data.

1.2.6 Determine the molecular formula when given both the empirical formula and experimental data.

1.3 Chemical equations

1.3.1 Deduce chemical equations when all reactants and products are given.

1.3.2 Identify the mole ratio of any two species in a chemical equation.

1.3.3 Apply the state symbols (s), (l), (g) and (aq).

1.4 Mass and gaseous volume relationships in chemical reactions

1.4.1 Calculate theoretical yields from chemical equations.

1.4.2 Determine the limiting reactant and the reactant in excess when quantities of reacting substances are given.

1.4.3 Solve problems involving theoretical, experimental and percentage yield.

1.4.4 Apply Avogadro's law to calculate reacting volumes of gases.

1.4.5 Apply the concept of molar volume at standard temperature and pressure in calculations.

1.4.6 Solve problems involving the relationship between temperature, pressure and volume for a fixed mass of an ideal gas.

1.4.7 Solve problems using the ideal gas equation, $PV = nRT$.

1.4.8 Analyse graphs relating to the ideal gas equation.

1.5 Solutions

1.5.1 Distinguish between the terms *solute*, *solvent*, *solution* and *concentration* (g dm^{-3} and mol dm^{-3}).

1.5.2 Solve problems involving concentration, amount of solute and volume of solution.

1.1 The mole concept and Avogadro's constant

Measurement and units

Scientists search for order in their observations of the world. Measurement is a vital tool in this search. It makes our observations more objective and helps us find relationships between different properties. The standardization of measurement of mass and length began thousands of years ago when kings and emperors used units of length based on the length of their arms or feet. Because modern science is an international endeavour, a more reliable system of standards, the **Système International** is needed.

Scientists have developed the SI system – from the French *Système International*, to allow the scientific community to communicate effectively both across disciplines and across borders.

A lot of experimental chemistry relies on the accurate measurement and recording of the physical quantities of mass, time, temperature and volume. The SI units for these are given below.

Property	Unit	Symbol for unit
mass	kilogram	kg
time	second	s
temperature	kelvin	K
volume	cubic metre	m^3
pressure	pascal	Pa or $N\,m^{-2}$

◀ Base SI units of some physical quantities used in chemistry; volume is a derived unit as it depends on length.

These units are however not always convenient for the quantities typically used in the laboratory. Volumes of liquids and gases, for example, are measured in cubic centimetres.

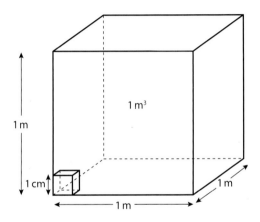

◀ **Figure 1.1** A cube of 1 m^3. This has a volume of 100 cm × 100 cm × 100 cm = 1000 000 cm^3. A typical gas syringe has a volume of 100 cm^3 so ten thousand of these would be needed to measure a gas with this volume.

Property	Unit	Symbol for unit
mass	gram	g
time	minute	min
temperature	degree celsius	°C
volume	cubic centimetre	cm^3
pressure	atmosphere	atm

◀ Other units used in chemistry.

Amounts of substance

Chemists need to measure quantities of substances for many purposes. Pharmaceutical companies need to check that a tablet contains the correct amount of the drug. Food manufacturers check levels of purity. In the laboratory, reactants need to be mixed in the correct ratios to prepare the desired product. We measure mass and volume routinely in the lab but they are not direct measures of amount. Equal quantities of apples and oranges do not have equal masses or equal volumes but equal numbers. The chemist adopts the same approach. As all matter is made up from small particles (see Chapter 2), we measure amount by counting particles. If the substance is an **element** we usually count **atoms**, if it is a **compound** we count molecules or ions.

 A chemical species may be an atom, a molecule or an ion.

A standard unit of amount can be defined in terms of a sample amount of any substance. Shoes and socks are counted in pairs, eggs in dozens and atoms in **moles**. A mole is the amount of a substance which contains the same number of chemical species as there are atoms in exactly 12 grams of the isotope carbon-12 (see Chapter 2). The *mole* is a SI unit with the symbol *mol*. The word derives from the Latin for heap or pile.

> **A mole is the amount of a substance which contains the same number of chemical species as there are atoms in exactly 12 g of the isotope carbon-12.**

As the average relative mass of a carbon atom is actually greater than 12 owing to the presence of heavier isotopes (see Chapter 2), one mole of the element carbon has a mass of 12.01 g. The mass of one mole of atoms of an element is simply the relative atomic mass (see page 41 in Chapter 2) expressed in grams. One mole of hydrogen atoms has a mass of 1.01 g, one mole of helium 4.00 g and so on.

One mole of carbon-12. ▶

> - **The mass of one mole of a species is called the molar mass. It is the relative mass expressed in g and has units of g mol⁻¹.**
> - **The molar mass of an element which exists as atoms is the relative atomic mass expressed in g.**
> - **The relative molecular mass (M_r) is defined as the sum of the relative atomic masses of the atoms in the molecular formula. The molar mass (M) of a compound is the relative molecular mass expressed in g.**

Some elements exist as molecules not as individual atoms. The composition of a molecule is given by its **molecular formula**. Hydrogen gas, for example, is made from diatomic molecules and so has the molecular formula H_2. Water molecules are made from two hydrogen atoms and one oxygen atom and have the molecular formula H_2O. The **relative molecular mass (M_r)** is calculated by adding the relative atomic masses of the atoms making up the molecule.

Worked example

Calculate the relative molecular mass of ethanol C_2H_5OH.

Solution
The compound is made from three elements, carbon, hydrogen and oxygen.

Find the number of atoms of each element and their relative atomic masses from the Periodic Table.

	C	H	O
relative atomic mass	12.01	1.01	16.00
number of atoms in one molecule of compound	2	5 + 1 = 6	1

Calculate the relative molecular mass of the molecule.

Relative molecular mass $= (2 \times 12.01) + (6 \times 1.01) + 16.00 = 46.08$

The molar mass of ethanol is 46.08 g mol$^{-1.}$ The molar mass of a compound is calculated in the same way as that of the elements. It is the relative molecular mass in grams.

It is incorrect to use the term *relative molecular mass* for ionic compounds as they are made from ions not molecules. The term **relative formula mass** is used. It is calculated in the same way.

Once the molar mass is calculated and the mass is measured, the number of moles can be determined.

Worked example

Calculate the number of moles in 4.00 g of sodium hydroxide, NaOH.

Solution

The relative atomic masses are Na: 22.99, O: 16.00 and H: 1.01.

The relative formula mass = 22.99 + 16.00 + 1.01 = 40.00

$M = 40.00$ g mol^{-1}

$n = \dfrac{m}{M} = \dfrac{4.00}{40.00} = 0.100$ mol

It is important to be precise when calculating amounts. One mole of hydrogen **atoms** has a molar mass of 1.01 g mol^{-1} but one mole of hydrogen **molecules**, H_2, has a mass of $2 \times 1.01 = 2.02$ g mol^{-1}.

Counting particles

As the mass of an individual atom can be measured using a mass spectrometer (see Chapter 2), the mole is a counting unit.

From mass spectrometer measurements: mass of 1 atom of $^{12}C = 1.99252 \times 10^{-23}$ g

Number of atoms in one mole (12 g of ^{12}C) $= \dfrac{12}{1.99252 \times 10^{-23}}$

$= 602\,000\,000\,000\,000\,000\,000\,000.$

This is a big number. It is called **Avogadro's number (L)** and is more compactly written in scientific notation as 6.02×10^{23}. It is the number of atoms in one mole of an element and the number of molecules in one mole of a covalent compound.

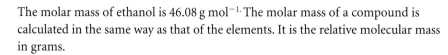

Imagine you emptied a glass of labelled water molecules into the sea and then allowed sufficient time for the molecules to disperse throughout the oceans. What is the probability that you could catch one of the original molecules if you placed the same glass into the sea? (*see the Answer section*). The magnitude of Avogadro's constant is beyond the scale of our everyday experience. This is one reason why 'moles' is a challenging subject and why natural sciences don't always come naturally!

Number of particles (*N*)
= number of moles (*n*) ×
Avogadro's constant (*L*)
N = *nL*

Although we could never count to L, even with the most powerful computer, we can prepare samples with this number of atoms. The atoms are counted in the same way as coins are counted in a bank; we use a balance:

3.01×10^{23} atoms of C $= \frac{1}{2}$ mol $= 0.5 \times 12.01$ g $= 6.005$ g.

3.01×10^{23} carbon atoms are 'counted out' when we prepare a sample of 6.005 g.

Worked example

Calculate the amount of water, H_2O, that contains 1.80×10^{24} molecules.

Solution

Use the shorthand notation: $N = nL$

$$n = \frac{N}{L}$$

$$= \frac{1.80 \times 10^{24}}{6.02 \times 10^{23}}$$

$$= 2.99 \text{ mol}$$

Note the answer should be given to 3 significant figures – the same precision as the data given in the question. If the amount given was 1.8×10^{24} the correct answer would be 3.0.

Worked example

Calculate how many hydrogen atoms are present in 3.0 moles of ethanol, C_2H_5OH.

Solution

In 1 molecule of ethanol there are 6 H atoms.

In 1 mole of ethanol molecules there are 6 moles of H atoms.

In 3 moles of ethanol there are 18 moles of H atoms.

Number of H atoms $= 18L = 6.01 \times 10^{23} \times 18 = 1.08 \times 10^{25}$

Exercises

1 Calculate how many hydrogen atoms are present in 0.040 moles of C_2H_6.

2 Calculate the molar mass of magnesium nitrate, $Mg(NO_3)_2$.

3 Calculate how many hydrogen atoms are contained in 2.3 g of C_2H_5OH ($M_r = 46$).

4 The relative molecular mass of a compound is 98.0. Calculate the number of molecules in a 4.90 g sample of the substance.

1.2 Formulas

Finding chemical formulas in the laboratory

When magnesium is burned in air its mass increases as it is combining with oxygen.

The mass change can be investigated experimentally.

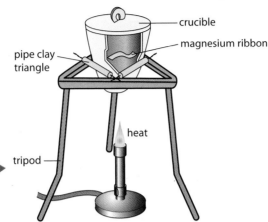

Figure 1.2 This apparatus reduces the chance of the product escaping when magnesium is heated.

Magnesium burns in air to produce a white residue of magnesium oxide.

● **Examiner's hint:** The uncertainties in all the measurements should be included in all data tables. This is discussed in Chapter 11.

Item	Mass/g (±0.001)
empty crucible	25.000
crucible with magnesium before heating	25.050
crucible with solid after heating	25.084

The masses of the magnesium and oxygen are then calculated.

◀ The precision of the calculated value is limited by the precision of the mass measurements to 2 significant figures.

Element	Mass/g (±0.002)	Moles
magnesium	$25.050 - 25.000 = 0.050$	$= \dfrac{0.050}{24.31} = 0.0021$
oxygen	$25.084 - 25.050 = 0.034$	$= \dfrac{0.034}{16.00} = 0.0021$

The ratio of magnesium : oxygen atoms $= 0.0021 : 0.0021 = 1:1$.

This is expressed as an **empirical formula**: MgO.

ⓘ The empirical formula gives the ratio of the atoms of different elements in a compound. It is the molecular formula expressed as its simplest ratio.

Worked example

A 2.765 g sample of a lead oxide was heated in a stream of hydrogen gas and completely converted to elemental lead with a mass of 2.401 g. What is the empirical formula of the oxide?

Solution

The mass loss is caused by a loss of oxygen.
Set out the calculation in a table.

	Pb	O
mass/g	2.401	$2.765 - 2.401 = 0.364$
moles	$= \dfrac{2.401}{207.19} = 0.01159$	$= \dfrac{0.364}{16.00} = 0.0228$
simplest ratio	$= \dfrac{0.01159}{0.01159} = 1$	$= \dfrac{0.0228}{0.01159} = 1.97 \approx 2$

Empirical formula: PbO_2

Worked example

A hydrocarbon contains 85.7% by mass of carbon. Deduce the empirical formula.

Solution

A hydrocarbon is a compound of carbon and hydrogen only (see Chapter 10). When data is given in percentages consider a 100 g sample.

	C	H
mass/g	85.7	$100 - 85.7 = 14.3$
moles	$= \dfrac{85.7}{12.01} = 7.14$	$= \dfrac{14.3}{1.01} = 14.16$
simplest ratio	$= \dfrac{7.14}{7.14} = 1$	$= \dfrac{14.16}{7.14} = 1.98 \approx 2$

Empirical formula: CH_2

Carry out your own carbon hydrogen analysis.
Now go to www.heinemann.co.uk/hotlinks, insert the express code 4259P and click on this activity.

Exercises

5   An oxide of sulfur contains 60% by mass of oxygen. Deduce the empirical formula.

6   Pure nickel was discovered in 1751. It was named from the German word 'kupfernickel', meaning 'devil's copper'. A compound of nickel was analysed and shown to have the following composition by mass: Ni 37.9%, S 20.7 %, O 41.4 %. Deduce the empirical formula.

The molecular formula shows the actual number of atoms of each element present in a molecule.

Molecular formula

The empirical formula does not give the actual number of atoms in the molecule. The hydrocarbon in the previous worked example had an empirical formula of CH_2 but no stable molecule with this formula exists. The molecular formula, which is a multiple of the empirical formula, can only be determined once the relative molecular mass is known. This can either be measured by a mass spectrometer (Chapter 2.2, page 40) or calculated from the ideal gas equation (Chapter 1.4, page 24).

State symbols indicate the state of a substance:
(s) is for solid, (l) is for liquid, (g) is for gas and (aq) is for aqueous – dissolved in water.

The molecular formulas of some compounds. The state symbols identify the state at room temperature and atmospheric pressure.

Substance	Formula	Substance	Formula
hydrogen	$H_2(g)$	carbon dioxide	$CO_2(g)$
oxygen	$O_2(g)$	ammonia	$NH_3(g)$
nitrogen	$N_2(g)$	methane	$CH_4(g)$
water	$H_2O(l)$	glucose	$C_6H_{12}O_6(s)$

Worked example

What is the empirical formula of glucose?

Solution

From the table above, the molecular formula = $C_6H_{12}O_6$

Express this as the simplest ratio: CH_2O.

Worked example

The compound with the empirical formula of CH_2 is analysed by a mass spectrometer and its relative molecular mass found to be 42.09. Deduce its molecular formula.

Solution

Empirical formula = CH_2

Molecular formula = C_nH_{2n} (where n is an integer)

$$M_r = 42.09 = (12.01n) + (2n \times 1.01) = 14.03n$$

$$n = \frac{42.09}{14.03} = 3$$

Molecular formula: C_3H_6

● **Examiner's hint:** Practise empirical formula calculations. All steps in the calculation must be shown. 'Keep going' as errors are carried forward so that a correct method in a later part of the question is rewarded even if you have made earlier mistakes. One common problem is the use of too few significant figures in intermediate answers.

Exercises

7 Which formula can be determined by only using the percent mass composition data of an unknown compound?

I Molecular formula

II Empirical (simplest) formula

A I only

B II only

C Both I and II

D Neither I nor II

8 CFCs are compounds of carbon, hydrogen chlorine and fluorine which catalyse the depletion of the ozone layer. The composition of one CFC is shown below.

carbon	hydrogen	chlorine	fluorine
17.8%	1.5%	52.6%	28.1%

The value of its M_r is 135.

Determine the molecular formula of the CFC.

States of matter

If you were hit with 180 g of solid water (ice) you could be seriously injured, but you would be only annoyed if it was 180 g of liquid water. 180 g of gaseous water (steam) could also be harmful. These three samples are all made from same particles – 10 moles of water molecules. The difference in physical properties is explained by kinetic theory. The basic ideas are:

- All matter consists of particles (atoms or molecules) in motion.
- As the temperature increases, the movement of the particles increases.

The three states can be characterized in terms of the arrangement and movement of the particles and the forces between them.

Most substances can exist in all three states. The state at a given temperature and pressure is determined by the strength of the interparticle forces.

Figure 1.3 Comparison of the three states of matter.

▼

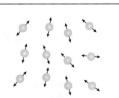
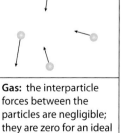

Solid: the particles are closely packed in fixed positions. The interparticle forces restrict the movement to vibration about a fixed position. Solids have a fixed shape.	**Liquid:** the particles are still relatively close together. The interparticle forces are sufficiently weak to allow the particles to change places with each other, but their movement is constrained to a fixed volume. Liquids can change shape but not volume.	**Gas:** the interparticle forces between the particles are negligible; they are zero for an ideal gas (see Section 1.4). The particles move freely occupying all the space available to them. Gases have no fixed shape or volume.

Changes of state

The movement or kinetic energy of the particles depends on the temperature. When the temperature increases enough for the particles to have sufficient energy to overcome the interparticle forces, a change of state occurs.

The heating curve below shows how the temperature changes as ice is heated from $-40°C$ to steam at $140°C$.

Figure 1.4 Heating curve for water. The phase change (l) →(g) needs more energy than (s)→(l) as all the inter-particle bonds are broken during this process.

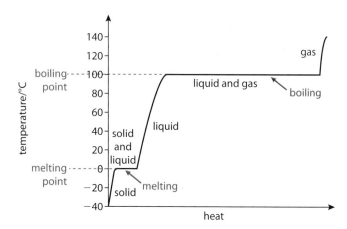

The Celsius scale of temperature is defined relative to the boiling and freezing points of water. The original scale, developed by the Swedish astronomer Anders Celsius, made the boiling point of water zero and the freezing point 100. This may now seem absurd but the modern scale is just as arbitrary.

To understand these changes it is more helpful to use the absolute or **Kelvin** scale of temperature.

Consider a sample of ice at $-40°C = 233$ K. The water molecules vibrate at this temperature about their fixed positions.

- As the ice is heated, the vibrational energy of its particles increases and so the temperature increases.
- At the melting point of 273 K, the vibrations are sufficiently energetic for the molecules to move away from their fixed positions and liquid water starts to form. The added energy is needed to break the bonds between the molecules – the **intermolecular bonds**. There is no increase in kinetic energy so there is no increase in temperature.

The kelvin is the *SI* unit of temperature.
Temperature in kelvin =
temperature in °C + 273
Temperature differences measured on either the Celsius or Kelvin scale are the same.
The absolute temperature of a substance is proportional to the average kinetic energy of its particles.
Absolute zero = 0 K. This is the temperature of minimum kinetic energy.

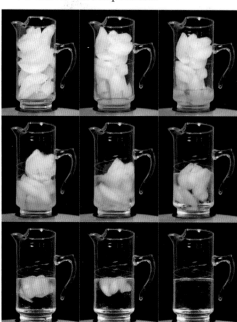

- As the water is heated, the particles move faster and so the temperature increases.
- Some molecules will have sufficient energy to break away from the surface of the liquid so some water evaporates.
- At the boiling point of water, there is sufficient energy to break all the intermolecular bonds. The added energy is used for this process, not to increase the kinetic energy, and so the temperature remains constant.
- As steam is heated, the average kinetic energy of the molecules increases and so the temperature increases.

Ice cubes melting over a period of 4 hours. The water is absorbing heat from the surroundings to break some of the intermolecular bonds.

Worked example

In which sample do molecules have the greatest average kinetic energy?
A He at 100 K
B H_2 at 200 K
C O_2 at 300 K
D H_2O at 400 K

Solution

Answer = D. The sample at the highest temperature has the greatest kinetic energy.

Some substances change directly from a solid to gas at atmospheric pressure. This change is called **sublimation**.

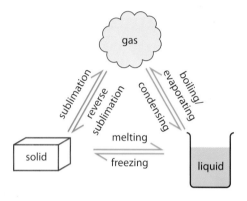

Some substances change directly from a solid to gas at atmospheric pressure.

> The kinetic energy of a particle depends on its mass (*m*) and speed (*v*). All gases have the same kinetic energy at the same temperature, so particles with smaller mass move at faster speeds. Kinetic energy $= \frac{1}{2}mv^2$.

◀ **Figure 1.5** The different phase changes.

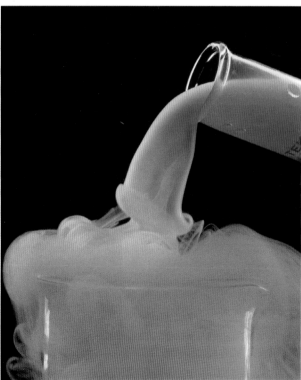

◀ Sublimation is the conversion of a solid directly to a vapour state. Dry ice, $CO_2(s)$, sublimes when it is mixed with water producing thick clouds of fog.

> The coldest place in nature is in the depths of outer space at a temperature of 3 K. The 2001 Nobel Prize in Physics was awarded to a team who cooled a sample of helium atoms down to only a few billionths (0.000 000 001) of a degree above absolute zero. Under these conditions helium atoms crawl along at a speed of only about 3 mm s⁻¹!

Exercise

9 When a small quantity of perfume is released into the air, it can be detected several metres away in a short time. Use the kinetic theory to explain why this happens.

We can smell perfumes because they evaporate at body temperature. In a mixture of molecules, the most volatile evaporate first and the least volatile last. The skill of the perfumer is to use the laws of chemistry to make sure that chemicals are released steadily in the same proportions.

The Celsius scale gives an artificial description of temperature and the Kelvin scale a natural description. Do the units we use help or hinder our understanding of the natural world?

Worked example

A flask contains water and steam at boiling point. Distinguish between the two states on a molecular level by referring to the average speed of the molecules and the relative intermolecular distances.

Solution

As the two phases are at the same temperature, they have the same average kinetic energy and are moving at the same speed. The separation between the particles in a gas is significantly larger than that in a liquid.

Exercise

10 Which of the following occur when a solid sublimes?

  I The molecules increase in size.

  II The distances between the molecules increase.

  A I only

  B II only

  C Both I and II

  D Neither I nor II

Chemical equations

Chemical equations: the language of chemistry

Atoms cannot be created or destroyed during a chemical reaction, they are simply rearranged. A **chemical equation** provides a balance sheet which allows us to monitor these changes as **reactants** are transformed into **products**. The number of atoms of each element must be the same on both sides of the equation.

For example, the formation of liquid water involves two molecules of hydrogen gas combining with one molecule of oxygen gas to produce two molecules of liquid water. This information can be expressed in a more concise form:

$$2H_2(g) + O_2(g) \rightarrow 2H_2O(l)$$

The reactants H_2 and O_2 are on the left-hand side and the product H_2O is on the right-hand side. There are 4 atoms of H and 2 atoms of O on both sides. The only change is in how these atoms are bonded to each other.

Since the mole is a counting unit, equations can also be interpreted in terms of moles:

$$2H_2(g) + O_2(g) \rightarrow 2H_2O(l)$$
$$\text{2 moles} \quad \text{1 mole} \quad \text{2 moles}$$

Two moles of water can be formed from one mole of oxygen and two moles of hydrogen. One mole of water is formed from half a mole of oxygen and one mole of hydrogen. The coefficients in front of each of the molecules give the molar ratios of the reactants and products. As the physical states of the reactants and products can affect the energy change and rate of reaction, it is good practice to include them in chemical equations.

 The coefficients in an equation give the molar ratios of the reactant and products.

Balancing equations

Trying to balance chemical equations can be very frustrating so it is important to follow a systematic method. Consider the unbalanced equation for the reaction between methane and oxygen to form carbon dioxide and water:

$$\_\_\_CH_4(g) + \_\_\_O_2(g) \rightarrow \_\_\_CO_2(g) + \_\_\_H_2O(l)$$

It is a good idea to start with the elements that are present in the least number of substances: in this case C and H.

Balance the C:

$$CH_4(g) + \_\_\_O_2(g) \rightarrow CO_2(g) + \_\_\_H_2O(l); \text{ 1 mole of C atoms on both sides}$$

Balance the H:

$$CH_4(g) + \_\_\_O_2(g) \rightarrow CO_2(g) + 2H_2O(l), \text{ 4 moles of H atoms on both sides.}$$

Balance the element which occurs in the most substances last: in this case O.

Changing the product side would change the C or H which are already balanced so we change the reactant side. Balance the O:

$$CH_4(g) + 2O_2(g) \rightarrow CO_2(g) + 2H_2O(l), \text{ 4 mol of O atoms on both sides.}$$

 Chemical equations are the sentences in the language of chemistry and they are written in moles. It is a universal language which transcends cultural and national boundaries.

● **Examiner's hint:** Practise writing and balancing a wide range of equations. Make sure that you do not change any formulas. Check that everything balances as it is very easy to make careless mistakes.

Worked example

Balance the equation for the combustion of ethane shown below:

$$\_\_C_2H_6(g) + \_\_O_2(g) \rightarrow \_\_CO_2(g) + \_\_H_2O(l)$$

Solution

Balance the C: 2 moles of atoms are needed on the product side.

$$C_2H_6(g) + \_\_O_2(g) \rightarrow 2CO_2(g) + \_\_H_2O(l)$$

Balance the H: 6 moles of atoms needed on the product side which gives $3H_2O$ molecules.

$$C_2H_6(g) + \_\_O_2(g) \rightarrow 2CO_2(g) + 3H_2O(l)$$

Balance the O: $(4 + 3)$ moles on the product side. 7 moles of O atoms needed on the reactant side, which gives $3\frac{1}{2}$ moles of O_2 molecules.

$$\_\_C_2H_6(g) + 3\frac{1}{2}O_2(g) \rightarrow 2CO_2(g) + 3H_2O(l)$$

Sometimes it is more convenient to deal with whole numbers so we multiply the equation by 2.

$$2C_2H_6(g) + 7O_2(g) \rightarrow 4CO_2(g) + 6H_2O(l)$$

Exercise

11 (a) Nitrogen and oxygen react in the cylinders of car engines to form nitrogen monoxide (NO). Give a balanced equation for this reaction.
   (b) Nitrogen monoxide is a primary pollutant. After it escapes into the atmosphere, it reacts with oxygen to produce nitrogen dioxide. Give a balanced equation for this reaction.
   (c) Nitrogen dioxide is a secondary pollutant which can react further with oxygen and water in the atmosphere to produce nitric acid, $HNO_3(aq)$, one of the ingredients of acid rain. Give a balanced equation for the formation of nitric acid from nitrogen dioxide.

1.4 Mass and gaseous volume relationships in chemical reactions

General strategies

A balanced chemical reaction is a quantitative description of a chemical reaction and can be used to make numerical predictions. Consider the thermal decomposition of limestone ($CaCO_3$) to make lime (CaO):

$$CaCO_3(s) \rightarrow CaO(s) + CO_2(g)$$

This equation shows that one mole of calcium carbonate will produce one mole of calcium oxide, or expressing the relationship in terms of mass, 100 g of calcium carbonate will produce 56 g of calcium oxide. The interpretation of the coefficient of a balanced equation as the number of moles opens the door to a wide range of calculations discussed in this section. The general strategy for the solution of these problems is outlined below.

1 Write the equation for the reaction.
2 Write the amounts in moles of the relevant reactants and products of interest from the equation and show the relationship between them.
3 Convert the known data given into moles to find moles of the substance required. If the amounts of all reactants are given, work out which reactant is in **excess** and which is the **limiting reagent** (see next section).

4 Convert the number of moles to the required quantities (mass, volumes etc). Express the answer to the correct number of significant figures and include units.

You will need to carry out conversions between moles and masses and volumes. Earlier we met the relationship $n = \frac{m}{M}$. This can be rearranged to give $m = nM$.

mass m = number of
moles n × molar mass M

$m = nM$

Worked example

Ethyne is used in welding as its combustion gives a lot of heat. The reaction can be described by the equation:

$$2C_2H_2(g) + 5O_2(g) \rightarrow 4CO_2(g) + 2H_2O(l)$$

Calculate the mass of CO_2 produced from the complete combustion of 1.00 g of C_2H_2.

Solution

Care should be taken when using calculators as they can lead to unnecessary rounding errors. In the worked examples, the solution is a shown with a minimum number of calculation steps. The intermediate calculator answers are shown in the right-hand column. If you are more comfortable doing the calculation in a number of steps, this is perfectly acceptable but make sure you avoid transcription errors.

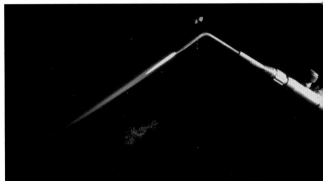

▲ The torch burns a mixture of oxygen and ethyne, C_2H_2 (acetylene) to produce a temperature of about 3300 °C. A common use for the tool is the cutting and welding of steel.

	Calculator values
Step 1 $2C_2H_2 + 5O_2 \rightarrow 4CO_2 + 2H_2O$ 2 moles 4 moles	
Step 2 $\frac{n(CO_2)}{n(C_2H_2)} = \frac{4}{2} = 2$ (*with experience you may choose to miss out this equation*) $n(CO_2) = 2n(C_2H_2)$ *The equation is written in the language of moles but you have been given the mass. To 'translate' from mass to moles, use $n = \frac{m}{M}$*	
Step 3 $M(C_2H_2) = (2 \times 12.01) + (2 \times 1.01)$ $n(C_2H_2) = \frac{m}{M} = \frac{1.00}{((2 \times 12.01) + (2 \times 1.01))}$ This gives: $n(CO_2) = 2 \times \left(\frac{1.00}{((2 \times 12.01) + (2 \times 1.01))}\right)$ *We now have to translate back into mass. Use $m = nM$*	$= 26.04$ $= \frac{1}{26.04} = 0.038\,402\,458$ $= 2 \times 0.038\,402\,458$ $= 0.076\,804\,916$
Step 4 $M(CO_2) = 12.01 + (2 \times 16.00)$ $m(CO_2) = nM$ $= \left(\frac{(12.01 + (2 \times 16.00)) \times 2 \times 1.00}{(2 \times 12.01) + (2 \times 1.01)}\right) = \textbf{3.38}\,\text{g}$	$= 44.01$ $= 44.01 \times 0.076\,804\,916$ $= 3.380\,184\,332$

Investigate combustion reactions
of the hydrocarbons.
Now go to www.heinemann.co.uk/
hotlinks, insert the express code
4295P and click on this activity.

Exercise

12 The combustion of hydrocarbon fuels is an environmental concern as it adds to the carbon
dioxide levels in the atmosphere. Calculate the mass of CO_2 produced when 100 g of propane is
burned according to the equation:

$$C_3H_8(g) + 5O_2(g) \rightarrow 3CO_2(g) + 4H_2O(l)$$

Using chemical equations: the theoretical yield

When you plan a meal you need to check that you have the correct amount of
ingredients to prepare the food in the required amounts. The chemist faces the
same problem when planning the synthesis of a new compound. A balanced
chemical reaction provides the recipe. You can use the strategy in the previous
worked example to predict how much product will be produced from given masses
of starting materials.

The language of chemistry is
precise and powerful, as it can be
used to solve numerical problems.
How do chemical equations direct
or limit our thinking?

Exercise

13 Iron is produced in the blast furnace by reduction of iron (III) oxide:

$$Fe_2O_3 + 3CO \rightarrow 2Fe + 3CO_2$$

Calculate the minimum mass of iron(III) oxide needed to produce 800 g of iron.

**The theoretical yield is the mass
or amount of product produced
according to the chemical
equation.**

Limiting reactants

The equation for the reduction of iron(III) oxide in the previous exercise shows
that one mole of iron(III) oxide reacts with three moles of carbon monoxide to
produce *two moles of iron*. The same amount of iron would be produced if we
had two moles of iron oxide and three moles of carbon monoxide because there
is insufficient carbon monoxide to reduce the additional iron(III) oxide. The
iron oxide is said to be in **excess**. The amount of iron produced is *limited* by the
amount of carbon monoxide. The carbon monoxide is the **limiting** reagent.

**The limiting reactant is the
reactant that determines the
theoretical yield of product.**

Worked example

A reaction vessel is filled with 4.04 g of hydrogen gas and 16.00 g of oxygen gas
and the mixture is exploded. Identify the limiting reagent and deduce the mass of
water produced.

Solution
Step 1
$$2H_2(g) + O_2(g) \rightarrow 2H_2O(l)$$

Step 2
2 moles of H_2 react with 1 mole of O_2 to produce 2 moles of H_2O.

Step 3
$$M(H_2) = (2 \times 1.01)$$
$$n(H_2) = \frac{m}{M} = \frac{4.04}{2 \times 1.01} = 2.00$$
$$M(O_2) = (2 \times 16.00)$$
$$n(O_2) = \frac{16.00}{(2 \times 16.00)} = 0.5000$$
2 moles of H_2 will react with 1 mole of O_2.

There is only 0.5000 moles of O_2 so this is the limiting reactant.

$n(H_2O) = 2 \times n(O_2) = 2 \times 0.5000 = 1.000$

0.5000 moles of O_2 produces 1.000 moles of H_2O.

Step 4

$M(H_2O) = (2 \times 1.01) + 16.00$

$m(H_2O) = nM = 1.000 \times ((2 \times 1.01) + 16.00) = 18.02$ g

This simulation will help you understand the concept of limiting reactant.

Now go to www.heinemann.co.uk/hotlinks, insert the express code 4259P and click on this activity.

Percentage yield

Few chemical reactions are completely efficient. The **experimental yield** is generally less than the **theoretical yield** predicted from the equation. There are several reasons for this:

- The reaction is incomplete.
- There are side reactions in which unwanted substances are produced.
- Complete separation of the product from reaction mixture is impossible.
- Product is lost during transfers of chemicals during the preparation.

The efficiency of the procedure can be quantified by the **percentage yield**.

Percentage yield

$= \dfrac{\textbf{experimental yield}}{\textbf{theoretical yield}} \times \textbf{100\%}$

Worked example

Aspirin, $C_9H_8O_4$, is made by reacting ethanoic anhydride $C_4H_6O_3$, with 2-hydroxybenzoic acid, $C_7H_6O_3$, according to the equation:

$$2C_7H_6O_3 + C_4H_6O_3 \rightarrow 2C_9H_8O_4 + H_2O$$

13.80 g of 2-hydroxybenzoic acid is reacted with 10.26 g of ethanoic anhydride.

(a) Determine the limiting reagent in this reaction.

(b) The mass obtained in this experiment was 10.90 g. Calculate the percentage yield of aspirin.

Solution

(a)

	Calculator values
Step 1 $2C_7H_6O_3 + C_4H_6O_3 \rightarrow 2C_9H_8O_4 + H_2O$ 2 moles 1 mole 2 moles	
Step 2 2 moles of $C_7H_6O_3$ react with 1 mole of $C_4H_6O_3$ to produce 2 moles of $C_9H_8O_4$	
Step 3 $M(C_7H_6O_3) = (7 \times 12.01) + (6 \times 1.01) + (3 \times 16.00)$ $n(C_7H_6O_3) = \dfrac{m}{M} = \dfrac{13.80}{((7 \times 12.01) + (6 \times 1.01) + (3 \times 16.00))}$ $= 0.1000$ (4 sf) $M(C_4H_6O_3) = (4 \times 12.01) + (6 \times 1.01) + (3 \times 16.00)$ $n(C_4H_6O_3) = \dfrac{10.26}{((4 \times 12.01) + (6 \times 1.01) + (3 \times 16.00))}$ $= 0.1000$ (4sf) 0.1000 mole of $C_7H_6O_3$ reacts with $\dfrac{0.1000}{2}$ moles of $C_4H_6O_3$ to produce a theoretical yield 0.1000 moles of $C_9H_8O_4$	$= 138.13$ $= \dfrac{13.80}{138.13}$ $= 0.099\,978\,281$ $= 102.64$ $= \dfrac{10.26}{102.64}$ $= 0.099\,905\,886$

$C_7H_6O_3$ is the limiting reactant.

(b)

Theoretical yield = 0.1000 mol of $C_9H_8O_4$	
Step 4 $M(C_9H_8O_4) = (9 \times 12.01) + (8 \times 1.01) + (4 \times 16.00)$ Theoretical mass $= nM = 0.1000 \times 180.17$	= 180.17 = 0.1 × 180.17 = 18.17
% yield $= \dfrac{10.90}{(0.1000 \times 180.17)} \times 100\%$	$= \dfrac{10.90}{18.17} \times 100$ = 0.599 889 928 × 100
$= 60.00\%$	= 59.988 9928

● **Examiner's hint:** Practise setting out calculations in a logical way, including a few words to indicate what process is being used.

See a video clip of the combustion of red phosphorus which illustrates the concepts of limiting and excess reagent.
Now go to www.heinemann.co.uk/hotlinks, insert the express code 4259P and click on this activity.

Exercises

14 The Haber process, which provides ammonia needed in the manufacture of fertilizers, has enabled us to increase food production to cater for the world's growing population. Ammonia is produced by the synthesis of nitrogen and hydrogen:

$$N_2(g) + 3H_2(g) \rightleftharpoons 2NH_3(g)$$

400 kg of N_2 is mixed with 200 kg of H_2 to produce 220 kg of NH_3. Calculate the percentage yield of ammonia.

Reacting gases

The balance is not always the most convenient instrument to measure quantity. Volume is often used for liquids and gases. Investigations into the relationship between the volumes of reacting gases were carried out by the French chemist Joseph Gay Lussac at the beginning of the 19th century. He observed that when gases react, their volumes and that of any products formed were in simple whole number ratios.

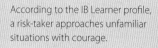

The scientist as risk-taker. Joseph Louis Gay-Lussac in a daring 1804 balloon ascent to investigate the composition of air at high altitude.

According to the IB Learner profile, a risk-taker approaches unfamiliar situations with courage.

A modern version of one of Gay Lussac's experiments is described in the worked example.

Worked example

Nitrogen monoxide, NO(g), reacts with oxygen, O_2(g), to form one product. This is a brown gas, nitrogen dioxide, NO_2(g).

Consider the apparatus below.

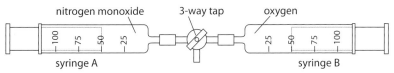

◀ **Figure 1.6** A modern version of one of Gay Lussac's experiments.

Syringe A contains $50\,cm^3$ of nitrogen monoxide. Syringe B contains $50\,cm^3$ of oxygen gas. In the experiment, $5.0\,cm^3$ portions of oxygen were pushed from syringe B into A. After each addition the tap was closed. After the gases had returned to their original temperature, the total volume of gases remaining was measured. The results are shown graphically on the right.

◀ **Figure 1.7** Results of a modern version of one of Gay Lussac's experiments.

(a) Deduce a balanced equation for the reaction.
(b) State the total volume of gases when the reaction is complete.
(c) Deduce the volume of oxygen that reacts with $50\,cm^3$ of nitrogen monoxide.
(d) Identify the limiting reagent in the reaction.
(e) Deduce the volume of nitrogen dioxide formed.
(f) Compare the volume ratios of the three gases involved in the reaction with their molar ratios. Suggest a reason for any relationships you find.

● **Examiner's hint:** Practise data response questions which involve the manipulation and interpretation of unfamiliar data – particularly if presented in graphical form.

Solution

(a) The unbalanced equation:

$$\_\_NO(g) + \_\_O_2(g) \rightarrow \_\_NO_2(g)$$

The N atoms are balanced. The only way to balance the O atoms without changing the N atoms is to change the coefficient of O_2:

$$NO(g) + \tfrac{1}{2}O_2(g) \rightarrow NO_2(g)$$

Multiply by 2:

$$2NO(g) + O_2(g) \rightarrow 2NO_2(g)$$

(b) The reaction is complete when the volume stops decreasing. Reading from the graph: total volume $= 75\,cm^3$.
(c) The reactions stops after $25\,cm^3$ of O_2 is added.
(d) The limiting reactant is nitrogen monoxide because the oxygen is left in excess.
(e) Volume of nitrogen dioxide $=$ total volume – volume of oxygen $= 75 - 25\,cm^3$ $= 50\,cm^3$.
(f) The ratio of the volumes of the gases $NO:O_2:NO_2$ is $50:25:50 = 2:1:2$. This is the same as the molar ratios expressed in the balanced equation. This implies that equal volumes correspond to equal amounts (NO and NO_2 in this example). The volume of NO is double the volume of oxygen as there is double the amount of NO compared to O_2.

One mole of each of the gases has the same volume.

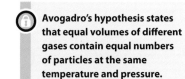

Avogadro's hypothesis states that equal volumes of different gases contain equal numbers of particles at the same temperature and pressure.

This explanation of Gay-Lussac results was first proposed by the Italian scientist Amedeo Avogadro. It is called **Avogadro's hypothesis**.

Amedeo Avogadro (1776–1856). His hypothesis was not widely accepted until after his death.

One of the reasons for the late acceptance of Avogadro's hypothesis was that it didn't agree with John Dalton's belief that all gaseous elements are made from atoms. Dalton was mistaken because some elements, as discussed earlier, exist as molecules. How does the spread of knowledge depend on the authority of the person proposing the new ideas?

● **Examiner's hint:** Problems involving volumes of gases can often be solved directly. There is no need for intermediate steps which calculate the number of moles.

STP = 273 K (0 °C) and 101.3 kPa (1 atm).

For a gas: number of moles
$$(n) = \frac{\text{volume } (V)}{\text{molar volume } (V_{molar})}$$
The molar gas volume at STP is 22.4 dm³. The molar gas volume at RTP is 24 dm³.

Worked example

40 cm^3 of carbon monoxide is reacted with 40 cm^3 of oxygen.

$$2CO(g) + O_2(g) \rightarrow 2CO_2(g)$$

What volume of carbon dioxide is produced? Assume all volumes are measured at the same temperature and pressure.

Solution
Step 1

$$2CO(g) + O_2(g) \rightarrow 2CO_2(g)$$
$$\text{2 moles} \quad \text{1 mole} \quad \text{2 moles}$$

Step 2
The ratio of the volumes is the same as the number of moles:

$$2CO(g) + O_2(g) \rightarrow 2CO_2(g)$$
$$40 \text{ cm}^3 \quad 20 \text{ cm}^3 \quad 40 \text{ cm}^3$$

The oxygen is in excess. 40 cm^3 of $CO_2(g)$ is produced.

Exercise

15 Assume all volumes are measured at the same temperature and pressure.
  (a) What volume of nitrogen forms when 100 cm^3 of ammonia, NH_3, decomposes completely into its elements.
$$2NH_3(g) \rightarrow N_2(g) + 3H_2(g)$$
  (b) What volume of oxygen is needed to react with 40 cm^3 of butane, C_4H_{10}, and what volume of carbon dioxide is produced?
$$2C_4H_{10}(g) + 13O_2(g) \rightarrow 8CO_2(g) + 10H_2O(l)$$

The molar volume of a gas

All gases have the same **molar volume** at the same temperature and pressure. The standard conditions of temperature and pressure (STP) are 273 K (0 °C) and 101.3 kPa (1 atm) pressure.

One mole of gas occupies $22\,400 \text{ cm}^3$ under these conditions. As this is such a large number it is often quoted in dm³ (1 dm = 10 cm, so 1 dm³ = 10^3cm^3). At the higher temperature of 298 K (room temperature) the molar volume is 24 dm³ (298 K and 101.3 kPa (1 atm) is called RTP).

The molar volume can be used to calculate the amount of gases in the same way as molar mass. Calculations are simpler as all gases have the same molar volume.

Worked example

Calculate the amount of chlorine in 44.8 cm^3 of the gas at STP.

Solution

$$n = \frac{V}{V_{molar}} = \frac{44.8}{22\,400} = 0.00200 \text{ mole}$$

Exercise

16 Calculate the volume occupied by 4.40 g of carbon dioxide at standard temperature and pressure.

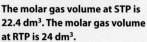

The volume of gaseous reactants and products in chemical reactions can be calculated using a similar strategy to that outlined earlier to calculate masses.

Worked example

What volume of hydrogen (H_2) is produced when 0.056 g of lithium (Li) reacts completely with water (H_2O):

$$2Li(s) + 2H_2O(l) \rightarrow 2LiOH(aq) + H_2(g)$$

Assume the volume is measured at STP.

Solution

	Calculator values
Step 1 $2Li(s) + 2H_2O(l) \rightarrow 2LiOH(aq) + H_2(g)$ 2 moles 1 mole	
Step 2 2 moles of Li react to produce 1 mole of H_2 $n(H_2) = \frac{1}{2} n(Li)$	
Step 3 $n(Li) = \frac{m}{M} = \frac{0.056}{6.94}$ $n(H_2) = \frac{1}{2}\left(\frac{0.056}{6.94}\right)$	$= 0.008\,069\,164$ $= 0.5 \times 0.008\,069\,164$ $= 0.004\,034\,582$
Step 4 Translate into volume. Use $V = nV_{mol}$ $V(H_2) = nV_{molar} = \frac{1}{2}\left(\frac{0.056}{6.94}\right) \times 22\,400 \text{ cm}^3$ $= 90 \text{ cm}^3$	$= 0.004\,034\,582 \times 22\,400$ $= 90.374\,639\,77$

---

17 Calcium reacts with water to produce hydrogen:

$$Ca(s) + 2H_2O(l) \rightarrow Ca(OH)_2(aq) + H_2(g)$$

Calculate the volume of gas, measured at STP produced when 0.200 g of calcium reacts completely with water.

 Pump gas molecules into a box and see what happens as you change the volume, add or remove heat, change gravity and more. Now go to www.heinemann.co.uk/hotlinks, insert the express code 4259P and click on this activity.

The gas laws

The gaseous state is the simplest state. All gases have the same molar volume and they respond in similar ways to changes in temperature, pressure and volume. The gas laws describe this behaviour.

Pressure

If you have ever pumped a bicycle tyre or squeezed an inflated balloon you have experienced the pressure of a gas. A gas produces a pressure when its particles collide with the walls of its container. An increase in the *frequency* or *energy* of these collisions will increase the pressure.

Relationship between volume and pressure for a gas

An increase in volume reduces the frequency of the collisions with the walls and so the pressure decreases. The relationship was studied experimentally by Robert Boyle in the 17th century. He found that if the temperature and amount of gas is kept constant, the pressure *halves* if the volume is *doubled*. The pressure is inversely proportional to the volume and the relationship can be expressed as:

$$P = \frac{k_1}{V}, \text{ where } k_1 \text{ is a constant.}$$

$$PV = k_1$$

Figure 1.8 The pressure of a gas is inversely proportional to the volume. A graph of P against $\frac{1}{V}$ produces a straight line through the origin.

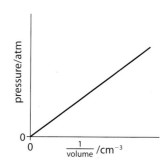

Investigate Boyle's Law using this simulation.
Now go to
www.heinemann.co.uk/hotlinks, insert the express code 4259P and click on this activity.

Relationship between temperature and pressure for a gas

You may have noticed that balloons have an increased tendency to 'pop' on hot summer days. An increase in temperature increases the average kinetic energy of the particles. The particles move faster and collide with the walls of the balloon with more energy and more frequency. Both factors lead to an increase in pressure. When the relationship is studied experimentally at constant volume, the following graphs are produced.

Figure 1.9 The pressure is proportional to the absolute temperature. The pressure of the gas is zero at absolute zero when the particles are not moving ($-273\,°C$).

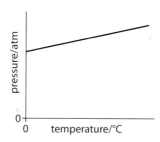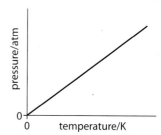

The pressure is proportional to the absolute temperature measured in kelvin (K).
$P = k_2 T$, where k_2 is a constant.

Effect of temperature on the gas volume

Combining the two previous relationships we can predict how the volume changes with absolute temperature. Consider the following sequence:

1 The temperature is *doubled* at fixed volume.
2 The volume is *doubled* at fixed temperature.

The changes are summarized below.

	Step 1	Step 2	Overall change
temperature	doubled	fixed	doubled
volume	constant	doubled	doubled
pressure	doubled due to increase in temperature	halved due to increase in volume	no change

The volume and the temperature of the gas have both doubled at fixed volume. This relationship is sometimes called Charles' law and is represented below.

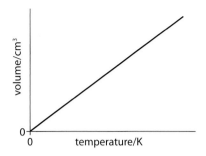

Figure 1.10 Charles' Law. The volume is proportional to the absolute temperature.

The volume of a gas is proportional to the absolute temperature. $V = k_3 T$, where k_3 is a constant.

Would there have been the gas laws without the work of Charles or Boyle?

In science, the individual scientist is irrelevant and all scientists contribute to a common body of knowledge. This should be contrasted with the arts. There could have been no *Hamlet* without Shakespeare, no *Guernica* without Picasso.

The combined gas law

We can combine the three gas laws into one expression:

$$V \propto T$$
$$P \propto T \quad \longrightarrow \quad PV \propto T$$
$$P \propto \frac{1}{V} \qquad \frac{PV}{T} = \text{constant}$$

The response of a gas to a change in conditions can be predicted by a more convenient form of the expression:

$$\frac{P_1 V_1}{T_1} = \frac{P_2 V_2}{T_2}$$

where 1 refers to the initial conditions and 2 the final conditions.

$\dfrac{P_1 V_1}{T_1} = \dfrac{P_2 V_2}{T_2}$

The temperature must be in kelvin.

Worked example

What happens to the volume of a fixed mass of gas when its pressure and its temperature (in kelvin) are both doubled?

Solution

The pressure and temperature are both doubled: $P_2 = 2P_1$, $T_2 = 2T_1$:

$$\frac{P_1 V_1}{T_1} = \frac{P_2 V_2}{T_2}$$

Substitute for P_2 and T_2:

$$\frac{P_1 V_1}{T_1} = \frac{2P_1 V_2}{2T_1}$$

P_1 and T_1 cancel from both sides:

$$V_1 = \frac{2V_2}{2}$$

$$V_1 = V_2$$

The volume does not change.

Blowing air molecules into a balloon increases the volume.

Use this simulation to investigate the gas laws.
Now go to www.heinemann.co.uk/ hotlinks, insert the express code 4259P and click on this activity.

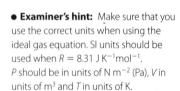

● **Examiner's hint:** Make sure that you use the correct units when using the ideal gas equation. SI units should be used when $R = 8.31$ J K^{-1}mol^{-1}. P should be in units of N m^{-2} (Pa), V in units of m^3 and T in units of K.

Exercises

18 The temperature in kelvin of 4.0 dm^3 of hydrogen gas is increased by a factor of three and the pressure is increased by a factor of four. Deduce the final volume of the gas.

19 The molar volume of a gas at STP is 22.4 dm^3. Use the combined gas equation to show that the molar volume of gas is 24 dm^3 at RTP.

The ideal gas equation

The combined gas equation refers to a fixed mass of gas. When you blow into a balloon you increase the number of particles and this increases the volume. When you pump up a bicycle tyre the added gases cause the pressure to increase. The number of moles can be included in the combined gas equation to give the ideal gas equation.

$\dfrac{PV}{nT} = R$ where R is the gas constant. When SI units are used R has the value 8.31 J K^{-1} mol^{-1}.

Gases which follow this equation exactly are called **ideal gases**. Real gases deviate from the equation at high pressure and low temperature owing to the effects of inter-particle forces.

Worked example

A helium party balloon has a volume of 18.0 dm^3. At room temperature (25 °C) the internal pressure is 1.05 atm. Calculate the number of moles of helium in the balloon and the mass needed to inflate it.

Solution

$PV = nRT$

$n = \dfrac{PV}{RT}$

Convert data into SI units:

$P = 1.05$ atm $= 1.05 \times 1.01 \times 10^5$ Pa (see Table 2 in the IB Data booklet)
$V = 18.0$ dm$^3 = 18.0 \times 10^{-3}$ m^3, $T = 25$°C $= (25 + 273)$ K $= 298$ K

$n = \dfrac{1.05 \times 1.01 \times 10^5 \times 18.0 \times 10^{-3}}{(8.31 \times 298)} = 0.771$ mole (calculator value: 0.770 842 924)

Mass $= nM = 0.771 \times 4.00 = 3.08$ g

Measuring the molar mass

The ideal gas equation can be used to find the molar mass of gases or volatile liquids.

$PV = nRT$

$n = \dfrac{m}{M}$

$PV = \left(\dfrac{m}{M}\right) RT$ when m is in g

$M = \dfrac{mRT}{PV}$

Density $\rho = \dfrac{m}{V}$

$M = \dfrac{\rho RT}{P}$, when density is in g m^{-3}

Worked example

A sample of gas has a volume of 432 cm³ and a mass of 1.500 g at a pressure of 0.974 atm and a temperature of 28 °C. Calculate the molar mass of the gas.

Solution

$$M = \frac{mRT}{PV}$$

Convert into SI units (the mass should be kept in g).

$T = 273 + 28$ K, $P = 0.974 \times 1.01 \times 10^5$ Pa, $V = 432 \times 10^{-6}$ m³

$$= \frac{1.500 \times 8.31 \times (273+28)}{(0.974 \times 1.01 \times 10^5 \times 432 \times 10^{-6})}$$

$= 88.3$ g mol⁻¹ (calculator value: 88.286 581 48)

Exercise

20 The density of a gaseous hydrocarbon with the empirical formula C_3H_7 is found to be 2.81 g dm⁻³ at 100 °C and 1.00 atm. Calculate the molar mass of the hydrocarbon and find its molecular formula.

1.5 Solutions

Liquids

Like gases it is often more convenient to measure the volume of a liquid instead of its mass. Unlike gases however there is no direct relationship between the volume of a liquid and its amount. The mass can be calculated from the volume if the density is known.

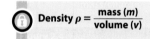

Density $\rho = \dfrac{\text{mass } (m)}{\text{volume } (v)}$

In the laboratory the volume of a liquid can be measured using different apparatus depending on the precision required. When the volume is known, volumetric flasks or pipettes are used. A 25 cm³ pipette has a typical uncertainty of ±0.75 cm³ and a 250 cm³ volumetric flask has an uncertainty of ±0.15 cm³. A burette is used when the volume is unknown. A 50 cm³ burette has a typical uncertainty of ±0.1 cm³. The uncertainty of measurements is discussed in more detail in Chapter 11.

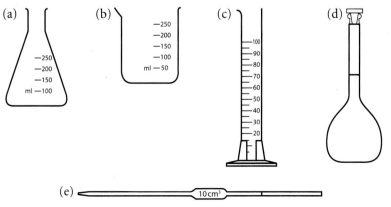

Figure 1.11 Different pieces of glassware used in the lab. (a) Conical or Erlenmeyer flask (250 cm³). The shape makes it easy to mix liquids as the flask can be easily swirled. (b) Beaker (250 cm³). (c) Measuring cylinder (100 cm³). (d) Volumetric flask (250 cm³). (e) Pipette (10 cm³). (f) Burette (50 cm³). The beaker and the conical flask are not generally used for measuring volume.

Solutions

The discussion so far has focused on pure substances but chemists often carry out reactions in **solution**. Solutions are mixtures of two components. The less abundant component is the **solute** and the more abundant the **solvent**. The solute can be solid, liquid or gas but the solvent is generally a liquid. Salt water is a solution with salt as the solute and water the solvent. Solutions in water are particularly important. These are called **aqueous** solutions and are given the state symbol (aq).

Concentration

The composition of a solution is generally expressed in terms of its **concentration**. As more and more solute dissolves in the solvent, the solution becomes more and more concentrated. When the solvent cannot dissolve any more solute, it is **saturated**.

The concentration is generally expressed in terms of the mass or amount of solute dissolved in $1\,dm^3$ of solution. The units are either $g\,dm^{-3}$ or $mol\,dm^{-3}$. One mole of sodium chloride for example has a mass of $22.99 + 35.45\,g = 58.44\,g$. When this amount of solute is added to water to make a $1\,dm^3$ solution, the concentration can either be expressed as $58.44\,g\,dm^{-3}$ or $1.00\,mol\,dm^{-3}$. Square brackets are used to represent concentrations, so this can be written [NaCl] $= 1.00\,mol\,dm^{-3}$. Concentrations in $mol\,dm^{-3}$ are generally used in solving problems involving chemical equations.

Concentration
$$= \frac{\text{number of moles } (n)}{\text{volume of solution } (V)}$$
The volume is in dm^3.
Square brackets are used to represent concentrations.

Worked example

A solution of sodium hydroxide has a concentration of $8.00\,g\,dm^{-3}$. What is its concentration in $mol\,dm^{-3}$?

Solution
To find number of moles use: $n = \dfrac{m}{M}$

$M = 22.99 + 1.01 + 16.00 = 40.00\,g$

$n = \dfrac{8.00}{40.00} = 0.200$

$[NaOH] = \dfrac{n}{V} = \dfrac{0.200}{1.00} = 0.200\,mol\,dm^{-3}$

Worked example

Calculate the concentration of a $0.0400\,mol\,dm^{-3}$ solution of sodium carbonate Na_2CO_3 in $g\,dm^{-3}$

Solution
To find the mass use: $m = nM$

$M = (22.99 \times 2) + 12.01 + (3 \times 16.00)$ (calculator value: 105.99)

$m = nM = 0.0400 \times ((22.99 \times 2) + 12.01 + (3 \times 16.00))$ (calculator value: 4.2396)

$[Na_2CO_3] = 4.24\,g\,dm^{-3}$

Standard solutions

A solution of known concentration is called a **standard solution**. The amount of solute needed can be calculated from the concentration and the volume required:

concentration $= \dfrac{n}{V}\,(dm^3)$

$n =$ concentration $\times V\,(dm^3)$

if the volume is in cm^3

$n = \dfrac{\text{concentration} \times V\,(cm^3)}{1000}$

The mass needed can then be calculated from $m = nM$.

Worked example

Calculate the mass of copper(II) sulfate pentahydrate, $CuSO_4 \cdot 5H_2O$, required to prepare 500 cm³ of a 0.400 mol dm⁻³ solution.

Solution

$n = \text{concentration} \times \dfrac{V}{1000}$

$\quad = 0.400 \times \dfrac{500}{1000}$ (calculator value: 0.2)

$m = nM$

$M = 63.55 + 32.06 + 4(16.00) + 5(16.00 + (2 \times 1.01))$

$\qquad$ (calculator value: 249.71)

Note there are five moles of H_2O in one mole of $CuSO_4 \cdot 5H_2O$ crystals.

$m = nM = \left(0.400 \times \dfrac{500}{1000} \right) \times (63.55 + 32.06 + 4(16.00)$

$\qquad + 5(16.00 + (2 \times 1.01)) = 49.8\,g$ (calculator value: $249.71 \times 0.2 = 49.942$)

> **Number of moles (n)**
>
> $= \dfrac{\text{concentration} \times \text{volume (V)}}{1000}$

Exercise

21 Calculate the mass of potassium hydroxide needed to prepare 250 cm³ of a 0.200 mol dm⁻³ solution.

Titrations

Standard solutions are used to find the concentration of other solutions. The analysis of composition by measuring the volume of one solution needed to react with a given volume of another solution is called **volumetric analysis**. One of the most important techniques is **titration**. Typically, a known volume of one solution is measured into a conical flask using a pipette. The other solution is then added from a burette to find the equivalence point – the volume when the reaction is just complete. In acid–base reactions the equivalence point can be detected by the colour change of an **indicator**.

◀ A pipette is used to measure a known volume of liquid accurately. Burettes and conical flasks, which are also used in the titrations, are in the background.

Worked example

What volume of hydrochloric acid with a concentration of 2.00 mol dm⁻³ would have to be added to 25.0 cm³ of a 0.500 mol dm⁻³ sodium carbonate solution to produce a neutral solution of sodium chloride?

Solution

Step 1

$$Na_2CO_3(aq) + 2HCl(aq) \rightarrow 2NaCl(aq) + H_2O(l) + CO_2(g)$$

1 mole   2 moles

Step 2

$$\frac{n(HCl)}{n(Na_2CO_3)} = \frac{2}{1}$$

$$n(HCl) = 2n(Na_2CO_3)$$

Step 3

$$n(Na_2CO_3) = \frac{\text{concentration} \times V}{1000} = \frac{(25.0 \times 0.500)}{1000}$$

$$n(HCl) = \frac{2.00 \times V(HCl)}{1000}$$

Substitute these amounts in the equation in step 2:

$$2.00 \times \frac{V(HCl)}{1000} = 2\left(\frac{25.0 \times 0.500}{1000}\right)$$

Find the unknown volume.

Step 4

$$V(HCl) = \frac{2 \times 25.0 \times 0.500}{2.00} = 12.5 \text{ cm}^3$$

Calculations involving solutions and gases

Worked example

Calculate the volume of carbon dioxide produced when 1.00 g of calcium carbonate reacts with 20.0 cm^3 of hydrochloric acid. Assume the volume of the gas is measured at 273K and 1 atm.

Solution

	Calculator values
Step 1 $CaCO_3(s) + 2HCl(aq) \rightarrow CaCl_2(aq) + H_2O(l) + CO_2(g)$ 1 mole 2 moles	
Step 2 1 mole of $CaCO_3(s)$ reacts with 2 moles of HCl to produce 1 mole of CO_2	
Step 3 $M(CaCO_3) = 40.08 + 12.01 + (3 \times 16.00)$ $n(CaCO_3) = \dfrac{1.00}{(40.08 + 12.01 + (3 \times 16.00))} = 0.0100$ $n(HCl) = \dfrac{[HCl] \times V(HCl)}{1000}$ $\qquad = \dfrac{2.00 \times 25.0}{1000} = 0.0500$ 0.0100 moles of $CaCO_3$ reacts with 2(0.0100) mol of HCl to produce a theoretical yield of 0.0100 mole of CO_2. $CaCO_3$ is the limiting reactant and HCl is in excess.	$= 100.09$ $= \dfrac{1}{100.09}$ $= 0.009\,991\,008$ 0.05
Step 4 $n(CO_2) = n(CaCO_3)$ $n(CO_2) = \dfrac{1.00}{(40.08 + 12.01 + (3 \times 16.00))}$ $V(CO_2) = nV_{molar}$ $\qquad = 22.4/(40.08 + 12.01 + (3 \times 16.00)) \text{ dm}^3$ $\qquad = 0.224 \text{ dm}^3 = 224 \text{ cm}^3$	$= \dfrac{1}{100.09}$ $= 0.009\,991\,008$ $= 0.009\,991\,008 \times 22.4$ $= 0.223\,798\,581$

Worked example

Calcium carbonate decomposes on heating:

$$CaCO_3(s) \rightarrow CaO(s) + CO_2(g)$$

What is the maximum volume (measured at RTP in dm^3) of CO_2 produced when 25 g of $CaCO_3$ is heated?

A 3.0 dm^3

B 6.0 dm^3

C 9.0 cm^3

D 12 dm^3

Solution

As this is a multiple choice question it should be answered without a calculator. You can use less precise values (the data is given only to 2 significant figures) for the relative atomic masses. This makes the arithmetic easier.

Step 1

$$CaCO_3(s) \rightarrow CaO(s) + CO_2(g)$$

    1 mole   1 mole

Step 2

1 mol of $CaCO_3(s)$ produces 1 mol of CO_2.

Step 3

$$n(CaCO_3) = \frac{25}{(40 + 12 + 3(16))} = 0.25$$

$n(CO_2) = 0.25$ mol

'Translate' back into volume. Use $V = nV_{molar}$

Step 4

$V(H_2) = 0.25 \times 24$ $dm^3 = 6.0$ dm^3

$Solution = B$

● **Examiner's hint:** In Paper 1 you can find the best solution with less precise relative atomic mass values. This makes the calculation easier and saves time. For papers 2 and 3 estimate the answer before you use a calculator. This will help you spot careless mistakes.

Exercise

22 25.00 cm^3 of 0.100 mol dm^{-3} sodium hydrogencarbonate solution was titrated with dilute sulfuric acid:

$$2NaHCO_3(aq) + H_2SO_4(aq) \rightarrow Na_2SO_4(aq) + 2H_2O(l) + 2CO_2(g)$$

15.2 cm^3 of the acid was needed to neutralize the solution.

(a) Calculate the concentration of the sulfuric acid.

(b) Calculate the volume of carbon dioxide, measured at STP produced during the titration.

Practice questions

1 What amount of oxygen, O_2, (in moles) contains 1.8×10^{22} molecules?

   A 0.0030   B 0.030   C 0.30   D 3.0

© International Baccalaureate Organization [2003]

2 ___$C_2H_2(g)$ + ___$O_2(g)$ → ___$CO_2(g)$ + ___$H_2O(g)$

  When the equation above is balanced, what is the coefficient for oxygen?

   A 2   B 3   C 4   D 5

© International Baccalaureate Organization [2003]

3 3.0 dm^3 of sulfur dioxide is reacted with 2.0 dm^3 of oxygen according to the equation below.

$$2SO_2(g) + O_2(g) \rightarrow 2SO_3(g)$$

What volume of sulfur trioxide (in dm^3) is formed? (Assume the reaction goes to completion and all gases are measured at the same temperature and pressure.)

A 5.0   B 4.0   C 3.0   D 2.0

© International Baccalaureate Organization [2003]

4 What volume of 0.500 mol dm^{-3} HCl(aq) is required to react completely with 10.0 g of calcium carbonate according to the equation below?

$$CaCO_3(s) + 2HCl(aq) \rightarrow CaCl_2(aq) + H_2O(l) + CO_2(g)$$

A 100 cm^3 B 200 cm^3 C 300 cm^3 D 400 cm^3

© International Baccalaureate Organization [2003]

5 The relative molecular mass of aluminium chloride is 267 and its composition by mass is 20.3% Al and 79.7% chlorine. Determine the empirical and molecular formulas of aluminium chloride.   (4)

© International Baccalaureate Organization [2003]

6 27.82 g of hydrated sodium carbonate crystals, $Na_2CO_3 \cdot xH_2O$, was dissolved in water and made up to 1.000 dm^3. 25.00 cm^3 of this solution was neutralized by 48.80 cm^3 of hydrochloric acid of concentration 0.1000 mol dm^{-3}.

(a) Write an equation for the reaction between sodium carbonate and hydrochloric acid.   (2)

(b) Calculate the molar concentration of the sodium carbonate solution neutralized by the hydrochloric acid.   (3)

(c) Determine the mass of sodium carbonate neutralized by the hydrochloric acid and hence the mass of sodium carbonate present in 1.000 dm^3 of solution.   (3)

(d) Calculate the mass of water in the hydrated crystals and hence find the value of x.   (4)

(*Total 12 marks*)

© International Baccalaureate Organization [2004]

7 Describe in molecular terms the processes that occur when:

(a) a mixture of ice and water is maintained at the melting point.   (2)

(b) a sample of a very volatile liquid (such as ethoxyethane) is placed on a person's skin.   (2)

(*Total 4 marks*)

© International Baccalaureate Organization [2004]

8 The percentage composition by mass of a hydrocarbon is C = 85.6% and H = 14.4%.

(a) Calculate the empirical formula of the hydrocarbon.   (2)

(b) A 100 g sample of the hydrocarbon at a temperature of 273 K and a pressure of 1.01 × 10^5 Pa (1.00 atm) has a volume of 0.399 dm^3.

  (i) Calculate the molar mass of the hydrocarbon.   (2)

  (ii) Deduce the molecular formula of the hydrocarbon.   (1)

(*Total 5 marks*)

© International Baccalaureate Organization [2005]

9 When a small quantity of strongly smelling gas such as ammonia is released into the air, it can be detected several metres away in a short time.

(a) Use the kinetic molecular theory to explain why this happens.   (2)

(b) State and explain how the time taken to detect the gas changes when the temperature is increased.   (2)

(*Total 4 marks*)

© International Baccalaureate Organization [2005]

2 Atomic structure

'All things are made from atoms.' This is one of the most important ideas that the human race has learned about the universe. Atoms are everywhere and they make up everything. You are surrounded by atoms – they make up the foods you eat, the liquids you drink and the fragrances you smell. Atoms make up you! To understand the world and how it changes you need to understand atoms.

The idea of the atom has its origins in Greek and Indian philosophy nearly 2500 years ago but it was not until the 19th century that there was experimental evidence to support their existence. Although atoms are too small ever to be seen directly by a human eye, they are fundamental to chemistry. All the atoms in a piece of gold foil, for example, have the same chemical properties. The atoms of gold, however, have different properties from the atoms of aluminium. This chapter will explain how they differ. We will explore their structure and discover that different atoms are made from different combinations of the same sub-atomic particles.

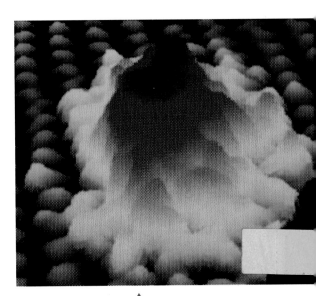

Picture of individual atoms. This is a scanning tunnelling micrograph of gold atoms on a graphite surface. The gold atoms are shown in yellow, red and brown and the graphite (carbon) atoms are shown in green.

Assessment statements

2.1 The atom
2.1.1   State the position of protons, neutrons and electrons in the atom.
2.1.2   State the relative masses and relative charges of protons, neutrons and electrons.
2.1.3   Define the terms *mass number (A)*, *atomic number (Z)* and *isotopes of an element*.
2.1.4   Deduce the symbol for an isotope given its mass number and atomic number.
2.1.5   Calculate the number of protons, neutrons and electrons in atoms and ions from the mass number, atomic number and charge.
2.1.6   Compare the properties of the isotopes of an element.
2.1.7   Discuss the uses of radioisotopes.

2.2 The mass spectrometer
2.2.1   Describe and explain the operation of a mass spectrometer.
2.2.2   Describe how the mass spectrometer may be used to determine relative atomic mass using the ^{12}C scale.
2.2.3   Calculate non-integer relative atomic masses and abundance of isotopes from given data.

2.3 Electron arrangement
2.3.1   Describe the electromagnetic spectrum.
2.3.2   Distinguish between a continuous spectrum and a line spectrum.
2.3.3   Explain how the lines in the emission spectrum of hydrogen are related to electron energy levels.
2.3.4   Deduce the electron arrangement for atoms and ions up to $Z = 20$.

 A billion of your atoms once made up Shakespeare, another billion made up Beethoven, another billion St. Peter and another billion the Buddha. Atoms can rearrange in chemical reactions but they cannot be destroyed.

2.1 The atom

Dalton's atom

An element is a substance that cannot be broken down into simpler substances by a chemical reaction.

One of the first great achievements of chemistry was to show that all matter is built from about 100 **elements**. The elements cannot be broken down into simpler components by chemical reactions. They are the simplest substances and their names are listed in your IB Data booklet. Different elements have different chemical properties but gold foil, for example, reacts in essentially the same away as a single piece of gold dust. Indeed if the gold dust is cut into smaller and smaller pieces, the chemical properties would remain essentially the same until we reached an **atom**. This is the smallest unit of an element. There are only 92 elements which occur naturally on earth and they are made up from only 92 different types of atom. (This statement will be qualified when isotopes are discussed later in the chapter.)

The word 'atom' comes from the Greek words for 'not able to be cut'.

(a)

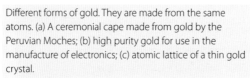
(b)

Different forms of gold. They are made from the same atoms. (a) A ceremonial cape made from gold by the Peruvian Moches; (b) high purity gold for use in the manufacture of electronics; (c) atomic lattice of a thin gold crystal.

(c)

Although John Dalton (1766–1844) was a school teacher from Manchester in England his name has passed into other languages. The internationally recognized term for colour-blindness, *Daltonisme* in French, for example, derives from the fact the he suffered from the condition.

The modern idea of the atom dates from the beginning of the 19th century. John Dalton noticed that the elements hydrogen and oxygen always combined together in fixed proportions. To explain this observation he proposed that:

- All matter is composed of tiny indestructible particles called atoms.
- Atoms cannot be created or destroyed.
- Atoms of the same element are alike in every way.
- Atoms of different elements are different.
- Atoms can combine together in small numbers to form **molecules**.

Using this model we can understand how elements react together to make new substances called **compounds**. The atoms of the different elements combine to form covalent molecules of the compound. The compound water, for example, is formed when two hydrogen atoms combine with one oxygen atom to produce one water molecule. If we repeat the reaction on a larger scale with $2 \times 6.02 \times 10^{23}$ atoms of hydrogen and 6.02×10^{23} atoms of oxygen, 6.02×10^{23} molecules of water will be formed. This leads to the conclusion (see Chapter 1) that 2 g of hydrogen will react with 16 g of oxygen to form 18 g of water. This is one of the observations Dalton was trying to explain.

Dalton was the first person to assign chemical symbols to the different elements.

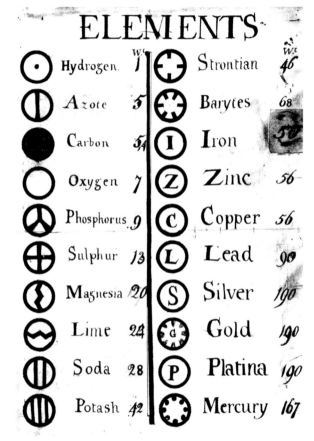

ELEMENTS

			w.t				w.t
⊙	Hydrogen	1		⊕	Strontian	46
	Azote	5			Barytes	68
●	Carbon	54	Ⓘ	Iron	50
○	Oxygen	7	Ⓩ	Zinc	56
	Phosphorus	9	Ⓒ	Copper	56
⊕	Sulphur	13	Ⓛ	Lead	90
	Magnesia	20	Ⓢ	Silver	190
	Lime	24		Gold	190
	Soda	28	Ⓟ	Platina	190
	Potash	42		Mercury	167

Following his example this can be written using modern notation:

$$2H + O \rightarrow H_2O$$

But what are atoms really like? It can be useful to think of them as hard spheres but this tells us little about how the atoms of different elements differ. To understand this, it is necessary to probe deeper.

'Dalton was a man of regular habits. For fifty-seven years… he measured the rainfall, the temperature… Of all that mass of data, nothing whatever came. But of the one searching, almost childlike question about the weights that enter the construction of simple molecules – out of that came modern atomic theory. That is the essence of science: ask an impertinent question: and you are on the way to the pertinent answer.' (J. Bronowski)
'What we observe is not nature itself but nature exposed to our mode of questioning.' (Werner Heisenberg)
How does the knowledge we gain about the natural world depend on the questions we ask and the experiments we perform?

The word 'molecule' comes from the Latin words for 'little mass'.

A compound is a substance made by chemically combining two or more elements.

John Dalton's symbols for the elements. It is now known that some of these substances are not elements but compounds. Lime for example is a compound of calcium and oxygen. Can you find any other examples?

A model of a water molecule made from two hydrogen atoms and one oxygen atom. Dalton's picture of the atom as a hard ball is the basis behind the molecular models we use today.

Sub-atomic particles

A hundred years or so after Dalton first proposed his model, experiments showed that atoms are themselves made up from smaller or **sub-atomic** particles. These particles are described by their *relative* masses and charges.

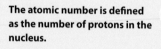

The masses and charges of sub-atomic particles are very small so it is simpler to consider only the relative values, which have no units.

Particle	Relative mass	Relative charge
proton	1	+
electron	0.0005	−
neutron	1	0

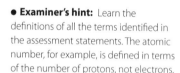

None of these sub-atomic particles can be (or ever will be) directly observed. Which ways of knowing do we use to interpret indirect evidence gained through the use of technology?

Atomic number and mass number

We are now in a position to understand how the atoms of different elements differ. They are all made from the same basic ingredients, the sub-atomic particles. The only difference is the recipe – how many of each of these sub-atomic particles are present in the atoms of different elements? If you look at the Periodic Table you will see that the elements are each given a number, which describes their relative position in the table. This is their **atomic number**. We now know that the atomic number is an important property. It tells us something about the structure of the atoms of the element. The atomic number is defined as the number of protons in the atom.

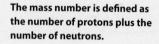

The atomic number is defined as the number of protons in the nucleus.

As an atom has no overall charge, the positive charge of the protons must be balanced by the negative charge of the electrons. The atomic number is also equal to the number of electrons.

● **Examiner's hint:** Learn the definitions of all the terms identified in the assessment statements. The atomic number, for example, is defined in terms of the number of protons, not electrons.

The electron has such a very small mass that it is essentially ignored in chemistry. The mass of an atom depends on the number of protons and neutrons only. The **mass number** is defined as the number of protons plus the number of neutrons. An atom is identified in the following way:

 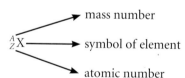

The mass number is defined as the number of protons plus the number of neutrons.

We can use these numbers to find the composition of any atom.

number of protons (p) = number of electrons = Z

number of neutrons (n) = A − number of protons = $A − Z$

Consider an atom of aluminium:

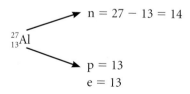

An aluminium atom is made from 13 protons and 13 electrons. An atom of gold on the other hand has 79 protons and 79 electrons. Can you find gold in the Periodic Table?

Structure of the atom

Ernest Rutherford (1871–1937) and his research team working at Manchester University in England showed that the atom is mostly empty space. Alpha particles which contain two protons and two neutrons were fired at a piece of gold foil. Most passed straight through, but a small number were repelled and bounced straight back. This led to the conclusion that the mass and positive charge of the atom, the protons and neutrons, are concentrated in a very small **nucleus**, with the electrons moving in orbits or energy levels around the nucleus. The arrangement of these energy levels is considered in more detail later in the chapter.

As you are made from atoms, you are also mainly empty space. The particles which make up your mass would occupy the same volume as a flea if they were all squashed together, but a flea with your mass. This gives you an idea of the density of the nucleus.

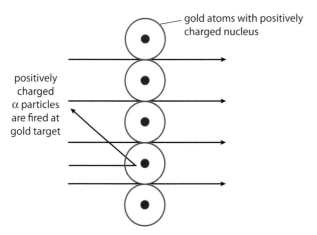

gold atoms with positively charged nucleus

positively charged α particles are fired at gold target

Figure 2.1 Fewer than one in 20 000 of the alpha particles were deflected back. Ernest Rutherford recalled that 'It was quite the most incredible thing that has happened to me. It was as if you had fired a (artillery) shell at a piece of tissue paper and it came back and hit you.'

See a simulation of Rutherford's experiment.
Now go to
www.heinemann.co.uk/hotlinks
insert the express code 4259P and click on this.

The fact that neutrons are not electrically charged is crucial for the stability of the nucleus. Without them, the protons would mutually repel each other as they have the same positive charge and the nucleus would fall apart.

Ions

The atomic number is defined in terms of number of protons because it is a fixed characteristic of the element. The number of protons identifies the element in the same way your fingerprints identify you. The number of protons and neutrons never changes during a chemical reaction. It is the electrons which are responsible for chemical change. Chapter 4 will examine how atoms can lose or gain electrons to form **ions**. When the number of protons is no longer balanced by the number of electrons, these particles have a non-zero charge. When an atom loses electrons it forms a positive ion or **cation** as the number of protons is now greater than the number of electrons. Negative ions or **anions** are formed when atoms gain electrons. The magnitude of the charge depends on the number of electrons lost or gained. The loss or gain of electrons makes a very big difference to the chemical properties. You swallow sodium ions, Na^+, every time you eat table salt, whereas as you will discover in Chapter 3 sodium atoms, Na, are dangerously reactive.

When an atom loses electrons, a positive ion is formed and when it gains electrons a negative ion is formed. Positive ions are called cations and negative ions are called anions.

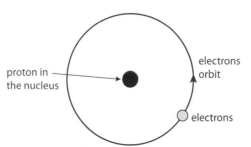

proton in the nucleus

electrons orbit

electrons

Figure 2.2 The simplest atom. Only one proton and one electron make up the hydrogen atom. The nuclear radius is 10^{-15} m and the atomic radius 10^{-10} m. Most of the volume of the atom is empty – the only occupant is the negatively charged electron. It is useful to think of the electrons orbiting the nucleus in a similar way to the planets orbiting the sun. The absence of a neutron is significant – it would be essentially redundant as there is only one proton.

An aluminium ion is formed when the atom loses three electrons. There is no change in the atomic or mass numbers of an ion because the number of protons and neutrons remains the same.

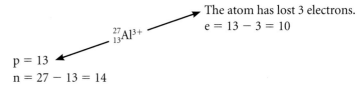

The atom has lost 3 electrons.
e = 13 − 3 = 10

$^{27}_{13}Al^{3+}$

p = 13
n = 27 − 13 = 14

Oxygen forms the oxide ion when the atom gains two electrons.

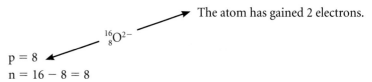

The atom has gained 2 electrons.

$^{16}_{8}O^{2-}$

p = 8
n = 16 − 8 = 8

Worked example

Identify the sub-atomic particles present in an atom of ^{226}Ra

The element radium was first discovered by the Polish–French scientist Marie Curie. She is the only person to win Nobel prizes in both physics and chemistry. The Curies were a remarkable family for scientific honours – Marie shared her first prize with husband Pierre, and her daughter Irène shared hers with her husband Frédéric. All the Curies' prizes were for work on radioactivity.

Solution

The number identifying the atom is the atomic number. We can find the atomic number from the IB Data booklet.
We have $Z = 88$ and $A = 226$
In other words, number of protons (p) = 88
number of electrons (e) = 88
number of neutrons (n) = 226 − 88 = 138

The Nobel Prize has been awarded to people and organizations every year since 1901, with a few exceptions such as during World War II. Alfred Nobel, the man behind the prize, invented dynamite and experimented with making synthetic rubber, leather and artificial silk. By the time of his death in 1896, he had acquired 355 patents. Play a game and find out about a Nobel Prize awarded for a discovery or work!
Now go to www.heinemann.co.uk/hotlinks, insert the express code 4259P and click on this activity.

Worked example

Most nutrient elements in food are present in the form of ions. The calcium ion $^{40}Ca^{2+}$ for example, is essential for healthy teeth and bones. Identify the sub-atomic particles present in the ion.

Solution

We can find the atomic number from the IB Data booklet.
We have $Z = 20$ and $A = 40$
i.e. number of protons (p) = 20
number of neutrons (n) = 40 − 20 = 20
As the ion has a positive charge of 2+ there are 2 more protons than electrons
number of electrons = 20 − 2 = 18

Worked example

Identify the species with 17 protons, 18 neutrons and 18 electrons.

Solution

The number of protons tells us the atomic number.
$Z = 17$ and the element is chlorine: Cl.
The mass number = p + n = 17 + 18 = 35: ^{35}Cl
The charge will be -1 as there is one extra electron: $^{35}_{17}Cl^-$.

Exercises

1 Use the Periodic Table to identify the sub-atomic particles present in the following species.

Species	No. of protons	No. of neutrons	No. of electrons
^7Li			
^1H			
^{14}C			
$^{19}F^-$			
$^{56}Fe^{3+}$			

2 Isoelectronic species have the same number of electrons. Identify the following isoelectronic species by giving the correct symbol and charge. You will need a Periodic Table.

The first one has been done as an example.

Species	No. of protons	No. of neutrons	No. of electrons
$^{40}Ca^{2+}$	20	20	18
	18	22	18
	19	20	18
	17	18	18

3 Which of the following species contain more electrons than neutrons?

A ^2_1H

B $^{11}_5B$

C $^{16}_8O^{2-}$

D $^{19}_9F^-$

Isotopes

Find chlorine in the Periodic Table. There are two numbers associated with the element.

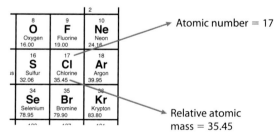

→ Atomic number = 17

→ Relative atomic mass = 35.45

How can an element have a fractional relative atomic mass if both the proton and neutron have a relative mass of 1? The reason is that atoms of the same element with different mass numbers exist and the Periodic Table gives the average values. To have different mass numbers the atoms must have different numbers of neutrons – both the atoms have the same number of protons as they are both chlorine atoms. Atoms of the same element with different numbers of neutrons are called **isotopes**.

 Isotopes are atoms of the same element with different mass numbers.

The isotopes show the same chemical properties, as a difference in the number of neutrons makes no difference to how they react and so they occupy the same place in the Periodic Table.

Chlorine exists as two isotopes, ^{35}Cl and ^{37}Cl. The average relative mass of the isotopes is however not 36, but 35.45. This value is closer to 35 as there are more ^{35}Cl atoms in nature – it is the more abundant isotope. In a sample of 100 chlorine atoms only 25 atoms of the heavier isotope would be present.

To work out the average mass of one atom we first have to calculate the total mass of the hundred atoms:

total mass = $(75 \times 35) + (25 \times 37) = 3550$

average mass = total mass/number of atoms = $\dfrac{3550}{100} = 35.5$

There is a more precise calculation later in the chapter.

The two isotopes are both atoms of chlorine with 17 protons and 17 electrons.
- ^{35}Cl; number of neutrons = $35 - 17 = 18$
- ^{37}Cl; number of neutrons = $37 - 17 = 20$

Although both isotopes essentially have the same chemical properties, the difference in mass does lead to different physical properties such as boiling and melting points. Heavier isotopes move more slowly at a given temperature and these differences can be used to separate isotopes.

The word 'isotope' derives from the Greek for 'same place'.

● **Examiner's hint:** A common error is to misunderstand the meaning of *physical property*. A difference in the number of neutrons is not a different physical property.

Exercise

4 State two physical properties other than boiling and melting point that would differ for the two isotopes of chlorine.

Uses of radioisotopes

The stability of a nucleus depends on the balance between the number of protons and neutrons. When a nucleus contains either too many or too few neutrons it changes to a more stable nucleus, by giving out radiation. This may be of several different forms which differ in ionization and penetration abilities. Alpha particles are composed of two protons and two neutrons, beta particles are electrons which have been ejected from the nucleus owing to neutron decay and gamma rays are a form of electromagnetic radiation (see page 43).

Radioactive isotopes can be used, for example, to:
- generate energy in nuclear power stations
- sterilize surgical instruments in hospitals
- preserve food
- fight crime
- detect cracks in structural materials.

They can be used either to kill or save human life.

Uranium exists in nature as two isotopes, uranium-235 and uranium-238. One key stage in the Manhatten project, which produced the first nuclear bomb, was the enrichment of uranium with the lighter and less abundant isotope as this is the atom which splits more easily. It is only 0.711% abundant in nature. First the uranium was converted to a gaseous compound (the hexafluoride UF_6). Gaseous molecules with the lighter uranium isotope move faster than those containing the heavier isotope at the same temperature and so the isotopes could be separated.

Carbon-14 dating

The most stable isotope of carbon ^{12}C has six protons and six neutrons. Carbon-14 has eight neutrons, which is too many to be stable. It can reduce the neutron-to-proton ratio when a neutron changes to a proton and an electron. The proton stays in the nucleus but the electron is ejected from the atom as a beta particle. (You do not need to worry about the details at this level.)

$$^{14}_{6}\text{C} \rightarrow {}^{14}_{7}\text{N} + {}^{0}_{-1}\text{e}$$

The relative abundance of carbon-14 present in living plants is constant as the carbon atoms are continually replenished from carbon present in carbon dioxide in the atmosphere. When organisms die, however, no more carbon-14 is absorbed and the levels of carbon-14 fall owing to nuclear decay. As this process occurs at a regular rate, it can be used to date carbon-containing materials. The rate of decay is measured by its **half-life**. This is the time taken for half the atoms to decay. The carbon-14 to carbon-12 ratio falls by 50% every 5730 years after the death of a living organism, a time scale which allows it to be used in the dating of archaeological objects.

Cobalt-60 used in radiotherapy

Radiotherapy, also called radiation therapy, is the treatment of cancer and other diseases with ionizing radiation. Cancerous cells are abnormal cells which divide at rapid rates to produce tumours that invade surrounding tissue. The treatment damages the genetic material inside a cell by knocking off electrons and making it impossible for the cell to grow. Although radiotherapy damages both cancer and normal cells, the normal cells are able to recover if the treatment is carefully controlled. Radiotherapy can treat localized solid tumours, such as cancers of the skin, tongue, larynx, brain, breast, or uterine cervix and cancers of the blood such as leukaemia. Cobalt-60 is commonly used as it emits very penetrating gamma radiation, when its protons and neutrons change their relative positions in the nucleus.

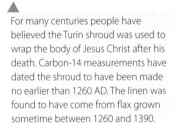

For many centuries people have believed the Turin shroud was used to wrap the body of Jesus Christ after his death. Carbon-14 measurements have dated the shroud to have been made no earlier than 1260 AD. The linen was found to have come from flax grown sometime between 1260 and 1390.

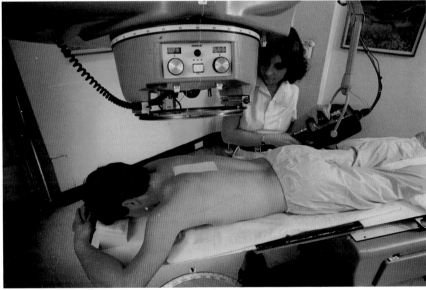

Cancer treatment with cobalt-60 gamma rays.

Iodine-131 as a medical tracer

Radioisotopes have the same chemical properties as any other atom of the same element and so they play the same role in the body. Their positions, unlike other isotopes, however, can be monitored by detecting radiation levels, making them suitable as medical tracers. Iodine-131, an emitter of both beta and gamma rays, can be used in the form of the compound sodium iodide to investigate the activity of the thyroid glands and diagnose and treat thyroid cancer. It has a short half-life of eight days so it is quickly eliminated from the body. Another isotope of iodine,

iodine-125, is used in the treatment of prostate cancer. Pellets of the isotope are implanted into the gland. It has a relatively longer half life of 80 days which allows low levels of beta radiation to be emitted over an extended period.

Despite the benefits, there are dangers arising from the use of unstable isotopes. Living organisms can be seriously affected if they are exposed to uncontrolled radiation which may result from excessive use in treatments or their release into the environment. There is a need for close international cooperation to ensure that the same high safety standards are applied both within and across borders.

2.2 The mass spectrometer

Principles of the mass spectrometer

The masses of the different isotopes and their relative abundance can be measured using a mass spectrometer.

Figure 2.3 A mass spectrometer can give information about the isotopic composition of different elements and the structure of molecules.

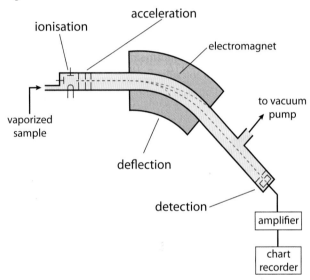

The mass spectrometer has five basic operations:
- **Vaporization**: A vaporized sample is injected into the instrument. This allows the individual atoms of the element to be analysed.
- **Ionization**: the atoms are hit with high energy electrons which knock out electrons producing positively charged ions:

$$X(g) + e^- \rightarrow X^+(g) + 2\ e^-$$

In practice, the instrument can be set up to produce only singly charged positive ions.
- **Acceleration**: the positive ions are attracted to negatively charged plates. They are accelerated by an **electric field** and pass through a hole in the plate.
- **Deflection**: the accelerated positive ions are deflected by a **magnetic field** placed at right angles to their path. The amount of deflection is proportional to the charge/mass ratio. Ions with smaller mass are deflected more than heavier ions. Ions with higher charges are deflected more as they interact more effectively with the magnetic field.
- **Detection**: positive ions of a particular mass/charge ratio are detected and a signal sent to a recorder. The strength of the signal is a measure of the number of ions with that charge/mass ratio that are detected.

The amount of deflection of an ion in a mass spectrometer is proportional to the charge/mass ratio.

Relative atomic masses of some elements

The mass spectrometer can be used to measure the mass of individual atoms. The mass of a hydrogen atom is 1.67×10^{-24} g and that of a carbon atom is 1.99×10^{-25} g. As the masses of all elements are in the range 10^{-24} to 10^{-22} g and these numbers are beyond our direct experience, it makes more sense to use relative values. The mass needs to be recorded relative to some agreed standard. As carbon is a very common element which is easy to transport and store because it is a solid, its isotope, ^{12}C, was chosen as the standard in 1961. This is given a relative mass of 12 exactly.

Element	Symbol	Relative atomic mass
carbon	C	12.011
chlorine	Cl	35.453
hydrogen	H	1.008
iron	Fe	55.845
carbon-12	^{12}C	12.000

Carbon-12 is the most abundant isotope of carbon but carbon-13 and carbon-14 also exist. This explains why the average value for the element is greater than 12.

Mass spectra

The results of the analysis by the mass spectrometer are presented in the form of a **mass spectrum**. The horizontal axis shows the mass/charge ratio of the different ions on the carbon-12 scale and the relative abundance of the ions is shown on the vertical axis.

The mass spectrum of gallium in Figure 2.4 shows that in a sample of 100 atoms, 60 have a mass of 69 and 40 have a mass of 71. We can use this information to calculate the relative atomic mass of the element.

total mass = $(60 \times 69) + (40 \times 71) = 6980$

average mass = total mass/number of atoms = $6980/100 = 69.80$

Worked example

Deduce the relative atomic mass of the element rubidium from the data given.

Solution

Consider a sample of 100 atoms.

total mass = $(85 \times 77) + (87 \times 23) = 8546$

relative atomic mass = average mass of atom

$$= \frac{\text{total mass}}{\text{number of atoms}}$$

$$= \frac{8546}{100} = 85.46$$

The relative atomic mass of an element (A_r) is the average mass of an atom of the element, taking into account all its isotopes and their relative abundance, compared to one atom of carbon-12.

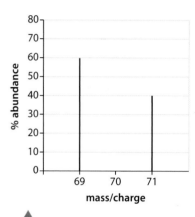

◀ Relative atomic masses of some elements compared to the carbon-12 standard.

▲ **Figure 2.4** Mass spectrum for gallium. The number of lines indicates the number of isotopes (two in this case), the value on the x axis indicates their mass number (69 and 71) and the y-axis shows the percentage abundance.

See a simulation of the mass spectrometer.
Now go to www.heinemann.co.uk/hotlinks, insert the express code 4259P and click on this activity.

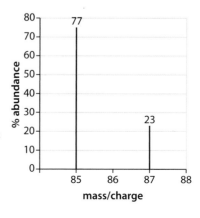

◀ **Figure 2.5** Mass spectrum for rubidium.

Worked example

Boron exists in two isotopic forms, ^{10}B and ^{11}B. ^{10}B is used as a control for nuclear reactors. Use your Periodic Table to find the abundances of the two isotopes.

Solution

Consider a sample of 100 atoms.

Let x atoms be ^{10}B atoms. The remaining atoms are ^{11}B.

number of ^{11}B atoms $= 100 - x$

total mass $= 10x + (100 - x)11 = 10x + 1100 - 11x = 1100 - x$

average mass $=$ total mass/number of atoms $= \dfrac{(1100 - x)}{100}$

From the Periodic Table

the relative atomic mass of boron $= 10.81$

$10.81 = \dfrac{(1100 - x)}{100}$

$1081 = 1100 - x$

$x = 1100 - 1081 = 19.00$

The abundances are $^{10}B = 19.00\%$ and $^{11}B = 81.00\%$

Exercises

5 Which ion would be deflected most in a mass spectrometer?

     A $^{35}Cl^+$ B $^{37}Cl^+$ C $^{37}Cl^{2+}$ D $(^{35}Cl^{37}Cl)^+$

6 What is the same for an atom of phosphorus-26 and at atom of phosphorus-27?

     A   atomic number and mass number   B   number of protons and electrons

     C   number of neutrons and electrons   D   number of protons and neutrons

7 Use the Periodic Table to find the percentage abundance of neon-20, assuming that neon has only one other isotope, neon-22.

In 1911, a 40 kg meteorite fell in Egypt. Isotopic and chemical analysis of oxygen extracted from this meteorite show a different relative atomic mass to that of oxygen normally found on Earth. This value matched measurements made of the Martian atmosphere by the Viking landing in 1976, proving that the meteorite had originated from Mars.

2.3   **Electron arrangement**

Some elements give out light of a distinctive colour when their compounds are heated in a flame or when an electric discharge is passed through their vapour. Our model of atomic structure is based on the analysis of light given out by the hydrogen atom.

Flame tests on the compounds of (a) sodium, (b) potassium and (c) copper.

 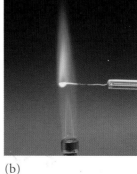 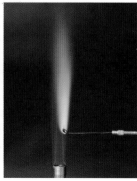

(a)   (b)   (c)

Flame colours can be used to identify unknown compounds. Now go to www.heinemann.co.uk/hotlinks, insert the express code 4259P and click on this activity.

To understand how the electrons are arranged in the atom we must consider the nature of electromagnetic radiation.

The electromagnetic spectrum

Electromagnetic radiation comes in different forms of differing energy. Gamma rays, as we have already discussed, are a particularly high energy form and the visible light we need to see the world is a lower energy form. All electromagnetic waves travel at the same speed (c) but can be distinguished by their different **wavelengths** (λ). Different colours of visible light have different wavelengths; red light, for example, has a longer wavelength than blue light.

 All electromagnetic waves travel at the same speed ($c = 3 \times 10^8 \, \mathrm{m\,s^{-1}}$). This is the cosmic speed limit, as according to Einstein's Theory of Relativity, nothing in the universe can travel faster than this.

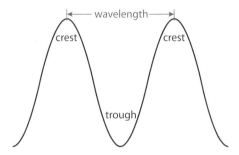

◀ **Figure 2.6** Snapshot of a wave at a given instant. The distance between successive crests or peaks is called the wavelength (λ)

The number of waves which pass a particular point in 1 s is called the **frequency** (f); the shorter the wavelength, the higher the frequency. Blue light has a higher frequency than red light.

The precise relation is $c = f\lambda$

White light is a mixture of light waves of differing wavelengths or colours. We see this when sunlight passes through a prism to produce a **continuous spectrum**.

 The distance between two successive crests (or troughs) is called the wavelength. The frequency of the wave is the number of waves which pass a point in one second. The wavelength and frequency are related by the equation $c = f\lambda$ where c is the speed of light.

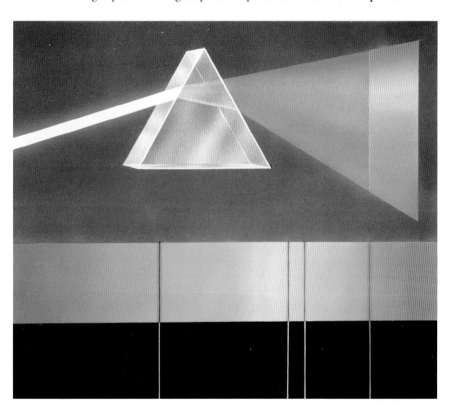

◀ A continuous spectrum is produced when white light is passed through a prism. The different colours merge smoothly into one another.

Visible light forms only a small part of the electromagnetic spectrum. Infrared waves have a longer wavelength than red light and ultraviolet waves a shorter wavelength than violet. The complete electromagnetic spectrum is shown overleaf.

Figure 2.7 The changing wavelength (in m) of electromagnetic radiation through the spectrum is shown by the trace across the top. At the short wavelength end (on the left) of the spectrum are gamma rays, X-rays and ultraviolet light. In the centre of the spectrum are wavelengths that the human eye can see, known as visible light. Visible light comprises light of different wavelengths, energies and colours. At the longer wavelength end of the spectrum (on the right) are infrared radiation, microwaves and radio waves. The visible spectrum gives us only a small window to see the world.

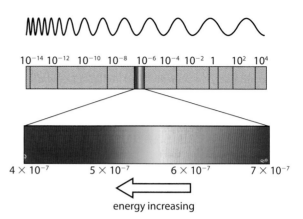

energy increasing

Visible emission spectrum of hydrogen. These lines form the Balmer series and you should note that they converge at higher energies. Similar series are found in the ultraviolet region – the Lyman Series and in the infrared region – the Paschen series.

Electromagnetic waves allow energy to be transferred across the universe. They also carry information. Low energy radio waves are used in radar and television, for example, and the higher energy gamma rays, as we have seen, are used as medical tracers. The precision with which we see the world is limited by the wavelengths of the colours we can see. This is why we will never be able to see an atom directly, as it is too small to interact with the relatively long waves of visible light. What are the implications of this for human knowledge?

The emission and absorption spectra are both the result of electron transitions. They can be used like barcodes to identify the different elements.
Now go to www.heinemann.co.uk/hotlinks, insert the express code 4259P and click on this activity.

Line spectra

When white light is passed through hydrogen gas, an **absorption** spectrum is produced. This is a **line spectrum** with some colours of the continuous spectrum missing. If a high voltage is applied to the gas, a corresponding **emission** line spectrum is produced.

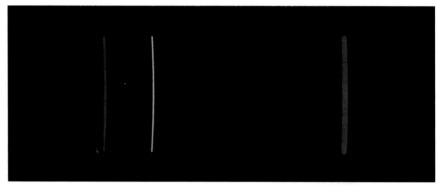

The colours present in the emission spectrum are the same as those that are missing from the absorption spectra. As different elements have different line spectra they can be used like barcodes to identify unknown elements. They give us valuable information about the arrangements of electrons in an atom.

The element helium was discovered in the Sun before it was found on Earth. Some unexpected spectral lines were observed when the absorption spectra of sunlight was analysed. These lines did not correspond to any known element. The new element was named after the Greek *helios* which means 'Sun'.

The hydrogen atom

How can a hydrogen atom absorb and emit energy? A simple picture of the atom was considered earlier with the electron orbiting the nucleus in a circular energy level. The Danish physicist Niels Bohr proposed that an electron moves into an orbit or higher energy level further from the nucleus when an atom absorbs energy. The **excited state** produced is however unstable and the electron soon falls back to the lowest level or **ground state**. The energy the electron gives out as it falls into lower levels is in the form of electromagnetic radiation. One packet of energy (quantum) or **photon**, is released for each electron transition. Photons of ultraviolet light have more energy than photons of infrared light. The energy of the photon is proportional to the frequency of the radiation.

The energy of the photon of light emitted is equal to the energy change in the atom: $\Delta E_{\text{electron}} = E_{\text{photon}}$

It is also related to the frequency of the radiation by Planck's equation: $E_{\text{photon}} = hf$. (This equation and the value of h (Planck's constant) are given in the IB Data booklet).

This leads to $\Delta E_{\text{electron}} = hf$

This is a very significant equation as it shows that line spectra allow us to glimpse the inside of the atom. The atoms emit photons of certain energies and lines of certain frequencies, because the electron can only occupy certain orbits. The energy levels can be thought of as a staircase. The electron cannot change its energy in a continuous way, in the same way that you cannot stand between steps, but can only change its energy by discrete amounts. This energy of the atom is quantized.

The hydrogen spectrum

The hydrogen atom gives out energy when an electron falls from a higher to a lower energy level. Hydrogen produces visible light when the electron falls to the second energy level ($n = 2$). The transitions to the first energy level correspond to a higher energy change and are in the ultraviolet region of the spectrum. Infrared radiation is produced when an electron falls to the third or higher energy levels.

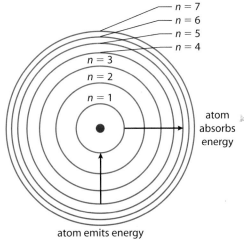

The pattern of the lines gives us a picture of the energy levels in the atom. The lines converge at higher energies because the energy levels inside the atoms are closer together. When an electron is at the highest energy $n = \infty$, it is no longer in the atom and the atom has been ionized. The energy needed to remove an electron from the ground state of each atom in a mole of gaseous atoms, ions or molecules is called the **ionization energy**. Ionization energies can also be used to support this model of the atom (see page 47).

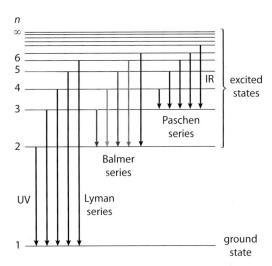

> The idea that electromagnetic waves can be thought of as a stream of photons or quanta is one aspect of quantum theory. The theory has implications for human knowledge and human technology. The key idea is that energy can only be transferred in discrete amounts or quanta. Quantum theory shows us that our everyday experience cannot be transferred to the microscopic world of the atom and has led to great technological breakthroughs such as the modern computer. It has been estimated that 30% of the gross national product of the USA depends on the applications of quantum theory.

◄ **Figure 2.8** When an electron is excited from a lower to a higher energy level, energy is absorbed and a line in the absorption spectrum is produced. When a electron falls from a higher to a lower energy level, radiation is given out by the atom and a line in the emission spectrum is produced.

> **The energy of a photon of electromagnetic radiation is directly proportional to its frequency and inversely proportional to its wavelength. It can be calculated from Planck's equation $E = hf$ given in the IB Data booklet.**

◄ **Figure 2.9** Energy levels of the hydrogen atom showing the transitions which produce the Lyman, Balmer and Paschen series. The transition $1 \rightarrow \infty$ corresponds to ionization:
$$H(g) \rightarrow H^+(g) + e^-.$$

> **The ionization energy is the minimum energy needed to remove an electron from the ground state of a gaseous atom, ion or molecule.**

How do the different electron transitions in the hydrogen atom produce lines of different energies? Now go to www.heinemann.co.uk/hotlinks, insert the express code 4259P and click on this activity.

● **Examiner's hint:** When asked to distinguish between a line and a continuous spectrum, answers have to be in terms of discrete energy levels or all colours/wavelengths/frequencies.

Building atoms

The chemical properties of an atom are dependent on the way its electrons are arranged. We are now in a position to explore the structures of the atoms beyond hydrogen. Building the atoms of these elements is like stacking a bookcase. Each energy level can hold a limited number of electrons. Electrons are placed in the lower energy level first and when this becomes complete we move on to the second energy level and so on. The helium atom $^4_2$He has two protons, two neutrons and two electrons. The protons and neutrons form the nucleus and the two electrons both occupy the lowest energy level.

The first energy level is now full as it can only hold two electrons. For the atom of the next element, lithium, we must use the second energy level.

Ne 2,8

▲ **Figure 2.12** The nucleus can be represented as a circle with the chemical symbol. Note the electrons in the second shell are shown in pairs. This makes it easy to count them. The electron arrangement is 2, 8.

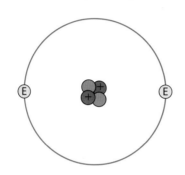

▲ **Figure 2.10** The helium atom. The two neutrons allow the two protons, which repel each other, to stay in the nucleus.

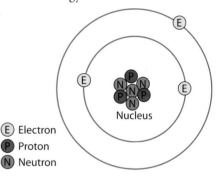

E Electron
P Proton
N Neutron

▲ **Figure 2.11** The lithium atom. There are two electrons in the first energy level and one in the second. This can be summarized by the shorthand 2, 1.

▲ **Figure 2.13** The electron arrangement for sodium is 2, 8, 1.

As the circumference of the second shell is larger than the first it can hold more mutually repelling electrons. There is space for a maximum of eight electrons in the second level. The number of electrons in the outer energy level increases by one for successive elements until a complete energy level is reached for an atom of neon.

Now for sodium we need to use the third energy level.

Although the picture becomes more complicated for higher elements, this method can be followed to find the electron arrangement for elements up to and including calcium. The third energy level also becomes full when it has eight electrons at argon and the fourth energy level starts to fill at potassium. Potassium has the electron arrangement 2,8,8,1 and calcium is 2,8,8,2.

▶ Electron arrangements of the first 20 elements.

Element	Electron arrangement	Element	Electron arrangement
H	1	Na	2, 8, 1
He	2	Mg	2, 8, 2
Li	2,1	Al	2, 8, 3
Be	2, 2	Si	2, 8, 4
B	2, 3	P	2, 8, 5
C	2, 4	S	2, 8, 6
N	2, 5	Cl	2, 8, 7
O	2, 6	Ar	2, 8, 8
F	2, 7	K	2, 8, 8, 1
Ne	2, 8	Ca	2, 8, 8, 2

The outer electrons are sometimes called **valence electrons**. The number of outer electrons follows a periodic pattern. See Chapter 3 for the full implications of this.

Patterns in successive ionization energy

Additional evidence for this description comes from looking at patterns of successive ionization energies. The first ionization energy is the energy needed to remove one mole of electrons from the ground state of one mole of the gaseous atom. For example, for aluminium we have:

$$Al(g) \rightarrow Al^+(g) + e^-$$

The second ionization energy corresponds to the change:

$$Al^+(g) \rightarrow Al^{2+}(g) + e^- \text{ and so on.}$$

The ionization energies for aluminium are shown below and they follow a similar 2, 8, 3 pattern to the electron arrangement.

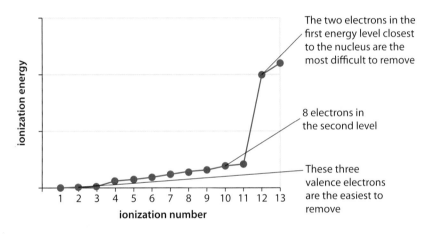

The two electrons in the first energy level closest to the nucleus are the most difficult to remove

8 electrons in the second level

These three valence electrons are the easiest to remove

This graph shows two key points.
- There is an increase in successive ionization energies. The first ionization energy involves the separation of an electron from a singly charged ion and the second the separation of an electron from a doubly charged ion. The process becomes more difficult as there is increasing attraction between the higher charged positive ions and the oppositely charged electron.
- There are jumps when electrons are removed from levels closer to the nucleus. The first three ionization energies involve the removal of electrons from the third level. An electron is removed from the second level for the fourth ionization energy. This electron is closer to the nucleus and is more exposed to the positive charge of the nucleus. It needs significantly more energy to be removed.

Ion	Electron arrangement	Energy level from which electron is removed when ionized
Al	2, 8, 3	third
Al$^+$	2, 8, 2	third
Al^{2+}	2, 8, 1	third
Al^{3+}	2, 8	second

Figure 2.14 Successive ionization energies for aluminium. Note the jumps between the 3rd and 4th and the 11th and 12th ionization energies as electrons are removed from lower energy levels.

What is the pattern in ionization energy for the other elements? Choose an element from the Periodic Table, and then find the link to ionization energies on the left hand margin.
Now go to www.heinemann.co.uk/hotlinks, insert the express code 4259P and click on this activity.

A number of people have played a part in the development of our understanding of the atom. Which qualities of the IB Learner Profile were the key to their contribution? The atomic model presented here is still not complete. Which qualities of the learner profile do you need to deepen your understanding of this topic?

Which of Dalton's five proposals (see p. 32) do we now hold to be 'true'? How does scientific knowledge change with time? Are the models and theories of science accurate descriptions of the natural world, or just useful interpretations to help predict and explain the natural world?

● **Examiner's hint:** Make sure that you understand the command term used in the examination question. *Deduce* means you are expected to make use of the information you are given and explain the reasons for a given result.

Worked example

1 Which is not a valid electron arrangement?
   A 2, 8   B 2, 3   C 2, 7, 2   D 2, 8, 8, 1

2 Deduce the electron arrangement of the Na^+ and O^{2-} ions.

Solution

1 C. Electrons fill the energy levels in order so an atom with 11 electrons would first fill the second level (8 electrons) before filling the third.

2 The Periodic Table shows that a sodium atom has 11 electrons. It forms a positive ion by losing one electron: 2, 8.

   An oxygen atom has 8 electrons and the electron arrangement 2, 6. It forms the oxide ion by gaining two electrons: 2, 8.

Exercise

8 How many energy levels are occupied when silicon is in its ground state?
   A 2   B 3   C 4   D 8

Practice questions

1 How many valence electrons are present in an atom of an element with atomic number 16?
   A 2   B 4   C 6   D 8

© International Baccalaureate Organization [2004]

2 Consider the composition of the species W, X, Y and Z below. Which species is an anion?

Species	Number of protons	Number of neutrons	Number of electrons
W	9	10	10
X	11	12	11
Y	12	12	12
Z	13	14	10

A W   B X   C Y   D Z

© International Baccalaureate Organization [2003]

3 Which statement is correct for the emission spectrum of the hydrogen atom?
   A The lines converge at lower energies.
   B The lines are produced when electrons move from lower to higher energy levels.
   C The lines in the visible region involve electron transitions into the energy level closest to the nucleus.
   D The line corresponding to the greatest emission of energy is in the ultraviolet region.

© International Baccalaureate Organization [2003]

4 What is the correct sequence for the processes occurring in a mass spectrometer?
   A vaporization, ionization, acceleration, deflection
   B vaporization, acceleration, ionization, deflection
   C ionization, vaporization, acceleration, deflection
   D ionization, vaporization, deflection, acceleration

© International Baccalaureate Organization [2003]

5 **(a)** Evidence for the existence of energy levels in atoms is provided by line spectra. State how a line spectrum differs from a continuous spectrum. (1)

(b) On the diagram below draw four lines in the visible line spectrum of hydrogen. (1)

$$\vdash\!\!-\!\!\dashv$$

Low energy   High energy

(c) Explain how the formation of lines indicates the presence of energy levels. (1)

(*Total 3 marks*)

© International Baccalaureate Organization [2004]

6 The diagram below (not to scale) represents some of the electron energy levels in the hydrogen atom.

———————————————————— $n = \infty$
———————————————————— $n = 6$
———————————————————— $n = 5$

———————————————————— $n = 4$

———————————————————— $n = 3$

———————————————————— $n = 2$

———————————————————— $n = 1$

(a) Draw an arrow on the diagram to represent the electron transition for the ionization of hydrogen. Label this arrow A. (2)

(b) Draw an arrow on the diagram to represent the lowest energy transition in the visible emission spectrum. Label this arrow B. (2)

(*Total 4 marks*)

© International Baccalaureate Organization [2003]

7 **(a)** Define the term *isotope*. (2)

(b) A sample of argon exists as a mixture of three isotopes.
- mass number 36, relative abundance 0.337%
- mass number 38, relative abundance 0.0630%
- mass number 40, relative abundance 99.6%

Calculate the relative atomic mass of argon. (2)

(c) State the number of electrons, protons and neutrons in the ion $^{56}Fe^{3+}$. (2)

electrons: protons: neutrons:

(*Total 6 marks*)

© International Baccalaureate Organization [2004]

8 **(a)** State a physical property that is different for isotopes of an element. (1)

(b) Chlorine exists as two isotopes, ^{35}Cl and ^{37}Cl. The relative atomic mass of chlorine is 35.45. Calculate the percentage abundance of each isotope. (2)

© International Baccalaureate Organization [2003]

9 **(a)** State the full electron arrangement for argon. (1)

(b) Give the formulas of **two** oppositely charged ions which have the same electron configuration as argon. (2)

(*Total 6 marks*)

© International Baccalaureate Organization [2004]

3 Periodicity

The Periodic Table is the 'map' of chemistry; it suggests new avenues of research for the professional chemist and is a guide for students, as it disentangles a mass of observations and reveals hidden order. Chemistry is not the study of a random collection of elements, but of the trends and patterns in their chemical and physical properties.

Mendeleyev grouped the known elements into families, leaving gaps corresponding to elements that should exist but which had not yet been discovered.

Mendeleyev is said to have made his discovery after a dream. When he awoke he set out his chart in virtually its final form. He enjoyed playing a form of patience (solitaire) and wrote the properties of each element on cards which he arranged into rows and columns.

The Periodic Table is a remarkable demonstration of the order of the subject. It was first proposed in 1869 by the Russian chemist Dmitri Mendeleyev. Previous attempts had been made to impose order on the then known 62 elements, but Mendeleyev had the insight to realize that each element has its allotted place, so he left gaps where no known elements fitted into certain positions. As a scientific idea it was extremely powerful as it made predictions about the unknown elements which fitted these gaps and which could be tested. When these were later discovered, the agreement between the predicted properties and the actual properties was remarkable.

Mendeleyev's Periodic Table of 1869. The noble gas elements had not been discovered. Reading from top to bottom and left to right, the first four gaps awaited scandium (1879), gallium (1875), germanium (1886) and technetium (1937).

				K = 39	Rb = 85	Cs = 133	—	—
				Ca = 40	Sr = 87	Ba = 137	—	—
				—	?Yt = 88?	?Di = 138?	Er = 178?	—
				Ti = 48?	Zr = 90	Ce = 140?	?La = 180?	Tb = 231
				V = 51	Nb = 94	—	Ta = 182	—
				Cr = 52	Mo = 96	—	W = 184	U = 240
				Mn = 55	—	—	—	—
Typische Elemente				Fe = 56	Ru = 104	—	Os = 195?	—
				Co = 59	Rh = 104	—	Ir = 197	—
				Ni = 59	Pd = 106	—	Pt = 198?	—
H = 1	Li = 7	Na = 23	Cu = 63	Ag = 108	—	Au = 199?	—
	Be = 9,4	Mg = 24	Zn = 65	Cd = 112	—	Hg = 200	—
	B = 11	Al = 27,3	—	In = 113	—	Tl = 204	—
	C = 12	Si = 28	—	Sn = 118	—	Pb = 207	—
	N = 14	P = 31	As = 75	Sb = 122	—	Bi = 208	—
	O = 16	S = 32	Se = 78	Te = 125?	—	—	—
	F = 19	Cl = 35,5	Br = 80	J = 127	—	—	—

What is the role of imagination and creativity in the sciences? To what extent might the formulation of a hypothesis be comparable to imagining and creating a work of art?

Which attributes of the IB Learner Profile are demonstrated by Mendeleyev's work on the Periodic Table?

Mendeleyev had no knowledge of the structure of the atom discussed in Chapter 2. With the benefit of hindsight it is clear that the periodicity of the elements is a direct consequence of the periodicity of the electron arrangements within the atom.

Assessment statements

3.1 The Periodic Table

3.1.1 Describe the arrangement of elements in the Periodic Table in order of increasing atomic number.

3.1.2 Distinguish between the terms *group* and *period*.

3.1.3 Apply the relationship between the electron arrangement of elements and their position in the Periodic Table up to $Z = 20$.

3.1.4 Apply the relationship between the number of electrons in the highest occupied energy level for an element and its position in the Periodic Table.

3.2 Physical properties

3.2.1 Define the terms *first ionization energy* and *electronegativity*.

3.2.2 Describe and explain the trends in atomic radii, ionic radii, first ionization energies, electronegativities and melting points for the alkali metals (Li→Cs) and the halogens (F→I).

3.2.3 Describe and explain the trends in atomic radii, ionic radii, first ionization energies and electronegativities for elements across Period 3.

3.2.4 Compare the relative electronegativity values of two or more elements based on their positions in the Periodic Table.

3.3 Chemical properties

3.3.1 Discuss the similarities and differences in the chemical properties of elements in the same group.

3.3.2 Discuss the changes in nature, from ionic to covalent and from basic to acidic, of the oxides across Period 3.

3.1 The Periodic Table

Periods and groups

If you have visited a large supermarket you will appreciate the importance of a classification system. Similar products are grouped together to help you find what you want. In the same way a chemist knows what type of element to find in different parts of the Periodic Table. The elements are placed in order of increasing atomic number (A), which we now know is a fundamental property of the element – the number of protons in the nucleus of its atoms. As there are no missing atomic numbers we can be confident that the search for new elements in nature is over.

The only way to extend the Periodic Table is by making elements artificially. Today there are over 110 elements recognized by the International Union of Pure and Applied Chemistry (IUPAC). The columns of the table are called **groups** and the rows **periods**.

In the IB Data booklet Periodic Table the main groups are numbered from 1 to 7, with the last column on the far right labelled '0'. The gap between Group 2 and Group 3 is filled by **transition elements** from the fourth period onwards.

The position of an element is related to the electron arrangement in its atom. The element sodium, for example, is in Period 3 as it has three occupied energy levels and in Group 1 as there is one electron in the outer shell.

 IUPAC is an international, non-governmental body with a membership made up of chemists which has the aim of fostering worldwide communication in chemistry.

Figure 3.1 The Periodic Table. The 'island' of elements from Ce – Lu and from Th – Lr is of little interest at this level.

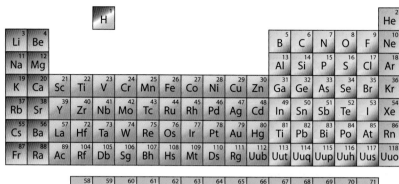

The columns in the Periodic Table are called groups. The group number gives the number of electrons in the outer shell. The rows in the Periodic Table are called periods. The period number gives the number of occupied electron shells.

The group number gives the number of electrons in the outer energy level (valence electrons). The period number gives the number of energy levels occupied. The electron arrangement of helium is exceptional and should be noted.

The discovery of the elements was an international endeavour. This is illustrated by some of their names. Some derive from the place where they were made, some derive from the origins of their discoverers and some derive from the geographical origins of the minerals from which they were first isolated. The Periodic Table of chemical elements hangs in front of chemistry classrooms and in science laboratories throughout the world.

Four elements derive their name from a small town Yttrium just outside Stockholm. Try to find their names.

Element	Period	Group	Electron arrangement
helium	1	0	2
lithium	2	1	2, 1
carbon	2	4	2, 4
aluminium	3	3	2,8, 3
chlorine	3	7	2, 8, 7
potassium	4	1	2, 8, 8, 1
calcium	4	2	2, 8, 8, 2

Although the model of electron arrangement discussed in Chapter 2 only works for the first 20 elements, the number of electrons in the outer shell of elements with higher atomic numbers can be deduced from the group number for all the elements.

Worked example

How many electrons are in the outer shell of iodine?

Solution

Find the element in the Periodic Table. It is Group 7 so it has seven electrons in its outer shell.

Exercises

1 Use the IB Periodic Table to identify the position of the following elements.

Element	Period	Group
helium		
chlorine		
barium		
francium		

2 Phosphorus is in Period 3 and Group 5 of the Periodic Table.
  (a) Distinguish between the terms period and group.
  (b) State the electron arrangement of phosphorus and relate it to its position in the Periodic Table.

3 How many valence (outer shell) electrons are present in the atoms of the element with atomic number 51?

Physical properties

The periodicity of the elements is reflected in their physical properties. The atomic and ionic radii, electronegativity and ionization energy are of particular interest as they explain the periodicity of the chemical properties.

Effective nuclear charge

The **nuclear charge** of the atom is given by the atomic number and so increases by one between successive elements in the table, as a proton is added to the nucleus. The outer electrons which determine many of the physical and chemical properties of the atom do not however experience the full attraction of this charge as they are **shielded** from the nucleus and repelled by the inner electrons. The **effective charge** is less than the full nuclear charge.

Consider the first four elements in Period 3 for example.

Element	Na	Mg	Al	Si
nuclear charge	11	12	13	14
electron arrangement	2, 8, 1	2, 8 2	2, 8, 3	2, 8, 4

As a period is crossed from left to right, one proton is added to the nucleus and one electron is added to the outer electron shell. The effective charge increases with the nuclear charge as there is no change in the number of inner electrons.

The changes down a group can be illustrated by considering the elements in Group 1.

Element	Nuclear charge	Electron arrangement
Li	3	2, 1
Na	11	2, 8, 1
K	19	2, 8, 8, 1

As we descend the group, the increase in the nuclear charge is largely offset by the increase in the number of inner electrons; both increase by eight between successive elements.

Atomic radius

The concept of atomic radius is not as straightforward as you may think as atoms are not hard spheres. For our purposes, however, it can be considered as the distance from the nucleus to the outermost electrons.

Table 8 in the IB Data booklet shows that atomic radii increase down a group and decrease across a period. To explain the trend down a group consider, for example, the Group 1 elements.

See different Periodic Table formats. Now go to www.heinemann.co.uk/hotlinks, insert the express code 4259P and click on this activity.

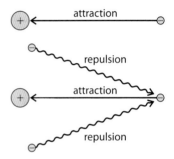

▲ **Figure 3.2** An electron in the hydrogen atom experiences the full attraction of the nuclear charge, but in a many-electron atom the attraction for the nucleus is reduced as the outer electron is repelled by inner electrons.

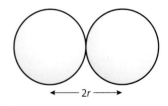

▲ **Figure 3.3** The atomic radius r is measured as half the distance between neighbouring nuclei.

The atomic radii of the Group 1 elements increase as we descend the group owing to the increase in number of electron shells.

Element	Electron arrangement	No. of occupied shells	Radius/nm	
Li	2, 1	2	0.152	
Na	2, 8, 1	3	0.186	
K	2, 8, 8, 1	4	0.231	
Rb	2, 8, 8,.., 1	5	0.244	
Cs	2, 8, 8,..,.., 1	6	0.262	

The atomic radii of the noble gases are not given in Table 8 of the IB Data booklet. Their inter-nuclei distances are difficult to measure as noble gases do not generally bond to other atoms.

The atomic radii increase down a group as the number of occupied electron shells, given by the period number, increases. The trend across a period is illustrated by the Period 3 elements.

Atomic radii of elements in Period 3. There is a significant decrease in size. A chlorine atom has a radius which is about half the size of a sodium atom.

Element	Na	Mg	Al	Si	P	S	Cl	Ar
atomic radius/10^{-12} m	186	160	143	117	110	104	99	–

All these elements have three occupied energy levels so there is a general decrease in atomic radii across the period. The attraction between the nucleus and the outer electrons increases as the nuclear charge increases.

Ionic radius

The atomic and ionic radii of the Period 3 elements are shown in the table below.

Atomic and ionic radii for the elements in Period 3.

Element	Na	Mg	Al	Si	P	S	Cl
atomic radius/10^{-12} m	186	160	143	117	110	104	99
ionic radius/10^{-12} m	98 (1+)	65 (2+)	45 (3+)	42 (4+); 271(4−)	212 (3−)	190 (2−)	181 (1−)

Five trends can be identified:
- Positive ions are smaller than their parent atoms.
  The formation of positive ions involves the loss of the outer shell. Na for example is 2, 8, 1 whereas Na^+ is 2, 8.
- Negative ions are larger than their parent atoms.
  The formation of negative ions involves the addition of electrons into the outer shell. Cl for example is 2, 8, 7 and Cl^- is 2, 8, 8. The increased electron repulsion between the electrons in the outer shell causes the electrons to move further apart and so increases the radius of the outer shell.
- The ionic radii decrease from groups 1 to 4 for the positive ions. The ions Na^+, Mg^{2+}, Al^{3+} and Si^{4+} all have the same electron arrangement 2, 8. The decrease in ionic radius is due to the increase in nuclear charge with atomic number across the period. The increased attraction between the nucleus and the electrons pulls the outer shell closer to the nucleus.

- The ionic radii decrease from groups 4 to 7 for the negative ions. The ions Si^{4-}, P^{3-}, S^{2-} and Cl^- have the same electron arrangement 2, 8, 8. The decrease in ionic radius is due to the increase in nuclear charge across the period, as explained above.
- The positive ions are smaller than the negative ions, as the former have only two occupied electron shells and the latter have three. This explains the big difference between the ionic radii of the Si^{4+} and Si^{4-} ions and the discontinuity in the middle of the table.

The ionic radii increase down a group as the number of electron shells increases.

Worked example

Describe and explain the trend in radii of the following species:

$$O^{2-}, F^-, Ne, Na^+ \text{ and } Mg^{2+}.$$

Solution

The ions have 10 electrons and the electron arrangement 2, 8. The nuclear charges increase with atomic number: O: $Z = +8$, F: $Z = +9$, Ne: $Z = +10$, Na: $Z = +11$ and Mg: $Z = +12$. The increase in nuclear charge results in increased attraction between the nucleus and the outer electrons. The ionic radii decrease as the atomic number increases.

The following animation illustrates atomic and ionic radii.
Now go to www.heinemann.co.uk/hotlinks, insert the express code 4259P and click on this activity.

Ionization energies

First ionization energies are a measure of the attraction between the nucleus and the outer electrons. They were defined in Chapter 2, where patterns in successive ionization energies of the same element provided evidence for the electron arrangement of the atom.

The first ionization energy of an element is the energy required to remove one mole of electrons from one mole of gaseous atoms.

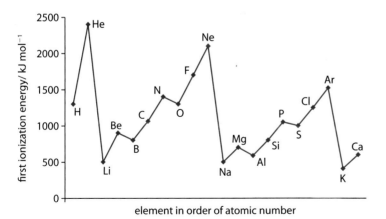

Figure 3.4 First ionization energies of the first 20 elements.

Two general trends can be identified from Fig 3.4:
- Ionization energies increase across a period. The increase in nuclear charge causes an increase in the attraction between the outer electrons and the nucleus and makes the electrons more difficult to remove.
- Ionization energies decrease down a group. The electron removed is from an electron shell furthest from the nucleus. Although the nuclear charges increase, the effective nuclear charge is about the same, owing to shielding of the inner electrons, and so the increased distance between the electron and the nucleus reduces the attraction between them.

The trend in ionization energy is the reverse of the trend in atomic radii. Both trends are an indication of the attraction between the nucleus for the outer electrons.

Electronegativity

Electronegativity is a term related to ionization energy as it is also a measure of the attraction between the nucleus and its outer electrons – in this case *bonding electrons.*

Electronegativity is the ability of an atom to attract electrons in a covalent bond.

An element with a high electronegativity has strong electron pulling power and an element with a low elctronegativity has weak pulling power. The concept was originally devised by the American chemist Linus Pauling and his values are given in the IB Data booklet. The general trends are the same as those for ionization energy:

- Electronegativity increases from left to right across a period owing to the increase in nuclear charge, resulting in an increased attraction between the nucleus and the bond electrons.

- Electronegativity decreases down a group. The bond electrons are furthest from the nucleus and so there is reduced attraction.

The most electronegative element is on the top right of the Periodic Table and the least electronegative element on the bottom left. As the concept does not apply to the group 0 elements which do not form covalent bonds, Pauling assigned the highest value of 4.0 to fluorine and the lowest value to of 0.7 to caesium.

Linus Pauling has the unique distinction of winning two *unshared* Nobel Prizes – one for Chemistry in 1954 and one for Peace in 1962. His Chemistry Prize was for improving our understanding of the chemical bond and his Peace Prize was for his campaign against nuclear weapons testing.

Although the general trends in ionization energy and electronegativity are the same, they are distinct properties. Ionization energies can be measured directly and are a property of gaseous atoms. Electronegativity is a property of an atom in a molecule and values are derived indirectly from experimental data.

Melting points

Comparisons between melting points of different elements are more complex as they depend on both the type of bonding and the structure (see Chapter 4). Trends down groups 1 and 7 can, however, be explained simply, as the elements within each group bond in similar ways.

Melting points of the group 1 and group 7 elements.

Element	Melting point (K)	Element	Melting point (K)
Li	454	F_2	54
Na	371	Cl_2	172
K	337	Br_2	266
Rb	312	I_2	387
Cs	302	At_2	575

See caesium melt. Now go to www.heinemann.co.uk/hotlinks, insert the express code 4259P and click on this activity.

Melting points decrease down Group 1. The elements have metallic structures which are held together by attractive forces between a delocalized outer electron and the positively charged ion. This attraction decreases with distance.

Melting points increase down Group 7. The elements have molecular structures which are held together by van der Waals intermolecular forces. These increase with the number of electrons in the molecule.

The melting points generally rise across a period and reach a maximum at Group 4. They then fall to reach a minimum at group 0. In Period 3, for example, the bonding changes from metallic (Na, Mg and Al) to giant covalent (Si) to weak van der Waals' attraction between simple molecules (P_4, S_8, Cl_2) and single atoms (Ar). All the Period 3 elements are solids at room temperature except chlorine and argon.

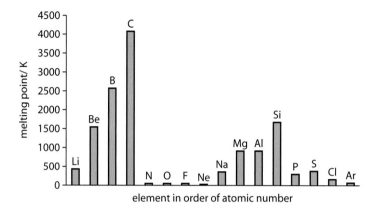

Figure 3.5 The melting points show a periodic pattern as the bonding changes from metallic, to giant covalent, to simple molecular.

Use a database from the Internet to investigate trends and variations in physical properties using a spreadsheet.
Now go to
www.heinemann.co.uk/hotlinks, insert the express code 4259P and click on this activity.

Exercises

4 Explain why sulfur has a higher melting point than phosphorus.

5 Which physical property generally increases down a group but decreases from left to right across a period?
  A melting point
  B electronegativity
  C ionization energy
  D atomic radius

6 The elements in the Periodic Table are arranged in order of increasing:
  A relative atomic mass
  B ionic radii
  C nuclear charge
  D ionization energy

7 What is the order of decreasing radii for the species Cl, Cl^+ and Cl^-?

8 Which one of the following elements has the highest electronegativity?
  A Be
  B Cl
  C Ca
  D Br

No one knows how high the atomic number of the elements will go, but it is expected that all new elements will fit into the current scheme. Could there ever be an 'end' to science? Could we reach a point where everything important in a scientific sense is known?

Here is another visual database of physical and thermochemical properties of the chemical elements.
Now go to
www.heinemann.co.uk/hotlinks, insert the express code 4259P and click on this activity.

3.3 Chemical properties

The chemical properties of an element are determined by the electron arrangement in its atoms. Elements of the same group have similar chemical properties as they have the same number of electrons in their outer shells. The alkali metals in Group 1, for example, all have one electron in their outer shell and the halogens in Group 7 have seven outer electrons. The trends in their chemical properties in a group can be accounted for by the trends in their physical properties discussed earlier.

Chemical properties of an element are largely determined by the number of electrons in the outer shell.

Group 0: the noble gases

To understand the reactivity of the elements it is instructive to consider Group 0 which contains the least reactive elements – the noble gases. This chemically aloof family of elements was only discovered at the end of the 19th century after Mendeleyev first published his table.

- They are colourless gases.
- They are monatomic; they exist as single atoms.
- They are very unreactive.

Their lack of reactivity can be explained by the inability of their atoms to lose or gain electrons. They have the highest ionization energies and extra electrons would have to be added to an empty outer shell where they would experience a negligible effective nuclear force, with the protons shielded by an equal number of inner electrons. With the exception of helium, they have complete outer shells of eight electrons; a **stable octet**.

Helium has a complete first shell of two electrons. The reactivity of elements in other groups can be explained by their unstable incomplete electron shells. They lose or gain electrons so as to achieve the electron arrangement of their nearest noble gas.

Elements in Groups 1 to 3 lose electrons to adopt the arrangement of the nearest noble gas with a lower atomic number. They are generally metals. Elements in Groups 5 to 7 gain electrons to adopt the electron arrangement of the nearest noble gas on their right in the Periodic Table. They are generally non-metals. Some elements in the middle of the table show intermediate properties and are called metalloids.

Group 0 used to be called the inert gases as it was thought that they were completely unreactive. No compounds of helium, neon or argon have ever been found. The first compound of xenon was made in 1962 and compounds of krypton have now been prepared. The most reactive element in the group has the lowest ionization energy as reactions involve the withdrawal of electrons from the parent atom.

Group 1: the alkali metals

All the elements are silvery metals that are too reactive to be found in nature and are usually stored in oil. The properties of the first three elements are summarized in the table.

Physical properties	Chemical properties
<ul><li>They are good conductors of electricity.</li><li>They have low densities.</li><li>They have grey shiny surfaces when freshly cut with a knife.</li></ul>	<ul><li>They are very reactive metals.</li><li>They form ionic compounds with non-metals.</li></ul>

Lithium is a soft reactive metal. When freshly cut, it has a metallic lustre. However, it rapidly reacts with oxygen in the air, giving it a dark oxide coat.

Sodium is softer and more reactive than lithium.

They form single charged ions M^+, with the stable octet of the noble gases when they react. Their outer electron can be lost relatively easily as they have low ionization energies. Reactivity increases down the group as the elements with the lower atomic number have lower ionization energies. Their ability to conduct electricity is also due to the availability of their outer electron.

Reaction with water

The alkali metals react with water to produce hydrogen and the metal hydroxide. When you drop a piece of one of the first three elements into a small beaker containing distilled water you may observe that:

- Lithium floats and reacts slowly, keeping its shape.
- Sodium reacts so vigorously that the heat produced is sufficient to melt the unreacted metal, which forms a small ball that moves around on the water surface.
- Potassium reacts even more vigorously to produce sufficient heat to ignite the hydrogen produced. It produces a lilac coloured flame and moves excitedly on the water surface.

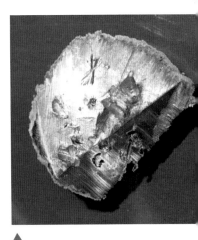

▲ Potassium is softer and more reactive than sodium.

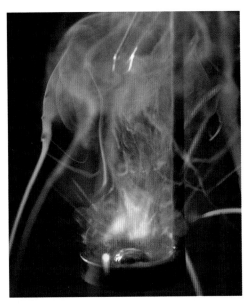

◀ Potassium reacting with water. The heat generated causes the hydrogen to ignite.

 It has been estimated that at any one time there are only 17 francium atoms on the earth.

 See the reaction of the group 1 metals with water.
Now go to www.heinemann.co.uk/hotlinks, insert the express code 4259P and click on this activity.

Note: there are 4 'hotlinks' here.

The metals are called alkali metals because the resulting solution is alkaline owing to the presence of the hydroxide ion.

For example with potassium:

$$2K(s) + 2H_2O(l) \rightarrow 2KOH(aq) + H_2(g)$$

As KOH is an ionic compound (see Chapter 4) which dissociates in water, it is more appropriate to write the equation as:

$$2K(s) + 2H_2O(l) \rightarrow 2K^+(aq) + 2OH^-(aq) + H_2(g)$$

The reaction becomes more vigorous as we descend the group. The most reactive element, caesium, has the lowest ionization energy and so forms positive ions most readily.

 Look carefully at the videos. Can you see any evidence that they are not what they claim to be? Can it ever be justified to mislead an audience?

● **Examiner's hint:** Observations must be something that can be observed. Note that the hydroxide is a product. A common mistake is to give the oxide as the product. You should learn the equation for the reaction of the Group 1 metals with water.

Exercise

9 State two observations you could make during the reaction between sodium and water. Give an equation for the reaction.

Group 7: the halogens

The Group 7 elements exist as diatomic molecules X_2.

The physical and chemical properties of halogens. ▶

Physical properties	Chemical properties
• They are coloured. • They show a gradual change from gases (F_2 and Cl_2), to liquid (Br_2) to solids (I_2 and At_2).	• They are very reactive as non-metals. • They form ionic compounds with metals or covalent compounds with other non-metals.

From left to right: chlorine (Cl_2), bromine (Br_2) and iodine (I_2). These are toxic and reactive non-metals. Bromine is a dark liquid at room temperature, although it readily produces a brown vapour. Iodine is a crystalline solid. ▶

 Two halogens are named by their colours: *chloros* is yellowish green and *ioeides* is violet in Greek, and one by its smell: *bromos* is the Greek word for stench.

 Chlorine was used as a chemical weapon during World War I. Should scientists be held morally responsible for the applications of their discoveries?

The halogens are a reactive group of non-metals. For example, see aluminium react with bromine. Now go to www.heinemann.co.uk/hotlinks, insert the express code 4259P and click on this activity.

The trend in reactivity can be explained by their readiness to accept electrons. As discussed earlier, their outer electrons experience a very high effective nuclear charge, which attracts an electron from atoms of other elements so as to complete their outer shell. The attraction is greatest for the smallest atom fluorine, which is the most reactive non-metal in the Periodic Table. Reactivity decreases down the group as the atomic radius increases and the attraction for outer electrons decreases.

Reaction with group 1 metals

The halogens react with the Group 1 metals to form ionic **halides**. The halogen atom gains one electron from the Group 1 elements to form a halide ion X^-. The resulting ions both have the stable octet of the noble gases. For example:

$$2Na(s) + Cl_2(g) \rightarrow 2NaCl(s)$$

The electrostatic force of attraction between the oppositely charged Na^+ and Cl^- ions bonds the ions together. The outer electron moves like a harpoon from the sodium to the chlorine. Once the transfer is complete the ions are pulled together by the mutual attraction of their opposite charges.

The most vigorous reaction occurs between the elements which are furthest apart in the Periodic Table: the most reactive alkali metal, francium, at the bottom of Group 1, with the most reactive halogen, fluorine, at the top of Group 7.

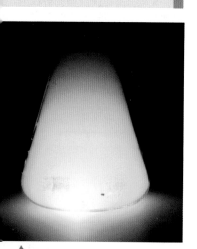

Sodium reacting with chlorine to form sodium chloride (NaCl, table salt). The violent reaction releases much heat.

Displacement reactions

The relative reactivity of the elements can also be seen by placing them in direct competition for an extra electron. When chlorine is bubbled through a solution of potassium bromide the solution changes from colourless to orange owing to the production of bromine:

$$2KBr(aq) + Cl_2(aq) \rightarrow 2KCl(aq) + Br_2(aq)$$

$$2Br^-(aq) + Cl_2(aq) \rightarrow 2Cl^-(aq) + Br_2(aq)$$

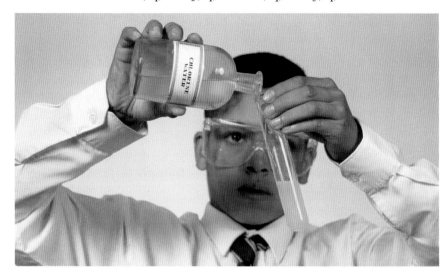

A chlorine nucleus has a stronger attraction for an electron than a bromine nucleus because of its smaller atomic radius and so takes the electron from the bromide ion. The chlorine has gained an electron and so forms the chloride ion, Cl^-. The bromide ion loses an electron to form bromine.

Other reactions are:

$$2I^-(aq) + Cl_2(aq) \rightarrow 2Cl^-(aq) + I_2(aq)$$

The colour changes from colourless to dark orange/brown owing to the formation of iodine.

$$2I^-(aq) + Br_2(aq) \rightarrow 2Br^-(aq) + I_2(aq)$$

The colour darkens owing to the formation of iodine. To distinguish between bromine and iodine more effectively, the final solution can be shaken with a hydrocarbon solvent. Iodine forms a violet solution and bromine a dark orange solution.

The halides

The halogens form insoluble salts with silver. Adding a solution containing the halide to a solution containing silver ions produces a **precipitate** which is useful in identifying the halide.

$$Ag^+(aq) + X^-(aq) \rightarrow AgX(s)$$

Exercises

10 How do the reactivities of the alkali metals and the halogens vary down the group?

11 Which property of the halogens increases from fluorine to iodine?
    A ionic charge
    B electronegativity
    C melting point of the element
    D chemical reactivity with metals.

ⓘ Group 1 and Group 7 are on opposite sides of the Periodic Table and show opposite trends in their reactivities and melting points.

◀ When chlorine water is added to the colourless potassium bromide solution, bromine (yellow/orange) is formed. Bromine is displaced from solution by the more reactive chlorine.

Ⓦ See the reaction of sodium with chlorine.
Now go to www.heinemann.co.uk/hotlinks, insert the express code 4259P and click on this activity.

ⓘ **The more reactive halogen displaces the ions of the less reactive halogen.**

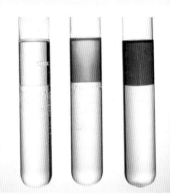

▲ Solutions of chlorine (left), bromine (middle) and iodine (right) in water (lower part) and cyclohexane (upper part). Chlorine dissolves in water, but the halogens are generally more soluble in non-polar solvents like cyclohexane.

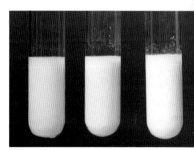

▲ Silver halide precipitates formed by reacting silver nitrate ($AgNO_3$) with solutions of halides. From left to right, these are silver chloride (AgCl), silver bromide (AgBr) and silver iodide (AgI).

Bonding of the Period 3 oxides

The transition from metallic to non-metallic character is illustrated by the bonding of the Period 3 oxides. Ionic compounds are generally formed between metal and non-metal elements and so the oxides of elements Na to Al have **giant ionic** structures. Covalent compounds are formed between non-metals, so the oxides of phosphorus, sulfur and chlorine are **molecular covalent**. The oxide of silicon, which is a metalloid, has a **giant covalent** structure.

The ionic character of a compound depends on the difference in electronegativity between its elements. Oxygen has an electronegativity of 3.5 so the ionic character of the oxides decreases from left to right, as the electronegativity values of the Period 3 elements approach this value.

The structure of the Period 3 oxides and their state at room temperature. ▶

Formula of higher oxide	$Na_2O(s)$	$MgO(s)$	$Al_2O_3(s)$	$SiO_2(s)$	$P_4O_{10}(s)$	$SO_3(l)$	$Cl_2O_7(l)$
Structure	giant ionic			giant covalent	molecular covalent		

Figure 3.6 Electronegativities increase across the period and approach 3.5, the value for oxygen. ▶

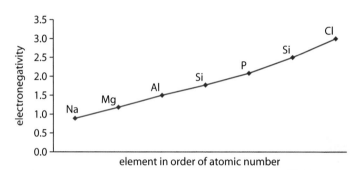

For the same reason the oxides become more ionic down a group, as the electronegativity decreases.

Acid–base character of the Period 3 oxides

The acid–base properties of the oxides are closely linked to their bonding. Metallic elements, which form ionic oxides, are basic and non-metal oxides, which are covalent, are acidic. Aluminium oxide, which can be considered as an ionic oxide with some covalent character, show **amphoteric** properties reacting with both acids and bases. The acid base properties of the period 3 oxides are shown below.

Acid–base properties of the period 3 oxides. ▶

Formula of oxide	$Na_2O(s)$	$MgO(s)$	$Al_2O_3(s)$	$SiO_2(s)$	$P_4O_{10}(s)/$ $P_4O_6(s)$	$SO_3(l)/$ $SO_2(g)$	$Cl_2O_7(l)/$ $Cl_2O(g)$
Acid–base character	basic		amphoteric		acidic		

Basic oxides

A basic oxide reacts with an acid to form a salt and water. The oxide ion combines with two H^+ ions to form water:

Amphoteric oxides show both acidic and basic properties.

$$O^{2-}(s) + 2H^+(aq) \rightarrow H_2O(l)$$
$$Li_2O(s) + 2HCl(aq) \rightarrow 2LiCl(aq) + H_2O(l)$$
$$MgO(s) + 2HCl(aq) \rightarrow MgCl_2(aq) + H_2O(l)$$

The Group 1 oxides dissolve in water to form alkaline solutions owing to the presence of hydroxide ions:

$$O^{2-}(s) + H_2O(l) \rightarrow 2OH^-(aq)$$

$$Na_2O(s) + H_2O(l) \rightarrow 2NaOH(aq)$$

$$MgO(s) + H_2O(l) \rightarrow Mg(OH)_2(aq)$$

Acidic oxides

Non-metallic oxides react with water to produce *acidic* solutions. Phosphorus oxide reacts with water to produce phosphoric acid:

$$P_4O_{10}(s) + 6H_2O(l) \rightarrow 4H_3PO_4(aq)$$

Sulfur trioxide reacts with water to produce sulfuric acid:

$$SO_3(l) + H_2O(l) \rightarrow H_2SO_4(aq)$$

Amphoteric oxides

Aluminium oxide does not affect the pH when it is added to water as it is essentially insoluble. It is amphoteric however as it shows both acid and base behaviour. It behaves as a base as it reacts with for example sulfuric acid:

$$Al_2O_3(s) + 6H^+(aq) \rightarrow 2Al^{3+}(aq) + 3H_2O(l)$$

$$Al_2O_3(s) + 3H_2SO_4(aq) \rightarrow Al_2(SO_4)_3(aq) + 3H_2O(l)$$

It behaves as an acid when it reacts with bases:

$$Al_2O_3(s) + 3H_2O(l) + 2OH^-(aq) \rightarrow 2Al(OH)_4{}^-(aq)$$

 Alkalis are bases which are soluble in water. They form hydroxide ions in aqueous solution.

 Oxides of metals are ionic and basic. Oxides of the non-metals are covalent and acidic. Oxides of some elements in the middle of the Periodic Table are amphoteric.

The Periodic Table has been called the most elegant classification chart ever devised. Is it a description or an explanation of periodic trends? Do other unifying systems exist in other areas of knowledge? To what extent do the classification systems we use affect the knowledge we obtain?

Exercises

12 An oxide of a Period 3 element is solid at room temperature and forms a basic oxide. Identify the element.
A Mg   B Al   C P   D S

13 Which pair of elements has the most similar chemical properties?
A N and S   B N and P   C P and Cl   D N and Cl.

Practice questions

1 For which element are the group number and the period number the same?

A Li   B Be   C B   D Mg

© International Baccalaureate Organization [2004]

2 Which properties of Period 3 elements increase from sodium to argon:
I   nuclear charge
II   atomic radius
III electronegativity?

A I and II only
B I and III only
C II and III only
D I, II and III

© International Baccalaureate Organization [2003]

3 Which pair of elements reacts most readily?

   A $Li + Br_2$ B $Li + Cl_2$ C $K + Br_2$ D $K + Cl_2$

                                      © International Baccalaureate Organization [2003]

4 Which of the reactions below occur as written?

   I $Br_2 + 2I^- \rightarrow 2Br^- + I_2$

   II $Br_2 + 2Cl^- \rightarrow 2Br^- + Cl_2$

   A   I only

   B   II only

   C   both I and II

   D   neither I nor II

                                        © International Baccalaureate Organization [2004]

5 Explain the following statements.

   (a)   The first ionization energy of sodium is:

       (i)   less than that of magnesium.   (2)

       (ii)   greater than that of potassium.   (1)

   (b)   The electronegativity of chlorine is higher than that of sulfur.   (2)

                                               (*Total 5 marks*)

                                       © International Baccalaureate Organization [2003]

6 Describe the acid–base character of the oxides of the period 3 elements Na to Ar. For sodium oxide and sulfur trioxide, write balanced equations to illustrate their acid–base character.   (4)

                                       © International Baccalaureate Organization [2003]

7 Atomic radii and ionic radii are found in the IB Data booklet.

   Explain why:

   (a)   the magnesium ion is much smaller than the magnesium atom.   (2)

   (b)   there is a large increase in ionic radius from silicon to phosphorus.   (2)

   (c)   the ionic radius of Na^+ is less than that of F^-.   (2)

                                               (*Total 6 marks*)

                                       © International Baccalaureate Organization [2003]

8 (a)   Classify each of the following oxides as acidic, basic or amphoteric.

       (i)   aluminium oxide   (1)

       (ii)   sodium oxide   (1)

       (iii)   sulfur dioxide   (1)

   (b)   Write an equation for each reaction between water and

       (i)   sodium oxide

       (ii)   sulfur dioxide.   (1)

                                               (*Total 4 marks*)

                                       © International Baccalaureate Organization [2005]

9 State and explain the trends in the atomic radius and the ionization energy

   (a)   for the alkali metals Li to Cs.   (4)

   (b)   for the Period 3 elements Na to Cl.   (4)

                                               (*Total 8 marks*)

                                       © International Baccalaureate Organization [2005]

10 The IB Data booklet gives the atomic and ionic radii of elements. State and explain the difference between

   (a)   the atomic radius of nitrogen and oxygen   (2)

   (b)   the atomic radius of nitrogen and phosphorus   (1)

   (c)   the atomic and ionic radius of nitrogen   (2)

                                               (*Total 5 marks*)

                                       © International Baccalaureate Organization [2004]

● **Examiner's hint:** Give explanations based on atomic level properties. Accounts based on the relative positions in the Periodic Table are not acceptable.

● **Examiner's hint:** Learn balanced equations for acid–base reactions of the Period 3 oxides.

● **Examiner's hint:** In dealing with questions of this nature, you need to find the 'crux' of the question. In (a), it is the loss of two electrons and the consequent loss of an energy level. In (b), it is the difference of a whole energy level and there should be some comment on the number of protons. In (c), it is the isoelectronic nature of the two ions and the difference in nuclear charge.

Bonding

We learned in Chapter 2 that all elements are made of atoms and that there are only about 100 chemically different types of atom. Yet we know that we live in a world made up of literally millions of different substances: somehow these must all have formed from just these 100 atomic building blocks. The extraordinary variety arises from the fact that atoms readily combine with each other and they do so in a myriad different ways. They come together in small numbers or large, with similar atoms or very different atoms, but the result of the combination is always a stable association known as a **bond**. Atoms linked together by bonds thus have very different properties from their parent atoms.

In this chapter we will study the main types of chemical bonds – the ionic bond, the covalent bond and the metallic bond and also consider other forces that help to hold substances together. We will learn that electrons are the key to the formation of all these bonds, so knowledge of electron arrangements in atoms (Periodicity, Chapter 3) will help you.

Chemical reactions take place when some bonds break and others reform. Being able to predict and understand the nature of the bonds within a substance is therefore central to explaining its chemical reactivity.

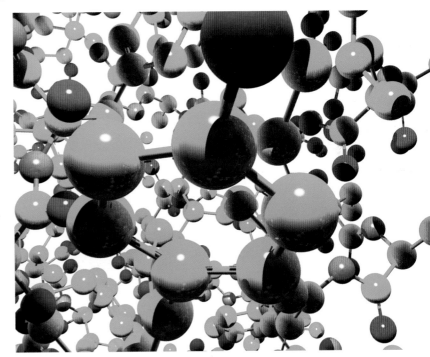

A molecule of insulin, the hormone essential for the regulation of glucose in the body. The ball and stick model shows all the atoms and bonds within the protein molecule. Insulin was the first protein to have its entire structure elucidated.

Assessment statements

4.1 Ionic bonding

4.1.1   Describe the ionic bond as the electrostatic attraction between oppositely charged ions.

4.1.2   Describe how ions can be formed as a result of electron transfer.

4.1.3   Deduce which ions will be formed when elements in Groups 1, 2 and 3 lose electrons.

4.1.4   Deduce which ions will be formed when elements in Groups 5, 6 and 7 gain electrons.

4.1.5   State that transition elements can form more than one ion.

4.1.6   Predict whether a compound of two elements would be ionic from the position of the elements in the Periodic Table or from their electronegativity values.

4.1.7   State the formula of common polyatomic ions formed by non-metals in Periods 2 and 3.

4.1.8   Describe the lattice structure of ionic compounds.

4.2 Covalent bonding

4.2.1   Describe the covalent bond as the electrostatic attraction between a pair of electrons and positively charged nuclei.

4.2.2   Describe how the covalent bond is formed as a result of electron sharing.

4.2.3   Deduce the Lewis (electron dot) structures of molecules and ions for up to four electron pairs on each atom.

4.2.4   State and explain the relationship between the number of bonds, bond length and bond strength.

4.2.5   Predict whether a compound of two elements would be covalent from the position of the elements in the Periodic Table or from their electronegativity values.

4.2.6   Predict the relative polarity of bonds from electronegativity values.

4.2.7   Predict the shape and bond angles for species with four, three and two negative charge centres on the central atom using the valence shell electron pair repulsion theory (VSEPR).

4.2.8   Predict whether or not a molecule is polar from its molecular shape and bond polarities.

4.2.9   Describe and compare the structure and bonding in the three allotropes of carbon (diamond, graphite and C_{60} fullerene).

4.2.10 Describe the structure of and bonding in silicon and silicon dioxide.

4.3 Intermolecular forces

4.3.1   Describe the types of intermolecular forces (attractions between molecules that have temporary dipoles, permanent dipoles or hydrogen bonding) and explain how they arise from the structural features of molecules.

4.3.2   Describe and explain how intermolecular forces affect the boiling points of substances.

4.4 Metallic bonding

4.4.1   Describe the metallic bond as the electrostatic attraction between a lattice of positive ions and delocalized electrons.

4.4.2   Explain the electrical conductivity and malleability of metals.

4.5 Physical properties

4.5.1   Compare and explain the properties of substances resulting from different types of bonding.

4.1 Ionic bonding

Ions form when electrons are transferred

All atoms are electrically neutral, even though they contain charged particles known as protons and electrons. This is because the number of protons ($+$) is equal to the number of electrons ($-$) and so their charges effectively cancel each other out. The positively charged protons, located within the nucleus of the atom, are not transferred during chemical reactions. Electrons, however, positioned outside the nucleus, can be transferred when atoms react together. When this happens the atom is no longer neutral, but instead carries an electric charge and is called an **ion**. The charge on the ion which forms will therefore be determined by how many electrons are lost or gained.

We learned in Chapter 3 that the group number in the Periodic Table is equal to the number of electrons in the outer shell of the atoms of all the elements in that group. We also learned that Group 0 elements, known as the noble gases, where the atoms all have full outer shells of electrons, are especially stable and have almost no tendency to react at all. This full outer shell behaves in a sense like the 'ultimate goal' for other atoms: they react to gain the stability associated with this by losing or gaining the appropriate number of electrons, whichever will be the easiest (in energetic terms). So elements that have a small number of electrons in their outer shells (groups 1, 2 and 3) will lose those electrons and form positive ions. These elements are the metals. Elements that have higher numbers of electrons in their outer shells (groups 5, 6 and 7) will gain electrons and form negative ions. These are the non-metals.

We are now able to summarize how the position of an element in the Periodic Table enables us to predict the type of ion that an element will form.

> You can follow an overview of bonding at this interactive site. Now go to www.heinemann.co.uk/hotlinks, insert the express code 4259P and click on this activity.

◄ Electric light bulb containing argon gas. As argon is a noble gas, it is very unreactive owing to its stable electron arrangement, so it will not react with the tungsten filament even when it becomes very hot.

> **An ion is a charged particle. Ions form from atoms or from groups of atoms by transfer of one or more electrons.**

> **When an atom loses electrons it forms a positive ion, also called a cation. When an atom gains electrons it forms a negative ion, also called an anion. The number of charges on the ion formed is equal to the number of electrons transferred.**

Group number	Example	Number of electrons in outer shell	Electrons lost or gained	Number of electrons transferred	Charge on ion formed	Type of element
1	sodium	1	lost	1	1+	metal
2	calcium	2	lost	2	2+	metal
3	aluminium	3	lost	3	3+	metal
4	carbon	4	–	–	–	non-metal
5	phosphorous	5	gained	3	3–	non-metal
6	oxygen	6	gained	2	2–	non-metal
7	bromine	7	gained	1	1–	non-metal

Note that elements in Group 4, having four electrons in their outer shell, do not have a tendency to gain or to lose electrons and so they generally do not form ions. This is because the energy involved in transferring four electrons would simply be too large to be favourable. These elements therefore react to form a different type of bond which we will discuss later in the chapter.

● **Examiner's hint:** It may help you to remember: CATion is PUSSYtive.

Worked example

Refer to the Periodic Table to deduce the charge on the ion formed when the following elements react:
  (i) lithium
 (ii) sulfur
(iii) argon

Solution
  (i) Lithium is in Group 1 so forms Li^+.
 (ii) Sulfur is in Group 6 so forms S^{2-}.
(iii) Argon is in Group 0 so does not form ions.

For some elements though, it is difficult to predict the ion that will form from its position in the Periodic Table. For example the so-called transition elements, which are metals occurring in the middle of the Periodic Table, have a somewhat unusual electron arrangement which enables them to form stable ions with different charges by losing different numbers of electrons. The transition element iron Fe can form Fe^{2+}, for example, by losing two electrons or Fe^{3+} by losing three electrons, depending on the reacting conditions. The two ions have distinct properties; for example, they form compounds with different colours.

▶ Compounds containing different ions of iron can be distinguished by colour: the left beaker contains $Fe^{2+}(aq)$ and the right beaker contains $Fe^{3+}(aq)$. Similar colour changes occur when iron rusts as it reacts with oxygen to form these different ions.

▲ Fehlings reagent uses the different colours of the copper ions to test for simple sugars. The left tube containing the blue Cu^{2+} ion changes to the red Cu^+ ion seen on the right when warmed with glucose and other 'reducing sugars'.

Likewise the element copper can exist as Cu^{2+} and Cu^+ and again these ions can be distinguished by colour.

Other examples of elements that form ions that are not obvious from their group number are:
  • lead, Pb, despite being in Group 4, forms a stable ion Pb^{2+}
  • silver, Ag, which forms the ion Ag^+.

Finally, there are some ions that are made up of more than one atom which together have experienced a loss or gain of electrons and so carry a charge. These species are called **polyatomic ions** and many of them are found in commonly occurring compounds. It will help you to become familiar with these few examples, as you will often use them when writing formulas and equations. (This information is not supplied in the IB Data booklet).

Polyatomic ion name	Charge on ion	Symbol	Example of compound containing this ion
nitrate	1−	NO_3^-	lead nitrate
hydroxide	1−	OH^-	barium hydroxide
hydrogencarbonate	1−	HCO_3^-	potassium hydrogencarbonate
carbonate	2−	CO_3^{2-}	magnesium carbonate
sulfate	2−	SO_4^{2-}	copper sulfate
phosphate	3−	PO_4^{3-}	calcium phosphate
ammonium	1+	NH_4^+	ammonium chloride

We will learn how to write the formulas for these compounds in the next section.

● **Examiner's hint:** When writing the symbol for ions, note the charge is written as a superscript with the number first and the charge next, for example, N^{3-}. When an ion X carries a charge of 1+ or 1− it is written just as X^+ or X^-.

● **Examiner's hint:** Note the common names of some compounds give a clue to their composition. Here you can see that the ending '-ate' refers to ions that contain oxygen bonded to another element.

Ionic compounds form when oppositely charged ions attract

Ions do not form in isolation. Rather the process of ionization – where electrons are transferred between atoms – can only occur when an atom that loses electrons passes them directly to an atom that gains them. Typically this means that electrons are transferred from a metal element to a non-metal element, for example sodium transfers an electron to chlorine when they react together.

Coloured scanning electron micrograph of crystals of table salt, sodium chloride NaCl. The very reactive elements sodium and chlorine have combined together to form this stable compound containing Na^+ and Cl^- ions.

$$Na\cdot \quad + \quad {}^{\times}_{\times}\overset{\times\times}{Cl}{}^{\times}_{\times} \quad \longrightarrow \quad [Na]^+ \quad [{}^{\times}_{\times}\overset{\times\times}{Cl}{}^{\times}_{\times}]^-$$

(2.8.1)	(2.8.7)	(2.8)	(2.8.8)
sodium atom	chlorine atom	sodium ion	chloride ion

Now the oppositely charged ions resulting from this ionization are attracted to each other and are held together by electrostatic forces. These forces are known as an **ionic bond** and ions held together in this way are known as **ionic compounds**.

Remember that in forming the ionic compound there is no net loss or gain of electrons, so the ionic compound, like the atoms that formed it, must be electrically neutral. Writing the formula for the ionic compound therefore involves *balancing the total number of positive and negative charges*, taking into account the different charges on each ion.

For example, magnesium oxide is made up of magnesium ions Mg^{2+} and oxide ions O^{2-}. Here each magnesium atom has transferred *two* electrons to each oxygen atom so that the compound contains equal numbers of each ion. It will have the formula $Mg^{2+}O^{2-}$, usually written as MgO. But when magnesium reacts with chlorine, each Mg loses *two* electrons, whereas Cl ionizes by gaining only *one* electron. So it will take two chlorine atoms to combine with each magnesium atom and the compound that results will therefore have the ratio $Mg:Cl = 1:2$. This is written as $Mg^{2+}(Cl^-)_2$ or $MgCl_2$.

● **Examiner's hint:** Note in many non-metal elements, the ending of the name changes to '-ide' when ionization occurs. For example, *chlorine* (the element) becomes *chloride* (the ion), *oxygen* becomes *oxide*, nitrogen becomes *nitride*, and so on.

You may find it helpful to use the following steps when working out the formulas of some ionic compounds.

Worked example

Write the formula for the compound that forms between aluminium and oxygen.

Solution

1 Check the Periodic Table for the ions that each element will form: aluminium in Group 3 will form Al^{3+}, oxygen in Group 6 will form O^{2-}.

2 Write the number of the charge above the ion:

     3   2
     Al   O

3 Cross-multiply these numbers:

     3   2
     Al   O

4 Write the final formula using subscripts to show the number of ions: Al_2O_3.

> **Examiner's hint:** Note that the formula of the compounds shows the *simplest ratio* of the ions it contains. So, for example
>
> Mg^{2+} O^{2-}
> Mg_2 O_2
>
> is written MgO

It is common practice to leave the charges out when showing the final formula. When dealing with polyatomic ions, if the formula contains more than one ion you will need to use brackets around the ion before the subscript. For example calcium hydroxide is written $Ca(OH)_2$ and ammonium sulfate is written $(NH_4)_2SO_4$.

> **Examiner's hint:** Note the convention in naming ionic compounds that the positive ion is written first and the negative ion second.

Exercise

1 Write the formula for each of the following compounds:
   (a) potassium bromide   **(b)** lead nitrate
   (c) sodium sulfate   **(d)** ammonium phosphate

Ionic character of compounds can be predicted from two factors

In order to form an ionic compound, the elements reacting together must have *very different tendencies to lose or gain electrons*. There are two ways of recognizing this.

1 Position of the elements in the Periodic Table

One element will usually be a metal on the left of the Periodic Table and the other a non-metal on the right. As well, we learned in Chapter 3 that the tendency to lose electrons and form positive ions increases *down* a group, whereas the tendency to gain electrons and form negative ions increases *up* a group. So the highest tendency to form ionic compounds will be between elements on the bottom left and those on the top right of the Periodic Table.

Figure 4.1 The pair of elements that react most easily to form ionic compounds are metals on the bottom left of the Periodic Table and non-metals on the top right, indicated by asterisks here.

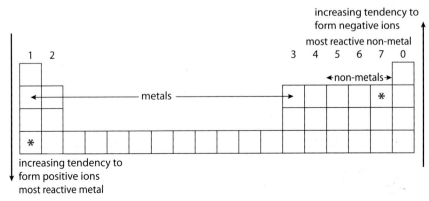

2 Electronegativity

Also in Chapter 3 we were introduced to the idea of electronegativity as a measure of the ability of an atom to attract electrons. So electronegativity values can also be used to determine whether an ionic compound will result from any two specific elements reacting together. Here the determining factor will be the *difference* in electronegativity values and it is generally recognized that a difference of 1.8 units or more on the Pauling scale will give a compound that is predominantly ionic.

Electronegativity values are given in Table 7 of the IB Data booklet

Exercises

2 Which fluoride is the most ionic?
   A NaF
   B CsF
   C MgF_2
   D BaF_2

3 Which pair of elements reacts most readily?
   A $Li + Br_2$
   B $Li + Cl_2$
   C $K + Br_2$
   D $K + Cl_2$

Ionic compounds have a lattice structure

The forces of electrostatic attraction between ions in a compound cause them to surround themselves with ions of opposite charge. As a result, the ionic compound takes on a predictable three-dimensional crystalline structure known as an **ionic lattice**. The details of the lattice's geometry vary in different compounds depending mainly on the sizes of the ions, but it always involves this fixed arrangement of ions based on a repeating unit.

For example, in the sodium chloride lattice, each Na^+ ion is surrounded by six Cl^- ions and each Cl^- ion is surrounded by six Na^+ ions.

Note that the lattice consists of a very large number of ions and it can grow indefinitely. As ionic compounds do not therefore exist as units with a fixed number of ions, their formulas are simply an expression of the *ratio* of ions present.

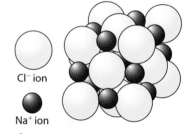

Cl^- ion

Na^+ ion

▲ **Figure 4.2** NaCl lattice built up from oppositely charged sodium and chloride ions.

● **Examiner's hint:** Make sure that you avoid the term 'molecule' when describing ionic compounds.

◄ Computer graphic of crystallized common salt NaCl. Small spheres represent Na^+ ions and larger spheres Cl^-. The lattice is arranged so that each Na^+ ion has six oppositely charged nearest neighbours and vice versa.

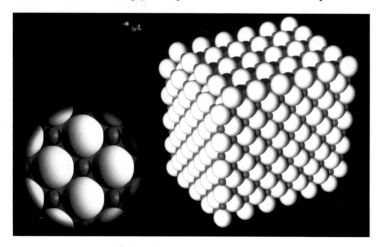

We will return to the lattice structure of ionic compounds when we discuss their characteristic physical properties at the end of this chapter.

(W) You can review the structure and properties of ionic compounds. Now visit www.heinemann.co.uk/hotlinks, insert the express code 4259P and click on this activity.

4.2 Covalent bonding

A covalent bond forms by atoms sharing electrons

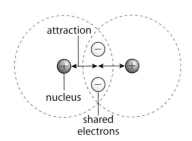

Figure 4.3 In a covalent bond the shared electrons are attracted to the nuclei of both atoms.

When atoms of two non-metals react together, each is seeking to gain electrons in order to achieve the stable electron structure of a noble gas. By sharing an electron pair they are effectively each able to achieve this. The shared pair of electrons is concentrated in the region between the two nuclei and is attracted to them both. It therefore holds the atoms together by electrostatic attraction and is known as a **covalent bond**. A group of atoms held together by covalent bonds forms a **molecule**.

For example two hydrogen atoms form a covalent bond as follows.

$$H^\times + {}_\bullet H \longrightarrow H^\times_\bullet H$$

two hydrogen atoms (2H) a molecule of hydrogen (H_2)

Note that in the molecule H_2 each hydrogen atom has a share of two electrons so it has gained the stability of the electron arrangement of the noble gas He.

Computer artwork of hydrogen molecules. Each molecule consists of two hydrogen atoms bonded covalently.

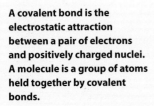

A covalent bond is the electrostatic attraction between a pair of electrons and positively charged nuclei. A molecule is a group of atoms held together by covalent bonds.

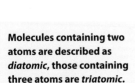

Molecules containing two atoms are described as *diatomic*, those containing three atoms are *triatomic*.

Similarly two chlorine atoms react together to form a chlorine molecule in which both atoms have gained a share of eight electrons in their outer shells (the electron arrangement of argon Ar). This tendency of atoms to form a stable arrangement of eight electrons in their outer shell is sometimes referred to as the **octet rule**.

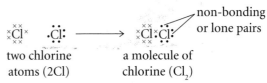

non-bonding or lone pairs

two chlorine atoms (2Cl) a molecule of chlorine (Cl_2)

Note that in the chlorine molecule, each atom has three pairs of electrons that are not involved in forming the bond. These are known as **non-bonding pairs**, or **lone pairs**, and as we will see later they play an important role in determining the shape of more complex molecules.

Atoms can share more than one pair of electrons to form multiple bonds

Sometimes it seems there are not enough electrons to achieve octets on all the atoms in the molecule. In these cases, the atoms will have to share more than one electron pair; in other words, form a multiple bond. A **double bond** forms when two electron pairs, a total of four electrons, are shared; a **triple bond** forms when three electron pairs, a total of six electrons, are shared.

For example, the two most abundant gases in the air, oxygen and nitrogen both exist as diatomic molecules containing multiple bonds.

$$\overset{\times\times}{\underset{\times}{O}} \overset{\times}{} : \overset{..}{O} : \quad \text{or} \quad \overset{\times\times}{\underset{\times}{O}} = \overset{..}{O} : \quad \text{double bond}$$

$$\overset{\times}{N} \overset{\times}{\underset{\times}{:}} N : \quad \text{or} \quad \overset{\times}{N} \equiv N : \quad \text{triple bond}$$

As shown above, it is often convenient to use a line to represent a shared pair of electrons, two lines to represent a double bond and three lines a triple bond.

Lewis diagrams are used to show the arrangement of electrons in covalent molecules

When describing the structure of covalent molecules, the most convenient method is known as a **Lewis structure**. This uses a simple notation to represent the outer

> The triple bond in nitrogen N_2 is difficult to break, making the molecule very stable. This is why, although nitrogen makes up about 78% of the atmosphere, it does not readily take part in chemical reactions and is only rarely used directly by organisms as their source of nitrogen for synthesis reactions.

◀ Gilbert Newton Lewis (1875–1946) was one of the greatest and most influential American chemists of the last century. He formulated the idea that the covalent bond consists of a shared pair of electrons, proposed the electron pair theory of acid–base reactions and was the first person to produce a pure sample of deuterium oxide (heavy water). He also published important theories on chemical thermodynamics and first coined the term 'photon' for the smallest unit of radiant energy. Since 1916, his dot diagrams for covalent structures have been used almost universally.

energy level, or valence shell, electrons of all the atoms in the molecule. It can be derived as follows:

1 Calculate the total number of valence electrons in the molecule by multiplying the group number of each element by the number of atoms of the element in the formula and totalling these.
2 Draw the skeletal structure of the molecule to show how the atoms are linked to each other.
3 Use a pair of crosses, dots or a single line to show one electron pair and put a pair in each bond between atoms.
4 Add more electron pairs to complete the octets (8 electrons) around the atoms (other than hydrogen which must have 2 electrons and the exceptions noted below).
5 If there are not enough electrons to complete the octets, form double bonds and if necessary triple bonds.
6 Check that the total number of electrons in your finished structure is equal to your calculation in step 1.

● **Examiner's hint:** Electron pairs can be represented by dots, crosses, a combination of dots and crosses or by a line. Use whichever notation you prefer, but be prepared to recognize all versions. The important thing is to be clear, consistent and to avoid vague and scattered dots.

Worked example

Draw the Lewis structure for the molecule CCl_4

Solution

1 Total number of valence electrons $= 4 + (7 \times 4) = 32$

2 Skeletal structure   3 Bonded pairs 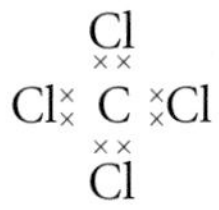   4 Completed Lewis structure

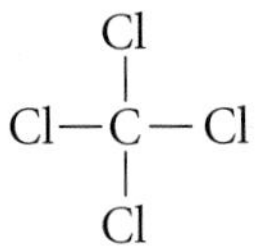

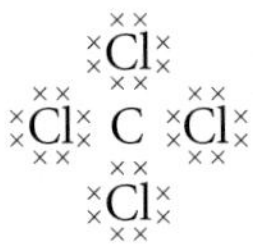

(32 electrons)

There are several different ways of drawing Lewis structures, and some alternative acceptable forms are shown below.

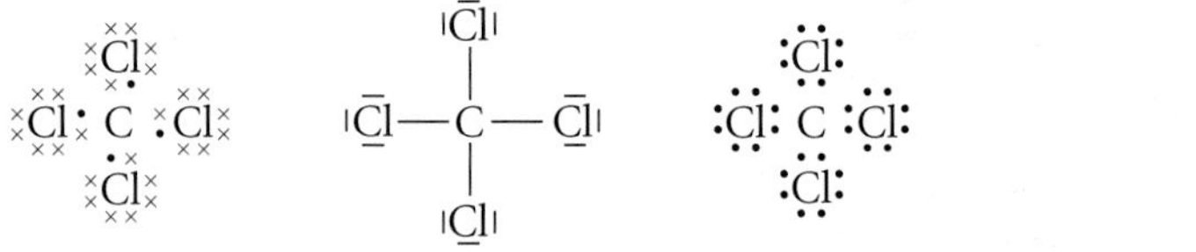

The table shows some examples of molecules with their Lewis structures.

Species	Total number of valence electrons	Lewis structure
CH_4	$4 + (1 \times 4) = 8$	
H_2O	$(1 \times 2) + 6 = 8$	
NH_3	$5 + (1 \times 3) = 8$	
CO_2	$4 + (6 \times 2) = 16$	
HCN	$1 + 4 + 5 = 10$	

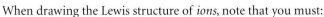

When drawing the Lewis structure of *ions*, note that you must:

- Total the valence electrons as above and then add one electron for each negative charge and subtract one electron for each positive charge.
- Put the Lewis structure in a square bracket with the charge shown outside.

For example OH^-: valence electrons = 6 + 1 + 1 = 8

$$\left[\overset{\times\times}{\underset{\times\times}{\times}}O \overset{\times}{} H \right]^-$$

and SO_4^{2-}: valence electrons = 6 + (6 × 4) + 2 = 32

$$\left[\begin{array}{c} \overset{\times\times}{O} \\ \times O \times S \times O \times \\ \overset{\times\times}{O} \end{array} \right]^{2-}$$

The octet rule is not always followed

There are a few molecules that are exceptions to the octet rule. For example, in small molecules such as $BeCl_2$ and BF_3 the limited space around the central atom would cause significant repulsion if there were four electron pairs. Instead their structures have less than an octet.

$BeCl_2$ valence electrons = 2 + (7 × 2) = 16 $\times \overset{\times\times}{\underset{\times\times}{Cl}} \times Be \times \overset{\times\times}{\underset{\times\times}{Cl}} \times$

BF_3 valence electrons = 3 + (7 × 3) = 24 $\times \overset{\times\times}{\underset{\times\times}{F}} \times B \times \overset{\times\times}{\underset{\times\times}{F}} \times$
$\overset{\times\times}{\underset{\times\times}{F}}$

Exercise

4 Draw the Lewis structures of:

(a) HF	**(b)** CF_3Cl	**(c)** C_2H_6	**(d)** NO_3^-
(e) SO_2	**(f)** C_2H_4	**(g)** C_2H_2	

● **Examiner's hint:** Remember to include *all lone pairs* in your diagram. Structures which show only bonded pairs, for example H–Cl, are structural formulas, not Lewis structures.

In dative bonds both shared electrons come from one atom

Most of the examples we have seen so far involve covalent bonds where each bonded atom contributes one electron to the shared pair. However, sometimes the bond forms by *both* the electrons in the pair originating from the same atom. This means that the other atom accepts and gains a share in a donated electron pair. Such bonds are called **dative bonds** (sometimes also known as coordinate bonds). An arrow is sometimes used to show a dative bond. For example:

H_3O^+

$$\left[\begin{array}{c} H \overset{\times\times}{\underset{\times\bullet}{\times}}O \times H \\ H \end{array} \right]^+ \qquad \left[\begin{array}{c} H - \overset{\times\times}{O} \rightarrow H \\ | \\ H \end{array} \right]^+$$

NH_4^+

$$\left[\begin{array}{c} H \\ H \overset{\times\bullet}{\underset{\times\bullet}{\times}}N \times H \\ H \end{array} \right]^+ \qquad \left[\begin{array}{c} H \\ | \\ H - N \rightarrow H \\ | \\ H \end{array} \right]^+$$

CO $:C \overset{\times\times}{\underset{\times\times}{:}} O \times$ $:C \equiv O \times$

Note that in CO the triple bond consists of two bonds which involve sharing an electron from each atom and the third bond is a dative bond where both electrons come from the oxygen. The three bonds are nonetheless identical to each other. This illustrates an important point about dative bonds: once they are formed they are no different from other covalent bonds. Understanding the origin of their electrons can be important, however, in interpreting some reactions such as Lewis acid–base behaviour (Chapter 8).

Short bonds are strong bonds

When we are comparing different covalent bonds it is often useful to refer to data on their bond length and bond strength. Bond length is a measure of the distance between the two bonded nuclei. Bond strength, usually described in terms of bond enthalpy, which will be discussed in Chapter 5, is effectively a measure of the energy required to break the bond.

Multiple bonds have a greater number of shared electrons and so have a stronger force of electrostatic attraction between the bonded nuclei. Thus there is a greater pulling power on the nuclei, bringing them closer together, resulting in bonds that are shorter and stronger than single bonds. We can see this by comparing different bonds involving the same atoms.

For example using data from Tables 9 and 10 in the IB Data booklet to compare three different hydrocarbons:

	C_2H_6 ethane	C_2H_4 ethene	C_2H_2 ethyne
	H—C—C—H (with H above and below each C)	H₂C=CH₂ structure	H—C≡C—H
Type of bond between carbons	single	double	triple
Bond length (nm)	0.154	0.134	0.120
Bond enthaply (kJ mol^{-1})	348	612	837

Also we can compare two different carbon–oxygen bonds within the molecule CH_3COOH:

	C—O	C=O
Bond length (nm)	0.143	0.122
Bond enthalpy (kJ mol^{-1})	360	743

single bonds   double bonds   triple bonds

→

decreasing length
increasing strength

Polar bonds result from unequal sharing of electrons

Not all sharing is equal. It may be the case that you share this textbook with a class mate, but if you have it for more than half the time, it clearly belongs more to you than to your friend. So it is with electron pairs. In simple terms if they spend more time with one atom than the other, they are not equally shared. This occurs when there is a difference in the electronegativities of the bonded atoms, as the more electronegative atom exerts a greater pulling power on the shared electrons and so gains more 'possession' of the electron pair. The bond is now unsymmetrical with respect to electron distribution and is said to be **polar**. The term **dipole** is often used to indicate the fact that this type of bond has two separated opposite electric charges. The more electronegative atom, with the greater share of the electrons, has become partially negative or δ^- and the less electronegative atom has become partially positive or δ^+.

For example, in HCl the shared electron pair is pulled more strongly by the Cl than the H, resulting in a polar molecule.

$$\overset{\delta^+}{H} \overset{\times}{\underset{\bullet}{\rule{2cm}{0.4pt}}} \overset{\delta^-}{Cl}$$

partially   partially
positive   negative

In water, the difference in electronegativity between O and H results in polar bonds:

$$\overset{\delta^+}{H} \rightarrowtail \overset{\delta^-}{O} \leftarrowtail \overset{\delta^+}{H}$$

Bonds are more polar when the *difference* in electronegativity between the bonded atoms is greater. For example, H–F is more polar than H–Cl, as F is more electronegative than Cl. Note, however, that both fluorine F–F and chlorine Cl–Cl are non-polar as here the difference is zero.

Polar bonds with their partial separation of opposite charges thus introduce some ionic nature into covalent bonds. They are therefore considered to be intermediate in relation to non-polar bonds and ionic bonds. In fact, the boundaries between these types of bonds are somewhat 'fuzzy', so it is often appropriate to describe substances as being somewhere on the scale using terms like 'predominantly' covalent or ionic, or of being 'strongly' polar and so on. Thus bond types can be better considered as a continuous range rather than as two distinct types, a concept known as the 'bonding continuum'. It is summarized in the table below.

● **Examiner's hint:** Note that the symbol δ (Greek letter d, pronounced delta) is used to represent a *partial charge*. This has no fixed value, but is always less than the unit charge associated with an ion such as X^+ or X^-.

● **Examiner's hint:** There are several ways to denote the polar nature of the bond in a structure. One is to write δ^+ and δ^- over the less electronegative and more electronegative atom, respectively. Another is to use an arrow on the line representing the bond, indicating the pull on the electrons by the more electronegative atoms. As you can see in the diagram of water here, it is quite acceptable to show both ways together.

The nature of a bond between two atoms, that is, whether it is covalent, polar or ionic can be predicted from the positions of the elements in the Periodic Table or from their electronegativity values. The further apart on the Periodic Table they are, the more ionic; the closer together, the more covalent.

	Type of bond		
	Non-polar covalent	**Polar covalent**	**Ionic**
Electronegativity difference between bonded atoms (numbers refer to the Pauling scale).	Atoms are the same or have almost no difference in electronegativity.	Atoms differ in electronegativity by up to about 1.8.	Atoms differ in electronegativity by more than about 1.8.
Examples	H–H, Cl–Cl, C–H	H–Cl, O–H, C–Cl	Na^+Cl^-, $Ca^{2+}O^{2-}$

Exercise

5 For each of these molecules, identify any polar bonds and label the atoms using δ^+ and δ^- appropriately.
   (a) HBr   **(b)** CO_2 **(c)** ClF   **(d)** O_2 **(e)** NH_3

The shape of a molecule is determined by repulsion between electron pairs

> Most people find this topic easier to understand when they can build and study models of the molecules in three dimensions. Does this suggest different qualities to the knowledge we acquire in different ways?

Once we know the Lewis structure of a molecule, we can predict exactly how the bonds will be orientated with respect to each other in space, that is, its three-dimensional structure, known as the shape of the molecule. This is often a crucial feature of a substance in determining its reactivity. For example, biochemical reactions depend on a precise 'fit' between the enzyme, which controls the rate of the reaction and the reacting molecule known as the substrate. Anything which changes the shape of either of these may therefore alter the reaction dramatically: many drugs actually work in this way.

Predictions of molecular shape are based on the Valence Shell Electron Pair Repulsion (VSEPR) theory. As its name suggests, this theory states that *electron pairs found in the outer energy level or valence shell of atoms repel each other and thus position themselves as far apart as possible.*

The following points will help you apply this theory to predict the shape of molecules:

- The repulsion applies to both bonding and non-bonding pairs of electrons.
- Double and triple bonded electron pairs are orientated together and so behave in terms of repulsion as a single unit known as a 'negative charge centre'.
- The total number of charge centres around the central atom will determine the geometrical arrangement of the electrons.
- The shape of the molecule is determined by the angles between the bonded atoms.
- Because non-bonding pairs are not shared between two atoms they cause more repulsion than bonding pairs. The repulsion decreases in the following order:

  lone pair–lone pair > lone pair–bonding pair > bonding pair–bonding pair.

  As a result, molecules with lone pairs on the central atom have some distortions in their structure which reduce the angle between the bonded atoms.

Note that in the following diagrams non-bonding electrons on the surrounding atoms have been omitted for clarity – these are therefore *not* Lewis structures.

Species with two negative charge centres

Molecules with two charge centres will position them at 180° to each other. The molecule will therefore have a **linear** shape.

$BeCl_2$ Cl—Be—Cl

CO_2 O=C=O

C_2H_2 H—C≡C—H

} shape: linear
bond angle: 180°

Species with three negative charge centres

Molecules with three charge centres will position them at 120° to each other, giving a **planar triangular** shape to the distribution of electrons. If all three charge centres are bonding, the shape of the molecule will therefore also be planar triangular.

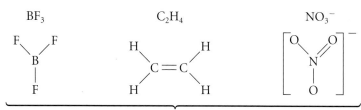

shape: planar triangular; bond angle: 120°

However, if one of the charge centres is a non-bonding pair, this will not be 'seen' in the overall shape of the molecule as it is part of the central atom. The final shape will be determined by the positions of the atoms fixed by the bonding pairs only, so it will appear **bent**. A further consideration is that non-bonding pairs cause slightly more repulsion than bonding pairs (as explained on page 78), so in their presence the angles are slightly altered.

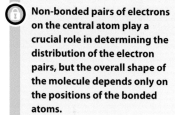
Non-bonded pairs of electrons on the central atom play a crucial role in determining the distribution of the electron pairs, but the overall shape of the molecule depends only on the positions of the bonded atoms.

Worked example

Describe the shape of the molecule SO_2

Solution

First work out its Lewis structure, following the steps on page 74.

$$\overset{\times\times}{\underset{\times\times}{O}} \overset{\times}{\underset{\times}{S}} \overset{\times\times}{\underset{\times\times}{O}}$$

So there are three charge centres around the central atom S, which will be arranged in a planar triangular shape.

bond angle 117°

The non-bonding pair of electrons distorts this shape slightly as it causes greater repulsion, resulting in an angle of 117°.

The shape of the molecule is determined by the relative positions of the bonded atoms, shown here as the red outline. Therefore the molecule is **bent** or **V shaped** with bond angle 117°.

Species with four negative charge centres

Molecules with four charge centres will position them at 109.5° to each other, giving a **tetrahedral** shape to the electron pairs. As before, if all the charge centres are bonding, the shape of the molecule will therefore be the same as this, that is tetrahedral.

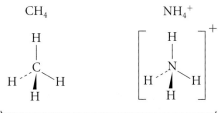

shape: tetrahedral; bond angle: 109.5°

View animated models of simple molecules.
Now go to www.heinemann.co.uk/hotlinks, insert the express code 4259P and click on this activity.

However, if one or more of the charge centres is a non-bonding pair, this will again influence the final shape of the molecule. Remember it is the position of the

You can test your knowledge of VSEPR theory.
Now go to www.heinemann.co.uk/hotlinks, insert the express code 4259P and click on this activity.

bonding pairs which determines the positions of the atoms. And again the non-bonding pairs will alter the bond angles by causing greater repulsion. For example:

NH_3 H—N—H   **pyramidal** 107°

H_2O H—O—H   bent or V-shaped 105°
              (2 non-bonding pairs cause greater repulsion here)

• **Examiner's hint:** Always draw the Lewis structure before attempting to predict the shape of a molecule as you have to know the number of bonding and non-bonding pairs around the central atom.

Exercise

6 Predict the shape and bond angles of the following molecules and ions:
  (a) H_2S **(b)** CF_4 **(c)** HCN   **(d)** NF_3 **(e)** CO_3^{2-}

Molecules with polar bonds are not always polar

We have learned that the polarity of a *bond* depends on the charge separation between its two bonded atoms. The polarity of a *molecule*, however, will depend on:

- the polar bonds that it contains
- the way in which such polar bonds are orientated with respect to each other, in other words on the shape of the molecule.

If the bonds are of equal polarity (i.e. involving the same elements) *and* are arranged symmetrically with respect to each other, their charge separations (dipoles) will oppose each other and so will effectively cancel each other out. In these cases the molecule will be non-polar, despite the fact that it contains polar bonds. It is a bit like a game of tug-of-war between players who are equally strong and symmetrically arranged.

These molecules are all non-polar because the dipoles cancel out.

$O = C = O$

Figure 4.4 Equal and opposite pulls cancel each other out.

The arrows in these structures represent the pull of electrons in the bonds. If, however, *either* the molecule contains bonds of different polarity, *or* its bonds are not symmetrically arranged, then the polarities will not cancel out and the molecule will be polar. Another way of describing this is to say that it has a net dipole moment which refers to its turning force in an electric field. This is what would happen in a tug of war if the players were not equally strong or were not pulling in exactly opposite directions.

These molecules are all polar because the dipoles do not cancel out:

CH₃Cl   NH₃   H₂O

Figure 4.5 When the pulls are not equal and opposite there is a net pull.

Exercise

7 By reference to the shape of their molecules, predict whether the following will be polar:
  (a) PH_3 **(b)** CF_4 **(c)** HCN

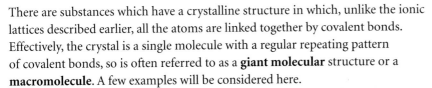

Some covalent substances form crystalline solids

There are substances which have a crystalline structure in which, unlike the ionic lattices described earlier, all the atoms are linked together by covalent bonds. Effectively, the crystal is a single molecule with a regular repeating pattern of covalent bonds, so is often referred to as a **giant molecular** structure or a **macromolecule**. A few examples will be considered here.

Allotropes of carbon

Allotropes are different forms of an element in the same physical state. Different bonding within these structures gives rise to distinct forms with different properties.

Carbon has three allotropes and these are described and compared in the table below.

Graphite	Diamond	Fullerene C_{60}
Each C atom is covalently bonded to 3 others, forming hexagons in parallel layers with bond angles of 120°. The layers are held only by weak van der Waals' forces (described later in this chapter) so they can slide over each other.	Each C atom is covalently bonded to 4 others tetrahedrally arranged in a regular repetitive pattern with bond angles of 109.5°. It is the hardest known natural substance.	Each C atom is bonded in a sphere of 60 carbon atoms, consisting of 12 pentagons and 20 hexagons. Structure is a closed spherical cage in which each carbon is bonded to 3 others.
density 2.26 g cm^{-3}	density 3.51 g cm^{-3}	density 1.72 g cm^{-3}
contains one non-bonded, delocalized electron per atom; conducts electricity	all electrons are bonded; non-conductor of electricity	easily accepts electrons to form negative ions
non-lustrous, grey solid	lustrous crystal	yellow crystalline solid, soluble in benzene
used as lubricant and in pencils	polished for jewellery and ornamentation; used in tools and machinery for grinding and cutting glass	reacts with K to make superconducting crystalline material; related forms are used to make nanotubes for the electronics industry, catalysts and lubricants

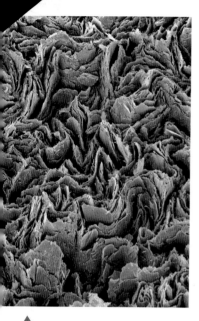

Coloured scanning electron micrograph of layers making up the core of a graphite pencil. Because graphite is a soft form of carbon, the tip of the pencil disintegrates under pressure leaving marks on the paper.

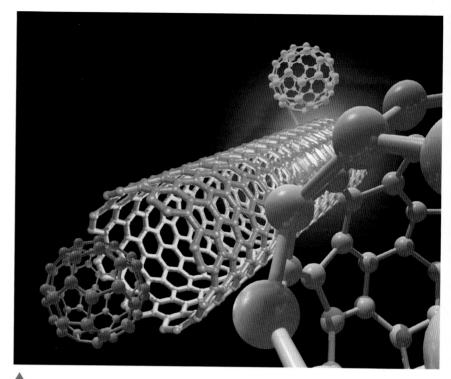

Computer artwork of spherical and cylindrical fullerenes – buckyballs and carbon nanotubes. These substances are being investigated for a wide range of technical and medical uses. Here the carbon nanotubes have been engineered to have a diameter just large enough to allow buckyballs to pass through them.

Cut and polished diamond. Diamond is a naturally occurring form of carbon that has crystallized under great pressure. It is the hardest known mineral. Splendid crystals are found in South Africa, Russia, Brazil and Sierra Leone.

The discovery of fullerenes in 1985 was the result of collaboration between scientists with different experience and research objectives. Harold Kroto from England was interested in red giant stars and how carbon might polymerize near them. Robert Curl and Richard Smalley working in Texas, USA had developed a technique using a laser beam for evaporating and analysing different substances. When they worked together and applied this technique to graphite, clusters of stable C_{60} and C_{70} spheres were formed. The three scientists shared the Nobel Prize in Chemistry for 1996.

The name 'fullerene' was given to the newly discovered spheres C_{60} in honour of the American architect R. Buckminster Fuller. He had designed the World Exhibition building in Montreal, Canada on the same concept of hexagons and a small number of pentagons to create a curved surface known as a geodesic dome. The dome of the Epcot Center in Disney World, Florida is similarly designed. Perhaps more familiarly it is also the structure of a European soccer ball. The term 'buckyballs' has slipped into common usage, derived from the full name of the structure 'buckminsterfullerene'.

View some models and photographs of carbon's allotropes.
Now go to www.heinemann.co.uk/hotlinks, insert the express code 4259P and click on this activity.

Silicon and silicon dioxide

Silicon is the most abundant element in the Earth's crust after oxygen, occurring as silica (SiO_2) in sand and in the silicate minerals. Since silicon is just below carbon in Group 4, the possibility of silicon-based life has been proposed. But unlike carbon, silicon is not able to form long chains, multiple bonds or rings so cannot compete with the diversity possible in organic chemistry, based on carbon. However, there is some evidence that the first forms of life were forms of clay minerals that were probably based on the silicon atom.

Like carbon, silicon is a Group 4 element and so its atoms have four valence shell electrons. In the elemental state, each silicon atom is covalently bonded to four others in a tetrahedral arrangement. This results in a giant lattice structure much like diamond.

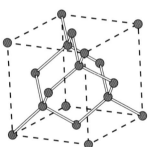

Figure 4.6 Silicon crystal structure and arrangement of bonds around a central silicon atom.

SiO_2, commonly known as silica or quartz, also forms a giant covalent structure. This is a similar tetrahedrally bonded structure, but here the bonds are between Si and O atoms. Each Si atom is covalently bonded to four oxygen atoms and each O to two Si atoms.

◀ Quartz crystals coloured scanning electron micrograph. Quartz is a form of silica (SiO_2) and the most abundant mineral in the Earth's crust. Quartz is used in optical and scientific instruments and in electronics such as quartz watches.

Figure 4.7 The structure of quartz, SiO₂.

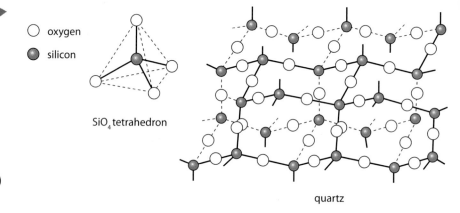

○ oxygen

● silicon

SiO₄ tetrahedron

quartz

Compare some covalent crystal structures.
Now got to www.heinemann.co.uk/hotlinks, insert the express code 4259P and click on this activity.

Note here the formula SiO_2 refers to the *ratio* of atoms within the giant molecule – the actual number of atoms present will be a very large multiple of this. The structure is strong, insoluble in water, has a high melting point and does not conduct electricity or heat. These are all properties we associate with glass and sand – different forms of silica.

4.3 Intermolecular forces

● **Examiner's hint:** Note that the prefix *intra-* refers to *within*, whereas the prefix *inter-* refers to *between*. For example an inter-national competition occurs between different nations, an intra-national contest within one nation.

Covalent bonds hold atoms together *within* molecules, but of course molecules do not exist in isolation. A gas jar full of chlorine Cl_2, for example, will contain millions of molecules of chlorine. So what are the forces that exist *between* these molecules, the so-called **intermolecular forces**? The answer depends on the structure and bonding of the molecules involved, so will vary for different molecules. We will consider three types here and see how they differ from each other in origin and in strength.

The strength of intermolecular forces will play a particularly important role in determining the volatility of a substance. Changing state from solid to liquid (melting) and from liquid to gas (boiling) both involve separating particles by overcoming the forces between them. It follows that the stronger the intermolecular forces, the more energy will be required to do this and so the higher will be the substance's melting and boiling points.

Van der Waals' forces

Johannes van der Waals (1837–1923), from the Netherlands, established himself as an eminent physicist on the publication of his very first paper, his PhD thesis. His study of the continuity of the gas and liquid state from which he put forward his 'equation of state' led James Clerk Maxwell to comment, 'There can be no doubt that the name of van der Waals will soon be among the foremost in molecular science.' Van der Waals did indeed fulfil this early promise, being awarded the Nobel Prize in Physics in 1910.

Non-polar molecules such as chlorine Cl_2 have no permanent separation of charge within their bonds because the shared electrons are pulled equally by the two chlorine atoms. In other words they do not have a permanent dipole.

However, because electrons behave somewhat like mobile clouds of negative charge, the density of this cloud may at any one moment be greater over one atom than the other. When this occurs the bond will have some separation of charge – a weak dipole known as a **temporary or instantaneous dipole**. This will not last for more than an instant as the electron density is constantly changing, but it may influence the electron distribution in the bond of a neighbouring molecule, causing an **induced dipole**.

| CI   CI | | |
| Electron cloud evenly distributed; no dipole. | At some instant, more of the electron cloud happens to be at one end of the molecule than the other; molecule has an instantaneous dipole. | Dipole is induced in a neighbouring molecule. |

This attraction is a van der Waals' force.

Figure 4.8 Temporary dipoles in Cl_2 cause van der Waals' forces between them.

As a result, weak forces of attraction, known as **van der Waals' forces**, will occur between opposite ends of these two temporary dipoles in the molecules. These are the weakest form of intermolecular force. Their strength increases as the number of electrons within a molecule increases, that is, with increasing M_r, as this increases the probability of temporary dipoles developing.

Substances that are held together by van der Waals' forces generally have low melting and boiling points, because relatively little energy is required to break the forces and separate the molecules from each other. This is why many elements and compounds with non-polar bonds are gases at room temperature, for example O_2, Cl_2 and CH_4. Boiling point data show how the strength of van der Waals' forces increases with increasing molecular mass. For example, comparing the boiling points of the halogens (Group 7 elements) and of the group of hydrocarbons known as the alkanes.

Element	M_r	Boiling point/°C	State at room temperature
F_2	38	−188	gas
Cl_2	71	−34	gas
Br_2	160	59	liquid
I_2	254	185	solid

Boiling point increases with increasing M_r.

Alkane	M_r	Boiling point/°C
CH_4	16	−164
C_2H_6	30	−89
C_3H_8	44	−42
C_4H_{10}	58	−0.5

Boiling point increases with increasing M_r.

Dipole–dipole attraction

Molecules such as HCl have a permanent separation of charge within their bonds as a result of the difference in electronegativity of the bonded atoms – one end of the molecule has a partial positive charge (δ^+) while the other end has a partial negative charge (δ^-). This is known as a **permanent dipole**. It results in opposite charges on neighbouring molecules attracting each other, generating a force known as a **dipole–dipole attraction**.

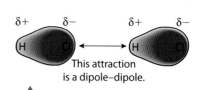

This attraction is a dipole–dipole.

Figure 4.9 Permanent dipoles in HCl cause forces of dipole–dipole attraction between them.

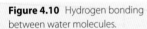

If you compare two covalent substances of similar molecular mass, the more polar substance will have the higher boiling point.

The strength of this intermolecular force will vary depending on the degree of polarity within the bond. For example, it will decrease in strength in the order: HCl>HBr>HI as the degree of polarity within the molecules decreases.

Dipole–dipole forces, however, are always stronger than van der Waals' forces. As a result, the melting and boiling points of polar compounds are higher than those of non-polar substances of comparable molecular mass.

Hydrogen bonding

When a molecule contains hydrogen covalently bonded to a very electronegative atom (fluorine, nitrogen or oxygen), these molecules are attracted to each other by a particularly strong type of intermolecular force called a **hydrogen bond**. The hydrogen bond is in essence a particular case of dipole–dipole attraction. The large electronegativity difference between hydrogen and the bonded fluorine, oxygen or nitrogen, results in the electron pair being pulled away from the hydrogen. Given its small size and the fact that it has no other electrons to shield the nucleus, the hydrogen now exerts a strong attractive force on a lone pair in the electronegative atom of a neighbouring molecule. This is the hydrogen bond.

Figure 4.10 Hydrogen bonding between water molecules.

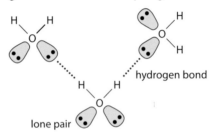

Hydrogen bonding only occurs between molecules which contain hydrogen bonded directly to fluorine, nitrogen or oxygen.

Hydrogen bonds are the strongest form of intermolecular attraction. Consequently they cause the boiling points of substances that contain them to be significantly higher than would be predicted from their M_r. We can see this in the graph below in which boiling points of the hydrides of Groups 4–7 are compared across the Periodic Table.

Figure 4.11 Periodic trends in the boiling points of the hydrides of Groups 4–7.

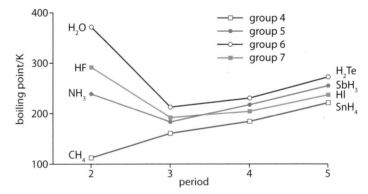

In all four groups there is an observable trend of boiling point increasing down the group as M_r increases. The anomalies are NH_3, HF and H_2O which have much higher boiling points than expected from their M_r. This can only be explained by the presence of hydrogen bonding in these molecules. If it wasn't for the fact that it is hydrogen bonded, H_2O would be a gas not a liquid at room temperature!

Likewise, when we compare the boiling points of some organic molecules that have similar or equal values of M_r we find a higher value where hydrogen bonding occurs between the molecules. For example, comparing two different forms (isomers) of C_2H_6O both with $M_r = 46$:

CH$_3$–O–CH$_3$	CH$_3$CH$_2$–O–H
methoxymethane $M_r = 46$ does not form hydrogen bonds boiling point $-23\,°C$	ethanol $M_r = 46$ forms hydrogen bonds boiling point $79\,°C$

Water makes a particularly interesting case for the study of hydrogen bonding. Here, because of the two hydrogen atoms in each molecule and the two lone pairs on the oxygen atom, each H$_2$O can form up to *four* hydrogen bonds with neighbouring molecules. Liquid water will contain fewer than this number, but in the solid form, ice, each H$_2$O will be maximally hydrogen bonded in this way. The result is a tetrahedral arrangement that holds the molecules a fixed distance apart, forming a fairly open structure which is actually *less* dense than the liquid. This is a remarkable fact – in nearly all other substances the solid form with closer packed particles is *more* dense than its liquid. The fact that ice floats on water is evidence therefore of the power of hydrogen bonds in holding the molecules together in ice. This density change means that water expands on freezing, which can lead to all kinds of problems such as burst pipes if not monitored. The same force of expansion is at work in the Earth's crust, fragmenting and splitting rocks, ultimately forming sand and soil particles. The humble hydrogen bond is truly responsible for massive geological changes!

● **Examiner's hint:** Make sure you realize that although hydrogen bonds are strong in relation to other types of intermolecular force, they are very much weaker (about 15–20 times) than covalent bonds and ionic bonds.

◀ Snowflake. This is an ice crystal that forms in air and has a temperature near the freezing point of water.

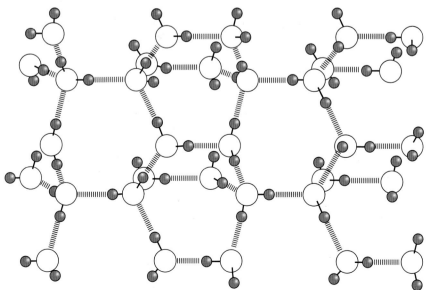

◀ **Figure 4.12** Arrangement of water molecules in ice. Each molecule is held by hydrogen bonds to four other molecules in a tetrahedral arrangement.

Worked example

Put the following molecules in order of increasing boiling point and explain your choice:

$$CH_3CHO, CH_3CH_2OH, CH_3CH_2CH_3$$

● **Examiner's hint:** Watch out for molecules, like CH_3CHO that contain H and O, but cannot form hydrogen bonds as the H is not directly bonded to the O.

Solution

First check the M_r of each molecule:

$CH_3CHO = 44$

$CH_3CH_2OH = 46$

$CH_3CH_2CH_3 = 44$, so they are all very similar.

Now consider the type of bonding and intermolecular attractions:

CH_3CHO	CH_3CH_2OH	$CH_3CH_2CH_3$

$$CH_3 - C \begin{smallmatrix} \diagup\diagup O \\ \diagdown H \end{smallmatrix}$$

$$CH_3 - \overset{\overset{\textstyle H}{|}}{\underset{\underset{\textstyle H}{|}}{C}} - O - H$$

polar bonds, therefore dipole–dipole   O–H bond, therefore H bonding   non-polar bonds, therefore van der Waals' forces

So the order starting with the lowest boiling point will be:

$$CH_3CH_2CH_3 < CH_3CHO < CH_3CH_2OH$$

In these examples, we have looked at hydrogen bonding as an intermolecular force, that is, *between* molecules. There are some important examples of it also occurring *within* large molecules where it plays a key role in determining properties. Proteins, for example, are fundamentally influenced by hydrogen bonding – you can read about this in Chapter 13, Option B Human Biochemistry. And a fascinating example is DNA (deoxyribose nucleic acid) which, as the chemical responsible for storing the genetic information in cells, is able to replicate itself exactly, a feat only possible because of its use of hydrogen bonding.

Computer artwork of a DNA molecule replicating. DNA is composed of two strands, held together by hydrogen bonds and twisted into a double helix. During replication the strands separate from each other by breaking the hydrogen bonds and each strand then acts as a template for the synthesis of a new molecule of DNA.

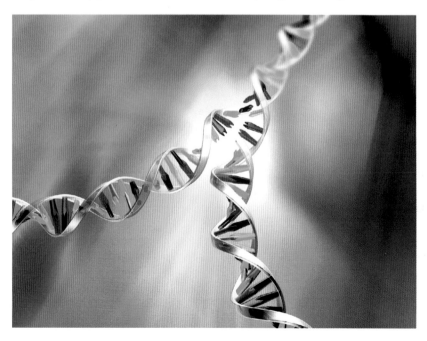

4.4 Metallic bonding

Metals are found on the left of the Periodic Table and have a small number of electrons in their outer shell. These are atoms with low ionization energies and so typically react with other elements by losing those electrons and forming positive ions. In other words, these are elements characterized by having a loose control over their outer shell electrons.

In the elemental state, when there is no other element present to accept the electrons and form an ionic compound, the outer electrons held only loosely by the atom's nucleus tend to 'wander off' or, more correctly, become **delocalized**. This means that they are no longer associated closely with any one metal nucleus but instead can spread themselves through the metal structure. The metal atoms without these electrons become positively charged ions and form a regular lattice structure through which these electrons can move freely.

You can think of it like a close neighbourhood of families where the children do not belong specifically to any one set of parents but are free to wander between the homes. This arrangement causes a close association between the families. Likewise in metals there is a force of electrostatic attraction between the lattice of positive ions and the delocalized electrons and this is known as **metallic bonding**. Understanding its origin helps to explain the physical properties of metals.

'pool' of delocalized electrons

lattice of positive ions

Figure 4.13 Model of metallic bonding.

Metals are good conductors of electricity because the delocalized electrons are highly mobile and can move through the metal structure in response to an applied voltage. This mobility of electrons is responsible for the fact that they are also very good conductors of heat. Furthermore the movement of electrons is non-directional – their movement is essentially random through the cation lattice – so they are not unduly disturbed by a change in the conformation of the metal through applied pressure. This property means that metals can be shaped under pressure so they are said to be **malleable**. A related property is that metals are **ductile**, meaning that they can be drawn out into threads. These properties are key reasons why metals are so widely used in objects as diverse as cars, electric wires and cutlery.

Copper is one of the oldest metals ever used. It is malleable, ductile and a good conductor of heat and electricity. Brass and bronze are copper alloys.

Alloys are produced by melting a metal, then adding controlled amounts of other metals or carbon, so that the different atoms can mix and bind by metallic bonding. They often have greater strength than their component elements and are used widely in manufacturing industries. Steel is an alloy of iron with varying amounts of carbon.

Steel manufacture is one of the world's largest industries and is sometimes used as a measure of a country's development and economic progress. Many countries are investing in technologies to become self-sufficient in steel making. It is estimated that by 2010 China's total steel output will be significantly above 500 million tonnes, with India and Russia also becoming increasingly productive. Steel is the most recycled material in the world and, in developed countries, recycling accounts for almost half of the steel produced.

Follow an animated summary of metallic bonding. Now go to www.heinemann.co.uk/hotlinks, insert the express code 4259P and click on this activity.

Physical properties

We have already seen how the nature of the bonds within a substance can predict and explain some of its properties. This is particularly true for physical properties, that is, those properties that can be examined without chemically altering the substance. We will consider three of these in more detail here.

Melting and boiling points

Ionic compounds tend to have high melting and boiling points as the forces of electrostatic attraction between the ions in the lattice are strong and thus require high energy to break. These compounds are thus solids at room temperature and will only melt at very high temperatures. NaCl, for example, remains solid until about 800 °C. This becomes an economic consideration in many industrial processes, such as the electrolysis of molten ionic compounds (Chapter 9), as it can be very expensive to maintain such high temperatures.

Macromolecular or giant covalent structures also have high melting and boiling points as covalent bonds must be broken for these changes of state to occur. They also exist as solids at room temperature. Diamond, for example, remains solid until about 4000 °C.

Covalent substances have lower melting and boiling points than ionic compounds as the forces that need to be overcome to separate the molecules are the relatively weak intermolecular forces. Consequently many covalent substances are liquids or gases at room temperature. As we have learned, however, the strength of the intermolecular forces varies widely in different molecules and the stronger they are, the higher will be the melting and boiling points. Remember that these forces will increase with:

- increasing molecular mass
- the extent of polarity within the bonds of the molecules.

These are the features to consider in predicting relative melting and boiling points.

Solubility

Solubility refers to the ease with which a solid (the solute) becomes dispersed through a liquid (the solvent) and forms a solution. Some substances like NaCl do this very readily in water, but much less readily in other liquids such as oil. On the other hand, we know that substances like sand and chlorophyll do not dissolve in water at all (otherwise think what would happen when it rained). So why the difference? There are several factors involved but, in general, solubility is determined by the degree to which the separated particles of solute are able to form bonds or attractive forces with the solvent.

Dry cleaning is a process where clothes are washed without water. Instead an organic liquid is used which may be a better solvent for stains caused by large non-polar molecules such as those in grass and grease.

Consider an ionic compound being placed in water. At the contact surface, partial charges in the water molecules are attracted to ions of opposite charge in the lattice, which may cause them to dislodge from their position. Ions separated from the lattice in this way become surrounded by water molecules and are said to be **hydrated**. When this happens, the solid is dissolved.

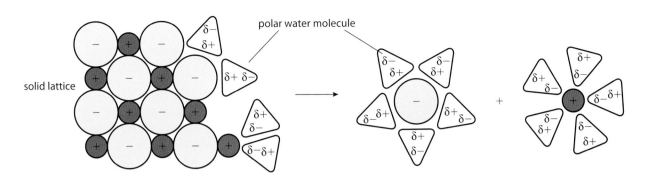

Figure 4.14 Polar solvent molecules are attracted to the ions in a solid lattice.

Similarly, many polar compounds are soluble owing to attraction between their dipoles and those in water. Sugar and ethanol, for example, are readily water soluble as they are able to form hydrogen bonds with water. The solubility of polar compounds is, however, more limited when we consider larger molecules in which the polar bond is only a small part of the total structure. Here the non-polar parts of the molecule, unable to associate with water, render it insoluble. We will explore such trends characteristic of homologous series in Organic Chemistry, Chapter 10.

Predictably, this inability of non-polar groups to associate with water means that non-polar covalent substances are not readily soluble in water. Nitrogen N_2, for example, has very low solubility in water at normal pressure, as do hydrocarbons such as candle wax.

The situation is reversed when we consider the pattern with a non-polar solvent such as hexane, C_6H_{14}. Here ionic compounds will not be soluble, as the ions, lacking any attraction to the solvent, will remain tightly bound to each other in the lattice. Similarly, polar compounds will have limited solubility, remaining held to each other by their dipole–dipole attractions. Non-polar substances, on the other hand, will be soluble owing to their ability to interact with the non-polar solvent by van der Waals' forces. For example, the halogens, all non-polar diatomic molecules (e.g. Br_2) are readily soluble in the non-polar solvent paraffin oil.

And so it appears that solubility trends are based on the similar chemical nature of the solute and solvent, as this is most likely to lead to successful interactions between them. The expression 'like dissolves like' is often used to capture this notion. It is summarized in the table below. (Note though that these are only generalized statements and somewhat over-simplified as there are some important exceptions.)

	Ionic compounds	Polar covalent compounds	Non-polar covalent compounds
solubility in polar solvent, e.g. water	soluble	solubility increases as polarity increases	non-soluble
solubility in non-polar solvent, e.g. hexane	non-soluble	solubility increases as polarity decreases	soluble

Electrical conductivity

Condom conductivity test. Condoms are tested for holes by being filled with water and placed in a solution of NaCl and then attached to electrodes. The current will not be conducted across the insulating material of the condom, but if there is a hole it will be conducted into the salty water, triggering an alarm. All condoms are conductivity tested in this way.

The ability of a compound to conduct electricity depends on whether it contains ions that are able to move and carry a charge. Ionic compounds are not able to conduct electricity in the solid state as the ions are firmly held within the lattice and so cannot move. However, when the ionic compound is either present in the liquid state (molten), or dissolved in water (aqueous solution), the ions *will* be able to move. Therefore ionic compounds as liquids or aqueous solutions do show electrical conductivity.

Covalent compounds do not contain ions and so are not able to conduct electricity in the solid or liquid state.

Practice questions

1 Which molecule is linear?

A SO_2 B CO_2

C H_2S D Cl_2O

© International Baccalaureate Organization [2004]

2 Why is the boiling point of PH_3 lower than that of NH_3?

A PH_3 is non-polar whereas NH_3 is polar.

B PH_3 is not hydrogen bonded whereas NH_3 is hydrogen bonded.

C Van der Waals' forces are weaker in PH_3 than in NH_3.

D The molar mass of PH_3 is greater than that of NH_3.

© International Baccalaureate Organization [2004]

3 Element X is in Group 2 and element Y is in Group 7, of the Periodic Table. Which ions will be present in the compound formed when X and Y react together?

A X^+ and Y^- B X^{2+} and Y^-

C X^+ and Y^{2-} D X^{2-} and Y^+

© International Baccalaureate Organization [2003]

4 What is the Lewis (electron dot) structure for sulfur dioxide?

A :Ö:S::Ö:

B :Ö:S̈:Ö:

C :Ö::S::Ö:

D :Ö::S̈:Ö:

5 How do bond length and bond strength change as the number of bonds between two atoms increases?

	Bond length	Bond strength
A	increases	increases
B	increases	decreases
C	decreases	increases
D	decreases	decreases

6 Which of the following is true for CO_2?

	$C=O$ bond	CO_2 molecule
A	polar	non-polar
B	non-polar	polar
C	polar	polar
D	non-polar	non-polar

7 The molar masses of C_2H_6, CH_3OH and CH_3F are very similar. How do their boiling points compare?

A $C_2H_6 < CH_3OH < CH_3F$

B $CH_3F < CH_3OH < C_2H_6$

C $CH_3OH < CH_3F < C_2H_6$

D $C_2H_6 < CH_3F < CH_3OH$

8 Which statement is true for most ionic compounds?

A They contain elements of similar electronegativity.

B They conduct electricity in the solid state.

C They are coloured.

D They have high melting and boiling points.

9 When the following bond types are listed in decreasing order of strength (strongest first), what is the correct order?

A covalent > hydrogen > van der Waals'

B covalent > van der Waals' > hydrogen

C hydrogen > covalent > van der Waals'

D van der Waals' > hydrogen > covalent

10 Which substance is most soluble in water (in mol dm^{-3}) at 298 K?

A　CH_3CH_3

B　CH_3OCH_3

C　CH_3CH_2OH

D　$CH_3CH_2CH_2CH_2OH$

© International Baccalaureate Organization [2004]

11 What is the valence shell electron pair repulsion (VSEPR) theory used to predict?

A　the energy levels in an atom

B　the shapes of molecules and ions

C　the electronegativities of elements

D　the type of bonding in compounds

© International Baccalaureate Organization [2005]

12 Which substance has the lowest electrical conductivity?

A　Cu(s)

B　Hg(l)

C　H_2(g)

D　LiOH(aq)

© International Baccalaureate Organization [2005]

13 Which molecule is non-polar?

A　H_2CO

B　SO_3

C　NF_3

D　$CHCl_3$

© International Baccalaureate Organization [2004]

14 (a)　**(i)** Draw Lewis (electron dot) structures for CO_2 and H_2S showing all valence electrons. (2)

　　(ii) State the shape of each molecule and explain your answer in terms of VSEPR theory.

　　　CO_2

　　　H_2S (4)

　　(iii) State and explain whether each molecule is polar or non-polar. (2)

(b) Identify the strongest type of intermolecular force in each of the following compounds.

　　CH_3Cl

　　CH_4

　　CH_3OH (3)

(*Total 11 marks*)

© International Baccalaureate Organization [2004]

15 (a) Draw the Lewis structure of methanoic acid, HCOOH. (1)

(b) In methanoic acid, predict the bond angle around the

　　(i) carbon atom

　　(ii) oxygen atom bonded to the hydrogen atom. (2)

(c) State and explain the relationship between the length and strength of the bonds between the carbon atom and the two oxygen atoms in methanoic acid. (3)

(*Total 6 marks*)

© International Baccalaureate Organization [2003]

16 (a) The letters W, X, Y and Z represent four consecutive elements in the Periodic Table. The number of electrons in the highest occupied energy levels are: W: 3, X: 4, Y: 5, Z: 6 Write the formula for:

　　(i) an ionic compound formed from W and Y, showing the charges (2)

　　(ii) a covalent compound containing X and Z. (1)

(b) State the number of protons, electrons and neutrons in the ion $^{15}_{7}N^{3-}$. (2)

(c) State the type of bonding in the compound $SiCl_4$. Draw the Lewis structure for this compound. (3)

(d) Outline the principles of the valence shell electron pair repulsion (VSEPR) theory. (3)

(e) **(i)** Use the VSEPR theory to predict and explain the shape and the bond angle of each of the molecules SCl_2 and C_2Cl_2. (6)

  (ii) Deduce whether or not each molecule is polar, giving a reason for your answer. (3)

(Total 20 marks)

17 (a) The boiling points of the hydrides of the group 6 elements are shown below.

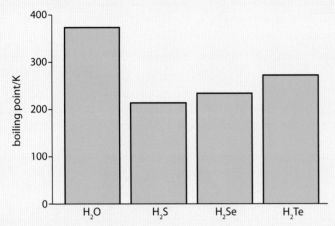

(i) Explain the trend in boiling points from H_2S to H_2Te. (2)

(ii) Explain why the boiling point of water is higher than would be expected from the group trend. (2)

(b) **(i)** State the shape of the electron distribution around the oxygen atom in the water molecule and state the shape of the molecule. (2)

  (ii) State and explain the value of the HOH bond angle. (2)

(c) Explain why the bonds in silicon tetrachloride, $SiCl_4$, are polar, but the molecule is not. (2)

The diagrams below represent the structures of iodine, sodium and sodium iodide.

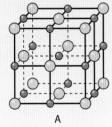 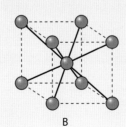 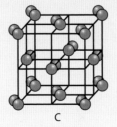

A B C

(d) **(i)** Identify which of the structures (A, B and C) correspond to iodine, sodium and sodium iodide. (1)

  (ii) State the type of bonding in each structure. (3)

(e) **(i)** Sodium and sodium iodide can both conduct electricity when molten, but only sodium can conduct electricity when solid. Explain this difference in conductivity in terms of the structures of sodium and sodium iodide. (4)

  (ii) Explain the high volatility of iodine compared to sodium and sodium iodide. (2)

(Total 20 marks)

 5 Energetics

All chemical reactions are accompanied by energy changes. Energy changes are vital. Our body's processes are dependent on the energy changes which occur during respiration, when glucose reacts with oxygen, and modern lifestyles are dependent on the transfer of energy that occurs when fuels burn. Energy changes are also important as they offer a signpost for the direction of change. They deepen our understanding of why things happen. In this chapter we will see how creative thinking, accurate calculations and careful observations and measurement can lead to a deeper understanding of the relationship between heat and chemical change. The calculations we encounter will allow us to assess the energy changes that occur both in real and potential chemical reactions.

▲ Conifer trees on fire during a forest fire at Stanley, Idaho, USA. This chapter will show how to calculate the energy changes in such exothermic combustion reactions.

Assessment statements

5.1 Exothermic and endothermic reactions
5.1.1 Define the terms *exothermic reaction*, *endothermic reaction* and *standard enthalpy change of reaction* ($\Delta H^{\ominus}$).
5.1.2 State that combustion and neutralization are exothermic processes.
5.1.3 Apply the relationship between temperature change, enthalpy change and the classification of a reaction as endothermic or exothermic.
5.1.4 Deduce, from an enthalpy level diagram, the relative stabilities of reactants and products and the sign of the enthalpy change for the reaction.

5.2 Calculation of enthalpy changes
5.2.1. Calculate the heat energy change when the temperature of a pure substance is changed.
5.2.2 Design suitable experimental procedures for measuring the heat energy changes of reactions.
5.2.3 Calculate the enthalpy change for a reaction using experimental data on temperature changes, quantities of reactants and mass of water.
5.2.4 Evaluate the results of experiments to determine enthalpy changes.

5.3 Hess's law
5.3.1 Determine the enthalpy change of a reaction that is the sum of two or three reactions with known enthalpy changes.

5.4 Bond enthalpies
5.4.1 Define the term *average bond enthalpy*.
5.4.2 Explain, in terms of average bond enthalpies, why some reactions are exothermic and others are endothermic.

▲ James Prescott Joule (1818–1889) was devoted to accurate measurements of heat. The SI unit of energy is named after him.

5.1 Exothermic and endothermic reactions

Energy and heat

Energy is a measure of the ability to do **work**, that is to move an object against an opposing force. It comes in many forms and includes heat, light, sound, electricity and chemical energy – the energy released or absorbed during chemical reactions. This chapter will focus on reactions which involve heat changes. Heat is a form of energy which is transferred as a result of a temperature difference and produces an increase in disorder in how the particles behave. Heat increases the average kinetic energy of the molecules in a disordered fashion. This is to be contrasted with work, which is a more ordered process. When you do work on a beaker of water, by lifting it from a table, for example, you raise all the molecules above the table in the same way.

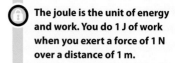
System and surroundings

Chemical and physical changes take place in many different environments such as test tubes, polystyrene cups, industrial plants and living cells. It is useful in these cases to distinguish between the **system** – the area of interest and the **surroundings** – in theory everything else in the universe. Most chemical reactions take place in an open system.

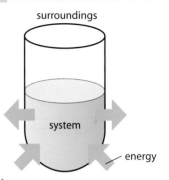

Figure 5.1 The system is the sample or reaction vessel of interest. The surroundings make up the rest of the universe.

Exothermic and endothermic reactions

Most chemical reactions, including all **combustion** and **neutralization** reactions are **exothermic**, as they result in a transfer of heat energy from the system to the surroundings. As heat is given out during the reaction, the products have less energy or heat content than the reactants. The heat content of a substance is called its **enthalpy**, a name which comes from the Greek word for 'heat inside'. It is like the reservoir of heat contained within a substance, which can be released as heat when it reacts. The heat content of a system decreases during an exothermic reaction and we can say that the enthalpy change, **ΔH**, is negative.

An open system can exchange energy and matter with the surroundings. A closed system can exchange energy but not matter with the surroundings.

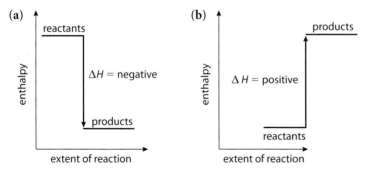

The combustion of methane can be described by the thermochemical equation:

$$CH_4(g) + 2O_2(g) \rightarrow CO_2(g) + 2H_2O(l) \qquad \Delta H = -890 \text{ kJ mol}^{-1}$$

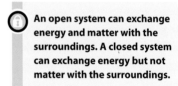

Figure 5.2 (a) An exothermic reaction: The enthalpy of the products is less than the enthalpy of the reactants. (b) An endothermic reaction: The enthalpy of the products is greater than the enthalpy of the reactants.

How important are technical terms such as *enthalpy* in different areas of knowledge? Is their correct use a necessary or sufficient indicator of understanding?

This is a shorthand way of expressing the information that *one mole* of methane gas reacts with *two moles* of oxygen gas to give *one mole* of gaseous carbon dioxide and *two moles* of liquid water and *releases* 890 kJ of heat energy.

A few reactions are **endothermic** as they result in an energy transfer from the surroundings to the system. In this case the products have more heat content than the reactants and ΔH is positive.

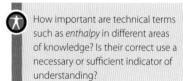

The thermite reaction between powdered aluminium and iron oxide:

$$2Al(s) + Fe_2O_3(s) \rightarrow Al_2O_3(s) + 2Fe(s)$$

releases 841 kJ mol^{-1} of heat energy. This is sufficient energy to melt the iron produced. The reaction is used in incendiary weapons and in underwater welding.

See the thermite reaction. Now go to www.heinemann.co.uk/hotlinks, insert the express code 4259P and click on this activity.

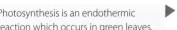

It is important to give the state symbols in thermochemical equations as the energy changes depend on the state of the reactants and the products.

Photosynthesis is an endothermic reaction which occurs in green leaves.

See some unorthodox applications of the thermite reaction, *which were done under carefully controlled conditions.*
Now go to
www.heinemann.co.uk/hotlinks,
insert the express code 4259P and
click on this activity.

What are the differences between the two videos of the thermite reaction? Which video is the most entertaining? What responsibilities do film makers have towards their audience?

For exothermic reactions heat is given out by the system and ΔH is negative.
For endothermic reactions heat is absorbed by the system and ΔH is positive.

The reaction

$Ba(OH)_2.8H_2O(s) + 2NH_4SCN(s) \rightarrow$
$Ba(SCN)_2(aq) + 2NH_3(g) + 10H_2O(l)$

causes water around the beaker to freeze.
Now go to
www.heinemann.co.uk/hotlinks,
insert the express code 4259P and
click on this activity.

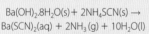

The standard conditions for enthalpy changes are:
- a temperature of 298 K or 25 °C
- a pressure of 101.3 kPa (1 atm)
- concentrations of 1 mol dm⁻³ for all solutions
- all the substances in their standard states.

The thermochemical equation for photosynthesis, for example, can be represented as:

$$6CO_2(g) + 6H_2O(l) \rightarrow C_6H_{12}O_6(aq) + 6O_2(g) \qquad \Delta H = +2802.5 \text{ kJ mol}^{-1}$$

Exercises

1 When a sample of NH_4SCN is mixed with solid $Ba(OH)_2.8H_2O$ in a glass beaker, the mixture changes to a liquid and the temperature drops sufficiently to freeze the beaker to the table. Which statement is true about the reaction?
   A The process is endothermic and ΔH is $-$
   B The process is endothermic and ΔH is $+$
   C The process is exothermic and ΔH is $-$
   D The process is exothermic and ΔH is $+$

2 Which one of the following statements is *true* of all exothermic reactions?
   A They produce gases.
   B They give out heat.
   C They occur quickly.
   D They involve combustion.

As the enthalpy change for a reaction depends on the conditions under which the reaction occurs **standard enthalpy changes** $\Delta H^\ominus$ are given in the literature.

Heat and temperature

The temperature of an object is a measure of the average kinetic energy of the particles (see page 10). If the same amount of heat energy is added to two different objects, the temperature change will not be the same, as the average kinetic energy of the particles will not increase by the same amount. The object with the smallest number of particles will experience the larger temperature increase. In general, the increase in temperature when an object is heated depends on:
- the mass of the object
- the heat added
- the nature of the substance.

Different substances need different amounts of heat to increase the temperature of unit mass of material by 1 K.

heat change = mass (m) × specific heat capacity (c) × temperature change (ΔT)

This relationship allows the heat change in a material to be calculated from the temperature change.

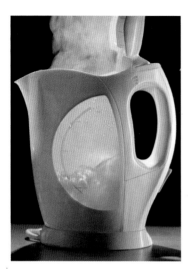 

◀ The water in the kettle has a higher temperature but the water in the swimming pool has more heat energy. Temperature is a measure of the average kinetic energy of the molecules.

> The specific heat capacity (c) is defined as the heat needed to increase the temperature of unit mass of material by 1 K. Specific heat capacity
>
> c = heat change/($m \times \Delta T$)
>
> where m is mass and ΔT is temperature change

> A temperature rise of 1 K is the same as the temperature rise of 1 °C.

Worked example

How much heat is released when 10.0 g of copper with a specific heat capacity of 0.385 J g^{-1}°C^{-1} is cooled from 85.0 °C to 25.0 °C?

Solution

Heat change = $m \times c \times \Delta T$
= $-10.0 \times 0.385 \times 60.0$ (the value is negative as the Cu has lost heat) = -231 J

> It takes more heat energy to increase the temperature of a swimming pool by 5 °C than boil a kettle of water from room temperature. The swimming pool contains more water molecules and has a larger heat capacity.

Exercises

3 If 500 J of heat is added to 100.0 g samples of each of the substances below, which will have the largest temperature increase?

		Specific heat capacity/J g^{-1} K^{-1}
A	gold	0.129
B	silver	0.237
C	copper	0.385
D	water	4.18

4 The specific heat of metallic mercury is 0.138 J g^{-1} C^{-1}. If 100.0 J of heat is added to a 100.0 g sample of mercury at 25.0 °C, what is the final temperature of the mercury?

> Heat change = $m \times c \times \Delta T$
> Heat change (J) = m (g) × c (J g^{-1} K^{-1}) ΔT (K)
> When the heat is absorbed by water, $c = 4.18$ J K^{-1} g^{-1}. This value is given in the IB Data booklet.

W Determine the specific heat capacity of ethanol from this simulation.
Now go to www.heinemann.co.uk/hotlinks, insert the express code 4259P and click on this activity.

Enthalpy changes and the direction of change

There is a natural direction for change. When we slip on a ladder, we go down not up. The direction of change is in the direction of lower stored energy. In a similar way, we expect methane to burn when we strike a match and form carbon dioxide and water. The chemicals are changing in a way which reduces their enthalpy.

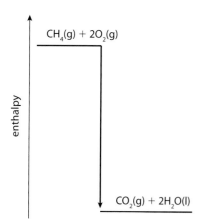

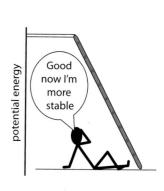

Figure 5.3 An exothermic reaction can be compared to a person falling off a ladder. Both changes lead to a reduction in stored energy. The state of lower energy is more stable.

There are many examples of exothermic reactions and we generally expect a reaction to occur if it leads to a reduction in enthalpy. In the same way that a ball is more stable on the ground than in mid air, we can say that the products in an exothermic reaction are more stable than the reactants. It is important to realize that stability is a relative term. Hydrogen peroxide, for example, is stable with respect to its elements but unstable relative to its decomposition to water and oxygen.

Figure 5.4 Hydrogen peroxide is stable relative to the hydrogen and oxygen but unstable relative to water.
$$\Delta H_1 + \Delta H_2 = \Delta H_3$$

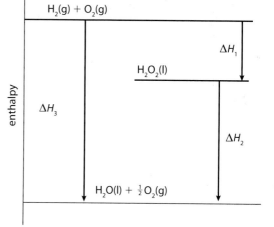

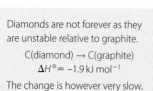

Diamonds are not forever as they are unstable relative to graphite.
$$C(diamond) \rightarrow C(graphite)$$
$$\Delta H^\ominus = -1.9 \text{ kJ mol}^{-1}$$
The change is however very slow.

The sign of ΔH is a guide for the likely direction of change but it is not completely reliable. We do not expect a person to fall up a ladder but some endothermic reactions can occur. For example, the reaction:

$$6SOCl_2(l) + FeCl_3.6H_2O(s) \rightarrow FeCl_3(s) + 6SO_2(g) + 12HCl(g)$$
$$\Delta H^\ominus = +1271 \text{ kJ mol}^{-1}$$

is extremely endothermic. Endothermic reactions are less common and occur when there is an increase in disorder of the system, for example owing to the production of gas. It is not necessary to know the details at this level.

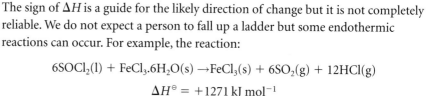
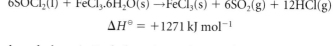

Diamond is a naturally occurring form of carbon that has crystallized under great pressure. It is unstable relative to graphite.

Calculation of enthalpy changes

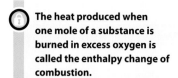
The heat produced when one mole of a substance is burned in excess oxygen is called the enthalpy change of combustion.

Heat of combustion

For liquids such as ethanol, the enthalpy change of combustion can be determined using the simple apparatus shown in Figure 5.5.

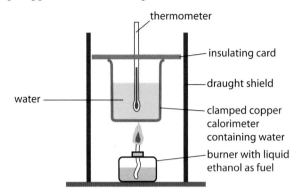

thermometer

insulating card

draught shield

water

clamped copper calorimeter containing water

burner with liquid ethanol as fuel

The temperature of the water increases as it has increased in heat content, owing to the heat released by the combustion reaction.

Figure 5.5 The heat produced by the combustion of the fuel is calculated from the temperature change of the water in the metal calorimeter. Copper is a good conductor of heat, so heat from the flame can be transferred to the water.

● **Examiner's hint:** It is important to state all assumptions when processing data. Simple treatments of heat of combustion reactions assume that all the heat is absorbed by the water, but the heat absorbed by the copper calorimeter can also be calculated.

Exercise

5 The mass of the burner and its content is measured before and after the experiment. The thermometer is read before and after the experiment. What are the expected results?

	Mass of burner and contents	Reading on thermometer
A	decreases	increases
B	decreases	stays the same
C	increases	increases
D	increases	stays the same

Calculating heats of reaction from temperature changes

When the heat released by an exothermic reaction is absorbed by water, the temperature of the water increases. The heat produced by the reaction can be calculated if it is assumed that all the heat is absorbed by the water.

$$\text{Heat change of reaction} = -\text{ heat change of water}$$
$$= -m_{H_2O} \times c_{H_2O} \times \Delta T_{H_2O}$$

As the water has gained the heat produced by the reaction, the heat change of reaction is negative when the temperature of the water increases.

During an endothermic reaction, the heat absorbed by the reaction is taken from the water and so the temperature of the water decreases. As the water has lost the heat absorbed by the reaction, the heat change of reaction is positive when the temperature of the water decreases.

As the heat change observed depends on the amount of reaction, for example the number of moles of fuel burned, enthalpy change reactions are usually expressed in kJ mol^{-1}.

Sherbet contains sodium hydrogen carbonate and tartaric acid. When sherbet comes into contact with water on the tongue an endothermic reaction takes place. The sherbet draws heat energy from the water on the tongue creating a cold sensation.

Worked example

Calculate the enthalpy of combustion of ethanol from the following data. Assume all the heat from the reaction is absorbed by the water. Compare your value with the IB Data booklet value and suggest reasons for any differences.

Mass of water in copper calorimeter/g	200.00
Temperature increase in water/°C	13.00
Mass of ethanol burned/g	0.45

Solution

Number of moles of ethanol $= \dfrac{m_{C_2H_5OH}}{M_{C_2H_5OH}}$

$M_{C_2H_5OH} = (12.01 \times 2) + (6 \times 1.01) + 16.00 = 46.08 \text{ g mol}^{-1}$

Heat change of reaction $= -m_{H_2O} \times c_{H_2O} \times \Delta T_{H_2O}$

$\Delta H_{combustion}$ (J mol^{-1}) = heat change of reaction for one mole of ethanol

$$= -m_{H_2O} \times c_{H_2O} \times \frac{\Delta T_{H_2O}}{\text{number of moles of ethanol}}$$

$$= -m_{H_2O} \times c_{H_2O} \times \frac{\Delta T_{H_2O}}{\left(\dfrac{m_{C_2H_5OH}}{46.08}\right)} \text{ J mol}^{-1}$$

$$= -200.00 \times 4.18 \times \frac{13.00}{\left(\dfrac{0.45}{46.08}\right)} \text{ J mol}^{-1}$$

$$= -1112\,883 \text{ J mol}^{-1} = -1112.883 \text{ kJ mol}^{-1}$$

$$= -1100 \text{ kJ mol}^{-1}$$

The precision of the final answer is limited by the precision of the mass of the ethanol (see Chapter 11).

The IB Data booklet value is -1371 kJ mol^{-1}. Not all the heat produced by the combustion is transferred to the water. Some is needed to heat the copper calorimeter can and some has passed to the surroundings. The combustion of the ethanol is unlikely to be complete owing to the limited oxygen available, as assumed by the literature value.

● **Examiner's hint:** It is important that you record qualitative as well as quantitative data when measuring enthalpy changes, for example, evidence of incomplete combustion in an enthalpy of combustion determination. When asked to evaluate experiments and suggest improvements, avoid giving trivial answers such as incorrect measurement. Incomplete combustion, for example, can be reduced by burning the fuel in oxygen. Heat loss can be reduced by insulating the apparatus.

All combustion reactions are exothermic, so $\Delta H_{combustion}$ values are always negative.

Exercise

6 The heat released from the combustion of 0.0500 g of white phosphorus increases the temperature of 150.00 g of water from 25.0 °C to 31.5 °C. Calculate a value for the enthalpy change of combustion of phosphorus. Discuss possible sources of error in the experiment.

The combustion of fossil fuel, which meets many of our energy needs, produces carbon dioxide which is a greenhouse gas. It is important we are aware of how our lifestyle contributes to global warming. It is a global problem but we need to act locally.

● **Examiner's hint:** A common error when calculating heat changes is using the incorrect mass of substance heated.

Enthalpy changes of reaction in solution

The enthalpy changes of reaction in solution can be calculated by carrying out the reaction in an insulated system, for example, a polystyrene cup. The heat released or absorbed by the reaction can be measured from the temperature change of the water.

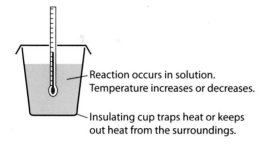

Reaction occurs in solution.
Temperature increases or decreases.

Insulating cup traps heat or keeps out heat from the surroundings.

Figure 5.6 A simple calorimeter. The polystyrene is a very good thermal insulator with a low heat capacity.

In the previous calculation, we assumed that all the heat produced in the reaction is absorbed by water. One of the largest sources of error in experiments conducted in a polystyrene cup are heat losses to the environment. Consider for example the exothermic reaction between zinc and aqueous copper sulfate:

$$Cu^{2+}(aq) + Zn(s) \rightarrow Cu(s) + Zn^{2+}(aq)$$

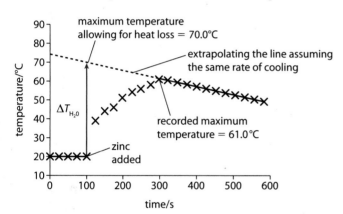

Figure 5.7 A known volume of copper sulfate solution is added to the calorimeter and its temperature measured every 25 s. Excess zinc powder is added after 100 s and the temperature starts to rise until a maximum after which it falls in an approximately linear fashion.

Heat is lost from the system as soon as the temperature rises above the temperature of the surroundings, in this case 20°C.

The maximum recorded temperature is lower than the true value obtained in a perfectly insulated system. We can make some allowance for heat loss by extrapolating the cooling section of the graph to the time when the reaction started.

$$\Delta H_{system} = 0 \text{ (assuming no heat loss)}$$
$$\Delta H_{system} = \Delta H_{water} + \Delta H_{reaction} \text{ (assuming all heat goes to the water)}$$
$$\Delta H_{reaction} = -\Delta H_{water}$$

For an exothermic reaction, $\Delta H_{reaction}$ is negative as heat has passed from the reaction into the water.

Heat transferred to water $= m_{H_2O} \times c_{H_2O} \times \Delta T_{H_2O}$

The limiting reactant must be identified in order to determine the molar enthalpy change of reaction.

Molar heat change of reaction $= -m_{H_2O} \times c_{H_2O} \times \dfrac{\Delta T_{H_2O}}{\text{(no. of moles limiting reagent)}}$

As the zinc was added in excess, the copper sulfate is the limiting reagent:

$$\text{number of moles } (n) = \text{concentration } ([\;]) \times \frac{\text{volume (cm}^3)\;(V)}{1000}$$

$$\text{number of moles of CuSO}_4\;(n_{\text{CuSO}_4}) = [\text{CuSO}_4] \times \frac{V_{\text{CuSO}_4}\;(\text{cm}^3)}{1000}$$

$$\text{molar heat change} = -m_{\text{H}_2\text{O}} \times c_{\text{H}_2\text{O}} \times \frac{\Delta T_{\text{H}_2\text{O}}}{n_{\text{CuSO}_4}}$$

$$= -m_{\text{H}_2\text{O}} \times c_{\text{H}_2\text{O}} \times \frac{\Delta T_{\text{H}_2\text{O}}}{([\text{CuSO}_4] \times V_{\text{CuSO}_4}/1000)}$$

If the solution is dilute, we can assume that

$$V_{\text{CuSO}_4} = V_{\text{H}_2\text{O}}$$

$$\text{molar heat change} = -m_{\text{H}_2\text{O}} \times c_{\text{H}_2\text{O}} \times \frac{\Delta T_{\text{H}_2\text{O}}}{([\text{CuSO}_4] \times V_{\text{H}_2\text{O}}/1000)}$$

$$= -c_{\text{H}_2\text{O}} \times \frac{\Delta T_{\text{H}_2\text{O}}}{([\text{CuSO}_4]/1000)}\;\text{J}$$

(assuming water has a density of 1.00 gm cm^{-3})

$$= -c_{\text{H}_2\text{O}} \times \frac{\Delta T^{\text{H}_2\text{O}}}{[\text{CuSO}_4]}\;\text{kJ}$$

Exercise

7 Calculate the molar enthalpy change from the data in Figure 5.7. The copper sulfate has a concentration of 1.00 mol dm^{-3}.

Worked example

The neutralization reaction between solutions of sodium hydroxide and sulfuric acid was studied by measuring the temperature changes when different volumes of the two solutions were mixed. The total volume was kept constant at 120 cm^3 and the concentrations of the two solutions were both 1.00 mol dm^{-3}.

Figure 5.8 Temperature changes produced when different volumes of sodium hydroxide and sulfuric acid are mixed.

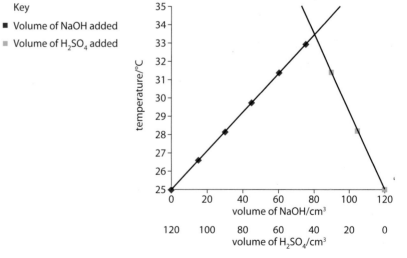

(a) Determine the volumes of the solutions which produce the largest increase in temperature.

(b) Calculate the heat produced by the reaction when the maximum temperature was produced.

(c) Calculate the heat produced for one mole of sodium hydroxide.

(d) The literature value for the enthalpy of neutralization is $-57.5\,\text{kJ mol}^{-1}$. Calculate the percentage error value and suggest a reason for the discrepancy between the experimental and literature values.

Solution

(a) From the graph: $V_{\text{NaOH}} = 80.0\,\text{cm}^3$

$V_{\text{H}_2\text{SO}_4} = 120.0 - 80.0 = 40.0\,\text{cm}^3$

(b) Assuming $120.0\,\text{cm}^3$ of the solution contains $120.0\,\text{g}$ of water and all the heat passes into the water.

heat produced $= -m_{\text{H}_2\text{O}} \times c_{\text{H}_2\text{O}} \times \Delta T_{\text{H}_2\text{O}}$

$= 120.0 \times 4.18 \times (33.5 - 25.0)$

$= 4264\,\text{J}$

(c) heat produced/mol $= \dfrac{4264}{n_{\text{NaOH}}}\,\text{J}$

$= \dfrac{4264}{(1.00 \times 80.0/1000)}\,\text{J}$

$= 53.3\,\text{kJ mol}^{-1}$

$\Delta H = -53.3\,\text{kJ mol}^{-1}$

(d) % error $= \dfrac{(-57.5 - 53.3)}{-57.5} \times 100\% = 7\%$

The calculated value assumes:
- no heat loss from the system
- all heat is transferred to the water
- the solutions contain $120\,\text{g}$ of water.

There are also uncertainties in the temperature, volume and concentration measurements.

The literature value assumes standard conditions.

What criteria do we use in judging whether discrepancies between experimental and theoretical values are due to experimental limitations or theoretical assumptions? Being a risk taker is one element of the IB Learner Profile. When is a scientist justified in rejecting the literature value in favour of their experimentally determined value?

● **Examiner's hint:** A common error is to miss out or incorrectly state the units and to miss out the negative sign for ΔH.

Determine the molar enthalpy of neutralization from this simulation. Now go to www.heinemann.co.uk/hotlinks, insert the express code 4259P and click on this activity.

5.3 Hess's Law

Standard enthalpy of formation

The **standard enthalpy of formation** of a substance is the enthalpy change that occurs when one mole of the substance is formed from its elements in their standard states under standard conditions.

Worked example

The enthalpy of formation of ethanol is given in table 11 of the IB Data booklet. Give the thermochemical equation which represents the standard enthalpy of formation of ethanol.

The standard enthalpy of formation of a substance is the enthalpy change that occurs when one mole of the substance is formed from its elements in their standard states under standard conditions.

Solution

The value from the IB Data booklet $= -278\,\text{kJ mol}^{-1}$

Ethanol (C_2H_5OH) is made from the elements carbon (C(graphite)), hydrogen ($H_2(g)$) and oxygen ($O_2(g)$).

___C(graphite) + ___$H_2(g)$ + ___$O_2(g) \rightarrow C_2H_5OH(l)$ $\Delta H^{\ominus} = -278\,\text{kJ mol}^{-1}$

Balancing the Cs, Hs and the Os:

$2C$(graphite) + $3H_2(g) + \frac{1}{2}O_2(g) \rightarrow C_2H_5OH(l)$ $\Delta H^{\ominus} = -278\,\text{kJ mol}^{-1}$

The standard enthalpy change of formation for an element $\Delta H^{\ominus}_{\text{form}} = 0$. There is no chemical change and so no enthalpy change when an element is formed from itself.

Exercise

8 Which of the following does *not* have a standard heat of formation value of *zero* at 25 °C and 1.00 atm?

A $Cl_2(g)$ B $I_2(s)$ C $Br_2(g)$ D Na(s)

Enthalpy cycles

Unfortunately, it is usually difficult to measure the enthalpy change of formation of compounds such as ethanol directly. Chemists have, however, found an indirect route for calculating enthalpy changes. Consider the following **energy cycle** in which the elements carbon, hydrogen and oxygen are combined to form carbon dioxide and water.

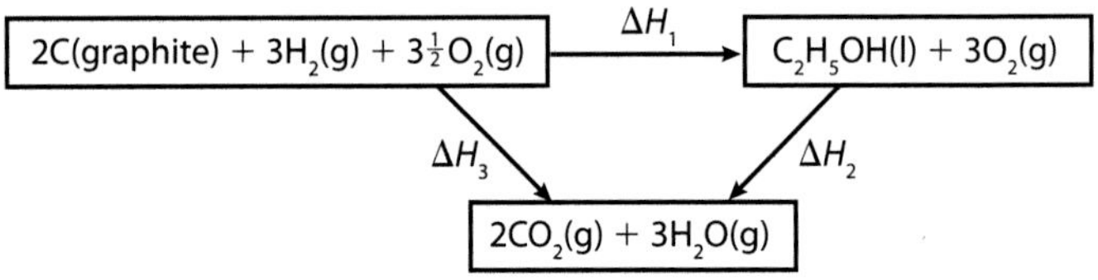

Figure 5.9 In the clockwise route the elements are first combined to form ethanol and then ethanol is burned. In the anticlockwise route the elements are burned separately.

Worked example

Use the IB Data booklet to find the values for the enthalpy changes ΔH_1, ΔH_2 and ΔH_3 and show that $\Delta H_1 + \Delta H_2 = \Delta H_3$.
Explain the relationship between the values.

Solution

Consider the clockwise route:

$\Delta H_1 = \Delta H^{\ominus}{}_{\text{form}}(C_2H_5OH(l)) = -278\ \text{kJ mol}^{-1}$

$\Delta H_2 = \Delta H^{\ominus}{}_{\text{combustion}}(C_2H_5OH(l)) = -1371\ \text{kJ mol}^{-1}$

$\Delta H_1 + \Delta H_2 = -1649\ \text{kJ mol}^{-1}$

Consider the anticlockwise route:

$\Delta H_3 = 2\Delta H^{\ominus}{}_{\text{combustion}}(\text{C(graphite)}) + 3\Delta H^{\ominus}{}_{\text{combustion}}(H_2(g))$

$= 2(-394) + 3(-286)\ \text{kJ mol}^{-1}$

$= -1646\ \text{kJ mol}^{-1}$

Given the uncertainty of the experimental values we can conclude that:

$$\Delta H_3 = \Delta H_1 + \Delta H_2$$

The values are the same as both changes correspond to the combustion of two moles of carbon and three moles of hydrogen. The result is a consequence of the law of conservation of energy, otherwise it would be possible to devise cycles in which energy was created or destroyed.

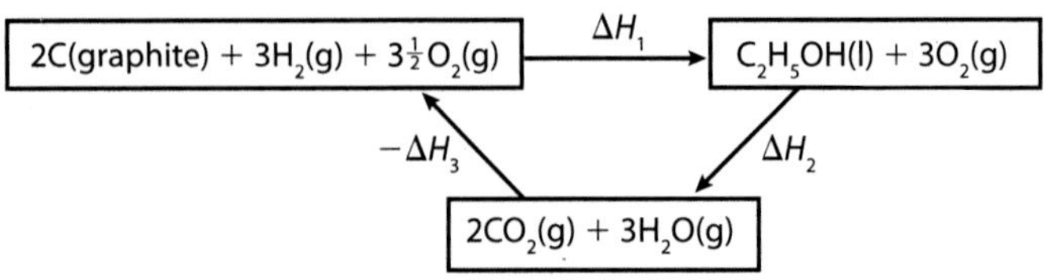

Figure 5.10 There is no net chemical change as the starting reactants and final products are the same.

From the law of conservation of energy:

$$\text{the enthalpy change in a complete cycle} = 0 = \Delta H_1 + \Delta H_2 - \Delta H_3$$

$$\text{therefore } \Delta H_1 + \Delta H_2 = \Delta H_3$$

Hess's Law is a natural consequence of the law of conservation of energy. If you know the law of conservation of energy, do you automatically know Hess's law?

This result can be generalized and is known as **Hess's law**.

Using Hess's law

Hess's law states that the enthalpy change for any chemical reaction is independent of the route provided the starting conditions and final conditions, and reactants and products, are the same.

The importance of Hess's law is that it allows us to calculate the enthalpy changes of reactions that we cannot measure directly in the laboratory. For example, although the elements carbon and hydrogen do not combine directly to form propane, the enthalpy change for the reaction:

$$3C(graphite) + 4H_2(g) \rightarrow C_3H_8(g)$$

can be calculated from the enthalpy of combustion data of the elements and the compound.

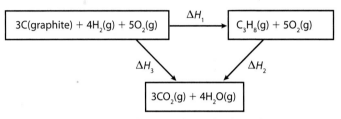

The steps in an enthalpy cycle may be hypothetical. The only requirement is that the individual chemical reactions in the sequence must balance. The relationship between the different reactions is clearly shown in an energy level diagram.

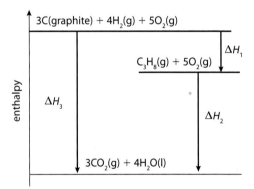

 Hess's law states that the enthalpy change for any chemical reaction is independent of the route, provided the starting conditions and final conditions, and reactants and products, are the same.

◀ **Figure 5.11** $\Delta H_1 + \Delta H_2 = \Delta H_3$, therefore $\Delta H_1 = \Delta H_3 - \Delta H_2$ Although ΔH_1 cannot be measured directly it can be calculated from the enthalpy of combustion of carbon, hydrogen and propane.

◀ **Figure 5.12** Energy level diagram used to obtain the enthalpy of formation of propane indirectly.

 Reversing the direction of a reaction reverses the sign of ΔH.

Worked example

Calculate the enthalpy change, $\Delta H^{\ominus}$, for the reaction:

$$S(s) + O_2(g) \rightarrow SO_2(g)$$

From the information below:

$$S(s) + \tfrac{3}{2}O_2(g) \rightarrow SO_3(g) \qquad \Delta H^{\ominus} = -395 \text{ kJ} \quad \text{I}$$
$$SO_2(g) + \tfrac{1}{2}O_2(g) \rightarrow SO_3(g) \qquad \Delta H^{\ominus} = -98 \text{ kJ} \quad \text{II}$$

Solution

We can think of the reaction as a journey from S(s) to $SO_2(g)$. As the enthalpy change cannot be measured directly, we must go by an alternative route suggested by the equations given.

Reaction I starts from the required starting point:

$$S(s) + \tfrac{3}{2}O_2(g) \rightarrow SO_3(g) \qquad \Delta H^{\ominus} = -395 \text{ kJ}$$

Reaction II relates $SO_3(g)$ to $SO_2(g)$. To finish with the required product we reverse the chemical change and the sign of enthalpy change:

$$SO_3(g) \rightarrow SO_2(g) + \tfrac{1}{2}O_2(g) \qquad \Delta H^{\ominus} = +98 \text{ kJ}$$

Use Hess's Law to find the enthalpy change of combustion of magnesium.
Now go to
www.heinemann.co.uk/hotlinks,
insert the express code 4259P and
click on this activity.

We can now combine these equations:

$$S(s) + \tfrac{3}{2}O_2(g) + SO_3(g) \rightarrow SO_3(g) + SO_2(g) + \tfrac{1}{2}O_2(g)$$
$$\Delta H^\ominus = -395 + 98 \text{ kJ}$$

Simplifying:

$$S(s) + \tfrac{3}{2}1O_2(g) + \cancel{SO_3(g)} \rightarrow \cancel{SO_3(g)} + SO_2(g) + \cancel{\tfrac{1}{2}O_2(g)} \quad \Delta H^\ominus = -297 \text{ kJ}$$
$$S(s) + O_2(g) \rightarrow SO_2(g) + \cancel{\tfrac{1}{2}O_2(g)} \quad \Delta H^\ominus = -297 \text{ kJ}$$

Exercise

9 Calculate the enthalpy change, $\Delta H^\ominus$, for the reaction:

$$2NO(g) + O_2(g) \rightarrow 2NO_2(g)$$

Using information below:

$$N_2(g) + O_2(g) \rightarrow 2NO(g) \quad \Delta H^\ominus = +180.5 \text{ kJ}$$
$$N_2(g) + 2O_2(g) \rightarrow 2NO_2(g) \quad \Delta H^\ominus = +66.4 \text{ kJ}$$

Using standard enthalpy changes of formation

Standard enthalpy changes of formation can be used to calculate the standard enthalpy change of any reaction. Consider the following general energy cycle:

Figure 5.13 The chemical change elements→products can either occur directly or indirectly. The total enthalpy change must be the same for both routes. Σ means 'the sum of'.

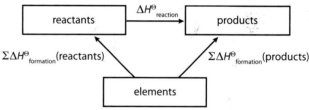

We have from the diagram

$$\Sigma\Delta H^\ominus_{\text{formation}}(\text{products}) = \Sigma\Delta H^\ominus_{\text{formation}}(\text{reactants}) + \Delta H^\ominus_{\text{reaction}}$$

This gives the general expression for $\Delta H^\ominus_{\text{reaction}}$ of any reaction.

$$\Delta H^\ominus_{\text{reaction}} = \Sigma\Delta H^\ominus_{\text{formation}}(\text{products}) - \Sigma\Delta H^\ominus_{\text{formation}}(\text{reactants})$$

$\Delta H^\ominus_{\text{reaction}} =$
$\Sigma\Delta H^\ominus_{\text{formation}}(\textbf{products}) -$
$\Sigma\Delta H^\ominus_{\text{formation}}(\textbf{reactants})$

Worked example

Calculate the enthalpy change for the reaction:

$$C_3H_8(g) + 5O_2(g) \rightarrow 3CO_2(g) + 4H_2O(g)$$

from the following standard enthalpy changes of formation.

	$\Delta H^\ominus_{\text{formation}}$/kJ mol^{-1}
$C_3H_8(g)$	-104
$CO_2(g)$	-394
$H_2O(l)$	-286

Solution

First write down the equation with the corresponding enthalpies of formation underneath:

$$C_3H_8(g) + 5O_2(g) \rightarrow 3CO_2(g) + 4H_2O(g)$$
$$-104 \qquad 0 \qquad 3(-394) \qquad 4(-286)$$

As the standard enthalpies of formation are given per mole they should be multiplied by the number of moles in the balanced equation, added in bold above.

Write down the general expression for the $\Delta H^\ominus{}_{reaction}$.

$$\Delta H^\ominus{}_{reaction} = \Sigma\Delta H^\ominus{}_{formation}(\text{products}) - \Sigma\Delta H^\ominus{}_{formation}(\text{reactants})$$

and express $\Delta H^\ominus{}_{reaction}$ in terms of the data given:

$$\Delta H^\ominus{}_{reaction} = 3(-394) + 4(-286) - (-104) = -2222\ \text{kJ mol}^{-1}$$

W Determine the molar enthalpy change of combustion for methane and use the value to calculate the molar enthalpy change of formation.
Now go to www.heinemann.co.uk/hotlinks, insert the express code 4259P and click on this activity.

Exercises

10 Calculate $\Delta H^\ominus$ (in kJ mol^{-1}) for the reaction:

$$Fe_3O_4(s) + 2C(\text{graphite}) \rightarrow 3Fe(s) + 2CO_2(g)$$

from the data below:

	$\Delta H^\ominus{}_{formation}$/kJ mol^{-1}
$Fe_3O_4(s)$	−1118
$CO_2(g)$	−394

11 Calculate $\Delta H^\ominus$ (in kJ mol^{-1}) for the reaction:

$$2NO_2(g) \rightarrow N_2O_4(g)$$

from the data below:

	$\Delta H^\ominus{}_{formation}$/kJ mol^{-1}
$NO_2(g)$	+33.2
$N_2O_4(g)$	+9.2

5.4 Bond enthalpies

Chemical reactions involve the breaking and making of bonds. To understand the energy changes in a chemical reaction we need to look at the energies needed to break the bonds that hold the atoms together in the reactants and the energy released when new bonds are formed in the products.

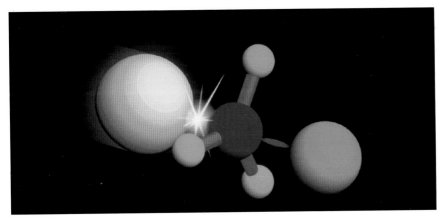

A chemical reaction involves the breaking and making of bonds. 500 to 1000 kJ of heat are typically needed to break one mole of chemical bonds. This image shows a change in the bond between the atoms represented by the yellow and the dark blue.

The bond enthalpy is the energy needed to break one mole of bonds in gaseous molecules under standard conditions.

Breaking bonds is an endothermic process

A covalent bond is due to the electrostatic attraction between the shared pair of electrons and the positive nucleus. Energy is needed to separate the atoms in a bond.

The bond enthalpy is the energy needed to break one mole of bonds in gaseous molecules under standard conditions.

● **Examiner's hint:** Learn the definition of bond enthalpy. A common error is to fail to indicate that all the species have to be in the gaseous state.

The energy change, for example, during the formation of two moles of chlorine atoms from one mole of chlorine molecules can be represented as:

$$Cl_2(g) \rightarrow 2Cl(g) \qquad \Delta H^\ominus = +242 \text{ kJ mol}^{-1}$$

The situation is complicated in molecules which contain more than two atoms. Breaking the first O—H bond in a water molecule requires more heat energy than breaking the second bond:

$$H_2O(g) \rightarrow H(g) + OH(g) \qquad \Delta H^\ominus = +502 \text{ kJ mol}^{-1}$$
$$OH(g) \rightarrow H(g) + O(g) \qquad \Delta H^\ominus = +427 \text{ kJ mol}^{-1}$$

Similarly the energy needed to break the O—H in other molecules such as ethanol, C_2H_5OH is different. In order to compare bond enthalpies which exist in different environments **average bond enthalpies** are tabulated.

Using Hess's Law:

$$H_2O(g) \rightarrow H(g) + OH(g) \qquad \Delta H^\ominus = +502 \text{ kJ mol}^{-1}$$
$$OH(g) \rightarrow H(g) + O(g) \qquad \Delta H^\ominus = +427 \text{ kJ mol}^{-1}$$
$$H_2O(g) \rightarrow H(g) + H(g) + O(g) \qquad \Delta H^\ominus = +502 +427 \text{ kJ mol}^{-1}$$

$$E(\text{O–H}) = \frac{(+502 +427)}{2} \text{ kJ mol}^{-1} = \frac{929}{2} = 464.5 \text{ kJ mol}^{-1}$$

This value should be compared with the bond enthalpies given in the table below which are calculated from a wide range of molecules.

Multiple bonds generally have higher bond enthalpies and are shorter than single bonds.

Bond	$E(X-Y)/\text{kJ mol}^{-1}$	Bond length/10^{-9}m
H—H	+436	0.074
C—C	+348	0.154
C=C	+612	0.134
C—H	+412	0.109
O=O	+496	0.121
O—H	+463	0.096
C=O	+743	0.122
Cl—Cl	+242	0.199

All bond enthalpies refer to reactions in the gaseous state so that the enthalpy changes caused by the formation and breaking of **intermolecular** forces can be ignored.

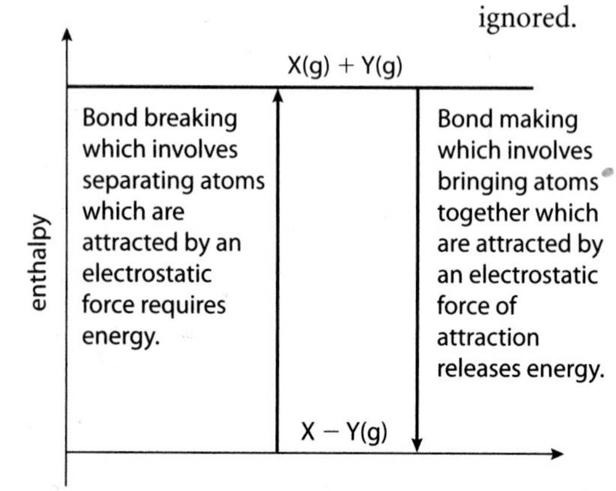

enthalpy

X(g) + Y(g)

Bond breaking which involves separating atoms which are attracted by an electrostatic force requires energy.

Bond making which involves bringing atoms together which are attracted by an electrostatic force of attraction releases energy.

X — Y(g)

Making bonds is an exothermic process

The same amount of energy is absorbed when a bond is broken as is given out when a bond is made. For example:

$$H(g) + H(g) \rightarrow H_2(g) \qquad \Delta H^\ominus = -436 \text{ kJ mol}^{-1}$$

Figure 5.14 The energy changes that occur when bonds are broken and bonds are formed.

Worked example

Which of the following processes are endothermic?
A $2Cl(g) \rightarrow Cl_2(g)$
B $Na(g) \rightarrow Na^+(g) + e^-$
C $Na^+(g) + Cl^-(g) \rightarrow NaCl(s)$
D $Na(g) \rightarrow Na(s)$

Solution

Only one of the processes involves the separation of particles:

$$Na(g) \rightarrow Na^+(g) + e^-$$

In this case, a negatively charged electron is separated from a positive ion Na^+.
Answer = B

 Endothermic processes involve the separation of particles which are held together by a force of attraction. Exothermic processes involve the bringing together of particles which have an attractive force between them.

Exercise

12 Which of the following processes is/are endothermic?
  I $H_2O(s) \rightarrow H_2O(g)$
  II $CO_2(g) \rightarrow CO_2(s)$
  III $O_2(g) \rightarrow 2O(g)$

Energy changes in reactions

We are now in a position to understand how energy changes occur in chemical reactions. Consider, for example, the complete combustion of methane which occurs in a Bunsen burner.

$$\begin{matrix} & H & & & & & \\ & | & & & & & \\ H- & C & -H + 2O{=}O \rightarrow O{=}C{=}O + 2H-O-H \\ & | & & & & & \\ & H & & & & & \end{matrix}$$

Energy is needed to break the C—H and O=O bonds in the reactants, but energy is given out when the C=O and O—H bonds are formed. The reaction is exothermic overall as the bonds which are formed are stronger than the bonds which are broken. A reaction is endothermic when the bonds broken are stronger than the bonds which are formed.

Using bond enthalpies to calculate the enthalpy changes of reaction

Worked example

Use bond enthalpies to calculate the heat of combustion of methane, the principal component of natural gas.

Solution

1 Write down the equation for the reaction showing all the bonds. This has already been done above.
2 Draw a table which shows the bonds which are broken and those that are formed during the reaction with the corresponding energy changes.

• **Examiner's hint:** Don't confuse
the different methods of calculating
enthalpy changes. A common error
when using bond enthalpies is the
reversal of the sign.
The correct expression is:
$\Delta H = \Sigma$ (bonds broken) $- \Sigma$ (bonds
formed). This should be contrasted with
the expression using standard enthalpies
of formation:
$\Delta H^{\ominus}_{reaction} = \Sigma\Delta H^{\ominus}_{formation}(products)$
$\qquad - \Sigma\Delta H^{\ominus}_{formation}(reactants)$

Bonds broken	ΔH/kJ mol^{-1} (endothermic)	Bonds formed	ΔH/kJ mol^{-1} (exothermic)
4 C—H	4 (+412)	2 C=O	2 (−743)
2 O=O	2(+496)	4 O—H	4(−463)
total	= 2640		= −3338

$\Delta H = 2640 - 3338 \text{ kJ mol}^{-1} = -698 \text{ kJ mol}^{-1}$

The value calculated from the bond enthalpies should be compared with the experimental value of −890 kJ mol^{-1} measured under standard conditions given in Table 13 of the IB Data booklet. The values are different, because the standard state of water is liquid and the bond enthalpy calculation assumes that the reaction occurs in the gaseous state. The use of average bond enthalpies is an additional approximation.

Comparing fuels

The enthalpy change of combustion of methane and methanol are compared in the table below.

Fuel	Graphical formula	$\Delta H_{combustion}$
methane	H | H—C—H | H	−890
methanol	H | H—C—O—H | H	−715

• **Examiner's hint:** Make sure that you
select the correct values for the bond
enthalpies. For example don't confuse
C=C with C–C, and use the correct
coefficients for the number of bonds
broken and formed.

Methanol has a lower enthalpy of combustion, because when it reacts only three O—H bonds are formed, compared to the combustion of methane, in which four O—H bonds are formed. Methanol already has one O—H.

Exercises

13 Which of the following is equivalent to the bond enthalpy of the carbon–oxygen bond in carbon monoxide?

A $CO(g) \rightarrow C(s) + O(g)$ B $CO(g) \rightarrow C(g) + O(g)$

C $CO(g) \rightarrow C(s) + \frac{1}{2}O_2(g)$ D $CO(g) \rightarrow C(g) + \frac{1}{2}O_2(g)$

14 Use the bond enthalpies below to calculate ΔH for the reaction:

$$H_2C{=}CH_2 + H_2 \rightarrow H_3C{-}CH_3$$

	Bond enthalpy/kJ mol^{-1}
C—C	+348
C=C	+612
H—H	+436
C—H	+412

15 Use the bond enthalpies below to calculate ΔH for the reaction:

$$2H_2(g) + O_2(g) \rightarrow 2H_2O(g)$$

	Bond enthalpy/kJ mol^{-1}
O=O	+496
H—H	+436
O—H	+463

1 What energy changes occur when chemical bonds are formed and broken?
  A Energy is absorbed when bonds are formed and when they are broken.
  B Energy is released when bonds are formed and when they are broken.
  C Energy is absorbed when bonds are formed and released when they are broken.
  D Energy is released when bonds are formed and absorbed when they are broken.

© International Baccalaureate Organization [2003]

2 The temperature of a 2.0 g sample of aluminium increases from 25 °C to 30 °C.
How many joules of heat energy were added? (Specific heat capacity of Al = 0.90 J g^{-1} K^{-1})

  A 0.36   B 2.3   C 9.0   D 11

© International Baccalaureate Organization [2003]

3 Using the equations below:

$$C(s) + O_2(g) \rightarrow CO_2(g) \qquad \Delta H = -390 \text{ kJ}$$
$$Mn(s) + O_2(g) \rightarrow MnO_2(s) \qquad \Delta H = -520 \text{ kJ}$$

What is ΔH (in kJ) for the following reaction?

$$MnO_2(s) + C(s) \rightarrow Mn(s) + CO_2(g)$$

  A +910   B +130   C −130   D −910

© International Baccalaureate Organization [2003]

4 What is ΔH for the reaction below in kJ?

$$CS_2(g) + 3O_2(g) \rightarrow CO_2(g) + 2SO_2(g)$$

ΔH_f /kJ mol^{-1}: $CS_2(g)$ 110, $CO_2(g)$ −390, $SO_2(g)$ −290

  A −570   B −790   C −860   D −1080

© International Baccalaureate Organization [2003]

5 The average bond enthalpies for O—O and O=O are 146 and 496 kJ mol^{-1}
respectively. What is the enthalpy change, in kJ, for the reaction below?

$$H-O-O-H(g) \rightarrow H-O-H(g) + \tfrac{1}{2}O=O(g)$$

  A −102   B +102   C +350   D +394

© International Baccalaureate Organization [2003]

6 Define the term *standard enthalpy of formation* and write the equation for the standard
enthalpy of formation of ethanol.   (5)

© International Baccalaureate Organization [2004]

● **Examiner's hint:** Learn the definition of enthalpy of formation. Be precise; it is an enthalpy *change* when *one mole* of the substance is formed from its elements in their *standard* states.

7 The standard enthalpy change of formation of $Al_2O_3(s)$ is −1669 kJ mol^{-1} and the
standard enthalpy change of formation of $Fe_2O_3(s)$ is −822 kJ mol^{-1}.
  (a) Use these values to calculate $\Delta H^{\ominus}$ for the following reaction:

$$Fe_2O_3(s) + 2Al(s) \rightarrow 2Fe(s) + Al_2O_3(s)$$

State whether the reaction is exothermic or endothermic.   (3)

  (b) Draw an enthalpy level diagram to represent this reaction. State the conditions under
  which standard enthalpy changes are measured.   (2)

(*Total 5 marks*)

© International Baccalaureate Organization [2004]

● **Examiner's hint:** Be sure to label the axes in enthalpy diagrams.

6 Kinetics

The word **kinetics** – derived from the Greek word *kinesis* – refers to movement. In fact the word cinema (kine-ma), used to describe the 'movies', has the same origin. In chemistry, the term kinetics is used to describe the study of how fast a reaction goes.

Imagine you are cooking in the kitchen. As you drop an egg into the hot fat in the pan it immediately changes to a white solid; meanwhile a container of milk that was left out of the refrigerator is slowly turning sour. We observe a similar variation in the rate of reactions that we study in the laboratory. Knowing and understanding why this is so helps us to make important decisions, such as choosing what apparatus and quantities to use, and helps to inform safety considerations. In industry, it can help chemists to choose the conditions that will give the most efficient and economic outcome for a process. But there are also times when we may want to slow down a reaction, or know how long certain reactants will continue to react. For example, when considering radioactive waste disposal, it is essential to know how long the radioactive effect of the reaction will continue. Similarly, in reactions involving pollutants in the atmosphere, one goal would be to find ways of slowing down reactions that cause the formation of new pollutants such as smog.

This chapter begins by studying reaction rates and considers how we can measure these in different situations. We then learn *how* reactions happen at the molecular level, by studying so-called collision theory. This will enable us to understand the effect that different factors have on reaction rates and so choose the most appropriate conditions for any particular reaction.

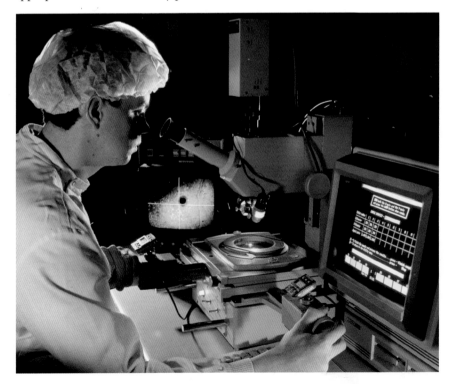

Pharmaceutical researcher monitoring the rate of release of a drug from a capsule. A laser has been used to drill a hole in the drug capsule, seen on the screen at centre left. A computer records results from a machine that is testing the rate at which the drug dissolves. Slow release drugs can be used to spread the effect of a drug over time, usually by embedding them in a polymer which slowly dissolves and gradually releases the drug. Understanding the factors that control reaction rates is essential for this research.

6.1 Rates of reaction
6.1.1 Define the term *rate of reaction*.
6.1.2 Describe suitable experimental procedures for measuring rates of reactions.
6.1.3 Analyse data from rate experiments.

6.2 Collision theory
6.2.1 Describe the kinetic theory in terms of the movement of particles whose average energy is proportional to temperature in kelvins.
6.2.2 Define the term *activation energy, E_a*.
6.2.3 Describe the collision theory.
6.2.4 Predict and explain, using the collision theory, the qualitative effects of particle size, temperature, concentration and pressure on the rate of a reaction.
6.2.5 Sketch and explain qualitatively the Maxwell–Boltzmann energy distribution curve for a fixed amount of gas at different temperatures and its consequences for changes in reaction rate.
6.2.6 Describe the effect of a catalyst on a chemical reaction.
6.2.7 Sketch and explain Maxwell–Boltzmann curves for reactions with and without catalysts.

● **Examiner's hint:** Because time and rate are reciprocal values, as one increases the other decreases. So in the example here, the racer with the *shortest time* of course wins the race because they had the *fastest rate*.

6.1 Rates of reaction

When we are interested in how quickly something happens, the factor that we usually measure is **time**. For example, in a sports race, the competitors are judged by the time it takes them to reach the finishing line. However, if we want to compare their performance in different races over different distances, we would need to express this as a **rate** – in other words how they performed *per unit time*.

Rate takes the reciprocal value of time, so is expressed *per unit time* or in SI units *per sec* (symbol $= s^{-1}$).

$$\text{Rate} = \frac{1}{\text{time}} = \frac{1}{s} = s^{-1}$$

In the study of chemical reactions we use the concept of **rate of reaction** to describe how quickly a reaction happens. As the reaction proceeds, reactants are converted into products and so the concentration of reactants decreases as the concentration of products increases. The graphs in Figures 6.1 and 6.2 show typical data from reactions.

The rate of reaction will depend on how quickly the concentration of either reactant or product changes with respect to time. It can be defined as follows:

The rate of a chemical reaction is a measure of the amount of reactants being converted into products per unit amount of time.

$$\text{Rate of reaction} = \frac{\text{increase in product concentration}}{\text{time taken}}$$

$$\text{or} = \frac{\text{decrease in reactant concentration}}{\text{time taken}}$$

It is expressed as: *change in concentration per unit time* or *mol dm^{-3} s^{-1}*.

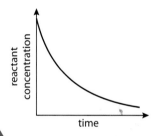

▲ **Figure 6.1** Concentration of reactants against time.

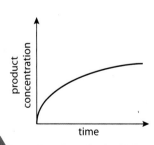

▲ **Figure 6.2** Concentration of products against time.

ℹ **The rate of a chemical reaction is a measure of the amount of reactants being converted into products per unit amount of time.**

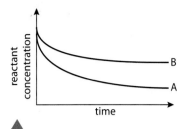

Figure 6.3 Graph showing reactant concentration against time for two different reactions A and B.

Imagine graphs of two different reactions showing the change in concentration of reactant against time. We can see in Figure 6.3 that the concentration of reactants is decreasing more quickly in reaction A than in reaction B – the curve is steeper. The steepness, or gradient, of the curve is a measure of the change in concentration per unit time, in other words, the rate of the reaction. This is what must be determined. However, because the graphs are curves and not straight lines, the gradient must be determined by drawing a tangent to the curve at a particular value of time and measuring its gradient. This is shown in Figure 6.4 – it will give the rate at that chosen value of time.

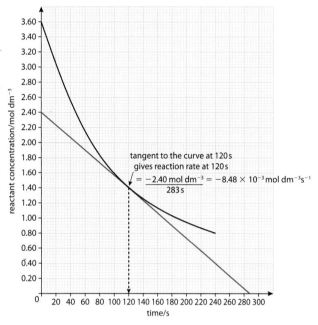

Figure 6.4 Measuring the gradient of the tangent to the curve at an interval of time $t = 120s$.

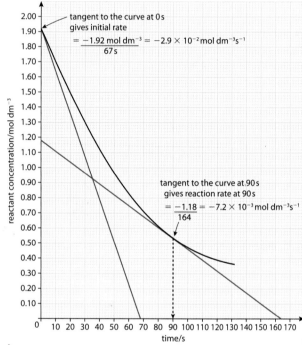

Figure 6.5 Graph showing calculation of the initial rate and the rate at 90 s during a reaction. The reaction proceeds more quickly at the start.

The fact that the graphs are curves indicates that the rate of the reaction is not constant during the reaction, but is usually fastest at the start and slows down as the reaction proceeds. (This is because of the effect that concentration has on the rate of reaction, which we will discuss later.) Therefore when we compare rates of reactions under different conditions it is common to compare the **initial rate** of each reaction by taking the tangent to the curve at $t = 0$.

Measuring rates of reaction

Choosing whether to measure the change in concentration of reactants or products and the technique with which to measure that change really depends on what will be easiest. This is different for different reactions. In most cases the concentration is not measured directly, but by means of a signal that is related to the changing concentration. If, for example, a reaction produces a coloured precipitate as product, change in colour could be measured; if a reaction gives off a gas, then the change in volume could be measured. Data logging devices can be used in many of these experiments. The raw data collected using these 'signals' will be in a variety of units, rather than as concentration measured in mol dm^{-3} directly. This is not generally a problem as it still enables us to determine the rate of the reaction. Some examples of common techniques are given below.

1 Change in volume of gas produced

This is a convenient method if one of the products is a gas. Collecting the gas and measuring the change in volume at regular time intervals enables a graph to be plotted of volume against time. A **gas syringe** is the apparatus best suited to this purpose. It consists of a ground glass barrel and plunger, which moves outwards as the gas collects and is calibrated to record the volume directly. If a gas syringe is not available, the gas can be collected by displacement of water in an inverted burette or measuring cylinder, but this method is limited as it can only be used if the gas collected has low solubility in water. For example:

$$Mg(s) + 2HCl(aq) \rightarrow MgCl_2(aq) + H_2(g)$$

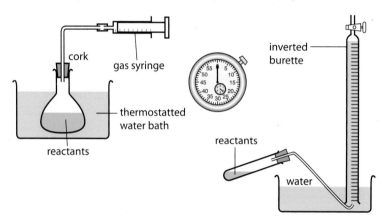

2 Change in mass

Many reactions involve a change in mass and it may be convenient to measure this directly. If the reaction is giving off a gas, the corresponding decrease in mass can be measured by standing the reaction mixture directly on a balance. This method is unlikely to work well where the evolved gas is hydrogen, as it is too light to give significant changes in mass. The method allows for continuous readings, so a graph can be plotted directly of mass against time. For example:

$$CaCO_3(s) + 2\,HCl(aq) \rightarrow CaCl_2(aq) + CO_2(g) + H_2O(l)$$

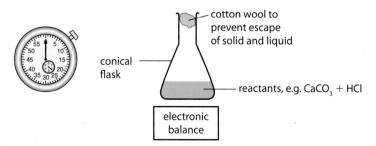

▲ **Figure 6.8** Experiment to measure rate of reaction by following change in mass against time.

When you take a glass of cold water from the refrigerator and leave it by your bed overnight, you may notice bubbles of gas have formed by morning. This is because the gas (mostly dissolved oxygen) has become less soluble as the temperature of the water has increased.

● **Examiner's hint:** Most gases are less soluble in warm water than in cold water. You can take advantage of this fact in the laboratory if you are collecting a gas by the displacement of water: use warm water to decrease the solubility of the gas.

◀ **Figure 6.6** Experiments to measure rate of reaction by following change in volume against time.

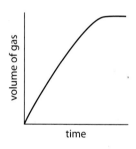

▲ **Figure 6.7** Graph of volume of gas against time.

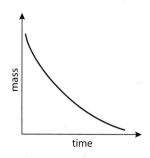

▲ **Figure 6.9** Graph of mass of reactant against time.

3 Change in transmission of light: colorimetry/spectrophotometry

This technique can be used if one of the reactants or products is coloured and so will give characteristic absorption in the visible region (i.e. wavelengths about 320–800 nm). Sometimes an indicator can be chosen to generate a coloured compound that can be followed in the reaction. A colorimeter or spectrophotometer passes light of a selected wavelength through the solution being studied and measures the light absorbed by the reaction components. As the concentration of the coloured compound increases, it absorbs proportionally more light, so less is transmitted. A photocell generates an electric current according to the amount of light transmitted and this is recorded on a meter or connected to a computer (see Chapter 12). For example, in the decomposition reaction:

$$2HI(g) \rightarrow H_2(g) + I_2(g)$$
colourless   colourless   coloured

Iodine is the only coloured component here. As its concentration increases during the reaction there will be an increase in absorbance of light of the appropriate wavelength.

Figure 6.10 Main components of a colorimeter.

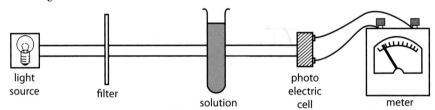

light source   filter   solution   photo electric cell   meter

The method allows for continuous readings to be taken, so a graph of absorbance against time can be plotted directly. It is possible to convert the absorbance values into concentration using a standard curve based on readings of known concentrations. Often, however, it is sufficient to record absorbance (or transmittance which is inversely proportional) itself as a function against time.

4 Change in concentration measured using titration

In some reactions it may be possible to measure the concentration of one of the reactants or products by titrating it against a known 'standard' (see Chapter 1). However, because this technique involves chemically changing the reaction mixture, it cannot be done continuously as the reaction proceeds. Instead samples must be withdrawn from the reaction mixture at regular time intervals and then analysed by titration. A problem here is that the process of titration takes a little while, during which time the reaction mixture in the sample will continue to react. To overcome this, a technique known as 'quenching' can be used, where a substance is introduced which effectively stops the reaction in the sample at the moment it is withdrawn. It is a rather like obtaining a 'freeze frame' shot of the reaction at a particular interval of time. In order to see how the concentration changes as the reaction proceeds, it is necessary to repeat this process at several intervals of time. For example, the reaction between H_2O_2 and acidified KI yields I_2, which can be titrated against $Na_2S_2O_3$ to determine its concentration:

$$H_2O_2(l) + 2H^+(aq) + 2I^-(aq) \rightarrow I_2(aq) + 2H_2O(l)$$

5 Change in concentration measured using conductivity

The total electrical conductivity of a solution depends on the total concentration of its ions and on their charges. If this changes when reactants are converted

● **Examiner's hint:** In all these reactions the goal is to measure change in concentration against time. Therefore you can use these methods to compare reaction rates under different conditions. Note that because the rate is dependent on the temperature, it is essential to control the temperature throughout these experiments. This can best be done by carrying out the reaction in a thermostatically controlled water bath.

to products, it can provide a convenient method to follow the progress of the reaction. Conductivity can be measured directly using a conductivity meter which involves immersing inert electrodes in the solution. As with colorimetry, the apparatus can be calibrated using solutions of known concentrations so that readings can be converted into the concentrations of the ions present. For example:

$$BrO_3^-(aq) + 5Br^-(aq) + 6H^+(aq) \rightarrow 3Br_2(aq) + 3H_2O(l)$$

The sharp decrease in the concentration of ions (12 on the reactants side and 0 on the products side) will give a corresponding decrease in the electrical conductivity of the solution as the reaction proceeds.

6 Non-continuous methods of detecting change during a reaction: 'clock reactions'

Sometimes it is difficult to record the continuous change in the rate of a reaction. In these cases, it may be more convenient to measure the time it takes for a reaction to reach a certain chosen fixed point – that is, something observable which can be used as an arbitrary 'end point' by which to stop the clock. The time taken to reach this point for the same reaction under different conditions can then be compared and used as a means of judging the different rates of the reaction.

For example, the following can be measured:

- the time taken for a certain size of magnesium ribbon to react completely (no longer visible) with dilute acid:

$$Mg(s) + 2HCl(aq) \rightarrow MgCl_2(aq) + H_2(g)$$

- the time taken for a solution of sodium thiosulfate with dilute acid to become opaque by the precipitation of sulfur, so that a cross viewed through paper is no longer visible:

$$Na_2S_2O_3(aq) + 2HCl(aq) \rightarrow 2NaCl(aq) + SO_2(aq) + H_2O(l) + S(s)$$

Recording increase in opaqueness during a reaction. Sodium thiosulfate (left) is a clear solution, which reacts with hydrochloric acid (upper centre) to form an opaque mixture (right). A cross (left) drawn onto paper is placed under the reaction beaker to show when the end point is reached. The experiment is timed from when the reactants are mixed until the cross disappears from sight.

See a simulation of the basics of kinetic molecular theory.
Now go to www.heinemann.co.uk/hotlinks, insert the express code 4259P and click on this activity.

Exercise

1 Consider the following reaction:

$$2MnO_4^-(aq) + 5C_2O_4^{2-}(aq) + 16H^+(aq) \rightarrow 2Mn^{2+}(aq) + 10CO_2(g) + 8H_2O(l)$$

Describe three ways in which you could measure the rate of this reaction.

6.2 Collision theory

Kinetic energy and temperature

Temperature in kelvins is proportional to the average kinetic energy of the particles in a substance.

Since the early 18th century, theories have been developed to explain the fact that gases exert a pressure. These theories developed alongside a growing understanding of the atomic and molecular nature of matter and were extended to include the behaviour of particles in all states of matter. Today they are summarized as the 'kinetic–molecular theory of matter' (see Chapter 1).

There is more heat in an iceberg than in a cup of boiling coffee. As heat is a form of energy, the total heat in the iceberg will be the sum of all the energy of all its particles. Although the particles will, on average, have lower kinetic energy than those in a cup of boiling coffee (the iceberg's *temperature* is much less than that of the coffee), there are vastly more of them in the iceberg. The net result is that the *total* energy in the iceberg will exceed that in the coffee.

The essence of kinetic–molecular theory is that particles in a substance move randomly as a result of the **kinetic energy** that they possess. However, because of the random nature of these movements and collisions, not all particles in a substance at any one time have the same values of kinetic energy, but will have instead a range of values that are reasonably close to each other. A convenient way to describe the kinetic energy of a substance is therefore to take the *average* of these values and this is related directly to its **absolute temperature**.

Increasing temperature therefore means an increase in the average kinetic energy of the particles of a substance. As we supply a substance with extra energy through heating it, we raise the average kinetic energy of the particles and so also raise its temperature. When we compare the behaviour of the particles in the three states of matter, from solid, through liquid, to gas, the differences are a result of this increase in the average kinetic energy of the particles.

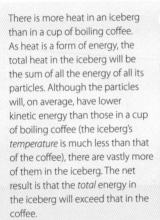

Change of state for a given substance:

solid   liquid   gas

INCREASING KINETIC ENERGY

INCREASING TEMPERATURE

The Maxwell–Boltzmann distribution curve

The fact that particles in a gas at a particular temperature show a range of values of kinetic energy is expressed by the **Maxwell–Boltzmann distribution curve**.

Figure 6.11 The Maxwell–Boltzmann distribution curve.

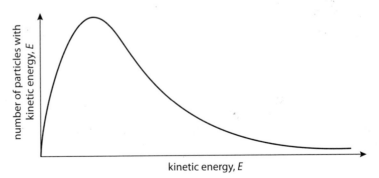

See a colourful simulation of the relationship between molecular speeds and their distribution.
Now go to www.heinemann.co.uk/hotlinks, insert the express code 4259P and click on this activity.

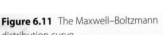

Like other distribution curves, this shows the number of particles that have a particular value of kinetic energy (or the probability of that value occurring) plotted against the values for kinetic energy. The area under the curve represents the total number of particles in the sample.

Although their names are linked in the famous energy distribution curve discussed here, James Clerk Maxwell and Ludwig Boltzmann were two people with very different outlooks on life. Maxwell was a Scottish physicist, known for his insatiable curiosity and overflowing humour. His wife worked alongside him in many of his experiments. Boltzmann, an Austrian, was prone to depression and eventually took his own life while on a family holiday, seemingly believing that his work was not valued. Nonetheless, as peers during the 19th century, both seeking to explain the observed properties of gases, they refined and developed each other's ideas, culminating in the distribution curve that bears both their names.

How reactions happen

When reactants are placed together, the kinetic energy that their particles possess causes them to collide with each other. The energy of these collisions may result in some bonds between the reactants being broken and some new bonds forming. As a result, products form and the reaction 'happens'.

It follows that the rate of the reaction will depend on the number of collisions between particles which are 'successful', that is, which lead to the formation of products. However, a very important point is that *not all collisions will be successful* and there are two reasons for this: energy of collision and geometry of collision.

1 Energy of collision

In order for a collision to lead to reaction, the particles must have a certain minimum value for their kinetic energy. This energy is necessary to overcome repulsion between molecules and often to break some bonds in the reactants before they can react. When this energy is supplied, the reactants achieve the **transition state** from which products can form. The energy required represents an energy barrier for the reaction and is known as the **activation energy**.

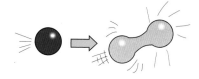

Figure 6.12 Particles react by colliding.

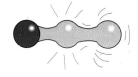

Figure 6.13 Diagram showing energy path of a reaction with the activation energy for both endothermic (a) and exothermic (b) reactions. * represents the transition state.

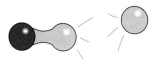

 Activation energy (E_a) is defined as the minimum value of kinetic energy which particles must have before they are able to react.

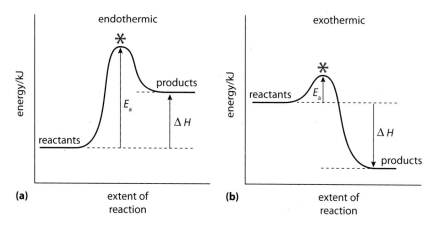

(a)

(b)

We can think of this as a 'threshold value' – a bit like a pass mark in an examination: values greater than this mark achieve a pass, lower values do not achieve a pass. It is the same for particles in a reaction, where the threshold value is the activation energy. Only particles which have a kinetic energy value greater than the activation energy will be able to achieve reaction – in other words will have successful collisions. Particles with kinetic energy lower than this will not have enough energy to achieve reaction, even though they may still collide with each other, but these collisions will not be 'successful' in the sense of causing a reaction.

Note that the value of activation energy varies greatly from one reaction to another and the magnitude of this value plays an important part in determining the overall rate of a reaction.

Figure 6.14 The Maxwell–Boltzmann distribution showing how E_a distinguishes between particles that have greater or lesser values of kinetic energy.

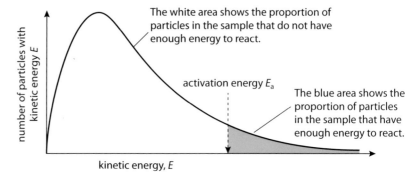

It therefore follows that the rate of the reaction depends on the proportion of particles that have values of kinetic energy greater than the activation energy.

2 Geometry of collision

Because collisions between particles are random, they are likely to occur with the particles in many different orientations. In some reactions, this can be crucial in determining whether or not the collisions will be successful and therefore what proportion of collisions will lead to a reaction.

Figure 6.15 Reactants with the correct collision geometry must collide if products are to be formed.

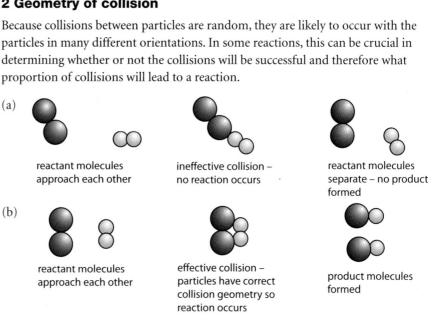

We can now summarise the collision theory as follows. The rate of a reaction will depend on the frequency of collisions which occur between particles possessing both:

- values of kinetic energy greater than the activation energy
- appropriate collision geometry.

In order to react, particles must have kinetic energy greater than the activation energy and the correct collision geometry.

Understanding this theory will help us to investigate and explain why certain factors increase the rate of reaction.

Exercise

2 Which statement is correct for a collision between reactant particles leading to a reaction?
   A   Colliding particles must have different energy.
   B   All reactant particles must have the same energy.
   C   Colliding particles must have a kinetic energy higher than the activation energy.
   D   Colliding particles must have the same velocity.

Factors affecting rate of reaction

1 Temperature

Increasing the temperature increases the rate of all reactions. This is because temperature is a measure of the average kinetic energy of the particles and so a higher temperature represents an increase in their average kinetic energy. This means that a larger number of particles will have energies exceeding the activation energy. We can see this effect in the Maxwell–Boltzmann distribution curves for a sample of gas at different temperatures.

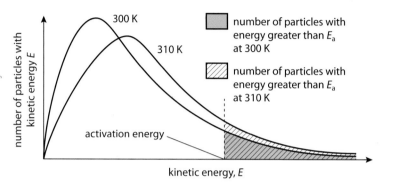

Examiner's hint: Be careful not to confuse the question of 'how fast' a reaction goes with the question of 'how far' it goes. We are discussing only the first question here. The question of how far a reaction goes, which influences the *yield* of the reaction, will be discussed in Chapter 7, Equilibrium.

Figure 6.16 Maxwell–Boltzmann distribution curves for a sample of gas at two different temperatures showing the proportion of particles with kinetic energy exceeding the activation energy at each temperature.

Note that the area under the two curves here is the same. This is because the area is proportional to the total number of particles and this is a constant in the sample under study. But with increasing temperature the peak of the curve shifts to the right. As a result there will be:

- an increase in collision frequency
- more collisions involving particles with higher values of kinetic energy, specifically higher than the activation energy.

Consequently there is an increase in the number of *successful* collisions and hence an increase in the rate of reaction. Many reactions double their reaction rate for every 10 °C increase in temperature.

W For simulations of experiments illustrating the effect of different factors on reaction rates, go to www.heinemann.co.uk/hotlinks, insert the express code 4259P and click on this activity.

i Specimens of the extinct mammal, the mammoth, dated as 10 000 years old, have been found perfectly preserved in the Arctic ice, whereas only the bones remain of individual specimens of a similar age found in California. This is an illustration of the effect that the cold temperature in the Arctic has in decreasing the rate of the reactions of decay. The same concept is used in refrigerating or freezing food to preserve it.

2 Concentration

Increasing the concentration of reactants increases the rate of reaction. This is because as concentration increases, the frequency of collisions between reactant particles increases, so that the frequency of successful collisions increases too. We can see the effect of concentration by following the rate of a reaction as it progresses. As reactants are used up, their concentration falls and the rate of the reaction decreases, giving the typical rate curve we saw in Figure 6.1.

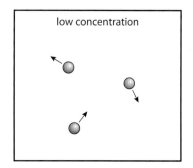
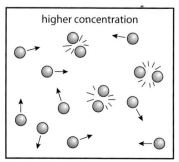

When particles are closer together they have a greater chance of reacting.

Figure 6.17 Effect of concentration on collision frequency.

Effect of concentration on the rate of reaction between zinc and sulfuric acid. The tube on the left has a more concentrated solution of the acid, the one on the right a more dilute solution. The product hydrogen gas is seen collecting much more quickly in the presence of the more concentrated acid.

A catalyst is a substance that increases the rate of a chemical reaction without itself undergoing permanent change.

Figure 6.18 Effect of catalyst on lowering the activation energy.

Milk powder dropped onto a flame. The fine particles in the powder expose a huge surface area to the flame, leading to very fast burning.

3 Particle size

Decreasing the particle size increases the rate of reaction. This is because subdividing a large particle into smaller parts increases the total surface area and therefore allows more contact and a higher probability of collisions between the reactants. You know, for example, how much easier it is to start a fire using small pieces of wood, rather than a large log – it's because there is more contact between the small pieces of the wood and the oxygen with which it is reacting. In reactions involving solutions, stirring may help to decrease particle size and so increase the rate.

The effect of particle size can be demonstrated in the reaction between marble ($CaCO_3$) and hydrochloric acid. When marble chips are replaced with powder, the effervescence caused by release of carbon dioxide is much more vigorous.

This effect of particle size on reaction rate can be quite dramatic. It has been responsible for many industrial accidents involving explosions of flammable dust powders – for example coal dust in mines and flour in mills.

4 Pressure

For reactions involving gases, increasing pressure increases the rate of reaction. This is because the higher pressure compresses the gas, effectively increasing its concentration. This will increase the frequency of collisions.

5 Catalyst

A catalyst is a substance that increases the rate of a reaction without itself undergoing permanent change.

Most catalysts work by providing an alternate route for the reaction, which has a lower activation energy.

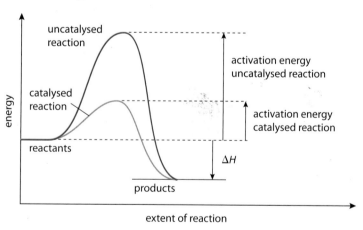

This means that without increasing the temperature, a larger number of particles will now have values of kinetic energy greater than the activation energy and so will be able to undergo successful collisions. Thinking again of activation energy as being like the pass mark in an examination, the effect of the catalyst could be likened to lowering the pass mark. This means that with the same work in the tests, a higher number of people would be able to achieve a pass!

Figure 6.19 uses the Maxwell–Boltzmann distribution to show how a catalyst increases the proportion of particles that have values for kinetic energy greater than the activation energy.

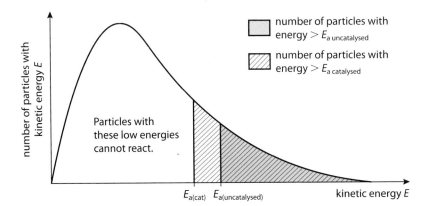

number of particles with energy $> E_{a \text{ uncatalysed}}$

number of particles with energy $> E_{a \text{ catalysed}}$

Particles with these low energies cannot react.

$E_{a(\text{cat})}$ $E_{a(\text{uncatalysed})}$

kinetic energy E

Figure 6.19 Effect of catalyst on increasing the proportion of particles able to react.

Exercise

3 Which change of condition will decrease the rate of the reaction between excess zinc granules and dilute hydrochloric acid?
   A increasing the amount of zinc
   B increasing the concentration of the acid
   C pulverizing the zinc granules into powder
   D decreasing the temperature

The development of the process of *catalytic reforming*, by which linear hydrocarbons are converted into branched or cyclic molecules which burn more smoothly, is often credited with having played a major role in World War II. Aircraft fuel using such hydrocarbons increased the performance of the European allies' planes to the point where they were able to gain victory in the skies.

Catalysts have an equal effect on both the forward and the reverse reactions and so they do not change the position of equilibrium or the yield (see Chapter 7). However, because of their ability to increase the rate of reactions and hence the rate that product is obtained, they play an essential role in many industrial processes and have a big impact on both efficiency and feasibility. Without catalysts, many reactions would proceed too slowly, or would have to be conducted at such high temperatures that they would simply not be worthwhile. This is why the discovery of the 'best' catalyst for a particular reaction is a very active area of research and often the exact specification of a catalyst used in an industrial process is a matter of secrecy.

Every *biological* reaction is controlled by a catalyst, known as an **enzyme**. Thousands of different enzymes exist as they are each specific for a particular reaction. Enzymes are finding increasingly widespread uses in many domestic and industrial processes, from biological detergents to acting as 'biosensors' in medical studies. Some of these applications, like cheese making, are centuries old, but others are developing rapidly, constituting the field known as 'biotechnology'.

A catalytic converter: this device catalyses reactions which convert the toxic emissions from an internal combustion engine into less harmful ones. It is estimated that catalytic converters can reduce pollution emission by 90% without loss of engine performance or fuel economy.

Exercise

4 Catalytic converters are now used in most cars to convert some components of exhaust gases into less environmentally damaging molecules. One of these reactions converts carbon monoxide and nitrogen monoxide into carbon dioxide and nitrogen. The catalyst usually consists of metals such as platinum or rhodium.

   (a) Write an equation for this reaction.
   (b) Explain why it is important to reduce the concentrations of carbon monoxide and nitrogen monoxide released into the atmosphere.
   (c) Why do you think the converter sometimes consists of small ceramic beads coated with the catalyst?
   (d) Suggest why the converter usually does not work effectively until the car engine has warmed up.
   (e) Discuss whether the use of catalytic converters in cars solves the problem of car pollution.

Practice questions

1 The reaction between calcium carbonate and hydrochloric acid, carried out in an open flask, can be represented by the following equation:

$$CaCO_3(s) + 2HCl(aq) \rightarrow CaCl_2(aq) + H_2O(l) + CO_2(g)$$

Which of the measurements below could be used to measure the rate of the reaction?
  I the mass of the flask and contents
  II the pH of the reaction mixture
  III the volume of carbon dioxide produced

  A I and II only
  B I and III only
  C II and III only
  D I, II and III

© International Baccalaureate Organization [2005]

2 For a given reaction, why does the rate of reaction increase when the concentrations of the reactants are increased?
  A The frequency of the molecular collisions increases.
  B The activation energy increases.
  C The average kinetic energy of the molecules increases.
  D The rate constant increases.

© International Baccalaureate Organization [2004]

3 Based on the definition for rate of reaction, which units are used for a rate?
  A $mol \ dm^{-3}$
  B $mol \ time^{-1}$
  C $dm^3 \ time^{-1}$
  D $mol \ dm^{-3} \ time^{-1}$

© International Baccalaureate Organization [2004]

4 Excess magnesium was added to a beaker of aqueous hydrochloric acid on a balance. A graph of the mass of the beaker and contents was plotted against time (line 1).

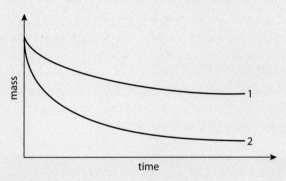

What change in the experiment could give line 2?
  I the same mass of magnesium but in smaller pieces
  II the same volume of a more concentrated solution of hydrochloric acid
  III a lower temperature

  A I only
  B II only
  C III only
  D None of the above

© International Baccalaureate Organization [2003]

5 The rate of a reaction between two gases increases when the temperature is increased and a catalyst is added. Which statements are both correct for the effect of these changes on the reaction?

	Increasing the temperature	Adding a catalyst
A	Collision frequency increases	Activation energy increases
B	Activation energy increases	Activation energy does not change
C	Activation energy does not change	Activation energy decreases
D	Activation energy increases	Collision frequency increases

© International Baccalaureate Organization [2003]

6 Consider the reaction between solid $CaCO_3$ and aqueous HCl. The reaction will be speeded up by an increase in which of the following conditions?
 I   concentration of the HCl
 II size of the $CaCO_3$ particles
 III temperature
 A I only
 B I and III only
 C II and III only
 D I, II and III

© International Baccalaureate Organization [2003]

7 Which of the following is (are) important in determining whether a reaction occurs?
 I   energy of the molecules
 II orientation of the molecules
 A I only
 B II only
 C both I and II
 D neither I nor II

© International Baccalaureate Organization [2003]

8 The reaction between ammonium chloride and sodium nitrite in aqueous solution can be represented by the following equation:

$$NH_4Cl(aq) + NaNO_2(aq) \rightarrow N_2(g) + 2H_2O(l) + NaCl(aq)$$

The graph below shows the volume of nitrogen gas produced at 30 second intervals from a mixture of ammonium chloride and sodium nitrite in aqueous solution at 20 °C.

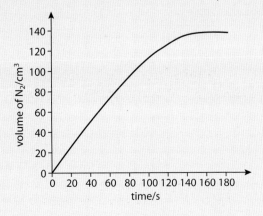

(a) (i) State how the rate of formation of nitrogen changes with time. Explain your answer in terms of collision theory. (2)

(ii) Explain why the volume eventually remains constant. (1)

(b) (i) State how the rate of formation of nitrogen would change if the temperature were increased from 20°C to 40°C. (1)

(ii) State **two** reasons for the change described in (b) (i) and explain which of the two is more important in causing the change. (3)

(iii) The reaction between *solid* ammonium chloride and aqueous sodium nitrite can be represented by the following equation:

$$NH_4Cl(s) + NaNO_2(aq) \rightarrow N_2(g) + 2H_2O(l) + NaCl(aq)$$

State and explain how the rate of formation of nitrogen would change if the same amount of ammonium chloride were used as large lumps instead of as a fine powder. (2)

(Total 9 marks)

© International Baccalaureate Organization [2004]

9 (a) Define the term *rate of reaction*. (1)

(b) The reaction between gases C and D is slow at room temperature.

(i) Suggest **two** reasons why the reaction is slow at room temperature. (2)

(ii) A relatively small increase in temperature causes a relatively large increase in the rate of this reaction. State **two** reasons for this. (2)

(iii) Suggest **two** ways of increasing the rate of reaction between C and D other than increasing temperature. (2)

(Total 7 marks)

© International Baccalaureate Organization [2005]

10 (a) Identify **two** features of colliding molecules that react together in the gas phase. (2)

(b) For many reasons, the rate approximately doubles for a 10 °C rise in temperature. State **two** reasons for this increase and identify which of the two is the more important. (3)

(Total 5 marks)

© International Baccalaureate Organization [2005]

11 When excess lumps of magnesium carbonate are added to dilute hydrochloric acid the following reaction takes place:

$$MgCO_3(s) + 2HCl(aq) \rightarrow MgCl_2(aq) + CO_2(g) + H_2O(l)$$

(a) Outline **two** ways in which the rate of this reaction could be studied. In each case sketch a graph to show how the value of the chosen variable would change with time. (4)

(b) State and explain **three** ways in which the rate of this reaction could be increased. (6)

(c) State and explain whether the total volume of carbon dioxide produced would increase, decrease or stay the same if:

(i) more lumps of magnesium carbonate were used. (2)

(ii) the experiments were carried out at a higher temperature. (2)

(Total 14 marks)

© International Baccalaureate Organization [2004]

7 Equilibrium

Imagine that you are part way along an escalator (a moving staircase) that is moving up and you decide to run down. If you can run down at exactly the same speed as the escalator is moving up, you will have no *net* movement. So if someone were to take a picture of you at regular time intervals it would seem as if you were not moving at all. Of course in reality both you and the escalator *are* moving, but because there is no net change neither movement is observable. In chemical reactions a similar phenomenon occurs when a reaction takes place at the same rate as its reverse reaction, so no net change is observed. This is known as the equilibrium state.

In this chapter we will explore some of the features of the equilibrium state and

learn how this enables us to predict how far reactions will proceed under different conditions. Understanding equilibria can help in determining such diverse things as how long drugs will remain active in the body, what conditions will maximize the yield in chemical manufacturing industries and how certain chemicals in the atmosphere might react together forming pollutants and contributing to climate change.

Electron micrograph of a section through human lung tissue, showing air spaces called alveoli. Equilibrium considerations help us to understand how oxygen and carbon dioxide are exchanged between the blood and the air in these spaces.

Assessment statements

7.1 Dynamic equilibrium
7.1.1   Outline the characteristics of chemical and physical systems in a state of equilibrium.

7.2 The position of equilibrium
7.2.1   Deduce the equilibrium constant expression (K_c) from the equation for a homogeneous reaction.

7.2.2   Deduce the extent of a reaction from the magnitude of the equilibrium constant.

7.2.3   Apply Le Chatelier's principle to predict the qualitative effects of changes of temperature, pressure and concentration on the position of equilibrium and on the value of the equilibrium constant.

7.2.4   State and explain the effect of a catalyst on an equilibrium reaction.

7.2.5   Apply the concepts of kinetics and equilibrium to industrial processes.

7.1 Dynamic equilibrium

Physical systems

Consider what happens when some bromine is placed in a sealed container at room temperature.

As bromine is a **volatile** liquid, with a boiling point close to room temperature, a significant number of particles (molecules of Br_2) will have enough energy to escape from the liquid state and form vapour in the process known as evaporation. At the same time, some of these vapour molecules will collide with the surface of the liquid, lose energy and become liquid in the process known as condensation.

$$\text{evaporation}$$
$$Br_2(l) \rightleftharpoons Br_2(g)$$
$$\text{condensation}$$

▲ Bromine stored in a sealed jar. The system is in dynamic equilibrium, so the concentrations of liquid and vapour do not change at constant temperature.

Figure 7.1 Establishing dynamic equilibrium in the evaporation of bromine. Equilibrium is established when the rate of evaporation equals the rate of condensation.

— $Br_2(g)$ —

— $Br_2(l)$ —

initial   at equilibrium

There will, however, come a time when the rate of evaporation is *equal* to the rate of condensation and at this point there will be no net change in the amounts of liquid and gas present. We say that the system has reached **equilibrium**.

Chemical systems

Consider the reaction of dissociation between hydrogen iodide HI and its elements hydrogen H_2 and iodine I_2. Iodine is released as a purple gas, whereas hydrogen and hydrogen iodide are colourless, so this helps us to see what is happening.

$$2HI(g) \rightleftharpoons H_2(g) + I_2(g)$$

If we carry out this reaction starting with hydrogen iodide in a sealed container, there will at first be an increase in the purple colour owing to the production of iodine gas. But after a while this increase in colour will stop and it may appear that the reaction too has stopped. In fact what has happened is that the rate of the dissociation of HI has become equal to the rate of the reverse reaction of association between H_2 and I_2. In other words equilibrium has been reached. No net change is observed even though both reactions are still occurring.

If we were to analyse the contents of the flask at this point, we would find HI, H_2 and I_2 would all be present and that if there were no change in conditions, their concentration would remain constant over time. We refer to this as the **equilibrium mixture**.

If we reversed the experiment and started with H_2 and I_2 instead of HI, we would find that eventually an equilibrium mixture would again be achieved in which the concentrations of H_2, I_2 and HI would remain constant.

▲ Iodine gas in a stoppered flask. Iodine is a crystalline solid at room temperature but sublimes on heating to form a purple gas.

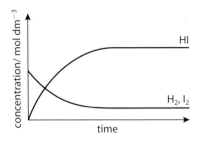

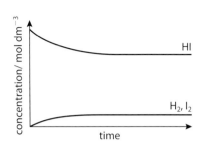

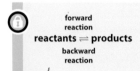

Figure 7.2 Equilibrium is reached when the concentrations of reactants and products become constant. Note the same equilibrium mixture is reached starting from pure HI or from a mixture of H_2 and I_2.

In studies of equilibria we are dealing with reversible reactions – those that occur in both directions. The convention is to describe the reaction from left to right (reactants to products) as the **forward reaction** and the reaction from right to left (products to reactants) as the **backward** or **reverse reaction**. The symbol $\rightleftharpoons$ is used to denote the fact that the reaction is an equilibrium reaction.

> **forward reaction**
> **reactants $\rightleftharpoons$ products**
> **backward reaction**

Characteristics of the equilibrium state

The examples discussed above have shown that *at equilibrium the rate of the forward reaction is equal to the rate of the backward reaction.*

These reactions have also shown some of the main features of the equilibrium state and these can now be summarized as they apply to *all* reactions at equilibrium.

> Strictly speaking, all reactions can be considered as equilibrium reactions. However, in many cases the equilibrium mixture consists almost entirely of products, that is, it is considered to have gone virtually to completion. By convention we use the symbol $\rightarrow$ rather than the equilibrium symbol $\rightleftharpoons$ in these cases. In other reactions there may be so little product formed that it is undetectable and the reaction is considered effectively not to have happened.

	Feature of equilibrium state	Explanation
1	Equilibrium is dynamic.	The reaction has not stopped but both forward and backward reactions are still occurring.
2	Equilibrium is achieved in a closed system.	A closed system prevents exchange of matter with the surroundings, so equilibrium is achieved where both reactants and products can react and recombine with each other.
3	The concentrations of reactants and products remain constant at equilibrium.	They are being produced and destroyed at an equal rate.
4	At equilibrium there is no change in macroscopic properties.	This refers to observable properties such as colour and density. These do not change as they depend on the concentrations of the components of the mixture.
5	Equilibrium can be reached from either direction.	The same equilibrium mixture will result under the same conditions, no matter whether the reaction is started with all reactants, all products, or a mixture of both.

● **Examiner's hint:** Make sure that you use the equilibrium symbol $\rightleftharpoons$ when writing equations for reactions where the reverse reactions are significant. For example it must be used when explaining the behaviour of weak acids and bases (Chapter 8).

 At what point is it true to say that when we cannot measure the quantity of a substance, it does not exist?

It is important to understand that even though the concentrations of reactant and product are *constant* at equilibrium, this in no way implies that they are *equal*. In fact, most commonly there will be a much higher concentration of either reactant or product in the equilibrium mixture, depending both on the reaction and on the conditions.

Thinking back to the analogy in the introduction to this chapter of you running in the opposite direction on a moving staircase where the top and bottom

> **At equilibrium, the rate of the forward reaction is equal to the rate of the backward reaction.**

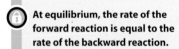

represent reactants and products respectively, it would be possible for you to be 'at equilibrium' near the top of the staircase, near the bottom or anywhere in between. As long as you were moving at the same speed as the staircase, you would still have no net change in position.

The proportion of reactant and product in the equilibrium mixture is referred to as its **equilibrium position**. Reactions where the mixture contains predominantly products are said to 'lie to the right', and reactions with predominantly reactants are said to 'lie to the left'. It is, however, often useful to be able to capture this information mathematically to help compare the equilibrium mixtures of different reactions and the effect of different conditions. In the next section we will look at how this is done.

In reality, it is not possible to achieve a completely closed system experimentally. Consider to what extent this is a limitation in interpreting equilibrium theory.

● **Examiner's hint:** Sometimes you may see the equilibrium sign written with unequal arrows such as ⇌. This is used to represent the reaction that lies in favour of products.

Likewise ⇌ is used to represent a reaction that lies in favour of reactants.

7.2   The position of equilibrium

The equilibrium constant K_c

Consider now the reaction:

$$H_2(g) + I_2(g) \rightleftharpoons 2HI(g)$$

If we were to carry out a series of experiments on this reaction with different starting concentrations of H_2, I_2 and HI, we could wait until each reaction reached equilibrium and then measure the composition of each equilibrium mixture. Here are some possible results when measured at 440 °C.

Experiment I

	Initial concentration/mol dm^{-3}	Equilibrium concentration/mol dm^{-3}
H_2	0.100	0.0222
I_2	0.100	0.0222
HI	0.000	0.156

Experiment II

	Initial concentration/mol dm^{-3}	Equilibrium concentration/mol dm^{-3}
H_2	0.000	0.0350
I_2	0.0100	0.0450
HI	0.350	0.280

Experiment III

	Initial concentration/mol dm^{-3}	Equilibrium concentration/mol dm^{-3}
H_2	0.0150	0.0150
I_2	0.000	0.0135
HI	0.127	0.100

At a glance these data may not appear to show any pattern. However, there is a predictable relationship between the different compositions of these equilibrium mixtures and the key to discovering it is in the stoichiometry of the reaction equation.

If we take the *equilibrium* concentrations and process them in the following way:

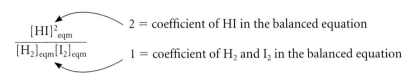

$$\frac{[HI]^2_{eqm}}{[H_2]_{eqm}[I_2]_{eqm}}$$

2 = coefficient of HI in the balanced equation

1 = coefficient of H_2 and I_2 in the balanced equation

Square brackets [ ] are commonly used to show concentration in mol dm^{-3}

we find the following results:

Experiment I	Experiment II	Experiment III
$\dfrac{(0.156)^2}{0.0222 \times 0.0222}$	$\dfrac{(0.280)^2}{0.035 \times 0.0450}$	$\dfrac{(0.100)^2}{0.0150 \times 0.0135}$
= 49.4	= 49.8	= 49.4

Clearly this way of processing the equilibrium data produces a constant value within the limits of experimental accuracy. This constant is known as the **equilibrium constant** K_c. It has a fixed value for this reaction *at a specified temperature.*

In fact every reaction has its own particular value of K_c which can be derived in a similar way. First we use the balanced equation to write the equilibrium constant expression.

For the reaction: $aA + bB \rightleftharpoons cC + dD$

the equilibrium constant expression is:

$$\frac{[C]^c_{eqm}[D]^d_{eqm}}{[A]^a_{eqm}[B]^b_{eqm}} = K_c$$

The value for K_c can thus be determined by substituting the equilibrium concentrations into this equation.

Note:
- The equilibrium constant expression has the concentrations of products in the numerator and the concentrations of reactants in the denominator.
- Each concentration is raised to the power of its coefficient in the balanced equation. (Where it is equal to one it does not have to be given.)
- Where there is more than one reactant or product the terms are multiplied together.

 Use this simulation to derive K_c with different starting concentrations of reactant and product.
Now go to www.heinemann.co.uk/hotlinks, insert the express code 4259P and click on this activity.

 The equilibrium constant K_c has a fixed value for a particular reaction at a specified temperature. The only thing that changes the value of K_c for a reaction is the temperature.

Worked example

Write the equilibrium expression for the following reactions.
(i) $2H_2(g) + O_2(g) \rightleftharpoons 2H_2O(g)$
(ii) $Cu^{2+}(aq) + 4NH_3(aq) \rightleftharpoons [Cu(NH_3)_4]^{2+}(aq)$

Solution

(i) $K_c = \dfrac{[H_2O]^2}{[H_2]^2[O_2]}$

(ii) $K_c = \dfrac{[[Cu(NH_3)_4]^{2+}]}{[Cu^{2+}][NH_3]^4}$

● **Examiner's hint:** The equilibrium expression will only give the value K_c when the concentrations used in the equation are the *equilibrium* concentrations for all reactants and products. Strictly speaking the subscript 'eqm' should always be used in the equation, but by convention this is generally left out. However, make completely sure that the only values you substitute into the equation are the equilibrium concentrations.

● **Examiner's hint:** The equilibrium constant expressions described here apply to homogeneous reactions, that is reactions where reactants and products are in the same phase, as gases, liquids or in solution. It is good practice always to include state symbols in your equations.

Exercises

1 Write the equilibrium constant expression for the following reactions:
   (a) $2NO(g) + O_2(g) \rightleftharpoons 2NO_2(g)$
   (b) $CH_3COOH(l) + C_3H_7OH(l) \rightleftharpoons CH_3COOC_3H_7(l) + H_2O(l)$
   (c) $4NH_3(g) + 7O_2(g) \rightleftharpoons 4NO_2(g) + 6H_2O(g)$

2 Write the equations for the reactions represented by the following equilibrium constant expressions:

   (a) $K_c = \dfrac{[NO_2]^2}{[N_2O_4]}$

   (b) $K_c = \dfrac{[CO][H_2]^3}{[CH_4][H_2O]}$

Magnitude of K_c

Different reactions have different values of K_c. What does this value tell us about a particular reaction?

As the equilibrium constant expression puts products on the numerator and reactants on the denominator, a high value of K_c will mean that at equilibrium there are proportionately more products than reactants. In other words, such an equilibrium mixture lies to the right and the reaction goes almost to completion. By contrast, a low value of K_c must mean that there are proportionately less products with respect to reactants, so the equilibrium mixture lies to the left and the reaction has barely taken place.

Consider the following three reactions and their K_c values measured at 550 K:
$$H_2(g) + I_2(g) \rightleftharpoons 2HI(g) \qquad K_c = 2$$
$$H_2(g) + Br_2(g) \rightleftharpoons 2HBr(g) \qquad K_c = 10^{10}$$
$$H_2(g) + Cl_2(g) \rightleftharpoons 2HCl(g) \qquad K_c = 10^{18}$$

The large range in their K_c values tells us about the differing extents of these reactions. Here we can deduce that the reaction between H_2 and Cl_2 has taken place the most fully at this temperature, while H_2 and I_2 have reacted the least.

A good rule of thumb to apply to these values is that if $K_c >> 1$, the reaction is considered to go almost to completion (very high conversion of reactants into products) and if $K_c << 1$, the reaction hardly proceeds.

The magnitude of the equilibrium constant, K_c, gives information about how far a reaction goes at a particular temperature, but not about how fast it will achieve the equilibrium state.

When equilibrium is disrupted

A system remains at equilibrium as long as the rate of the forward reaction equals the rate of the backward reaction. But as soon as this balance is disrupted by any change in conditions that unequally affects the rates of these reactions, the equilibrium condition will no longer be met. It has been shown, however, that equilibria respond in a predictable way to such a situation, based on a principle known as **Le Chatelier's principle**. This states that *a system at equilibrium when subjected to a change will respond in such a way as to minimize the effect of the change*. Simply put, this means that whatever we do to a system at equilibrium, the system will respond in the opposite way. Add something and the system will react to remove it, remove something and the system will react to replace it. After a while a new equilibrium will be established and this will have a different composition from the earlier equilibrium mixture. Applying the principle therefore enables us to predict the qualitative effect of typical changes that occur to systems at equilibrium.

When a system at equilibrium is subjected to a change, it will respond in such a way as to minimize the effect of the change.

Henri-Louis Le Chatelier was a French chemist who published his equilibria principle in 1884. Amongst other research, he also investigated the possibility of the synthesis of ammonia, but abandoned his efforts after suffering a devastating explosion in his laboratory. After Haber's later elucidation of the conditions required in the reaction, Le Chatelier realized that he had been very close to the discovery himself. Late in his life he wrote 'I let the discovery of the ammonia synthesis slip through my hands. It was the greatest blunder of my career'. We can only speculate on how history might have been re-written if this discovery had in fact been made in France rather than in Germany before World War I.

Changes in concentration

Suppose an equilibrium is disrupted by an increase in the concentration of one of the reactants. The system will respond to reduce this concentration by favouring the forward reaction, in other words shifting the equilibrium to the right. Equilibrium will later be re-established with new concentrations of all reactants and products. The value of K_c will be unchanged.

Similarly, the equilibrium could be disrupted by a decrease in the concentration of product by removing it from the equilibrium mixture. The system will respond by increasing the concentration of product, again by shifting the equilibrium to the right. A different equilibrium position will now be achieved, but the value of K_c will be unchanged.

Often in an industrial process the product will be removed as it forms. This ensures that the equilibrium is continuously pulled to the right, hence increasing the yield of product.

Applying Le Chatelier's principle, can you think what concentration changes would cause an equilibrium to shift to the left? The answer is either an increase in concentration of product or a decrease in concentration of reactant.

▲ Experiment to show the effect of changing the concentration of chloride ions on the cobalt chloride equilibrium:

$$[Co(H_2O)_6]^{2+}(aq) + 4Cl^-(aq) \rightleftharpoons CoCl_4^{2-}(aq) + 6H_2O(l)$$

The flask on the left has a low concentration of chloride ions, giving the pink colour of the complex ion with water. As the concentration of chloride ions is increased, the equilibrium shifts to the right, changing the colour from pink to blue. Adding water would shift the equilibrium in the opposite direction. Cobalt chloride is often used to test for the presence of water because of this colour change.

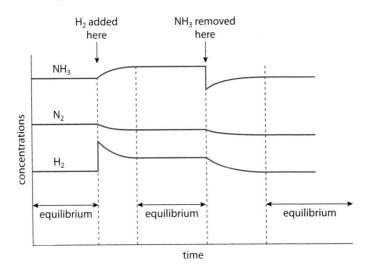

◀ **Figure 7.3** Effects of the addition of reactant and removal of product on the equilibrium:

$$N_2(g) + 3H_2(g) \rightleftharpoons 2NH_3(g)$$

When H_2 is added some N_2 reacts and more NH_3 is formed as the equilibrium shifts to the right. When NH_3 is removed, more N_2 reacts with H_2 as the equilibrium again shifts to the right. After each change a new equilibrium mixture is achieved.

 Changes in pressure or volume will affect the position of equilibrium of a reaction if it involves a change in the number of gas molecules.

Changes in pressure

Equilibria involving gases will be affected by a change in pressure if the reaction involves a change in the number of molecules. This is because there is a direct relationship between the number of molecules and the pressure exerted by a gas in a fixed volume. So if such a reaction at equilibrium is subject to an increase in pressure, the system responds to decrease this pressure by favouring the side with the smaller number of molecules. Conversely, a decrease in pressure will cause a shift in the equilibrium position to the side with the larger number of molecules. A different equilibrium position will be achieved but the value of K_c will be unchanged, as long as the temperature remains the same.

For example, consider the reaction used in the production of methanol:

$$CO(g) + 2H_2(g) \rightleftharpoons CH_3OH(g)$$

There are a total of three molecules of gas on the left side and one molecule of gas on the right side. So here high pressure will shift the equilibrium to the right, in favour of the smaller number of molecules, so increasing the production of CH_3OH.

Changes in temperature

We have noted that K_c is temperature dependent meaning that changing the temperature will change K_c. However, in order to predict *how* it will change we must examine the enthalpy changes (see Chapter 5) of the forward and backward reactions. Remember that an exothermic reaction releases heat, whereas an endothermic reaction absorbs heat. So we can apply Le Chatelier's principle, thinking of heat as a product in an exothermic reaction and as a reactant in an endothermic reaction. Note also that the enthalpy changes of the forward and backward reactions are equal and opposite to each other.

Consider the reaction:

$$2NO_2(g) \rightleftharpoons N_2O_4(g) \qquad \Delta H = -24 \text{ kJ mol}^{-1}$$
$$\text{brown} \qquad\quad \text{colourless}$$

The negative sign of ΔH tells us that the forward reaction is exothermic and so releases heat. If this reaction at equilibrium is subjected to a decrease in temperature, the system will respond by producing heat and favouring the exothermic reaction. This means that the equilibrium will shift to the right, in favour of products. A new equilibrium mixture will be achieved and the value of K_c will increase. So here we can see that the reaction will give a higher yield of products at a *lower temperature*. Can you think of what might be a disadvantage of carrying out such a reaction at a low temperature? (Hint: see Chapter 6, Kinetics) The answer is that at low temperatures the reaction will proceed more *slowly* and so although a higher yield will be produced eventually, it may simply take too long to achieve this. We will come back to this point later in this chapter.

Now consider the following reaction:

$$N_2(g) + O_2(g) \rightleftharpoons 2NO(g) \qquad \Delta H = +181 \text{ kJ mol}^{-1}$$

In this case we can see that the forward reaction is endothermic and so absorbs heat. So here the effect of a decreased temperature will be to favour the backward exothermic reaction. Hence the equilibrium will shift to the left, in favour of reactants and K_c will decrease. At higher temperatures, the forward reaction is favoured; this takes place in motor vehicles where the heat released by the combustion of the fuel is sufficient to cause the nitrogen and oxygen gases from the air to combine together in this way. Unfortunately, the product NO is toxic and, worse still, quickly becomes converted into other toxins that form the components of acid rain and smog. It is therefore of great interest to car manufacturers to find ways of lowering the temperature during combustion in order to reduce the production of NO in the reaction above.

Addition of a catalyst

As we learned in Chapter 6, a catalyst speeds up the rate of a reaction by lowering its activation energy (E_a) and so increases the number of particles that have sufficient energy to react without raising the temperature.

When ΔH is given for an equilibrium reaction, by convention its sign refers to the forward reaction. So a negative sign for ΔH means that the forward reaction is exothermic and the backward reaction is endothermic.

Experiment to show the effect of temperature on the conversion of NO_2 to N_2O_4. As the temperature is increased more NO_2 is produced and the gas becomes darker as seen in the tube on the left.

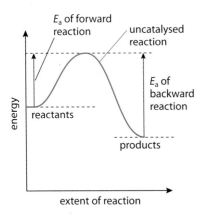

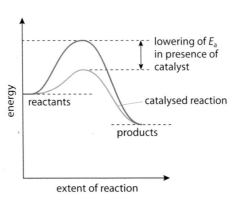

Figure 7.4 Effect of a catalyst in lowering the activation energy of both forward and backward reactions.

The diagrams show that the effect of the catalyst in lowering the activation energy is the same for both the forward and backward reactions. Hence the rate of both these reactions will be increased by the same amount. The catalyst will therefore have no effect on the position of equilibrium, or on the value of K_c. In other words the catalyst will not increase the yield of product in a reaction. It will, however, speed up the attainment of the equilibrium state and so cause products to form more quickly.

We can now summarize the effects of concentration, pressure, temperature and catalyst on the position of equilibrium and on the value of K_c.

Effect of:	Position of equilibrium	Value of K_c
1 concentration	changes	no change
2 pressure	changes if reaction involves a change in the number of gas molecules	no change
3 temperature	changes	changes
4 catalyst	no change	no change

Industrial applications

In reactions involving the manufacture of a chemical, it is obviously a goal to obtain as high a yield of product as possible. Applying Le Chatelier's principle to the reactions involved enables us to maximize the yield by choosing conditions that will cause the equilibrium to lie to the right.

However, the *yield* of a reaction is only part of the consideration. The *rate* is also clearly of great significance. It would, for example, be of limited value if a process were able to claim a 95% yield of product, but to take several years to achieve this! Clearly the economics of the process will depend on considerations of both the equilibrium and the kinetics of the reaction, in other words how far and how fast the reaction will proceed. Sometimes these two criteria work against each other and so chemists must choose the best compromise between them.

Catalysts do not change the position of the equilibrium or the yield of a reaction, but they enable equilibrium to be achieved more quickly.

A particular reaction at a specified temperature can have many different possible equilibrium positions but only one value for the equilibrium constant K_c.

Carry out virtual experiments by changing the conditions of reactions and seeing how the equilibrium shifts in different reactions.
Now go to www.heinemann.co.uk/hotlinks, insert the express code 4259P and click on this activity.

Remember: The *only* thing which changes the value of K_c for a particular reaction is the temperature.

Fritz Haber (1886–1934).

 Fritz Haber was born in what is now Poland but moved to Germany early in his career. Together with Carl Bosch, also of Germany, he developed the process for the industrial synthesis of ammonia from its elements and the first factory for ammonia production opened in Germany in 1913, just before World War I. This development had enormous significance for the country at war; it enabled the continued production of explosives despite the fact that imports were barred through the blockaded ports and thus effectively enabled Germany to continue its war efforts for another four years. Haber was awarded the Nobel prize in chemistry in 1918. In many ways history has recorded this as a controversial choice – not only had Haber helped to prolong the war, he had also been responsible for the development and usage of chlorine as the first poison gas. Ironically, despite his evident patriotism towards Germany, he was expelled from the country in 1933 when the rising tide of anti-semitism conflicted with his Jewish ancestry.

The Haber process: the production of ammonia NH_3

Ammonia, NH_3, is a chemical used on an enormous scale worldwide. Fertilizers such as ammonium nitrate, many plastics such as nylon, refrigerants and powerful explosives are all derived from it. Its synthesis is therefore of great economic importance and it is estimated that about 120 million tonnes are produced worldwide each year, with China being responsible for nearly one-third of this. Approximately 80% of the ammonia is used to make fertilizers.

Tractor applying a chemical solution of fertilizer to the soil. Ammonium salts such as ammonium nitrate and sulfate are particularly effective fertilizers as they supply nitrogen needed by plants and are readily soluble. The use of ammonium fertilizers has transformed world food production.

The process is based on the reaction:

$$N_2(g) + 3H_2(g) \rightleftharpoons 2NH_3(g) \qquad \Delta H = -93\,kJ\,mol^{-1}$$

The following information can be derived from this equation:
- All reactants and products are gases and there is a change in the number of molecules as the reaction proceeds: four gas molecules on the left and two on the right.
- The forward reaction is exothermic and so releases heat; the backward reaction is endothermic and so absorbs heat.

Applying Le Chatelier's principle, we can therefore consider the optimum conditions for this reaction:
- Concentration: the reactants nitrogen and hydrogen are supplied in the molar ratio 1 : 3 in accordance with their stoichiometry in the equation. The product ammonia is removed as it forms, thus helping to pull the equilibrium to the right and increasing the yield.

- Pressure: as the forward reaction involves a decrease in the number of molecules, it will be favoured by a *high pressure*. The usual pressure used in the Haber process is about 200 atmospheres.
- Temperature: as the forward reaction is exothermic, it will be favoured by a lower temperature. However, too low a temperature would cause the reaction to be uneconomically slow and so a *moderate temperature* of about 450 °C is used.
- Catalyst: although a catalyst will not increase the yield of ammonia, it will speed up the rate of production and so help to compensate for the moderate temperature used. A catalyst of finely divided iron is used, with small amounts of aluminium and magnesium oxides added to improve its activity.

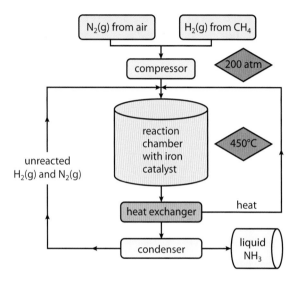

Figure 7.5 Summary of the Haber process for ammonia synthesis.
$$N_2(g) + 3H_2(g) \rightleftharpoons 2NH_3(g)$$

The Contact process: the production of sulfuric acid H_2SO_4

Sulfuric acid, H_2SO_4, has the highest production of any chemical in the world. It is used in the production of fertilizers, detergents, dyes, explosives, drugs, plastics and in many other chemical industries. An estimated 150 million tonnes are manufactured every year globally.

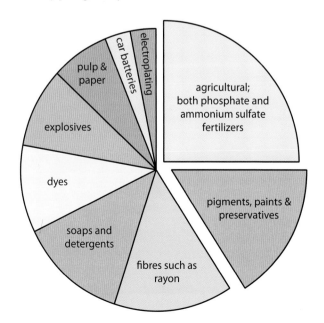

Figure 7.6 The uses of sulfuric acid.

The process gets its name the *Contact process* from the fact that molecules of the gases O_2 and SO_2 react in *contact* with the surface of the solid catalyst V_2O_5.

Its production, known as the Contact process, involves a series of three simple reactions:

(i) The combustion of sulfur $\qquad$ $S(s) + O_2(g) \rightarrow SO_2(g)$

(ii) The oxidation of sulfur dioxide $\qquad$ $2SO_2(g) + O_2(g) \rightleftharpoons 2SO_3(g)$

(iii) The combination of sulfur trioxide with water. This usually takes place indirectly by first absorbing the sulfur trioxide into a flowing solution of concentrated sulfuric acid and then allowing the product of this reaction to react with water. This avoids the problem caused by the violent nature of the direct reaction between sulfur trioxide and water:

$$SO_3(g) + H_2SO_4(l) \rightarrow H_2S_2O_7(l) + H_2O(l) \rightarrow 2H_2SO_4(l)$$

It has been shown that the overall rate of the process depends on step (ii). So applying Le Chatelier's principle to this, we can predict the conditions that will most favour the formation of product. These are summarized below:

$$2SO_2(g) + O_2(g) \rightleftharpoons 2SO_3(g) \qquad \Delta H = -196 \text{ kJ mol}^{-1}$$

	Influence on reaction	Condition used
pressure	forward reaction involves reduction in the number of molecules of gas: high pressure will favour product	2 atm (this gives a very high yield, so still higher pressure is not needed)
temperature	forward reaction is exothermic: low temperature will increase the yield, but decrease the rate	450 °C
catalyst	increases the rate of reaction	vanadium (V) oxide

Land contaminated by waste impurities from an old sulfuric acid plant close to a residential area in Bilbao, Spain. The waste largely derives from smelting and combustion processes. Today the full consideration of any industrial process must include an assessment of its impact on the environment, both locally and globally.

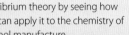

Practise your understanding of equilibrium theory by seeing how you can apply it to the chemistry of ethanol manufacture.

Now go to www.heinemann.co.uk/hotlinks, insert the express code 4259P and click on this activity.

1 Which statements are correct for a reaction at equilibrium?

I The forward and reverse reactions both continue.

II The rates of the forward and reverse reactions are equal.

III The concentrations of reactants and products are equal.

A I and II only

B I and III only

C II and III only

D I, II and III

2 Which statement is always true for a chemical reaction that has reached equilibrium?

A The yield of product(s) is greater than 50%.

B The rate of the forward reaction is greater than the rate of the reverse reaction.

C The amounts of reactants and products do not change.

D Both forward and reverse reactions have stopped.

3 $I_2(g) + 3Cl_2(g) \rightleftharpoons 2ICl_3(g)$

What is the equilibrium constant expression for the reaction above?

A $K_c = \dfrac{[ICl_3]}{[I_2][Cl_2]}$

B $K_c = \dfrac{2[ICl_3]}{3[I_2][Cl_2]}$

C $K_c = \dfrac{2[ICl_3]}{[I_2] + 3[Cl_2]}$

D $K_c = \dfrac{[ICl_3]^2}{[I_2][Cl_2]^3}$

4 The manufacture of sulfur trioxide can be represented by the equation below:

$$2SO_2(g) + O_2(g) \rightleftharpoons 2SO_3(g) \qquad \Delta H^\theta = -197\ kJ\ mol^{-1}$$

What happens when a catalyst is added to an equilibrium mixture from this reaction?

A The rate of the forward reaction increases and that of the reverse reaction decreases.

B The rates of both forward and reverse reactions increase.

C The value of ΔH° increases.

D The yield of sulfur trioxide increases.

5 What will happen to the position of equilibrium and the value of the equilibrium constant when the temperature is increased in the following reaction?

$$Br_2(g) + Cl_2(g) \rightleftharpoons 2BrCl(g) \qquad \Delta H^\theta = +14\ kJ$$

	Position of equilibrium	Value of equilibrium constant
A	shifts towards the reactants	decreases
B	shifts towards the reactants	increases
C	shifts towards the products	decreases
D	shifts towards the products	increases

6 Which changes will shift the position of equilibrium to the right in the following reaction?

$$2CO_2(g) \rightleftharpoons 2CO(g) + O_2(g)$$

I adding a catalyst

II decreasing the oxygen concentration

III increasing the volume of the container.

A I and II only

B I and III only

C II and III only

D I, II and III

7 Which statement(s) is/are true for a mixture of ice and water at equilibrium?

I The rates of melting and freezing are equal.

II The amounts of ice and water are equal.

III The same position of equilibrium can be reached by cooling water and heating ice.

A I only

B I and III only

C II only

D III only

8 In the Haber process for the synthesis of ammonia, what effects does the catalyst have?

	Rate of formation of $NH_3(g)$	Amount of $NH_3(g)$ formed
A	increases	increases
B	increases	decreases
C	increases	no change
D	no change	increases

9 $$2SO_2(g) + O_2(g) \rightleftharpoons 2SO_3(g) \qquad \Delta H^{\ominus} = -200\,kJ$$

According to the above information, what temperature and pressure conditions produce the greatest amount of SO_3?

	Temperature	Pressure
A	low	low
B	low	high
C	high	high
D	high	low

10 Consider the following equilibrium reaction:

$$2SO_2(g) + O_2(g) \rightleftharpoons 2SO_3(g) \qquad \Delta H = -198\,kJ$$

Using Le Chatelier's Principle, state and explain what will happen to the position of equilibrium if:

(a) the temperature increases (2)

(b) the pressure increases. (2)

(*Total 4 marks*)

11 The table below gives information about the percentage yield of ammonia obtained in the Haber process under different conditions.

Pressure/atmosphere	Temperature/°C			
	200	300	400	500
10	50.7	14.7	3.9	1.2
100	81.7	52.5	25.2	10.6
200	89.1	66.7	38.8	18.3
300	89.9	71.1	47.1	24.4
400	94.6	79.7	55.4	31.9
600	95.4	84.2	65.2	42.3

(a) From the table, identify which combination of temperature and pressure gives the highest yield of ammonia. (1)

(b) The equation for the main reaction in the Haber process is:

$$N_2(g) + 3H_2(g) \rightleftharpoons 2NH_3(g) \qquad \Delta H \text{ is negative}$$

Use this information to state and explain the effect on the yield of ammonia of

   (i) increasing the pressure (2)

   (ii) increasing the temperature (2)

(c) In practice, typical conditions used in the Haber process are a temperature of 500 °C and a pressure of 200 atmospheres. Explain why these conditions are used rather than those that give the highest yield. (2)

(d) Write the equilibrium constant expression, K_c, for the production of ammonia. (1)

(Total 8 marks)

12 The equation for one reversible reaction involving oxides of nitrogen is shown below:

$$N_2O_4(g) \rightleftharpoons 2NO_2(g) \qquad \Delta H^\theta = +58 \text{ kJ}$$

Experimental data for this reaction can be represented on the following graph:

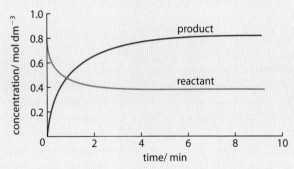

(a) Write an expression for the equilibrium constant K_c, for the reaction. Explain the significance of the horizontal parts of the lines on the graph. State what can be deduced about the magnitude of K_c for the reaction, giving a reason. (4)

(b) Use Le Chatelier's principle to predict and explain the effect of increasing the temperature on the position of equilibrium. (2)

(c) Use Le Chatelier's principle to predict and explain the effect of increasing the pressure on the position of equilibrium. (2)

(d) State and explain the effects of a catalyst on the forward and reverse reactions, on the position of equilibrium and on the value of K_c. (6)

(Total 10 marks)

© International Baccalaureate Organization

8 Acids and bases

The burning feeling of acid indigestion, the sour taste of grapefruit and the vinegary smell of wine that has been exposed to the air are just some of the everyday encounters we have with acids. Likewise alkalis, or bases, are familiar substances – for example in baking soda, in household cleaners that contain ammonia and in medication against indigestion. So what are the defining properties of these two groups of substances?

This question has intrigued chemists for centuries. The word 'acid' is derived from the Latin word *acetum* meaning sour – early tests to determine whether a substance was acidic were based on tasting! But it was learned that acids had other properties in common too: for example, they changed the colour of the dye litmus from blue to red and corroded metals. Similarly, alkalis were known to have distinctive properties such as being slippery to the touch, being able to remove fats and oils from fabrics and turning litmus from red to blue. The name alkali comes from the Arabic word for plant ash, *alkalja*, where they were first identified. Early theories about acids and alkalis focused only on how they reacted together – it was actually suggested that the sourness of acids came from their possession of sharp angular spikes which became embedded in soft, rounded particles of alkali!

The last 120 years have seen the evolution of our understanding of acids and bases, within the framework of increasing knowledge of atomic structure. Theories have arisen and been disproved, while others have stood the test of time and experimentation. It is a fascinating tale of the scientific method in action and has given us today a basis for interpreting, measuring and using the properties of these high-profile substances. Understanding acid–base theory is central to topics such as air and water pollution, how global warming may affect the chemistry of the oceans, the action of drugs in the body and many other aspects of cuting-edge chemistry research. Much of acid theory is dependent on interpreting equilibria, so it will help if you have first studied Chapter 7.

Food scientist testing a sample of orange juice in a factory in France. pH measurements are an important part of the quality control of the product.

Theories of acids and bases

Early theories

The famous French chemist Lavoisier proposed in 1777 that oxygen was the 'universal acidifying principle'. He believed that an acid could be defined as a compound of oxygen and a non-metal. In fact the name he gave to the newly discovered gas *oxygen* means 'acid-former'. This theory, however, had to be dismissed when the acid HCl was proved to be made of hydrogen and chlorine only – with no oxygen. To hold true, of course any definition of an acid has to be valid for *all* acids.

A big step forward came in 1887 when the Swedish chemist Arrhenius suggested that an acid could be defined as a substance that dissociates in water to form hydrogen ions (H^+) and anions, while a base dissociates into hydroxide ions (OH^-) and cations. He also recognized that the hydrogen and hydroxide ions could form water and the cations and anions form a salt. In a sense, Arrhenius was very close to the theory that is widely used to explain acid and base properties today, but his focus was only on aqueous systems and hence somewhat limited. A broader theory was needed to account for reactions occurring without water and especially for the fact that some insoluble substances show base properties.

Reaction between vapours of HCl and NH_3 forming the white smoke of ammonium chloride NH_4Cl.

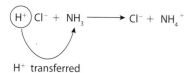

H^+ transferred

Figure 8.1 HCl transfers a H^+ to NH_3.

A Brønsted–Lowry acid is a proton (H^+) donor.
A Brønsted–Lowry base is a proton (H^+) acceptor.

Svante August Arrhenius (1859–1927) wrote up his ideas on acids dissociating into ions in water as part of his doctorate thesis while a student at Stockholm University. But his theory was not well received and he was awarded the lowest possible class of degree. Later his work gradually gained recognition and he received one of the earliest Nobel Prizes in Chemistry in 1903.

Arrhenius may be less well known as the first person documented to predict the possibility of global warming as a result of human activity. In 1896, aware of the rising levels of CO_2 caused by increased industrialization, he calculated the likely effect of this on the temperature of the Earth. Today, over 100 years later, the significance of this relationship between increasing CO_2 and global temperatures has become a subject of major international concern.

Brønsted–Lowry: a theory of proton transfer

In 1923 two chemists, Martin Lowry of Cambridge, England and Johannes Brønsted of Copenhagen, Denmark, independently published similar conclusions regarding the definitions of acids and bases. Their findings overcame the limitations of Arrhenius' work and have become established as the **Brønsted–Lowry theory**.

This theory focuses on the transfer of H^+ ions during an acid–base reaction: acids donate H^+ while bases accept H^+. For example, in the reaction between HCl and NH_3:

$$HCl + NH_3 \rightleftharpoons NH_4^+ + Cl^-$$

HCl transfers H^+ to NH_3 and so acts as an acid, NH_3 accepts the H^+ and so acts as a base.

Hydrogen atoms contain just one proton and one electron, so when they ionize by losing the electron, all that is left is the proton. Therefore *H^+ is equivalent to a proton* and we will use the two terms interchangeably here.

The theory can therefore be stated as:
- A Brønsted–Lowry acid is a proton (H^+) donor.
- A Brønsted–Lowry base is a proton (H^+) acceptor.

Conjugate pairs

The act of donating cannot happen in isolation – there must always be something present to play the role of acceptor. In Brønsted–Lowry theory, an acid can therefore only behave as a proton donor if there is also a base present to accept the proton.

Let's consider the acid–base reaction between a generic acid HA and base B:

$$HA + B \rightleftharpoons A^- + BH^+$$

We can see that HA acts as an acid, donating a proton to B while B acts as a base, accepting the proton from HA. But if we look also at the reverse reaction, we can pick out another acid–base reaction: here BH^+ is acting as an acid, donating its proton to A^- while A^- acts as a base accepting the proton from BH^+. In other words acid HA has reacted to form the base A^-, while base B has reacted to form acid BH^+.

conjugate acid–base pair

$$HA + B \rightleftharpoons A^- + BH^+$$

conjugate acid–base pair

So acids react to form bases and vice versa. The acid–base pairs related to each other in this way are called **conjugate acid–base pairs** and you can see that they *differ by just one proton*. It is important to be able to recognize these pairs in a Brønsted–Lowry acid–base reaction.

One example of a conjugate pair is H_2O and H_3O^+ which is found in all acid–base reactions in aqueous solution. The reaction $H_2O + H^+ \rightleftharpoons H_3O^+$ occurs when a proton released from an acid readily associates with H_2O molecules forming H_3O^+. In other words, protons become hydrated. H_3O^+ is variously called the hydroxonium ion, the oxonium ion or the hydronium ion and is always the form of hydrogen ions in aqueous solution. However, for most reactions it is convenient simply to write it as $H^+(aq)$. Note that in this pair H_3O^+ is the conjugate acid and H_2O its conjugate base.

You can follow a clear summary of conjugate acid–base pairs with examples.
Now go to www.heinemann.co.uk/hotlinks, insert the express code 4259P and click on this activity.

Worked example

Label the conjugate acid–base pairs in the following reaction:

$$CH_3COOH(aq) + H_2O(l) \rightleftharpoons CH_3COO^-(aq) + H_3O^+(aq)$$

Lowry described the ready hydration of the proton as 'the extreme reluctance of the hydrogen nucleus to lead an isolated existence.'

Solution

The fact that in a conjugate pair the acid always has one proton more than its conjugate base makes it easy to predict the formula of the corresponding conjugate for any given acid or base.

Worked examples

1 Write the conjugate base for each of the following:

   (a) HF   (b) HNO_2 (c) H_3O^+

   (d) NH_3 (e) $H_2PO_4^-$ (f) H_2CO_3

2 What is the conjugate acid of the following?

   (a) CN^- (b) PO_4^{3-} (c) H_2O

   (d) OH^- (e) CO_3^{2-} (f) NH_3

To form a conjugate acid, add one H^+ to its base; to form a conjugate base, remove one H^+ from its acid.

Solution

1 The question implies that these act as acids and so will form conjugate bases by the removal of one proton. Remember to adjust the charge for the $1+$ of the H^+ removed.

   (a) F^- (b) NO_2^- (c) H_2O

   (d) NH_2^- (e) HPO_4^{2-} (f) HCO_3^-

2 Here the question implies that these act as bases, so will form conjugate acids with one additional proton. Again remember to account for the $1+$ charge of the H^+ added.

   (a) HCN   (b) HPO_4^{2-} (c) H_3O^+

   (d) H_2O (e) HCO_3^- (f) NH_4^+

Some species can act as acids and as bases

You may be surprised to see water described in the answers above to Q1 part (c) as a base and to Q2 part (d) as an acid, as you are probably not used to thinking

You can watch an animation of the amphoteric behaviour of water. Now go to www.heinemann.co.uk/hotlinks, insert the express code 4259P and click on this activity.

Amphoteros is a Greek word meaning 'both'. For example amphibians are adapted both to water and to land.

of water as an acid, or as a base, but rather as a neutral substance. The point is that Brønsted–Lowry theory describes acids and bases in terms of how they react together, so it all depends on what water is reacting with. Consider the following:

$$CH_3COOH(aq) + H_2O(l) \rightleftharpoons CH_3COO^-(aq) + H_3O^+(aq)$$
$$\quad\text{acid}\qquad\qquad\text{base}\qquad\qquad\text{base}\qquad\qquad\text{acid}$$

$$NH_3(aq) + H_2O(l) \rightleftharpoons NH_4^+(aq) + OH^-(aq)$$
$$\quad\text{base}\qquad\quad\text{acid}\qquad\quad\text{acid}\qquad\quad\text{base}$$

So with CH_3COOH, water acts as a Brønsted–Lowry base, but with NH_3 it acts as a Brønsted–Lowry acid.

Notice that water is not the only species that appears here as both an acid and a base, for example NH_3 and HCO_3^- do likewise. Substances which can act as acids and bases in this way are said to be **amphoteric** or **amphiprotic**. What are the features that enable these species to have this 'double identity'?

We know that to act as a Brønsted–Lowry acid substances must be able to dissociate and release H^+; to act as a Brønsted–Lowry base they must be able to accept H^+. In order to do this they must have a lone pair of electrons.

Worked example

Write equations to show HCO_3^- acting (a) as an acid and (b) as a base.

Solution

(a) To act as an acid, it donates H^+

$$HCO_3^-(aq) + H_2O(l) \rightleftharpoons CO_3^{2-}(aq) + H_3O^+(aq)$$

(b) To act as a base, it accepts H^+

$$HCO_3^-(aq) + H_2O(l) \rightleftharpoons H_2CO_3(aq) + OH^-(aq)$$

Exercises

1 Deduce the formula of the conjugate acid of the following:
   (a) SO_3^{2-} **(b)** CH_3NH_2 **(c)** $C_2H_5COO^-$
   (d) NO_3^- **(e)** F^- **(f)** HSO_4^-

2 Deduce the formula of the conjugate base of the following:
   (a) H_3PO_4 **(b)** CH_3COOH **(c)** H_2SO_3
   (d) HSO_4^- **(e)** OH^- **(f)** HBr

3 For each of the following reactions, identify the Brønsted–Lowry acids and bases and the conjugate acid–base pairs:
   (a) $CH_3COOH(aq) + NH_3(aq) \rightleftharpoons NH_4^+(aq) + CH_3COO^-(aq)$
   (b) $CO_3^{2-}(aq) + H_3O^+(aq) \rightleftharpoons H_2O(l) + HCO_3^-(aq)$
   (c) $NH_4^+(aq) + NO_2^-(aq) \rightleftharpoons HNO_2(aq) + NH_3(aq)$

Lewis: a theory of electron pairs

Gilbert Lewis, whose name famously belongs to electron dot structures for representing covalent bonding (Chapter 4), used such structures in interpreting Brønsted–Lowry theory. Realizing that the base must have a lone pair of electrons, he reasoned that the entire reaction could be viewed in terms of the electron pair rather than in terms of proton transfer. For example, the reaction previously described in which ammonia acts as a base can be represented as follows:

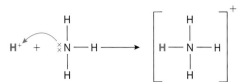

The curly arrow is a convention used to show donation of a pair of electrons. H^+ is acting as an electron pair acceptor and the nitrogen atom in ammonia as an electron pair donor. From such thinking Lewis developed a new, broader definition of acids and bases.

- A Lewis acid is an electron pair acceptor.
- A Lewis base is an electron pair donor.

Lewis bases and Brønsted–Lowry bases are therefore the same group, in other words, the same compounds simply described differently. By either definition they will include species that have a lone pair of electrons.

However, the Lewis definition of acids is broader than the Brønsted–Lowry theory; no longer restricted just to H^+, an acid by Lewis definition will now describe any species capable of accepting a lone pair of electrons. Of course this *includes* H^+ with its vacant energy level or orbital (hence all Brønsted–Lowry acids *are* Lewis acids) – but will also include molecules that have an incomplete valence shell or a vacant valence orbital. Lewis acid–base reactions result in the formation of a covalent bond, which will always be a **dative bond** because both the electrons come from the base. For example,

BF$_3$ has an incomplete octet so is able to act as a Lewis acid and accept a pair of electrons; NH$_3$ acts as a Lewis base, donating its lone pair of electrons. The arrow on the covalent bond denotes the fact that it is a dative bond with both electrons donated from the nitrogen.

Other good examples of Lewis acid–base reactions are found in the chemistry of the transition elements. These are metals found in the middle of the Periodic Table that often form ions with vacant orbitals. Thus they are able to act as Lewis acids and accept lone pairs of electrons. The Lewis base, which donates the lone pair, is called a **ligand** and usually surrounds the ion in a fixed number ratio. Dative bonds form between the metal ion and the ligands, resulting in a **complex ion** that has a characteristic colour.

For example, Cu^{2+} in aqueous solution reacts as follows:

$$Cu^{2+}(aq) + 4H_2O(l) \rightarrow [Cu(H_2O)_4]^{2+}(aq)$$

Typical ligands found in complex ions include H_2O, CN^- and NH_3. Note that these all possess lone pairs of electrons, the defining feature of their Lewis base properties.

▲ Copper ions (Cu^{2+}) forming different complex ions with distinct colours. From left to right the ligands are H_2O, Cl^-, NH_3 and the organic group EDTA. The Cu^{2+} ion has acted as the Lewis acid, the ligands as Lewis bases.

Exercises

4 For each of the following reactions identify the Lewis acid and the Lewis base:
 (a) $4NH_3(aq) + Zn^{2+}(aq) \rightarrow [Zn(NH_3)_4]^{2+}(aq)$
 (b) $2Cl^-(aq) + BeCl_2(aq) \rightarrow [BeCl_4]^{2-}(aq)$
 (c) $Mg^{2+}(aq) + 6H_2O(l) \rightarrow [Mg(H_2O)_6]^{2+}(aq)$

5 Which of the following could not act as a ligand in a complex ion of a transition metal?
 A Cl^- B NCl_3 C PCl_3 D CH_4

Comparison of Brønsted–Lowry and Lewis theories of acids and bases

Theory	Definition of acid	Definition of base
Brønsted–Lowry	proton donor	proton acceptor
Lewis	electron pair acceptor	electron pair donor

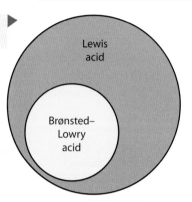

Figure 8.2 Relationship between Brønsted–Lowry acids and Lewis acids.

- Although all Brønsted–Lowry acids are Lewis acids, not all Lewis acids are Brønsted–Lowry acids. The term Lewis acid is usually reserved for those species which can *only* be described by Lewis theory, that is those that do not release H^+.
- Many reactions cannot be described as Brønsted–Lowry acid–base reactions, but do qualify as Lewis acid–base reactions. These are reactions where no transfer of H^+ occurs.

Exercise

6 Which of the following reactions represents an acid–base reaction according to Lewis theory but not according to Brønsted–Lowry theory.
  A $NH_3(g) + HCl(g) \rightleftharpoons NH_4Cl(s)$
  B $2H_2O(l) \rightleftharpoons H_3O^+(aq) + OH^-(aq)$
  C $Cu^{2+}(aq) + 4NH_3 \rightleftharpoons [Cu(NH_3)_4]^{2+}(aq)$
  D $BaO(s) + H_2O(l) \rightleftharpoons Ba^{2+}(aq) + 2OH^-(aq)$

You can follow a summary of the nature of acids and bases and test your understanding in this online pH tutorial.
Now go to
www.heinemann.co.uk/hotlinks, insert the express code 4259P and click on this activity.

8.2 Properties of acids and bases

While we have seen that ideas regarding the defining nature of acids and bases have been long debated, the recognition of what these substances *do* has been known for centuries.

● Examiner's hint: In acid–base theory the words ionization and dissociation are often used interchangeably as acid dissociation always leads to ion formation.

We will look here at some typical reactions of acids and bases in aqueous solutions where H^+ is the ion common to all acids. The bases considered here are those that neutralize acids to produce water and these include metal oxides and hydroxides, ammonia, soluble carbonates (Na_2CO_3 and K_2CO_3) and hydrogen carbonates ($NaHCO_3$ and $KHCO_3$).

Figure 8.3 The relationship between alkalis and bases.

The soluble bases are known as **alkalis**. When dissolved in water they all release the hydroxide ion OH^-. For example:

$$K_2O(s) + H_2O(l) \rightarrow 2K^+(aq) + 2OH^-(aq)$$
$$NH_3(aq) + H_2O(l) \rightleftharpoons NH_4^+(aq) + OH^-(aq)$$
$$CO_3^{2-}(aq) + H_2O(l) \rightleftharpoons HCO_3^-(aq) + OH^-(aq)$$
$$HCO_3^-(aq) \rightleftharpoons CO_2(g) + OH^-(aq)$$

BASES
substances which accept H^+ ions

ALKALIS
substances which form OH^- ions in solution

Alkalis are bases that dissolve in water to form the hydroxide ion OH^-.

Acids and bases can be distinguished using indicators

Indicators tell us what is going on by changing in some obvious way. In chemistry the most widely used are **acid–base indicators** that change colour reversibly according to the concentration of H^+ ions in the solution. This happens because of a shift in the equilibrium position of their dissociation reaction. Indicators are generally used either as aqueous solutions or absorbed onto 'test paper'.

Probably the best known acid–base indicator is **litmus**, a dye derived from lichens, which turns pink in the presence of acid and blue in the presence of alkalis. It is widely used to test for acids or alkalis, but is not so useful in distinguishing between different strengths of acid or alkali.

Other indicators give different colours in different solutions of acid and alkali. Some common examples are given in the table here and there are more in Table 16 of your IB Data booklet.

Litmus indicator compared in acid and alkali solutions.

Indicator	Colour in acid	Colour in alkali
litmus	pink	blue
methyl orange	red	yellow
phenolphthalein	colourless	pink

● **Examiner's hint:** Be careful not to assume that indicator tests always show acids as pink and alkalis as blue. This is true with litmus, but other indicators give many different colours including pink in alkali.

Many of these indicators are derived from natural substances such as extracts from flower petals and berries. A common indicator in the laboratory is **universal indicator**, which is formed by mixing together several indicators and so changes colour many times across a range of different acids and alkalis. It can therefore be used to measure the concentration of H^+ on the pH scale. We will discuss this later in the chapter.

Acids react with metals, bases and carbonates to form salts

The term **salt** refers to the compound formed when the hydrogen of an acid is replaced by a metal or another positive ion. The familiar example NaCl, known as common salt, is derived from the acid HCl in this way. The term **parent acid** is sometimes used to describe this relationship between an acid and its salt.

There are three main types of reaction by which acids react to form salts.

1 Acid + metal → salt + hydrogen

$$2HCl(aq) + Zn(s) \rightarrow ZnCl_2(aq) + H_2(g)$$

$$H_2SO_4(aq) + Fe(s) \rightarrow FeSO_4(aq) + H_2(g)$$

$$2CH_3COOH(aq) + Mg(s) \rightarrow Mg(CH_3COO)_2(aq) + H_2(g)$$

Magnesium reacting with HCl. The tiny bubbles are hydrogen gas being liberated.

We can also write these as ionic equations. For example:

$$2H^+(aq) + 2Cl^-(aq) + Zn(s) \rightarrow Zn^{2+}(aq) + 2Cl^-(aq) + H_2(g)$$

Species which do not change during the reaction, like Cl^- here, are called **spectator ions** and can be cancelled out. So the net reaction is:

$$2H^+(aq) + Zn(s) \rightarrow Zn^{2+}(aq) + H_2(g)$$

These reactions of metals with acids are the reason why acids have corrosive properties on most metals and why, for example, it is important to keep car battery acid well away from the metal bodywork of the car.

You can demonstrate the release of hydrogen from acids in simple experiments by dropping a small piece of metal into a dilute solution of the acid. There is a big range, however, in the reactivity of metals in these reactions. More reactive metals, such as sodium and potassium in group 1, would react much too violently, while copper and other less reactive metals such as silver and gold will not react at all. This is partly why these less reactive metals are so valuable – they are much more resistant to corrosion. We will consider this differing reactivity in Chapter 9. Another point to note is that although the common acid, nitric acid HNO_3, does react with metals, it usually does not release hydrogen owing to its oxidizing properties (Chapter 9).

You can view an animation of a neutralization reaction.
Now go to www.heinemann.co.uk/hotlinks, insert the express code 4259P and click on this activity.

2 Acid + base → salt + water

$$HCl(aq) + NaOH(aq) \rightarrow NaCl(aq) + H_2O(l)$$
$$HNO_3(aq) + NH_4OH(aq) \rightarrow NH_4NO_3(aq) + H_2O(l)$$
$$2CH_3COOH(aq) + CuO(s) \rightarrow Cu(CH_3COO)_2(aq) + H_2O(l)$$

These reactions are the classic **neutralization** reactions between acids and bases. They can all be represented by one common ionic equation that shows the reaction clearly:

$$H^+(aq) + OH^-(aq) \rightarrow H_2O(l)$$

This reaction is often used in the laboratory to calculate the exact concentration of an acid or an alkali when the other is known. The technique, known as **titration**, involves reacting together a carefully measured volume of one of the solutions and adding the other solution gradually until the so-called **equivalence point** is reached where they exactly neutralize each other. The process is known as **standardization** of an acid or an alkali.

Figure 8.4 Simple titration apparatus.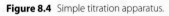

You can carry out a virtual titration and calculate the concentration of acid and alkali.
Now go to www.heinemann.co.uk/hotlinks, insert the express code 4259P and click on this activity.

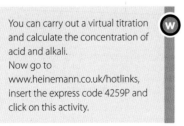

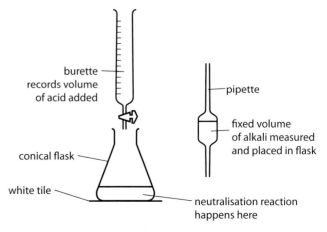

There are times when it is useful to be able to reduce the effect of an acid or a base through the neutralization reaction. For example, in places where the soil has become too acidic, the growth of many plants will be restricted. Adding a weak alkali such as lime (CaO) can help to reduce the acidity and hence increase the fertility of the soil. And treatment for acid indigestion often involves using 'antacids' which contain a mixture of weak alkalis such as magnesium hydroxide and aluminium hydroxide (see Chapter 15).

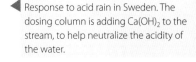
Response to acid rain in Sweden. The dosing column is adding $Ca(OH)_2$ to the stream, to help neutralize the acidity of the water.

Bee stings are slightly acidic and so have traditionally been treated by using a mild alkali such as baking soda, $NaHCO_3$. Wasp stings on the other hand are claimed to be alkali and so are often treated with the weak acid, ethanoic acid, CH_3COOH, in vinegar. Whether these claims are valid, however, is open to dispute as the pH of wasp stings is actually very close to neutral. Nonetheless the healing powers of vinegar are well documented and vigorously defended.

3 Acid + carbonate → salt + water + carbon dioxide

$$2HCl(aq) + CaCO_3(s) \rightarrow CaCl_2(aq) + H_2O(l) + CO_2(g)$$

$$H_2SO_4(aq) + Na_2CO_3(s) \rightarrow Na_2SO_4(aq) + H_2O(l) + CO_2(g)$$

$$CH_3COOH(aq) + KHCO_3(s) \rightarrow KCH_3COO(aq) + H_2O(l) + CO_2(g)$$

These reactions can also be represented as an ionic equation:

$$2H^+(aq) + CO_3^{2-}(aq) \rightarrow H_2O(l) + CO_2(g)$$

The reactions, like the reaction of acids with metals, involve a gas being given off, visibly producing bubbles, known as **effervescence**.

Limestone rock shaped by natural chemical erosion in Switzerland. Rain water, a weak solution of H_2CO_3, reacts with the calcium carbonate, slowly dissolving it.

Rain water dissolves some carbon dioxide from the air to form a weak solution of carbonic acid, H_2CO_3. Greater pressure, such as that found in capillary beds of limestone ($CaCO_3$) rocks, increases the tendency of CO_2 to dissolve giving rise to a more acidified solution. This then reacts on the limestone as follows:

$$H_2CO_3(aq) + CaCO_3(s) \rightleftharpoons Ca(HCO_3)_2(aq)$$

The soluble product calcium hydrogen carbonate washes away, leading to erosion of the rocks. This is why caves commonly form in limestone regions. Inside the cave where the pressure is lower, the reaction above may be reversed, as less CO_2 dissolves. In this case $CaCO_3$ comes out of solution and precipitates, giving rise to the formations known as stalactites and stalagmites.

Similar reactions of rain water dissolving $CaCO_3$ rocks can give rise to water supplies with elevated levels of Ca^{2+} ions, known as 'hard water'.

Under normal conditions rain water is slightly acidic, with a pH close to 5.6 owing to dissolved CO_2. However, over the last 30 years or so the presence of other acidic gases in the atmosphere has caused the acidity of rainwater to increase, dropping the pH to about 4.5. This is the phenomenon known as *acid rain*. The gases responsible are chiefly oxides of sulfur and nitrogen released from industrial processes, particularly the burning of coal and oil. The effects of the increased acidity of rainfall include massive loss of forests, poisoning of lakes and untold destruction of historical marble buildings and monuments worldwide. Alleviation of the problem will have to come from reducing acidic emissions – an enormous challenge that must be faced on a global scale (see Chapter 16).

Exercise

7 Write equations for the following reactions:
   (a) sulfuric acid + copper oxide
   (b) nitric acid + sodium hydrogen carbonate
   (c) phosphoric acid + potassium hydroxide
   (d) ethanoic acid + aluminium

Marble statue damaged by acid rain.

8.3 Strong and weak acids and bases

We have seen that the reactions of acids and bases are dependent on the fact that they dissociate in solution, acids to produce H^+ ions and bases to produce OH^- ions. As a result, their aqueous solutions exist as equilibrium mixtures containing both the undissociated form and the ions. As we will see, the position of this equilibrium is what defines the strength of an acid or a base.

Consider the acid dissociation reaction:

$$HA \rightleftharpoons H^+ + A^-$$

If this equilibrium lies to the right, it means that the acid has dissociated fully and is said to be a **strong acid**. In this case, it will exist virtually entirely as ions in solution. For example:

$$HCl \rightleftharpoons H^+ + Cl^-$$

In this case, the reverse reaction can be considered to be negligible so it is usually written $HCl \rightarrow H^+ + Cl^-$.

If, on the other hand, the equilibrium lies to the left, it means that the acid has dissociated only partially and is said to be a **weak acid**. Here it will exist almost entirely in the undissociated form. For example:

$$CH_3COOH \rightleftharpoons H^+ + CH_3COO^-$$

The strength of an acid is therefore a measure of how readily it dissociates in aqueous solution. This is an inherent property of a particular acid, dependent on its bonding. Do not confuse acid *strength* with its *concentration*, which is a variable depending on the number of moles per unit volume, according to how much solute has been added to the water. Note for example that it is possible for an acid to be strong but present in a dilute solution, or weak and present in a concentrated solution.

In a similar way, bases can be described as strong or weak on the basis of the extent of their dissociation. For example, the strong base NaOH dissociates fully, so its equilibrium lies to the right, producing a high concentration of ions:

$$NaOH \rightleftharpoons Na^+ + OH^-$$

which is usually written $NaOH \rightarrow Na^+ + OH^-$

Watch this animation to see the difference in ionization of a strong acid and a weak acid.
Now go to www.heinemann.co.uk/hotlinks, insert the express code 4259P and click on this activity.

● **Examiner's hint:** Be careful not to confuse two different pairs of opposites. Strong and weak acids or bases refer to their extent of dissociation; concentrated and dilute refer to the amount of water added to the solution.

On the other hand, a weak base such as NH_3 ionizes only partially, so its equilibrium lies to the left and the concentration of ions will be low:

$$NH_3 + H_2O \rightleftharpoons NH_4^+ + OH^-$$

Weak acids and bases are much more common than strong acids and bases

It is often useful to know which of the acids and bases we come across are strong and which are weak. Fortunately this is quite easy as there are very few common examples of strong acids and bases, so this short list can be committed to memory. You will then know that any other acids and bases you come across are likely to be weak.

You can view animations of the ionization of strong and weak acids and bases.
Now go to www.heinemann.co.uk/hotlinks, insert the express code 4259P and click on this activity.

	Acid		Base	
common examples of *strong* forms	HCl	hydrochloric acid	LiOH	lithium hydroxide
	HNO_3	nitric acid	NaOH	sodium hydroxide
	H_2SO_4	sulfuric acid	KOH	potassium hydroxide
			$Ba(OH)_2$	barium hydroxide
some examples of *weak* forms	CH_3COOH other organic acids	ethanoic acid	NH_3	ammonia
	H_2CO_3	carbonic acid	$C_2H_5NH_2$ other amines	ethylamine
	H_3PO_4	phosphoric acid		

Note that amines such as ethylamine can be considered as derivatives of NH_3 in which one of the hydrogen atoms has been replaced by an alkyl (hydrocarbon) group. There are literally hundreds of acids and bases in organic chemistry (Chapter 10), all of which are weak in comparison with the strong inorganic acids listed here. For example the amino acids, the building blocks of proteins, as their name implies contain both the basic $-NH_2$ amino group and the $-COOH$ acid group. And the 'A' in DNA, the store of genetic material, stands for 'acid', in this case the acid present is phosphoric acid.

 Strong acids and bases dissociate almost completely in solution; weak acids and bases dissociate only partially in solution.

Distinguishing between strong and weak acids and bases

Owing to their greater dissociation in solution, strong acids and strong bases will contain a *higher concentration of ions* than weak acids and weak bases. This then can be used as a means of distinguishing between them. Note though that such comparisons will only be valid when solutions of the same concentration (mol dm^{-3}) are compared at the same temperature. We will consider here three properties that depend on the concentration of ions and so can be used for this purpose.

1 Electrical conductivity

Electrical conductivity of a solution depends on the concentration of mobile ions. Strong acids and strong bases will therefore show higher conductivity than weak acids and bases. This can be measured using a conductivity meter.

2 Rate of reaction

The reactions of acids described in Section 8.2 depend on the concentration of H^+ ions. They will therefore happen at a faster rate with stronger acids. This may be an important consideration, for example, regarding safety in the laboratory, but usually does not provide an easy means of quantifying data to distinguish between weak and strong acids.

3 pH

As we will learn in the next section, the pH scale is a measure of the H^+ concentration and so can be used directly to compare the strengths of acids (providing they are of equal molar concentration.) It is a scale in which the higher the H^+ concentration, the lower the pH value. Universal indicator or a pH meter can be used to measure pH.

Exercise

8 Which of the following 1 mol dm^{-3} solutions will be the poorest conductor of electricity?

A   HCl

B CH_3COOH

C   NaOH

D   NaCl

8.4 The pH scale

The Danish chemist Sörensen (1868–1939) developed the pH concept in 1909, originally proposing that it be formulated as p_H. He did not account for his choice of the letter 'p'. It has been suggested to originate from the German word *potenz* for power, although could equally well derive from the Latin, Danish or French terms for the same word.

Chemists realized a long time ago that it would be useful to have a quantitative scale of acid strength based on the concentration of hydrogen ions. As the majority of acids encountered are weak, the hydrogen ion concentration expressed directly as mol dm^{-3} produces numbers with large negative exponents; for example, the H^+ concentration in our blood is 4.6×10^{-8} mol dm^{-3}. Such numbers are not very user-friendly when it comes to describing and comparing acids. The introduction of the pH scale in 1909 by Sörensen led to wide acceptance owing to its ease of use. It is defined as follows:

- **pH $= -\log_{10}[H^+]$**

  In other words pH is the negative number to which the base 10 is raised to give the $[H^+]$ or

- **$[H^+] = 10^{-pH}$.**

  So a solution that has $[H^+] = 0.1$ mol dm^{-3} has $[H^+] = 10^{-1}$ mol dm^{-3} therefore pH = 1.

  And a solution that has $[H^+] = 0.01$ mol dm^{-3} has $[H^+] = 10^{-2}$ mol dm^{-3} therefore pH = 2.

The pH scale can be considered to be an artificial or an arbitrary scale. To what extent is this true of all scales used in measuring?

 pH $= -\log_{10}[H^+]$

This shows us some of the features of the pH scale that help to make it so convenient:

1 *pH numbers are usually positive and have no units*
   Although the pH scale is theoretically an infinite scale (and can even extend into negative numbers), most acids and bases encountered will have positive pH values and fall within the range 0–15, corresponding to $[H^+]$ from 1 mol dm^{-3} to 10^{-15} mol dm^{-3}.

2 *The pH number is inversely related to the $[H^+]$*
   Solutions with a higher $[H^+]$ have a lower pH and vice versa. So stronger and more concentrated acids have a lower pH, weaker and more dilute acids have a higher pH.

3 *A change of one pH unit represents a 10 fold change in $[H^+]$*
   This means increasing the pH by one unit represents a decrease in $[H^+]$ by 10 times; and decreasing by one pH unit represents an increase in $[H^+]$ by 10 times.

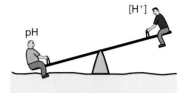

Figure 8.5 The reciprocal relationship between pH and $[H^+]$.

Worked example

If the pH of a solution is changed from 3 to 5, deduce how the hydrogen ion concentration changes.

Solution

$$pH = 3$$
so $[H^+] = 10^{-3}$ mol dm^{-3}
$$pH = 5$$
so $[H^+] = 10^{-5}$ mol dm^{-3}

Therefore $[H^+]$ has changed by 10^{-2} or decreased by 100

Exercise

9 What happens to the pH of an acid when 10 cm^3 of it is added to 90 cm^3 of water?

Because the pH scale is logarithmic, this means that it compresses a very wide range of hydrogen ion concentrations into a much smaller scale of numbers; a small pH change therefore represents a dramatic difference in the acidity of a solution. Keep this in mind when you read reports of changes in the pH of rainfall, for example, as a result of pollution. A reported change from pH 5.5 to pH 4.5 may not sound much, but you can see its huge significance in terms of the change in hydrogen ion concentration and hence in acid properties. In our blood, the pH is carefully controlled to remain at 7.4; a change of only half a pH unit on either side of this is known to be fatal.

The pH scale is a measure of $[H^+]$ and at first glance may appear to be more suitable for the measurement of acids than of bases. But we can in fact use the same scale to describe the alkalinity of a solution. This is because the relationship between $[H^+]$ and $[OH^-]$ is inverse in aqueous solutions and so lower $[H^+]$ (higher pH) means higher $[OH^-]$ and vice versa. Thus the scale of pH numbers represents a range of values from strongly acidic through to strongly alkaline.

In the last 40 years, researchers have developed so-called 'super acids' by mixing together various substances. These are several orders of magnitude more acidic than conventional acids and one example known as 'magic acid' is even able to dissolve candle wax.

	at 25 °C
Acid solutions are defined as those in which $[H^+] > [OH^-]$	**pH < 7**
Neutral solutions are defined as those in which $[H^+] = [OH^-]$	**pH = 7**
Alkaline solutions are defined as those in which $[H^+] < [OH^-]$	**pH > 7**

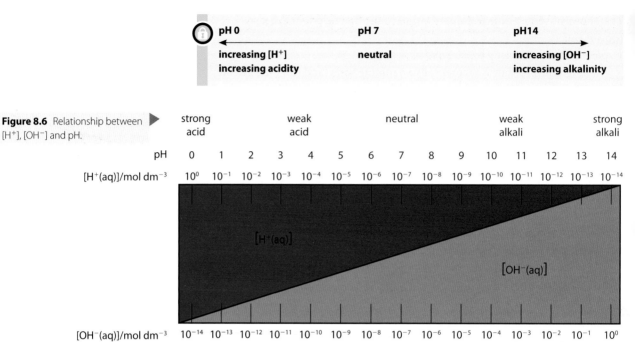

Figure 8.6 Relationship between [H⁺], [OH⁻] and pH.

Measuring pH

An easy way to measure pH is with universal indicator paper or solution. The substance tested will give a characteristic colour, which can then be compared with a colour chart supplied with the indicator. Narrower range indicators give a more accurate reading than broad range, but they always depend on the ability of the user's eyes to interpret the colour.

A more objective and usually more accurate means is by using a pH meter that directly reads the H⁺ concentration through a special electrode. pH meters can record to an accuracy of several decimal points. They must, however, be calibrated before each use with a buffer solution and standardized for the temperature.

pH is a temperature-dependent measurement; owing to the ionization of water, its value decreases with increasing temperature. Water at 50 °C has a pH of 6.6 and at 0 °C a pH of 7.5. Note these solutions are still neutral because $[H^+] = [OH^-]$: water does not become acidic when you boil it!

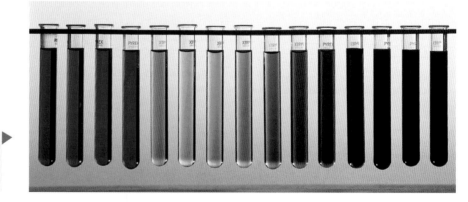

The pH scale and universal indicator. The tubes contain universal indicator added to solutions of pH 0–14 from left to right.

Exercise

10 Put the following substances in order of increasing pH:

$CH_3COOH(aq)$, $NaOH(aq)$, $NaCl(aq)$, $HCl(aq)$, $C_2H_5NH_2(aq)$

1 Consider the following equilibria in 0.10 mol dm^{-3} carbonic acid.

$$H_2CO_3(aq) \rightleftharpoons H^+(aq) + HCO_3^-(aq)$$
$$HCO_3^-(aq) \rightleftharpoons H^+(aq) + CO_3^{2-}(aq)$$

Which species is present in the highest concentration?

A $H_2CO_3(aq)$

B $H^+(aq)$

C $HCO_3^-(aq)$

D $CO_3^{2-}(aq)$

© International Baccalaureate Organization [2004]

2 Which substance can be dissolved in water to give a 0.1 mol dm^{-3} solution with a high pH and a high electrical conductivity?

A HCl

B NaCl

C NH_3

D NaOH

© International Baccalaureate Organization [2004]

3 An aqueous solution of which of the following reacts with magnesium metal?

A ammonia

B hydrogen chloride

C potassium hydroxide

D sodium hydrogencarbonate

© International Baccalaureate Organization [2003]

4 What will happen if $CO_2(g)$ is allowed to escape from the following reaction mixture at equilibrium?

$$CO_2(g) + H_2O(l) \rightleftharpoons H^+(aq) + HCO_3^-(aq)$$

A The pH will decrease.

B The pH will increase.

C The pH will remain constant.

D The pH will become zero.

© International Baccalaureate Organization [2004]

5 Four aqueous solutions, I, II, III and IV, are listed below.

 I 0.100 mol dm^{-3} HCl

 II 0.010 mol dm^{-3} HCl

 III 0.100 mol dm^{-3} NaOH

 IV 0.010 mol dm^{-3} NaOH.

What is the correct order of **increasing** pH of these solutions?

A I, II, III, IV

B I, II, IV, III

C II, I, III, IV

D II, I, IV, III

© International Baccalaureate Organization [2003]

6 Which of the following is/are formed when a metal oxide reacts with a dilute acid?

 I a metal salt

 II water

 III hydrogen gas

A I only

B I and II only

C II and III only

D I, II and III

© International Baccalaureate Organization [2003]

7 The pH of a solution is 2. If its pH is increased to 6, how many times greater is the [H⁺] of the original solution?

A 3

B 4

C 1000

D 10000

8 The pH of solution X is 1 and that of Y is 2. Which statement is correct about the hydrogen ion concentrations in the two solutions?

A $[H^+]$ in X is half that in Y.

B $[H^+]$ in X is twice that in Y.

C $[H^+]$ in X is one tenth that in Y.

D $[H^+]$ in X is ten times that in Y.

9 When the following 1.0 mol dm⁻³ solutions are listed in increasing order of pH (lowest first), what is the correct order?

A $HNO_3 < H_2CO_3 < NH_3 < Ba(OH)_2$

B $NH_3 < Ba(OH)_2 < H_2CO_3 < HNO_3$

C $Ba(OH)_2 < H_2CO_3 < NH_3 < HNO_3$

D $HNO_3 < H_2CO_3 < Ba(OH)_2 < NH_3$

10 Lime was added to a sample of soil and the pH changed from 4 to 6. What was the corresponding change in the hydrogen ion concentration?

A increased by a factor of 2

B increased by a factor of 100

C decreased by a factor of 2

D decreased by a factor of 100

11 A 0.01 mol dm⁻³ solution of hydrochloric acid has a pH value of 2. Suggest, with a reason, the pH values of:

(a) 0.10 mol dm⁻³ hydrochloric acid   (2)

(b) 0.10 mol dm⁻³ ethanoic acid   (2)

12 (a) Define the terms *strong acid* and *weak acid*. Using hydrochloric and ethanoic acid as examples, write equations to show the dissociation of each acid in aqueous solution.   (4)

(b) (i) Calcium carbonate is added to separate solutions of hydrochloric acid and ethanoic acid of the same concentration. State **one** similarity and **one** difference in the observations you could make.   (2)

(ii) Write an equation for the reaction between hydrochloric acid and calcium carbonate.   (2)

(iii) Determine the volume of 1.50 mol dm⁻³ hydrochloric acid that would react with exactly 1.25 g of calcium carbonate.   (3)

(iv) Calculate the volume of carbon dioxide, measured at 273 K and 1.01 × 10⁵ Pa, which would be produced when 1.25 g of calcium carbonate reacts completely with the hydrochloric acid.   (2)

(Total 13 marks)

⑨ Oxidation and reduction

Oxygen makes up only about 20% of the air, yet is the essential component for so many reactions. Without it fuels would not burn, iron would not rust and we would be unable to obtain energy from our food molecules through respiration. Indeed animal life on the planet did not evolve until a certain concentration of oxygen had built up in the atmosphere over 600 million years ago. The term **oxidation** has been in use for a long time to describe these and other reactions where oxygen is added. Oxidation, though, is only half of the story, as it is always accompanied by the opposite process **reduction**, which was originally thought of in terms of loss of oxygen.

Later, however, the terms widened to include a much broader range of reactions. We now define these two processes, oxidation and reduction, as occurring whenever electrons are transferred from one reactant to another – and many of these reactions do not involve oxygen at all. For example, photosynthesis, the process by which plants store chemical energy from light energy, involves oxidation and reduction reactions although oxygen itself is not used.

Transferring electrons from one substance to another leads to a flow of electrons, in other words an electric current. Thus chemical reactions can be used to generate electricity – a simple battery works by using a reaction of oxidation and reduction in this way. As we will see, we can also reverse the process and use an electric current to drive a reaction of oxidation and reduction – this is the process known as electrolysis. Since the discovery of electrolysis in the early 1800s, it has developed to become one of the most important industrial processes on which we depend. Reactive metals such as potassium, sodium, magnesium, lithium and aluminium are only effectively isolated through electrolysis and the process is also the source of important chemicals such as chlorine and hydrogen. An understanding of oxidation and reduction is therefore at the heart of understanding a large branch of chemistry both in the laboratory and beyond.

View of a row of large electrolytic cells at a copper refinery plant. This modern plant in Germany uses electrolysis to produce about 170 000 tonnes of pure copper from impure copper each year. Electrolysis uses an electric current to drive oxidation and reduction reactions that do not happen spontaneously.

9.1 Introduction to oxidation and reduction

9.1.1 Define *oxidation* and *reduction* in terms of electron loss and gain.
9.1.2 Deduce the oxidation number of an element in a compound.
9.1.3 State the names of compounds using oxidation numbers.
9.1.4 Deduce whether an element undergoes oxidation or reduction in reactions using oxidation numbers.

9.2 Redox equations

9.2.1 Deduce simple oxidation and reduction half equations given the species involved in a redox reaction.
9.2.2 Deduce redox equations using half equations.
9.2.3 Define the terms *oxidizing agent* and *reducing agent*.
9.2.4 Identify the oxidizing and reducing agents in redox equations.

9.3 Reactivity

9.3.1 Deduce a reactivity series based on the chemical behaviour of a group of oxidizing and reducing agents.
9.3.2 Deduce the feasibility of a redox reaction from a given reactivity series.

9.4 Voltaic cells

9.4.1 Explain how a redox reaction is used to produce electricity in a voltaic cell.
9.4.2 State that oxidation occurs at the negative electrode (anode) and reduction occurs at the positive electrode (cathode).

9.5 Electrolytic cells

9.5.1 Describe, using a diagram, the essential components of an electrolytic cell.
9.5.2 State that oxidation occurs at the positive electrode (anode) and reduction occurs at the negative electrode (cathode).
9.5.3 Describe how current is conducted in an electrolytic cell.
9.5.4 Deduce the products of the electrolysis of a molten salt.

Magnesium ribbon burning in air. It forms mostly magnesium oxide with small amounts of magnesium nitride.

9.1 Introduction to oxidation and reduction

When magnesium is burned in air, it gives a bright white flame and produces a white powder, magnesium oxide:

$$2Mg(s) + O_2(g) \rightarrow 2MgO(s)$$

The fact that magnesium gains oxygen in this reaction makes it easy to see why we say it is an **oxidation** reaction and that magnesium has been oxidized. However, during the same reaction a small amount of the magnesium will combine with the nitrogen of the air too, forming magnesium nitride. It may be less obvious that this is also an oxidation reaction and that again magnesium is oxidized:

$$3Mg(s) + N_2(g) \rightarrow Mg_3N_2(s)$$

What do these two reactions have in common which means that they can both be defined in this way? If we divide them into so-called half equations, each showing what happens to one reactant, we can examine what is happening in terms of electrons:

$$2Mg(s) \rightarrow 2Mg^{2+}(s) + 4e^-$$
$$O_2(g) + 4e^- \rightarrow 2O^{2-}(s)$$
$$\overline{2Mg(s) + O_2(g) \rightarrow 2MgO(s)}$$

$$3Mg(s) \rightarrow 3Mg^{2+}(s) + 6e^-$$
$$N_2(g) + 6\,e^- \rightarrow 2N^{3-}(s)$$
$$\overline{3Mg(s) + N_2(g) \rightarrow Mg_3N_2(s)}$$

In both reactions Mg is forming Mg^{2+} by losing electrons, while N and O respectively are forming O^{2-} and N^{3-} by gaining electrons. It is this transfer of electrons that defines oxidation and its opposite reaction, reduction.

Oxidation is the loss of electrons, reduction is the gain of electrons.

So in the reactions above, magnesium is oxidized while oxygen and nitrogen are respectively reduced. Clearly each process is dependent on the other, so oxidation and reduction will always occur together and reactions of this type are known as **redox** reactions. They include a large number of interesting reactions, making up a branch of chemistry known as electrochemistry.

The free radical theory of ageing suggests that the physiological changes associated with ageing are the result of oxidative reactions in cells causing damage to membranes and large molecules such as DNA. These changes accumulate with time and may explain the increase in degenerative diseases such as cancer with age. The theory suggests that supplying cells with anti-oxidants will help to slow down the damaging oxidative reactions. Anti-oxidants are particularly abundant in fresh fruit and vegetables, as well as in red wine, tea and cocoa. Although there is strong evidence that anti-oxidant supplementation may help protect against certain diseases, it has not yet been shown to produce a demonstrated increase in the lifespan of humans.

Fresh fruits and vegetables are good sources of anti-oxidants, which may help prevent damaging oxidative reactions in cells.

Oxidation numbers

In reactions involving ions such as the examples above, it is easy to identify the electron transfers occurring. But what about a reaction where electrons are not transferred but instead are shared in the covalent bond, such as the combination of hydrogen and oxygen? Can oxidation and reduction be identified here too?

$$2H_2(g) + O_2(g) \rightarrow 2H_2O(l)$$

The answer is yes, through the introduction of the concept of **oxidation number**. This is a value we assign to each atom in a compound that is a measure of the electron control or possession it has relative to the atom in the pure element. It is as if we exaggerate the unequal sharing in a covalent bond to the point where each atom has complete gain or loss of the electrons shared. This enables us to keep track of the relative electron density in a compound and how it changes during a reaction. There are two parts to the oxidation number:

- the sign: a + sign means the atom has lost electron control; a − sign means it has gained electron control.
- its value: this refers to the number of electrons over which control has changed.

The oxidation number is written with the sign first, followed by the number, e.g. +2 or −3.

Oxidation numbers are a contrived means of communicating information about oxidation and reduction as they do not have a structural basis. For example, Mn with oxidation number +7 does not mean that the Mn atom has lost 7 electrons. Consider therefore the extent to which they may help enhance or confuse understanding.

Strategy for assigning oxidation numbers

When you first use oxidation numbers, it is useful to follow these few simple rules:

1 Atoms in the elemental state have an oxidation number of zero.

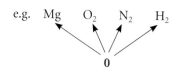

e.g.   Mg O_2 N_2 H_2

0

2 In simple ions, the oxidation number is the same as the charge on the ion.

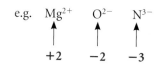

e.g. Mg^{2+} O^{2-} N^{3-}

+2   −2   −3

3 The oxidation numbers of all the atoms in a neutral (uncharged) compound must add up to zero, e.g. H_2SO_4, sum of oxidation numbers = 0.

4 The oxidation numbers of all the atoms in a polyatomic ion must add up to the charge on the ion, e.g. SO_4^{2-}, sum of oxidation numbers = −2.

5 The usual oxidation number for an element is the same as the charge on its most common ion, e.g. group 1 elements have an oxidation number of +1. This means that for many elements their oxidation state can usually be predicted from the Periodic Table. The following are useful to remember:

Element	Usual oxidation state	Exceptions
Na, K	+1	
F	−1	
O	−2	peroxides such as H_2O_2 where it is −1; OF_2 where it is +2
H	+1	metal hydrides such as NaH, where it is −1
Cl	−1	when it is combined with O or F

6 Some elements have oxidation states that vary in different compounds depending on the other elements present. Common examples include: N, P, S, all transition elements, Sn, Pb.

It is usually best to assign the oxidation numbers to the atoms that are easy to predict first, then use rules 3 and 4 above to find the more unpredictable elements by subtraction.

Worked examples

Assign oxidation numbers to sulfur in (a) H_2SO_4 and (b) SO_3^{2-}.

Solution

(a) We can assign H and O as follows: H_2SO_4

+1 −2

Note that the oxidation numbers apply to each atom and that here the sum of all the oxidation numbers must be zero as H_2SO_4 is electrically neutral.

Therefore $2\,(+1) + S + 4\,(-2) = 0$

so $S = +6$

(b) Here start by assigning O: SO_3^{2-}

$$\uparrow$$
$$-2$$

Note that here the oxidation numbers must add up to -2, the charge on the ion.

Therefore $S + 3(-2) = -2$ so $S = +4$

---

1 Assign oxidation numbers to all elements in the following compounds and ions:

(a) NH_4^+ (b) $CuCl_2$ (c) H_2O (d) SO_2

(e) Fe_2O_3 (f) NO_3^- (g) MnO_2 (h) PO_4^{3-}

(i) $K_2Cr_2O_7$ (j) MnO_4^-

Interpreting oxidation numbers

We can see that an element like sulfur can have a wide range of oxidation numbers in different compounds:

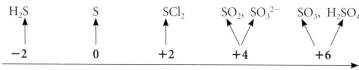

increasing oxidation number

What is the significance of these different values? Because the oxidation number is a measure of the electron control that an atom has, we can see that the higher the positive number, the more the atom has lost control over electrons, in other words the more oxidized it is. Likewise the greater the negative number, the more it has gained electron control, hence the more reduced it is. It follows that any change in oxidation numbers during a reaction is an indication that redox processes are occurring: increase in oxidation number represents oxidation, decrease in oxidation number represents reduction.

So going back to the hydrogen–oxygen reaction discussed earlier, we can now clearly follow the redox process:

 A redox reaction is a chemical reaction in which changes in the oxidation numbers occur.

$$2H_2(g) + O_2(g) \rightarrow 2H_2O(l)$$

$$\uparrow \quad\quad \uparrow \quad\quad \uparrow \quad \uparrow$$
$$0 \quad\quad 0 \quad\quad +1 \; -2$$

Hydrogen has been oxidized (increased from $0 \rightarrow +1$) and oxygen has been reduced (decreased from $0 \rightarrow -2$).

 Oxidation occurs when there is an increase in oxidation number of an element, reduction occurs when there is a decrease in oxidation number of an element.

Worked example

Use oxidation numbers to deduce which species has been oxidized and which has been reduced in the following reactions:

(a) $Ca(s) + Sn^{2+}(aq) \rightarrow Ca^{2+}(aq) + Sn(s)$

(b) $4NH_3(g) + 5O_2(g) \rightarrow 4NO(g) + 6H_2O(l)$

Solution

(a) $Ca(s) + Sn^{2+}(aq) \rightarrow Ca^{2+}(aq) + Sn(s)$
       0   **+2**   **+2**   **0**

Ca is oxidized because its oxidation number increases from 0 to $+2$, Sn^{2+} is reduced because its oxidation number decreases from $+2$ to 0.

(b) $4NH_3(g) + 5O_2(g) \rightarrow 4NO(g) + 6H_2O(l)$
     −3 +1   **0**   **+2 −2**   **+1 −2**

N is oxidized because its oxidation number increases from -3 to $+2$, O is reduced because its oxidation number decreases from 0 to -2

Electron micrograph of the head of a rusty nail. Rust is hydrated iron oxide resulting from electrochemical reactions between iron and atmospheric water vapour and oxygen. The flaky structures seen are the head of the nail which has been degraded and weakened by the rusting process. Rusting will spontaneously cause iron to revert to its more stable oxidized state, unless this is prevented by protecting the iron. It is estimated that corrosion costs for maintenance and repair in the USA alone are over 300 billion dollars a year.

Exercise

2 Use oxidation numbers to deduce which species is oxidized and which is reduced in the following reactions:

(a) $Sn^{2+}(aq) + 2Fe^{3+}(aq) \rightarrow Sn^{4+}(aq) + 2Fe^{2+}(aq)$

(b) $Cl_2(aq) + 2NaBr(aq) \rightarrow Br_2(aq) + 2NaCl(aq)$

(c) $2FeCl_2(aq) + Cl_2(aq) \rightarrow 2FeCl_3(aq)$

(d) $2H_2O(l) + 2F_2(aq) \rightarrow 4HF(aq) + O_2(g)$

(e) $I_2(aq) + SO_3^{2-}(aq) + H_2O(l) \rightarrow 2I^-(aq) + SO_4^{2-}(aq) + 2H^+(aq)$

Systematic names of compounds use oxidation numbers

We have seen that elements such as sulfur exhibit different oxidation numbers in different compounds. In these cases it is useful to give information about the oxidation number in the name. Traditional names used descriptive language that became associated with a particular oxidation number. For example, ferrous and ferric iron oxides referred to FeO and Fe_2O_3 in which Fe has oxidation numbers $+2$ and $+3$, respectively.

The IUPAC system founded in 1919 introduced a nomenclature using oxidation numbers to make the names more recognizable and unambiguous. This involves inserting a Roman numeral corresponding to the oxidation number after the name of the element. Compounds that have elements with different oxidation numbers are said to be in different **oxidation states**. The table shows some common examples.

Formula of compound	Oxidation number	Name using oxidation state
FeO	Fe $+2$	iron(II) oxide
Fe_2O_3	Fe $+3$	iron(III) oxide
Cu_2O	Cu $+1$	copper(I) oxide
CuO	Cu $+2$	copper(II) oxide
MnO_2	Mn $+4$	manganese(IV) oxide
MnO_4^-	Mn $+7$	manganate(VII) ion
$K_2Cr_2O_7$	Cr $+6$	potassium dichromate(VI)

Although this nomenclature can theoretically be used in the naming of all compounds, it is really only worthwhile when an element has more than one common oxidation state. For example, Na_2O could be called sodium(I) oxide, but as we know Na always has oxidation number $+1$, it is perfectly adequate to call it simply sodium oxide.

The IUPAC system aims to help chemists communicate more easily in all languages by introducing systematic names into compounds. However its success in achieving this will be determined by how readily it is adopted. What do you think might prevent chemists using exclusively the 'new names'?

.2 Redox equations

Writing half equations

Although we have seen that oxidation cannot take place without reduction and vice versa, it is sometimes useful to separate out the two processes from a redox equation and write separate equations for the oxidation and reduction processes. These are thus called **half equations**. Electrons are added on one side of each equation to balance the charges.

Worked example

Deduce the two half equations for the following reaction:

$$Zn(s) + Cu^{2+}(aq) \rightarrow Zn^{2+}(aq) + Cu(s)$$

Solution

Assign oxidation numbers so you can see what is being oxidized and what is reduced.

$$Zn(s) + Cu^{2+}(aq) \rightarrow Zn^{2+}(aq) + Cu(s)$$
$$\ 0 \qquad\ +2 \qquad\quad +2 \qquad\quad 0$$

Here we can see that Zn is being oxidized and Cu^{2+} is being reduced.

Oxidation $Zn(s) \rightarrow Zn^{2+}(aq) + 2e^-$ electrons are lost

Reduction $Cu^{2+}(aq) + 2e^- \rightarrow Cu(s)$ electrons are gained

Note there must be equal numbers of electrons in the two half equations, so that when they are added together they cancel out.

Exercise

3 Deduce the half equations of oxidation and reduction for the following reactions:
 (a) $Ca(s) + 2H^+(aq) \rightarrow Ca^{2+}(aq) + H_2(g)$
 (b) $2Fe^{2+}(aq) + Cl_2(aq) \rightarrow 2Fe^{3+}(aq) + 2Cl^-(aq)$
 (c) $Sn^{2+}(aq) + 2Fe^{3+}(aq) \rightarrow Sn^{4+}(aq) + 2Fe^{2+}(aq)$
 (d) $Cl_2(aq) + 2Br^-(aq) \rightarrow 2Cl^-(aq) + Br_2(aq)$

Writing redox equations using half equations

Sometimes you may know the species involved in a redox reaction, but not the overall equation so you will need to work this out, making sure it is balanced for both atoms and charge. A good way to do this is by writing half equations for the oxidation and reduction processes separately and then adding these two together to give the overall reaction. Many of these reactions take place in acidified solutions and you will therefore use H_2O and/or H^+ ions to balance the half equations. The process is best broken down into a series of steps as in the next worked example.

Worked example

Write an equation for the reaction in which NO_3^- and Cu react together in acidic solution to produce NO and Cu^{2+}.

Solution

1. Assign oxidation numbers to determine which atoms are being oxidized and which are being reduced.

$$NO_3^-(aq) + Cu(s) \rightarrow NO(g) + Cu^{2+}(aq) \quad\quad \text{unbalanced}$$
$$\;\;+5\;-2 \quad\quad\quad 0 \quad\quad +2\;-2 \quad\quad +2$$

   Cu is being oxidized ($0 \rightarrow +2$) and N is being reduced ($+5 \rightarrow +2$)

2. Write half equations for oxidation and reduction as follows:

   (a) Balance the atoms other than H and O

   Oxidation $Cu(s) \rightarrow Cu^{2+}(aq)$

   Reduction $NO_3^-(aq) \rightarrow NO(g)$ in this example the nitrogen is already balanced.

   (b) Balance each half equation for O by adding H_2O as needed.
   Here the reduction equation needs two more O atoms on the right side so add $2H_2O$.

   Reduction $NO_3^-(aq) \rightarrow NO(g) + 2H_2O(l)$

   (c) Balance each half equation for H by adding H^+ as needed.
   Here the reduction equation needs 4H atoms on the left side so add $4H^+$:

   Reduction $NO_3^-(aq) + 4H^+(aq) \rightarrow NO(g) + 2H_2O(l)$

   (d) Balance each half equation for charge by adding electrons to the sides with the more positive charge. (Electrons will be products in the oxidation equation and reactants in the reduction equation).

   Oxidation $Cu(s) \rightarrow Cu^{2+}(aq) + 2e^-$

   Reduction $NO_3^-(aq) + 4H^+(aq) + 3e^- \rightarrow NO(g) + 2H_2O(l)$

   Now check that each half equation is balanced for atoms and for charge.

3. Equalize the number of electrons in the two half equations by multiplying each appropriately.

   Here the equation of oxidation must be multiplied by 3 and the equation of reduction by 2, to give six electrons in both equations.

   Oxidation $3Cu(s) \rightarrow 3Cu^{2+}(aq) + 6e^-$

   Reduction $2NO_3^-(aq) + 8H^+(aq) + 6e^- \rightarrow 2NO(g) + 4H_2O(l)$

4. Add the two half equations together, cancelling out anything that is the same on both sides.

$$3Cu(s) + 2NO_3^-(aq) + 8H^+(aq) \rightarrow 3Cu^{2+}(aq) + 2NO(g) + 4H_2O(l)$$

   Your final equation should be balanced for atoms and charge and have no electrons.

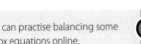

You can practise balancing some redox equations online.
Now go to
www.heinemann.co.uk/hotlinks, insert the express code 4259P and click on this activity.

Summary of steps in writing redox equations:
1. **Assign oxidation numbers to determine which atoms are being oxidized and which are being reduced.**
2. **Write half equations for oxidation and reduction as follows:**
   (a) **Balance the atoms other than H and O.**
   (b) **Balance each half equation for O by adding H_2O as needed.**
   (c) **Balance each half equation for H by adding H^+ as needed.**
   (d) **Balance each half equation for charge by adding electrons to the sides with the more positive charge.**
3. **Equalize the number of electrons in the two half equations by multiplying each appropriately.**
4. **Add the two half equations together, cancelling out anything that is the same on both sides.**

Exercise

4 Write balanced equations for the following reactions which occur in acidic solutions:

(a) $Zn(s) + SO_4^{2-}(aq) \rightarrow Zn^{2+}(aq) + SO_2(g)$

(b) $I^-(aq) + HSO_4^-(aq) \rightarrow I_2(aq) + SO_2(g)$

(c) $NO_3^-(aq) + Zn(s) \rightarrow NH_4^+(aq) + Zn^{2+}(aq)$

(d) $I_2(aq) + OCl^-(aq) \rightarrow IO_3^-(aq) + Cl^-(aq)$

(e) $MnO_4^-(aq) + H_2SO_3(aq) \rightarrow Mn^{2+}(aq) + SO_4^{2-}(aq)$

Oxidizing and reducing agents

We have seen that redox reactions *always* involve the simultaneous oxidation of one reactant with the reduction of another as electrons are transferred between them. The reactant that accepts electrons is called the **oxidizing agent** as it brings about oxidation of the other reactant. In the process it becomes reduced. Likewise the reactant that supplies the electrons is known as the **reducing agent**, because it brings about reduction and itself becomes oxidized.

For example, in the reaction where iron Fe is extracted from its ore Fe_2O_3:

$$\underset{+3}{\underset{\text{oxidizing} \atop \text{agent}}{Fe_2O_3(s)}} + \underset{0}{\underset{\text{reducing} \atop \text{agent}}{3C(s)}} \rightarrow \underset{0}{2Fe(s)} + \underset{+2}{3CO(g)}$$

(The oxidation number of O is not shown as it does not change during the reaction.)

The reducing agent C brings about the reduction of Fe from +3 in Fe_2O_3 to 0 in Fe, while the carbon is oxidized from zero in the element to +2 in CO. The oxidizing agent Fe_2O_3 brings about the oxidation of C, and is itself reduced to Fe.

 In a redox equation the substance that is reduced is the oxidizing agent, the substance that is oxidized is the reducing agent.

Worker standing in front of a blast furnace used in the steel-making industry. Iron is extracted from its ore Fe_2O_3 by reducing it with carbon in the form of coke. Although blast furnaces existed in China from about the 5th century BC and were widespread across Europe, a major development occurred in England in 1709. Substitution of the reducing agent charcoal for coke produced a less brittle form of iron. This accelerated the iron trade, which was a key factor in the British Industrial Revolution (for more details, see Chapter 14).

Exercise

5 Identify the oxidizing agents and the reducing agents in the following reactions:

(a) $H_2(g) + Cl_2(g) \rightarrow 2HCl(g)$

(b) $2Al(s) + 3PbCl_2(s) \rightarrow 2AlCl_3(s) + 3Pb(s)$

(c) $Cl_2(aq) + 2KI(aq) \rightarrow 2KCl(aq) + I_2(aq)$

(d) $CH_4(g) + 2O_2(g) \rightarrow CO_2(g) + 2H_2O(l)$

A strip of zinc metal half submerged in a solution of copper(II) sulfate. Solid copper which appears brown is deposited and the blue colour fades as the copper ions are reduced by the zinc. Zinc is shown to be the stronger reducing agent.

Figure 9.1 Reaction of zinc with Cu(II) sulfate solution. ▶

More reactive metals are stronger reducing agents than less reactive metals.

9.3 Reactivity

More reactive metals are stronger reducing agents

Of course not all oxidizing and reducing agents are of equal strength. Some will be stronger than others depending on their relative tendencies to lose or gain electrons. We learned in Chapters 3 and 4 that metals have a tendency to lose electrons and form positive ions, so they will act as reducing agents, pushing their electrons on to another substance. More reactive metals lose their electrons more readily and so we might expect they will be stronger reducing agents than less reactive metals.

We can check this out by seeing if one metal is able to reduce the ions of another metal in solution. If we immerse zinc in a solution of copper sulfate, a reaction occurs. The blue colour of the solution fades, the pinkish-brown colour of copper metal appears and there is a rise in temperature. What is happening is that the Cu^{2+} ions are being **displaced** from solution as they are reduced by Zn. At the same time Zn dissolves as it is oxidized to Zn^{2+}.

$$Zn(s) + CuSO_4(aq) \rightarrow Cu(s) + ZnSO_4(aq)$$

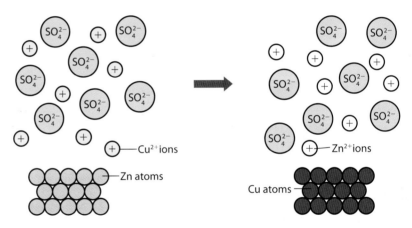

We can write this as an ionic equation without showing the sulfate ions as these act as spectator ions and are not changed during the reaction.

$$Zn(s) + Cu^{2+}(aq) \rightarrow Zn^{2+}(aq) + Cu(s)$$

So zinc has acted as the reducing agent − it is therefore the more reactive metal. We can think of it as having the reducing strength to 'force' copper ions to accept the electrons.

We could confirm this by trying the reaction the other way round, with copper metal immersed in a solution of zinc ions. Can you predict what will happen? The answer is there will be no reaction, because Cu is not a strong enough reducing agent to reduce Zn^{2+}. This is another way of saying that it is a less reactive metal, less able to push the electrons onto Zn^{2+}.

By comparing **displacement** reactions like these between different combinations of metals and their ions, we can build up a list of relative strengths of the metals as reducing agents. This is called a **reactivity series** and it enables us to predict whether a particular redox reaction will be feasible between a metal and the ions of another metal. It is referred to extensively in industries where processes for the extraction of metals often involve choosing a suitable reducing agent to reduce a metal ore.

Here is a small part of the reactivity series of metals:

Mg | strongest reducing agent, most readily becomes oxidized
Al
Zn
Fe
Pb
Cu
Ag ↓ weakest reducing agent, least readily becomes oxidized

It is not important that you learn a list like this, but you should be able to interpret it and to deduce it from given data.

Worked example

Refer to the reactivity series given above to predict whether the following reactions will occur:

(a) $ZnCl_2(aq) + 2Ag(s) \rightarrow 2AgCl(s) + Zn(s)$
(b) $2FeCl_3(aq) + 3Mg \rightarrow 3MgCl_2(aq) + 2Fe(s)$

Solution

(a) This reaction would involve Ag reducing Zn^{2+} in $ZnCl_2$. But Ag is a weaker reducing agent than Zn so this will not occur.

(b) This reaction involves Mg reducing Fe^{3+} in $FeCl_3$. Mg is a stronger reducing agent than Fe so this will occur.

We can investigate how some non-metals such as carbon and hydrogen would fit into this reactivity series of metals by similar types of displacement reactions. All metals above hydrogen in the reactivity series displace H^+ ions from dilute acids to release hydrogen gas. As noted in Chapter 8, copper cannot do this, as it is below hydrogen in the reactivity series. Carbon is able to reduce the oxides of iron and metals below it in the series, providing one of the most effective means for the extraction of these metals (see Chapter 14).

More reactive non-metals are stronger oxidizing agents

In a similar way, the different strengths of non-metals as oxidizing agents can be compared. For example the halogens (Group 7 elements) react by gaining electrons and forming negative ions, so acting as oxidizing agents, removing electrons from another substance. We learned in Chapter 3 that their tendency to do this decreases down the group, so we would expect the following trend:

F_2 | strongest oxidizing agent, most readily becomes reduced
Cl_2
Br_2
I_2 ↓ weakest oxidizing agent, least readily becomes reduced

Again this can be verified by reacting one halogen with solutions containing the ions of another halogen (known as halide ions).
For example:

$$Cl_2(aq) + 2KI(aq) \rightarrow 2KCl(aq) + I_2(aq)$$

Chlorine gas bubbling through a colourless solution of potassium iodide KI. The solution is turning brown owing to the formation of iodine in solution, as chlorine oxidizes the iodide ions and forms chloride ions.

A more reactive metal is able to reduce the ions of a less reactive metal.

See a simulation of metal/metal ion reactions.
Now go to www.heinemann.co.uk/hotlinks, insert the express code 4259P and click on this activity.

Redox reactions between a metal and the oxide of a less reactive metal can also confirm the reactivity series. Here magnesium metal and copper oxide react together vigorously when heated to produce magnesium oxide and copper.
$Mg(s) + CuO(s) \rightarrow MgO(s) + Cu(s)$

A more reactive non-metal is able to oxidize the ions of a less reactive non-metal.

Here the K^+ ions are spectator ions so we can write the ionic equation without showing them:

$$Cl_2(aq) + 2I^-(aq) \rightarrow 2Cl^-(aq) + I_2(aq)$$

The reaction occurs because Cl is a stronger oxidizing agent than I and is able to remove electrons from it. In simple terms, you can think of it as a competition for electrons where the stronger oxidizing agent, in this case chlorine, will always 'win'.

Exercises

6 Use the two reactivity series given to predict whether reactions will occur between the following reactants and write equations where relevant.
   (a) $CuCl_2(aq) + Ag(s)$ **(b)** $Fe(NO_3)_2(aq) + Al(s)$
   (c) $NaI(aq) + Br_2(aq)$ **(d)** $KCl(aq) + I_2(aq)$

7 **(a)** Use the following reactions to deduce the order of reactivity of the elements w, x, y, z putting the most reactive first.
     $w + x^+ \rightarrow w^+ + x;$ $y^+ + z \rightarrow$ no reaction
     $x + z^+ \rightarrow x^+ + z;$ $x + y^+ \rightarrow x^+ + y$
   (b) Which of the following reactions would you expect to occur according to the reactivity series you established in (a)?
     (i) $w^+ + y \rightarrow w + y^+$ **(ii)** $w^+ + z \rightarrow w + z^+$

9.4   Voltaic cells

Italian physicist Count Alessandro Volta (1745–1827) demonstrated his newly invented battery or 'voltaic pile' to Napoleon Bonaparte in 1801. Constructed from alternating discs of zinc and copper with pieces of cardboard soaked in brine between the metals, his voltaic pile was the first battery that produced a reliable, steady current of electricity.

INVENTIONS ILLUSTRES
La pile de Volta

Let us consider again the reaction we discussed in Section 9.3 in which zinc reduced copper ions. Remember that here zinc was the reducing agent and became oxidized while copper ions were reduced. When the reaction is carried out in a single test tube, as shown in the photo on page 170, the electrons flow spontaneously from the zinc to the copper ions in the solution and, as we noted, energy is released in the form of heat. There is, however, a different way of organizing this reaction so that the energy released in the redox reaction, instead of being lost as heat, is available as electrical energy. It is really a case of separating the two half reactions:

oxidation $Zn(s) \rightarrow Zn^{2+}(aq) + 2e^-$ and
reduction $Cu^{2+}(aq) + 2e^- \rightarrow Cu(s)$

into so-called **half cells** and allowing the electrons to flow between them only through an external circuit. This is known as an electrochemical, galvanic or a **voltaic cell** and we will see how it is constructed in the next section.

Half cells generate electrode potentials

There are many types of half cell but probably the simplest is made by putting a strip of metal into a solution of its ions.

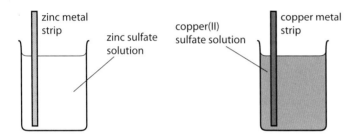

In the zinc half cell, zinc atoms will form ions by releasing electrons that will make the surface of the metal negatively charged with respect to the solution.

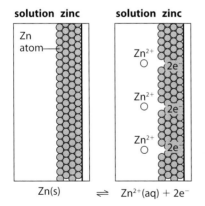

There will therefore be a charge separation, known as an **electrode potential**, between the metal and its ions in solution. At the same time ions in the solution gain electrons to form Zn atoms, so an equilibrium exists as follows:

$$Zn^{2+}(aq) + 2e^- \rightleftharpoons Zn(s)$$

The position of this equilibrium will determine the size of the electrode potential in the half cell and will depend on the reactivity of the metal.

So because copper is a less reactive metal, in its half cell the equilibrium position for the equivalent reaction: $Cu^{2+}(aq) + 2e^- \rightleftharpoons Cu(s)$ lies further to the right, in other words copper has less of a tendency to lose electrons than zinc. Consequently there are fewer electrons on the copper metal strip, so it will develop a larger (or less negative) electrode potential than the zinc half cell.

Copper half cell consisting of a piece of copper metal dipping into a solution of a copper salt. An equilibrium is set up between the Cu metal and its ions.

$$Cu^{2+}(aq) + 2e^- \rightleftharpoons Cu(s)$$

◀ **Figure 9.2** Copper and zinc half cells.

◀ **Figure 9.3** Zinc atoms form zinc ions by releasing electrons. An equilibrium is set up between the metal and its solution of ions.

Figure 9.4 The zinc half cell develops a negative potential with respect to the copper half cell.

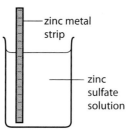

zinc metal strip

zinc sulfate solution

$$Zn^{2+}(aq) + 2e^- \rightleftharpoons Zn(s)$$

Some zinc atoms from the metal strip release electrons, giving it a negative charge.

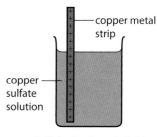

copper metal strip

copper sulfate solution

$$Cu^{2+}(aq) + 2e^- \rightleftharpoons Cu(s)$$

Some copper ions in the solution accept electrons from the copper rod giving a positive charge

In general, the more reactive a metal, the more negative its electrode potential in its half cell.

Oxidation always occurs at the anode; reduction always occurs at the cathode. In the voltaic cell, the anode has a negative charge and the cathode has a positive charge.

Two connected half cells make a voltaic cell

If we now connect these two half cells by an external wire, electrons will have a tendency to flow spontaneously from the zinc half cell to the copper half cell because of their different electrode potentials. The half cells connected in this way are often called **electrodes** and their name gives us information about the type of reaction that occurs there. The electrode where oxidation occurs is called the **anode**, in this case it is the zinc electrode:

$$Zn(s) \rightarrow Zn^{2+}(aq) + 2e^- \quad \text{and it has a negative charge.}$$

The electrode where reduction occurs is called the **cathode**, in this case it is the copper electrode:

$$Cu^{2+}(aq) + 2e^- \rightarrow Cu(s) \quad \text{and it has a positive charge.}$$

A potential difference will, however, only be generated between the electrodes when the circuit is complete.

Figure 9.5 This cell has an incomplete circuit – no voltage is generated. A salt bridge must be added to allow ions to flow between the two electrodes.

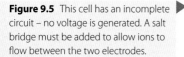

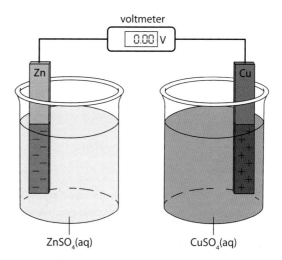

voltmeter

0.00 V

Zn

Cu

$ZnSO_4(aq)$

$CuSO_4(aq)$

Zinc–copper voltaic cell showing a copper half cell and a zinc half cell connected by a salt bridge which appears white. Electrons flow from the zinc electrode to the copper electrode through the electrical wires, while ions flow through the salt bridge to complete the circuit. The voltmeter is showing 1.10 V, the potential difference of this cell.

The voltaic cell therefore must have the following connections between the half cells:

- An electrical wire, connected to the metal electrode in each half cell. A voltmeter can also be attached to this external circuit to record the voltage generated. Electrons will flow from the anode to the cathode through the wire.

- A salt bridge that completes the circuit. The salt bridge is a glass tube or strip of absorptive paper that contains an aqueous solution of ions that enables negative charge to be carried in the opposite direction to that of the electrons (from cathode to anode). This ion movement will neutralize any build up of charge and maintain the potential difference. The solution chosen is often $NaNO_3$ or KNO_3 as these will not interfere with the reactions at the electrodes. Without a salt bridge no voltage will be generated.

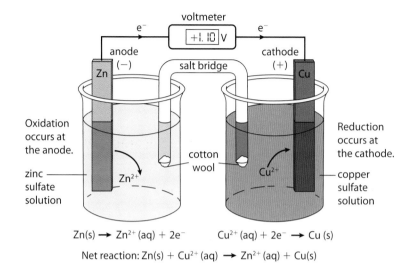

$$Zn(s) \rightarrow Zn^{2+}(aq) + 2e^- \qquad Cu^{2+}(aq) + 2e^- \rightarrow Cu(s)$$

Net reaction: $Zn(s) + Cu^{2+}(aq) \rightarrow Zn^{2+}(aq) + Cu(s)$

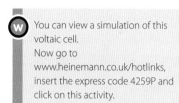

Figure 9.6 A copper−zinc voltaic cell.

(W) You can view a simulation of this voltaic cell.
Now go to www.heinemann.co.uk/hotlinks, insert the express code 4259P and click on this activity.

(i) You may be familiar with the sensation of a mild electric shock if you happen to bite some aluminium foil on a tooth that has a filling. The filling is made of an amalgam of mercury and either tin or silver and creates a voltaic cell when it touches the foil. Aluminium is the anode, the filling is the cathode and the saliva is the electrolyte 'salt bridge'. A weak current flows between the electrodes and is detected by the sensitive nerves in the teeth.

(i) **Electrons always flow in the external circuit from anode to cathode.**

Different half cells make voltaic cells with different voltages

Any two half cells can be connected together similarly to make a voltaic cell. For any such cell, the direction of electron flow and the voltage generated will be determined by the *difference* in reducing strength of the two metals. In most cases this can be judged by the relative position of the metals in the reactivity series. For example, if we changed the copper half cell in the example above to a silver half cell, a larger voltage would be produced because the difference in electrode potentials of zinc and silver is greater than between that of zinc and copper. Electrons will flow from zinc (anode) to silver (cathode).

◀ **Figure 9.7** A silver−zinc voltaic cell.

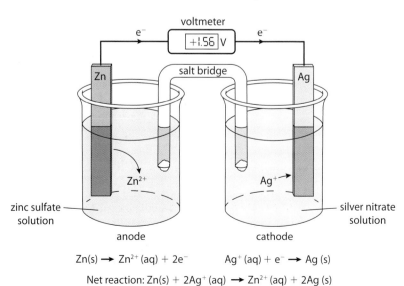

$$Zn(s) \rightarrow Zn^{2+}(aq) + 2e^- \qquad Ag^+(aq) + e^- \rightarrow Ag(s)$$

Net reaction: $Zn(s) + 2Ag^+(aq) \rightarrow Zn^{2+}(aq) + 2Ag(s)$

If we now make a voltaic cell with one copper electrode and one silver electrode, the direction of electron flow would be *away* from copper towards silver. In other words, copper will be the anode and silver the cathode. This is due to the greater reducing power of copper − it has the lower electrode potential.

Figure 9.8 A silver–copper voltaic cell. ▶

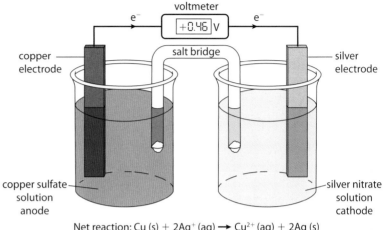

Net reaction: Cu (s) + 2Ag⁺ (aq) ➝ Cu²⁺ (aq) + 2Ag (s)

We can now summarize the parts of a voltaic cell and the direction of movement of electrons and ions.

Figure 9.9 Summary of the components of a voltaic cell showing the ion and electron movements. ▶

You can simulate different voltaic cells and see the effect of changing conditions.
Now go to
www.heinemann.co.uk/hotlinks, insert the express code 4259P and click on this activity.

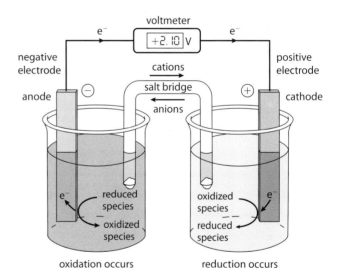

Batteries are an application of a voltaic cell, making electrical energy available as a source of power. Our reliance on batteries increases as we develop more and more portable energy-hungry electronic devices such as camera phones and high performance portable computers. The global market for batteries is over 60 billion US dollars and rising sharply, especially in China, India, Brazil, Czech Republic and South Korea. While demand for batteries looks set to continue, concern over toxicity and environmental damage from battery disposal has meant that mercury and cadmium batteries are being phased out in many places. The different types of batteries and their relative advantages are explained more fully in Option C, Chapter 14.

An assortment of different types, sizes and brands of batteries. The output and effective life of a battery depends on which chemicals it uses to produce the electric current. ▶

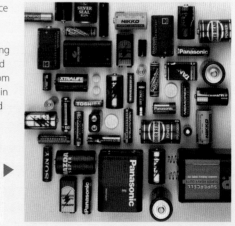

8 Use the metal reactivity series given earlier to predict which electrode will be the anode and which will be the cathode when the following half cells are connected. Write half equations for the reactions occurring at each electrode.
(a) Zn/Zn^{2+} and Fe/Fe^{2+}
(b) Fe/Fe^{2+} and Mg/Mg^{2+}
(c) Mg/Mg^{2+} and Cu/Cu^{2+}

9 Draw a voltaic cell with one half cell consisting of Mg and a solution of Mg^{2+} ions and the other consisting of Zn and a solution of Zn^{2+} ions. Label the electrodes with name and charge, the direction of electron and ion movement and write equations for the reactions occurring at each electrode.

10 Predict what would happen if an iron spatula was left in a solution of copper sulfate overnight.

9.5 Electrolytic cells

We have just learned that a voltaic cell takes the energy of a spontaneous redox reaction and harnesses it to produce electric voltage. An electrolytic cell does the reverse: it uses an external source of voltage to bring about a redox reaction that would otherwise be non-spontaneous. You can think of it in terms of an external power supply effectively pumping electrons into the electrolytic cell, driving redox reactions. As a result, electrolysis enables neutral elements to be released from ionic compounds, by **discharging** the ions (removing their charge) through oxidation and reduction reactions. This is why it is such an important large-scale process in industry, used in the manufacture of many chemicals.

An electrolytic cell has the following components:

- The source of electric power, for example a battery or a dc power source. This is always shown in diagrams as ┃┃ where the longer line represents the positive terminal and the shorter line the negative terminal.
- The **electrolyte**. This is a liquid that conducts electricity and undergoes chemical change as a result. Electrolytes are commonly molten ionic compounds, or aqueous solutions of ionic compounds.
- The **electrodes**. These are always made from a conducting substance (a metal or graphite) that is immersed in the electrolyte and connected to the power supply. They must not touch each other!
- Electrical conductors (wires) to connect the power supply to the electrodes.

 Michael Faraday, the English physicist and chemist (1791–1867), first defined and introduced the names electrolyte, electrode, anode, cathode, ion, anion and cation, all of which are derived from Greek, into scientific language in 1834. He recognized the need to clarify the terminology, seeing the electrodes as surfaces where the current enters (anode) and leaves (cathode) the 'decomposing body' (electrolyte). He was referring to the established convention that current direction is always stated in reverse direction to electron flow. Faraday rather modestly suggested his names would be used only when necessary to avoid confusion, saying, 'I am fully aware that names are one thing and science another'.

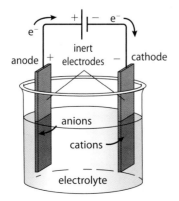

◀ **Figure 9.10** Components of an electrolytic cell.

 You can read Michael Faraday's paper 'On electrical decomposition'. Now go to www.heinemann.co.uk/hotlinks, insert the express code 4259P and click on this activity.

At the anode, negative ions lose electrons; at the cathode, positive ions gain electrons.

You can view a simulation of electrolytic cells.
Now go to heinemann.co.uk/ hotlinks, insert the express code 4259P and click on this activity.

Conduction of the current through the electrolytic cell

The power source pushes electrons towards the negative electrode where they enter the electrolyte. They are released at the positive terminal and returned to the source. The current is passed through the electrolyte by the ions as they migrate to the electrodes.

Redox reactions occur at the electrodes

The ions in the electrolyte migrate to the electrodes by the attraction of opposite charges. The negative electrode attracts positive ions (cations) while the positive electrode attracts negative ions (anions). At the electrodes redox reactions occur which result in the ions being discharged and released as neutral products.

At the negative electrode (cathode): $M^+ + e^- \rightarrow M$
Cations gain electrons and so are reduced.

At the positive electrode (anode): $A^- \rightarrow A + e^-$
Anions lose electrons and so are oxidized.

You will notice that the charges on the electrodes are inverted in an electrolytic cell compared with an electrochemical cell. This is because it is the nature of the redox reaction not the electrical charge which defines the electrode — oxidation always occurs at the anode and reduction at the cathode. So electrons flow from anode to cathode. This never changes.

	Voltaic cell		Electrolytic cell	
anode	oxidation occurs here	negative	oxidation occurs here	positive
cathode	reduction occurs here	positive	reduction occurs here	negative

Knowing the chemical nature of the electrolyte enables us to deduce the electrode reactions that will occur and hence the products that will be released from the electrolytic cell.

Electrolysis of molten NaCl

Worked example

Write half equations for the electrode reactions that occur when molten NaCl is electrolysed.

Solution

(a) Deduce the ions present and to which electrode they will be attracted.

$$NaCl \rightarrow Na^+ \text{ and } Cl^-$$

to cathode   to anode

(b) Write half equations for the reactions in which these ions will be discharged at each electrode and what might be observed.
At the anode: oxidation:

$$2Cl^-(l) \rightarrow Cl_2(g) + 2e^-$$

Figure 9.11 Electrolysis of molten sodium chloride.

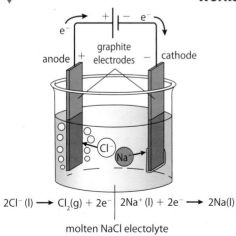

$2Cl^-(l) \rightarrow Cl_2(g) + 2e^-$ | $2Na^+(l) + 2e^- \rightarrow 2Na(l)$

molten NaCl electolyte

We know that Cl atoms will combine to make Cl_2 as this is the most stable form of chlorine.

At the cathode: reduction:

$$Na^+(l) + e^- \rightarrow Na(l)$$

In the cell there must be an equal number of electrons released at the anode as are taken up at the cathode, so here we need to double the equation at the cathode:

$$2Na^+(l) + 2e^- \rightarrow 2Na(l)$$

So a pale green gas will collect around the anode and a metallic liquid (at the temperature of this cell) will form at the cathode.

Overall reaction: $2NaCl(l) \rightarrow 2Na(l) + Cl_2(g)$

Electroplating is a process using electrolysis to deposit a layer of one metal on top of another metal. This is done to cover a metal with a decorative, more expensive or corrosion-resistant layer of another metal. For example, silver plating a spoon uses a silver anode and an iron spoon cathode. Galvanizing iron involves depositing a layer of zinc on top of the iron to help protect it from corrosion as the zinc will be preferentially oxidized. This is sometimes called sacrificial protection.

Exercise

11 Write half equations for the electrode reactions occurring during the electrolysis of the following molten salts:

(a) KBr   **(b)** MgF_2 **(c)** ZnS

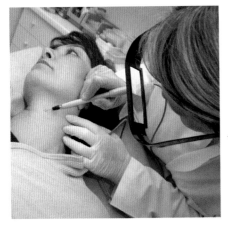

Technician inspecting components that have been electroplated with chromium. The process used an electrolytic cell containing chromium ions in the electrolyte which were reduced and deposited at the cathode, which was made of the components to be coated.

Electrolysis is used to remove unwanted hairs permanently. The needle is inserted into the hair shaft and passes an electric current through the follicle. Electrolytic reactions result in the production of NaOH, which destroys the hair follicle.

Aluminium is a unique metal: strong, flexible, lightweight, corrosion-resistant and 100% recyclable. Its commercial manufacture began in the 1880s when electrolysis made it possible to extract it from its ore, bauxite, Al_2O_3. It is therefore a young metal in contrast to tin, lead and iron which have been in use for thousands of years, but in this short time it has become the world's second most used metal after steel. Aluminium production is, however, very energy intensive and also is associated with the production of perfluorocarbons (PFCs), strong greenhouse gases. A major emphasis must therefore be placed on recycling the metal as this uses only 5% of the energy and has only 5% of the greenhouse gas emissions compared with aluminium production. Recycling of old scrap now saves an estimated 84 million tonnes of greenhouse gas emissions per year.

The aluminium drink can is the world's most recycled container. More than 63% of all cans are recycled worldwide.

Practice questions

1 Which statement is correct?
A Oxidation involves loss of electrons and a decrease in oxidation state.
B Oxidation involves gain of electrons and an increase in oxidation state.
C Reduction involves loss of electrons and an increase in oxidation state.
D Reduction involves gain of electrons and a decrease in oxidation state.

© International Baccalaureate Organization [2003]

2 What are the oxidation numbers of the elements in sulfuric acid, H_2SO_4?

	Hydrogen	Sulfur	Oxygen
A	+1	+6	−2
B	+1	+4	−2
C	+2	+1	+4
D	+2	+6	−8

© International Baccalaureate Organization [2005]

3 The following information is given about reactions involving the metals X, Y and Z and solutions of their sulfates.

$$X(s) + YSO_4(aq) \rightarrow \text{no reaction}$$
$$Z(s) + YSO_4(aq) \rightarrow Y(s) + ZSO_4(aq)$$

When the metals are listed in decreasing order of reactivity (most reactive first), what is the correct order?
A Z>Y>X   B X>Y>Z   C Y>X>Z   D Y>Z>X

© International Baccalaureate Organization [2005]

4 Which equations represent reactions that occur at room temperature?
I $2Br^-(aq) + Cl_2(aq) \rightarrow 2Cl^-(aq) + Br_2(aq)$
II $2Br^-(aq) + I_2(aq) \rightarrow 2I^-(aq) + Br_2(aq)$
III $2I^-(aq) + Cl_2(aq) \rightarrow 2Cl^-(aq) + I_2(aq)$

A I and II only   B I and III only   C II and III only   D I, II and III

© International Baccalaureate Organization [2005]

5 Which equation represents a redox reaction?
A $KOH(aq) + HCl(aq) \rightarrow KCl(aq) + H_2O(l)$
B $Mg(s) + 2HCl(aq) \rightarrow MgCl_2(aq) + H_2(g)$
C $CuO(s) + 2HCl(aq) \rightarrow CuCl_2(aq) + H_2O(l)$
D $ZnCO_3(s) + 2HCl(aq) \rightarrow ZnCl_2(aq) + CO_2(g) + H_2O(l)$

© International Baccalaureate Organization [2005]

6 The following reactions are spontaneous as written:
$Fe(s) + Cd^{2+}(aq) \rightarrow Fe^{2+}(aq) + Cd(s)$
$Cd(s) + Sn^{2+}(aq) \rightarrow Cd^{2+}(aq) + Sn(s)$
$Sn(s) + Pb^{2+}(aq) \rightarrow Sn^{2+}(aq) + Pb(s)$

Which of the following pairs will react spontaneously?
I $Sn(s) + Fe^{2+}(aq)$
II $Cd(s) + Pb^{2+}(aq)$
III $Fe(s) + Pb^{2+}(aq)$

A I only   B II only   C III only   D II and III only

© International Baccalaureate Organization [2004]

7 The oxidation number of chromium is the same in all the following compounds **except**

A $Cr(OH)_3$

B Cr_2O_3

C $Cr_2(SO_4)_3$

D CrO_3

8 What occurs during the operation of a voltaic cell based on the following reaction?

$Ni(s) + Pb^{2+}(aq) \rightarrow Ni^{2+}(aq) + Pb(s)$

	External circuit	Ion movement in solution
A	electrons move from Ni to Pb	$Pb^{2+}(aq)$ move away from $Pb(s)$
B	electrons move from Ni to Pb	$Pb^{2+}(aq)$ move toward $Pb(s)$
C	electrons move from Pb to Ni	$Ni^{2+}(aq)$ move away from $Ni(s)$
D	electrons move from Pb to Ni	$Ni^{2+}(aq)$ move toward $Ni(s)$

9 In which change does oxidation occur?

A $CH_3CHO \rightarrow CH_3CH_2OH$

B $CrO_4^{2-} \rightarrow Cr_2O_7^{2-}$

C $SO_4^{2-} \rightarrow SO_3^{2-}$

D $NO_2^- \rightarrow NO_3^-$

10 What happens at the positive electrode in a voltaic cell and in an electrolytic cell?

	Voltaic cell	Electrolytic cell
A	oxidation	reduction
B	reduction	oxidation
C	oxidation	oxidation
D	reduction	reduction

11 What species are produced at the positive and negative electrodes during the electrolysis of molten sodium chloride?

	Positive electrode	Negative electrode
A	$Na^+(l)$	$Cl_2(g)$
B	$Cl^-(l)$	$Na^+(l)$
C	$Na(l)$	$Cl_2(g)$
D	$Cl_2(g)$	$Na(l)$

12 Which processes occur during the electrolysis of molten sodium chloride?

I   Sodium and chloride ions move through the electrolyte.

II Electrons move through the external circuit.

III Oxidation takes place at the positive electrode (anode).

A I and II only

B I and III only

C II and III only

D I, II and III

© International Baccalaureate Organization [2003]

13 Consider the following reaction.

$$H_2SO_3(aq) + Sn^{4+}(aq) + H_2O(l) \rightarrow Sn^{2+}(aq) + HSO_4^-(aq) + 3H^+(aq)$$

Which statement is correct?

A H_2SO_3 is the reducing agent because it undergoes reduction.

B H_2SO_3 is the reducing agent because it undergoes oxidation.

C Sn^{4+} is the oxidizing agent because it undergoes oxidation.

D Sn^{4+} is the reducing agent because it undergoes oxidation.

© International Baccalaureate Organization [2004]

14 Consider the following redox equation:

$$5Fe^{2+}(aq) + MnO_4^-(aq) + 8H^+(aq) \rightarrow 5Fe^{3+}(aq) + Mn^{2+}(aq) + 4H_2O(l)$$

(a) **(i)** Determine the oxidation numbers for Fe and Mn in the reactants and in the products. (2)

(ii) Based on your answer to (i), deduce which substance is oxidized. (1)

(iii) The compounds CH_3OH and CH_2O contain carbon atoms in different oxidation states. Deduce the oxidation states and state the kind of chemical change needed to make CH_2O from CH_3OH. (3)

(b) A part of the reactivity series of metals, in order of decreasing reactivity, is shown below.

magnesium

zinc

iron

lead

copper

silver

If a piece of copper metal were placed in separate solutions of silver nitrate and zinc nitrate:

(i) Determine which solution would undergo reaction. (1)

(ii) Identify the type of chemical change taking place in the copper and write the half-equation for this change. (2)

(iii) State, giving a reason, what visible change would take place in the solutions. (2)

(c) **(i)** Solid sodium chloride does not conduct electricity but molten sodium chloride does. Explain this difference, and outline what happens in an electrolytic cell during the electrolysis of molten sodium chloride using carbon electrodes. (4)

(ii) State the products formed and give equations showing the reactions at each electrode. (4)

(iii) State what practical use is made of this process. (1)

(*Total 20 marks*)

© International Baccalaureate Organization [2004]

10 Organic chemistry

Organic chemistry is one of the major branches of chemistry. It includes the study of:

- all biological molecules
- all fossil fuels – including oil, coal and natural gas
- nearly all synthetic materials – such as nylon, Lycra and Gore-Tex®
- many domestic and industrial products such as paints, detergents and refrigerants.

So what defines an organic compound? Simply, it is one which contains carbon and, in nearly all cases, also hydrogen in a covalently bonded structure. Other elements such as oxygen, nitrogen, chlorine and sulfur are often also present, but carbon is the key. Amazingly, this single element is able to form a larger number of compounds than all the other elements put together.

This chapter will start by considering how we organize the study of organic compounds. We will then investigate some specific groups of organic compounds, with an emphasis on their characteristic reactions and the applications of these processes in today's world.

◀ False-colour scanning electron micrograph (SEM) of a Velcro hook. Velcro is a nylon material manufactured in two separate pieces, one with a hooked surface and the other with a smooth surface made up of loops. When the two surfaces are brought together they form a strong bond, allowing for quick closure on clothing. Velcro is an example of a product of research and development in organic chemistry.

Assessment statements

10.1 Introduction

10.1.1 Describe the features of a homologous series.

10.1.2 Predict and explain the trends in boiling points of members of a homologous series.

10.1.3 Distinguish between *empirical*, *molecular* and *structural* formulas.

10.1.4 Describe structural isomers as compounds with the same molecular formula but with different arrangements of atoms.

10.1.5 Deduce structural formulas for the isomers of the non-cyclic alkanes up to C_6.

10.1.6 Apply IUPAC rules for naming the isomers of the non-cyclic alkanes up to C_6.

10.1.7 Deduce structural formulas for the isomers of the straight-chain alkenes up to C_6.

10.1.8 Apply IUPAC rules for naming the isomers of the straight-chain alkenes up to C_6.

10.1.9 Deduce structural formulas for compounds containing up to six carbon atoms with one of the following functional groups: alcohol, aldehyde, ketone, carboxylic acid and halide.

10.1.10 Apply IUPAC rules for naming compounds containing up to six carbon atoms with one of the following functional groups: alcohol, aldehyde, ketone, carboxylic acid and halide.

10.1.11 Identify the following functional groups when present in structural formulas: amino (NH_2), benzene ring (⬡) and esters (RCOOR).

10.1.12 Identify primary, secondary and tertiary carbon atoms in alcohols and halogenoalkanes.

10.1.13 Discuss the volatility and solubility in water of compounds containing the functional groups listed in 10.1.9.

10.2 Alkanes

10.2.1 Explain the low reactivity of alkanes in terms of bond enthalpies and bond polarity.

10.2.2 Describe, using equations, the complete and incomplete combustion of alkanes.

10.2.3 Describe, using equations, the reactions of methane and ethane with chlorine and bromine.

10.2.4 Explain the reactions of methane and ethane with chlorine and bromine in terms of a free-radical mechanism.

10.3 Alkenes

10.3.1 Describe, using equations, the reactions of alkenes with hydrogen and halogens.

10.3.2 Describe, using equations, the reactions of symmetrical alkenes with hydrogen halides and water.

10.3.3 Distinguish between *alkanes* and *alkenes* using bromine water.

10.3.4 Outline the polymerization of alkenes.

10.3.5 Outline the economic importance of the reactions of alkenes.

10.4 Alcohols

10.4.1 Describe, using equations, the complete combustion of alcohols.

10.4.2 Describe, using equations, the oxidation reactions of alcohols.

10.4.3 Determine the products formed by the oxidation of primary and secondary alcohols.

10.5 Halogenoalkanes

10.5.1 Describe, using equations, the substitution reactions of halogenoalkanes with sodium hydroxide.

10.5.2 Explain the substitution reactions of halogenoalkanes with sodium hydroxide in terms of S_N1 and S_N2 mechanisms.

10.6 Reaction pathways

10.6.1 Deduce reaction pathways given the starting materials and the product. The compound and reaction types in this topic are summarized in the scheme, shown in Figure 10.3 on page 210.

0.1 Introduction

The total number of organic compounds that exist on Earth is so large that it is impossible to estimate with any accuracy. In any case, it is increasing all the time as new materials are synthesized. But we do know that there are at least five million different organic molecules currently on the planet and every one of them is unique in its chemical structure and specific properties. Of course it is not possible or necessary to study the chemistry of all of the compounds in this vast array of organic chemicals, but it is useful instead to introduce a system of classification.

Homologous series

Organic compounds are classified into 'families' or series of compounds, which are closely related to each other. The members of such a series differ from each other in the number of carbon atoms they contain and are known collectively as a **homologous series**.

Consider this example of a homologous series, where the carbons are all bonded by single covalent bonds:

CH_4 C_2H_6 C_3H_8 C_4H_{10}

methane   ethane   propane   butane

This homologous series is known as the **alkanes**. It can be seen that these compounds differ from each other by a CH_2 group. As a result, all members of the series can be described by the general formula: C_nH_{2n+2}.

Other homologous series are all characterized by the presence of a particular **functional group**. This is usually a small group of atoms attached to a carbon atom in a molecule, which will give characteristic properties to the compound. So by studying the characteristic reactions of each functional group, it becomes possible to predict the properties of all members of the series.

For example, consider the homologous series where the members contain the functional group OH:

CH_3OH C_2H_5OH C_3H_7OH C_4H_9OH

methanol   ethanol   propanol   butanol

This homologous series is known as the **alcohols**.

Again it can be seen that the difference between successive members of the group is the CH_2 unit. And again there is a general formula to describe the series: $C_nH_{2n+1}OH$.

In all organic compounds the part of the molecule containing only carbon and hydrogen, is known as the **hydrocarbon skeleton** and it is this which increases

For a long time it was believed that organic molecules were unique to living things and could not therefore be synthesized outside a living organism. However, in 1828, the German chemist Friedrich Wohler synthesized urea from inorganic reactants, commenting in a letter to Berzelius, 'I must tell you that I can make urea without the use of kidneys, either man or dog. Ammonium cyanate is urea'. This discovery (which like many great scientific discoveries was actually made by accident) destroyed the former belief in 'vitalism' and opened the door to the exploration of organic synthesis reactions. The development of new organic compounds is responsible for many of the innovations in our world today.

as we go up the series. As the molecules get larger, the hydrocarbon chain plays a larger part in the properties of the compound. This is reflected in a gradual trend in the physical properties of the members of the series. For example, the effect of the length of the carbon chain on the boiling point of the alkanes is shown in the table below:

Alkane	Boiling point (°C)	
methane, CH_4	−164	gases at room temperature
ethane, C_2H_6	−89	
propane, C_3H_8	−42	
butane, C_4H_{10}	−0.5	
pentane, C_5H_{12}	36	liquids at room temperature
hexane, C_6H_{14}	69	
heptane, C_7H_{16}	98	
octane, C_8H_{18}	125	

The data show that the effect of the successive addition of each CH_2 group is to increase the boiling point. This is because of the increased temporary dipoles causing stronger van der Waals' forces as their relative molecular mass increases (see Chapter 4). Note, though, that the increase is not linear, but steeper near the beginning as the influence of the increased chain length is proportionally greater for small molecules. This trend in boiling points is of great significance in the oil industry, making it possible to separate the many components of crude oil into 'fractions' containing molecules of similar molecular mass on the basis of their boiling points. Other physical properties that show this predictable trend with increasing carbon number are density and viscosity.

Oil products. Containers of crude oil and various products obtained from crude oil. In the background is a silhouetted oil refinery which is where crude oil is separated (refined) into fractions. The hydrocarbons in oil vary in size, and as the crude oil is heated, the lighter fractions boil off first. These are arranged here in order of boiling point from left (lowest) to right (highest): liquid petroleum gas (a mix of butane and propane), petrol (gasoline), jet fuel (kerosene), diesel, lubricating oils (light and heavy), fuel oil, crude oil and bitumen. These oil products are used as fuels, industrial lubricants and to make products such as plastics in the chemical industry.

The different members of each homologous series will have similar chemical properties, as indicated by the presence of the same functional group. For example, because of their –OH functional group, the alcohols can all be oxidized to form organic acids. The alkanes, lacking this functional group, are not able to react in this way.

We can now summarize some of the main features of a homologous series.

- Members of a homologous series have the same functional group and can be represented by the same general formula.
- Successive members of the series have an additional CH_2 group.
- The members of a series show a gradation in their physical properties.
- The members of a series have similar chemical properties.

Empirical, molecular and structural formulas

The **empirical formula** of a compound is the simplest whole number ratio of the atoms it contains (see Chapter 1). For example, the empirical formula of the alkane C_2H_6 shown above is CH_3. This formula can be derived from its percentage composition data obtained from combustion analysis. It is, however, of rather limited use on its own as it does not tell us the actual number of atoms in the molecule.

The **molecular formula** of a compound is the actual number of atoms of each type present in a molecule. For example, the molecular formula of ethane is C_2H_6 and of ethanoic acid is $C_2H_4O_2$. The molecular formula is therefore a multiple of the empirical formula and so can be deduced if we know both the empirical formula and the relative molecular mass M_r. The relationship can be expressed as:

M_r = (molecular mass of empirical formula)$_n$, where n = an integer

So for example, if we know that the empirical formula of ethane is CH_3 and if it is known that M_r = 30, using the formula above:

$$30 = (\text{mass of } CH_3)_n, \text{ so } 30 = (12 + (3 \times 1))_n, \text{ therefore } n = 2.$$

Therefore the molecular formula is $(CH_3)_2$ or C_2H_6.

Worked example

The empirical formula of glucose is CH_2O and its M_r = 180. Calculate its molecular formula.

Solution
M_r = (mass of $CH_2O)_n$, so $180 = (12 + (2 \times 1) + 16)_n$,
so $180 = (30)_n$, therefore $n = 6$.

Therefore the molecular formula is six times bigger than the empirical formula, giving $(CH_2O)_6$ or $C_6H_{12}O_6$

However, the molecular formula is also of quite limited value as the properties of a compound are determined not only by the atoms it contains, but also by how they are arranged in relation to each other and in space. We therefore need a representation of the molecule showing exactly how the atoms are bonded to each other. This is known as the **structural formula**.

A **full structural formula** (graphic formula or displayed formula) shows every bond and atom; a **condensed structural formula** often omits bonds where they can be assumed and groups atoms together. The important thing about any structural formula is that it must be a non-ambiguous representation of the arrangement of the atoms – in other words there is only one possible structure that could be described by this formula.

The table below gives some examples of these different formulas applied to three compounds:

Compound	Empirical formula	Molecular formula	Full structural formula	Condensed structural formula
ethane	CH_3	C_2H_6		CH_3CH_3
ethanoic acid	CH_2O	$C_2H_4O_2$		CH_3COOH
glucose	CH_2O	$C_6H_{12}O_6$		$CHO(CHOH)_4CH_2OH$

● **Examiner's hint:** Be careful to mark all the hydrogen atoms with –H when drawing structural formulas. Leaving these out gives only a 'skeletal' structure and is not acceptable.

Sometimes we do not need to show the exact details of the hydrocarbon, or alkyl, part of the molecule, so we can abbreviate this to 'R'. For molecules which contain a benzene ring – aromatic compounds – we use ⬡ to show the ring.

Most commonly, structural formulas use 90° and 180° angles to show the bonds, because this is the clearest representation on a two-dimensional page. It does not, however, represent the true geometry of the molecule. Note that when carbon forms four single bonds, the arrangement is tetrahedral with the bonds at 109.5° to each other. When it forms a double bond, the arrangement is triangular planar, with bonds at 120° (see Chapter 4).

In some cases it is useful to show the relative positions of atoms or groups around carbon in three dimensions and such a formula is known as a **stereochemical formula**. The convention here is that a bond sticking forwards from the page is shown as a solid, enlarging wedge, whereas a bond sticking behind the page is shown as a dotted line.

Organic chemistry uses many models to represent molecular structures and these differ from each other in the amount of detail. Discuss the values and limitations of these models. What assumptions do they include?

For example: methanol, CH_3OH

ethene, C_2H_4

Nomenclature of organic compounds: the IUPAC system

One of the challenges of organic chemistry is being able to describe each compound clearly by giving it a specific, non-ambiguous name. For over a hundred years, chemists have realized the need to develop a specific set of rules for naming organic compounds and this has given rise to the IUPAC (International Union of Pure and Applied Chemistry) system of nomenclature. It is based on a few simple rules, which you will quickly learn and be able to apply to any organic compound that you encounter. This will enable you to communicate precisely and clearly with chemists working anywhere else in the world. It will also help you to know something about the compounds described on everyday labels such as those on toothpaste and glue sticks.

Rule 1: Identify the longest straight or continuous chain of carbon atoms; this gives the **stem** of the name as follows.

To what extent is chemistry a unique language?
What are the main differences between the language of chemistry and that of your 'mother tongue'?

Number of carbon atoms in longest chain	Stem for IUPAC name
1	meth-
2	eth-
3	prop-
4	but-
5	pent-
6	hex-

What do you think is the significance of chemists having internationally agreed names of compounds?

Be careful when identifying the longest straight chain not to be confused by the way the molecule is drawn on paper, as sometimes the same molecule can be represented differently owing to the free rotation around the carbon–carbon single bonds. For example:

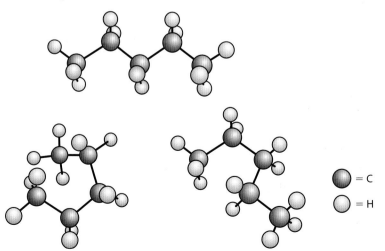

= C
= H

▶ **Figure10.1** Models showing different representations of pentane, C_5H_{12}.

These are all representations of the same molecule C_5H_{12}, pentane, rotated in different positions.

Rule 2: Use the functional group ending as the last part or **suffix** of the name.

These are summarized in the table below.

Homologous series	Functional group	Suffix for IUPAC name
alkane		–ane
alkene	—C=C—	–ene
alcohol	—OH	–anol
aldehyde	—CHO 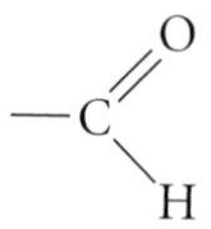	–anal
ketone	—CORR′ 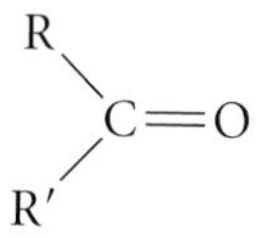	–anone
carboxylic acid	—COOH 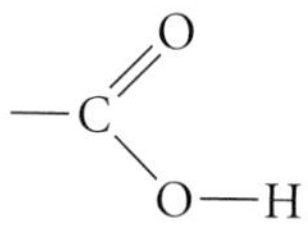	–anoic acid

Rule 3: Name the side chains or substituent groups as the first part or **prefix** of the name. The common ones are summarized below.

Side chain/substituent group	Prefix for IUPAC name
—CH$_3$	methyl
—C$_2$H$_5$	ethyl
—C$_3$H$_7$	propyl
—F, —Cl, —Br, —I	fluoro, chloro, bromo, iodo
—NH$_2$	amino
—OH	hydroxy

The position of these substituent groups is shown by a number, followed by a dash, which refers to the number of the carbon atom to which it is attached. The carbon chain is numbered starting at the end which will give the substituent groups the smallest number, for example:

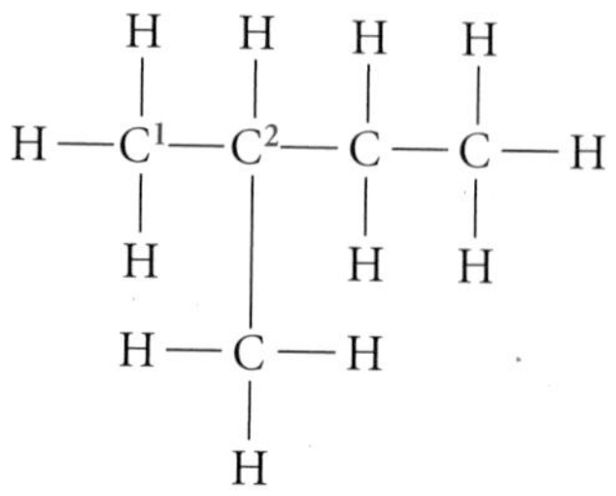

2-methylbutane

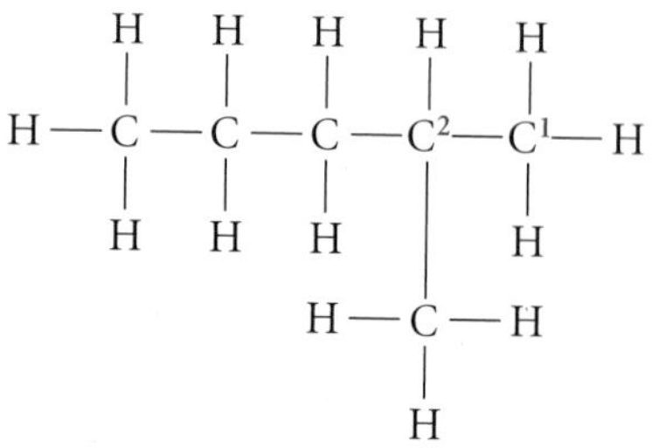

2-methylpentane

(here we start numbering carbons from the right hand side so that the number of the side chain will be 2, not 4)

If there is more than one side chain of the same type, we use the prefixes di-, tri-, tetra- and so on, to show this. If there are several side chains within a molecule we put them in alphabetical order, separated by dashes.

For example:

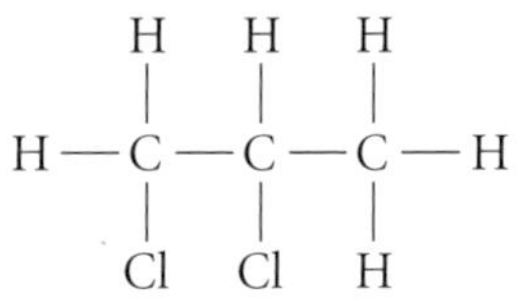

1,2-dichloropropane 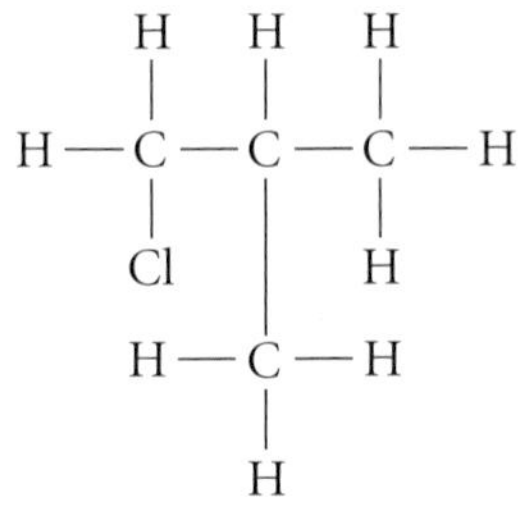   1-chloro-2-methylpropane

We use a similar process of numbering carbon atoms to show the position of a functional group. In this case we use the number followed by a dash immediately before the functional group ending.

For example:

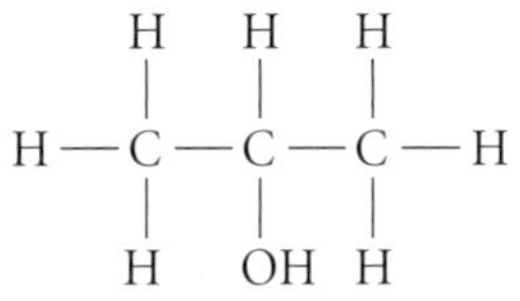

propan-2-ol 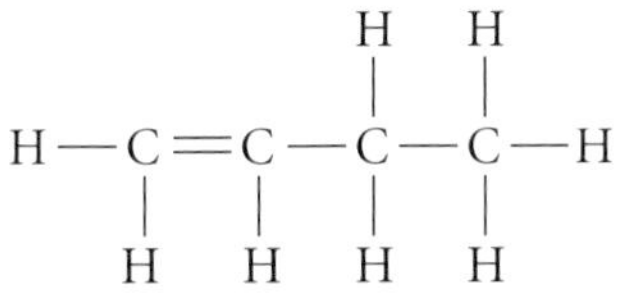   but-1-ene

Sometimes a functional group can only be in one place and in these cases we do not need to give a number to show its position.

For example:

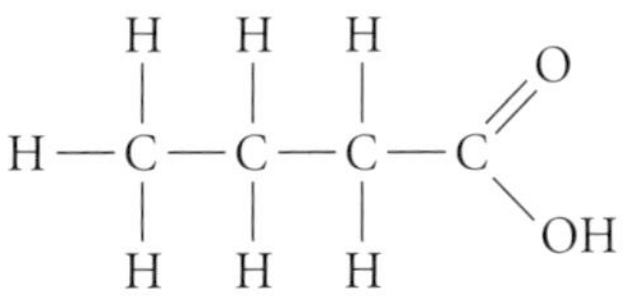

butanoic acid 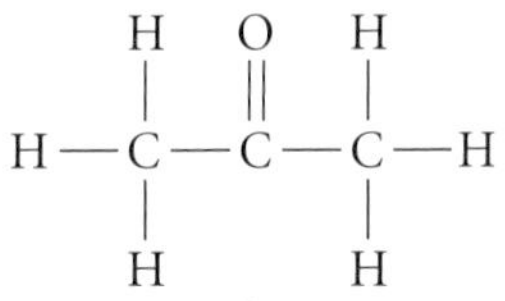   propanone

Worked examples

1 Name the following:
   (a) $CH_3CH_2CH_2COOH$
   (b) $CHCl_2CH_2CH_3$
   (c) $CH_3CH_2COCH_3$

2 Draw the structural formulas of the following molecules:
   (a) hexanoic acid
   (b) butanal

Solution

1 (a) This has four carbon atoms and the carboxylic acid is the functional group, so it is called butanoic acid.
   (b) The molecule has three carbon atoms so the stem is prop- and there are two chlorine atoms on the first carbon atom, so it is 1,1-dichloropropane.
   (c) When you draw the full structural formula you will see that the four-carbon has a ketone functional group, so it is butanone. We do not need to put a number here because in butanone, the carbonyl carbon ($C=O$) must be bonded to two other carbons so this is the only possible position.

● **Examiner's hint:** In counting the longest carbon chain, don't forget to include the carbon that is part of a functional group like —COOH.

● **Examiner's hint:** When trying to name a compound from a condensed structural formula, it is often easier if you draw the full structural formula first.

2 (a) This will have six carbon atoms and the acid functional group which must be terminal so

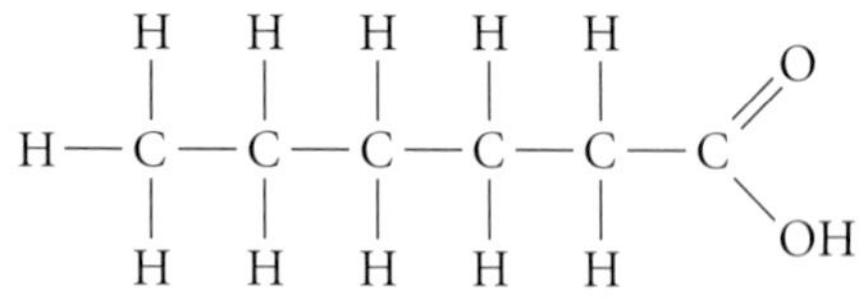

(b) This will have four carbon atoms and the aldehyde is the functional group.

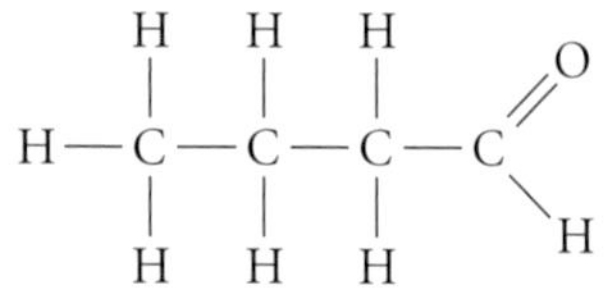

Ester functional group

Esters are organic compounds which form when organic acids react with alcohols. In effect they are organic salts. These occur naturally in many fats and are also important in the manufacture of soap. Their functional group is:

RCOOR' or

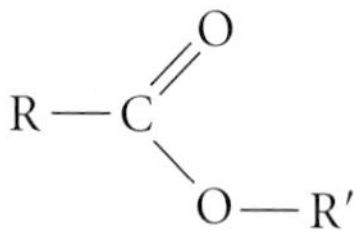

● **Examiner's hint:** When you are naming esters, remember that they are derived from acids with the hydrogen being replaced by an alkyl group. So the salt of ethanoic acid with sodium is *sodium ethanoate* and with methanol is *methyl ethanoate*.

For example methyl ethanoate

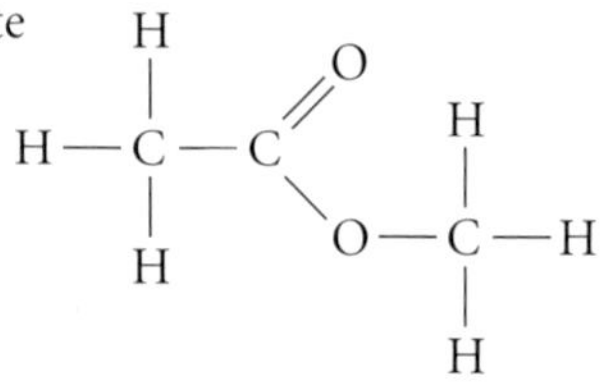

contains the *methyl* group from the alcohol methanol and *ethanoate* derived from ethanoic acid.

Worked example

Name the following ester.

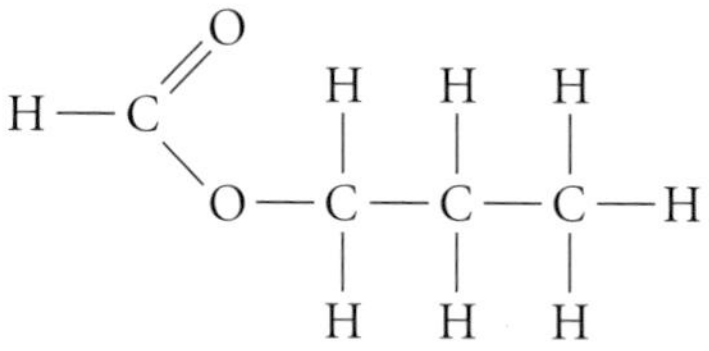

Solution

The ester is derived from methanoic acid and contains the C_3H_7 alkyl group – so it is called *propyl methanoate*.

Aromatic compounds

Aromatic compounds are those which contain the benzene ring C_6H_6,

Benzene is a planar molecule in which the six carbon atoms share electrons with themselves and with the six hydrogen atoms in a symmetrical arrangement. (This is known as **delocalization** of the electron clouds and makes the molecule particularly stable). Many derivatives of benzene exist in which one or more of the hydrogen atoms are substituted by different groups. For example, the well known explosive TNT (trinitrotoluene) is a derivative of benzene containing one methyl and three nitro substituted groups.

Exercises

1 Name the following molecules:

(a)

```
Cl   H
 |   |
 C = C
 |   |
 H   H
```

(b)

```
  H          H         O
   \         |        //
    N — C — C
   /         |        \
  H          H         OH
```

2 Draw the structural formulas of the following molecules

(a) ethyl ethanoate   **(b)** 1,1,1-trichloroethane

Structural isomers

As we noted earlier, molecular formulas show only part of the information about a molecule. In fact, sometimes one molecular formula can describe more than one molecule, in which the same atoms are bonded together in different arrangements. Such molecules are known as **structural isomers** of each other, that is **molecules possessing the same molecular formula but different arrangement of atoms and therefore different structural formulas.** Isomers are quite distinct in their physical and chemical properties.

> **Structural isomers are compounds which have the same molecular formula but different arrangements of atoms.**

Structural isomers in alkanes

For example the molecular formula C_4H_{10} describes the two isomers:

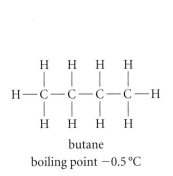

```
      H   H   H   H
      |   |   |   |
H —  C — C — C — C  — H
      |   |   |   |
      H   H   H   H

          butane
   boiling point −0.5 °C
```

```
        H   H   H
        |   |   |
   H — C — C — C — H
        |   |   |
        H   |   H
            |
        H — C — H
            |
            H

    2-methylpropane
 boiling point −11.7 °C
```

When we study the larger alkanes, we find there is an increasing number of isomers as the carbon number increases.

Worked example

Draw the structural formulas and give the IUPAC names of the isomers of C_5H_{12}.

Solution

Start with the longest straight chain isomer – there is only one possibility for this, a five-carbon chain

```
      H   H   H   H   H
      |   |   |   |   |
H —  C — C — C — C — C  — H
      |   |   |   |   |
      H   H   H   H   H

          pentane
```

Now draw the isomers with a chain of four carbon atoms and one carbon in a side chain. How many positions are possible for this side chain?

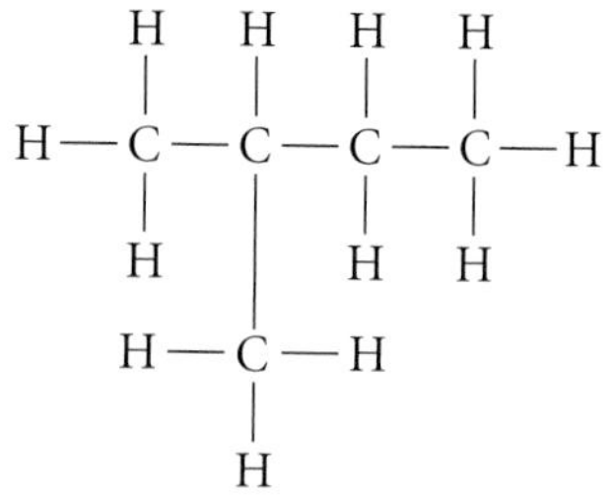

2-methylbutane (there is only one position for the side chain)

Now consider isomers with a chain of three carbon atoms and two carbons in side chains. How many possibilities are there?

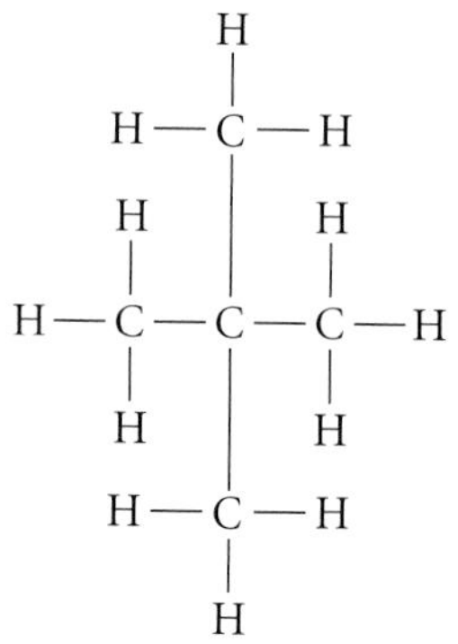

2,2-dimethylpropane (again there is only one possibility for the three-carbon chain molecule)

So in total there are *three* possible isomers for C_5H_{12}.

Worked example

Follow the same process to draw the structures and give the IUPAC names for all the isomers of C_6H_{14}.

Solution

A good exercise is to give the names that you have given your molecules to one of your classmates to see if they can draw the structures correctly. There should be only one possible answer for each name!

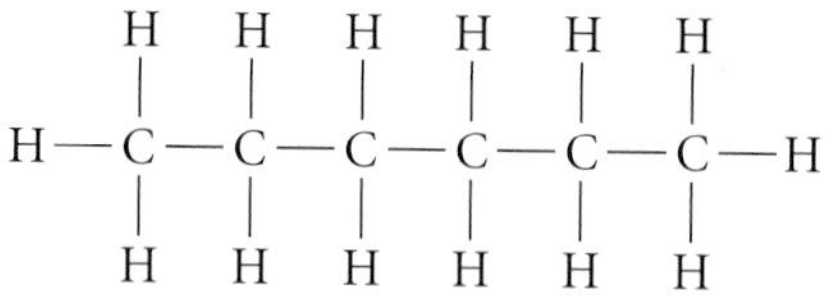

hexane

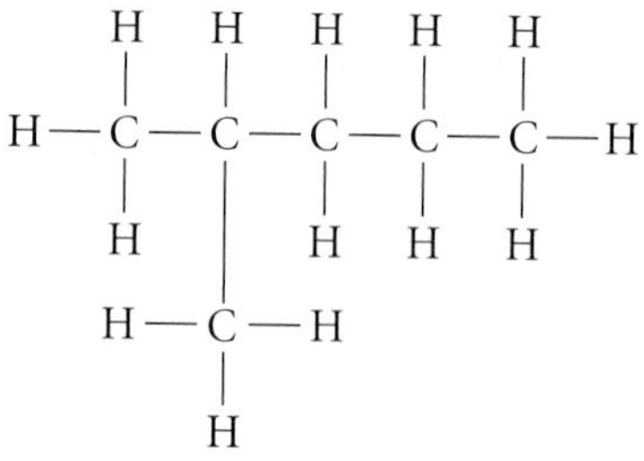

2-methylpentane

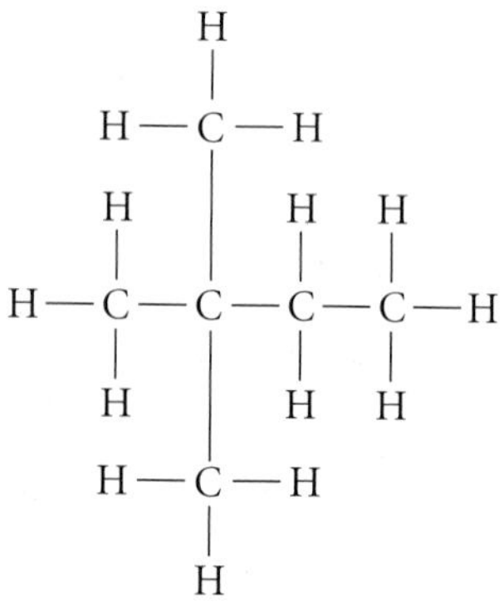

2, 2 -dimethylbutane

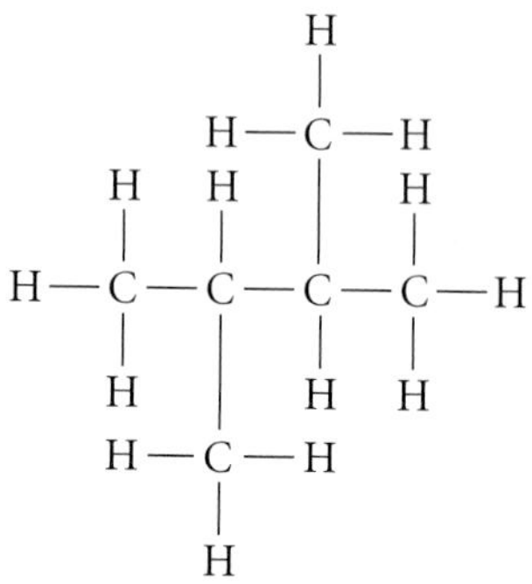

2, 3-dimethylbutane

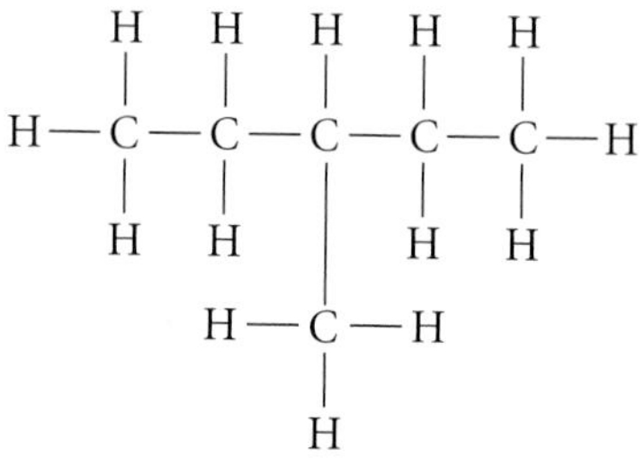

3-methylpentane

The existence of these different straight-chain and branched-chain isomers of the alkanes is of great significance in the petroleum industry. It has been found that branched chain isomers generally burn more smoothly in internal combustion engines than straight chain isomers and so oil fractions with a higher proportion of these branched chain isomers are considered to be of 'better grade'. This is often referred to as a higher 'octane number' and means that you pay more for it at the pump.

Structural isomers in alkenes

In alkenes, a different type of structural isomer occurs when the double bond is found in different positions. For example:

$$\underset{\text{but-1-ene}}{\begin{array}{c}\text{H}\quad \text{H}\quad \text{H}\quad \text{H}\\ |\quad\ |\quad\ |\quad\ |\\ \text{C}=\text{C}-\text{C}-\text{C}-\text{H}\\ |\qquad\ |\quad\ |\\ \text{H}\qquad \text{H}\quad \text{H}\end{array}}\quad\text{is different from}\quad\underset{\text{but-2-ene}}{\begin{array}{c}\text{H}\quad \text{H}\quad \text{H}\quad \text{H}\\ |\quad\ |\quad\ |\quad\ |\\ \text{H}-\text{C}-\text{C}=\text{C}-\text{C}-\text{H}\\ |\qquad\qquad\ |\\ \text{H}\qquad\qquad \text{H}\end{array}}$$

Note that the molecules are named using the smallest numbered carbon that is part of the double bond.

Now consider the straight chain isomers of C_5H_{10} with their IUPAC names:

pent-1-ene

pent-2-ene

Note that H—C—C—C=C—C—H is also pent-2-ene, the same molecule rotated through 180°, so there are only two isomers here.

Worked example

Draw the straight chain isomers of C_6H_{12} and give them their IUPAC names.

Solution

hex-1-ene

hex-2-ene

hex-3-ene

As we can see here, the number of isomers that exist for a molecular formula increases as the molecular size increases. In fact, the increase is exponential; there are 75 possible isomers of $C_{10}H_{22}$ and 366 319 of $C_{20}H_{42}$!

Starting in 1923, a compound called tetraethyl lead – marketed as 'ethyl' from America – was added to petroleum in most parts of the world. It proved to be a very successful 'anti-knock agent', that is, it allowed lower grades of fuel to be used in combustion engines without causing premature burning known as 'knocking'. Many decades and thousands of tons of lead emissions later, mounting concern about the effect of rising lead levels in the atmosphere led to the additive being banned in most countries from about 1986 onwards. Lead is a neurotoxin which is linked to many health effects, particularly brain damage. Since it was phased out from petroleum, blood levels of lead have fallen dramatically but still remain about 600 times higher than they were a century ago.

The person who researched and patented tetraethyl lead as a petroleum additive was the same person who later was responsible for the discovery and marketing of chlorofluorocarbons (CFCs) as refrigerants. Thomas Midgley of Ohio, USA did not live to know the full extent that the long-term impact his findings would have on the Earth's atmosphere. Ironically he died aged 55 from 'accidental strangulation' after becoming entangled in ropes and pulleys he had devised to get himself in and out of bed following loss of use of his legs caused by polio. Perhaps his epitaph should have been 'the solution becomes the problem'.

● **Examiner's hint:** When drawing structural formulas, double check that you have not drawn the same thing twice by drawing it the other way round, as in pent-2-ene above, for example.

Classes of compounds

Sometimes the activity of a functional group is influenced by its position in the carbon chain and so it is useful to describe these different positions exactly. This is done as follows.

A **primary carbon atom** is attached to the functional group and also to at least two hydrogen atoms. Molecules with this arrangement are known as primary molecules, for example:

ethanol is a primary alcohol, C_2H_5OH.

$$H-\overset{\displaystyle H}{\underset{\displaystyle H}{C}}-\overset{\displaystyle H}{\underset{\displaystyle H}{C}}-OH$$

primary carbon atom

A **secondary carbon atom** is attached to the functional group and also to one hydrogen atom and two alkyl groups. These molecules are known as secondary molecules, for example:

propan-2-ol is a secondary alcohol, $CH_3CH(OH)CH_3$.

$$H-\overset{\displaystyle H}{\underset{\displaystyle H}{C}}-\overset{\displaystyle H}{\underset{\displaystyle OH}{C}}-\overset{\displaystyle H}{\underset{\displaystyle H}{C}}-H$$

secondary carbon atom

A **tertiary carbon atom** is attached to the functional group and is also bonded to three alkyl groups so has no hydrogen atoms. These molecules are known as tertiary molecules, for example:

2-methylpropan-2-ol, $C(CH_3)_3OH$

$$H-\overset{\displaystyle H}{\underset{\displaystyle H}{C}}-\overset{\overset{\displaystyle H}{\underset{\displaystyle |}{\overset{\displaystyle C}{|}}}}{\underset{\displaystyle OH}{C}}-\overset{\displaystyle H}{\underset{\displaystyle H}{C}}-H$$

tertiary carbon atom

Secondary alcohol molecule. This is butan-2-ol. Note that there is only one hydrogen atom on the carbon attached to the —OH group. Carbon atoms are represented as black, hydrogen atoms as white and oxygen atoms as red.

Tertiary alcohol molecule. This is 2-methyl propan-2-ol. Note that there are no hydrogen atoms on the carbon attached to the —OH group. Carbon atoms are represented as black, hydrogen atoms as white and oxygen atoms as red.

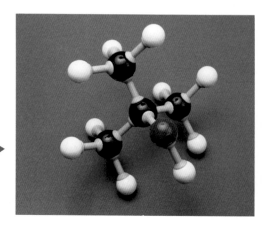

3 Draw and name the structures of the smallest primary, secondary and tertiary chloroalkanes.

Trends in physical properties

As the members of each homologous series have the same functional group, we would expect them to have many similar properties, but to show a trend in these properties with increasing carbon number. Some examples of physical properties are discussed here.

Volatility

This is a measure of how easily the substance changes into the gaseous state – high volatility means that the compound has a low boiling point. Remember (Chapter 4) that volatility depends on overcoming the forces *between* the molecules, so the stronger the intermolecular forces, the higher the boiling point. There are generally three factors to consider here.

1 As we saw earlier in this chapter as we go up a series, the M_r increases by the addition of a CH_2 unit and this results in stronger van der Waals' forces between the molecules, which will therefore raise the boiling point. So for all series at room temperature, the lower members are likely to be gases or liquids, while the higher members will be more likely to be solids.

2 Branching of the chain also has an effect on the volatility, as it influences the strength of the intermolecular forces. Think how tree logs with lots of branches sticking out are going to be much less closely stacked than a pile of logs which have no branches. Similarly, branched chain isomers are going to have less contact with each other than straight chain isomers, so will have weaker intermolecular forces and hence lower boiling points.

3 The presence of a functional group will influence volatility according to its effect on the intermolecular forces. Groups which are polar will develop dipole–dipole interactions between the molecules so these will have higher boiling points. Groups which enable hydrogen bonds to form will have even stronger forces between the molecules, giving rise to even higher boiling points.

 View an animated tutorial on the boiling and melting points of alkanes.
Now go to
www.heinemann.co.uk/hotlinks,
insert the express code 4259P and
click on the activity.

Remember that when you are comparing boiling points of molecules in different homologous series, it is important to compare molecules that have similar M_r values – which may mean comparing molecules with different numbers of carbon atoms. For example, ethanol, C_2H_5OH, has an M_r of 46 and a boiling point of 78 °C and can be usefully compared with propane, C_3H_8, whose M_r is 44 and boiling point is −42 °C. Here we can clearly see that the higher boiling point in ethanol is due to the presence of the –OH group which causes hydrogen bonding between the molecules.

We can summarize the effect on volatility of the different functional groups as follows:

Most volatile   Least volatile

alkane > halogenoalkane > aldehyde > ketone > alcohol > carboxylic acid

van der Waals → dipole–dipole interaction → hydrogen bonding

increasing strength of intermolecular attraction ⟶

increasing boiling point ⟶

Solubility in water

There are two factors to consider when determining the solubility of an organic compound in water.

1 The length of the hydrocarbon chain: as this part of the molecule is non-polar, it does not facilitate the solubility of the molecule in water and so solubility will decrease as the chain length increases.

2 The nature of the functional group: solubility is determined by the extent to which this part of the molecule is able to interact with water, for example through forming hydrogen bonds.

Considering these two factors, we can see that the lower members of the following homologous series are quite soluble in water:

alcohols, aldehydes, ketones and carboxylic acids

Halogenoalkanes are not soluble in water as, despite their polarity, they are unable to form hydrogen bonds with water.

Worked example

Which compound has the lowest boiling point?
A $CH_3CH_2CH(CH_3)CH_3$
B $(CH_3)_4C$
C $CH_3CH_2CH_2CH_2CH_3$
D $CH_3CH_2OCH_2CH_3$

Solution

First check and note that the M_r of all four of these molecules is approximately equal. Now compare their structures: of the three hydrocarbons B is the most branched molecule and therefore will have the lowest boiling point.

10.2 Alkanes

- General formula is C_nH_{2n+2}.
- Alkanes are **saturated hydrocarbons**.
- **Saturated** means that all the carbon–carbon bonds are single bonds.
- **Hydrocarbons** refers to compounds which contain carbon and hydrogen *only*.

Alkanes. Molecular representation of the first three alkanes: methane (CH_4 top left), ethane (C_2H_6 top right) and propane (C_3H_8). Carbon atoms (C) are shown in blue and hydrogen atoms in (H) purple. Alkanes are members of a group of hydrocarbons that have the general formula C_nH_{2n+2}, where n is an integer number. The first four alkanes, methane, ethane, propane and butane are colourless gases, the higher members are liquids and those above $C_{16}H_{34}$ are waxy solids. Alkanes are insoluble in water but soluble in chloroform and benzene. They are very important fuels.

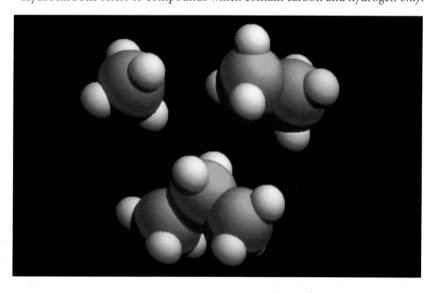

Alkanes have low chemical reactivity

Alkanes contain only C—C and C—H bonds. These are both strong bonds (C—C, 348 kJ mol^{-1} and C—H, 412 kJ mol^{-1}), so these molecules will only react in the presence of a strong source of energy, strong enough to break these bonds. As a result, alkanes are stable under most conditions and can be stored, transported and even compressed safely – which is partly why they are such useful compounds.

The C—C and C—H bonds are also characteristically non-polar, so these molecules are not susceptible to attack by most common reactants. These two factors taken together mean that alkanes are generally of very low reactivity.

There are, however, two reactions involving alkanes that we will consider here.

Combustion: alkanes as fuels

Alkanes are widely used as fuels, in internal combustion engines and household heating for example, because they release significant amounts of energy when they burn, in other words the reactions of combustion are highly exothermic. This is mainly because of the large amount of energy released in forming the double bonds in CO_2 and the bonds in H_2O (remember bond forming releases energy, Chapter 5).

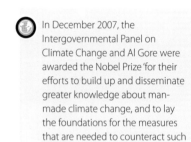

In December 2007, the Intergovernmental Panel on Climate Change and Al Gore were awarded the Nobel Prize 'for their efforts to build up and disseminate greater knowledge about man-made climate change, and to lay the foundations for the measures that are needed to counteract such change'.

Alkanes burn in the presence of excess oxygen to produce carbon dioxide and water, for example:

$$C_3H_8(g) + 5O_2(g) \rightarrow 3CO_2(g) + 4H_2O(g) \quad \Delta H = -2220\,\text{kJ mol}^{-1}$$

However, when the oxygen supply is limited, carbon monoxide and water will be produced, for example:

$$2C_3H_8(g) + 7O_2(g) \rightarrow 6CO(g) + 8H_2O(g)$$

In conditions when oxygen is extremely limited, carbon will also be produced, for example:

$$C_3H_8(g) + 2O_2(g) \rightarrow 3C(s) + 4H_2O(g)$$

The products of all these reactions have a serious impact on the environment, which is why the burning of these and other 'fossil fuels' on a very large scale is now widely recognised as a global problem. Carbon dioxide and water are both so-called 'greenhouse gases', which means that they absorb infrared radiation and so contribute to global warming. Rising levels of carbon dioxide are being largely implicated in the significant increase in average world temperatures. The Intergovernmental Panel on Climate Change (IPCC) meeting in Paris in January 2007 acknowledged that 11 of the preceding 12 years have been the warmest since 1850.

▶ Aeroplane landing with exhaust behind. Burning hydrocarbon fuels releases large amounts of carbon dioxide, as well as carbon monoxide and other pollutants into the atmosphere.

Carbon monoxide is a toxin because it combines irreversibly with the haemoglobin in the blood and prevents it from carrying oxygen. This is a particular problem in regions of high traffic densities like inner cities, as the slow idling car engines produce higher concentrations of CO. It is also the reason why it is very important to have adequate ventilation when these fuels are being burned – there have been many cases, for example, of people dying from carbon monoxide poisoning from using a gas heater in a confined space where the oxygen supply is limited.

Unburned carbon is released into the air as particulates, which have a direct effect on human health, especially the respiratory system. In addition, these particulates act as catalysts in forming smog in polluted air and have recently been targeted as the source of another serious environmental problem known as 'global dimming'.

Substitution reactions of alkanes: halogenation

As alkanes are saturated molecules, the main type of reaction which they can undergo is **substitution** in which an incoming species will take the place of a hydrogen atom. Halogen molecules are able to act in this way under conditions in which they are split into separate atoms, known as **free radicals**, which have an unpaired electron. Once formed, these radicals will lead to a chain reaction in which a mixture of products including the halogenoalkanes is formed. We can divide the reaction into the following steps, known as the **reaction mechanism**:

Initiation

For example: $Cl_2 \xrightarrow{\text{UV light}} 2Cl\cdot$ radicals

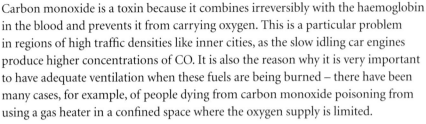

2 chlorine radicals

This process occurs in the presence of ultraviolet light. It is known as **homolytic fission** because the bond between the chlorine atoms is broken, leaving one of the bonding electrons with each atom. *Homo* meaning 'the same' refers to the fact that the two products have an equal assignment of electrons from the bond.

Propagation

For example: $Cl\cdot + CH_4 \rightarrow CH_3\cdot + HCl$

$CH_3\cdot + Cl_2 \rightarrow CH_3Cl + Cl\cdot$

$CH_3Cl + Cl\cdot \rightarrow CH_2Cl\cdot + HCl$

$CH_2Cl\cdot + Cl_2 \rightarrow CH_2Cl_2 + Cl\cdot$

These reactions are called propagation because they both use and produce free radicals and so allow the reaction to continue. This is why the reaction is often called a **chain reaction**.

Termination

For example: $Cl\cdot + Cl\cdot \rightarrow Cl_2$

$CH_3\cdot + Cl\cdot \rightarrow CH_3Cl$

$CH_3\cdot + CH_3\cdot \rightarrow C_2H_6$

These reactions remove free radicals from the reaction by causing them to react together and pair up their electrons. Hence we can see that the reaction mixture may contain mono- and di-substituted halogenoalkanes, as well as HCl and larger alkanes. A similar reaction occurs with other alkanes and with bromine. Because UV light is needed to produce the radicals, alkanes will not react with halogens in the dark.

View the highly acclaimed BBC documentary on global dimming. Now go to www.heinemann.co.uk/hotlinks, insert the express code 4259P and click on this activity.

Now that we are aware of so many of the negative environmental effects associated with the burning of fossil fuels, how can we make changes in our lifestyles to lessen these impacts?

A free radical contains an unpaired electron and so is very reactive.

Alkanes are saturated hydrocarbons and undergo substitution reactions.

● **Examiner's hint:** Make sure that you understand the difference between a *free radical* and an *ion*. A free radical has an unpaired electron but no net charge; an ion carries a charge.

Exercise

4 Write equations showing possible steps leading to a mixture of products in the reaction between bromine and ethane reacting together in UV light.

Alkenes

- General formula is C_nH_{2n}
- Alkenes are **unsaturated hydrocarbons** containing a carbon–carbon double bond.

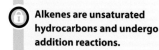

The carbon–carbon double bond is actually made up of two different bonds, one is called sigma, σ and the other is called pi, π. The carbon atoms which form the double bond have an arrangement of groups around them which is trigonal planar with angles of 120° (see Chapter 4).

Addition reactions of alkenes

The double bond represents the site of reactivity of the molecule. The π bond is a weaker bond than the σ bond so it is relatively easily broken. This creates two new bonding positions on the carbon atoms, enabling alkenes to undergo **addition reactions** and giving rise to a range of different saturated products. These are described below.

> **Alkenes are unsaturated hydrocarbons and undergo addition reactions.**

With hydrogen

Hydrogen reacts with alkenes to form alkanes in the presence of a nickel catalyst at about 150 °C, for example:

$$CH_3CHCH_2 + H_2 \longrightarrow CH_3CH_2CH_3$$
propene   Ni catalyst,   propane
150 °C

This process, known as **hydrogenation**, is used in the margarine industry to convert oils containing many unsaturated hydrocarbon chains into more saturated compounds which have higher melting points. This is done so that margarine will be a solid at room temperature. However, there are now widespread concerns about the health effects of some of the fats produced in this way, known as *trans* fats (see Chapters 13 and 17).

> **Examiner's hint:** Be careful not to confuse the terms *hydrogenation* (addition of hydrogen) with *hydration* (addition of water).

With halogens

Halogens react with alkenes to produce dihalogeno compounds. These reactions happen quickly at room temperature and are accompanied by the loss of colour of the reacting halogen. Note that because these reactions involve the halogen atoms becoming attached to the two carbons of the double bond, the name and structure of the product must indicate these positions.

For example:

$$CH_3CHCH_2 + Br_2 \longrightarrow CH_3CHBrCH_2Br$$
propene   1,2-dibromopropane

With hydrogen halides

Hydrogen halides (HCl, HBr, etc.) react with alkenes to produce halogenoalkanes. These reactions take place rapidly in solution at room temperature.

For example:

$$CH_2CH_2 + HCl \longrightarrow CH_3CH_2Cl$$
ethene   chloroethane

All the hydrogen halides are able to react in this way, but the reactivity is in the order HI>HBr>HCl owing to the decreasing strength of the hydrogen halide bond down Group 7 (see Chapter 3). So HI, with the weakest bond, reacts the most readily.

With water

The reaction with water is known as **hydration** and converts the alkene into an alcohol. In the laboratory, it can be achieved using concentrated sulfuric acid as a catalyst. The reaction involves an intermediate in which both H^+ and HSO_4^- ions are added across the double bond. This is quickly followed by hydrolysis with replacement of the HSO_4^- by OH^- and reformation of the H_2SO_4.

$$CH_2CH_2 \xrightarrow{H_2SO_{4\,(conc)}} CH_3CH_2(HSO_4) \xrightarrow{H_2O} CH_3CH_2OH + H_2SO_4$$
ethene   ethyl hydrogensulfate   ethanol

Conditions: heat with steam and catalyst of concentrated H_2SO_4

The hydration of ethene is of industrial significance because ethanol is a very important solvent and hence is manufactured on a large scale.

Test to distinguish between alkanes and alkenes

We can use the fact that alkenes readily undergo addition reactions, whereas alkanes will not (and will only undergo substitution reactions in UV light), as the basis of tests to distinguish between the two homologous series. If separate samples of an alkane and an alkene are shaken together with bromine water at room temperature, you will see that the red-brown colour of the bromine water is immediately decolourized by the alkene but remains coloured in the alkane.

Alkenes also differ from alkanes in the colour of the flame when they burn. Because they have a higher ratio of carbon to hydrogen, alkenes contain much more unburned carbon than alkanes when they burn in similar conditions. This gives them a much dirtier, smokier flame. By comparison aromatic compounds – those containing the benzene ring – are highly unsaturated and so burn with an even smokier flame.

Polymerization of alkenes

Because alkenes readily undergo addition reactions by breaking their double bonds, they can be joined together to produce long chains known as **polymers**. The alkene used in this reaction is known as the **monomer** and its chemical nature will determine the properties of the polymer. Polymers, typically containing thousands of molecules of the monomer, are a major product of the organic chemical industry. Indeed many of our most common and useful plastics are polymers of alkenes.

For example, ethene polymerizes to form poly-ethene, commonly known as polythene. This molecule was first synthesized in 1935, in a process which was discovered largely by accidental contamination of the reactants with oxygen. It has excellent electrical insulating properties and played an essential role in the development of radar during the Second World War. It is commonly used in household containers, carrier bags, water tanks and piping.

Alkene test. Demonstration of the result of testing an alkane (hexane) and an alkene (hex-1-ene) with bromine water. The brown colour of the bromine water has been decolourized by the alkene, because it reacted with the carbon–carbon double bond in an addition reaction. No colour change occurs with the alkane, as it is a saturated molecule and is unable to undergo an addition reaction with bromine.

Figure 10.2 People cannot form a chain until they unfold their arms to release their hands. In the same way, alkenes must break their double bonds in order to join with other molecules in the polymer.

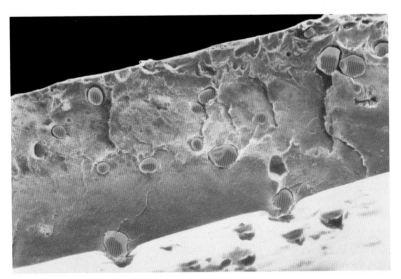

Coloured scanning electron micrograph of a section through a sheet of a biodegradable plastic. Many granules of starch (orange) can be clearly seen embedded in the plastic. When the plastic is buried in soil, the starch grains take up water and expand. This breaks the plastic into many small fragments, increasing the contact area with bacteria in the soil which digest the plastic. Such plastics help to address the major problem of waste plastic disposal.

$$n \ \underset{\substack{| \\ H}}{\overset{\substack{H \\ |}}{C}}=\underset{\substack{| \\ H}}{\overset{\substack{H \\ |}}{C}} \xrightarrow{\text{polymerization}} \left(\underset{\substack{| \\ H}}{\overset{\substack{H \\ |}}{C}} - \underset{\substack{| \\ H}}{\overset{\substack{H \\ |}}{C}} \right)_n$$

ethene   the repeating unit

Similarly propene polymerizes to form polypropene, often called polypropylene. This polymer is used in the manufacture of clothing, especially thermal wear for outdoor activities.

Worked example

Show the reaction of polymerization of the monomer chloroethene, identifying the repeating unit.

Solution

$$\underset{\substack{| \\ H}}{\overset{\substack{H \\ |}}{C}}=\underset{\substack{| \\ H}}{\overset{\substack{Cl \\ |}}{C}} + \underset{\substack{| \\ H}}{\overset{\substack{H \\ |}}{C}}=\underset{\substack{| \\ H}}{\overset{\substack{Cl \\ |}}{C}} \longrightarrow \left(\underset{\substack{| \\ H}}{\overset{\substack{H \\ |}}{C}} - \underset{\substack{| \\ H}}{\overset{\substack{Cl \\ |}}{C}} \right) \underset{\substack{| \\ H}}{\overset{\substack{H \\ |}}{C}} - \underset{\substack{| \\ H}}{\overset{\substack{Cl \\ |}}{C}} -$$

repeating unit

Polychloroethene is also known as PVC (poly vinyl chloride) and is very widely used in all forms of construction materials, packaging, electrical cable sheathing and so on. It is one of the world's most important plastics. Its widespread use is, however, somewhat controversial as its synthesis is associated with some toxic by-products known as dioxins, which are linked to reproductive disorders and a variety of cancers. The environmentalist group Greenpeace has advocated the global phase out of PVC.

Another interesting polymer is known as PTFE – polytetrafluoroethene. Because of its non-adhesive surface properties, it is widely used in non-stick pans under registered trademark names such as Teflon®. It also comprises one of the layers in the manufacture of waterproof and breathable fabrics such as Gore-Tex®. Its structure is:

$$\left(\underset{\substack{| \\ F}}{\overset{\substack{F \\ |}}{C}} - \underset{\substack{| \\ F}}{\overset{\substack{F \\ |}}{C}} \right)_n$$

● **Examiner's hint:** Note that when you are drawing these polymerization reactions, it is easiest to put the double bond in the *middle* of the structure, with the other groups above and below

like this
$$\underset{\substack{| \\ H}}{\overset{\substack{H \\ |}}{C}}=\underset{\substack{| \\ H}}{\overset{\substack{CH_3 \\ |}}{C}}$$

not like this
$$H - \underset{\substack{| \\ H}}{\overset{\substack{ \\ }}{C}}=\underset{\substack{| \\ H}}{\overset{\substack{ \\ }}{C}} - CH_3$$

Then you can see how they can link together when the double bond breaks. Draw the two monomers side by side with exactly the same representation (as if you had used the 'copy' and 'paste' functions of a computer). Then just bond them together and see the repeating pattern.

Take part in 'The great PVC controversy'. Now go to www.heinemann.co.uk/hotlinks, insert the express code 4259P and click on this activity.

◀ Waste dumping of PVC – a major environmental problem.

Coloured scanning electron micrograph of Gore-Tex® fabric used to make water-proof clothing. The pink layers on top and bottom are nylon, while the filling shown in yellow/white is made from Teflon. This forms a microporous membrane containing pores less than a micrometre in diameter, 20 000 times smaller than a *drop* of water but 700 times larger than a water *molecule*. So the fabric allows water vapour to move outwards from the body, without allowing the penetration of liquid water inwards. Clothing made from this fabric is thus known as 'breathable waterproofing'.

Summary of reactions of alkenes

- Alkenes readily undergo addition reactions.
- They are used as starting materials in the manufacture of many industrially important chemicals.

10.4 Alcohols

- General formula $C_nH_{2n+1}OH$
- Alcohols have the –OH functional group. As this is a polar group, it increases the solubility in water of the molecules relative to the corresponding alkanes. The most common alcohol, ethanol C_2H_5OH, is readily soluble in water, as we know from its presence in alcoholic drinks.

Combustion

Like the hydrocarbons, alcohols burn in oxygen to form carbon dioxide and water with the release of significant amounts of energy. Indeed, alcohols are an important source of fuel and are used in alcohol burners and similar heaters. The amount of energy released per mole of alcohol increases as we go up the homologous series, chiefly due to the increasing number of carbon dioxide molecules produced.

For example, the burning of methanol can be represented as follows:

$$2CH_3OH(l) + 3O_2(g) \rightarrow 2CO_2(g) + 4H_2O(g)$$

which means it has a 1:1 ratio of CO_2:alcohol and $\Delta H^{\theta}_c = 726.1$ kJ mol^{-1}, whereas the burning of pentanol can be represented as follows:

$$2C_5H_{11}OH(g) + 15O_2(g) \rightarrow 10CO_2(g) + 12H_2O(g)$$

which means it has a 5:1 ratio of CO_2:alcohol and $\Delta H^{\theta}_c = 3330.9$ kJ mol^{-1}.

Alcohol burner: the flame is burning on a wick that is soaked in ethanol. Alcohols burn with a relatively clean (non-sooty) flame so are useful as fuels.

Methanol is considered to be a potential candidate to replace fuels based on crude oil. It can be burned directly as a fuel, or used in the production of hydrogen for fuel cells. It is synthesized on a large scale by the reduction of carbon dioxide and carbon monoxide.

As is the case with the hydrocarbons, in the presence of a limited supply of oxygen alcohols will produce carbon monoxide instead of carbon dioxide.

In New York City, a methanol-powered bus drives down the street. Methanol, CH_3OH, is a clear and colourless liquid used as a hydrogen carrier for fuel cells. Methanol fuel cells will reduce the dependence on petroleum and improve urban air quality.

Oxidation

Although combustion involves the *complete* oxidation of the alcohol molecules, it is also possible for them to react with oxidizing agents which selectively oxidize the carbon atom attached to the −OH group, keeping the carbon skeleton of the molecule intact. In this way, alcohols can be oxidized into other organic compounds of significance. The exact nature of these reactions is determined by the class of alcohol, as we described in Section 10. 1.

Various oxidizing agents can be used for these reactions, but the one most commonly used in the laboratory is acidified potassium dichromate(VI) (see Chapter 9 for an explanation of oxidation numbers). This is a bright orange solution (owing to the presence of Cr(VI)). When the reaction mixture is heated, an obvious colour change is observed as the Cr(VI) is reduced to Cr(III) which is green, while the alcohol is oxidized. When writing these reactions it is often easier to show the oxidizing agent simply as +[O]. The oxidation reactions of the different alcohols are as follows.

Primary alcohols

Primary alcohols are oxidized in a two-step reaction, first forming the **aldehyde**, which is then oxidized further to the **carboxylic acid**.

For example:

$$\underset{\substack{\text{ethanol} \\ \text{primary alcohol}}}{\text{H}-\overset{\overset{\displaystyle H}{|}}{\underset{\underset{\displaystyle H}{|}}{C}}-\overset{\overset{\displaystyle H}{|}}{\underset{\underset{\displaystyle H}{|}}{C}}-\text{OH}} \xrightarrow{\text{+[O], heat}} \underset{\substack{\text{ethanal} \\ \text{aldehyde}}}{\text{H}-\overset{\overset{\displaystyle H}{|}}{\underset{\underset{\displaystyle H}{|}}{C}}-\text{C}\underset{\diagdown H}{\overset{\diagup\!\!\!\!O}{}}} \xrightarrow[\text{reflux}]{\text{+[O], heat}} \underset{\substack{\text{ethanoic acid} \\ \text{carboxylic acid}}}{\text{H}-\overset{\overset{\displaystyle H}{|}}{\underset{\underset{\displaystyle H}{|}}{C}}-\text{C}\underset{\diagdown OH}{\overset{\diagup\!\!\!\!O}{}}}$$

This is why, when we leave a bottle of wine exposed to the air, bacteria slowly oxidize the ethanol to ethanoic acid, giving the smell of vinegar.

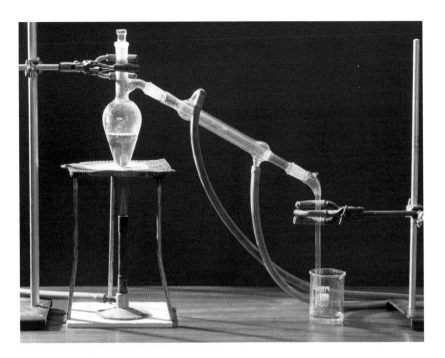

Student heating a pear-shaped flask using a bunsen burner and a reflux condensor. This apparatus is used to oxidize a primary alcohol to completion – to the carboxylic acid. It is designed to collect and condense vapours that would escape from the reaction mixture, so enabling the volatile components to remain in the reaction for long enough to complete their reaction.

If we want to obtain the aldehyde as the product, it is possible to remove it from the reaction mixture by distilling it off as it forms. This is possible because aldehydes have lower boiling points than either alcohols or carboxylic acids, owing to the fact that they do not have hydrogen bonding between their molecules. If, on the other hand, we want to obtain the carboxylic acid as the product, we must leave the aldehyde in contact with the oxidizing agent for a prolonged period of time. This will be achieved most efficiently if apparatus called a **reflux condensor** is used.

Secondary alcohols

Secondary alcohols are oxidized to the **ketone** by a similar process of oxidation, for example:

CH₃CHOHCH₃
propan-2-ol

(CH₃)₂CO
propanone

Tertiary alcohols

Tertiary alcohols are not readily oxidized under comparable conditions, as this would involve breaking the carbon skeleton of the molecule, which requires significantly more energy. Therefore we will not see a colour change in the potassium dichromate(VI) oxidizing agent when it is reacted with a tertiary alcohol, for example:

2-methylpropan-2-ol

no reaction

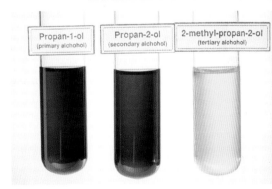

Oxidation of alcohols. Completed oxidation reactions of three alcohols with potassium dichromate solution ($K_2Cr_2O_7$, yellow). The dichromate is a strong oxidizing agent that is reduced when it reacts to form a green solution. Primary and secondary alcohols can be oxidized, forming carboxylic acids and ketones, respectively. Tertiary alcohols are not oxidized and do not react.

10.5 Halogenoalkanes

- General formula $C_nH_{2n+1}X$, where X = halogen.
- Halogenoalkanes contain an atom of fluorine, chlorine, bromine or iodine bonded to the carbon skeleton of the molecule. The halogen group can be replaced by other atoms or groups in **substitution reactions**. As a result, halogenoalkanes can be used in synthetic pathways leading to a large number of important organic products.

Halogenoalkanes have also been widely used directly in many products. In particular, the group of compounds known as CFCs (chlorofluorocarbons), which contain more than one halogen atom per molecule, were widely used in refrigerants and aerosol propellants in many parts of the world from the 1930s. The growing awareness of their role in breaking down the stratospheric **ozone layer**, which is a vital shield for the existence of life on Earth, has led to regulations concerning their distribution. Sadly, the stability of these molecules is such that even though they are no longer being released in large quantities they are likely to remain active and hence destructive in the atmosphere for generations.

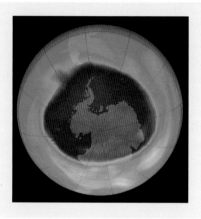

Antarctic ozone hole 2005. Coloured satellite image of low atmospheric ozone levels over Antarctica on 11th September 2005. The ozone hole (dark blue) is 27 million km² in size. The largest hole was 29.2 million km² in 2000. Ozone levels are colour-coded, from dark blue (lowest), through cyan and green to yellow (highest). Ozone absorbs harmful ultraviolet (UV) radiation from the Sun, but its levels are reduced by chlorofluorocarbons (CFCs) and other compounds. CFC production was restricted in 1987, but the hole will take decades to heal. Data are from the Ozone Monitoring Instrument on the Aura satellite.

The carbon–halogen bond is polar owing to the greater electronegativity of the halogen atom, which results in charge distribution as follows:

$$-\overset{|}{\underset{|}{C}} \overset{\delta+}{\Longrightarrow} \overset{\delta-}{Cl}$$

We can see that the carbon atom attached to the halogen therefore has a partial positive charge and it is described as being **electron deficient**. This makes it susceptible to attack by a group of chemicals called **nucleophiles** – species which are themselves electron rich and hence are attracted to a region of electron deficiency. Nucleophiles have a lone pair of electrons and may also be negatively charged.

As halogenoalkanes are saturated molecules, the type of reaction they undergo (like alkanes) is substitution. A good example of this is the substitution reaction by the hydroxide ion OH⁻ from alkalis such as NaOH. In this reaction, OH⁻ is the nucleophile and this will take the place of (substitute) the halogen, so converting the halogenoalkane into an alcohol. These reactions are commonly described as S_N reactions, standing for substitution nucleophilic.

The exact mechanism of these reactions depends on the class of the halogenoalkane – whether it is primary, secondary or tertiary – as this influences

Visit NASA's site for an excellent summary of the history and politics of the role of CFCs in ozone depletion.
Now go to www.heinemann.co.uk/hotlinks, insert the express code 4259P and click on this activity.

In relation to environmental concerns of global significance, discuss the balance between the responsibility of the individual and that of governments.

the environment of the carbon–halogen bond. In organic reaction mechanisms, it is customary to use **curly arrows** shown here in blue to represent the movement of electron pairs. We will now look at examples of these.

Primary halogenoalkanes: S_N2 mechanism

For example: $CH_3Cl + OH^- \quad CH_3OH + Cl^-$

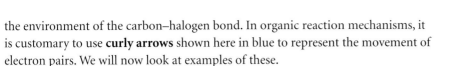

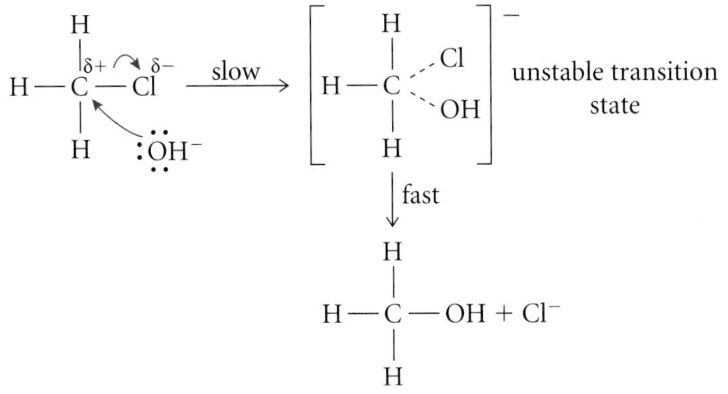

The first step in this reaction is the slow step, in which the OH^- ion attacks the electron-deficient carbon atom, leading to the formation of an unstable transition state in which both the OH^- and the Cl^- are partially bonded to the carbon atom. This then quickly breaks down, releasing the chloride ion, forming the alcohol. Because the slow step of this reaction – known as the rate-determining step – depends on the concentration of *two* reactants (halogenoalkane and the hydroxide ion), it is known as a **bimolecular** reaction. Therefore this mechanism is fully described as S_N2 (substitution nucleophilic bimolecular).

Tertiary halogenoalkanes: S_N1 mechanism

For example: $C(CH_3)_3Cl + OH^- \rightarrow C(CH_3)_3OH + Cl^-$

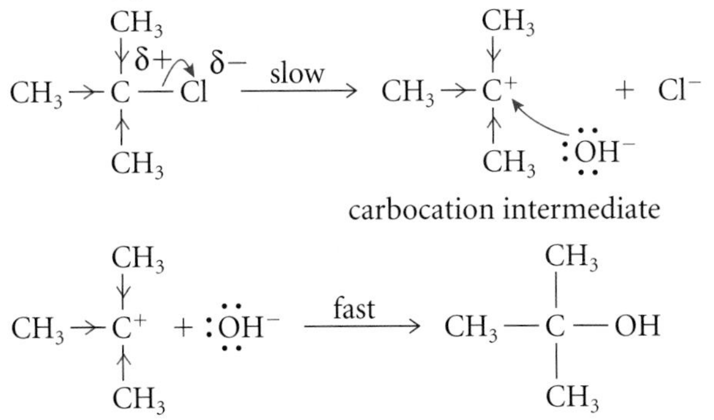

This reaction has a different mechanism for several reasons. The presence of the three alkyl groups around the carbon of the carbon–halogen bond, causes what is called **steric hindrance**, meaning that these bulky groups make it difficult for an incoming group to attack this carbon atom. Instead, the first step of the reaction involves the halogenoalkane ionizing by breaking its carbon–halogen bond. This happens in such a way that the pair of electrons in the bond both end up in the halogen, forming the halide ion and leaving a temporary positive charge on the carbon atom, which is known as a **carbocation**.

Another reason which favours this mechanism is that the carbocation is stabilized by the presence of the three alkyl groups, as each of these has an electron-donating (sometimes called a positive inductive) effect, shown by the arrows in the structure above.

> **Homolytic fission is when a bond breaks producing free radicals with unpaired electrons**
> $$X:X \rightarrow X\cdot + X\cdot$$
> **Heterolytic fission is when a bond breaks producing two oppositely charged ions**
> $$X:X \rightarrow X:^- + X^+$$

Because the slow step of this reaction is determined by the concentration of only *one* reactant (the halogenoalkane), it is described as a **unimolecular** reaction. Thus this reaction mechanism is described as S_N1 (substitution nucleophilic unimolecular).

Note that both mechanisms involve the **heterolytic fission** of the carbon–chlorine bond releasing Cl^-.

Secondary halogenoalkanes

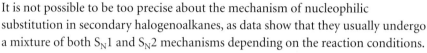

View a more in depth tutorial on S_N1 and S_N2 mechanisms. Now go to www.heinemann.co.uk/hotlinks, insert the express code 4259P and click on this activity.

It is not possible to be too precise about the mechanism of nucleophilic substitution in secondary halogenoalkanes, as data show that they usually undergo a mixture of both S_N1 and S_N2 mechanisms depending on the reaction conditions.

The relative reactivity of the different halogens in these reactions depends on the strength of their bonds with carbon and this decreases as we go down the halogen group. So we find that the iodoalkane with the weakest carbon–halogen bond is the most reactive and the fluoroalkane is the least reactive.

10.6 Reaction pathways

We can now summarize some of the reactions we have studied in this chapter and see how they are inter-related.

Figure 10.3 Some pathways of conversion of organic compounds.

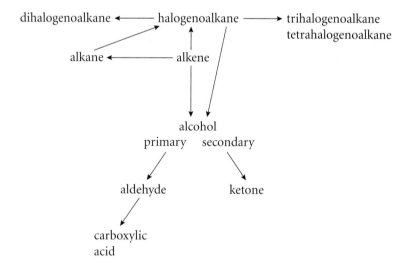

The development of new organic compounds – from drugs to dyes, clothing to construction materials – represents a major part of modern industrial chemistry. The oil industry is the main source of organic compounds for these processes, but it does not generally yield the required proportion of desired compounds. Therefore organic chemists typically have to convert compounds from one form into another, often by linking reactions such as those given above in several steps, known as a **reaction pathway**. Deciding on a 'reaction route' between starting compound and desired product is something that you can now do on the basis of the reactions we have studied here.

Worked example

You are required to convert the compound 1-chlorobutane into butanoic acid. Describe the steps you would use, giving reagents, conditions and equations for each stage.

Solution

Step 1: Hydrolyze the 1-chlorobutane by heating it with sodium hydroxide solution:

$$CH_3(CH_2)_2CH_2Cl + NaOH \rightarrow CH_3(CH_2)_2CH_2OH + NaCl$$

1-chlorobutane   butan-1-ol

Conditions: aqueous solution, dilute alkali $NaOH(aq)$

Step 2: Oxidize the butan-1-ol with acidified potassium dichromate solution:

$$CH_3(CH_2)_2CH_2OH + [O] \rightarrow CH_3(CH_2)_2COOH$$

butan-1-ol   butanoic acid

Conditions: heat with acidified potassium dichromate(VI) solution, use reflux condensor and allow the reaction to go to completion.

Practice questions

1 Which statement about neighbouring members of all homologous series is correct?

   A   They have the same empirical formula.

   B   They differ by a CH_2 group.

   C   They possess different functional groups.

   D   They differ in their degree of unsaturation.

                   © International Baccalaureate Organization [2004]

2 Which compound is a member of the same homologous series as 1-chloropropane?

   A   1-chloropropene

   B   1-chlorobutane

   C   1-bromopropane

   D   1,1-dichloropropane

                   © International Baccalaureate Organization [2005]

3 Which type of compound must contain a minimum of three carbon atoms?

   A   an aldehyde

   B   a carboxylic acid

   C   an ester

   D   a ketone

                   © International Baccalaureate Organization [2004]

4 What is the IUPAC name for $CH_3CH_2CH(CH_3)_2$?

   A   1,1-dimethylpropane

   B   2-methylbutane

   C   isopentane

   D   ethyldimethylmethane

                   © International Baccalaureate Organization [2004]

5 How many structural isomers are possible with the molecular formula C_6H_{14}?

   A   4

   B   5

   C   6

   D   7

                   © International Baccalaureate Organization [2005]

6 Which compound is a member of the aldehyde homologous series?

 A CH_3COCH_3

 B $CH_3CH_2CH_2OH$

 C CH_3CH_2COOH

 D CH_3CH_2CHO

7 Which formulas represent butane or its isomer?

 I $CH_3(CH_2)_2CH_3$

 II $CH_3CH(CH_3)CH_3$

 III $(CH_3)_3CH$

 A I and II only

 B I and III only

 C II and III only

 D I, II and III

8 Which substance(s) could be formed during the incomplete combustion of a hydrocarbon?

 I   carbon

 II hydrogen

 III carbon monoxide

 A I only

 B I and II only

 C I and III only

 D II and III only

9 What product results from the reaction of $CH_2{=}CH_2$ with Br_2?

 A CHBrCHBr

 B CH_2CHBr

 C CH_3CH_2Br

 D CH_2BrCH_2Br

10 What is the final product formed when CH_3CH_2OH is refluxed with acidified potassium dichromate(VI)?

 A CH_3CHO

 B $CH_2{=}CH_2$

 C CH_3COOH

 D $HCOOCH_3$

11 The alkanes are a homologous series of saturated hydrocarbons.

 (a) State the meaning of each of the following terms.

  (i) homologous series   (2)

  (ii) hydrocarbon   (1)

  (iii) saturated   (1)

(b) **(i)** State and explain the trend in the boiling points of the first five alkanes. (2)

     (ii) Explain why the enthalpies of combustion of alkanes are negative values. (1)

(c) State the products of the complete combustion of alkanes (2)

(Total 9 marks)

© International Baccalaureate Organization [2004]

12 Give the structural formulas for the isomers of molecular formula C_4H_{10} and state the name of each one. (4)

© International Baccalaureate Organization [2005]

13 Ethene, propene and but-2-ene are members of the alkene homologous series.

(a) Describe three features of members of a homologous series. (3)

(b) State and explain which compound has the highest boiling point. (3)

(c) Draw the structural formula and give the name of an alkene containing five carbon atoms. (2)

(d) Write an equation for the reaction between but-2-ene and hydrogen bromide, showing the structure of the organic product. State the type of reaction occurring. (3)

(e) Propene can be converted to propanoic acid in three steps:

$$\text{propene} \xrightarrow{\text{step 1}} \text{propan-1-ol} \xrightarrow{\text{step 2}} \text{propanal} \xrightarrow{\text{step 3}} \text{propanoic acid}$$

State the type of reaction occurring in steps 2 and 3 and the reagents needed. Describe how the conditions of the reaction can be altered to obtain the maximum amount of propanal, and in a separate experiment, to obtain the maximum amount of propanoic acid. (5)

(f) Identify the strongest type of intermolecular force present in each of the compounds propan-1-ol, propanal and propanoic acid. List these compounds in decreasing order of boiling point. (4)

(Total 20 marks)

© International Baccalaureate Organization [2005]

14 The percentage composition of a hydrocarbon is C = 85.6% and H = 14.4%.

(a) Calculate the empirical formula of the hydrocarbon. (2)

(b) A 100 g sample of the hydrocarbon at a temperature of 273 K and a pressure of 1.01×10^5 Pa (1.00 atm) has a volume of 0.399 dm³.

     (i) Calculate the molar mass of the hydrocarbon. (2)

     (ii) Deduce the molecular formula of the hydrocarbon. (1)

(c) Explain why the *incomplete* combustion of hydrocarbons is harmful to humans. (2)

(Total 7 marks)

© International Baccalaureate Organization [2005]

15 (a) List *three* characteristics of an homologous series, and explain the term **functional group**. (3)

(b) Ethanol and ethanoic acid can be distinguished by their melting points. State and explain which of the two compounds will have a higher melting point. (2)

(Total 5 marks)

© International Baccalaureate Organization [2003]

11 Measurement and data processing

The scales on two pieces of measuring glassware. The white numbers (left) belong to a measuring cylinder, while the black numbers (centre) mark out much smaller volumes on the side of a graduated pipette. A greater degree of measuring accuracy can be obtained by using the pipette rather than the cylinder.

Science is a communal activity and it is important that information is shared openly and honestly. An essential part of this process is the way the international scientific community subjects the findings of scientists to intense critical scrutiny through the repetition of experiments and the peer review of results in journals and at conferences. All measurements have uncertainties and it is important these are reported when data is exchanged, as these limit the conclusions that can be legitimately drawn. Science has progressed and is one of the most successful enterprises in our culture because these inherent uncertainties are recognized. Chemistry provides us with a deep understanding of the material world but it does not offer absolute certainty.

Data collected from investigations are often presented in graphical form. A graph is a useful tool as it shows relationships between variables and identifies data points which do not fit the general trend and so gives another measure of the reliability of the data.

Scientists need to be principled and act with integrity and honesty.

'One aim of the physical sciences has been to give an exact picture of the material world. One achievement ... has been to prove that this aim is unattainable.'
(J. Bronowski)
What are the implications of this claim for the aspirations of science?

Assessment statements

11.1 Uncertainty and error in measurement
11.1.1 Describe and give examples of random uncertainties and systematic errors.
11.1.2 Distinguish between *precision* and *accuracy*.
11.1.3 Describe how the effects of random uncertainties may be reduced.
11.1.4 State random uncertainty as an uncertainty range ($\pm$).
11.1.5 State the results of calculations to the appropriate number of significant figures.

11.2 Uncertainties in calculated results
11.2.1 State uncertainties as absolute and percentage uncertainties.
11.2.2 Determine the uncertainties in results.

11.3 Graphical techniques
11.3.1 Sketch graphs to represent dependences and interpret graph behaviour.
11.3.2 Construct graphs from experimental data.
11.3.3 Draw best-fit lines through data points on a graph.
11.3.4 Determine the values of physical quantities from graphs.

Uncertainty and error in measurement

Uncertainty in measurement

Measurement is an important part of chemistry. In the laboratory you will use different measuring apparatus and there will be times when you have to select the instrument that is most appropriate for your task from a range of possibilities. Suppose, for example, you wanted 25 cm³ of water, you could choose from measuring cylinders, pipettes, burettes, volumetric flasks of different sizes, or even an analytical balance if you know the density. All of these could be used to measure a volume of 25 cm³, but with different levels of uncertainty.

Uncertainty in analogue instruments

An uncertainty range applies to any experimental value. Some pieces of apparatus state the degree of uncertainty, in other cases you will have to make a judgement. Suppose you are asked to measure the volume of water in the measuring cylinder shown in Figure 11.1. The bottom of the meniscus of a liquid usually lies between two graduations and so the final figure of the reading has to be estimated. The smallest division in the measuring cylinder is 4 cm³ so we should report the volume as 62 ±2 cm³. The same considerations apply to other equipment such as burettes and alcohol thermometers that have analogue scales. The uncertainty of an analogue scale is ± half the smallest division.

An analytical balance is one of the most precise instruments in a school laboratory. This is a digital instrument.

Exercise

1 What is the uncertainty range in the measuring cylinder in the close up photo below?

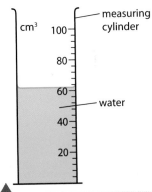

Figure 11.1 The volume reading should be taken from the bottom of the meniscus. You could report the volume as 62 cm³ but this is not an exact value.

◄ An alcohol thermometer with a smallest division of 1 °C. The uncertainty is 0.5 °C so the temperature should be recorded as 25.0 ±0.5 °C.

ⓘ The uncertainty of an analogue scale is ± half the smallest division.

215

The mass of the water is recorded as 100.00 ±0.01 g.

The uncertainty of a digital scale is ± the smallest scale division.

Measure your reaction time. Now go to www.heinemann.co.uk/ hotlinks, insert the express code 4259P and click on this activity.

Uncertainty in digital instruments

A top pan balance has a digital scale. The mass of the sample of water shown here is 100.00 g but the last digit is uncertain. The degree of uncertainty is ±0.01 g: the smallest scale division. The uncertainty of a digital scale is ± the smallest scale division.

Other sources of uncertainty

Chemists are interested in measuring how properties change during a reaction and this can lead to additional sources of uncertainty. When time measurements are taken for example, the reaction time of the experimenter should be considered.

Similarly there are uncertainties in judging, for example the point that an indicator changes colour when measuring the end-point of a titration, or what is the temperature at a particular time during an exothermic reaction, or what is the voltage of an electrochemical cell. These extra uncertainties should be noted even if they are not actually quantified when data are collected in experimental work.

Exercise

2 A reward is given for a missing diamond, which has a reported mass of 9.92 ±0.05 g. You find a diamond and measure its mass as 10.1 ±0.2 g. Could this be the missing diamond?

Significant figures in measurements

The digits in the measurement up to and including the first uncertain digit are the **significant figures** of the measurement. There are two significant figures, for example, in 62 cm^3 and five in 100.00 g. The zeros are significant here as they signify that the uncertainty range is ± 0.01 g. The number of significant figures may not always be clear. If a time measurement is 1000 s, for example, are there one, two, three or four significant figures? As it is not clear, it is useful to use scientific notation to avoid any confusion with one non-zero digit on the left of the decimal point. 0.98 for example is written as 9.8×10^{-1}.

Measurements	Significant figures	Measurements	Significant figures
1000 s	unspecified	0.45 mol dm^{-3}	2
1×10^3 s	1	4.5×10^{-1} mol dm^{-3}	2
1.0×10^3 s	2	4.50×10^{-1} mol dm^{-3}	3
1.00×10^3 s	3	4.500×10^{-1} mol dm^{-3}	4
1.000×10^3 s	4	4.5000×10^{-1} mol dm^{-3}	5

Exercises

3 Express the following in standard notation:
  (a) 0.04 g   **(b)** 222 cm^3 **(c)** 0.030 g   **(d)** 30 °C
4 What is the number of significant figures in each of the following?
  (a) 15.50 cm^3 **(b)** 150 s   **(c)** 0.0123 g   **(d)** 150.0 g

Experimental errors

The experimental error in a result is the difference between the recorded value and the generally accepted or literature value. Errors can be categorized as **random** or **systematic**.

● **Examiner's hint:** You should compare your results to literature values where appropriate.

Random errors

When an experimenter approximates a reading, there is an equal probability of being too high or too low. This is a random error.

Random errors are caused by:
- the readability of the measuring instrument
- the effects of changes in the surroundings such as temperature variations and air currents
- insufficient data
- the observer misinterpreting the reading.

As they are random, the errors can be reduced through repeated measurements. This is why it is good practice to duplicate experiments when designing experiments. If the same person duplicates the experiment with the same result the results are **repeatable**, if several experimenters duplicate the results they are **reproducible**.

Suppose the mass of a piece of magnesium ribbon is measured several times and the following results obtained:

0.1234 g,   0.1232 g,   0.1233 g,   0.1234 g,   0.1235 g,   0.1236 g

$$\text{The average value} = \frac{(0.1234 + 0.1232 + 0.1233 + 0.1234 + 0.1235 + 0.1236)}{6} \text{ g}$$
$$= 0.1234 \text{ g}$$

The mass is reported as 0.1234 ± 0.0002 g as it is in the range 0.1232–0.1236 g.

Systematic errors

Systematic errors occur as a result of poor experimental design or procedure. They cannot be reduced by repeating the experiments. Suppose the top pan balance was incorrectly zeroed in the previous example and the following results were obtained:

0.1236 g,   0.1234 g,   0.1235 g,   0.1236 g,   0.1237 g,   0.1238g

All the values are too high by 0.0002 g.

$$\text{Average mass} = \frac{(0.1236 + 0.1234 + 0.1235 + 0.1236 + 0.1237 + 0.1238)}{6} \text{ g}$$
$$= 0.1236 \text{ g}$$

● **Examiner's hint:** When evaluating investigations, distinguish between systematic and random errors.

Examples of systematic errors:
- Measuring the volume of water from the top of the meniscus rather than the bottom will lead to volumes which are too high.
- Overshooting the volume of a liquid delivered in a titration will lead to volumes which are too high.
- Heat losses in an exothermic reaction will lead to smaller temperatures changes.

Systematic errors can be reduced by careful experimental design.

Accuracy and precision

The smaller the systematic error, the greater will be the **accuracy**. The smaller the random uncertainties, the greater will be the **precision**. The masses of magnesium in the earlier example are measured to the same precision but the first set of values is more accurate.

 Precise measurements have small random errors and are reproducible in repeated trials. Accurate measurements have small systematic errors and give a result close to the accepted value.

Precise measurements have small random errors and are reproducible in repeated trials. Accurate measurements have small systematic errors and give a result close to the accepted value.

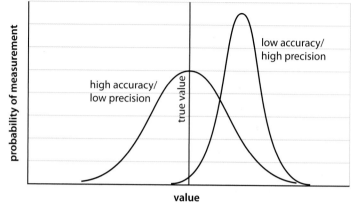

Exercise

5 Repeated measurements of a quantity can reduce the effects of:
   I   random errors
   II systematic errors

   A   I only
   B   II only
   C   I and II
   D   neither I or II.

11.2 Uncertainties in calculated results

Significant figures in calculations

Uncertainties in the raw data lead to uncertainties in processed data and it is important that these are propagated in a consistent way.

Multiplication and division

Consider a sample of sodium chloride with a mass of 5.00 ± 0.01 g and a volume of 2.3 ± 0.1 cm^3. What is its density?

Using a calculator:

$$\text{density } \rho = \frac{\text{mass}}{\text{volume}} = \frac{5.00}{2.3} = 2.173913043 \text{ g cm}^{-3}$$

Can we claim to know the density to such precision when the value is based on less precise raw data?

The value is misleading as the mass lies in the range 4.99–5.01 g and the volume is between 2.2–2.4 cm^3. The best we can do is to give a range of values for the density.

The maximum value is obtained when the maximum value for the mass is combined with the minimum value of the volume.

$$\rho_{max} = \frac{5.01}{2.2} = 2.277273 \text{ g cm}^{-3}$$

and the minimum value is obtained by combining the minimum mass with a maximum value for the volume.

$$\rho_{min} = \frac{4.99}{2.4} = 2.079167 \text{ g cm}^{-3}$$

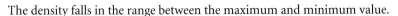

The density falls in the range between the maximum and minimum value.

The second significant figure is uncertain and the reported value must be reported to this precision as 2.2 g cm^{-3}. The precision of the density is limited by the volume measurement as this is the least precise.

This leads to a simple rule. Whenever you multiply or divide data, the answer should be quoted to the same number of significant figures as the least precise data.

> **Whenever you multiply or divide data, the answer should be quoted to the same number of significant figures as the least precise data.**

Addition and subtraction

When values are added or subtracted, the number of decimal places determine the precision of the calculated value.

Suppose we need the total mass of two pieces of zinc of mass 1.21 g and 0.56 g.

The total mass = 1.77 g can be given to two decimal places as the balance was precise to $\pm$ 0.01 in both cases.

Similarly when calculating a temperature increase from 25.2 °C to 35.2 °C. Temperature increase = 35.2–25.2 °C = 10.0 °C

> **Whenever you add or subtract data, the answer should be quoted to the same number of decimal places as the least precise value.**

Worked example

Report the total mass of solution prepared by adding 50 g of water to 1.00 g of sugar. Would the use of a more precise balance for the mass of sugar result in a more precise total mass?

● **Examiner's hint:** When evaluating procedures you should discuss the precision and accuracy of the measurements. You should specifically look at the procedure and use of equipment.

Solution

Total mass = 50 + 1.00 g = 51 g

The precision of the total is limited by the precision of the mass of the water. Using a more precise balance for the mass of sugar would have not improved the precision.

Percentage uncertainties and errors

An uncertainty of 1 s is more significant for time measurements of 10 s than it is for 100 s. It is helpful to express the uncertainty using absolute, fractional or percentage values.

The fractional uncertainty = absolute uncertainty/measured value.

This can be expressed as a percentage (see Key fact box below).

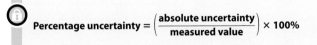

> **Percentage uncertainty** $= \left(\dfrac{\text{absolute uncertainty}}{\text{measured value}} \right) \times 100\%$

Percentage uncertainty should not be confused with **percentage error**. Percentage error is a measure of how close the **experimental value** is to the literature or accepted value.

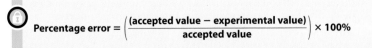

> **Percentage error** $= \left(\dfrac{\text{(accepted value − experimental value)}}{\text{accepted value}} \right) \times 100\%$

Propagation of uncertainties

Addition and subtraction

Consider two burette readings:
Initial reading/$\pm0.05\,cm^3$ = 15.05
Final reading/$\pm0.05\,cm^3$ = 37.20

What value should be reported for the volume delivered?
The initial reading is in the range: 15.00–15.10
The final reading is in the range: 37.15–37.25

> **When adding or subtracting measurements, the uncertainty is the sum of the absolute uncertainties.**

The maximum volume is formed by combining the maximum final reading with the minimum initial reading:
$$vol_{max} = 37.25–15.00 = 22.25\,cm^3$$

The minimum volume is formed by combining the minimum final volume with the maximum initial reading:
$$vol_{min} = 37.15–15.10 = 22.05\,cm^3$$
therefore vol = 22.15 $\pm0.1\,cm^3$

The volume depends on two measurements and the uncertainty is the sum of the two absolute uncertainties.

This result can be generalized.

When adding or subtracting measurements, the uncertainty is the sum of the absolute uncertainties.

Multiplication and division

Working out the uncertainty in calculated values can be a time-consuming process. Consider the density calculation:

	Value	Absolute uncertainty	% Uncertainty
mass/g	24.0	±0.5	$= \left(\frac{0.5}{24.0}\right) \times 100\% = 2\%$
volume/cm^3	2.0	±0.1	$= \left(\frac{0.1}{2.0}\right) \times 100 = 5\%$

> **When multiplying or dividing measurements, the total percentage uncertainty is the sum of the individual percentage uncertainties. The absolute uncertainty can then be calculated from the percentage uncertainty.**

	Value	Maximum value	Minimum value
density/g cm^{-3}	$= \frac{24.0}{2.0} = 12.00$	$= \frac{24.5}{1.9} = 12.89$	$= \frac{23.5}{2.1} = 11.19$

	Value	Absolute uncertainty	% Uncertainty
density/g cm^{-3}	12	$= 12.89 – 12.00 = \pm0.89$	$= \left(\frac{0.89}{12.00}\right) \times 100\%$ $= 7.4\%$

As discussed earlier the density should only be given to two significant figures given the uncertainty in the mass and volume values. The uncertainty in the calculated value of the density is 7% (given to one significant figure). This is equal to the **sum** of the uncertainties in the mass and volume values: (5 + 2% to the same level of accuracy). This approximate result provides us with a simple treatment of propagating uncertainties when multiplying and dividing measurements

When multiplying or dividing measurements, the total percentage uncertainty is the sum of the individual percentage uncertainties. The absolute uncertainty can then be calculated from the percentage uncertainty.

Worked example

The lengths of the sides of a wooden block are measured and the diagram shows the measured values with their uncertainties.

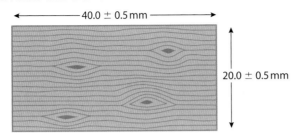

40.0 ± 0.5 mm

20.0 ± 0.5 mm

What is the percentage uncertainty in the calculated area of the block?

Solution

Area = 40.0×20.0 mm^2 = 800 mm^2 (area is given to three significant figures)
(% uncertainty of area) = (% uncertainty of length) + (% uncertainty of breadth)
% uncertainty of length = $(0.5/40.0) \times 100\%$ = 1.25%
% uncertainty of breadth = $(0.5/20.0) \times 100\%$ = 2.5%
% uncertainty of area = $1.25 + 2.5 = 3.75 = 4\%$
Absolute uncertainty = $(3.75/100) \times 800$ mm^2 = 30 mm^2
Area = 800 ± 30 mm^2

 To find the absolute uncertainty in a calculated value for ab or $\frac{a}{b}$:

1 Find the percentage uncertainty in a and b.
2 Add the percentage uncertainties of a and b to find the percentage uncertainty in the calculated value.
3 Convert this percentage uncertainty to an absolute value.

● **Examiner's hint:** The calculated uncertainty is generally quoted to not more than one significant figure if it is greater or equal to 2% of the answer and to not more than two significant figures if it is less than 2%. Intermediate values in calculations should not be rounded off to avoid unnecessary imprecision.

Exercise

6 The concentration of a solution of hydrochloric acid = 1.00 ± 0.05 mol dm^{-3} and the volume = 10.0 ± 0.1 cm^3. Calculate the number of moles and give the absolute uncertainty.

Discussing errors and uncertainties

An experimental conclusion must take into account any systematic errors and random uncertainties. You should recognize when the uncertainty of one of the measurements is much greater than the others as this will then have the major effect on the uncertainty of the final result. The approximate uncertainty can be taken as being due to that quantity alone. In thermometric experiments, for example, the thermometer often produces the most uncertain results, particularly for reactions which produce small temperature differences.

Can the difference between the experimental and literature value be explained in terms of the uncertainties of the measurements or were other systematic errors involved? This questions needs to be answered when evaluating an experimental procedure. Heat loss to the surroundings, for example, accounts for experimental enthalpy changes for exothermic reactions being lower than literature values. Suggested modifications, such as improved insulation to reduce heat exchange between the system and the surroundings, should attempt to reduce these errors. This is discussed in more detail in Chapter 5.

Exercise

7 What is the main source of error in experiments carried out to determine enthalpy changes in a school laboratory?
A uncertain volume measurements
B heat exchange with the surroundings
C uncertainties in the concentrations of the solutions
D impurities in the reagents

● **Examiner's hint:** There should be no variation in the precision of raw data measured with the same instrument and the same number of decimal places should be used. For data derived from processing raw data (for example, averages), the level of precision should be consistent with that of the raw data.

11.3 Graphical techniques

A graph is often the best method of presenting and analysing data. It shows the relationship between the **independent variable** plotted on the horizontal axis and the **dependent variable** on the vertical axis and gives an indication of the reliability of the measurements.

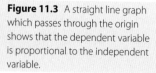

The independent variable is the *cause* and is plotted on the horizontal axis. The dependent variable is the *effect* and is plotted on the vertical axis.

Plotting graphs

When you draw a graph you should:

- Give the graph a title.
- Label the axes with both quantities and units.
- Use the available space as effectively as possible.
- Use sensible linear scales – there should be no uneven jumps.
- Plot all the points correctly.
- A line of best fit should be drawn smoothly and clearly. It does not have to go through all the points but should show the overall trend.
- Identify any points which do not agree with the general trend.
- Think carefully about the inclusion of the origin. The point $(0, 0)$ can be the most accurate data point or it can be irrelevant.

The 'best-fit' straight line

In many cases the best procedure is to find a way of plotting the data to produce a straight line. The 'best-fit' line passes as near to as many of the points as possible. For example, a straight line through the origin is the most appropriate way to join the set of points in Figure 11.3:

Figure 11.3 A straight line graph which passes through the origin shows that the dependent variable is proportional to the independent variable.

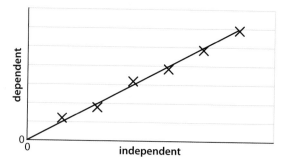

The best-fit line does not necessarily pass through any of the points plotted.

Two properties of a straight line are particularly useful: the gradient and the intercept.

Finding the gradient and the intercept

The equation for a straight line is $y = mx + c$.

x is the independent variable, y is the dependent variable, m is the gradient and c is the intercept on the vertical axis.

The gradient of a straight line is the increase in the dependent variable divided by the increase in the independent variable. The triangle used to calculate the gradient should be as large as possible.

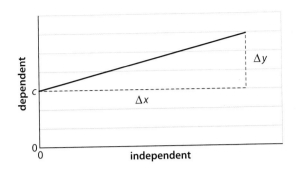

Figure 11.4

$$m = \frac{\Delta y}{\Delta x}$$

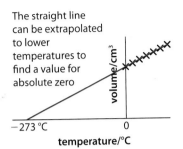

The straight line can be extrapolated to lower temperatures to find a value for absolute zero

Figure 11.5

The gradient of a straight line has units; the units of the vertical axis divided by the units of the horizontal axis. Sometimes a line has to be extended beyond the range of measurements of the graph. This is called **extrapolation**. Absolute zero, for example, can be found by extrapolating the volume/temperature graph for an ideal gas.

The process of assuming that the trend line applies between two points is called **interpolation**. The gradient of a curve at any point is the gradient of the tangent to the curve at that point.

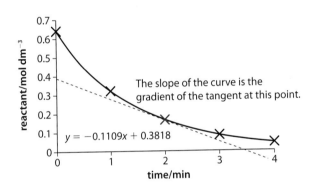

Figure 11.6 This graph shows how the concentration of a reactant decreases with time. The gradient of a slope is given by the gradient of the tangent at that point. The equation of the tangent was calculated by computer software. The rate at the point shown is -0.11 mol dm^{-3} min^{-1}. The negative value shows that that reactant concentration is decreasing with increasing time.

Errors and graphs

Systematic errors and random uncertainties can often be recognized from a graph. A graph combines the results of many measurements and so minimizes the effects of random uncertainties in the measurements.

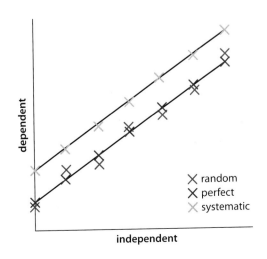

Figure 11.7 A systematic error produces a displaced straight line. Random uncertainties lead to points on both sides of the perfect straight line.

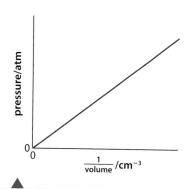

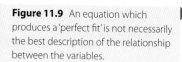

Figure 11.8 This straight line graph shows that the pressure is inversely proportional to the volume.

Choosing what to plot to produce a straight line

In many cases, the best way to analyse measurements is to find a way of plotting the data to produce a straight line.

For example the ideal gas equation:

$$PV = nRT$$

can be rearranged to give a straight line graph:

$$P = nRT\left(\frac{1}{V}\right)$$

The pressure is **inversely proportional** to the volume. This relationship is clearly seen when a graph of $1/V$ against P gives a straight line passing through the origin at constant temperature.

Using spreadsheets to plot graphs

There are many software packages which allow graphs to be plotted and analysed; the equation of the best fit line can be given and other properties calculated. For example, the tangent to the curve in Figure 11.6 has the equation:

$$y = -0.1109x + 0.3818$$

so the gradient of the tangent at that point $= -0.11$ mol dm^{-3} min^{-1}.

Care should, however, be taken when using these packages.

Figure 11.9 An equation which produces a 'perfect fit' is not necessarily the best description of the relationship between the variables. ▶

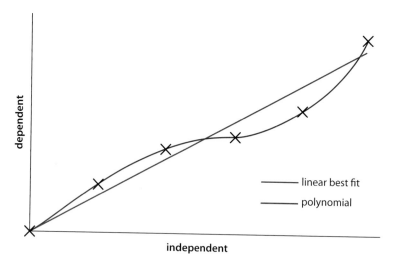

The set of data points can either be joined by a best fit straight line which does not pass through any point except the origin:

$$y = 1.6255x \ (R^2 = 0.9527)$$

or a polynomial which gives a perfect fit as indicated by the R^2 value of 1.

$$y = -0.0183x^5 + 0.2667x^4 - 1.2083x^3 + 1.7333x^2 + 1.4267x$$
$$(R^2 = 1)$$

The polynomial equation is unlikely, however, to be physically significant as any series of random points can fit a polynomial of sufficient length, just as any two points define a straight line.

1 The volume V, pressure P and temperature T and number of moles of an ideal gas are related by the ideal gas equation: $PV = nRT$. If the relationship between pressure and volume at constant temperature of a fixed amount of gas is investigated experimentally, which one of the following plots would produce a linear graph?

A P against V

B P against $\frac{1}{V}$

C $\frac{1}{P}$ against $\frac{1}{V}$

D No plot can produce a straight line.

2 The mass of an object is measured as 1.652 g and its volume 1.1 cm³. If the density (mass per unit volume) is calculated from these values, to how many significant figures should it be expressed?

A 1

B 2

C 3

D 4

3 The time for a 2.00 cm sample of magnesium ribbon to react completely with 20.0 cm³ of 1.00 mol dm⁻³ hydrochloric acid is measured four times by a student. The readings lie between 48.8 and 49.2 s. This measurement is best recorded as:

A 48.8 ± 0.2 s

B 48.8 ± 0.4 s.

C 49.0 ± 0.2 s

D 49.0 ± 0.4 s

4 A student measures the volume of water incorrectly by reading the top instead of the bottom of meniscus. This error will affect:

A neither the precision nor the accuracy of the readings

B only the accuracy of the readings

C only the precision of the readings

D both the precision and the accuracy of the readings

5 A known volume of sodium hydroxide solution is added to a conical flask using a pipette. A burette is used to measure the volume of hydrochloric acid needed to neutralize the sodium hydroxide. Which of the following would lead to a systematic error in the results?

I   the use of a wet burette

II the use of a wet pipette

III the use of a wet conical flask

A I and II only

B I and III only

C II and III only

D I, II and III

6 The number of significant figures that should be reported for the mass increase which is obtained by taking the difference between readings of 11.6235 g and 10.5805 g is:

A 3

B 4

C 5

D 6

7 A 0.266 g sample of zinc added to hydrochloric acid. 0.186 g of zinc is later recovered from the acid. What is the percentage mass loss of the zinc to the correct number of significant figures?

  A 30%

  B 30.1%

  C 30.07%

  D 30.08%

8 Which type of errors can cancel when differences in quantities are calculated?

  I random errors

  II systematic errors

  A I only

  B II only

  C I and II

  D neither I or II

9 The enthalpy change of the reaction:

$$CuSO_4(aq) + Zn(s) \rightarrow ZnSO_4(aq) + Cu(s)$$

was determined using the procedure outlined on page 103.

Assuming:

- zinc is in excess
- all the heat of reaction passes into the water

The molar enthalpy change can be calculated from the temperature change of the solution using the expression:

$$\Delta H = -c_{H_2O} \times \frac{(T_{final} - T_{initial})}{[CuSO_4]} \text{ kJ mol}^{-1}$$

where c_{H_2O} is the specific heat capacity of water, $T_{initial}$ is the temperature of the copper sulfate before zinc was added and T_{final} is the maximum temperature of the copper sulfate solution after the zinc was added.

The following results were recorded:

$T_{final} \pm 0.1/°C$	$T_{final} \pm 0.1/°C$
21.2	43.2

$[CuSO_4] = 0.500 \text{ mol dm}^{-3}$

(a) Calculate the temperature change during the reaction and give the absolute uncertainty.

(b) Calculate the percentage uncertainty of this temperature change.

(c) Calculate the molar enthalpy change of reaction.

(d) Assuming the uncertainties in any other measurements are negligible, determine the percentage uncertainty in the experimental value of the enthalpy change.

(e) Calculate the absolute uncertainty.

(f) The literature value for the standard enthalpy change of reaction $= -217 \text{ kJ mol}^{-1}$. Comment on any differences between the experimental and literature values.

10 The literature value for the enthalpy change of reaction between copper sulfate and zinc is -217 kJ mol^{-1}. An IB student followed the procedure outlined on page 103 to obtain an experimental value of -210 kJ mol^{-1}. Calculate the percentage error.

Modern analytical chemistry: Option A

Analytical chemistry plays a significant role in today's society. It is used in forensic, medical and industrial laboratories and helps us monitor our environment and check the quality of the food we eat and the materials we use. Early analysts relied on their senses to discover the identity of unknown substances, but we now have the ability to probe the structure of substances using electromagnetic radiation beyond the visible region. This has allowed us to discover how atoms are bonded in different molecules, and to detect minute quantities of substances in mixtures down to levels of parts per billion. No one method supplies us with all the information we need, so a battery of tools and range of skills have been developed. Many of the methods are automated, involving computers and robotics, but there is still room for more classical approaches. One of the most effective techniques for separating mixtures is chromatography, a method you probably first used to separate the pigments in different coloured inks. This chapter will discuss the underlying chemical principles of the different methods and show how chemists need to interpret information from different sources in their detective work.

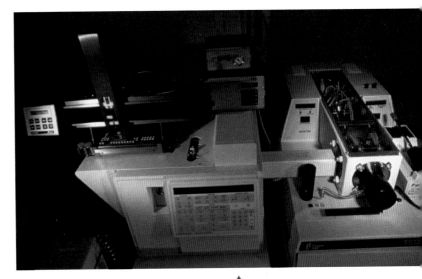

▲ A gas chromatography machine (left) connected to a mass spectrometer (right) in a forensic laboratory. This equipment is sensitive enough to detect minute quantities of illegal drugs in the hair of a suspect – weeks after any drugs were taken.

Assessment statements

A.1 Analytical techniques
A.1.1 State the reasons for using analytical techniques.
A.1.2 State that the structure of a compound can be determined by using information from a variety of analytical techniques singularly or in combination.

A.2 Principles of spectroscopy
A.2.1 Describe the electromagnetic spectrum.
A.2.2 Distinguish between absorption and emission spectra and how each is produced.
A.2.3 Describe the atomic and molecular processes in which absorption of energy takes place.

A.3 Infrared (IR) spectroscopy
A.3.1 Describe the operating principles of a double-beam IR spectrometer.
A.3.2 Describe how information from an IR spectrum can be used to identify bonds.
A.3.3 Explain what occurs at a molecular level during the absorption of IR radiation by molecules.
A.3.4 Analyse IR spectra of organic compounds.

A.4 Mass spectrometry

A.4.1   Determine the molecular mass of a compound from the molecular ion peak.

A.4.2   Analyse fragmentation patterns in a mass spectrum to find the structure of a compound.

A.5 Nuclear magnetic resonance (NMR) spectroscopy

A.5.1   Deduce the structure of a compound given information from its ^{1}H NMR spectrum.

A.5.2   Outline how NMR is used in body scanners.

A.6. Atomic absorption (AA) spectroscopy

A.6.1   State the uses of AA spectroscopy.

A.6.2   Describe the principles of atomic absorption.

A.6.3   Describe the use of each of the following components of the AA spectrophotometer: fuel, atomizer, monochromatic light source, monochromatic detector, read-out.

A.6.4   Determine the concentration of a solution from a calibration curve.

A.7 Chromatography

A.7.1   State the reasons for using chromatography.

A.7.2   Explain that all chromatographic techniques involve adsorption on a stationary phase and partition between a stationary phase and a mobile phase.

A.7.3   Outline the use of paper chromatography, thin-layer chromatography (TLC) and column chromatography.

 # **A.1 Analytical techniques**

Chemical analysts identify and characterize unknown substances, determine the composition of a mixture and identify impurities. Their work can be divided into:

- **Qualitative analysis:** the detection of the *presence* but not the quantity of a substance in a mixture, for example, forbidden substances in an athlete's blood.
- **Quantitative analysis:** the measurement of the *quantity* of a particular substance in a mixture, for example, the alcohol levels in a driver's breath, or the toxic metal levels in a sample of river water.
- **Structural analysis:** a description of how the atoms are arranged in molecular structures, for example, the determination of the structure of a naturally occurring or artificial product.

Many instruments are available to provide structural analysis but they generally work by analysing the effect of different forms of energy on the substance analysed.

- **Infrared spectroscopy** is used to identify the bonds in a molecule.
- **Mass spectrometry** is used to determine relative atomic and molecular masses. The fragmentation pattern can be used as a fingerprint technique to identify unknown substances or for evidence for the arrangements of atoms in a molecule.

- **Nuclear magnetic resonance spectroscopy** is used to show the chemical environment of certain atoms (hydrogen, carbon, phosphorus and fluorine) in a molecule and so gives vital structural information.

No one method is definitive, but a combination of techniques can provide strong evidence for the structure.

A.2 Principles of spectroscopy

The electromagnetic spectrum

Spectroscopy is the main method we have of probing into the atom and the molecule. There is a type of spectroscopy for each of the main regions of the electromagnetic spectrum. As discussed in Chapter 2, electromagnetic radiation is a form of energy transferred by waves and characterized by its:

- **wavelength (λ)**: the distance between successive crests or troughs
- **frequency (f)**: the number of waves which pass a point every second.

The energy of electromagnetic radiation is carried in packets of energy called **photons** or quanta. The energy of the radiation is related to the frequency by Planck's equation: $E = hf$, where h is Planck's constant (6.63×10^{-34} J s).

The physical analytical techniques now available to us are due to advances in technology. How does technology extend and modify the capabilities of our senses? What are the knowledge implications of this?

The energy of a photon of radiation is related its frequency $E = hf$

Worked example

Calculate the energy of a photon of visible light with a frequency of 3.0×10^{14} s^{-1}. Express your answer in kJ mol^{-1}

Solution

$E = hf$

$E = 6.63 \times 10^{-34}$ J s $\times 3.0 \times 10^{14}$ s^{-1}

$\quad = 1.989 \times 10^{-19}$ J

The energy of one mole of photons $= 6.02 \times 10^{23} \times 1.989 \times 10^{-19}$ J mol^{-1}

$\quad = 120$ kJ mol^{-1}

The distance between two successive crests (or troughs) is called the wavelength. The frequency of the wave is the number of waves which pass a point in one second. The wavelength and frequency are related by the equation $c = f\lambda$ where c is the speed of the wave.

Exercises

1 A radio station transmits a frequency of 1.0×10^5 s^{-1}. What is the energy of one mole of photons at this frequency?

2 A beam of IR radiation has energy of 4.00×10^{-20} J per photon. Calculate the frequency of the radiation.

The electromagnetic spectrum is summarized below.

Type of electromagnetic radiation	Typical frequency (f)/s^{-1}	Typical wavelength (λ)/m
radio waves (low energy)	3×10^6	10^2
microwaves	3×10^{10}	10^{-2}
infrared	3×10^{12}	10^{-4}
visible	3×10^{14}	10^{-6}
ultraviolet	3×10^{16}	10^{-8}
X rays	3×10^{17}	10^{-9}
gamma rays	greater than 3×10^{18}	less than 10^{-10}

It should be noted from the table that $f \times \lambda = 3.0 \times 10^8$ m s$^{-1} = c$, the speed of light. This gives $f = \dfrac{c}{\lambda}$.

In infrared spectroscopy, the frequency of radiation is often measured as number of waves per centimetre (cm^{-1}), also called the **wavenumber**.

Worked example

Calculate the wavenumber in cm^{-1} for an IR wave with a frequency of $3 \times 10^{13}\ s^{-1}$.

Solution

$$\frac{1}{\lambda} = \frac{f}{c} = \frac{3 \times 10^{13}}{3 \times 10^{8}} = 1 \times 10^{5}\ m^{-1} = 1000\ cm^{-1}$$

As well as transferring energy, the electromagnetic radiation can also be viewed as a carrier of information. Different regions give different types of information, by interacting with substances in different ways.

- **Radio waves** can be absorbed by certain nuclei causing them to reverse their spin. They are used in NMR and can give information about the environment of certain atoms.
- **Microwaves** cause molecules to increase their rotational energy. This can give information about bond lengths. It is not necessary to know the details at this level.
- **Infrared radiation** is absorbed by certain bonds causing them to stretch or bend. This gives information about the bonds in a molecule.
- **Visible and ultraviolet light** can produce electronic transitions and give information about the electronic energy levels within the atom or molecule.
- **X rays** are produced when electrons make transitions between inner energy levels. They have wavelengths of the same order of magnitude as the inter-atomic distances in crystals and produce diffraction patterns which provide direct evidence of atomic structure. It is not necessary to know the details at this level.
- **Gamma rays** cause changes in the energy of atomic nuclei. They are not of direct concern to the analytical chemist.

Microwave cookers heat food very quickly as the radiation penetrates deep into the food. The frequency used corresponds to the energy needed to rotate water molecules, which are present in most food. The radiation absorbed by the water molecules makes them rotate faster. As they bump into other molecules the extra energy is spread throughout the food and the temperature rises.

Exercises

3 Suggest why the absorptions obtained from ^{1}H NMR spectroscopy occur at much lower frequencies than those obtained from IR spectroscopy.

4 Which of the following types of electromagnetic radiation has photons of the highest energy?
   A gamma rays   B IR radiation   C microwaves   D UV light

Absorption and emission spectra

When electromagnetic radiation is passed through a collection of atoms or molecules, some of the radiation is absorbed and used to excite the atoms or molecules from a lower energy level to a higher energy level. The spectrometer analyses the transmitted radiation relative to the incident radiation and an **absorption spectrum** is produced. Electrons move to higher energy levels, for example, when radiation from the ultraviolet and visible region are absorbed. Molecules increase their vibrational energy by moving to a higher vibrational energy level when infrared radiation is absorbed.

Figure 12.1 The origin of emission and absorption spectra. An emission spectrum is produced when a molecule moves from a higher to a lower level. An absorption spectra shows the radiation absorbed as atoms/molecules move from a lower to a higher energy level.

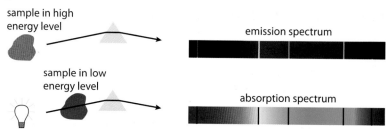

sample in high
energy level

emission spectrum

sample in low
energy level

absorption spectrum

An **emission spectrum** is produced when the radiation from an excited sample is analysed. The line spectra of hydrogen, produced when excited electrons fall from higher to lower energy levels was discussed in Chapter 2. Each element produces its own distinctive emission spectrum which can be used as a 'fingerprint' to identify the element.

A.3 Infrared (IR) spectroscopy

The natural frequency of a chemical bond

A chemical bond can be thought of as a spring. Each bond vibrates and bends at a natural frequency which depends on the bond strength and the masses of the atoms. Light atoms, for example, vibrate at higher frequencies than heavier atoms and multiple bonds vibrate at higher frequencies than single bonds.

Simple diatomic molecules such as HCl, HBr and HI, can only vibrate when the bond stretches. The HCl bond has the highest frequency of these three as it has the largest bond energy and the halogen atom with the smallest relative atomic mass.

In more complex molecules, different types of vibration can occur, such as bending, so that a complex range of frequencies is present.

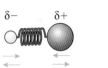

Figure 12.2 IR radiation can cause a bond to stretch or bend.

Using infrared radiation to excite molecules

The energy needed to excite the bonds in a molecule to make them vibrate with greater amplitude, occurs in the IR region. A bond will only interact with the electromagnetic infrared radiation, however, if it is polar. The presence of separate areas of partial positive and negative charge in a molecule allows the electric field component of the electromagnetic wave to excite the vibrational energy of the molecule. The change in the vibrational energy produces a corresponding change in the dipole moment of the molecule. The intensity of the absorptions depends on the polarity of the bond. Symmetrical non-polar bonds in $N\equiv N$ and $O=O$ do not absorb radiation, as they cannot interact with an electric field.

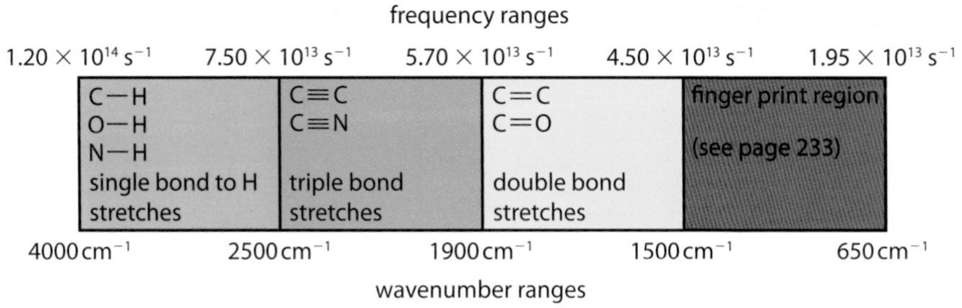

frequency ranges

1.20×10^{14} s^{-1}	7.50×10^{13} s^{-1}	5.70×10^{13} s^{-1}	4.50×10^{13} s^{-1}	1.95×10^{13} s^{-1}
C—H O—H N—H single bond to H stretches	C≡C C≡N triple bond stretches	C=C C=O double bond stretches	finger print region (see page 233)	
4000 cm^{-1}	2500 cm^{-1}	1900 cm^{-1}	1500 cm^{-1}	650 cm^{-1}

wavenumber ranges

Figure 12.3 The natural frequencies of some covalent bonds.

The double-beam IR spectrometer

Many spectroscopic methods use a double-beam method, in which one beam is passed through the sample under investigation and the other through a reference sample. In the double-beam IR spectrometer, IR radiation from a heated filament is split into two parallel beams. Radiation is absorbed by the sample when it has the same frequency as any of the natural bond frequencies in the sample molecules. Other frequencies simply pass through the sample. The sample and reference beams are analysed and differences in the intensities of the two beams measured by the detector at each wavenumber and fed into the recorder, which produces a spectrum. When the radiation is not absorbed by the sample, the transmittance is 100% but when radiation is absorbed the transmittance falls to lower values. The baseline of the spectrum corresponds to 100% transmittance and signals are recorded when the transmittance falls as the radiation is absorbed.

Figure 12.4 Design of a typical double beam infrared spectrometer. The radiation is split into two beams. One is passed through the sample and the other through a reference. The detector measures the absorbance of radiation.

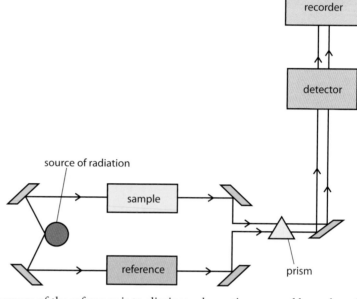

Scientists using an IR spectrometer. The plot of absorption across the infrared spectrum is displayed on the screen.

The purpose of the reference is to eliminate absorptions caused by carbon dioxide and water vapour in the air, or absorptions from the bonds in the solvent used.

Matching wavenumbers with bonds

The absorption of particular wavenumbers of IR radiation helps the chemist to identify the bonds in a molecule. The precise position of the absorption depends on the environment of the bond, so a range of wavenumbers is used to identify different bonds.

Table 1 Characteristic infrared absorption bands.

Bond	Wavenumber/cm^{-1}
C—O	1050–1410
C=C	1610–1680
C=O	1700–1750
C≡C	2100–2260
O—H (hydrogen bonded in acids)	2500–3300
C—H	2850–3100
O—H (hydrogen bonded in alcohols)	3200–3600
N—H	3300–3500

Explore the relationship between the IR spectra and molecular vibrations in different compounds. Now go to www.heinemann.co.uk/hotlinks, insert the express code 4259P and click on this activity.

You are not expected to remember the characteristic wavenumbers. A more complete list is given in Table 17 of the IB Data booklet.

Exercise

5 A molecule absorbs IR at a wavenumber of 1720 cm^{-1}. Which functional group could account for this absorption?
  I aldehydes
  II esters
  III ethers

As hydrogen bonding broadens the absorptions, its presence can also be detected. For example, hydrogen bonding between hydroxyl groups changes the O—H vibration; it makes the absorption much broader and shifts it to a lower frequency. Molecules with several bonds can vibrate in many different ways and with many different frequencies. The complex pattern can be used as a fingerprint to be matched against the recorded spectra of known compounds in a database. A comparison of the spectra of a sample with that of a pure compound can also be used as a test of purity.

● **Examiner's hint:** It is important to note that IR allows you to identify the bonds present in a molecule but it is not always able to distinguish between different functional groups which may contain the same bonds.

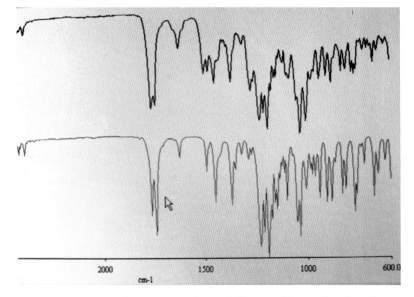

◀ IR spectrum of the illegal drug heroin (blue) compared to that of an unknown sample (black). The near perfect match indicates that the sample contains a high percentage of heroin. Spectral analysis such as this can identify unknown compounds in mixtures or from samples taken from clothing or equipment. The technique is widely used in forensic science.

Consider the spectrum of propanone shown below. As discussed earlier, the base line at the top corresponds to 100% transmittance and the key features are the troughs which occur at the natural frequencies of the bonds present in the molecule.

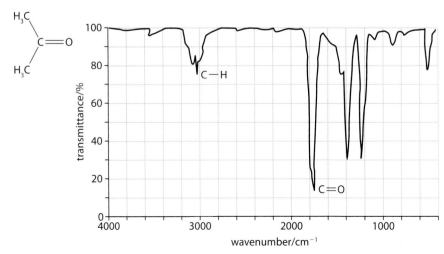

◀ **Figure 12.5** The molecular structure and spectrum of propanone.

The absorption at just below 1800 cm^{-1} shows the presence of the C=O bond and the absorption at just below 3000 cm^{-1} is due to the presence of the C—H bond. The more polar C=O bond produces the more intense absorption. The presence of the C—H bond can again been seen at just below 3000 cm^{-1} in the spectrum of ethanol shown below. The broad peak at just below 3400 cm^{-1} shows the presence of hydrogen bonding which is due to the hydroxyl (OH) group.

Figure 12.6 Infrared spectrum of ethanol. Note that the horizontal axis has a non-linear scale. This is common for many instruments, so you should always take care when reading off values for the wavenumbers of the absorptions.

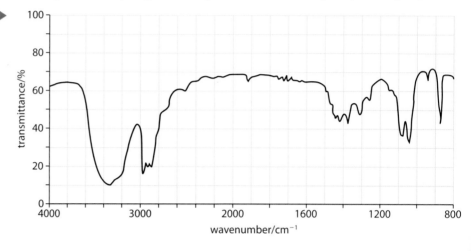

Exercises

6 A bond has an IR absorption of 2100 cm^{-1}. What is the wavelength of the radiation and the natural frequency of the bond?

7 State what occurs at the molecular level when infrared radiation is absorbed.

8 Cyclohexane and hex-1-ene are isomers. Suggest how you could use infrared spectroscopy to distinguish between the two compounds.

9 The intoximeter, used by the police to test the alcohol levels in their breath, measures the absorbance at 2900 cm^{-1}. Identify the bond which causes ethanol to absorb at this wavenumber.

10 A molecule has the molecular formula C_2H_6O. The infrared spectrum shows an absorption band at 1000–1300 cm^{-1}, but no absorption bands above 3000 cm^{-1}. Deduce its structure.

Access this AIST database to see the spectra of many organic compounds.
Now go to www.heinemann.co.uk/hotlinks, insert the express code 4259P and click on this activity.

The Spectra Database for Organic Compounds was opened in 1997 and has given the public free access to the spectra of many organic compounds. The total accumulated number of visits reached 146 million by the end of August 2006 and the database has sent information from Japan to all over the world. The open exchange of information is a key element of scientific progress.

A.4 Mass spectrometry

Determining the molecular mass of a compound

The mass spectrometer was introduced in Chapter 2 where we saw it was used to find the mass of individual atoms and the relative abundances of different isotopes. The instrument can be used in a similar way to find the relative molecular mass of a compound. If the empirical formula is also known from compositional analysis, the molecular formula can be determined. The technique also provides useful clues about the molecular structure.

Exercise

11 An unknown compound has the following mass composition:

C, 40.0 %;   H, 6.7%;   O, 53.3%.

The largest mass recorded on the mass spectra of the compound corresponds to a relative molecular mass of 60. Calculate the empirical formula and determine the molecular formula of the compound.

The IR spectrum shows an absorption band at 1700 cm^{-1} and a very broad band between 2500−3300 cm^{-1}. Deduce its molecular structure.

Fragmentation patterns

As we discussed in Chapter 2, the ionization process in the mass spectrometer involves an electron from an electron gun hitting the incident species and removing an electron:

$$X(g) + e^- \rightarrow X^+(g) + 2e^-$$

The collision can be so energetic that it causes the molecule to break up into different fragments. The largest mass peak in the previous exercise corresponded to a parent ion passing through the instrument unscathed, but other ions, produced as a result of this break up, are also detected.

This **fragmentation pattern** can provide useful evidence for the structure of the compound. A chemist pieces together the fragments to form a picture of the complete molecule, in the same way an archaeologist finds clues about the past from the pieces they find in the ground.

The molecular ion or parent ion is formed when a molecule loses one electron but otherwise remains unchanged.

The structure of ethanol and its mass spectrum are shown below.

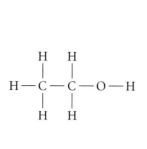

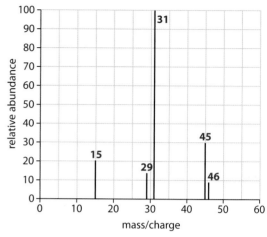

The molecular ion corresponds to the peak at 46. The ion that appears at a relative mass of 45, one less than the parent ion, corresponds to the loss of a H atom. A fragmentation path which explains the spectra is shown below.

Figure 12.7 Possible fragmentation pattern produced when ethanol is bombarded with high energy electrons.

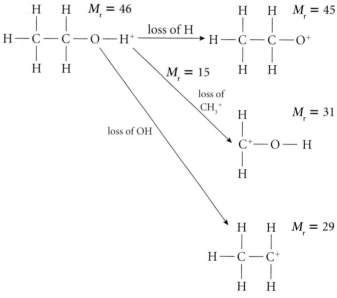

The parent ion can break up into smaller ions in a mass spectrometer. A compound is characterized by this fragmentation pattern.

For each fragmentation, one of the products keeps the positive charge. So, for example, if the C—C bond breaks in the ethanol molecules, two outcomes are possible:

Figure 12.8 Two possible ways in which the C—C bond can break in ethanol. Only the charged species can be detected, as electric and magnetic fields have no effect on neutral fragments.

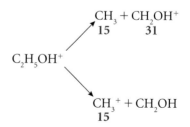

This explains the presence of peaks at both 15 and 31. Generally the fragment that gives the most stable ion is formed. The cleavage of the C—O bond leads to the formation of the $C_2H_5^+$ ion in preference to the OH^+ ion in the example above, so there is an observed peak at 29 but not at 17.

Full analysis of the mass spectrum can be a complex process. We make use of the mass difference between the peaks to identify the pieces which have fallen off. You are expected to recognize the following mass fragments.

Mass difference	Possible group
15	CH_3^+
29	$C_2H_5^+$ or CHO^+
31	CH_3O^+
45	$COOH^+$

● **Examiner's hint:** Don't forget the positive charge on the ions when identifying different fragments.

Worked example

A molecule with an empirical formula CH_2O has the simplified mass spectrum below. Deduce the molecular formula and possible structure of the compound.

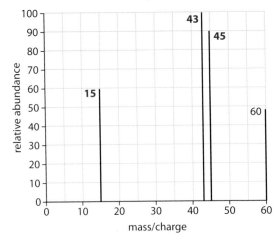

Solution

Empirical formula = CH_2O; molecular formula = $C_nH_{2n}O_n$

We can see that the parent ion has a relative mass of 60.

$M_r = n(12.01) + 2n(1.01) + n(16.00) = 30.03n$

$n = \dfrac{60}{30.03} = 2$

Molecular formula = $C_2H_4O_2$

From the spectrum we can identify the following peaks:

Peaks	Explanation
15 (60–45)	presence of CH_3^+ loss of COOH from molecule
43 (60–17)	presence of $C_2H_3O^+$ loss of OH from molecule
45 (60–15)	presence of $COOH^+$ loss of CH_3 from molecule

The structure consistent with this fragmentation pattern is:

$$\begin{array}{ccc} H & O & \\ | & || & \\ H-C-C-O-H^+ \\ | & & \\ H & & \end{array}$$

Exercises

12 The mass spectra of two compounds are shown below. One is propanone (CH_3COCH_3) and the other is propanal (CH_3CH_2CHO). Identify the compound in each case and explain the similarities and differences between the two spectra.

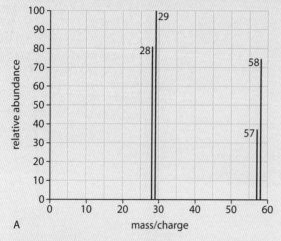

A   mass/charge

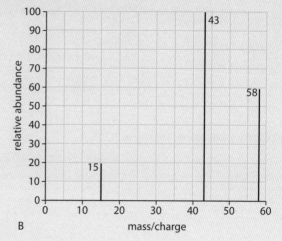

B   mass/charge

13 The simplified mass spectrum of a compound with empirical formula C_2H_5 is shown below.
  (a) Explain which ions give rise to the peaks shown.
  (b) Deduce the molecular structure of the compound.

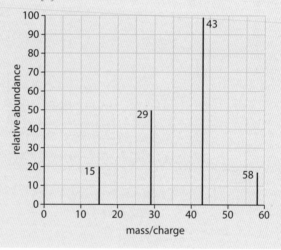

mass/charge

Screen display of a nuclear magnetic resonance spectrum. In the background, a scientist is seen loading a sample into the NMR spectrometer's magnet.

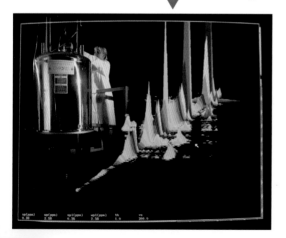

A.5 # Nuclear magnetic resonance (NMR) spectroscopy

The principles of NMR

Nuclear magnetic resonance spectroscopy, a powerful technique for finding the structure and shape of molecules, depends on a combination of nuclear physics and chemistry. The nuclei of atoms with an odd number of protons such as ^1H, ^{13}C, ^{19}F and ^{31}P, spin and behave like tiny bar magnets. If placed in an external magnetic field, some of these nuclei will line up with an applied field and, if they have sufficient energy, some will line up against it. This arrangement leads to two nuclear energy levels; the energy needed for the nuclei to reverse their spin and change their orientation in a magnetic field can be provided by radio waves.

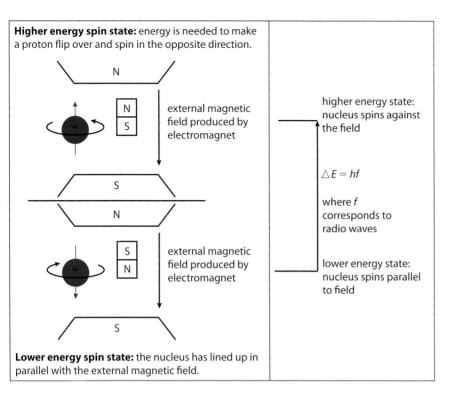

Higher energy spin state: energy is needed to make a proton flip over and spin in the opposite direction.

external magnetic field produced by electromagnet

external magnetic field produced by electromagnet

higher energy state: nucleus spins against the field

$$\triangle E = hf$$

where f corresponds to radio waves

lower energy state: nucleus spins parallel to field

Lower energy spin state: the nucleus has lined up in parallel with the external magnetic field.

Figure 12.9 A spinning nucleus can be thought of as a small bar magnet. The energy between the two states depends on the strength of the external magnetic field applied by an electromagnet and the chemical environment of the nucleus.

In practice, a sample is placed in an electromagnet. The field strength is varied until the radio waves have the exact frequency needed to make the nuclei flip over and spin in the opposite direction. This is called **resonance** and can be detected electronically and recorded in the form of a spectrum.

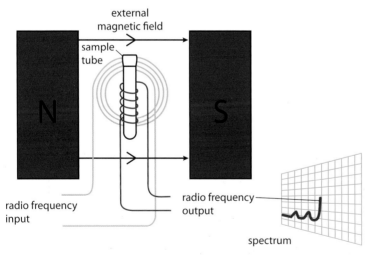

external magnetic field

sample tube

radio frequency input

radio frequency output

spectrum

Figure 12.10 Simplied diagram of a NMR spectrometer. The strength of the magnetic field is varied until the radio waves cause the nuclei to flip from one energy level to another. NMR spectroscopy is non-invasive as the small quantities of the sample are recovered unharmed after the experiment.

The chemical shift

As electrons shield the nucleus from the full effects of external magnetic field, differences in electron distribution produce different energy separations between the two spin energy levels. The technique is a very useful analytical tool, as nuclei in different **chemical environments** produce different signals in the spectrum. Proton or ^{1}H NMR is particularly useful. The hydrogen nuclei, present in all organic molecules, effectively act as spies and give information about their position in a molecule.

The signals are measured against the standard signal produced by the twelve hydrogen nuclei in tetramethylsilane (**TMS**) the structure of which is shown opposite.

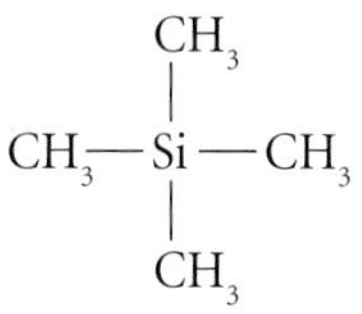

$$CH_3 - Si - CH_3$$
(with CH_3 above and CH_3 below the Si)

Figure 12.11 Tetramethylsilane (TMS). Each of the twelve hydrogen atoms is bonded to a carbon, which in turn is bonded to two other hydrogen atoms and a silicon atom, which is bonded to three methyl groups. They are all in the same environment so one signal is recorded.

The position of the NMR signal relative to this standard is called the **chemical shift** of the proton. Hydrogen nuclei in particular environments have characteristic chemical shifts. Some examples are given below. A more complete list is given in the Table 17 of the IB Data booklet.

Type of proton	Chemical shift δ/ppm
TMS	0
R—CH₃	0.9–1.0
R—C(=O)—H	9.4–10.0
R—C(CH₃)(=O)	2.2–2.7
R—OH	0.5–6.5*
R—CH₂—O	3.6
R—CH₂—R	1.3–1.4

* Signals from the hydrogen atoms in the —OH groups are very variable owing to hydrogen bonding.

Interpreting ¹H NMR spectra

The NMR spectrum of ethanal is shown below.

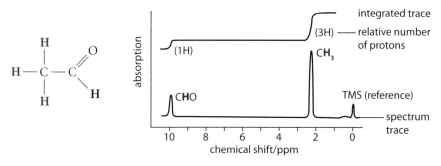

Figure 12.12 The NMR spectrum of ethanal shows two peaks because the hydrogen atoms are in two different environments. The **integrated trace** indicates the relative number of hydrogen atoms in the two environments.

● **Examiner's hint:** Avoid losing marks through carelessness. The number of peaks does not simply give the number of different chemical environments – it gives the number of different chemical environments in which hydrogen atoms are located.

The spectrum trace has a peak at 9.7, which corresponds to the CHO proton and a peak at 2.1 which corresponds the three protons in the CH₃ group. The area under the CH₃ peak is three times larger than that under the CHO peak as it indicates the relative number of protons in the different environment. The integrated trace gives this information more directly, as it goes up in steps which are proportional to the number of protons.

Worked example

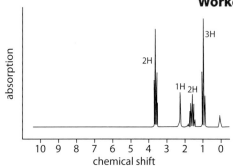

The NMR spectrum of a compound which has the molecular formula C₃H₈O is shown on the left.

(a) Draw the full structural formulas and give the names of the three possible isomers of C₃H₈O.

(b) Identify the substance responsible for the peak at 0 ppm and state its purpose.

(c) Identify the unknown compound from the number of peaks in the spectrum.

(d) Identify the group responsible for the signal at 0.9 ppm.

Solution

(a) The structures and names are:

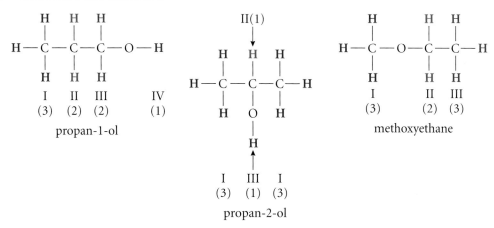

propan-1-ol

propan-2-ol

methoxyethane

(b) Tetramethylsilane is used as a reference standard.

(c) For each structure, I–IV identifies the different environments of the H atoms in the molecule. 1–3 represents the number of atoms in each environment. There are four peaks in the spectrum. Propan-1-ol has four peaks with the correct areas.

(d) Peaks at 0.9 pmm correspond to the CH_3 group.

Exercises

14 How many peaks will the following compounds show in their ^1H NMR spectra?

(a)
$$CH_3-\overset{\overset{\displaystyle O}{\|}}{C}-O-CH_3$$

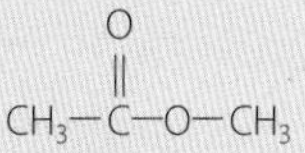

(b) CH_3-O-CH_3

(c)
$$CH_3-\overset{\overset{\displaystyle CH_3}{|}}{\underset{\underset{\displaystyle CH_3}{|}}{C}}-CH_3$$

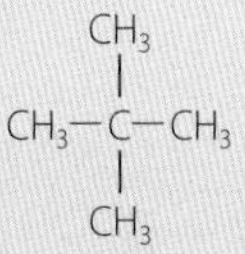

(d)
$$CH_3-\overset{\overset{\displaystyle CH_3}{|}}{\underset{\underset{\displaystyle Cl}{|}}{C}}-H$$

● **Examiner's hint:** Include all H atoms when asked to draw a molecular structure.

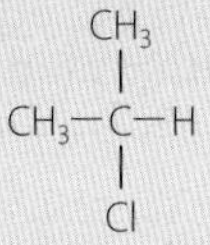

15 The NMR spectrum of a hydrocarbon with empirical formula C_3H_7 is shown. Use the NMR spectrum to identify the compound.

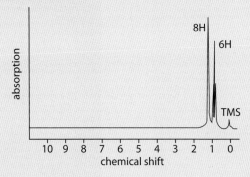

16 Describe and explain the ^1H NMR spectrum of CH_3CH_2OH.

Magnetic resonance imaging

NMR is the basis of the diagnostic medical tool known as **magnetic resonance imaging**. It is known as **MRI**, a label chosen to reduce possible public concerns about nuclear technology. The water which makes up about 70% of the human body is in very different environments and these differences can be measured using NMR. As discussed earlier, the technique is non-invasive and unlike the medical use of X-rays, it is extremely sensitive to differences in parts of the body with high water content. It is used to study blood flow, tissues, muscles and other soft parts of the body. The hydrogen atoms in carbohydrates, proteins and fats are also sources of information. Radio waves are low energy waves with no known side effects.

The patient is placed in a strong magnetic field chamber and bombarded with pulses of radio waves. The signals produced are decoded by a computer to produce a two- or three-dimensional image. MRI is ideal for detecting brain tumours, infections in the brain, spine and joints, and in diagnosing strokes and multiple sclerosis.

MRI produces 'slice' images through the body. The patient lies beneath a powerful magnet, which makes the nuclei of the hydrogen atoms in the patient's body line up parallel to each other. Radio wave pulses emitted by the scanner knock the hydrogen nuclei out of alignment. MRI is useful for studying soft tissues like the brain and spinal cord.

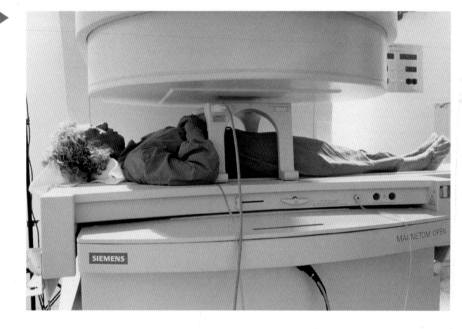

Exercise

17 The image on the right is of the human brain. Such images are used to study soft tissues and muscles. State how the image was produced and give one advantage of the technique.

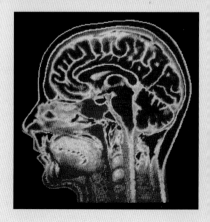

A.6 Atomic absorption (AA) spectroscopy

The principles of atomic absorption

We saw in Chapter 2 that an emission spectrum is produced when electrons fall from a higher to lower energy levels and an absorption spectrum is produced when electrons are excited from a lower to a higher energy level. If light from the emission spectrum of an element is passed through a sample, it will be absorbed if it meets atoms of the same element in its path. The degree of absorption gives a measure of the concentration of the atoms present in the sample. As the sample is vaporized and broken into atoms by a flame, **atomic absorption spectroscopy** allows us to determine the concentration of atoms irrespective of how they are combined together. It is an extremely sensitive method, allowing concentrations as low as one part per billion to be measured. Atomic absorption spectroscopy is also quicker than conventional methods such as volumetric analysis. It is used to determine the concentration of metals in, for example, water, soils, food and blood.

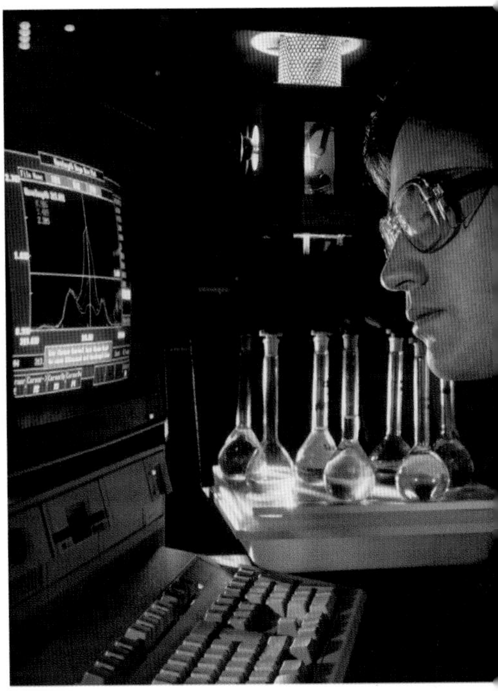

Scientist using an atomic absorption (AA) spectrometer to analyse water samples. Concentrations of one part of metal (lead, for example) in a million million parts can be measured. The method can be used to detect pollution of water by heavy metals.

Atomic absorption spectrometer

A simplified diagram of an atomic absorption spectrometer is shown below:

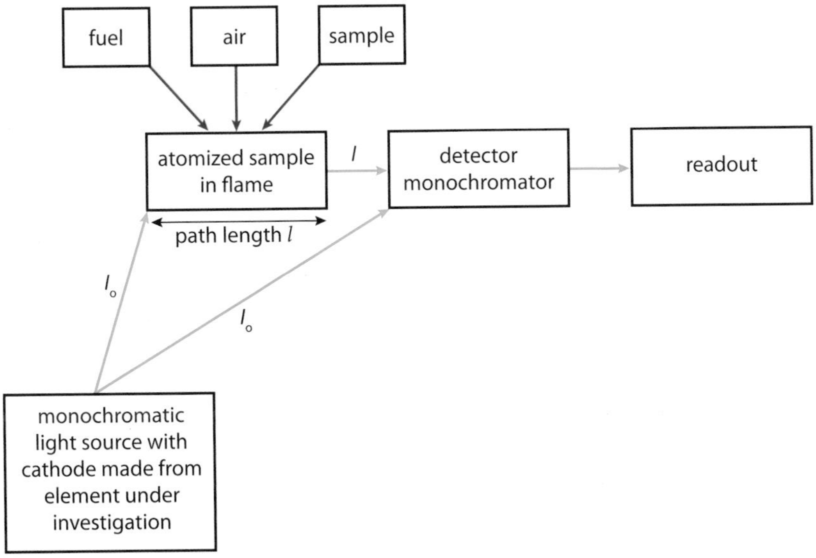

Figure 12.13 The blue lines show the path of the light through the spectrometer. Monochromatic light of intensity I_0 enters the atomized sample. The intensity falls to I as some of the light is absorbed by atoms in the sample.

The monochromatic source

The source lamp has a hollow cathode containing the vapour of the element under investigation. For example, if the concentration of manganese in the sample is measured, the source lamp will have a hollow manganese cathode. The light emitted by the manganese atoms in the cathode will be absorbed by any manganese atoms in the flame. If the concentrations of different elements in the sample are needed, the light source is changed. The monochromator is used to select light of one particular frequency emitted by the element. The wavelength of maximum absorbance (λ_{max}) for the element under investigation is generally used.

The atomizer

The red lines in Fig 12.13 outline how the flame is atomized:

- A solution of the sample enters the apparatus as a fine spray.
- The spray is mixed with fuel (e.g. ethyne, C_2H_2) and air and carried into the flame.
- At temperatures above 2000 K the solvent evaporates and gaseous atoms of the sample are formed.

The temperature of the flame needs to be controlled otherwise ions which have a different spectra will be produced.

Detection

Modern machines use the double beam principle discussed in Section A.3. One beam from the hollow cathode passes through the flame and the other does not. The difference between these beams is detected by converting it into an electrical signal by a photomultiplier. This is the amount of light absorbed by atoms in the flame.

Determining the concentration of an element from a calibration curve

The amount of light absorbed by atoms can be used to measure the concentration of the element in a sample. Beer–Lambert's Law relates the absorbance (A) to the concentration (c) and path length (l), for dilute solutions.

$$\text{absorbance, } A = \log_{10}\left(\frac{I_0}{I}\right) = \varepsilon c l$$

where ε, the molar absorptivity, is the absorbance of a 1.0 mol dm^{-3} solution in a 1 cm cell. It depends on the wavelength of the incident radiation. It is usual to carry out experiments involving the Beer–Lambert law at the wavelength of maximum absorption ε_{max}.

This law cannot be used directly to calculate the concentration because of variations in the atomization efficiency, and the concentration and path length of the sample atoms. Instead a calibration curve is used. The absorbance of standard solutions with a range of concentrations is measured and plotted on a graph. The concentration of the atoms in the sample can then be read off once the absorbance is known.

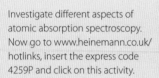

This animation shows details of each step in atomic adsorption spectroscopy.
Now go to www.heinemann.co.uk/hotlinks, insert the express code 4259P and click on this activity.

Investigate different aspects of atomic absorption spectroscopy.
Now go to www.heinemann.co.uk/hotlinks, insert the express code 4259P and click on this activity.

Figure 12.14 A calibration curve used to find the concentration of an element in a sample. The graph is linear for low concentrations in agreement with the Beer–Lambert Law.

In the 19th century, Robert Bunsen and Gustav Kirchhoff invented spectroscopic analysis, by atomizing samples of elements in a Bunsen burner. They discovered the elements rubidium and caesium by this method.

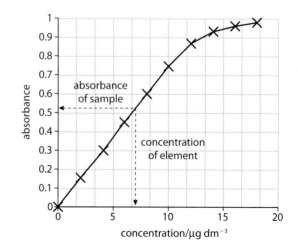

18 The presence of chromium in sea water has been linked to the skin disorder dermatitis. A sample of sea water was analysed using AA spectroscopy, along with six standard solutions. Use a calibration curve to find the concentration of the chromium in the sea water.

Chromium concentration/μg dm^{-3}	Absorbance at $\lambda = 358$ nm
1.00	0.062
2.00	0.121
3.00	0.193
4.00	0.275
5.00	0.323
6.00	0.376
sample	0.215

A.7 Chromatography

Chromatography is a technique for separating and identifying the components of a mixture. Many different forms of chromatography are used but they all work on the same principle. The components have different affinities for two phases: a **stationary phase** and a **mobile phase** and so are separated as the mobile phase moves through the stationary phase. A component which has a strong attraction for the mobile phase will move quickly, whereas a component with a strong attraction for the stationary phase will be held back.

If the stationary and mobile phases are carefully chosen, the different components will move at different speeds and so be separated effectively. Polar compounds, for example, are more likely to move quickly when the mobile phase is a polar solvent.

> A phase is a homogeneous part of a system that is physically distinct. It is separated from other phases by a boundary.

Gas chromatography being used by a forensic scientist. He is preparing a sample for analysis. The display screen shows the output from the detector, showing the chemical composition of a sample. This allows small traces of both known and unknown materials to be detected. For example, drugs can be detected in hair samples.

Adsorption and partition chromatography

There are two main types of chromatography: **partition** and **adsorption** chromatography.

Adsorption chromatography

Chromatography which uses a solid stationary phase and a mobile liquid or gas phase is known as **adsorption chromatography**. Some components of the mixture are attracted to the solid surface and the other components which are less strongly bonded travel faster with the mobile phase. **Thin-layer chromatography** is an example. As the stationary phase is generally a polar solid, the more polar solutes are more readily adsorbed than the less polar solutes.

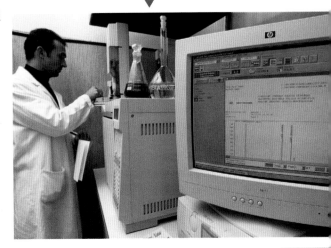

A substance is **adsorbed** when it adheres to the surface of a material. It is **absorbed** when it enters pores in the material.

Partition chromatography

Chromatography using a non-volatile liquid stationary phase held on an inert solid surface is known as partition chromatography. The components distribute themselves between the two phases according to their relative solubility. Paper chromatography and gas liquid chromatography are examples. The more soluble or volatile the component the faster it will move.

Partition chromatography depends on differences between the solubilities of components in the mobile and stationary phases.

Exercise

19 Distinguish between adsorption and partition chromatography by stating which states of matter are used in the stationary and mobile phases.

Paper chromatography

You probably first used this method to separate the different colours in black ink on a piece of filter paper. The different colours in the ink move at different rates over the paper and so separate.

Small spots of solutions containing the samples tested are placed on the base line. The paper is suspended in a closed container to ensure that the paper is saturated. The different components have different affinities for the water in the paper and the solvent and so separate as solvent moves up the paper.

(a)

(b)

This is a simple form of partition chromatography used mainly for qualitative analysis. Paper contains about 10% water and this forms the stationary phase. Water is adsorbed by forming hydrogen bonds with the OH groups in the cellulose of the paper. The mobile phase is the liquid solvent, such as water or ethanol.

R_f = distance moved by component above the base line ÷ distance moved by the solvent front.

When some of the solvent has almost reached the top of the paper, the paper is removed from the solvent and dried. The resulting **chromatogram** is treated with a dye, or ultraviolet light if the different components are not visible. The organic dye **ninhydrin**, for example, is used to identify the different amino acids produced when a protein molecule has been hydrolysed (see Chapter 13). Exposure to iodine vapour for 5–10 min can also be used in some procedures. The different components appear as brown spots.

● **Examiner's hint:** One common error when calculating R_f values is to measure the heights from the bottom of the paper rather than from where the samples were spotted originally.

The different components are identified by their R_f value (retention factor) which compares the distance they have moved relative to the maximum distance moved by the solvent, the **solvent front**.

Components with a high R_f value are attracted to the solvent and so move quickly through the system. Components with a low R_f value are more strongly bonded to the water adsorbed in the paper and so do not move as far.

 See an animation which explains the method of paper chromatography.
Now go to www.heinemann.co.uk/hotlinks, insert the express code 4259P and click on this activity.

Exercise

20 A student wanted to investigate the green colour in some leaves by paper chromatography using the organic solvent ethanol. The results are shown on the right.

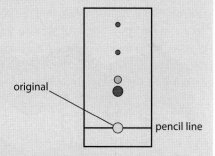

original

pencil line

(a) Suggest why the student used ethanol and not water in her investigation.
(b) State and explain the conclusion which the student can make about the colouring matter in the leaves.
(c) Explain why some of the coloured material had not moved from the original spot.
(d) Explain why a pencil and not a pen is used to draw the base line.
(e) Suggest why repeating the experiment with a different solvent may give more information.
(f) Identify the mobile and stationary phase in the separation technique.

 A chromatogram is the result of the separation process by chromatography.

Thin-layer chromatography (TLC)

Thin-layer chromatography is an example of adsorption chromatography. It follows the same procedure as paper chromatography, with small spots of the test solutions placed on the base line using a capillary tube. The stationary phase is a thin layer of absorbent particles of alumina or silica supported on a glass or thin plastic plate and the mobile phase is a liquid solvent. The different components separate and can be identified. The technique is used in qualitative analysis to determine whether a substance is pure. TLC has four advantages over paper chromatography:

- It is about three times quicker than paper chromatography.
- It is more efficient – it works on very small samples and the separated components can be easily recovered in a pure form.
- The results are more easily reproduced.
- A range of mixtures can be separated by changing the mobile and stationary phases.

 Thin-layer chromatography is used in forensic testing, quality control and clinical diagnosis.

 Watch a movie showing how the components of a mixture are separated using thin-layer chromatography.
Now go to www.heinemann.co.uk/hotlinks, insert the express code 4259P and click on this activity.

Exercise

21 Three compounds were separated using thin-layer chromatography on a silica gel stationary phase.

Compound	Distance travelled/cm
A	2.5
B	7.5
C	10.0
solvent	15.0

Calculate the R_f values and comment on the relative polarity of the components.

 See an animation which explains thin-layer chromatography.
Now go to www.heinemann.co.uk/hotlinks, insert the express code 4259P and click on this activity.

● **Examiner's hint:** Column chromatography is preferred when larger amounts of the sample are being separated.

Figure 12.15 The mixture to be separated is added at the top of the column (left). The individual components flow downwards at different rates (right).

Column chromatography is used to separate the various components from a mixture of chemicals. During this process, the mixture is put in the top of the column. The mixture passes through a porous substance which selectively hinders the movement of each of the components. This means that some components will travel further in a given time than others, allowing each of them to be individually collected.

Column chromatography

This technique is essentially TLC on a large scale, with a column filled with an adsorbent material such as silica or alumina. The tap at the bottom is first closed so that the column can be saturated with the solvent. The sample to be separated is dissolved in a minimum volume of solvent and added to the column from the top. Fresh solvent is added in the same way to wash the sample down the stationary phase and the tap is opened. The different components are separated as they pass through the column at different rates and collected at the bottom as different fractions. In the laboratory this method is used to obtain small quantities of pure compounds. In industry, columns several metres high are used to obtain larger quantities of materials.

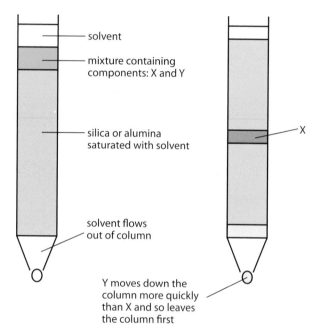

solvent

mixture containing components: X and Y

silica or alumina saturated with solvent

solvent flows out of column

X

Y moves down the column more quickly than X and so leaves the column first

Analytical chemistry depends on combining information

The techniques discussed in this chapter provide the analytical chemist with different types of information. The skill of the analyst is to combine these methods to give a complete description of the structure of the substance studied. For example, chromatography can be used to separate the different components of a mixture, which can then be analysed by a mass spectrometer.

Similarly, infrared spectroscopy gives some information about the bonds present in a molecule, but often this information needs to be supplemented with data from other sources to give a complete structure of the molecule.

Worked example

(a) An unknown compound is found to have the following composition:

	% composition by mass
C	85.6
H	14.4

Deduce the empirical formula of the compound.

(b) The mass spectrum of the compound is shown below. Deduce the molecular formula of the compound. Is the molecule likely to contain a CH_3 group? Explain your answer.

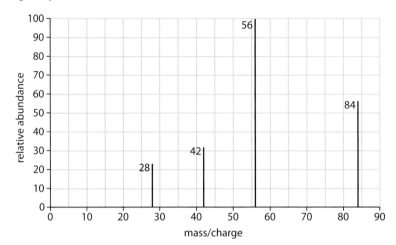

(c) The infrared spectrum shows one absorption close to 2900 cm^{-1}, but there is no absorption close to 1600 cm^{-1}. State what can be deduced from this information.

(d) Deduce the molecular structure from the ^1H NMR spectrum shown.

Solution

(a) To find the empirical formula calculate the relative number of moles:

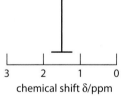

	C	H
mass/g	85.6	14.4
moles	= 85.6/12.01 = 7.13	= 14.4/1.01 = 14.3
simple ratio	= 7.13/7.13 = 1	= 14.4/7.13 = 2.00

The empirical formula is CH_2

(b) The mass spectrum shows a parent ion at 84.

The molecular formula is C_nH_{2n}

$n(12.01) + 2n(1.01) = 84$

$14.03n = 84$

$n = 84/14.03 = 5.99$; therefore the molecular formula is C_6H_{12}.

The absence of peaks at 15 or 69 (84–15) suggests that the molecule probably does not contain a methyl group.

249

(c) The absorption close to 2900 cm^{-1} is due to the C—H bond. The absence of an absorbance at 1600 cm^{-1} suggests that the molecule does not contain a C=C bond. It has a ring structure.

(d) The NMR spectra shows only one peak as all the hydrogen atoms are in the same chemical environment. This confirms that the molecule has a ring structure. It is cyclohexane.

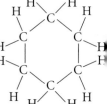

Practice questions

1 Organic compounds are often identified by using more than one analytical technique. Some of these techniques were used to identify the compounds in the following reaction.

$$C_3H_8O \rightarrow C_3H_6O$$
$$\quad A \qquad B$$

(a) Using H_2O as an example, describe what happens, at a molecular level, during the absorption of infrared radiation. (3)

(b) The infrared spectrum of A showed a broad absorption at 3350 cm^{-1}. The infrared spectrum of B did not show this absorption, but instead showed an absorption at 1720 cm^{-1}. Explain what these results indicate about the structures of A and B. (2)

(c) Draw the two possible structures of B. (2)

(d) Fragmentation of B in a mass spectrometer produced lines with $\frac{m}{z}$ values of 15 and 28, but none at values of 14 or 29. Identify B and explain how you used this information to do so. (2)

(e) State the number of lines in the ^1H NMR spectrum of each of the structures in (c). (2)

(*Total 11 marks*)

© International Baccalaureate Organization [2003]

2 A student used the technique of ascending paper chromatography in an experiment to investigate some permitted food dyes (labelled P1–P5). The result is shown below.

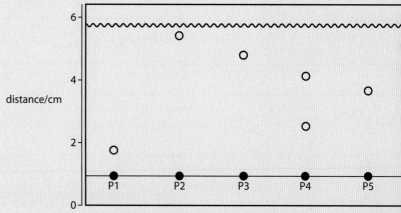

(a) By reference to the diagram above, describe how the experiment would be carried out and explain the meaning of the terms *stationary phase*, *mobile phase*, *partition*, *solvent front* and R_f *value*. (8)

(b) (i) Calculate the R_f value of P1. (2)

(ii) State, giving a reason, whether P4 is a single substance or a mixture. (1)

(*Total 11 marks*)

© International Baccalaureate Organization [2003]

3 Explain the following observation:
Hydrogen iodide is infrared active whereas iodine is infrared inactive. (2)
© International Baccalaureate Organization [2003]

4 A student wanted to determine a more accurate value for the concentration of a solution of $Mn^{2+}(aq)$ which was known to be between 0.10 and 0.010 mol dm^{-3}. She was provided with a solution of 1.00 mol dm^{-3} manganese(II) sulfate, $MnSO_4$. Describe how she could determine the unknown concentration using a visible spectrometer and explain the importance of the Beer–Lambert law in the method used. (5)
© International Baccalaureate Organization [2003]

5 There are four isomeric alcohols with the molecular formula $C_4H_{10}O$. They can be distinguished using a variety of analytical techniques.
(a) The structures of two of the alcohols (**A** and **B**) are shown below. Draw a structure for each of the other two alcohols (**C** and **D**). (2)

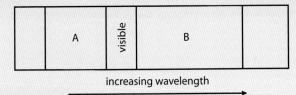

alcohol **A**
$CH_2—CH_2—CH_2—CH_3$
$|$
OH

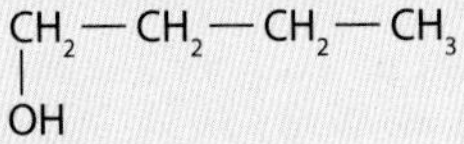

alcohol **B**
$CH_3—CH—CH_2—CH_3$
$|$
OH

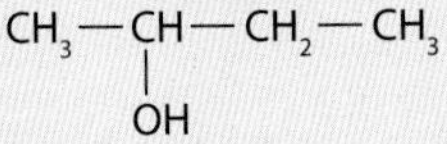

(b) Explain why the four compounds could not easily be distinguished by looking at their infrared spectra. (1)
(c) The ^{1}H NMR spectra of **A** and **B** both show the same number of peaks, but with a different ratio of areas under the peaks.
(i) State what can be deduced from the number of peaks in an ^{1}H NMR spectrum. (1)
(ii) Deduce the number of peaks in the ^{1}H NMR spectra of **A** and **B**. (1)
(iii) Determine the ratio of areas under the peaks for **A** and **B**. (2)
(d) Explain the following features of the mass spectra of **A** and **B**.
(i) Both spectra show a peak at $\frac{m}{z} = 74$. (1)
(ii) One spectrum shows a prominent peak at $\frac{m}{z} = 45$ but the other shows a prominent peak at $\frac{m}{z} = 31$. (2)
(*Total 10 marks*)
© International Baccalaureate Organization [2004]

6 The figure below depicts the visible region of the electromagnetic spectrum and the two regions nearest to it.

A | visible | B

increasing wavelength

(a) Name the regions labelled A and B, identify the atomic or molecular processes associated with each region and compare the energies of the photons involved in these processes. (5)
(b) State, giving a reason, which region (A or B) could be used to:
(i) test for metal ions (1)
(ii) obtain information about the strengths of bonds. (1)
(*Total 7 marks*)
© International Baccalaureate Organization [2005]

13 Human biochemistry: Option B

In recent years many of the Nobel prizes in chemistry – generally considered to be the most prestigious recognition of leading research in the subject – have been given to scientists working in the field of biochemistry. Prizes have been awarded for major advances made in our understanding of proteins, of communication across membranes and the detailed action of DNA. Biochemistry is evidently a rapidly advancing area of knowledge and applications of biochemical research are found in the fields of health, diet and medicine as well as in new technologies.

In this chapter we will focus on some aspects of human biochemistry, the study of biological molecules found in the human body. As in many ways it is true that 'we are what we eat', we will include a consideration of the components of a healthy diet which is the source of these molecules.

Conceptual image of a meal of dietary supplements. Vitamin and mineral pills like these are actively marketed in many parts of the world and available in a bewildering array of choice. However, they will never replace the need for a diet balanced with respect to chemical composition and energy provision.

Throughout this study our focus will be on the relationship between molecular structure and function in the human body. Biological properties will be explained through chemical concepts such as bonding, energetics and acid–base theory, so it will be easier if you already have some knowledge of these topics covered in earlier chapters. In particular, as biochemical molecules are all organic in nature, it will be especially useful if you have first studied Chapter 10, Organic chemistry.

Assessment statements

B.1 Energy
B.1.1 Calculate the energy value of a food from enthalpy of combustion data.

B.2 Proteins
B.2.1 Draw the general formula of 2-amino acids.
B.2.2 Describe the characteristic properties of 2-amino acids.
B.2.3 Describe the condensation reaction of 2-amino acids to form polypeptides.

B.2.4 Describe and explain the primary, secondary (α-helix and β-pleated sheets), tertiary and quaternary structure of proteins.

B.2.5 Explain how proteins can be analysed by chromatography and electrophoresis.

B.2.6 List the major functions of proteins in the body.

B.3 Carbohydrates

B.3.1 Describe the structural features of monosaccharides.

B.3.2 Draw the straight chain and ring structural formulas of glucose and fructose.

B.3.3 Describe the condensation of monosaccharides to form disaccharides and polysaccharides.

B.3.4 List the major functions of carbohydrates in the human body.

B.3.5 Compare the structural properties of starch and cellulose, and explain why humans can digest starch but not cellulose.

B.3.6 State what is meant by the term *dietary fibre*.

B.3.7 Describe the importance of a diet high in dietary fibre.

B.4 Lipids

B.4.1 Compare the composition of the three types of lipids found in the human body.

B.4.2 Outline the difference between HDL and LDL cholesterol and outline its importance.

B.4.3 Describe the difference in structure between saturated and unsaturated fatty acids.

B.4.4 Compare the structures of the two essential fatty acids, linoleic (omega-6 fatty acid) and linolenic (omega-3 fatty acid) and state their importance.

B.4.5 Define the term *iodine number* and calculate the number of $C=C$ double bonds in an unsaturated fat/oil using addition reactions.

B.4.6 Describe the condensation of glycerol and three fatty acid molecules to make a triglyceride.

B.4.7 Describe the enzyme-catalysed hydrolysis of triglycerides during digestion.

B.4.8 Explain the higher energy value of fats compared to carbohydrates.

B.4.9 Describe the important roles of lipids in the body and the negative effects that they can have on health.

B.5 Micronutrients and macronutrients

B.5.1 Outline the difference between micronutrients and macronutrients.

B.5.2 Compare the structures of retinol (vitamin A), calciferol (vitamin D) and ascorbic acid (vitamin C).

B.5.3 Deduce whether a vitamin is water- or fat-soluble from its structure.

B.5.4 Discuss the causes and effects of nutrient deficiencies in different countries and suggest solutions.

B.6 Hormones

B.6.1 Outline the production and function of hormones in the body.

B.6.2 Compare the structures of cholesterol and the sex hormones.

B.6.3 Describe the mode of action of oral contraceptives.

B.6.4 Outline the use and abuse of steroids.

Energy

The human body, in common with that of other living organisms, is made of structural units called cells. Each cell contains literally thousands of different biological molecules involved in very complex interlinked reactions. The sum total of all these reactions in the body is referred to as **metabolism**. Biochemistry is therefore largely the study of metabolic processes and, as in the study of all chemical reactions, this includes a consideration of the energy changes involved.

Energy is made available in cells through a complex series of oxidation reactions known as **respiration**. This process usually begins with the simple sugar molecule glucose. Other energy-rich molecules are usually first converted into glucose or intermediates by metabolic processes.

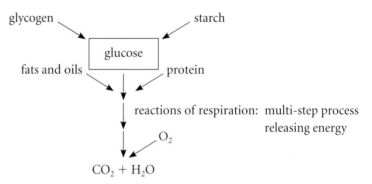

The body is therefore dependent on a continuous supply of energy-rich molecules to drive the reactions of metabolism. The source of these molecules is our diet and knowing the energy content of different food types is thus of great importance. It is estimated that a moderately active woman requires about 9200 kJ per day and a moderately active man about 12 600 kJ per day. When we take in a greater quantity of energy-rich food than our body needs, most of it is converted into storage molecules such as fat for later use. The concept of 'dieting' effectively reverses this process by ensuring that we take in less energy-rich food than the body needs, so that these stored molecules are used up to provide the energy.

Labels on food packaging usually provide data on the energy value of its food content. This is expressed in calories or in joules (or kilojoules) per unit serving, which may be quoted by mass or by volume. For example:

Food type	Unit serving	Energy
mixed nuts	38 g	1000 kJ
cereal grain + milk	40 g + 125 cm³	590 kJ
pancake mix	34 g/62.5 cm³	460 kJ
tinned tuna	55 g/62.5 cm³	250 kJ

These values are obtained by combustion analysis. In Chapter 5 you learned how to calculate enthalpy changes for reactions by measuring the temperature change in a pure substance. The apparatus used to carry out this type of measurement is called a calorimeter. A **bomb calorimeter** is a special type of calorimeter used to measure the heat of combustion of a particular reaction.

The energy for this athlete to run is derived from the chemical oxidation of food molecules occurring in all cells in his body.

 Although different countries use different units for measuring energy, the accepted unit in the SI system is the joule (J). In studies of food analysis and diet the energy value is often expressed in calories and so for our purposes here this must be converted into joules or kilojoules: 1 calorie = 4.18 J. Somewhat confusingly, manufacturers generally use the term 'Calorie' (upper case) to represent kilocalorie.

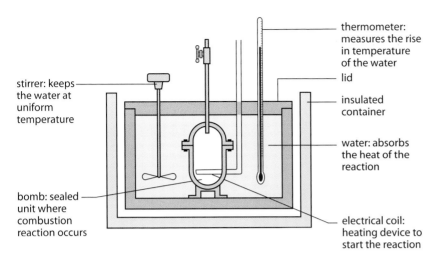

Figure 13.1 The bomb calorimeter.

thermometer: measures the rise in temperature of the water

lid

insulated container

water: absorbs the heat of the reaction

electrical coil: heating device to start the reaction

stirrer: keeps the water at uniform temperature

bomb: sealed unit where combustion reaction occurs

The food is burned to completion after being ignited electrically (the bomb) and the heat released as it burns is measured by recording the temperature rise in a known mass of pure water. As we know the specific heat capacity of the water (the amount of energy required to raise the temperature of 1 g by 1 K), we can scale this value by the actual mass of the water and the temperature change using the following relationship:

$$q = mc\,\Delta T$$

where: q = the energy evolved (J)
$\quad\quad m$ = the mass of the water (g)
$\quad\quad c$ = the specific heat capacity of the water = $4.18\,\text{J}\,\text{g}^{-1}\text{K}^{-1}$
$\quad\quad \Delta T$ = the temperature change in the water (K)

When done accurately, the calculation must include a factor known as the 'bomb factor' which allows for the temperature rise in the metal bomb parts and must also make a small correction to account for the electrical energy input and the burning fuse. However, in our calculations here we will not include these terms.

Worked example

A 0.78 g sample of a food substance was combusted in a bomb calorimeter and raised the temperature of 105.10 g of water from 15.4 °C to 30.6 °C. Calculate the energy value of the food in kJ g^{-1}.

Solution

The temperature rise in the water is 30.6 − 15.4 = 15.2 °C or 15.2 K

Specific heat capacity of water = $4.18\,\text{J}\,\text{g}^{-1}\,\text{K}^{-1}$ (from IB Data booklet, Table 2)

$$q = mc\,\Delta T = (105.10\,\text{g})\,(4.18\,\text{J}\,\text{g}^{-1}\text{K}^{-1})\,(15.2\,\text{K})$$

$$= 6677.63\,\text{J per } 0.78\,\text{g of sample heated}$$

so energy value = $\dfrac{6677.63\,\text{J}}{0.78\,\text{g}}$ = 8561.1 J g^{-1} or 8.56 kJ g^{-1}

A question may sometimes require you to express your answer in J mol^{-1}, in which case you will need to multiply the answer in J g^{-1} by the molar mass (g mol^{-1}).

● **Examiner's hint:** In calculations involving the bomb calorimeter, remember it is the *water* that is experiencing the temperature rise, so this is the mass that must be used in the equation. Be careful not to confuse this with the mass of the food sample burned.

 This tutorial has an animation of how a bomb calorimeter works and gives you a chance to practise the calculations.

Now go to www.heinemann.co.uk/hotlinks, insert the express code 4259P and click on this activity.

Scroll to Section 11.8 Calorimetry and click on 'view tutorial'.

Exercise

1 1.50 g of glucose, $C_6H_{12}O_6$, was completely combusted in a bomb calorimeter. The heat evolved raised the temperature of 225.00 g of water from 18.50 °C to 27.96 °C. Calculate the energy value of glucose in kJ mol^{-1}.

B.2 Proteins

The functions of proteins

Proteins are one of the major groups of biological molecules. In many ways they are the most remarkable of the chemical substances found in the human body as they have such amazingly diverse roles, which we can divide roughly into two main types. First, proteins are largely responsible for the *structure* of the body: from protective structures like hair and fingernails, to connective tissue such as tendons, to contractile structures in muscles. We are mostly built from proteins.

Second, proteins act as the *tools* that operate on the molecular level: they act as catalysts (known as enzymes) which speed up metabolic reactions, as carrier molecules for transporting oxygen in the blood, as structures in blood cells able to help fight disease and in some cases as messengers known as hormones. We depend on proteins to drive the reactions of metabolism.

In all of these and many other cases, each function is carried out by specific proteins so it is useful to know the names of some of these. The table below summarizes the major functions of proteins in the body with an example of each .

Role of protein	Named example of protein	Specific function
structural	keratin	protective covering in hair and finger nails
structural	collagen	connective tissue in skin and tendons
structural	myosin	contractile action in muscles to bring about movement
enzyme (catalyst)	lactase	hydrolyses lactose into glucose and galactose
hormone	insulin	controls and maintains the concentration of glucose in the blood
protective mechanisms	immunoprotein	act as antibodies which help destroy foreign proteins (e.g. from bacteria) in the blood
transport molecules	haemoglobin	carries oxygen from the lungs to all respiring cells
storage molecules	casein	food substance in milk
lubrication	mucoproteins	mucous secretions to reduce friction in many parts of the body, e.g. the knee joint

How can it be that this same type of molecule can be used for both the walls of the reactor and the reactions within? The answer lies in the fact that proteins are as diverse and unique in their structures as they are in their functions and that this variety is rooted in their molecular building blocks.

The structure of proteins

Amino acids are the building blocks of proteins

Proteins are polymers – long chain molecules – of monomer units called **amino acids**. Each amino acid contains an amino group ($-NH_2$) and a carboxylic acid group ($-COOH$) bonded to the same carbon atom.

They are called 2-amino acids because the carbon of the acid $-COOH$ group is denoted 1, so the carbon to which the amino group is attached is carbon 2. Note that this carbon atom is also bonded to a hydrogen atom and to a group usually known as 'R'. The R group differs from one amino acid to the next and is therefore the feature that defines the amino acid. About 20 different amino acids are found in naturally occurring proteins. Each is given a standard three letter abbreviation, for example the smallest amino acid glycine is known as Gly.

Coloured scanning electron micrograph (SEM) of hair shafts growing from the surface of human skin. Hair is made from the fibrous protein keratin, anchored in hair follicles. The outer layer of skin consists of dead keratinized cells that become detached giving this flaky appearance.

◀ **Figure 13.2** Structure of glycine, where R = H.

A complete list of all the amino acids is given in Table 19 of the IB Data booklet. Amino acids can be classified according to the chemical nature of their R group, usually on the basis of its different polarities, as shown in the examples below.

Type of amino acid	R group contains	Named example	Structure
non-polar/hydrophobic	hydrocarbon	alanine Ala	$H_2N-CH-COOH$ $\quad\quad\quad CH_3$
polar but uncharged	alcohol $-OH$ or sulfhydryl $-SH$ or amide $-CONH_2$	serine Ser	$H_2N-CH-COOH$ $\quad\quad\quad CH_2-OH$
basic (positively charged at pH 6.0–8.0)	amino $-NH_2$	lysine Lys	$H_2N-CH-COOH$ $\quad\quad\quad CH_2-CH_2-CH_2-CH_2-NH_2$
acidic (negatively charged at pH 6.0–8.0)	acid $-COOH$	aspartic acid Asp	$H_2N-CH-COOH$ $\quad\quad\quad CH_2-COOH$

In addition to the 20 common amino acids of proteins, over 150 other amino acids occur in biology in different forms other than in proteins. Fungi and higher plants have a particularly large variety of non-protein amino acids, some of which are toxic to other forms of life.

Amino acids are crystalline compounds with high melting points, usually above 200 °C, and have much greater solubility in water than in non-polar solvents. These properties are typical of ionic compounds and suggest that amino acids exist as dipolar ions (having both positive and negative charges on the same group of atoms) known as **zwitterions**. The fact that amino acids usually move in an electric field is further evidence of the existence of charges within their structure. The formation of the zwitterion is the result of an internal acid–base reaction, with the transfer of a proton (H^+) from the acid —COOH group to the basic $-NH_2$ group in the same amino acid.

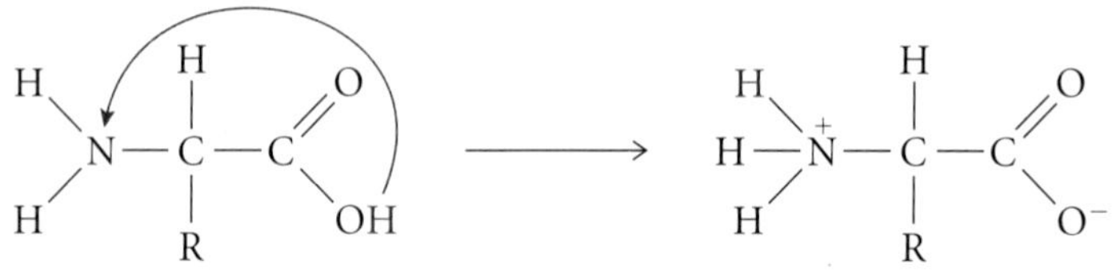

undissociated form zwitterion

As amino acids contain both an acid and a basic group, they are also able to react with both bases and acids, a property known as being **amphoteric**. Note that in the zwitterion it is the conjugates of the acid and the base that are responsible for this property. In aqueous solution, they will accept and donate H^+ according to changes in the pH of the medium as shown below.

As an acid, donating H^+:

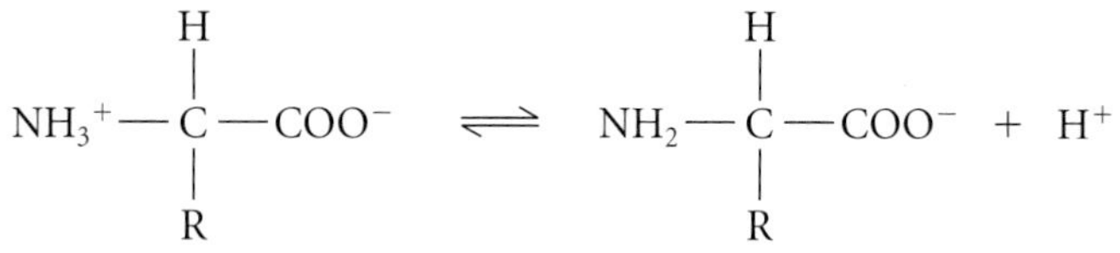

As a base, accepting H^+:

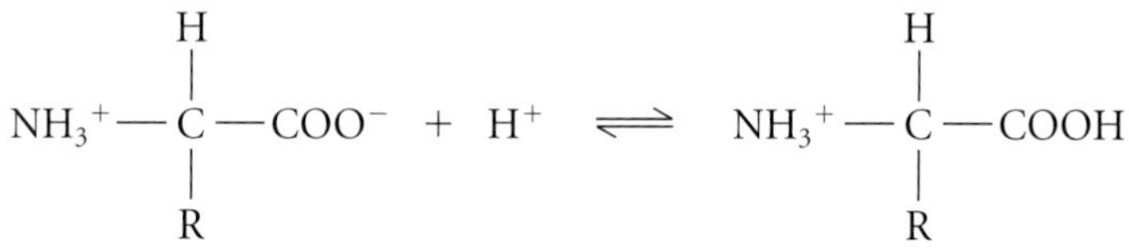

Because pH is a measure of the H^+ concentration, usually adding H^+ or OH^- ions to a solution brings about a dramatic change in the pH. However, the equations above show that in the presence of an amino acid the added H^+ and OH^- ions are effectively removed by their reaction with the amino acid. Consequently the pH will change only very little. This property of amino acids, where they are able to maintain a relatively constant pH despite the addition of small amounts of acid or alkali, is known as **buffering**. This is a crucial feature of biological solutions, as many of the protein components – especially enzymes – are extremely sensitive to changes in pH and can be destroyed by significant fluctuations. For example, human blood has a pH of 7.4 and an increase or a decrease of more than 0.5 pH units can be fatal. Clearly, effective buffering is a must! There are several different buffer systems at work in the human body and amino acids may play an important role as part of these.

A buffer is a solution which resists changes in pH on the addition of a small amount of acid or alkali.

The effect of pH on an amino acid is shown in the equilibria expressions on the next page. This example assumes that the R group is an uncharged group, for example, the amino acid alanine.

$$\underset{\text{positive ion}}{\overset{\displaystyle H}{\underset{\displaystyle CH_3}{H_3N^+\!-\!\overset{|}{\underset{|}{C}}\!-\!COOH}}} \rightleftharpoons \underset{\text{neutral}}{\overset{\displaystyle H}{\underset{\displaystyle CH_3}{H_3N^+\!-\!\overset{|}{\underset{|}{C}}\!-\!COO^-}}} \rightleftharpoons \underset{\text{negative ion}}{\overset{\displaystyle H}{\underset{\displaystyle CH_3}{NH_2\!-\!\overset{|}{\underset{|}{C}}\!-\!COO^-}}}$$

$$\underset{\text{Decreasing pH}}{\longleftarrow} \quad \overline{\text{ISO ELECTRIC POINT}} \quad \underset{\text{Increasing pH}}{\longrightarrow}$$

We can see that the pH determines the net charge that the amino acid carries: it is positively charged at low pH and negatively charged at high pH. The intermediate pH at which the amino acid is electrically neutral is known as its **isoelectric point**. With no net charge at this pH, amino acids will not move in an electric field. Also at this point, the molecules will have minimum mutual repulsion and so be the least soluble. Table 19 in the IB Data booklet gives the pH of the isoelectric point of each amino acid alongside its structure. You can see that amino acids like alanine and glycine, which have uncharged R groups, all have nearly identical isoelectric points (pH 6.0), but where there is an R group which itself changes its charge with changing pH, the isoelectric points are very different, for example, lysine (pH 9.7) and aspartic acid (pH 2.8). This difference can be exploited in techniques for separating amino acids which will be discussed later.

Common name	Symbol	Structural formula	pH of isoelectric point
glycine	Gly	$H_2N\!-\!CH\!-\!COOH$	6.0
alanine	Ala	$H_2N\!-\!CH\!-\!COOH$ $\quad\quad\;\; \vert$ $\quad\quad\; CH_3$	6.0
lysine	Lys	$H_2N\!-\!CH\!-\!COOH$ $\quad\quad\;\; \vert$ $\quad CH_2\!-\!CH_2\!-\!CH_2\!-\!CH_2\!-\!NH_2$	9.7
aspartic acid	Asp	$H_2N\!-\!CH\!-\!COOH$ $\quad\quad\;\; \vert$ $\quad\;\; CH_2\!-\!COOH$	2.8

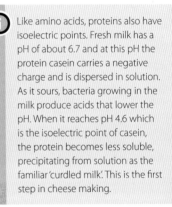

Like amino acids, proteins also have isoelectric points. Fresh milk has a pH of about 6.7 and at this pH the protein casein carries a negative charge and is dispersed in solution. As it sours, bacteria growing in the milk produce acids that lower the pH. When it reaches pH 4.6 which is the isoelectric point of casein, the protein becomes less soluble, precipitating from solution as the familiar 'curdled milk'. This is the first step in cheese making.

A trough of curdled milk in a cheese-making factory. The curd is solidified milk formed by lowering the pH and so precipitating the protein at its isoelectric point.

Amino acids link together through condensation reactions

Amino acids are able to react together in a condensation reaction in which a molecule of water is eliminated and a new bond is formed between the acid group of one amino acid and the amino group of the other. This bond is a substituted amide link known as a **peptide bond** and two amino acids linked in this way are known as a **dipeptide**. By convention the free $-NH_2$ group (known as the N-terminal) is put on the left of the sequence and the free $-COOH$ group (C-terminal) on the right.

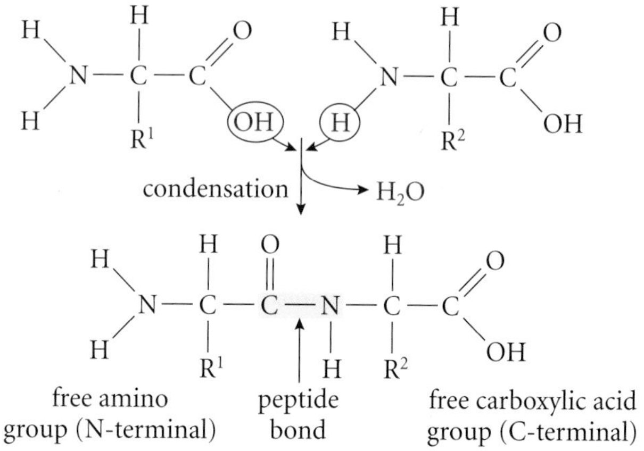

Figure 13.3 Formation of a dipeptide by condensation of two amino acids.

We can see that the dipeptide still has a functional group at each end of the molecule — NH_2 at one end and $-COOH$ at the other – so it can react again by condensation reactions, forming a **tripeptide** and eventually a chain of linked amino acids known as a **polypeptide**.

Worked example

Draw a tripeptide with the following sequence:

Cys–Val–Asn

Solution

Look up the structures (the R groups) of the amino acids in Table 19 of the IB Data booklet and draw them out in the same order as given in the question.

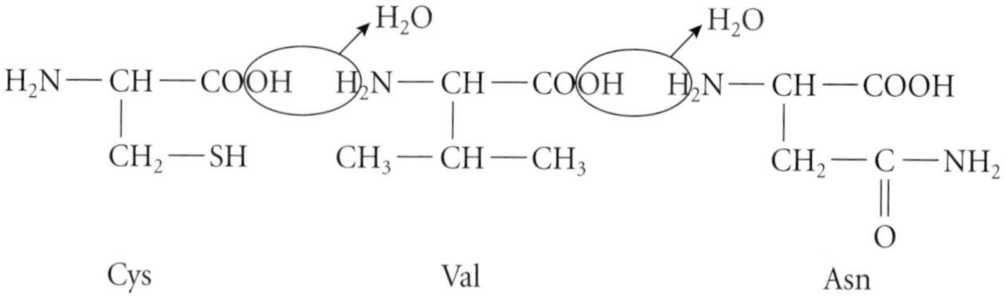

Now draw peptide bonds between the carbon of the $-COOH$ group and the nitrogen of the $-NH_2$ group, ensuring that H_2O is released and that each atom has the correct number of bonds in the final structure.

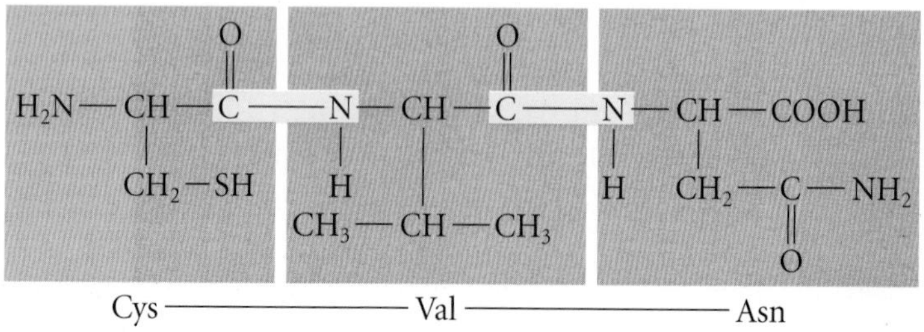

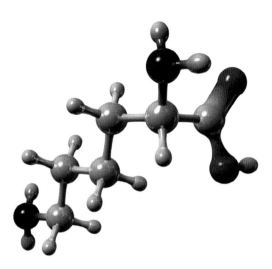

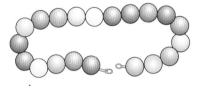

Molecular model of the amino acid lysine $NH_2(CH_2)_4CH(NH_2)COOH$. Lysine is known as an 'essential' amino acid because it cannot be synthesized by the body and so must be obtained in the diet. Carbon atoms are shown in blue, hydrogen in gold, oxygen in red and nitrogen in dark blue.

In just the same way as letters linked together in different orders make different words (e.g. eat, ate, tea), so amino acids linked together in different sequences make different peptides. The three amino acids above could also have been linked for example as: Asn — Cys — Val or Cys — Asn — Val, all of which would be different tripeptides with different properties.

The sequence in which the amino acids are linked to form the chain is of tremendous significance as it will determine the exact nature of the polypeptide. This is where the extraordinary variety of protein structures comes from.

Consider making a necklace by joining together 20 different colours of beads, with each colour being used as many times as you like. In every position you would have a choice of 20 different possibilities, so just imagine how many different combinations of beads you could have! Building polypeptides from amino acids presents a similar situation – at any point in the chain there are 20 different possibilities. If it was only a tripeptide there would be $20 \times 20 \times 20 = 8000$ different possible combinations. But proteins are typically made from polypeptide chains with 50 or more amino acids, so the number of possible structures becomes enormous, in this case 20^{50} – literally millions.

We will now move on to look at how the sequence of amino acids in the polypeptide uniquely determines the structure and therefore the function of the protein. Understanding protein structure can seem quite complex, so for convenience it is divided into four levels of organization.

Figure 13.4 Different coloured beads can be strung together in different combinations to make a wide variety of different necklaces. In a similar way, different sequences of amino acids link together to give rise to an almost infinite variety of proteins.

The primary structure of a protein is the amino acid sequence

The primary structure of a protein refers to the number and sequence of amino acids in its polypeptide chain. Held together by peptide bonds, this forms the covalent backbone of the molecule. Interestingly, once the primary structure has been determined, all the other levels of protein structure will follow – so it really does dictate the entire structure and function of the protein. So crucial is the primary structure that the alteration of just one amino acid can completely change the functioning of the protein, as is the case in the disease sickle-cell anaemia. This condition occurs when the protein haemoglobin is not able to carry oxygen efficiently, the result of a single amino acid change in its chain of 146 amino acids. The primary structure is of key interest to biochemists and is now routinely analysed in laboratories. It is also the aspect of protein structure used in studies of biochemical evolution exploring the relationships between organisms.

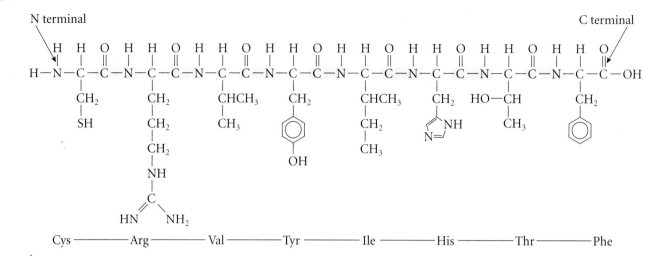

Figure 13.5 Primary structure of a small polypeptide. Peptide bonds are highlighted in blue.

So what determines the primary structure of a protein? The answer to this question when it came in the early 1960s was considered to be one of the most important discoveries of molecular biology. DNA (deoxyribose nucleic acid), which determines genetic information, acts by dictating to cells the primary structure of their proteins. Simply put, the expression of our genes is through the proteins that we synthesize. So it is the primary structure of our proteins that gives each of us our unique genetic characteristics.

The secondary structure of proteins is regular hydrogen bonding

The secondary structure refers to folding of the polypeptide chain as a result of hydrogen bonding between peptide groups along its length. Hydrogen bonds can form between the $-C=O$ group of one peptide bond and the $-N-H$ group of another peptide bond further along the chain which will cause the chain to fold. The exact configuration of this will be influenced by the R groups along the chain and so differs in different proteins and even in different sections of the same protein. We can distinguish two main types of secondary structure, the **α-helix** and the **β-pleated sheet**.

The α-helix is a regular coiled configuration of the polypeptide chain resulting from hydrogen bonds forming between two peptide bonds four amino acid units apart. This twists the chain into a tightly coiled helix, much like a spiral staircase, with 3.6 amino acids per turn.

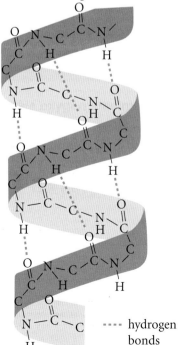

Figure 13.6 α-helical secondary structure of keratin. The amino acid backbone winds in a spiral, held by hydrogen bonds shown in blue.

···· hydrogen bonds

Often considered the father of modern molecular biology, Fred Sanger of Cambridge, England, is one of the few people to have been awarded two Nobel Prizes. In 1958 he was awarded the prize for establishing the sequence of the 51 amino acids in insulin chain B. This was the first protein to have its primary structure elucidated in this way and it was the culmination of 12 years of work. In 1980 Sanger shared the Nobel Prize for similar work on the base sequencing of nucleic acids.

You can watch an interview with Fred Sanger reflecting on his achievements in research and on his life philosophy.

Now go to www.heinemann.co.uk/hotlinks, insert the express code 4259P and click on this activity.

The α-helix is flexible and elastic because the *intra-chain* hydrogen bonds easily break and reform as the molecule is stretched. A good example of the α-helix is found in keratins – structural proteins found in hair, skin and nails.

The β-pleated sheet is a structure composed of 'side by side' polypeptides which are in extended form, that is, not tightly coiled as in the α-helix. The polypeptides are arranged in pleated sheets that are cross-linked by *inter-chain* hydrogen bonds.

Human hair (made of the protein keratin) grows approximately 15 cm in one year, which means that 9.5 turns of the α-helix must be produced every second.

◀ **Figure 13.7** β-pleated sheet secondary structure of silk fibroin. The polypeptides run parallel to each other, held in place by hydrogen bonds.

Hair stretches to almost double its length when exposed to moist heat but contracts to its normal length on cooling. This is why hair is often much curlier in humid conditions.

---- hydrogen bonds

Spider's web with drops of morning dew. The web fibres are made of the protein fibroin containing a β-pleated sheet secondary structure and spun from special secreting glands. A typical web may contain 20 m of fibroin.

The β-pleated sheet is flexible but inelastic. It is found in the fibres spun by spiders and silkworms and in the beaks and claws of birds.

Proteins that have a well-defined secondary structure such as those described here are known as **fibrous** proteins. They are physically tough and insoluble in water.

The tertiary structure of proteins is the result of interactions between the R groups

The tertiary structure refers to the further twisting, folding and coiling of the polypeptide chain as a result of interactions between the R groups, known as **side chains**. The structure that results will be a very specific compact three-dimensional structure, known as the protein's **conformation**. It is the most stable arrangement of the protein, taking into account all the possible interactions along the entire length of the polypeptide. Note that the interactions between the R groups are all *intra*-molecular forces, as they occur within the one polypeptide chain.

The conformation is particularly important in the so-called **globular** proteins, which include all the enzymes and protein hormones. They are water soluble because their structure positions nearly all of the polar (or hydrophilic) R groups on the outer surface of the molecules where they can interact with water and most

Computer artwork showing the structure of the protein albumen from human blood. The spiral regions of α-helical structure can be clearly seen as well as the overall three-dimensional conformation. ▶

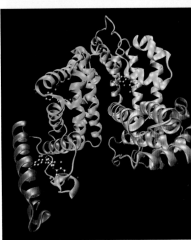

of the non-polar (or hydrophobic) R groups in the interior out of contact with water. The interactions that stabilize this conformation are of the following types.

(a) Hydrophobic interactions – between non-polar side chains
For example, between two alkyl side chains in valine; these weak interactions, based on van der Waals' forces between induced dipoles, produce non-polar regions in the interior of the protein.

(b) Hydrogen bonding – between polar side chains
For example, between the $-CH_2OH$ group in serine and the $-CH_2COOH$ group in aspartic acid.

(c) Ionic bond – between side chains carrying a charge
For example, between the $-(CH_2)_4 NH_3^+$ group in lysine and the $-CH_2 COO^-$ group in aspartic acid.

(d) Disulfide bridges – between the sulfur atoms in the amino acid cysteine
These are covalent bonds and hence the strongest of these interactions.

These different interactions which are responsible for maintaining the tertiary structure are summarized in the diagram below.

Figure 13.8 Summary of interactions contributing to tertiary structure. ▶

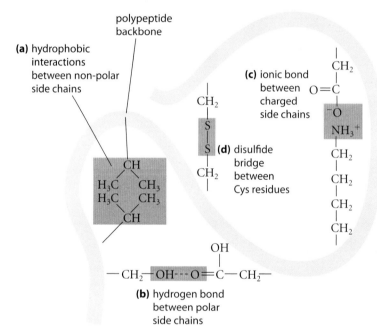

The process of 'perming' which introduces more curls into hair involves first breaking the disulfide bridges between the cysteine residues in the keratin using a reducing agent. New disulfide bridges are formed when the hair is chemically re-oxidized while it is twisted around rollers. The size of the roller determines the position of the new disulfide bridges that form. As these are covalent bonds they do not break on normal treatments like washing and combing, so are said to be 'permanent'. Similar processes are used in straightening curly hair.

These interactions can all be upset by changes in the medium, such as changes in temperature or pH. When a protein loses its specific tertiary structure as a result of such disruptions, it is said to be **denatured**. The familiar sight of the white of an egg solidifying on heating is an example of this. Denaturation of enzymes renders them biologically inactive, which is one of the reasons why intracellular conditions must be tightly controlled.

The quaternary structure of a protein is the association between different polypeptides

Some proteins comprise more than one polypeptide chain and in these cases the association between these chains is known as the quaternary structure. For example, the protein collagen, which is found in skin and tendons and is actually the most abundant protein in the human body, is a triple helix of three polypeptide chains, with inter-chain hydrogen bonds between them. This helps to give it a stable rope-like structure that is resistant to stretching.

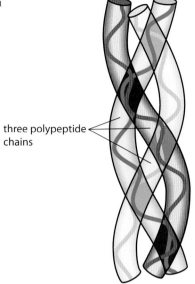

◀ **Figure 13.9** Triple helical quaternary structure of collagen.

three polypeptide chains

Another example is the protein haemoglobin that is responsible for carrying oxygen in the blood. It is made up of four polypeptide chains, known as α and β chains, which fit together tightly in the protein assembly.

β_2 β_1

α_2 α_1

◀ **Figure 13.10** Quaternary structure of haemoglobin, an assembly of four polypeptides.

 The four polypeptide chains in adult haemoglobin are two α chains and two β chains. Before birth, haemoglobin in the foetus has a different structure with two α chains and two γ chains. This form has a higher affinity for oxygen and so is able to extract it from the maternal blood. After birth, the foetal haemoglobin levels decline and by six months adult haemoglobin becomes the predominant form.

Many proteins consist of only one polypeptide chain and so do not have a quaternary structure.

Analysis of proteins

The analysis of a protein is typically begun by determining its amino acid composition. (Note that this is not the same as its primary structure, as the *sequence* of the amino acids will not be known). This involves first chemically separating the amino acids from each other by breaking the peptide bonds between them through **hydrolysis** reactions usually using acid. These reactions reverse the condensation reactions discussed earlier and occur in the body during enzyme-catalysed protein digestion in the intestine.

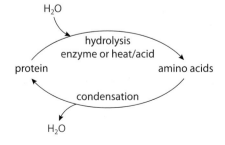

H_2O

hydrolysis
enzyme or heat/acid

protein   amino acids

condensation

H_2O

 You can follow an illustrated summary of the four levels of protein structure.

Now go to www.heinemann.co.uk/hotlinks, insert the express code 4259P and click on this activity.

Separation of the resulting amino acid mixture into its components can then be achieved in two ways.

(i) Chromatography

Chromatography (described in Chapter 12, page 245) is a useful technique for separating and identifying the components of a mixture, particularly when they are coloured. Amino acids, though colourless in solution, take on colour when treated with a **locating reagent**.

The procedure is simple to run. A small sample of the amino acid mixture is spotted near the bottom of some chromatographic paper and this position, known as the **origin**, clearly marked (in pencil so as not to interfere with the experiment). The paper is then suspended in a chromatographic tank containing a small volume of solvent, ensuring that the spot is above the level of the solvent.

As the solvent rises up the paper by capillary action it will pass over the spot. Amino acids in the spot will distribute themselves between two phases – the stationary phase (the water in the paper) and the mobile phase (the solvent) to different extents and so move up the paper at different speeds. They will therefore become spread out according to their different solubilities.

Figure 13.11 Apparatus used to separate amino acids by paper chromatography.

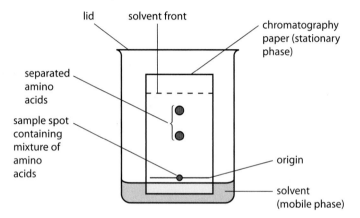

When the solvent reaches almost to the top of the paper, its final position is marked and is known as the **solvent front**. The paper is removed from the tank and developed by spraying it with the locating reagent **ninhydrin**. Most amino acids will now take a purple colour and can be distinguished as separate isolated spots up the length of the paper.

The position of each amino acid can be expressed as an R_f value (retention factor), calculated as follows:

Figure 13.12 Calculation of R_f values in chromatography.

$$R_f = \frac{\text{distance moved by amino acid}}{\text{distance moved by solvent}}$$

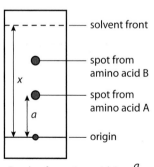

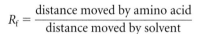

Specific amino acids have characteristic R_f values when measured under the same conditions, so can be identified by comparing the values obtained with data tables. It is helpful to spot known amino acids alongside the mixture to act as markers for the experiment.

(ii) Electrophoresis

Electrophoresis is a technique for the analysis and separation of a mixture based on the movement of charged particles in an electric field. As we learned earlier, amino acids carry different charges depending on the pH and so can be separated by this means when placed in a buffered solution.

In gel electrophoresis, the medium is a gel, typically made of polyacrylamide. The amino acid mixture is placed in wells in the centre of the gel and an electric field is applied. Depending on the pH of the buffer used, different amino acids will move at different rates towards the oppositely charged electrodes. At their isoelectric point, amino acids will not move as they carry no net charge. When separation is complete they can be detected by a stain or made to fluoresce under UV light and identified from their position using data tables.

Electrophoresis can also be used to separate and identify intact proteins according to their different rates of migration towards the poles.

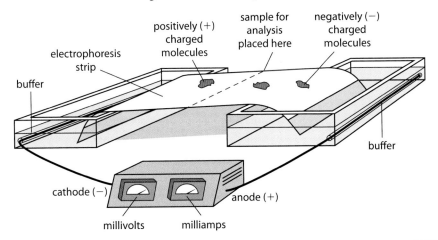

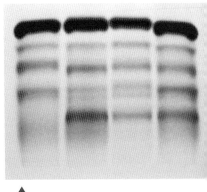

Electrophoresis of human blood serum. The charged protein molecules in a buffer solution have separated according to their different attractions to opposite electrical poles across the polyacrylamide gel (Polyacryl Amide Gel Electrophoresis or PAGE). The bands have been stained, so the separated proteins can be identified from their position. This technique is used to detect whether proteins associated with particular diseases are found in the blood.

▲ **Figure 13.13** Electrophoresis apparatus for amino acid or protein separation.

Exercises

Make reference to Table 19 in the IB Data booklet to answer these questions.

2 Explain why in gel electrophoresis the amino acid isoleucine migrates towards the anode at high pH and towards the cathode at low pH.

3 You are attempting to separate a mixture of glutamic acid and histidine by gel electrophoresis. Give a suggested pH for an appropriate buffer solution to use and say in which direction each amino acid would migrate.

W You can do a virtual experiment on gel electrophoresis.

Now go to www.heinemann.co.uk/hotlinks, insert the express code 4259P and click on this activity.

B.3 Carbohydrates

Carbohydrates (literally *hydrated-carbon*) are composed of the three elements carbon, hydrogen and oxygen, with the hydrogen and oxygen always in the same ratio as in water i.e. 2:1. They therefore can be expressed by the general formula $C_x(H_2O)_y$. There are two main types of carbohydrate – simple sugars or **monosaccharides** and condensation polymers of these known as **polysaccharides**.

Functions of carbohydrates

The monosaccharides, for example **glucose** and **fructose**, are readily soluble in water and are mostly taken up by cells quite rapidly. They are used as the main substrate for respiration, releasing energy for all cell processes. They also act as precursors in a large number of metabolic reactions, leading to the synthesis of other molecules such as fats, nucleic acids and amino acids. Polysaccharides, being insoluble, are used as the storage form of carbohydrates, mostly in the form of **glycogen** stored in the liver and muscles. The human body makes very little use of carbohydrates for structural materials, although by contrast plant cells depend on carbohydrates for their structure and support, particularly the polysaccharide **cellulose** that is claimed to be the most abundant organic compound on Earth.

Structure of carbohydrates

Monosaccharides are simple sugars

The monosaccharides are the simplest form of carbohydrates and are usually classified according to the number of carbon atoms that they contain. Some of the most common are the triose sugars (C3), the pentose sugars (C5) and the hexose sugars (C6).

> Monosaccharides contain a carbonyl group (C=O) and at least two —OH groups. They have the empirical formula CH_2O.

These sugar molecules all have two or more alcohol groups (—OH) and a carbonyl group (—C=O). Their large number of polar hydroxyl groups is responsible for their ready solubility in water. All monosaccharides can be represented by the empirical formula CH_2O. So hexose sugars, for example, all have the molecular formula $C_6H_{12}O_6$. However, as we have seen with other organic compounds (Chapter 10), there are many isomers representing different structural arrangements of the same number and type of atoms in different molecules. Two of the most common isomers of $C_6H_{12}O_6$ are glucose and fructose, shown below:

Figure 13.14 Straight chain forms of glucose and fructose, structural isomers of $C_6H_{12}O_6$. The brown highlight shows the position of the carbonyl group, which determines whether it is an aldose (aldehyde sugar) or a ketose (ketone sugar).

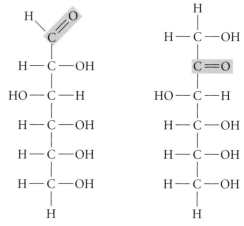

glucose: an aldose sugar   fructose: a ketose sugar

These are the so-called straight chain forms of these sugars, but in aqueous solution the sugars undergo an internal reaction resulting in more familiar ring structures.

Figure 13.15 Ring forms of glucose and fructose. Note that these abbreviated structures omit the carbons in the ring.

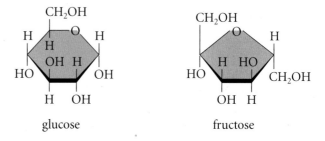

glucose   fructose

The formation of the ring in glucose and fructose makes possible another type of isomer, as it restricts the rotation around the carbon atoms and fixes the groups relative to each other. Look at the difference in the positions of the —OH groups at carbon-1 in the structures below. These two forms are known as α-glucose and β-glucose and as we shall see the difference between them has a significant effect on the properties of their polymers.

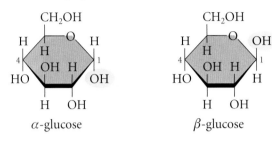

α-glucose β-glucose

◀ **Figure 13.16** The difference between α-glucose and β-glucose.

Disaccharides are two simple sugars linked together

Disaccharides form by linking two monosaccharides together in a condensation reaction in which a molecule of water is eliminated as an —OH group from each sugar molecule react together. The resulting bond between the monosaccharides is known as a **glycosidic link**. Disaccharides are all soluble molecules that can be hydrolysed into two monosaccharides by acid hydrolysis or by enzyme-catalysed reaction. Combining different monosaccharides will produce different disaccharides.

For example, two α-glucose molecules condense to form the disaccharide maltose as shown here. The glycosidic link is known as 1–4 because C_1 in one molecule is bonded to C_4 in the other molecule.

In α-glucose the —OH group at C1 is below the plane of the ring; in β-glucose the —OH group at C1 is above the plane of the ring.

CH₂OH   CH₂OH   →   CH₂OH   1–4 glycosidic   CH₂OH   + H₂O
                              linkage

α-glucose α-glucose   maltose

The most familiar disaccharides are shown in the table below.

Name of disaccharide	Monosaccharide units	Occurrence in the body
lactose	β-glucose + β-galactose	found in milk
maltose	α-glucose + α-glucose	product from starch digestion
sucrose	α-glucose + β-fructose	cane sugar; the most common form of sugar added to food

 Many people suffer from 'lactose intolerance', which is usually a genetic condition, characterized by an inability to digest lactose owing to a lack of the enzyme lactase. The condition is more prevalent in many Asian and South African cultures where dairy products (containing lactose) are less traditionally part of the adult diet. By contrast, people with ancestry in Europe, the Middle East and parts of East Africa, where mammals are often milked for food, typically maintain lactase production throughout life.

You can find the full structures of lactose and sucrose in Table 21 of the IB Data booklet. Note that the molecular formula of all these disaccharides is $C_{12}H_{22}O_{11}$.

Polysaccharides are the polymers of sugars

Polysaccharides form by repetitions of the reaction shown above, leading to a long chain of monosaccharide units held together by glycosidic bonds. Polysaccharides are all insoluble molecules and so make an ideal storage form of the energy-rich carbohydrates. There are three common glucose-based polysaccharides that differ from each other in the isomer of glucose used and in the amount of cross-linking in the chain.

(i) Starch

Starch is a polymer of α-glucose, used as the main storage carbohydrate in plants. Therefore many forms of food derived from plants are rich sources of starch – such as potatoes, rice and flour. Starch is actually a mixture of two separate polysaccharides – amylose and amylopectin. Amylose is a straight chain polymer with 1–4 α-glucose linkages.

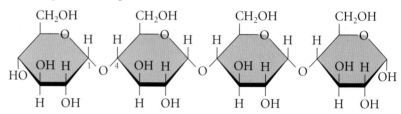

amylose: 1–4 linkage of α-glucose monomers

Amylopectin is a branched polymer with both 1–4 and 1–6 α-glucose linkages.

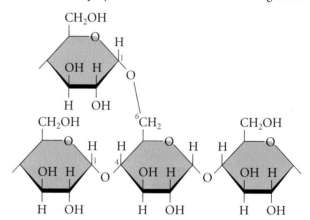

amylopectin: 1–4 and 1–6 linkages of α-glucose monomers

These two forms enable starch to be a relatively compact spiral structure, stored as **starch grains** in plant cells.

(ii) Glycogen

Also a polymer of α-glucose, glycogen is sometimes called 'animal starch' as it is the main storage carbohydrate in animals, found in the liver and muscles. It has a structure very similar to that of amylopectin shown above, but with many more 1–6 branches.

(iii) Cellulose

A polymer of β-glucose, cellulose is used as a structural material in plant cell walls. It is a linear polymer with 1–4 links known as β-glycosidic links. These position the sugars at a different angle from the α-glycosidic links found in amylose and amylopectin so the cellulose chain forms an uncoiled linear structure with alternate glucose monomers 'upside down' with respect to each other. This enables the hydroxyl groups to form hydrogen bonds with the hydroxyls of other cellulose molecules lying parallel.

cellulose: 1–4 linkage of β-glucose monomers

Consequently cellulose forms cables, known as **microfibrils**, of parallel chains that give it its rigid structure. This is one of the main sources of support in plant cells and is why wood, which is rich in cellulose, is such a useful building material.

Digestion of polysaccharides

Polysaccharides, being insoluble, cannot be transported in the blood but must first be broken down to their monosaccharide units in the reactions of digestion. This involves hydrolysis reactions (the reverse of condensation) in which the glycosidic links are broken producing soluble monosaccharides. The reactions are controlled by enzymes and these are very specific in their action.

The human body produces enzymes to digest starch and glycogen, so these polysaccharides are readily broken down into glucose molecules that are then absorbed by the body. However, the body does *not* produce the enzyme required for the breakdown of the different glycosidic links found in cellulose and in related molecules such as hemicellulose, waxes, lignin and pectin, also components of plant cell walls. The required enzyme is known as **cellulase** which may be secreted in small amounts by bacteria living in the gut. But in general these substances will not be digested and so will pass through the gut largely chemically intact, contributing to the bulk of the faeces.

Coloured scanning electron micrograph of cellulose microfibrils in a plant cell wall. Microfibrils measure between 5 nm and 15 nm in diameter.

Dietary fibre describes substances that cannot be digested

Substances such as cellulose, which cannot be digested by the body, are known as **dietary fibre**. They might at first glance be considered to be of no use in nutrition, as they do quite literally 'pass straight through'. However, substantial medical data have indicated that in fact dietary fibre is of great benefit, particularly to the health of the large intestine. The cellulose fibrils abrade the wall of the digestive tract and stimulate the lining to produce mucus. This helps in the smooth passage of undigested food through the gut and so helps to reduce conditions such as constipation and the related conditions haemorrhoids (bleeding of the wall of the rectum) and irritable bowel syndrome. There is also evidence that it may be helpful in preventing the development of colorectal cancer. Our growing understanding of this significance of fibre in the diet has led to an increase in the marketing of 'whole foods' such as grains and plant foods such as vegetables and salads. In general, foods derived from plants with little or no processing are likely to be a good source of fibre.

 The World Health Organization cites a low fruit and vegetable intake as a key risk factor in chronic diseases such as diabetes mellitus, obesity, Crohn's disease and cancers, principally of the digestive tract. Fruit and vegetable intake varies considerably among countries, largely reflecting the prevailing economic, cultural and agricultural environments. In developed countries fresh fruit and vegetable intake has decreased with increasing dependence on fast foods that are highly processed. It is estimated that globally 2.7 million deaths per year are attributable to low fruit and vegetable intake.

Exercise

4 **(a)** State the empirical formula of all monosaccharides.
  (b) The structural formula of lactose is shown in Table 21 of the IB Data booklet.
     (i) Deduce the structural formula of one of the monosaccharides that reacts to form lactose and state its name.
     (ii) State the name of the other monosaccharide.
  (c) State two major functions of polysaccharides in the body.

B.4 Lipids

The word *lipid* is used as an umbrella term for a range of biological molecules which are characterized by being hydrophobic or insoluble in water. They are nonetheless soluble in non-polar solvents and this property is often used in extracting them from cells. Lipids contain the elements carbon, hydrogen and oxygen, but the ratio of hydrogen to oxygen is greater than in carbohydrates – in other words they are less oxidized molecules. The most common lipids are fats and oils, steroids and phospholipids.

Functions and negative effects of lipids

Lipids are essential molecules in a variety of roles in the body. At the same time they, and in particular fats and some steroids, are associated with various health problems arising from excess intake in our diet. We will therefore consider both their uses and the potential problems associated with their excess intake.

Lipids contain stored energy that can be released when they are broken down in the reactions of respiration in cells. The reactions involve a series of oxidation steps, ultimately yielding CO_2 and H_2O. As noted above, lipids are less oxidized than carbohydrates and so can effectively undergo *more* oxidation and so release *more* energy per unit mass when used as a respiratory substrate. The difference is significant: a gram of lipid releases almost twice as much energy as a gram of carbohydrate. However, partly owing to their insolubility, the energy in lipids is not so readily available as it is in carbohydrates as more reactions are involved in their breakdown. This is why you are more likely to take a glucose tablet than suck a lump of cheese, for example, when you are running a marathon. But if you were going on an expedition to the Arctic, you would take lots of lipids like cheese and butter, because they make ideal storage molecules. The fat stores, known as **adipose tissue**, which we have in different parts of the body, serve as reservoirs of energy, swelling and shrinking as fat is deposited and withdrawn. In addition, this tissue helps to protect some body organs such as the kidneys and a layer of fat under the skin insulates the body.

Electron micrograph of lipid droplets shown in green in a fat cell. These cells form adipose tissue, which stores energy as an insulating layer of fat.

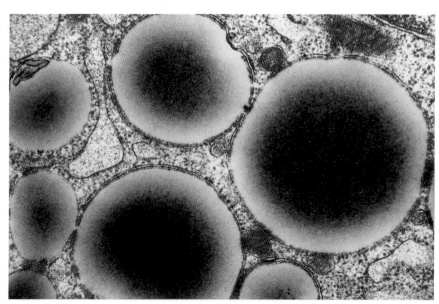

Some hormones, such as the sex hormones testosterone and estrogen, are made from lipids in the form of steroids. Bile acids, which aid digestion of fat in the intestine, are also steroid based.

Lipids also play an important structural role in the body. The phospholipids are a major component of membranes that bind cells. Here they help to determine the selective transport of metabolites across cell boundaries. In nerve cells a special layer of phospholipids called the myelin sheath gives electrical insulation to the nerves and speeds up nervous transmission. A different lipid molecule, cholesterol, is also important in plasma membrane structure, where it influences the fluidity and hence the permeability of the membrane. In addition, lipids help to absorb fat-soluble vitamins such as A, D, E and K.

Excess lipids in the diet are, however, increasingly linked with negative effects on health. These arise largely owing to the low solubility of the lipids that causes some of them to be deposited in the walls of the main blood vessels and this can restrict blood flow, a condition known as **atherosclerosis**. It is usually associated with high blood pressure and can lead to heart disease.

In addition, because of the body's ability to convert excess fats into adipose tissue for storage, a diet too rich in lipids can lead to **obesity**. This is linked to many other health issues including diabetes and a variety of cancers.

The molecule that for a long time has been considered to be the main culprit in the circulatory conditions described here is **cholesterol**. It is present in our diet particularly in animal fat and is also synthesized in the body. Understanding cholesterol's role in causing cardiovascular disease is made more complex by the fact that, because it is insoluble in blood, it is transported when bound in different lipoproteins, the most well known of which are LDL (low density lipoprotein) and HDL (high density lipoprotein). These have gained the somewhat simplistic terms 'bad cholesterol' and 'good cholesterol', respectively. The names reflect the fact that high levels of LDL cholesterol are associated with increased deposition in the walls of the arteries, while high levels of HDL cholesterol seem to protect against heart attack. It is believed that HDL tends to carry cholesterol away from the arteries, thus slowing its build-up. The main sources of LDL cholesterol are saturated fats and *trans* fats, the chemical nature of which will be discussed in the next section.

Clearly the type of fat consumed is as important as the total amount. In general an intake of polyunsaturated fats such as those found in fish, many nuts and corn oil is considered beneficial in lowering levels of LDL cholesterol. Also, a type of fatty acid known as omega-3-polyunsaturated fatty acid, found for example in fish oils and flax seeds, has been shown to be linked to reduced risk of cardiovascular disease as well as to optimum neurological development. These fatty acids cannot be manufactured by the body, so are known as **essential fatty acids** and must be taken in the diet. Their structure will also be discussed in the next section.

Magnified view of a slice through an artery showing a thick deposit caused by the disease atherosclerosis. The deposit is composed of a mixture of fats, cholesterol and dead muscle cells. It disrupts blood flow and can break off in fragments blocking smaller blood vessels, leading to strokes and heart disease.

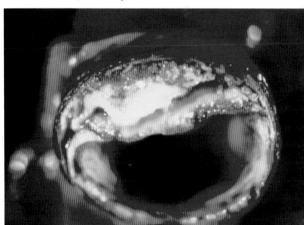

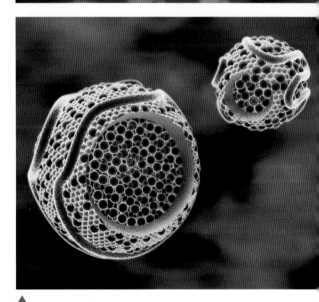

Computer artwork of LDL (right) and HDL (left) cholesterol, the major carriers of cholesterol in the blood. The purple spheres represent cholesterol molecules which are bonded to phospholipids, shown in yellow and protein shown as purple and pink strands. LDL cholesterol is associated with increased risk of heart disease.

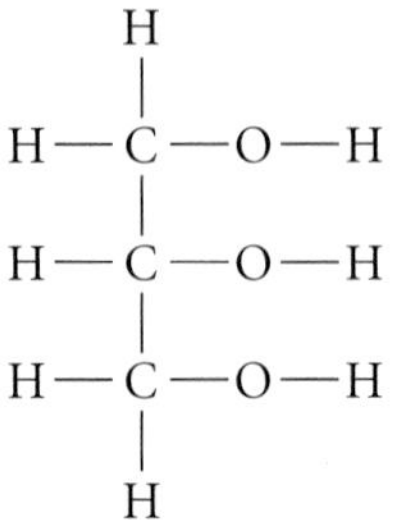

glycerol

Figure 13.17 The structure of glycerol.

Structure of the different lipids

The structures of the three main types of lipids – triglycerides, phospholipids and steroids – will be considered here in turn.

1 Structure of triglycerides – fats and oils

Triglycerides are the major constituent of fats and oils. They are esters formed by condensation reactions between **glycerol** and **three fatty acids**.

Glycerol is a molecule of three carbon atoms, each of which bears an alcohol group as shown in Figure 13.17. Following the guidelines in Chapter 10, see if you can give glycerol its systematic IUPAC name. The answer is propane-1,2,3-triol; however, we will continue to refer to it as glycerol here as this name is widely used.

Fatty acids are long chain carboxylic acids, R—COOH. For example, the fatty acid palmitic acid, $C_{15}H_{31}COOH$, has the following structure.

palmitic acid

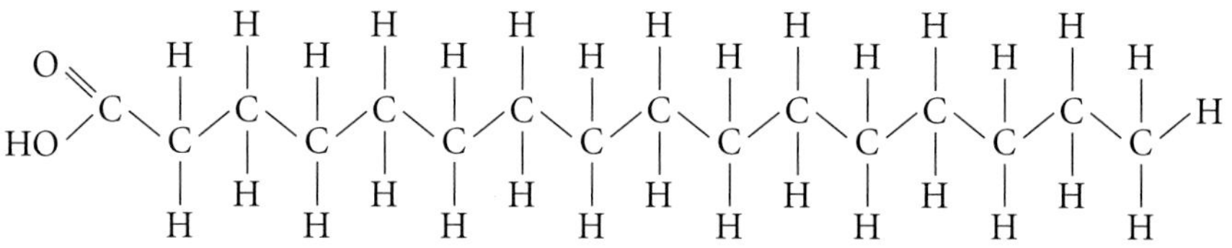

Figure 13.18 The structure of palmitic acid.

Until recently the American Food and Drug Administration (FDA) recommended that pregnant women and nursing mothers should limit their intake of fish to two servings per week, owing to concerns about mercury contamination. However, a study released in 2007 concluded that women who had eaten more than this amount of fish produced better-developed, more intelligent children and related this to increased omega-3-fatty acid intake. The obvious tension between these opposing recommendations leaves women with a difficult choice. One possible solution is to choose fish with low mercury levels such as salmon and sardines; another is to use omega-3-fatty acid dietary supplements.

An esterification reaction takes place between an acid —COOH group and each —OH group in glycerol, eliminating water as each ester link forms. So one glycerol condenses with *three* fatty acids to form the *tri*glyceride.

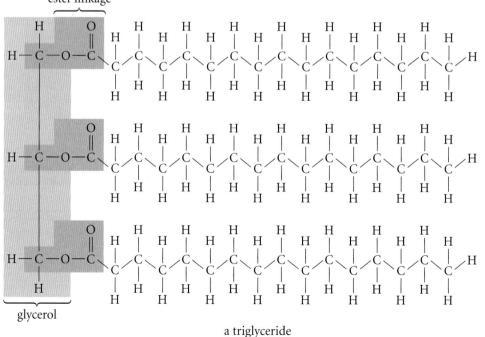

a triglyceride

Figure 13.19 A triglyceride.

In most natural oils and fats, the three fatty acids that form one triglyceride molecule are not all the same.

The fatty acids differ from each other in the following two ways which give rise to the specific properties of different fats and oils:

- The length of their hydrocarbon chain: the most abundant fatty acids have an even number of carbon atoms with chains between 14 and 22 carbons long.
- The number and position of carbon–carbon double bonds in the hydrocarbon chain: fatty acids with no double bonds are said to be **saturated**, those with just one double bond are described as **mono-unsaturated** and those with several double bonds are described as **polyunsaturated**.

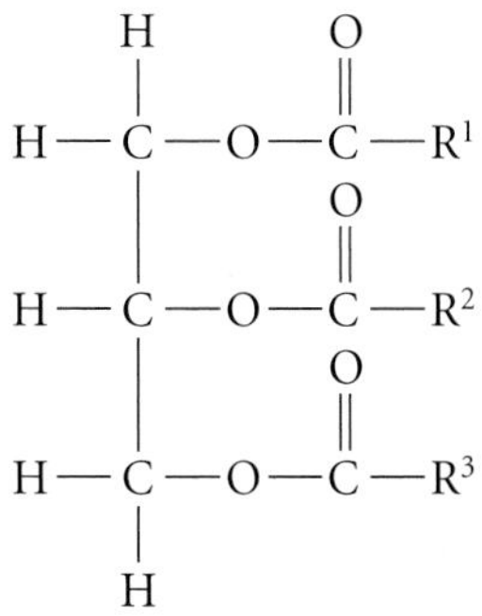

The nature of the fatty acids present in the triglyceride affects its melting point and some other important properties that we will discuss below. Because fats and oils usually contain a variety of fatty acids, they are classified according to the predominant types of unsaturation present.

Saturated fatty acids in which all carbon–carbon bonds are single have tetrahedral bond angles (109.5°) between their atoms. This allows the molecules to pack relatively closely together, leading to significant van der Waals' forces between them. As a result they form triglycerides with relatively high melting points that are solids at room temperature. They are known as **fats** and are derived mostly from animals. Common examples are butter and lard.

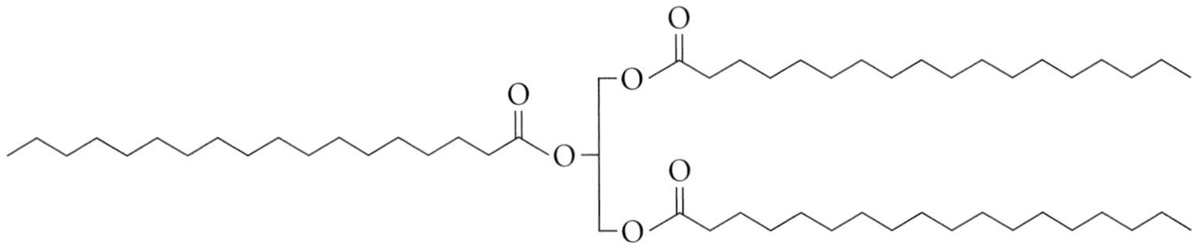

Figure 13.20 A triglyceride containing three different fatty acids, represented by R¹, R² and R³.

Saturated fatty acids contain all single carbon–carbon bonds; unsaturated fatty acids contain one or more double carbon–carbon bond in the hydrocarbon chain.

Figure 13.21 A saturated triglyceride. The zig-zag lines represent the hydrocarbon chains for each fatty acid.

saturated triglyceride

By contrast, the unsaturated fatty acids, containing one or more carbon–carbon double bonds with 120° bond angles, have kinks in the chains that make it more difficult for the molecules to pack closely together. So they form triglycerides with weaker intermolecular forces and hence lower melting points that are liquids at room temperature. They are known as **oils** and are found mostly in plants and fish. Common examples are corn oil and cod liver oil.

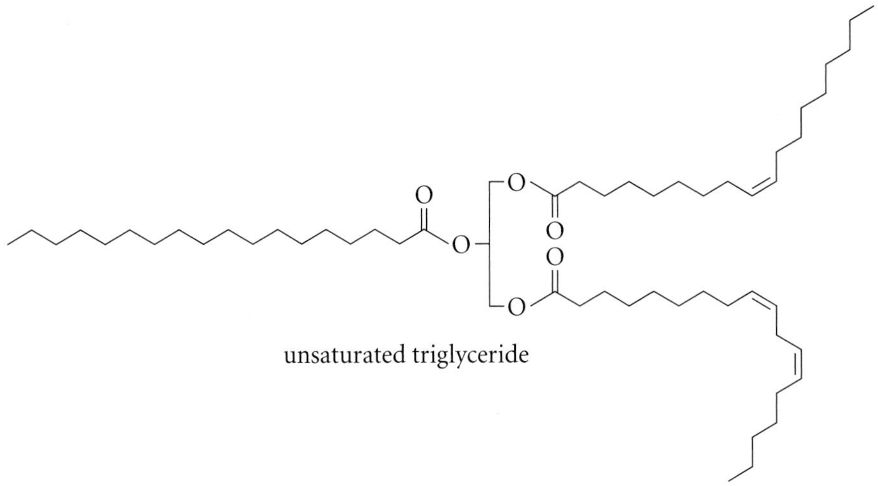

Figure 13.22 An unsaturated triglyceride. The double bonds put kinks in the hydrocarbon chains.

Fatty acids with an odd number of carbon atoms are rarely found in land-based animals, but are very common in marine organisms.

unsaturated triglyceride

As noted earlier, a strong correlation has been shown between diets rich in saturated fats and elevated levels of LDL cholesterol, with an associated increase in the incidence of heart disease.

Assortment of dietary oils (liquids) and fats (solids). Oils have a lower melting point because they contain unsaturated fatty acids. These lower the level of cholesterol in the blood.

When linoleic and linolenic fatty acids were first discovered to be essential nutrients in 1923, they were originally designated as Vitamin F. Like vitamins, they give rise to deficiency disorders when absent from the diet. However, later work showed that they are better classified with the fats than with the vitamins.

The iodine number of a fat is defined as the number of grams of iodine which reacts with 100 g of fat.

Essential fatty acids must be obtained in the diet

The body is able to synthesize the required saturated and mono-unsaturated fatty acids from other precursors, but is unable to make two polyunsaturated fatty acids, linoleic acid and linolenic acid. Their structures are as follows:

linoleic acid (omega-6-fatty acid)	$CH_3(CH_2)_4(CH=CHCH_2)_2(CH_2)_6COOH$
linolenic acid (omega-3-fatty acid)	$CH_3CH_2(CH=CHCH_2)_3(CH_2)_6COOH$

The terms omega-6 and omega-3 fatty acids refer to the position of the first double bond in the molecule relative to the terminal $-CH_3$ group. This is referred to as omega (the last letter in the Greek alphabet), to represent its distance from the $-COOH$ group. These structures (as condensed formulas) are given in Table 22 of the IB Data booklet.

Because they cannot be made in the body, these fatty acids must be obtained in the diet and are therefore known as **essential fatty acids**. They are obtained from plant and fish sources, for example, shellfish, leafy vegetables, canola oil and flaxseed oil. It has been shown that they play a part in many metabolic processes, including the synthesis of a group of lipids called prostaglandins which are involved in processes such as lowering blood pressure. As mentioned earlier in this section, there is also now evidence that these fatty acids, especially omega-3-fatty acids, play a role in lowering LDL cholesterol and hence help to protect against heart disease.

Determination of the degree of unsaturation in a fat uses iodine

Unsaturated fatty acids are able to undergo **addition reactions**, by breaking the double bond and adding incoming groups to the new bonding positions created on the carbon atoms. (This is a characteristic reaction of alkenes, described in Chapter 10.) Iodine (I_2) is able to react with unsaturated fats in this way.

$$\diagdown C=C\diagup + I_2 \longrightarrow -\overset{\overset{\textstyle I}{|}}{C}-\overset{\overset{\textstyle I}{|}}{C}-$$

The equation shows that one mole of iodine will react with each mole of double bonds in the fat. Therefore the higher the number of double bonds per molecule, the larger the amount of iodine that can react. This is expressed as the **iodine number**, defined as the number of grams of iodine which reacts with 100 grams of fat. It is therefore a measure of the amount of unsaturation in the fat.

Determination of the iodine number of a fat usually involves reacting a known amount of the fat with a known amount of iodine and waiting for the reaction to be completed. The amount of excess iodine remaining can then be calculated by titration with $Na_2S_2O_3(aq)$ from which the reacted iodine can be determined.

Worked example

Linoleic acid has the formula $C_{18}H_{32}O_2$. Determine the iodine number of linoleic acid.

Solution

The formula for linoleic acid can be expressed as $C_{17}H_{31}COOH$, from which we can deduce that it has two carbon–carbon double bonds.

Therefore 2 moles I_2 will react with 1 mole linoleic acid.

M_r for linoleic acid = $280 \, g \, mol^{-1}$ and M_r for I_2 = $254 \, g \, mol^{-1}$

Therefore 280 g linoleic acid reacts with 508 g I_2

So 100 g reacts with $\dfrac{508 \times 100}{280} = 181 \, g$

Therefore iodine number = 181

Exercise

5 A sample of fat containing 0.02 moles of fatty acid was found to react with 10.16 g of iodine. Determine the number of carbon–carbon double bonds present in the fatty acid.

Addition reactions to unsaturated fats are used in the food industry

You may have seen the term 'partially hydrogenated fat' on food labels. This refers to oils which have been chemically modified by addition reactions as described above, using hydrogen to add across double bonds and so decrease the degree of unsaturation. The outcome is a fat which, being more saturated, has a higher melting point and therefore is in a more convenient form for packing and storage as a solid or semi-solid. Fats made in this way also break down less easily under conditions of high temperature frying and usually have a longer shelf life than liquid oils. Most margarines and shortening come into this category.

Foods containing *trans* fats produced by hydrogenation. The process is used to solidify fats and extend their shelf life, but has been linked to increased risk of heart disease.

There is, however, a problem with this process. The chemical modifications involve heat and pressure treatments, during which a chemical change occurs affecting the positions of the groups around the remaining double bonds, altering them from the so-called *cis* position on the bond to the *trans* position. The resulting fats are therefore known as **trans fats**. They are particularly prevalent in processed foods and are always present when food is described as 'partially dehydrogenated'. Evidence shows that consuming *trans* fats raises the level of LDL cholesterol which is a risk factor for heart disease. Furthermore, *trans* fats reduce the blood levels of HDL cholesterol which protects against heart disease. So *trans* fats, like saturated fats and for the same reason, must clearly be reduced or eliminated from a healthy diet. Limiting the intake of commercially fried food and high fat bakery products is an important step in this process.

The growing awareness of the link between *trans* fats and heart disease has caused many different responses around the world. Denmark has the strictest *trans* fats legislation of all countries and since 2004 these fats have effectively been banned. Canada was the first country to introduce mandatory labelling of *trans* fats on food products and this had an effect on the food manufacturing industry, actively reducing the *trans* fat content of their food. In 2007 New York City banned restaurants from using them and other major American cities are likely to follow suit. The World Health Organization has recommended that all governments phase out use of *trans* fats if labelling alone does not spur significant reductions. The cost of this is, however, considerable as it will involve major changes in food formulations.

Digestion of fats

Fats and oils are insoluble molecules so cannot be transported in the blood. They are therefore broken down to their component molecules (fatty acids and glycerol) in the gut in the process of digestion. This involves hydrolysis reactions, in which water is used, under the control of enzymes known as **lipases**.

Lipases are secreted in different parts of the gut and act sequentially to complete the digestion of the lipid as it passes through. Typically these are the slowest molecules to be broken down in digestion and may take many hours before they are made soluble and can be absorbed into the blood. Lipases, being enzymes and hence made of protein, are very sensitive to changes in the pH of the medium. Controlling the pH in different parts of the gut is therefore one way in which the body controls lipid digestion.

2 Structure of phospholipids

Phospholipids are similar to triglycerides in that they are also derived from fatty acids and glycerol, but have only two fatty acids condensed onto the glycerol molecule. The third —OH position of the glycerol has, instead, condensed with a phosphate group. Different phospholipids vary in their fatty acid chains and in the group attached to the phosphate. One of the most common phospholipids is known as **lecithin** shown below.

Figure 13.23 Representations of the structure of phospholipids.

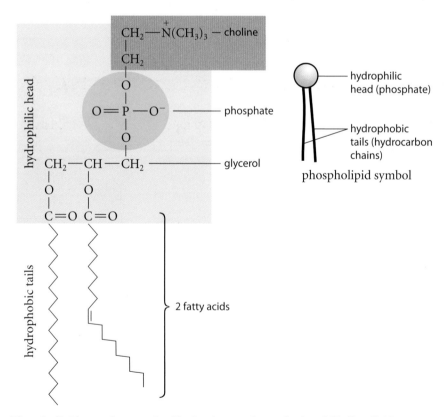

Phospholipids are characterized by having a polar, or hydrophilic 'head' (the phosphate group) and two non-polar, or hydrophobic 'tails' (the hydrocarbon chains of the fatty acids). As a result they will spontaneously form a **phospholipid bilayer** which maximizes the interactions between the polar groups and water, while creating a non-polar (hydrophobic) interior.

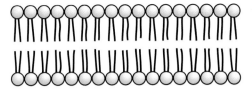

Figure 13.24 Phospholipid bilayer.

phospholipid bilayer

This phospholipid bilayer provides the basis of membrane structure.

3 Structure of steroids

Steroids are lipids with a structure consisting of four fused rings. One of the most important steroids is **cholesterol** which has the following structure.

Figure 13.25 Structure of cholesterol.

cholesterol

Cholesterol is the steroid used in the body in the synthesis of many other steroids, including the sex hormones. The uses and problems of cholesterol in the body were discussed earlier in this section.

W You can read a summary and test yourself on the biochemistry you have learned so far. There are links from here to other sites.

Now go to www.heinemann.co.uk/hotlinks, insert the express code 4259P and click on this activity.

B.5 Micronutrients and macronutrients

Nutrients are classified according to amounts needed

The term 'nutrients' refers to molecules that are required in the diet for absorption and use by the body. Given the complexity of metabolic processes, it is not surprising that we need an equally complex array of nutrients to maintain health. A key concept in the consideration of a healthy diet is *balance* between the different types of nutrients. It is convenient to classify nutrients roughly according to the amounts in which they are needed, usually expressed as the **recommended daily intake**.

Micronutrients are those needed in extremely small amounts, generally less than 0.005% of body mass. Their quantities are so small they are usually measured in mg or μg per day. These substances are needed to enable the body to produce enzymes, hormones and other substances essential for health. As tiny as the amounts are, however, the consequences of their absence are severe. Micronutrients include the **vitamins** and many so-called **trace minerals** such as Fe, Cu, Zn, I, Se, Mn, Mo, Cr, Co and B.

Macronutrients are those nutrients needed in relatively large amounts. They are used to provide energy in the body and to build and maintain its structure. They include the macromolecules described earlier in this chapter – carbohydrates, proteins and lipids – as well as some minerals needed on a larger scale such as Na, Mg, K, Ca, P, S and Cl.

i The average adult has 1.0–1.5 kg of calcium in their body, of which 99% is found in bones and teeth; the remainder is in body fluids and membranes.

Vitamins are organic micronutrients

Vitamins are organic compounds, needed in small amounts for normal growth and metabolism, which are not synthesized in the body. They are usually broken down by the reactions in which they are involved, so must be taken in the diet.

Vitamins vary in whether they are principally soluble in water or in fat. Water-soluble vitamins are transported directly in the blood and excesses are filtered out by the kidneys and excreted. Fat-soluble vitamins are slower to be absorbed and excesses tend to be stored in fat tissues where they can produce serious side-effects. Differences in their structure determine these solubility differences. Vitamins that are water soluble have polar bonds and the ability to form hydrogen bonds with water. Those that are fat soluble are mostly non-polar molecules with long hydrocarbon chains or rings. The structures of some important vitamins are given in Table 21 of the IB Data booklet, so they do not have to be learned. It is important, though, that you can explain their different solubilities through interpreting their structures.

Vitamin	Structure	Solubility and properties
A retinol		Fat soluble Hydrocarbon chain and ring are non-polar and influence the solubility more than the one —OH group. Involved in the visual cycle in the eye and particularly important for vision at low light intensity.
C ascorbic acid		Water soluble Several —OH groups enable hydrogen bonds to form with water. Acts as cofactor in some enzymic reactions and important in tissue regeneration following injury and also helps give resistance to some diseases.
D calciferol		Fat soluble Predominantly a hydrocarbon molecule with four non-polar rings and only one —OH group. Note its chemical similarity to cholesterol. Stimulates the uptake of calcium ions by cells and so is important in the health of bones and teeth.

Vitamin C contains several functional groups (—OH and —C=C—) that are relatively easily oxidized. This is why the vitamin is easily destroyed by most methods of food processing and storage and is hence best obtained from *fresh* fruits and vegetables.

Exercise

6 By referring to Table 21 in the IB Data booklet, identify one vitamin that is water soluble and one vitamin that is fat soluble. Explain the differences in solubility in terms of their structures and intermolecular forces.

Malnutrition is the result of deficiencies or imbalance in the diet

When people do not obtain a regular, balanced supply of the diverse nutrients needed in the diet, they suffer from **malnutrition**. This describes a broad spectrum of conditions that are always associated with compromised health and increased mortality. The main focus of malnutrition has traditionally been the large variety of nutrient-deficiency diseases and in particular the incidence of these in underdeveloped countries. But malnutrition is not uniquely the concern of poor countries. Increasingly the world is seeing a dramatic increase in diseases caused by high consumption of processed, energy-dense but micronutrient-poor foods. The term *malnutrition* can therefore also be used to describe the resulting chronic diseases such as obesity and diabetes particularly prevalent in industrialized countries.

Micronutrient deficiencies

The World Health Organization has identified iodine, vitamin A and iron deficiencies as the most important micronutrient deficiencies in global health terms, so these three will be discussed here.

Iodine is needed in the diet for the synthesis of the hormone thyroxine, which regulates the metabolic rate. It is present in most types of seafood and in some vegetables. A lack of iodine in the diet causes a swelling of the thyroid gland in the neck, known as **goitre**. In children, iodine deficiency is considered to be the world's largest cause of preventable mental retardation. The main strategy for the control of iodine deficiency is through adding it to salt, which has an extremely low cost.

Despite its extraordinary progress in reducing the rate of iodine deficiency in most parts of the world, the salt iodization programme has been much less successful in many parts of Europe. In addition, there is growing evidence that iodine deficiency is reappearing in some European countries where it was thought to have been eliminated. The reasons for these trends are currently the subject of research and policy review.

The lack of vitamin C in stored foods was the reason many sailors on long voyages suffered from a deficiency disease known as scurvy in the 1800s. The symptoms of this are bleeding gums, poor resistance to infection and dark spots on the skin; if untreated it is fatal. Because the concept of a disease resulting from the *lack* of a dietary component was not understood, it took a long time to establish the link between scurvy and vitamin C deficiency. Meanwhile, the British Navy found that supplementing the diet of the crew with limes prevented occurrence of the disease, which is why British people are sometimes still known as 'limeys' in America.

'Freedom from hunger and malnutrition is a basic human right and their alleviation is a fundamental prerequisite for human and national development.' World Health Organization

Bangladeshi woman with large goitre. This swelling of the neck is caused by enlargement of the thyroid gland owing to lack of iodine in the diet. Treatment includes an iodine-rich diet of fish and iodized salt.

Vitamin A (retinol) is needed in the diet for healthy skin (acne treatment), good eyesight and protection against some damaging effects of toxins, as it is an antioxidant. It is found in orange and yellow fruits and vegetables, spinach and egg yolks. A deficiency in vitamin A causes **xerophthalmia**, a condition characterized by dry eyes and also night blindness. Since it is a fat-soluble vitamin it has been found that it can be effectively added to margarine in a process known as 'vitamin A fortification'. The process is simple and inexpensive and has been found to reduce levels of xerophthalmia in many parts of the world. The potential of rice as a vehicle for vitamin A fortification is also being explored, given that rice is an important staple in many countries where the prevalence of vitamin A deficiency is high.

Iron deficiency is currently considered to be the most prevalent micronutrient deficiency in the world. Because iron is an essential part of haemoglobin, which is the pigment in red blood cells responsible for transporting oxygen around the body, its deficiency leads to a serious condition known as **anaemia**. The symptoms of this are fatigue, brittle nails, poor endurance and lowered immunity. Iron is found in red meats, green leafy vegetables, nuts and seeds. While its dietary deficiency is a cause of concern in many parts of the world, the question of how best to alleviate this is complicated by the fact that iron supplementation may increase the susceptibility to malaria, which is also widespread. Iron fortification has been found to be most effective when added with vitamin C to cereal flours and milk products.

Some other significant micronutrient deficiencies and their resulting diseases are summarized in the table below.

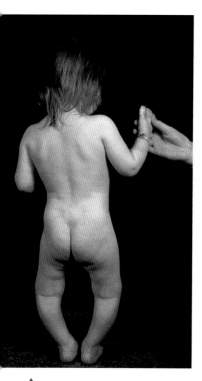

▲ Child suffering from rickets. Rickets is a disease in growing children in which the bones do not harden and are malformed owing to a deficiency in vitamin D which is necessary for the uptake of calcium.

Exposure to sunlight is an important source of vitamin D as ultraviolet rays trigger its synthesis in the skin. But increasingly it is becoming known that ultraviolet light also has a damaging effect on the skin and can be the cause of skin cancers (Chapter 16), which necessitates the use of sunscreens. Sunscreens with a protection factor of 8 or greater will block UV rays that produce vitamin D. This makes it even more important to include good sources of vitamin D in the diet when sun exposure is limited in this way.

Micronutrient	Deficiency condition or disease
niacin, vitamin B3	pellagra: dermatitis, diarrhoea and dementia
thiamin, vitamin B1	beriberi: weight loss, fatigue and swelling
ascorbic acid, vitamin C	scurvy: bleeding gums, lowered resistance to infection and dark spots on the skin
calciferol, vitamin D	rickets: softened and deformed bones
selenium	Kashin–Beck disease: atrophy and degeneration of cartilage. This occurs particularly in parts of northern Russia and China where the soil is Se deficient.

Macronutrient deficiencies

Severe malnutrition can include protein deficiency and when this is prolonged it is life threatening. Half of the 10.4 million deaths occurring in children younger than five years old in developing countries are associated with protein deficiencies.

Marasmus is a condition resulting from protein deficiency found mainly in infants from developing countries at the time of weaning or when a mother's milk is greatly reduced. It is characterized by failure to gain weight, followed by weight loss and emaciation. **Kwashiorkor** is a similar condition that affects young children whose diet is high in starch and low in protein.

Summary

In summary, we can see that the causes of malnutrition are varied and widespread. They include:
- lack of distribution of global resources
- depletion of nutrients in the soil and water cultures through soil erosion
- lack of education about, or understanding of, the importance of a balanced diet
- over-processing of food for transport and storage
- the use of chemical treatments such as herbicides in food production.

Equally, there are many possible solutions to the varying challenges of malnutrition. These include:
- fortification of different staple foods with micronutrients
- the availability of nutritional supplements in many forms
- possible improvements in nutrient content of food through genetic modification
- increased labelling of foods with content information
- education regarding the nature of a balanced diet and promotion of the importance of personal responsibility in dietary choices.

As we reach the end of this section on the chemistry of the molecules in your diet and how they affect your health, you may like to ask yourself in the light of what you have learned here, what changes to your diet do you think would be beneficial to your health? And how could you make those changes?

W You can visit the World Health Organization website to find out more about particular diseases of malnutrition by country. You can even view it in your own language. Now go to www.heinemann.co.uk/ hotlinks, insert the express code 4259P and click on this activity.

13.6 Hormones

Different parts of the body are specialized to perform particular functions, but must communicate with each other to ensure the health of the whole. There are two main methods of communication in the body: the nervous system, which uses electrochemical messages and the endocrine system, which is based on chemical messengers known as **hormones**. The latter is the system we will discuss here.

Hormones have a variety of chemical structures, including many of the types of molecules described earlier in this chapter. Some are proteins, others are steroids, and still others are modified amino acids or fatty acids. What they have in common is the fact that they are produced in glands known as **endocrine glands**, which have no duct and so secrete the hormone directly into the blood. Once in the bloodstream, the hormones circulate throughout the body but bring about responses only in cells that have receptors for them, known as **target cells**. It is a little bit like communicating by sending a radio message – the waves are transmitted everywhere, but only working radios tuned to the appropriate frequency will detect them.

The position of some important endocrine glands in the body is shown in Figure 13.26.

Figure 13.26 The human endocrine system.

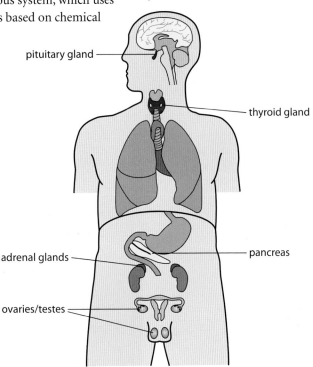

pituitary gland

thyroid gland

adrenal glands

pancreas

ovaries/testes

Some of the important hormones with their functions and target cells are summarized below.

Endocrine gland	Hormone name and structural type	Target cells	Functions
pituitary gland	anti-diuretic hormone (ADH); a short peptide	kidney tubules	increases uptake of water, so raises the concentration of urine; important in the control of osmotic potential of the blood
thyroid gland	thyroxine; modified amino acid containing iodine	all cells	regulation of the basal metabolic rate, growth and development
adrenal cortex	aldosterone; steroid	kidney tubules	increases uptake of Na^+ by the kidneys and so important in the control of Na^+ and K^+ ratios in fluids; raises blood pressure
adrenal medulla	adrenaline (epinephrine), modified amino acid	many parts of the body including muscles, brain, circulatory and digestive systems	raises blood glucose level, increases rate and force of heartbeat and increases blood supply to heart and skeletal muscles
pancreas	insulin; protein	all cells, especially liver	decreases blood glucose level by increasing uptake and utilization by cells; increases glucose to glycogen conversion in the liver
ovary	estrogen (estradiol) and progesterone; steroids	many parts of the body; especially the uterus lining during pregnancy	development of secondary female characteristics, control of menstrual cycle, growth and development of placenta and foetus
testes	testosterone; steroid	many parts of the body	development of male secondary sexual characteristics

Insulin pump attached to the abdomen of a woman who suffers from diabetes, caused by failure of her pancreas to secrete sufficient insulin. The insulin is delivered directly into her blood to control glucose levels. The dosage is altered according to her activity and dietary intake and must be constantly checked and adjusted.

Steroid-based hormones all have a common structure

We learned earlier that cholesterol is a steroid molecule, a lipid based on four fused hydrocarbon rings. By studying the structures shown below (which are given in Table 21 of the IB Data booklet) you can see that the hormones, known collectively as the 'sex hormones' are also based on this chemical framework. The different side chains and functional groups they possess give them their different properties.

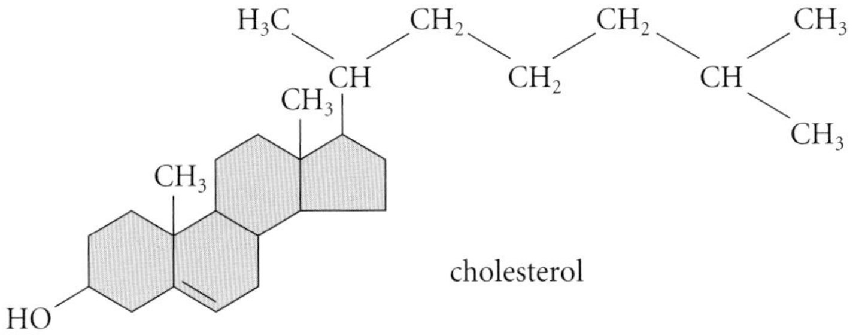

cholesterol

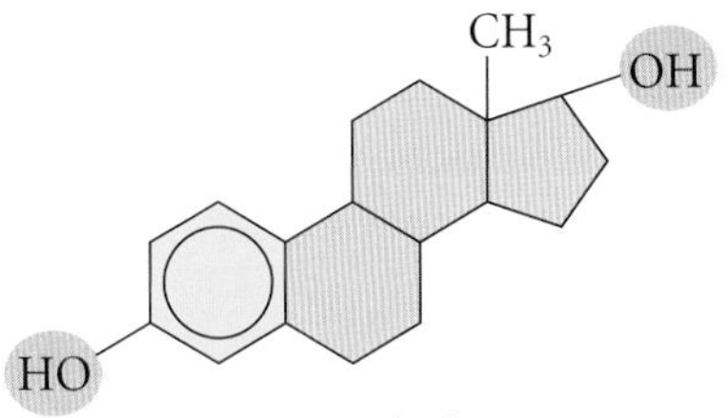

estradiol
(estrogen)

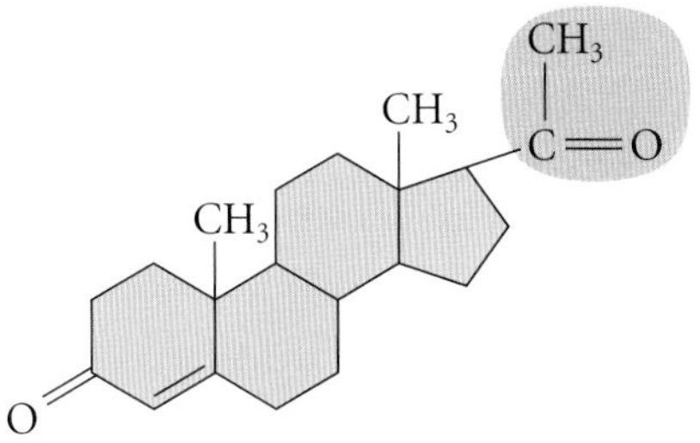

progesterone

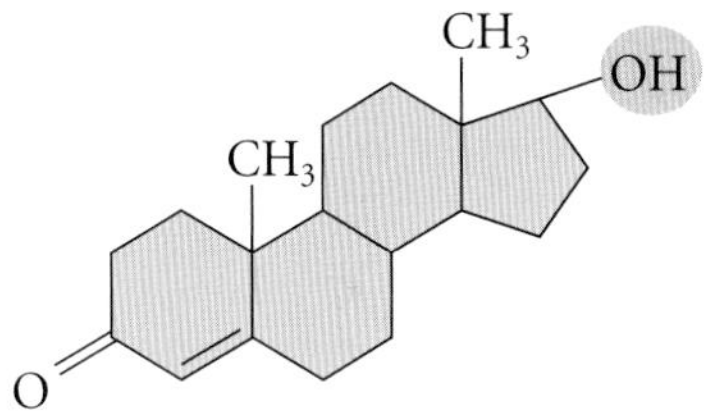

testosterone

The female sex hormone progesterone differs only slightly from the male sex hormone testosterone by having a ketone group in place of the alcohol group. The other female sex hormone estradiol differs from the other steroids in that it contains an aromatic ring (benzene structure). It also contains two alcohol groups which is why it is known as estradiol.

Figure 13.27 Comparison of the structures of cholesterol and the sex hormones.

Exercise

7 Refer to the structural formulas given above for cholesterol and testosterone.
  (a) Identify the class of compound to which cholesterol and testosterone belong.
  (b) State the names of two functional groups present in both cholesterol and testosterone.
  (c) Cholesterol and testosterone both contain a five-membered ring as part of their structures. Deduce the total number of hydrogen atoms joined directly to the carbon atoms in the ring.

Oral contraceptives

One of the most effective forms of contraception is the oral contraceptive pill which usually works by preventing ovulation, the release of an unfertilized ovum. The pill contains a mixture of the female hormones progesterone and estrogen and so acts to suppress the secretion of other hormones known as FSH (follicle stimulating hormone) and LH (luteinizing hormone) which normally act in tandem to trigger ovulation. In effect, it simulates the hormonal conditions of pregnancy. Many different versions of the contraceptive pill exist, but most commonly a pill is taken every day for three weeks and then stopped for one week during which menstruation happens. In many countries, the pill is available only by prescription from a doctor so that side-effects can be monitored. Other pills, known as 'morning after' pills, contain higher concentrations of the hormones progesterone and estrogen and may prevent pregnancy from occurring following unprotected intercourse. They are, however, intended only for emergency use.

Time Magazine named Margaret Sanger as one of the 100 most influential people of the last century for her fight in legalizing contraception. Working in the poorest neighbourhoods of New York City in the early 1900s, she saw women deprived of their health and ability to care for children already born. She had already witnessed her own mother's slow death, worn out after 18 pregnancies and 11 live births. At the time, contraceptive information was suppressed, so Sanger, in defying church and state in promoting the cause, was often arrested and involved in court battles. She coined the term 'birth control' in 1914 and lived to see the marketing of the first contraceptive pill in 1960. It is considered to be one of the most culturally and demographically significant medications in history, taken by millions of women worldwide.

To what extent do current societial belief systems, enshrined in the legal system of a country, constrain the development of new paradigms?

Uses and abuses of steroids

Female steroid hormones are used as described above in contraceptive pill formulations. They are also used in medications prescribed to women at menopause to alleviate some of the unpleasant symptoms. This is known as HRT (hormone replacement therapy) because the hormones replace those secreted in the body prior to menopause. In all these uses of hormones, possible side-effects must be monitored and ongoing research is essential to provide data about long term usage.

Male steroid hormones are collectively called **androgens**, of which testosterone is the most important. Medical uses of testosterone include treatment of disorders of the testes and breast cancer. These hormones are also known as **anabolic steroids** owing to their role in promoting tissue growth especially of muscles. Synthetic forms are used medically to help gain weight after debilitating diseases.

Modified synthetic forms of these anabolic steroids have been used by athletes to build up body muscles and supposedly to increase endurance. This has been particularly prevalent in sports like weight lifting and wrestling, as well as in running, swimming and cycling. However, there are serious medical and ethical issues concerning this practice and it is a continuing focus of major concern by national and international sporting authorities. Anabolic steroids can cause many changes in secondary sexual characteristics resulting from systemic hormone imbalances. Changes in hair distribution, sexual desire and fertility are common. Of greater danger to the individual is the fact that these hormones are toxic to the liver and have an associated increased risk of liver cancer. Their use is banned by most sporting bodies and regular 'drug testing' involving urine analysis is now widespread.

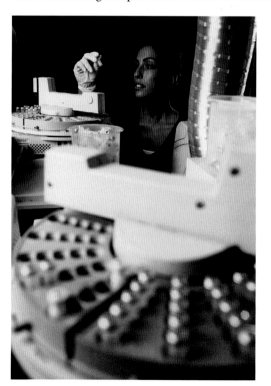

Scientist centrifuging samples sent for anti-doping testing at the laboratories of the Italian National Olympic Committee. The samples will be analysed for performance-enhancing drugs such as anabolic steroids. Drug testing like this has become a major industry associated with many sports.

1 (a) Draw the straight chain structure of glucose. (1)
   (b) The structure of α-glucose is shown right.

   Outline the structural difference between α-glucose and β-glucose. (1)
   (c) Glucose molecules can condense to form starch which can exist in two forms, amylose
       and amylopectin. Describe the structural differences between the two forms. (2)
   (d) 1.00 g of sucrose, $C_{12}H_{22}O_{11}$, was completely combusted in a food calorimeter. The
       heat evolved was equivalent to increasing the temperature of 631 g of water from
       18.36 °C to 24.58 °C. Calculate the calorific value of sucrose (in kJ mol^{-1}) given the
       specific heat capacity of water in Table 2 of the IB Data booklet. (3)
       (*Total 7 marks*)
       © International Baccalaureate Organization [2003]

2 Polypeptides and proteins are formed by the condensation reactions of amino acids.
   (a) Give the general structural formula of a 2-amino acid. (1)
   (b) Give the structural formula of the dipeptide formed by the reaction of alanine and
       glycine. State the other substance formed during this reaction. (2)
   (c) State two functions of proteins in the body. (2)
   (d) Electrophoresis can be used to identify the amino acids present in a given protein.
       The protein must first be hydrolysed.
       (i) State the reagent and conditions needed to hydrolyse the protein and
           identify the bond that is broken during hydrolysis. (4)
       (ii) Explain how the amino acids could be identified using electrophoresis. (4)
       (*Total 13 marks*)
       © International Baccalaureate Organization [2003]

3 The structures of the amino acids cysteine and serine are shown in Table 19 of the IB
   Data booklet. They can react with each other to form a dipeptide.
   (a) State the type of reaction occurring when amino acids react together and identify
       the other product of the reaction. (2)
   (b) Draw the structures of the two possible dipeptides formed in the reaction between
       one molecule each of cysteine and serine. (2)
   (c) Six tripeptides can be formed by reacting together one molecule of each of the
       amino acids arginine, histidine and leucine. Predict the primary structures of these
       six tripeptides using the symbols shown in Table 19 of the IB Data booklet to
       represent the amino acids. (3)
   (d) When many amino acid molecules react together a protein is formed. These proteins
       have primary, secondary and tertiary structures.
       (i) State the type of intermolecular force responsible for maintaining the
           secondary structure. (1)
       (ii) State **two** other ways in which the tertiary structure of the protein is
            maintained. (2)
       (*Total 10 marks*)
       © International Baccalaureate Organization [2004]

4 Fats and oils can be described as esters of glycerol, $C_3H_8O_3$.

  (a) **(i)** Draw the structure of glycerol. (1)

     (ii) Glycerol can react with three molecules of stearic acid, $C_{17}H_{35}COOH$, to form a triglyceride. Deduce the number of carbon atoms in one molecule of this triglyceride. (1)

    (iii) A triglyceride is also formed in the reaction between glycerol and three molecules of oleic acid, $C_{17}H_{33}COOH$. State and explain which of the two triglycerides (the one formed from stearic acid or the one formed from oleic acid) has the higher melting point. (3)

  (b) An oil sample containing 0.0100 mol of oil was found to react with 7.61 g of iodine, I_2. Determine the number of C=C double bonds present in each molecule of the oil. (2)

(Total 7 marks)

© International Baccalaureate Organization [2003]

5 **(a)** A brand of vegetable fat consists of 88% unsaturated fats and 12% saturated fats. State the major structural difference between unsaturated and saturated fats. (1)

  (b) Linoleic acid, $CH_3(CH_2)_4CH=CHCH_2CH=CH(CH_2)_7COOH$, and palmitic acid, $CH_3(CH_2)_{14}COOH$, are components of vegetable fat. Explain why palmitic acid has the higher melting point. (3)

  (c) The energy content of a vegetable oil was determined using a calorimeter. A 5.00 g sample of the oil was completely combusted in a calorimeter containing 1000 g of water at an initial temperature of 18.0 °C. On complete combustion of the oil, the temperature of the water rose to 65.3 °C.

    Calculate the calorific value of the oil in kJ g^{-1}. (4)

  (d) List **two** functions of fats in the human body. (2)

(Total 10 marks)

© International Baccalaureate Organization [2005]

6 Linoleic acid, $C_{17}H_{31}COOH$, ($M_r = 280$) and stearic acid, $C_{17}H_{35}COOH$, ($M_r = 284$) both contain 18 carbon atoms and have similar molar masses.

  (a) Explain why the melting point of linoleic acid is considerably lower than the melting point of stearic acid. (3)

  (b) Determine the maximum mass of iodine, I_2, ($M_r = 254$) that can add to:

    (i) 100 g of stearic acid (1)

    (ii) 100 g of linoleic acid (2)

  (c) Draw the simplified structural formula of a fat containing one stearic acid and two linoleic acid residues. (1)

(Total 7 marks)

© International Baccalaureate Organization [2003]

7 The structures of two sex hormones, progesterone and testosterone, are shown in Table 21 of the Data booklet.

  (a) State the names of **two** functional groups that are present in **both** hormones. (2)

  (b) Identify which of the two hormones is the female sex hormone and where in the human body it is produced. (2)

  (c) Outline the mode of action of oral contraceptives. (3)

(Total 7 marks)

© International Baccalaureate Organization [2004]

8 (a) State the name of a disease which results from the deficiency of each of the following vitamins. (2)

    vitamin A

    vitamin C

    vitamin D

(b) A person consumes an excess of both vitamin A and C. State, with a reason, which **one** is more likely to be stored in the body and which is more likely to be excreted. (2)

(Total 4 marks)

© International Baccalaureate Organization [2005]

9 (a) The structures of three important vitamins are shown in Table 21 of the IB Data booklet. State the name of each one and deduce whether each is water-soluble or fat-soluble, explaining your choices by reference to their structures. (5)

(b) Identify the metal ion needed for the maintenance of healthy bones and state the name of the vitamin needed for its uptake. (2)

(c) State the name of the vitamin responsible for maintaining healthy eyesight and the name of the functional group which is most common in this vitamin. (2)

(d) Identify **one** major function of vitamin C in the human body and state the name of the most common disease caused by deficiency of this vitamin. (2)

(e) Fresh fruits and vegetables are good sources of vitamin C. Explain why some meals made from these foods may contain little vitamin C. (2)

(Total 13 marks)

© International Baccalaureate Organization [2004]

10 (a) Using the three-letter word symbols for amino acids, show all the possible tripeptides that can form from the three amino acids tyrosine, valine and histidine. (3)

(b) Deduce the number of different peptides that could form from the four amino acids tyrosine, valine, histidine and proline. (2)

(Total 5 marks)

11 (a) List the interactions responsible for forming the tertiary structure of protein. (4)

(b) Give two conditions under which the tertiary structure can be disrupted, and for each explain the chemical basis of this effect. (4)

(Total 8 marks)

12 (a) Distinguish between the terms *micro* and *macro nutrient* and give three examples of each. (5)

(b) Give examples of three micronutrient deficiency diseases with reference to the dietary deficiency. (3)

(c) Suggest ways in which micronutrient deficiencies can be alleviated. (3)

(Total 11 marks)

14 Chemistry in industry and technology

Option C

The Iron Bridge spanning the River Severn in England was completed in 1779 and has come to be regarded as a symbol of the beginning of the British Industrial Revolution. It is now a World Heritage site.

One of the key roles of the chemist is to transform natural resources which are readily available into more useful forms of matter. Civilisations are sometimes characterized by the technology they have developed to accomplish this. The bronze age, for example, marks the time when the ancients were able to produce copper from smelted ores. The extraction of iron from its ore in the blast furnace is probably one of the most significant developments in the industrial revolution of the 18th century.

These technological advances, however, often came without a full understanding of the underlying scientific principles. Today chemists are able to use their understanding of the bonding and structure of materials to develop new substances with properties to serve modern needs. This chapter discusses traditional heavy industries related to the extraction of metals and the manufacture of plastics from crude oil and gives some indications of future developments, both in the materials and the sources of energy we use.

Computer graphic of a molecular tube. Nanotechnology, which has grown rapidly since the 1990s, involves the construction of such devices. It has been described as 'the science of the very small with big potential' and could revolutionize computing, medicine and manufacturing. Each of the coloured spheres represents a single atom: carbon (blue), oxygen (red) and hydrogen (yellow).

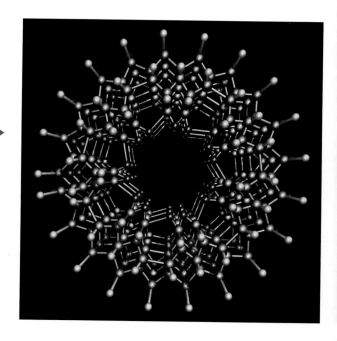

Assessment statements

C.1 Iron, steel and aluminium

C.1.1   State the main sources of iron.

C.1.2   Describe and explain the reactions that occur in the blast furnace.

C.1.3   Describe and explain the conversion of iron into steel using the basic oxygen converter.

C.1.4   Describe alloys as a homogeneous mixture of metals or a mixture of a metal and non-metal.

C.1.5   Explain how alloying can modify the properties of metals.

C.1.6   Describe the effect of heat treatment of steel.

C.1.7   Describe the properties and uses of iron and steel.

C.1.8   Describe and explain the production of aluminium by electrolysis of alumina in molten cryolite.

C1.9   Describe the main properties and uses of aluminium and its alloys.

C.1.10 Discuss the environmental impact of iron and aluminium production.

C.2 The oil industry

C.2.1   Compare the use of oil as an energy source and as a chemical feedstock.

C.2.2   Compare catalytic cracking, thermal cracking and steam cracking.

C.3 Addition polymers

C.3.1   Describe and explain how the properties of polymers depend on their structural features.

C.3.2   Describe the ways of modifying the properties of addition polymers.

C.3.3   Discuss the advantages and disadvantages of polymer use.

C.4 Catalysts

C.4.1   Compare the modes of action of homogeneous and heterogeneous catalysts.

C.4.2   Outline the advantages and disadvantages of homogeneous and heterogeneous catalysts.

C.4.3   Discuss the factors in choosing a catalyst for a process.

C.5 Fuel cells and rechargeable batteries

C.5.1   Describe how a hydrogen–oxygen fuel cell works.

C.5.2   Describe the workings of rechargeable batteries.

C.5.3   Discuss the similarities and differences between fuel cells and rechargeable batteries.

C.6 Liquid crystals

C.6.1   Describe the meaning of the term *liquid crystals*.

C.6.2   Distinguish between *thermotropic* and *lyotropic* liquid crystals.

C.6.3   Describe the liquid-crystal state in terms of the arrangement of the molecules and explain thermotropic behaviour.

C.6.4   Outline the principles of the liquid-crystal display device.

C.6.5   Discuss the properties needed for a substance to be used in liquid-crystal displays.

C.7 Nanotechnology

C.7.1   Define the term *nanotechnology*.

C.7.2   Distinguish between *physical* and *chemical* techniques in manipulating atoms to form molecules.

C.7.3   Describe the structure and properties of carbon nanotubes.

C.7.4   Discuss some of the implications of nanotechnology.

Iron, steel and aluminium

The ability to extract metals was an important technological step in the development of our civilisation. Some unreactive metals, such as gold and silver, occur in nature as the free element. More reactive metals are found in rocks or **ores** as compounds, combined with other elements present in the environment. These ores are usually oxides, sulfides or carbonates of the metal mixed with impurities. The extraction of metals from these ores, involves the reduction of the metal compounds (see Chapter 9) and the removal of impurities. Transition metal oxides can be reduced by chemical means using carbon. More reactive metals such as aluminium are extracted using electrolysis to reduce the metal ions.

Haematite is a variety of iron oxide (Fe_2O_3), mined as one of the main ores of iron.

Iron

Most of the metal around you is iron or steel. Iron is too reactive to be found naturally in its elemental form and is most commonly found as an oxide or sulfide. It is extracted, mainly from its ores **haematite** (Fe_2O_3) and **magnetite** (Fe_3O_4) in a **blast furnace**. Pyrites (FeS_2), although a common ore, is not usually used, as the sulfur dioxide produced under such conditions causes acid rain.

Figure 14.1 A blast furnace is a steel tower approximately 60 m high, lined with heat-resistant bricks.

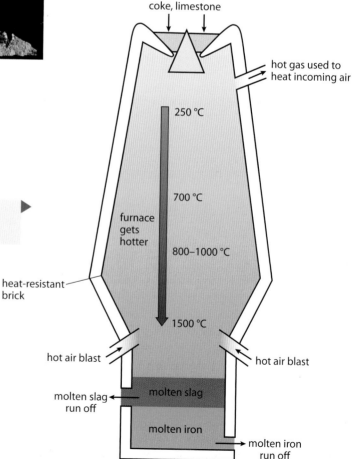

Iron ore, **coke** (an impure form of carbon formed by heating coal) and **limestone** ($CaCO_3$) are added at the top of the blast furnace and a blast of **hot air** is blown in from near the bottom. The iron ore is added in the form of small pellets, which have a large surface area to increase the rate of reaction.

The coke burns in the preheated air to form carbon dioxide:

$$C(s) + O_2(g) \rightarrow CO_2(g) \quad \Delta H = -298 \, kJ \, mol^{-1}$$

The heat produced in this reaction increases the temperatures at the bottom of the furnace. Under these conditions, the limestone, which is added to remove acidic impurities, decomposes to calcium oxide:

$$CaCO_3(s) \rightarrow CaO(s) + CO_2(g)$$

The carbon dioxide produced in both these reactions will react with more hot coke to produce carbon monoxide:

$$C(s) + CO_2(g) \rightarrow 2CO(g)$$

The carbon monoxide acts as the **reducing agent**. The gas reduces the iron(III) oxide as it rises up the furnace:

$$Fe_2O_3(s) + 3CO(g) \rightarrow 2Fe(l) + 3CO_2(g)$$

The iron produced is in the liquid state at the temperature of the furnace (700 °C).

The calcium oxide produced from the thermal decomposition of limestone reacts with silicon dioxide and aluminium oxides, the main impurities present in the ore, to form a liquid called **slag** which contains calcium silicate ($CaSiO_3$) and calcium aluminate ($Ca(AlO_2)_2$):

$$CaO(s) + SiO_2(s) \rightarrow CaSiO_3(l)$$
$$CaO(s) + Al_2O_3(s) \rightarrow Ca(AlO_2)_2(l)$$

Both the molten iron and the slag of impurities trickle to the bottom of the furnace where the less dense slag floats on the molten iron, allowing easy separation. The liquid iron can be run out of the bottom into moulds called pigs to produce **pig iron**.

The hot waste gases can be used to heat the incoming air and so reduce the energy costs of the process. They should not be released into the atmosphere as they contain the poisonous inflammable gas carbon monoxide. The slag can be used to make cement or build roads.

Steel

The iron produced by the blast furnace contains about 4% carbon. This high level of impurity makes the metal brittle and reduces its melting point. As this iron has limited uses the majority is converted into **steel**. There is no one material called steel. It is the general name for a mixture of iron and carbon and other metals. Small differences in the composition of the steel can produce a range of different properties. This makes steel a versatile material with properties that can be adjusted to suit its use.

Alloys

Steel is an **alloy**. An alloy is a homogeneous mixture containing at least one metal formed when liquid metals are added together and allowed to form a solid of

See an animation which shows the workings of an early blast furnace.

Now go to www.heinemann.co.uk/hotlinks, insert the express code 4259P and click on this activity.

Pig iron has a very high carbon content (typically 4%) which makes it very brittle and not very useful. It is formed in moulds which traditionally had a branching structure, similar in appearance to a litter of piglets suckling on a sow.

Watch this short video which describes the reactions occurring in a blast furnace.

Now go to www.heinemann.co.uk/hotlinks, insert the express code 4259P and click on this activity.

uniform composition. Alloys are useful because they have a range of properties that are different from the pure metal. The presence of other elements in the metallic structure changes the regular arrangement of the metals atoms in the solid, making it more difficult for atoms to slip over each other, and so change their shape. Alloys are generally stronger than the pure metal.

Figure 14.2 An alloy is a stronger, harder and less malleable metal than the pure metal.

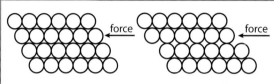

pure metal
The shape of a pure metal can be changed as the atoms can easily slip over each other.

alloy
The presence of atoms of different sizes disrupts the regular structure and prevents the atoms from slipping across each other.

Light micrograph of high carbon steel. It contains 0.65% carbon by mass alloyed with iron. It is very strong but brittle and is used for cutting tools, high-strength wires and springs.

An alloy is a homogeneous mixture containing at least one metal formed when liquid metals are added together and allowed to form a solid of *uniform* composition.

Basic oxygen steelmaking process

Steels are usually made by the **basic oxygen process** (**BOP**). The content of non-metal elements needs to be reduced and other metallic elements added. Oxygen is blown through a 7:3 mixture of molten and scrap iron and small quantities of alloying elements such as **nickel** and **chromium** are added. The oxygen combines with the unwanted carbon and sulfur to form the oxides which escape as gases:

Removal of carbon as carbon dioxide: $C(s) + O_2(g) \rightarrow CO_2(g)$

Removal of sulfur as sulfur dioxide: $S(s) + O_2(g) \rightarrow SO_2(g)$

Oxides of silicon and phosphorus are also formed:

$$4P(s) + 5O_2(g) \rightarrow P_4O_{10}(s)$$

$$Si(s) + O_2(g) \rightarrow SiO_2(s)$$

These combine with the lime (CaO) that is added to the converter to form a slag consisting of calcium phosphate, $Ca_3(PO_4)_2$ and calcium silicate, $CaSiO_3$.

Worked example

Give the balanced equation for the formation of calcium phosphate from lime (CaO) and P_4O_{10}

Solution

$6CaO + P_4O_{10} \rightarrow 2Ca_3(PO_4)_2$

As these redox reactions are very exothermic; the scrap iron is added to help to control the temperature. The percentage of carbon present has a dramatic effect on the properties and uses of the steel as shown below.

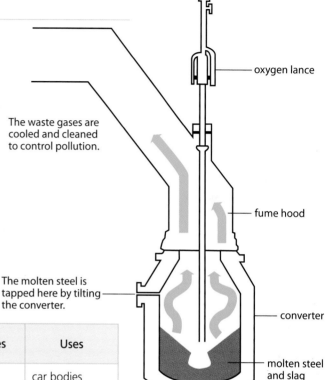

▲ **Figure 14.3** The basic oxygen furnace. Oxygen is blown through the molten iron and the impurities are oxidized and removed as waste gases or combined with CaO to form slag.

Type of steel	Percentage of carbon	Properties	Uses
low carbon (mild steel)	0.07–0.25	easily cold worked	car bodies
high carbon (carbon tool steel)	0.85–1.2	wear resistant	cutting tools, railway lines

The addition of small amounts of other transition metals changes the properties of the material even further.

Alloying element	Properties given to steel	Uses
cobalt	easily magnetized	magnets
molybdenum	maintains high strength at high temperature	high speed drill tips
manganese	tough	safes
stainless steel (nickel, chromium)	resists corrosion	surgical instruments, cutlery
titanium	withstands high temperatures	aircraft, turbine blades
vanadium	strong, hard	high speed tools

Oxygen dissolves in the steel during the process. This must be removed by adding controlled amounts of aluminium or silicon before the steel is suitable for casting or rolling.

● **Examiner's hint:** It is important that you distinguish clearly between the extraction of iron in a blast furnace and the conversion of iron to steel.

▲ The atoms in a piece of metal are not all arranged in a regular way. This is shown by the different orientation of the squares in the diagram above. Areas of regular structure are called 'crystal grains'. The grain structure of brass, an alloy of copper and zinc is shown below. The properties of an alloy depend on the size and orientations of the grain boundaries.
▼

Bauxite is the primary ore from which aluminium is obtained. ▶

Heat treatment of steel

Changing the composition of the steel is not the only way to adjust its properties. The steel can also be subjected to various degrees of heating and cooling, which change the structure of the metal.

Metals can be made softer by a process called **annealing**. The metal is heated to a temperature of about 1000 °C. The structure recrystallizes into many finer grains making the metal more malleable and ductile. **Quenching** describes the sudden immersion of a heated metal into cold water or oil. It is used to make the metal very hard. At high temperatures the alloying metals are dissolved in the iron, but if quenched, the alloying metals become trapped within the crystal grains, making the structure harder. Quenched steel is brittle and can be made more malleable and springy by a process known as **tempering**. The quenched steel is heated to a lower temperature (200–300 °C) with the colour of the steel ranging from yellow at 200 °C to dark blue at 300 °C, owing to an increasingly thick film of iron oxide on the surface of the metal. When the metal reaches the tempering temperature, it is slowly cooled. This removes internal stresses in the structure and replaces brittleness with toughness. The resulting steel is still hard but is more malleable and ductile. The only drawback to this procedure is that the metal must not be worked further above its tempering temperature.

Exercise

1 The iron produced in a blast furnace contains about 5% impurities.
   (a) State the major impurity.
   (b) This iron can be converted into steel. It is melted in a basic oxygen converter and two chemicals are added. State the two chemicals added.
   (c) Describe the essential chemical processes that take place during the conversion of iron into steel.

Aluminium

Aluminium is the most abundant metal in the Earth's crust and is found in the minerals **bauxite** and mica as well as in clay.

It was, however, not discovered until 1825 by H. C. Oersted in Denmark. It is a reactive metal which means that its compounds are extremely difficult to break down by chemical reactions.

Nowadays, aluminium is a relatively cheap metal. The extraction of aluminium from the mineral bauxite involves three stages:

- **Purification**: The mineral is treated with aqueous sodium hydroxide. Bauxite is an impure form of hydrated aluminium oxide: $Al_2O_3.xH_2O$. The amphoteric nature of the oxide allows it to be separated from other metal oxides. The soluble aluminium oxide is separated by filtration from the insoluble metal oxides (iron(III) oxide, titanium dioxide) and sand.

$$Al_2O_3(s) + 2OH^-(aq) + 3H_2O(l) \rightarrow 2Al(OH)_4^-(aq)$$

The reaction can be reversed when crystals of aluminium oxide are added to the solution.

- **Solvation**: The purified aluminium oxide is dissolved in molten cryolite – a mineral form of Na_3AlF_6. This reduces the melting point of aluminium oxide and so reduces the energy requirements of the process. Pure aluminium oxide would not be a suitable electrolyte because it has a very high melting point and it is a poor electrical conductor even when molten. Its bonding is intermediate between ionic and polar covalent.

- **Electrolysis**: The molten mixture is electrolysed. Graphite anodes are dipped into the molten electrolyte. The graphite lined steel cell acts as the cathode.

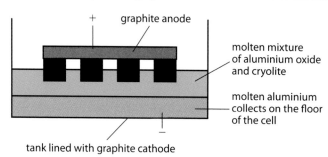

tank lined with graphite cathode

The negatively charged O^{2-} ions are attracted to the anode where they lose electrons and are oxidized to oxygen gas:

$$2O^{2-}(l) \rightarrow O_2(g) + 4e^-$$

At the high temperature of the process, the oxygen reacts with the graphite anode to form carbon dioxide:

$$C(s) + O_2(g) \rightarrow CO_2(g)$$

As the graphite is burned away, the anode needs to be regularly replaced.

The positive aluminium ions Al^{3+} ions are attracted to the cathode, where they gain electrons and are reduced to molten aluminium:

$$Al^{3+}(l) + 3e^- \rightarrow Al(l)$$

The electrolysis of aqueous compounds of aluminium cannot be used, as the less reactive element hydrogen present in the water would be produced in preference to the aluminium at the cathode.

The aluminium produced by this method is 99% pure with small amounts of silicon and iron impurities. As the electrolyte contains fluoride ions, fluorine gas is also produced in the process. This needs to be removed from the waste gases before they pass into the atmosphere as it would lead to environmental damage.

Napoleon III, the Emperor of France from 1848 to 1870, owned an aluminium dinner service which was said to be more precious than gold. The high value reflects the difficulty of extracting the metal at the time.

An amphoteric oxide is an oxide that can act either as an acid or a base.

Figure 14.4 The electrolysis of molten aluminium oxide.

In an electrolysis cell, the positive electrode is called the anode and the negative electrode is called the cathode.

The electrolytic extraction of aluminium was developed almost simultaneously by Charles Martin Hall and Paul Héroult, who worked independently on different sides of the Atlantic. They both discovered the process in the same year, 1886. Both were born in the same year (1863) and died in the same year (1914).

The need for high temperatures means that the process needs to be continuous to be economical. The cost of electricity is the most important factor to consider when deciding the location of an aluminium plant and they are often sited near hydroelectric power plants. The high energy demand emphasizes the importance of recycling. The energy requirements of recycling are less than 5% of that needed to extract the metal directly.

Figure 14.5 The first stage (left) is the production of alumina (Al_2O_3) from raw bauxite. The bauxite is crushed (top) and NaOH added. Alumina hydrate is precipitated (brown) and then heated to form pure alumina (yellow). The conveyor belt deposits the alumina in molten cryolite (green). Electrolysis (right) is used to obtain molten aluminium metal (grey, lower right pipe).

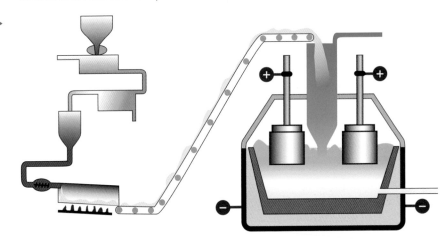

Watch this video which shows the extraction of aluminium from bauxite.
Now go to www.heinemann.co.uk/hotlinks, insert the express code 4259P and click on this activity.

Today we use aluminium in very large quantities. Although it is a reactive metal it is protected from corrosion by a stable oxide layer that forms on its surface. The thickness of the layer can be further increased by a process known as **anodizing**, in which sulfuric acid is electrolysed with an aluminium anode. The oxygen produced at the aluminium anode:

$$2H_2O(l) \rightarrow O_2(g) + 4H^+(aq) + 4e^-$$

combines with the metal to produce an oxide coating:

$$4Al(s) + 3O_2(g) \rightarrow 2Al_2O_3(s)$$

Aluminium is a malleable metal and can be shaped easily. It has a high thermal and electrical conductivity and a lower density than steel. It can be made stronger by alloying with other metals such as copper and magnesium. Some properties and uses are summarized in the table.

It is more economical to recycle aluminium than steel. The extraction of aluminium requires more energy than the extraction of iron.

The aluminium drink can is the world's most recycled container – more than 63% of all cans are recycled worldwide. You could watch three hours of television on the energy saved by recycling one aluminium can.

Property of Al	Use
low density/high strength	It is combined with copper in the alloy duralumin in aircraft bodies. It is combined with magnesium in the alloy magnalium in aircraft parts and kitchen utensils.
low density/high electrical conductivity	overhead electric cables
low density/resistant to corrosion	foil for food packaging
resistant to corrosion/high thermal conductivity	cooking pans

Exercise

2 (a) State the ore from which aluminium is extracted.

(b) Name the impurities which are removed in the purification of the ore.

(c) Explain why aluminium is not extracted from its oxide by carbon reduction in a blast furnace.

(d) Describe and explain how aluminium atoms are formed during the extraction process.

(e) Explain why aluminium cannot be obtained by electrolysis of an aqueous solution of an aluminium compound.

(f) Explain with chemical equations why the carbon anodes need to be replaced at regular intervals.

(g) Alloys of aluminium with nickel are used to make engine parts. Suggest why this alloy is used rather than pure aluminium.

The oil industry

Crude oil is one of the most important raw materials in the world today. This complex mixture of **hydrocarbons** supplies us with the fuel we need for transport and electricity generation and is an important **chemical feedstock** for the production of important organic compounds such as polymers, pharmaceuticals, dyes and solvents.

Crude oil was formed over millions of years from the remains of marine animals and plants, which were trapped under layers of rock. Under these conditions of high temperature and high pressure, organic matter decays in the presence of bacteria and the absence of oxygen. It is a limited resource and eventually reservoirs will be so depleted that chemists will need to consider other sources of carbon, both as a fuel and as a chemical feedstock.

Crude oil: a valuable fuel and chemical feedstock

There are risks and benefits in using oil as a source of energy or as a source of carbon to make new products. Petrol is a highly concentrated and convenient energy source for use in transport: a petrol pump supplies energy to a car at a rate of about 34×10^6 J s^{-1}. It could be argued, however, that burning hydrocarbons, with its resulting environmental side-effects such as smog and global warming, is a misuse of this valuable resource. When the great Russian chemist Dmitri Mendeleyev (see Chapter 3) visited the oils fields of Azerbaijan at the end of the 19th century, he is said to have likened the burning of oil as a fuel to 'firing up a kitchen stove with banknotes'. We still use about 90% of the refined product as a fuel, but as supplies decrease, this proportion may fall. Crude oil will last longer if we conserve energy and recycle materials such as plastics. It is the most convenient and economical option at the moment but alternative energy sources and feedstocks may be developed. Polymers, for example, could also be made from coal, of which there are still large reserves, and renewable biological materials such as wood, starch or cotton.

Petrochemical plants take crude oil, separate it into fractions and process it to make useful organic compounds.

Oil refining

Crude oil is of no use before it is **refined**. Sulfur impurities, mainly in the form of hydrogen sulfide, must first be removed as they would block the active sites of the catalysts used in later chemical processing. The acidic hydrogen sulfide is removed by dissolving it in basic potassium carbonate solution:

$$H_2S(g) + CO_3{}^{2-} (aq) \rightleftharpoons HS^-(g) + HCO_3^- (aq)$$

The hydrogen sulfide can be recovered from solution by later reversing the reaction. It is burned in air to form sulfur dioxide:

$$2H_2S(g) + 3O_2(g) \rightarrow 2SO_2(g) + 2H_2O(l)$$

The sulfur dioxide produced can then react with more hydrogen sulfide to produce elemental sulfur:

$$2H_2S(g) + SO_2(g) \rightarrow 3S(g) + 2H_2O(g)$$

This desulfurization step also reduces acid rain pollution which would result if the sulfur was burned.

The crude oil is then separated into different **fractions** on the basis of their boiling points. In this **fractional distillation** process the crude oil is heated to a temperature of about 400 °C. At this temperature all the different components of the mixture are vaporized and allowed to pass up a **distillation column**. The level at which the molecules condense depends on their size. The smaller molecules containing between one and four carbon atoms condense at the top as the **refinery gas** fraction. Molecules of successively larger molecular mass condense at lower levels corresponding to their higher boiling points.

Figure 14.6 The fractional distillation of crude oil.

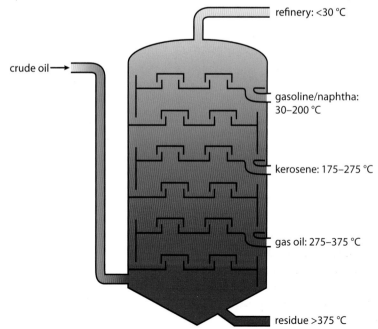

crude oil →

refinery: <30 °C

gasoline/naphtha: 30–200 °C

kerosene: 175–275 °C

gas oil: 275–375 °C

residue >375 °C

The different fractions and their uses are tabulated.

Fraction	Number of carbon atoms	Use
refinery gas	1–4	Used as fuel and as a feedstock for petrochemicals.
gasoline/naphtha	5–10	Gasoline (petrol) is used as fuel for cars. Naphtha is used as chemical feedstock.
kerosene	10–16	fuel for jets, paraffin for heating
gas oil	13–25	fuel for diesel engines, power plants and heating
residue	>25	oil-fired power stations, polishing waxes, lubricating oils, bitumen used to surface roads

Cracking

Fractional distillation is a physical process and although some of the compounds distilled can be used directly, further treatment is generally needed. The demand for the different fractions does not necessarily match the amounts present in the crude oil supplied and so the hydrocarbon molecules from the crude oil need to be chemically changed. Hydrocarbons with up to 12 carbon atoms are in the most demand as they are more easily vaporized and therefore make the best fuels. The supply of these molecules can be increased by breaking down or **cracking** larger molecules.

For example:

$$C_{16}H_{34} \rightarrow C_8H_{18} + C_8H_{16}$$

$$\underset{\text{alkane}}{C_{10}H_{22}} \rightarrow \underset{\text{alkane}}{C_8H_{18}} + \underset{\text{alkene}}{C_2H_4}$$

The cracking of a long hydrocarbon

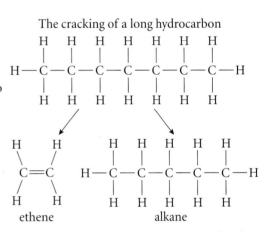

ethene   alkane

As we can see, the reaction produces the more useful alkenes (e.g. C_8H_{16} and C_2H_4), which can be used to make addition polymers (see later) and other important products.

Cracking also tends to produce branched chain alkanes, which burn more evenly in a car engine than their straight chain isomers. Straight chain molecules have a greater tendency to **auto-ignite** in the internal combustion engine as the fuel–air mixture is compressed by the piston. This reduces the power generated by the engine and so wastes fuel. The higher the **octane number** of a fuel, the less likely the fuel is to auto-ignite or **knock**. Cracking can be used to produce petrol of a higher octane number.

 The octane number indicates the resistance of a motor fuel to knock. Octane numbers are based on a scale on which 2,2,4-trimethylpentane (isooctane) is 100 (minimal knock) and hepane is 0 (maximum knock).

Thermal cracking

Thermal cracking is carried out by heating very long chain alkanes from very heavy fractions to temperatures of 800–850 °C at pressures of up to 70 atm ($70 \times 1.01 \times 10^5$ Pa) and then cooling rapidly. Under such conditions, a free radical (see page 200) reaction occurs and a mixture of products is produced including shorter chain alkanes, alkenes and coke. Ethene is a favoured product as it is the key starting material for the preparation of other chemicals.

Steam cracking

Steam cracking is a form of thermal cracking. The feedstock of ethane, butane and alkanes with eight carbon atoms is preheated, vaporized and mixed with steam at 1250–1400 °C. The steam dilutes the feedstock and produces a higher yield of ethene and other low molecular mass alkenes. The addition of steam also reduces the amount of carbon produced, which would otherwise line the cracker and reduce the amount of heat transferred to the reactants.

Catalytic cracking

The use of a catalyst allows the cracking process to occur at lower temperatures of 500 °C and helps to give the required product by controlling the **mechanism**. The reactions that occur are complicated but generally involve the formation of **carbocations** (see page 209), which are produced and then rearrange on the catalyst surface. Large and intermediate sized alkanes are passed over an alumina Al_2O_3 and silica SiO_2 catalyst, which is in powdered form to increase its surface area. The lower temperature requires less energy and so reduces the cost of the process. Zeolites, which are naturally occurring minerals of aluminium, silicon and oxygen, are also good catalysts for this process as their crystal structures contain an extensive network which offers the hydrocarbons a large surface area for reaction.

Catalytic cracking produces a mixture of alkanes, alkenes and compounds which contain the **benzene ring** (aromatics). The alkanes produced have high octane numbers as they have branched structures. They are used in high-quality petrol. Some carbon is, however, formed during the process and this can coat the catalyst and stop it working. The catalyst is cleaned or regenerated by separating it from the reaction mixture using steam jets. The carbon coat is then removed by heating. The heat produced from the combustion of this carbon can be used to sustain the cracking reaction.

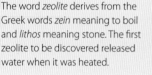

The word *zeolite* derives from the Greek words *zein* meaning to boil and *lithos* meaning stone. The first zeolite to be discovered released water when it was heated.

Hydrocracking

In this process, heavy hydrocarbon fractions are mixed with hydrogen at a pressure of about 80 atm ($80 \times 1.01 \times 10^5$ Pa) and cracked over palladium on a zeolite surface. A high yield of branched chain alkanes and cycloalkanes with some aromatic compounds with a high octane number is produced for use in high-quality petrol. The presence of hydrogen ensures that no unsaturated alkenes are produced.

Exercise

3 (a) Deduce an equation for the cracking of $C_{11}H_{24}$ in which an alkene and an alkane are formed in the ratio 3:1.
(b) Explain why cracking is a useful process.
(c) Although alkanes can be cracked with heat alone, it is more common for oil companies to use catalysts. Suggest two reasons for this.
(d) State the name of a catalyst used in catalytic cracking.

◄ Catalytic cracking uses high temperature and a catalyst to break down (crack) heavy oil fractions into lighter, more useful oils. The oil is heated to 500 °C and passed over a catalyst such as zeolite crystals. The vessel where the cracking takes places is the barrel-shaped grey one on the right.

Addition polymers

In the 1930s some British scientists were investigating the reactions of ethene with other carbon compounds under high pressure. In some of the experiments, a hard waxy solid was produced, which was found to consist of only carbon and hydrogen atoms in the ratio 1:2. This accidental discovery has had a profound effect on all our lives. They had made polyethene, the first **synthetic plastic**. Plastics are now the basis of many everyday materials. The **addition polymerization** reaction of ethene, in which many ethene molecules join together like a chain of paper clips is outlined in Chapter 10.

$$n \begin{pmatrix} H & H \\ \backslash & / \\ C = C \\ / & \backslash \\ H & H \end{pmatrix} \longrightarrow \begin{pmatrix} H & H \\ \backslash & / \\ C - C \\ / & \backslash \\ H & H \end{pmatrix}_n$$

monomer   polymer
ethene   polyethene

> An addition polymer is formed when the double bonds of many monomer molecules open up to form a long continuous chain.

The double bond in ethene breaks open and allows many molecules to link together to form a chain. The value of *n* varies with the reaction conditions but it is generally in the thousands. The strength and melting points of the polymers increase with chain length, as the intermolecular forces increase with molecular size.

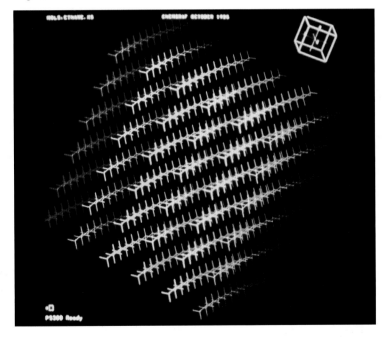

◀ Computer graphic representation of the packed chains of the polyethene molecule, a long chain hydrocarbon with a high molecular mass. Polyethene is made by the polymerization of C_2H_4, by heating under pressure in the presence of oxygen. It may be essentially considered to be a very long chain alkane.

Polymers, with different chemical compositions can be formed by changing the **monomer**: the formation of polyethene, polychlorethene, polypropene and polystyrene follow the same reaction scheme:

$$n \begin{pmatrix} H & H \\ \backslash & / \\ C = C \\ / & \backslash \\ H & X \end{pmatrix} \longrightarrow \begin{pmatrix} H & H \\ \backslash & / \\ C - C \\ / & \backslash \\ H & X \end{pmatrix}_n$$

monomer   polymer with a long straight
chain of carbon atoms

Monomer	Polymer	Monomer	Polymer
ethene	polyethene	propene	polypropene
$\begin{array}{c} H \quad\;\; H \\ \backslash \quad / \\ C{=}C \\ / \quad \backslash \\ H \quad\;\; H \end{array}$	$\left(\begin{array}{c} H \quad\;\; H \\ \mid \quad \mid \\ {-}C{-}C{-} \\ \mid \quad \mid \\ H \quad\;\; H \end{array}\right)_n$	$\begin{array}{c} H \quad\;\; H \\ \backslash \quad / \\ C{=}C \\ / \quad \backslash \\ H \quad\;\; CH_3 \end{array}$	$\left(\begin{array}{c} H \quad\;\; H \\ \mid \quad \mid \\ {-}C{-}C{-} \\ \mid \quad \mid \\ H \quad\;\; CH_3 \end{array}\right)_n$
chloroethene (vinyl chloride)	polychlorethene (PVC)	styrene	polystyrene
$\begin{array}{c} H \quad\;\; H \\ \backslash \quad / \\ C{=}C \\ / \quad \backslash \\ H \quad\;\; Cl \end{array}$	$\left(\begin{array}{c} H \quad\;\; H \\ \mid \quad \mid \\ {-}C{-}C{-} \\ \mid \quad \mid \\ H \quad\;\; Cl \end{array}\right)_n$	$\begin{array}{c} H \quad\;\; H \\ \backslash \quad / \\ C{=}C \\ / \quad \backslash \\ H \quad\;\; C_6H_5 \end{array}$	$\left(\begin{array}{c} H \quad\;\; H \\ \mid \quad \mid \\ {-}C{-}C{-} \\ \mid \quad \mid \\ H \quad\;\; C_6H_5 \end{array}\right)_n$

● Examiner's hint: Many students have difficulty drawing the structure of polypropene. It is important to note that it follows the general scheme with the methyl group as a side chain. Practice drawing structures for polymers with side groups (formed from monomers such as propene and chloroethene).

Changing the chemical composition of the monomer and the chain length is not the only strategy used to change the properties of a polymer. The description of a polymer as one straight chain is an oversimplification as branching can occur along the main chain. The relative orientation of all the groups along the chain can also affect the properties of the polymer.

Branching

The polyethene used to make plastic bags has very different properties from the polyethene used to make plastic buckets and toys. The carbon and hydrogen atoms are in the ratio 1:2 but the molecules have different molecular structures. If polyethene is polymerized at very high pressures, the reaction proceeds by a free radical mechanism and branched carbon chains are produced. This branching limits the interaction between neighbouring chains and the intermolecular forces are relatively weak. The resulting low density polymer has a low melting point and quite flexible carbon chains.

Figure 14.7 Low density polythene (LDPE). Branching limits the ability of the chains to pack closely. In this **amorphous** (non-crystalline) form the intermolecular interactions between the chains are weak.

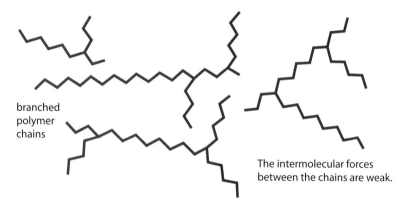

branched polymer chains

The intermolecular forces between the chains are weak.

When ethene is polymerized at a lower temperature in the presence of a catalyst (a Zeigler catalyst with metal–carbon bonds) the reaction occurs by an ionic mechanism and a more crystalline structure is produced. In this high-density form the molecules have straight chains. It is more rigid as the molecules are more closely packed with stronger intermolecular forces and has a higher melting point.

◀ The plastic used to make this bag was LDPE (low density polyethylene).

The intermolecular forces between the straight chains are relatively strong.

Figure 14.8 High density polyethene (HDPE). In this **crystalline** form the parallel chains are closely packed with relatively strong intermolecular bonds.

A range of polyethenes with varying properties can be produced by modifying the extent and location of branching in the low density form.

Orientation of side groups

The presence of a methyl group in propene introduces a structural feature into the polymer chain not found in polyethene. Methyl groups can be arranged with different orientations relative to the carbon backbone. The **isotactic** form of the polymer, with methyl groups arranged on one side is an example of a **stereoregular** polymer. It is crystalline and tough and can be moulded into different shapes. It is used to make car bumpers and plastic toys and can be drawn into fibres to make clothes and carpets.

Figure 14.9 Isotactic polypropene has a regular structure with the methyl groups pointing in the same direction making it crystalline and tough.

The **atactic** form, produced when the methyl groups are randomly orientated, is softer and more flexible. It is useful as a sealant and in other waterproof coatings.

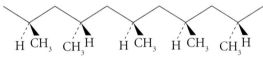

Figure 14.10 Atactic polypropene has an irregular structure, which prevents the chains from packing together. It is soft and flexible.

The product of the polymerization reaction of propene can be controlled by using catalysts allowing chemists to tailor-make polymers with precise properties. A free radical catalyst will produce the atactic polymer; a **Ziegler-Natta** catalyst, which leads to an ionic mechanism, will produce the more ordered isotactic form. The monomer binds to the catalyst surface with the correct orientation to produce the more ordered polymer. Other polymers with side chains such as PVC can also exist in isotactic and atactic forms.

Catalysts used to make stereoregular polymers are called Zeigler-Natta catalysts. The German chemist Karl Ziegler and Italian Guillio Natta shared the 1963 Noble Prize for their work in this field.

Exercise

4 (a) Draw a full structural formula showing the repeating unit in polypropene.
(b) Polypropene can exist in isotactic and atactic forms. Sketch the structure and name the stereoregular polymer.
(c) Explain why the more crystalline form can be used to make strong fibres for carpets.
(d) Deduce how many monomer units of propene could be joined together to make a polymer with an average relative molecular mass of 2.1×10^6.
(e) Explain why only an *average* value can be given for the relative molecular mass.

Modifying the properties of addition polymers

Polyvinyl chloride and plasticizers

The non-systematic name for chloroethene is vinyl chloride and so the polymer of this monomer is more commonly known as polyvinyl chloride or PVC. The presence of the polar $C^{\delta+}$—$Cl^{\delta-}$ bond in PVC gives it very different properties from both polyethene and polypropene. The molecule has a permanent dipole allowing a strong dipole/dipole intermolecular interaction to occur between neighbouring chains. The presence of the relatively large Cl atom also limits the ability of the chains to move across each other. The pure polymer is hard and brittle and has few uses. Its properties are radically improved, however, when **plasticizers**, such as di-(2-ethylhexyl)hexanedioate are added. The platicizer molecules fits in between and separates the polymer chains. This allows the chains to slip across each other more easily. The resulting plastic is softer and more flexible and is used, for example, to make credit cards. PVC with varying degrees of flexibility can be produced by varying the amount of platicizer.

Figure 14.11 The plasticizer molecules shown here in red separate the polymer chains. This allows them to move freely past each other.

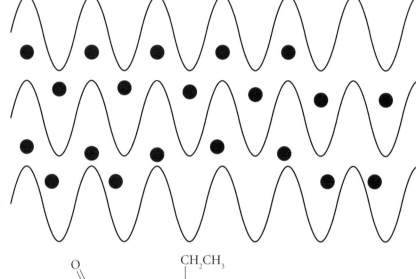

Figure 14.12 Di-(2-ethylhexyl)-hexanedioate is a common plasticizer. Note the presence of the two ester functional groups.

Light micrograph of fibres of PVC. PVC is a tough, white material, which softens with the application of a plasticizer.

Expanded polystyrene

Expanded polystyrene is made by **expansion moulding**. Polystyrene beads containing about 5% of a volatile hydrocarbon such as pentane are placed in a mould and heated. The heat causes the pentane to evaporate and bubbles of gas to form. The expansion of the gas causes the polymer to expand into the shape of the mould. The resulting plastic has a low density, is white, opaque and an excellent thermal insulator. These properties should be contrasted with the polystyrene made without a foaming agent, which is colourless, transparent and brittle.

Expanded polystyrene is widely used as a thermally insulating and protective packaging material.

Synthetic rope can be made from isotactic polypropene.

Thermoplastic and thermosetting polymers

The plastics we have discussed are all examples of **thermosoftening** or **thermoplastic** polymers. They are made from polymer chains which interact only weakly via intermolecular forces. When they are heated one chain can slip across another making the polymer soften. They can be reheated and remoulded many times. If the chains are allowed to line up, the intermolecular forces increase and a strong **fibre** is produced. Isotactic polypropene can be made into such a strong fibre.

Thermosetting plastics have very different properties. When they are first heated *covalent* bonds are formed between adjacent chains of the polymers. These strong covalent **cross-linkages** give the material increased strength and rigidity. The cross-links prevent the plastic from melting when reheated and so they cannot be softened or remoulded.

thermosoftening polymer   thermosoftening polymer in the form of a fibre   thermosetting polymer

Figure 14.13 Schematic of thermosoftening and thermosetting plastics.

The advantages and disadvantages of polymer use

Advantages

Plastics are relatively cheap to produce and, as outlined earlier, they have many useful properties. They are relatively unreactive, have low densities, are good electrical and thermal insulators, are flexible and can be easily coloured and moulded. They have taken over in recent years from traditional materials such as metals, glass and wood. Polymer fibres have replaced cotton and wool. Some properties and uses of addition polymers are summarized below.

Polymer	Properties	Uses
polyethene *(structure: —CH2—CH2— repeat unit with H, H on each carbon, shown as n)*	LDPE: thermoplastic, low density, lower melting point ($\approx 100\,°C$), opaque, excellent insulator, unreactive	plastic bags, cling film
	HDPE: thermoplastic, high density, higher melting point ($\approx 140\,°C$), high tensile strength, more opaque, excellent insulator, unreactive	buckets, plastic toys, water pipes
polychloroethene, polyvinylchloride *(structure: —CH2—CHCl— repeat unit, shown as n)*	rigid PVC: thermoplastic, transparent, high density, tough, high impact strength, excellent insulator, unreactive	used in electrical insulation, water pipes, floor tiles
	flexible PVC; thermoplastic, low tensile strength and density	raincoats, cling film
polypropene *(structure: —CH2—CHCH3— repeat unit, shown as n)*	atactic: thermoplastic, soft and flexible, unreactive	used in sealants and roofing
	isotactic: thermoplastic	automobile parts, plastic rope, carpeting and clothing
polyphenylethene, polystyrene *(structure: —CH2—CHC6H5— repeat unit, shown as n)*	thermoplastic, hard, transparent	rigid boxes, television and radio cabinets, toys, imitation glass
	expanded form: low density, opaque, good thermal insulator, opaque and shock absorber	disposable cups, insulation and packaging
polytetrafluoroethene, Teflon® *(structure: —CF2—CF2— repeat unit, shown as n)*	thermoplastic: highly water repellent, low friction	non-stick pans, Gore-Tex® fabric, hip joint replacements

● **Examiner's hint:** Learn the specific properties of the polymers in the table.

Some products made from PVC (polyvinyl chloride).

 It is said that the American space programme would have floundered without Teflon because the material was used to make so many things, from space suits to the bags used to hold samples of moon rock.

Disadvantages

Depletion of natural resources

The rapid growth of the plastics industry has, however, brought a number of problems that we will have to face up to in the future. Addition polymers are all currently produced from crude oil, which as discussed earlier is a limited resource. As reserves are used up, chemists will need to find other sources of carbon. Renewable sources of natural polymers such as starch and cellulose may offer the solution and future plastics may be made from wood and cotton.

Disposal of plastics

The problem of what to do with unreactive plastic waste won't go away because many polymers are not biodegradable. They are not broken down by bacteria. Much of our plastic waste has been used to **landfill** disused quarries. However suitable sites are becoming harder to find and reducing the amount of plastic dumped into landfills is a high priority.

 The discovery of the addition polymers polyethene and Teflon both included some elements of luck. What part does serendipity play in scientific discoveries?

'Dans les champs de l'observation le hazard ne favorise que les esprits préparés.' 'In the field of observation, fortune only favours the prepared mind.' (Louis Pasteur 1822–1895).

Many accidents and chance happenings occur in our everyday lives. It is the skill of the scientist to know which are significant.

Some possible strategies are:

- **Incineration**: The waste plastic can be burned and used as a fuel. As the addition polymers discussed are made up from mainly carbon and hydrogen they are a concentrated energy source and the energy produced can be used constructively. However there are problems. Carbon dioxide is a greenhouse gas and carbon monoxide produced during incomplete combustion is poisonous. The combustion of PVC poses a particular problem as the hydrogen chloride produced causes acid rain. It must be removed from the fumes before they are released into the atmosphere.

- **Recycling**: This is a way of reducing the amount of new plastics made. Thermoplastics can be melted down and remoulded. For the process to be successful and self-sustainable, however, the costs of recycling must be less than those needed to produce new materials. There are costs in sorting the different used plastics and melting them so that they can be reshaped. The recycled plastic is often of lower quality than the original and so has a limited range of uses.

Landfill sites are used to dispose of about 90% of the world's domestic waste.

Different countries have different recycling policies. For recycling to be successful, economic and political factors need to be considered. If it is not economical to recycle plastic at the moment perhaps we should bury the plastic separately so that future generations could recover it later. Plastic disposal is a global problem with local solutions.

Brooms made from recycled plastic.

Biodegradability

Polyalkenes are not biodegradable as bacteria do not have the enzymes needed to break them down. Some polyethene plastic bags, with added natural polymers such as starch, cellulose or protein, however, can be made to biodegrade. The bacteria in the soil decompose the natural polymer and so the bag is broken down into smaller pieces. The synthetic polymer chains that remain have an increased surface area which speeds up the rate of decay further. One problem with biodegradability is that conditions in a landfill are often not suitable. The need to make sites water tight to prevent soluble products leaking into the environment also limits the supply of oxygen, preventing the bacteria from acting.

Exercise

5 (a) Plastics have replaced many traditional materials. Suggest two properties which make plastic more suitable than wood for making children's toys.

(b) Increased use of polymers has led to problems of waste disposal. State one method of waste disposal and discuss issues other than cost associated with its use.

(c) Explain why synthetic polyalkenes are not generally biodegradable.

(d) Explain how a polyethene bag can be made more biodegradable.

C.4 Catalysts

Catalysts increase the rate of some reactions but they do not change the position of equilibrium. They are not chemically changed at the end of the reaction.

The word *catalyst* derives from the Chinese word for marriage broker.

Catalysts play an essential role in the chemical industry. Without them, many chemical processes would go too slowly to be economical. Catalysts work by providing reactions with alternative reaction mechanisms that have lower activation energies.

A catalyst can't make more of a product than would eventually be produced without it. It can however act *selectively* when two or more competing reactions are possible with the same starting materials, producing more of the desired product by catalysing only that reaction.

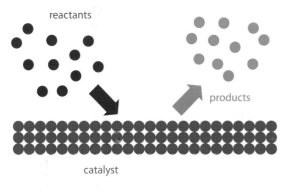

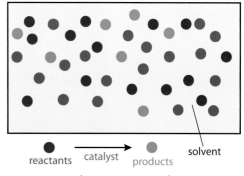

reactants

products

catalyst

heterogeneous catalysis

reactants → catalyst → products   solvent

homogeneous catalysis

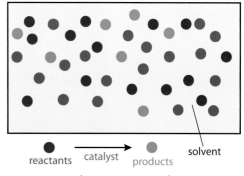
Figure 14.14 Diagram representing homogeneous and heterogeneous catalysis.

Homogeneous and heterogeneous catalysis

Chemists divide catalysts into two types: **homogeneous** and **heterogeneous**. Homogeneous catalysts are in the same state of matter as the reactants, whereas in heterogeneous catalysis, the catalyst and the reactants are in different states. For example, the catalyst may be a solid and the reactants gases or liquids.

The place on the catalyst where the reaction takes place is called the **active site**. In heterogeneous catalysis the reactant molecules can only collide with the active sites on the *surface*. For the reactions to go significantly faster there must be a significant drop in activation energy to compensate for this. There are more active sites available in homogeneous catalysed reactions and a small drop in activation energy can lead to a dramatic increase in rate. Heterogeneous catalysis is generally preferred in industrial processes, however, as the catalyst can be easily removed by filtration from the reaction mixture. The use of iron in the Haber Process and vanadium(V) oxide in the Contact Process is discussed in Chapter 7. The use of homogeneous catalysis, which often requires expensive separation techniques, is generally reserved for the production of complex organic molecules. As they have greater activity, they work under milder conditions with greater selectivity. Enzyme-catalysed reactions in cells, which take place in aqueous solution are examples of homogeneous catalysis.

> ℹ In the Haber Process, chemists can produce ammonia at an economical rate at temperatures of 525 °C and a pressure of 20 atm (2×10^6 Pa). To make one gram of ammonia, at the same temperature and pressure without a catalyst, would require a reactor 10 times the size of the Solar System.

Examples of catalysts: transition metals

Industrial process	Catalyst
Haber Process: $N_2(g) + 3H_2(g) \rightleftharpoons 2NH_3(g)$	finely divided iron
Contact Process: $2SO_2(g) + O_2(g) \rightleftharpoons 2SO_3(g)$	vanadium(V) oxide, platinum
hydrogenation of unsaturated oils to make margarine	nickel
reaction of CO and H_2 to make methanol: $CO(g) + 2H_2(g) \rightarrow CH_3OH(g)$	copper
catalytic cracking, e.g. $C_{10}H_{22}(g) \rightarrow C_4H_8(g) + C_6H_{14}(g)$	Al_2O_3/SiO_2, zeolites

> 🔒 **A substance is adsorbed when it is weakly attached to a surface. It is absorbed when it enters pores in the material.**

Many catalysts are either transition metals or their compounds. Transition metals show two properties that make them particularly effective as catalysts:

- They have variable oxidation states. They are particularly effective catalysts in redox reactions.
- They adsorb small molecules onto their surface. Transition metals are often good heterogeneous catalysts as they provide a surface for the reactant molecules to come together with the correct orientation.

Catalyst having variable oxidation state	Catalyst allowing adsorbtion onto surface
Vanadium(V) oxide as a catalyst: $V_2O_5(s) + SO_2(g) \rightarrow V_2O_4(s) + SO_3(g)$ $V_2O_4(s) + \frac{1}{2}O_2(g) \rightarrow V_2O_5(s)$ Overall reaction $SO_2(g) + \frac{1}{2}O_2(g) \rightarrow SO_3(g)$ Vanadium shows variable oxidation states. It is reduced from the +5 to the +4 and then oxidized back to the +5 state	The reactants are both gases.
	The reactants are both adsorbed on the Ni surface.
	Bonds are broken and formed on the surface.
	The product moves away from the surface.
	Nickel, shown in blue, adsorbs both C_2H_4 and H_2 and provides a surface for reaction. It brings the reactants together with the correct orientation for a successful addition reaction. C_2H_6 is the product.

Examples of catalysts: zeolites

The use of zeolites in catalytic cracking was discussed earlier in the chapter.

Zeolites are a family of aluminium silicates. Their open caged structures give them excellent catalytic properties:

- They offer a huge surface for reactants to be adsorbed. Almost every atom in the solid is at a surface and is therefore available as an active site.
- The shape and size of the channels makes them *shape selective* catalysts. Only reactants with the appropriate geometry can interact effectively with the active sites.

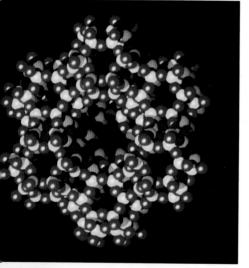

◀ Computer graphic representation of the structure of zeolite-Y, a mineral used in the catalytic cracking process. In this image, silicon and aluminium atoms are shown in yellow and oxygen atoms in red.

Some limitations

Some catalysts have a limited working life. The iron catalysts in the Haber Process work for between 5 and 10 years. The time depends on whether or not the catalyst encounters substances that poison the catalyst. Sulfur from traces of hydrogen sulfide in the natural gas used as the source of hydrogen presents the greatest problems. Similarly, the use of platinum as an effective catalyst for the Contact Process is affected by even the smallest amounts of arsenic. Catalytic poisons block the active sites because they are adsorbed on the surface more strongly than reactant molecules. Other catalytic poisons include mercury(II) salts, carbon monoxide and hydrogen cyanide.

The open structure of zeolites is illustrated by the fact that a teaspoon of zeolite has a surface area of two tennis courts.

Which catalyst?

The choice of catalyst will depend on a number of factors:
- Selectivity – does the catalyst give a high yield of the desired product?
- Efficiency– how much faster is the reaction with the catalyst?
- Life expectancy
- Environmental impact
- Ability to work under a range of conditions of temperature and pressure. A heterogeneous catalyst may melt and or become less effective if its operating temperatures are too high or its surface becomes coated with unwanted products.

Although some catalysts such as the transition metals platinum and palladium are very expensive, their use is economical. They reduce the energy costs of the process, increase yields and can be reused as they are not chemically changed.

Exercise

6 (a) Although many catalysts are very expensive, their use does allow the chemical industry to operate economically. Outline the advantages of using catalysts in industrial processes.
(b) Sulfur in crude oil must be removed before it is refined as it can poison the catalysts. Explain how the sulfur impurities poison the catalyst.

Fuel cells and rechargeable batteries

C.5

Some of the problems of burning our limited supplies of oil were discussed in Section C.2. Crude oil is a valuable feedstock for the chemical industry and the combustion of hydrocarbon releases large quantities of the greenhouse gas carbon dioxide into the atmosphere. It is clear that one of the most important challenges for the chemist is to develop other, more environmentally friendly, sources of energy. Electrochemistry is an important field of technological development in this area as it could offer a cleaner way of producing energy. Primary electrochemical cells, in which the electrons transferred in a spontaneous redox reaction produce electricity are discussed in Chapter 9. They are a useful way to store and transport relatively small amounts of energy, but as they cannot be recharged their disposal can pose environmental problems. Batteries are currently less efficient than fossil fuels as they must be manufactured using energy and every energy transformation includes an energy loss. This situation may change however in the future. In this section we will discuss **secondary cells**. These can be recharged and so have a longer life than primary cells.

A primary cell/battery is one that cannot be recharged. A secondary cell/battery is one that can be recharged.

The hydrogen fuel cell

Hydrogen is a possible alternative fuel to hydrocarbons. It could reduce our dependence on fossil fuels and reduce the emission of carbon dioxide released into the atmosphere. One mole of hydrogen can release 286 kJ of heat energy when it combines directly with oxygen:

$$H_2(g) + \tfrac{1}{2}O_2(g) \rightarrow H_2O(l) \qquad \Delta H = -286 \text{ kJ mol}^{-1}$$

As this is a redox reaction that involves the transfer of electrons from hydrogen to oxygen, it can be used to produce an electric current if the reactants are physically separated. This is the basis of a **fuel cell**, where the reactants can be continuously supplied to the electrodes. The hydrogen–oxygen fuel cell operates with either an acidic or alkaline **electrolyte**.

The hydrogen–oxygen fuel cell with an alkaline electrolyte

The hydrogen–oxygen fuel cell most commonly has an alkaline electrolyte.

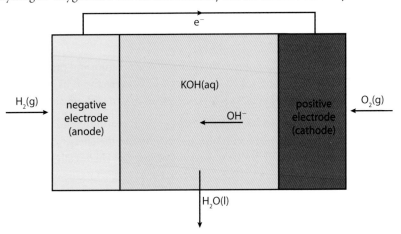

Half reaction at the negative electrode (anode)	Half reaction at the positive electrode (cathode)
$H_2(g)$ is oxidized at the anode:	$O_2(g)$ is reduced at the cathode:
$2H_2(g) + 4OH^-(aq) \rightarrow 4H_2O(l) + 4e^-$	$2H_2O(l) + O_2(g) + 4e^- \rightarrow 4OH^-(aq)$

The overall reaction is the sum of the oxidation and reduction half reactions:

$$2H_2(g) + \cancel{4OH^-(aq)} + 2H_2O(l) + O_2(g) + \cancel{4e^-} \rightarrow 4H_2O(l) + \cancel{4e^-} + \cancel{4OH^-(aq)}$$

$$2H_2(g) + O_2(g) \rightarrow 2H_2O(l)$$

The fuel cell will function as long as hydrogen and oxygen are supplied. The electrodes are often made of porous carbon with added transition metals such as nickel. The potassium hydroxide provides the hydroxide ions that are transferred across the cell.

The hydrogen–oxygen fuel cell with an acidic electrolyte

The hydrogen–oxygen fuel cell can also function in acidic solution. The **proton exchange membrane** fuel cell has a membrane usually made from the strong and durable plastic Teflon which allows H^+ ions to move from the anode to the cathode. Both electrodes are coated with tiny particles of platinum to catalyse the reaction.

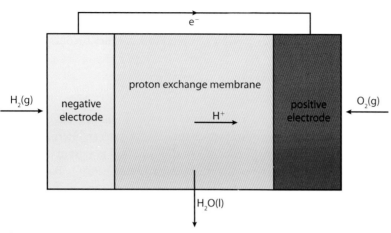

proton exchange membrane

$H_2(g)$

negative electrode

e^-

H^+

positive electrode

$O_2(g)$

$H_2O(l)$

Half reaction at the negative electrode (anode)	Half reaction at the positive electrode (cathode)
$H_2(g)$ is oxidized at the anode:	$O_2(g)$ is reduced at the cathode:
$2H_2(g) \rightarrow 4H^+(aq) + 4e^-$	$4H^+(aq) + O_2(g) + 4e^- \rightarrow 4H_2O(l)$

Again the overall reaction is the sum of the oxidation and reduction half reactions:

$$2H_2(g) + O_2(g) + \cancel{4H^+(aq)} + \cancel{4e^-} \rightarrow 2H_2O(l) + \cancel{4H^+(aq)} + \cancel{4e^-}$$
$$2H_2(g) + O_2(g) \rightarrow 2H_2O(l)$$

One of the problems with the hydrogen fuel cell is that hydrogen gas is almost never found as the element in nature and has to be extracted from other sources. Hydrocarbons, including fossil fuels and biomass (waste organic matter) for example, can be processed to break down into hydrogen and carbon dioxide. The alternative is to electrolyse water. For the whole process to be environmentally clean, the hydrogen should be generated using renewable resources such as wind power.

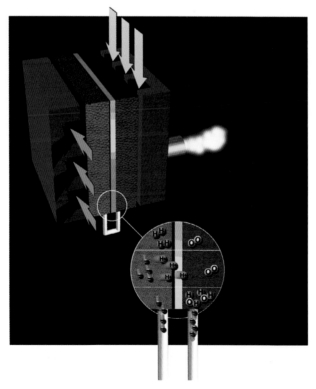

 A spacecraft needs a continuous supply of electrical energy. NASA developed efficient but expensive fuel cells for the Space Shuttle programme. The Challenger explosion in 1986 was due to a violent reaction between hydrogen and oxygen from the propellant system, not from the fuel cell.

◀ The hydrogen fuel cell is a clean and efficient power source. Hydrogen is pumped into the cell (blue arrows), where the hydrogen nuclei (blue, inset) are separated from their electrons (yellow, inset). The electrons flow around a conducting loop (beige) as an electric current which can be harnessed. The hydrogen nuclei pass through a membrane (yellow, inset) and combine with the electrons and oxygen from the air (pale blue arrows) to form steam (white).

● **Examiner's hint:** Learn the equations for the half reactions of the hydrogen fuel cell in alkaline and acid conditions.

 See a video about hydrogen fuel cells.

Now go to www.heinemann.co.uk/hotlinks, insert the express code 4259P and click on this activity.

Rechargeable batteries

Rechargeable batteries are expensive to buy at first but they become more economical with use.

Lead acid battery

Electricity is used in motor vehicles to provide the initial power to start the engine. Once the engine is running, the power from the engine is used to recharge the battery.

The lead acid battery is used for heavy power applications as it can deliver a high current for short periods of time, which is needed to start an internal combustion engine. The lead acid battery relies on the ability of lead to exist in two oxidation states: +2 and +4 and the insolubility of lead(II) sulfate: $PbSO_4$. Both the electrodes are made from lead, but the negative electrodes are additionally filled with a paste of lead(IV) oxide. The electrolyte is sulfuric acid. As each cell produces a voltage of 2 V, a battery of six cells is needed to produce the 12 V that is necessary for a car engine. The large density of lead does limit the uses of the battery.

Discharging a lead acid battery

Half reaction at the negative electrode	Half reaction at the positive electrode
Lead is oxidized to lead(II) sulfate: $Pb(s) + SO_4^{2-}(aq) \rightarrow PbSO_4(s) + 2e^-$	Lead(IV) oxide is reduced to lead(II) sulfate: $PbO_2(s) + 4H^+(aq) + SO_4^{2-}(aq) + 2e^- \rightarrow PbSO_4(s) + 2H_2O(l)$

Adding the two half reactions gives the complete reaction for the discharge of a lead battery:

$$Pb(s) + 2H_2SO_4(aq) + PbO_2(s) \rightarrow 2PbSO_4(s) + 2H_2O(l)$$

Note the sulfuric acid is used up during the discharge process.

Charging a lead acid battery

As the lead(II) sulfate produced in the discharging process is insoluble, it is not dispersed into the electrolyte and the process can be reversed. When the lead(II) sulfate on the two electrodes is connected to a dc supply, electrolysis occurs and one electrode is oxidized back to lead(IV) oxide while the other reduced to lead.

Reduction half reaction	Oxidation half reaction
$PbSO_4(s) + 2e^- \rightarrow Pb(s) + SO_4^{2-}(aq)$	$PbSO_4(s) + 2H_2O(l) \rightarrow PbO_2(s) + 4H^+(aq) + SO_4^{2-}(aq) + 2e^-$

● **Examiner's hint:** Learn the equations for the half reactions of the lead acid battery.

During the charging process some sulfuric acid is electrolysed to hydrogen and oxygen. The lead acid battery needs to be topped up with the acid at intervals to make up for this loss. This provides a convenient method for testing the state of a battery, as the density decreases as the acid is used up.

Nickel cadmium batteries

Rechargeable nickel cadmium batteries are used in electronics and toys. When the battery is discharged, the positive electrode is nickel hydroxide and the negative electrode is cadmium hydroxide. The electrolyte is aqueous potassium hydroxide.

During the charging process the cadmium(II) hydroxide is reduced to the element and nickel(II) hydroxide is oxidized to Ni^{3+} in the form of $NiO(OH)$.

Charging a nickel cadmium battery

Reduction half reaction	Oxidation half reaction
$Cd(OH)_2(s) + 2e^- \rightarrow Cd(s) + 2OH^-(aq)$	$Ni(OH)_2(s) + OH^-(aq) \rightarrow NiO(OH)(s) + H_2O(l) + e^-$

The reverse reactions occur when it is discharged. The discharge process can be summarized by the equation:

$$2NiO(OH)(s) + Cd(s) + 2H_2O(l) \rightarrow 2Ni(OH)_2(s) + Cd(OH)_2(s)$$

This reaction can be reversed as both metal hydroxides are insoluble.

These batteries have a **discharge memory**. If their normal cycle of use involves short periods of discharge followed by periods of recharge, they can be discharged for longer periods.

Nickel cadmium batteries must be disposed of responsibly as cadmium is a toxic metal.

The lithium ion battery

One of the most promising new reusable batteries is the lithium ion battery, which benefits from the lithium's low density and high reactivity. It can store a lot of electrical energy per unit mass. Two kinds of electrode are used, one made from a transition metal compound such as manganese dioxide and the other made from graphite. The electrode where oxidation takes place is made of lithium metal mixed with graphite. Lithium is also present at the electrode where reduction takes place. Here it is placed in the lattice of a metal oxide (MnO_2). A non-aqueous polymer-based electrolyte is used.

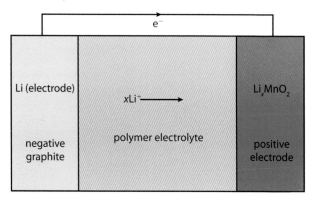

Discharging a lithium ion battery

negative electrode	positive electrode
Lithium is oxidized: $xLi \rightarrow xLi^+(polymer) + e^-$	Assuming Li is present as Li^+, it is the Mn which is reduced: $Li^+(polymer) + MnO_2(s) + e^- \rightarrow LiMnO_2(s)$

The two half reactions are reversed when the battery is recharged.

Worked example

Assuming Li has an oxidation number of $+1$, deduce the oxidation number of Mn in the mixed oxide: $LiMnO_2$ and hence show that the Mn has been reduced in the half reaction:

$$Li^+(polymer) + MnO_2(s) + e^- \rightarrow LiMnO_2(s)$$

Are oxidation numbers 'real' or are they artificial constructs invented by the chemist?

Solution

The oxidation number (ox) of Li = +1 and of O = −2

For the mixed oxide $LiMnO_2$: $+1 + ox\ (Mn) + 2(-2) = 0$

Therefore ox (Mn) = +3

The oxidation number of Mn has been reduced from +4 in MnO_2 to +3.

Lithium ion batteries are used in cell (mobile) phones, lap-tops and cameras.

Similarities and differences between fuel cells and rechargeable batteries

In a fuel cell the fuel is supplied continuously whereas in rechargeable batteries the energy is stored inside the batteries. Some advantages and disadvantages of the different systems are summarized below.

	Advantages	Disadvantages
fuel cell	more efficient than direct combustion as more chemical energy is converted to useful energy; no pollution; low density	hydrogen is a potentially explosive gas; hydrogen must be stored and transported in large/heavy containers; very expensive; technical problems due to catalytic failures, leaks and corrosion
lead acid	can deliver large amounts of energy over short periods	heavy mass; lead and sulfuric acid could cause pollution
cadmium nickel	longer life than lead acid batteries	cadmium is very toxic; produces a low voltage; very expensive
lithium ion	small density; high voltage; does not contain a toxic heavy metal	expensive; limited life span

Exercise

7 The reaction taking place when a lead acid storage battery discharges is:

$$Pb(s) + PbO_2(s) + 2H_2SO_4(aq) \rightarrow 2PbSO_4(s) + 2H_2O(l)$$

(a) Use oxidation numbers to explain what happens to the Pb(s) in terms of oxidation and reduction during this reaction.

(b) Write a balanced half equation for the reactions taking place at the negative terminal during this discharge process.

(c) Identify the property of $PbSO_4$ which allows this process to be reversed.

(d) State one advantage and one disadvantage of using a lead acid battery.

C.6 Liquid crystals

The liquid crystal state

The solid and liquid states are discussed in Chapter 1. When a solid crystal melts, the ordered arrangement of the particles breaks down, to be replaced by the disordered state of the liquid. Some crystals, however, melt to give a state which retains some of the order of the solid state. This intermediate state of matter with properties between the solid and liquid state is called the **liquid crystal** state. Liquid crystals have many of the physical properties of solid crystals, however these properties can be easily modified. In digital watches, for example, a small electric field can alter optical properties by changing the orientation of some of the molecules. Some areas of the display go dark and others remain light, allowing the shape of different digits to be displayed. Over the past 40 years liquid crystals have gone from being an academic curiosity to the basis of big business.

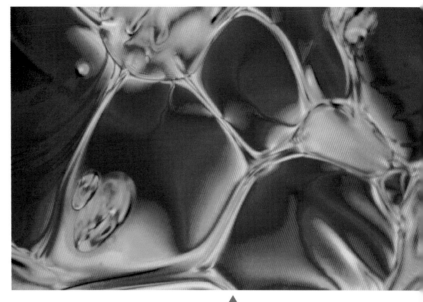

▲ Although liquid crystals (LC) flow like a fluid, there is some order in their molecular arrangement.

Liquid crystals typically all contain long, thin rigid polar organic molecules. Imagine a large number of pencils put into a rectangular box and shaken. When you open the box, the pencils will be facing in about the same direction, but will have no definite spatial organization. They are free to move, but generally line up in about the same direction. This gives a simple model for the **nematic** type of a liquid phase liquid state. The molecules are randomly distributed as in a liquid, but the intermolecular forces are sufficiently strong to hold the molecule in one orientation.

temperature increasing

Solid. The molecules have a regular arrangement and orientation.

Liquid crystal. The molecules have an irregular arrangement and a regular orientation.

Liquid. The molecules have an irregular arrangement and orientation.

Thermotropic liquid crystals are formed in a temperature range between the solid and liquid state.

The liquid crystal phase is only stable over a small range of temperatures. The directional order is lost and the liquid state is formed when the molecules have too much kinetic energy to be constrained in the same orientation by the intermolecular forces. The production of compounds which exist in the liquid phase at room temperature was one of the great challenges of organic chemistry.

Graphite, cellulose, DNA and the solution extruded by a spider to form silk form liquid crystal states under certain conditions.

Thermotropic and lyotropic liquid crystals

Liquid crystals formed by pure substances over a certain temperature range are called **thermotropic** liquid crystals. Some substances can form a different type of liquid crystal state in solution. Consider a solution containing some rod-like molecules as the solute. At low concentrations, the molecules generally have a disordered orientation and an irregular arrangement. If the concentration is increased sufficiently the molecules will adopt an ordered structure and solid crystals will form. At intermediate concentrations a **lyotropic** liquid crystal state may be possible where the molecules have an irregular arrangement with a regular orientation.

DNA crystals. DNA shows liquid crystal properties under certain conditions but it is not known how significant this is to their biological function.

The phase transitions of thermotropic liquid crystals depend on temperature, while those of lyotropic liquid crystals depend on both temperature and concentration.

Liquid crystal properties may play a central role in the processing of silk. The water-soluble silk molecules are stored in aqueous solution, but they can be assembled into rod-like units which form a liquid crystal state.

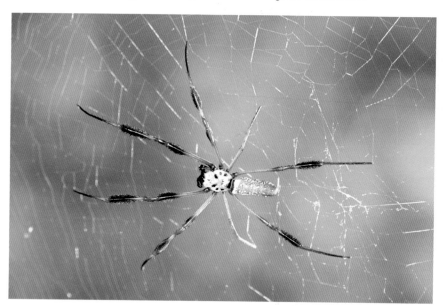

concentration decreasing

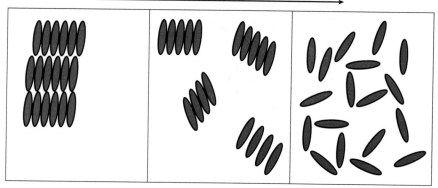

Solid. The molecules have a regular arrangement and orientation.

Liquid crystal. The molecules have an irregular arrangement and a regular orientation.

Liquid. The molecules have an irregular arrangement and orientation.

The phase transitions of lyotropic liquid crystals depend on both temperature and concentration.

The molecules that make up lyotropic liquid crystals generally consist of two distinct parts: a polar, often ionic, **head** and a non-polar, often hydrocarbon **tail**. When dissolved in high enough concentrations in aqueous solutions, the molecules arrange themselves so that the polar heads are in contact with a polar solvent in an arrangement called a **micelle**.

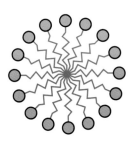

◀ **Figure 14.15** The formation of a micelle.

hydrophobic hydrocarbon chain

hydrophobic non-polar tail

hydrophilic polar head

A micelle is formed when the molecules group together to form a spherical arrangement. The hydrophilic heads are exposed to water, shielding the non-polar tails.

Lyotropic liquid crystals are found in many everyday situations. Soaps and detergents, for example, form lyotropic liquid crystals when they combine with water. Many biological membranes also display lyotropic liquid crystalline behaviour.

Liquid crystal display device

The structure of pentylcyanophenyl, a commercially available nematic crystal, is shown below.

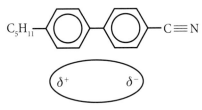

C_5H_{11}———C≡N

δ^+ δ^-

The molecule is polar as N has a greater electronegativity than carbon.

This rod-shaped molecule is suitable for liquid crystal displays as its ability to transmit light depends on its relative orientation. As the molecule is polar, its orientation can be controlled by the application of a small voltage across a small film of the material. When there is no applied voltage, light can be transmitted and the display appears light. When a small voltage is applied, the orientation of the molecules changes and light can no longer be transmitted through the film and the display appears dark. The areas of the display that are light and dark can thus be controlled, enabling different shapes to be displayed.

As discussed earlier, the nematic state for a thermotropic liquid crystal only exists within a small range of temperatures. This limits the operating temperatures of liquid crystal display devices. Pentylcyanophenyl is used in liquid crystal display devices as it has the following properties:
- It is chemically stable.
- It has a liquid crystal phase stable over a suitable range of temperatures.
- It is polar, making it able to change its orientation when an electric field is applied.
- It responds to changes of voltage quickly; it has a fast switching speed.

▲ The dark areas of the display correspond to areas where a small voltage changes the orientation of the liquid crystal molecules, preventing light from passing through the film.

W See an interview with George Gray one of the pioneers of the field of liquid crystals.

Now go to www.heinemann.co.uk/hotlinks, insert the express code 4259P and click on this activity.

Exercise

8 The molecule below has liquid crystal properties.

C_5H_{11} — ... — F, F

(a) Explain how the hydrocarbon chain adds to the chemical stability of the molecule.
(b) How does the presence of two fluorine atoms improve the liquid crystal properties?
(c) Compare the structures of the molecules below:

C_5H_{11} — ◯ — ◯ — $C\equiv N$

A

C_5H_{11} — ◯ — ◯ — ◯ — $C\equiv N$

B

Suggest why B has improved liquid crystals properties compared to A.

Richard Feynman (1918–1988). His article 'There's plenty of room at the bottom' made predictions about nanotechnology before it was possible practically.

 Read the complete article 'There's plenty of room at the bottom'.
Now go to www.heinemann.co.uk/hotlinks, insert the express code 4259P and click on this activity.

C.7 Nanotechnology

In 1959 the Nobel Prize winning physicist Richard Feynman gave a groundbreaking talk about the physical possibility of making, manipulating and visualizing things on a small scale and arranging atoms 'the way we want'. Feynman challenged scientists to develop a new field where devices and machines could be built from tens or hundreds of atoms. This field is now called **nanotechnology**, which has been described as 'the science of the very small with big potential'.

Individual silicon atoms (yellow) can be positioned to store data. This data can be written and read using a scanning tunnelling microscope.

It is theoretically possible to store the information in all the books of the world in a cube of material the size of the 'barest piece of dust that can be made out by the human eye'. See Feynman's article for more details.

  'Before you become too entranced with gorgeous gadgets ... let me remind you that information is not knowledge, knowledge is not wisdom, ...' (Arthur C Clarke)
What is the difference between knowledge and information?

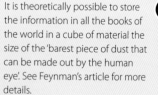

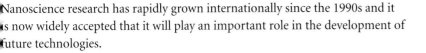

Nanoscience research has rapidly grown internationally since the 1990s and it is now widely accepted that it will play an important role in the development of future technologies.

What is nanotechnology?

Nanotechnology is defined as the research and technology development in the 1–100 nm range. Nanotechnology creates and uses structures that have novel properties because of their small size. It builds on the ability to control or manipulate matter on the atomic scale.

Nanotechnology is an interdisciplinary subject which covers chemistry, physics, biology and materials science. To the chemist, who is familiar with the world of molecules and atoms, 1 nm (10^{-9} m) is relatively large, whereas 1 μm (10^{-6} m) is considered small on an engineering scale. There are two general ways that are available to produce nanomaterials. The **top-down** approach starts with a bulk material and breaks it into smaller pieces. The **bottom up** approach builds the material from atomic or molecular species. It is important to understand that materials behave very differently to their bulk properties on the nanoscale. The rules are very different from those that apply to our everyday world. Quantum effects and the large surface-area-to-volume ratios can lead to the same material having a range of size-dependent properties. The colour of a material, for example, can depend on its size.

One of the first advances in nanotechnology was the invention of the **scanning tunnelling microscope** (STM). The scanning tunnelling microscope does not 'see' the atoms, but 'feels' them. An ultra-fine tip scans a surface and records a signal as the tip moves up and down depending on the atoms present. The STM also provides a physical technique for manipulating individual atoms. They can be positioned accurately in just the same way as using a pair of tweezers.

> Nanotechnology involves research and technology development in the 1–100 nm range. It creates and uses structures that have novel properties because of their small size and builds on the ability to control or manipulate on the atomic scale. One nanometre is 0.000 000 001 m. It can be written as 1 nm or 1×10^{-9} m.

◀ The head of a variable temperature scanning tunnelling microscope.

The use of the scanning tunnelling microscope has allowed us to 'see' individual atoms. Does technology blur the distinction between simulation and reality?

Simple molecules such as water and glucose, for example, are just below 1 nm in size. The synthesis of nanoscale materials, which are 10–100 times larger, is difficult from such molecules using conventional chemical methods. It would involve large numbers of molecules spontaneously self-assembling. The process

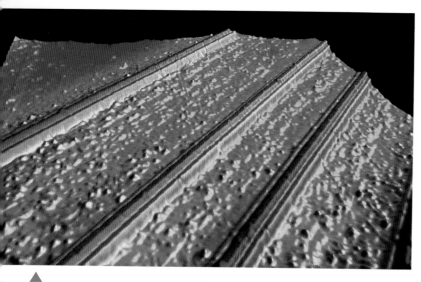

Coloured scanning tunnelling micrograph of nanowires. Just 10 atoms wide, these wires could be used in computers operating at the limits of miniaturization.

does, however, occur in nature where highly complex molecular structures such as proteins are built from the simple building blocks of 20 amino acids. This is possible as the amino molecules *recognize* and bind to each other by intermolecular interactions such as **hydrogen bonding** and **van der Waal's** forces. DNA-assisted assembly methods can be used in a similar way to make nanoscale materials. Strands of the molecule act as an 'intelligent sticky tape' allowing only certain base pairings to occur. Molecules can only bind to bases of the DNA when specific hydrogen bonding interactions occur. The field has developed in many directions with chemists synthesizing ever more complex and finely tuned super-molecules.

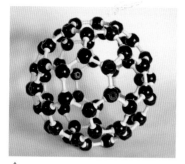

C_{60} has a structure consisting of interlinking hexagonal and pentagonal rings that form a hollow spherical shape similar to a soccer ball.

The carbon nanotube is capped owing to the presence of pentagons at the end of the structure.

In 1996 scientists at the IBM Research Laboratory in Zurich built the world's smallest abacus. Individual C_{60} molecules could be pushed back and forth by the ultra fine tip of a scanning tunnelling microscope.

Prof Harry Kroto (1939–) tells the story of the discovery of C_{60}.
Now go to www.heinemann.co.uk/hotlinks, insert the express code 4259P and click on this activity.

Carbon nanotubes

The structure of buckminsterfullerene C_{60} was discussed in Chapter 4. The addition of pentagons into the hexagonal structure of graphite allows the carbon atoms to form a closed spherical cage. The discovery of C_{60} was one of the key developments in nanochemistry.

The discovery of C_{60} led to the discovery of whole family of structurally related carbon nanotubes. These resemble a rolled-up sheet of graphite, with the carbon molecules arranged in repeating hexagons. The tubes, which have a diameter of 1 nm can be closed if pentagons are present in the structure.

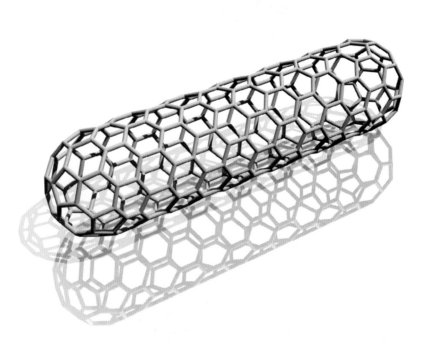

A whole series of molecules, including structures with multiple walls of concentric tubes have been produced. Carbon nanotubes have proved to have very useful properties. Bundles of carbon nanotubes have tensile strengths between 50 to 100 times that of iron, as there is strong covalent bonding within the walls of the nanotube. Different tubes have different electrical properties because at the nanoscale, the behaviour of electrons is very sensitive to the dimensions of the tube. Some tubes are conductors and some are semi-conductors.

Their properties can also be altered by trapping different atoms inside the tubes. Silver chloride, for example, can be inserted into a tube and then decomposed to form an inner coat of silver. The resulting tube is a thin metallic electrical conductor. As tubes have large surface areas and specific dimensions they have the potential to be very efficient and size-selective heterogeneous catalysts. Their mechanical (stiffness, strength, toughness), thermal and electrical properties allow a wide variety of applications, from batteries and fuel cells, to fibres and cables, to pharmaceuticals and biomedical materials.

The world's smallest test tube has been made from a carbon nanotube. One end of the tube is closed by a fullerene cap that contains both pentagons and hexagons. The tube has a volume of 10^{-24} dm^3.

Implications of nanotechnology

Nanotechnology has the potential to provide significant advances over the next 50 years. Applications will be broad, including healthcare, medicine, security, electronics, communications and computing.

	Current and potential uses
agriculture	nanoporous zeolites for slow release of water and fertilizers
healthcare/medicine	biological nanosensors as diagnostic tools
energy	nanoscale catalyst-enhanced fuels for better efficiency; nanomaterials for fuel cells/batteries/solar cells
electronics	carbon nanotube electronic components
ICT	flat panel flexible displays using nanotechnology; high-density data storage using nanomagnetic effects; faster processing using quantum computers
water treatment	nanomembranes for water treatment

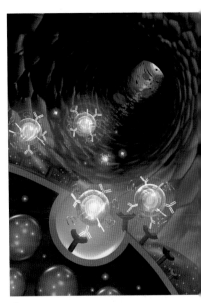

Quantum dot nanoparticle probes, used to target and image tumours through the incorporation of antibodies that bind to the target cancer cells.

While scientists are very excited about the potential of nanotechnology, there are some concerns about the problems that the new technologies might cause. New technologies always carry new risks and concerns. There are unknown health effects and concerns that the human immune system will be defenceless against nanoscale particles. As they have very different properties from their related bulk materials, they need to be handled differently. The toxicity of the materials, for example, depends on the size of particles. Many applications only require very small numbers of nanoparticles, so this reduces risks considerably. However some uses involve large quantities, for example sun screens. Large scale manufacture can lead to explosions. The small particle size and large surface area increase the rate of reactions to dangerous levels. Like any new chemical products, a full risk assessment is required, both for the production of new materials and their subsequent uses. It is the responsibility of scientists to carry out these trials, assess the risks and engage in debate with the public to ensure that concerns are addressed and the scientific facts of the technology are communicated.

Listen to this programme (2) which discusses some of the concerns of nanotechnology.
Now go to www.heinemann.co.uk/ hotlinks, insert the express code 4259P and click on this activity.

Will nanotechnology change the world, as some have promised? What's all this about molecular machines in our blood?

Now go to www.heinemann.co.uk/hotlinks, insert the express code 4259P and click on this activity.

Nanontechnology will have an impact on the ethical, legal and political issues that face the international community in the near future. It is important that international bodies such as UNESCO promote a dialogue between the public and the scientific communities.

● **Examiner's hint:** Match your answers to the number of marks allotted to the questions.

Exercise

9 (a) A carbon nanotube has a diameter of 1 nm and is 10 μm long. How many diameters does this length represent?

(b) These tubes are believed to be stronger than steel. Explain the tensile strength of the tubes on a molecular level.

(c) One problem in the synthesis of nanotubes is that a mixture of tubes with different lengths and orientations is produced. Suggest why this is a problem.

(d) The wavelength of UV light is in the range 1–400 nm. Many modern sunscreens contain nano-sized particles of titanium dioxide which do not absorb ultraviolet radiation. Suggest how these nano-particles are able to protect skin from ultraviolet radiation.

Practice questions

1 (a) Traditionally, the raw materials for the production of iron are iron ore, coke, limestone and preheated air. Iron oxides are reduced in a blast furnace by both carbon and carbon monoxide to form iron. Give the equation for the reduction of iron(III) oxide by carbon monoxide. (1)

(b) In many modern blast furnaces, hydrocarbons, (such as methane) are also added to the preheated air. This produces carbon monoxide and hydrogen. The hydrogen formed can also act as a reducing agent. Give the equation for the reduction of magnetite, Fe_3O_4, by hydrogen. (1)

(c) The iron produced in the blast furnace is known as 'pig iron'. It contains about 5% carbon, together with small amounts of other elements such as phosphorus and silicon. Explain the chemical principles behind the conversion of iron into steel using the basic oxygen converter. (6)

(d) State **one** element that must be added to the basic oxygen converter to produce stainless steel rather than ordinary steel. (1)

(Total 9 marks)

2 Several monomers are produced by the oil industry and used in polymer manufacture. Examples include propene, styrene and vinyl chloride.

(a) (i) Draw the structural formula of propene. (1)

(ii) Isotactic polypropene has a regular structure, while atactic polypropene does not. Draw the structure of isotactic polypropene, showing a chain of at least six carbon atoms. State and explain how its properties differ from those of atactic polypropene. (3)

(b) Styrene can be polymerized to polystyrene, which is a colourless, transparent, brittle plastic. Another form of the polymer is expanded polystyrene. Outline how expanded polystyrene is produced from polystyrene and state how its properties differ from those of polystyrene. (4)

(c) Many plastic materials are disposed of by combustion. State **two** disadvantages of disposing of polyvinyl chloride in this way. (2)

(Total 10 marks)

3 (a) The properties of polyvinyl chloride, PVC, may be modified to suit a particular use. State the main method of modifying PVC and the effect this has on its properties. (2)

(b) Outline **two** disadvantages of using polymers such as polypropene and PVC and give **one** disadvantage that is specific to PVC. (3)

(Total 5 marks)

4 Fuel cells have been described as the energy source of the future, because they are said to be non-polluting and can use renewable resources. One type uses hydrogen as the fuel and oxygen as the other substance consumed, with hot aqueous potassium hydroxide as the electrolyte. The overall equation for the process is $2H_2 + O_2 \rightarrow 2H_2O$, but the actual reactions taking place are different.

(a) Give the **two** half-equations for the reactions involving each reactant. (2)

(b) Each kilojoule of chemical energy released in the oxidation of hydrogen in the fuel cell costs more than that released in the combustion of gasoline. Explain why fuel cells are considered to be more economical than gasoline engines. (1)

(Total 3 marks)

5 (a) Distinguish between the liquid and the liquid crystal state. (2)

(b) Distinguish between a lyotropic and a thermotropic liquid crystal. (2)

(c) Outline how a micelle forms in a soap solution. (3)

(Total 7 marks)

6 (a) Explain why heterogeneous catalysts are generally used in industrial processes. (2)

(b) Suggest two reasons why carbon nanotubes could be effective catalysts. (2)

(c) Suggest a reason why it is difficult to regulate for the toxicity of nanoparticles. (2)

(Total 6 marks)

7 Outline the principles of a liquid crystal display device. (4)

8 Nanotechnology is currently a popular area for research.

(a) Define the term *nanotechnology*. (1)

(b) Discuss some of the positive and negative implications of *nanotechnology*. (4)

(Total 5 marks)

9 Aluminium is produced on a large scale by the electrolysis of alumina.

(a) Give the formula of alumina. (1)

(b) Explain why cryolite is used in the process. (2)

(c) Write an equation to show what happens to each of the following ions during electrolysis. (2)

Al^{3+}

O^{2-}

(d) Identify the material used for the positive electrodes (anodes) and explain, with the help of an equation, why it has to be replaced regularly. (3)

(e) Suggest why much more aluminium is recycled than iron. (1)

(Total 9 marks)

10 Electrical energy can be produced from chemical energy by the use of batteries.

(a) Explain the workings of the lead–acid storage battery. Your answer should include:

- the materials used for each electrode
- the identity of the electrolyte
- the half-equation for the reaction that occurs at each electrode. (5)

(b) Identify the type of reaction that occurs at the negative electrode (anode) and explain your answer. (2)

(Total 7 marks)

11 The most widely used polymer is polythene, which is made in low-density and high-density forms.

(a) Discuss the differences between these **two** forms by referring to the amount of branching, the forces between the polymer chains and the physical properties. (4)

(b) Both forms of polythene are described as *thermoplastics*. State the meaning of this term. (1)

(Total 5 marks)

© International Baccalaureate Organization – questions 1 to 4 and 9 to 11

15 Medicines and drugs:

Option D

Records from Egypt and from Greece written over three thousand years ago document medical properties in extracts from animal organs, plant tissue and minerals. Chinese medicine too has its roots in ancient times. These insights into the healing properties of natural substances, often based on knowledge of the local environment, have typically been passed on from generation to generation within communities. This continues to be an important aspect of health management for many people today.

The 20th century, however, saw a major new development in health care – that of the production of synthetic molecules specifically for the treatment of illnesses. Without question this has been one of the most significant achievements of the last 100 years. Development of targeted drugs and vaccines has meant that diseases such as smallpox have been eradicated, countless millions have survived infections such as malaria and tuberculosis, and other diseases like polio are on their way to extinction. Untold numbers of people today owe their lives to the action of medicines.

At the same time, and as with other great innovations, the pharmaceutical industry has brought its own challenges. Abuses, problems arising from excesses and new problems like antibiotic resistance all have to be faced. As global travel becomes more commonplace and new diseases such as avian 'flu and ebola appear, the potential exists for pandemics (epidemics across a large region of human population), as we have already seen with HIV. In addition, there are huge discrepancies in the availability of drugs in different parts of the world, which means that many diseases for which effective treatments exist are still inflicting suffering and death in some places.

As most medicines and drugs are organic in nature, you will gain a greater understanding of this chapter if you have first studied Chapter 10, Organic chemistry. It is hoped that this option will help you to apply your chemistry knowledge to the many topical issues discussed, as well as to be better prepared to make important decisions about the management of your own health.

Coloured scanning electron micrograph ▶ of MRSA (methicillin-resistant *Staphylococcus aureus*) bacteria. These bacteria are resistant to most commonly prescribed antibiotics and have become a serious problem in many hospitals. The search for new antibiotics to fight resistant bacteria is a major aspect of research by the pharmaceutical industry.

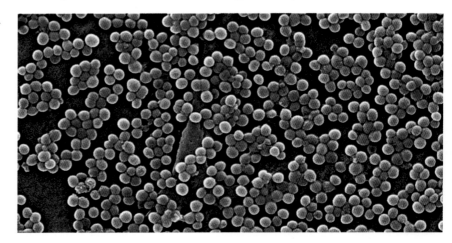

Assessment statements

D.1 Pharmaceutical products
D.1.1 List the effects of medicines and drugs on the functioning of the body.
D.1.2 Outline the stages involved in the research, development and testing of new pharmaceutical products.
D.1.3 Describe the different methods of administering drugs.
D.1.4 Discuss the terms *therapeutic window, tolerance* and *side-effects*.

D.2 Antacids
D.2.1 State and explain how excess acidity in the stomach can be reduced by the use of different bases.

D.3 Analgesics
D.3.1 Describe and explain the different ways that analgesics prevent pain.
D.3.2 Describe the use of derivatives of salicylic acid as mild analgesics and compare the advantages and disadvantages of using aspirin and paracetamol (acetaminophen).
D.3.3 Compare the structures of morphine, codeine and diamorphine (heroin, a semi-synthetic opiate).
D.3.4 Discuss the advantages and disadvantages of using morphine and its derivatives as strong analgesics.

D.4 Depressants
D.4.1 Describe the effects of depressants.
D.4.2 Discuss the social and physiological effects of the use and abuse of ethanol.
D.4.3 Describe and explain the techniques used for the detection of ethanol in the breath, the blood and urine.
D.4.4 Describe the synergistic effects of ethanol with other drugs.
D.4.5 Identify other commonly used depressants and describe their structures.

D.5 Stimulants
D.5.1 List the physiological effects of stimulants.
D.5.2 Compare amphetamines and epinephrine (adrenaline).
D.5.3 Discuss the short- and long-term effects of nicotine consumption.
D.5.4 Describe the effects of caffeine and compare its structure with that of nicotine.

D.6 Antibacterials
D.6.1 Outline the historical development of penicillins.
D.6.2 Explain how penicillins work and discuss the effects of modifying the side-chain.
D.6.3 Discuss and explain the importance of patient compliance and the effect of penicillin overprescription.

D.7 Antivirals
D.7.1 State how viruses differ from bacteria.
D.7.2 Describe the different ways in which antiviral drugs work.
D.7.3 Discuss the difficulties associated with solving the AIDS problem.

D.1 Pharmaceutical products

The human body has many natural systems of defence

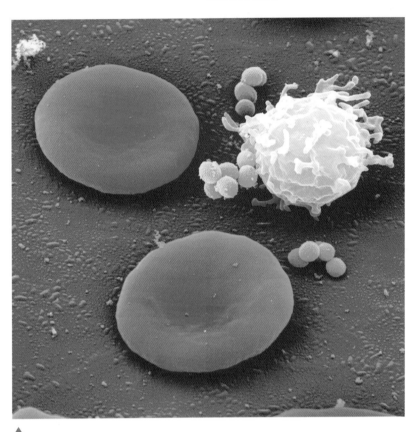

The functioning of the human body involves an incredibly intricate balance of thousands of different reactions occurring simultaneously. All of these must respond to the changing demands of the individual's activities and environment – it is truly complex chemistry! The remarkable fact is that for most people most of the time, the functioning of the body works effectively – the situation when we describe ourselves as 'healthy'. However, inevitably the system can suffer from many types of defect and breakdown, through injury, through genetically or environmentally caused abnormalities and through accumulated changes with age. In addition, we are constantly under attack from microorganisms which can enter the body, alter its functioning and so cause disease.

▲ Coloured scanning electron micrograph of bacteria, shown in yellow, in the blood alongside red blood cells and a white blood cell. The white blood cell will destroy the bacteria, protecting the body from disease.

Happily, the human body is well equipped with equally complex systems of defence and healing processes to try to minimize the effects of these challenges. Rather like in a battle in a war, we describe attacking microorganisms as **invaders** and the body's responses as different **lines of defence**, activated as the invaders penetrate more deeply. Some of the key aspects of the natural defence mechanisms are described in the table below.

Non-specific defence mechanisms		Specific defence mechanisms
First line of defence: *barriers to prevent entry*	*Second line of defence:* *attack invaders*	*Third line of defence:* *immune system*
• skin	• white blood cells engulf invaders (phagocytosis)	• white blood cells produce specific proteins called **antibodies** to recognize and destroy the invaders
• mucous membranes	• blood clotting to prevent loss of blood and further invasions	• memory cells enable the body to fight a repeat invasion of the same organism more effectively
• closures and secretions of natural openings such as lips, eyelids, ear wax etc.	• the inflammatory response	

Often the responses of the body to an invading organism manifest themselves as symptoms of disease. For example, we may experience excess mucus from the nasal passages, or a fever as the body raises its temperature to fight the infection of a common cold. Although these symptoms generally need to be monitored, as for example a high body temperature can be dangerous, they are not usually themselves cause for concern.

When considering how best to fight disease, it is essential that we keep the focus on maximizing the effectiveness of the body's natural defence systems, rather than in any way defeating it or inhibiting its effect. At best, medicines work by supplementing our natural healing processes.

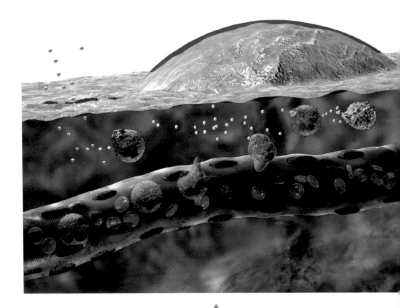

Computer artwork of the inflammatory response. Bacteria, shown in gold, are seen entering the body through a cut in the skin and the blood capillary beneath the site of entry is releasing white blood cells, shown in purple and green, into the tissue. These cells will destroy the bacteria and activate the immune response.

There are many different types of medicines and drugs

The terms 'medicines' and 'drugs' are sometimes used interchangeably and sometimes have slightly different meanings in different parts of the world. They are most clearly defined as follows.

Drug: a chemical that affects how the body works. This includes changes for the better and for the worse. The term is sometimes associated with substances which are illegal in many countries, such as cocaine, ecstasy and heroin, but its usage is not limited to these cases.

Medicine: a substance that improves health. Medicines, which may be natural or synthetic, therefore contain beneficial drugs. Synthetic medicines also contain other ingredients, which are non-active but help in the presentation and administration of the drug. The beneficial effect of a medicine is known as its **therapeutic** effect.

In general, the effects on the body of drugs include the following:
- alteration of the physiological state, including consciousness, activity level and coordination
- alteration of incoming sensory sensations
- alteration of mood or emotions.

Given the complexity of the chemical reactions in the body, most drugs have more than one effect and so can be difficult to classify precisely. However, the drugs considered in this chapter are those which primarily:
- target the nervous system and brain, including the perception of stimuli; these include **analgesics**, **stimulants** and **depressants**
- target metabolic processes; these include **antacids**
- aim to supplement the body's ability to fight disease-causing organisms; these include **antibacterials** and **antivirals**.

The word *placebo* is Latin for 'I will please'. The term *nocebo*, Latin for 'I will harm', is sometimes used to describe a condition worsened by a belief that a drug used is harmful. One example is a person dying of fright after being bitten by a non-venomous snake.

The placebo effect is when patients gain therapeutic effect from their belief that they have been given a useful drug, even when they have not.

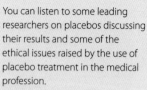

Studies on the placebo effect are fraught with difficulties of interpretation as there are many other factors that could have contributed to the claimed therapeutic effects. These include spontaneous improvement, fluctuation of symptoms, answers of politeness and patient misjudgement. Consider what other factors might be involved in interpreting such research and how experiments to produce reliable and reproducible data could be conducted.

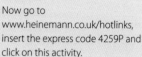

You can listen to some leading researchers on placebos discussing their results and some of the ethical issues raised by the use of placebo treatment in the medical profession.

Now go to www.heinemann.co.uk/hotlinks, insert the express code 4259P and click on this activity.

The placebo effect – the power of suggestion?

It has been known for years that a significant number of patients receive therapeutic and healing effects from medicines that are pharmacologically inert, when they *believe* they are taking an effective drug. This effect, called the **placebo effect**, has been the subject of much research and analysis, but remains controversial. To date, no rigorous clinical explanation exists for the placebo effect. Nonetheless, many medical reports validate the phenomenon, in particular the ability of placebos to reduce pain. Recent research using brain scans has shown that some patients who believed they were taking pain medication were actually releasing opioids or natural pain relief, so providing some biological basis to explain the effect. It is generally accepted that about one-third of a control group taking a placebo show some improvements, a fact used in all major clinical trials, which will be discussed below.

Drugs can be administered in several different ways

The manner in which a drug is delivered to the patient's body depends on many factors. These include the chemical nature of the drug, the condition of the patient and the most effective way of getting the drug to the target organ. For example, some chemicals (including proteins such as insulin) are decomposed by the action of the digestive enzymes in the gut, so they cannot be administered as pills, but must instead be injected directly into the blood. Likewise, a patient in a coma might be unable to swallow an ingested pill so the drug must be delivered in another way.

The following methods are all used to administer drugs.

Method of administering drug	Description	Example
oral	taken by mouth	tablets, capsules, pills, liquids
inhalation	vapour breathed in; smoking	medications for respiratory conditions such as asthma; some drugs of abuse such as nicotine and cocaine
skin patches	absorbed directly from the skin into the blood	some hormone treatments e.g. estrogen, nicotine patches
suppositories	inserted into the rectum	treatment of digestive illnesses, haemorrhoids
eye or ear drops	liquids delivered directly to the opening	treatments of infections of the eye or ear
parenteral – by injection (see diagram on the next page)	intramuscular	many vaccines
	intravenous: fastest method of injection	local anaesthetics
	subcutaneous	dental injections

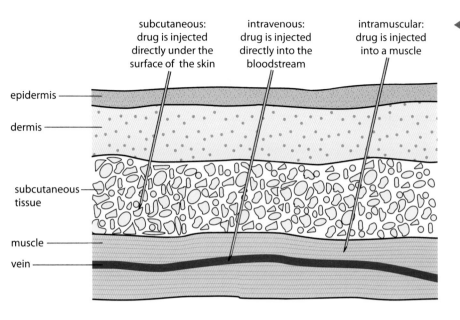

subcutaneous: drug is injected directly under the surface of the skin

intravenous: drug is injected directly into the bloodstream

intramuscular: drug is injected into a muscle

epidermis

dermis

subcutaneous tissue

muscle

vein

◀ **Figure 15.1** Methods of injection. (parenteral administration)

Physiological effects of drugs are complex and depend on the dosage

Because of the complexity of the chemical reactions in the body, a drug can interact in many different ways. This means that usually a drug will produce more than one physiological effect and these can be classified as follows:

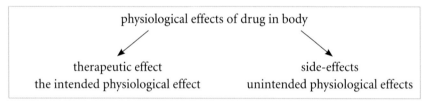

physiological effects of drug in body

therapeutic effect
the intended physiological effect

side-effects
unintended physiological effects

Side-effects are defined as physiological effects which are not intended and vary greatly from one drug to another and with the same drug in different people. Sometimes side-effects may be beneficial, such as the fact that aspirin, taken for pain relief, helps protect against heart disease. Other times, the side-effects may be relatively benign, such as causing drowsiness, nausea or constipation. But of greater concern are side-effects which are much more adverse, such as causing damage to organs. The impact of these side-effects must be evaluated throughout the drug treatment. Patients must also be made aware of the possible side-effects of a drug to help in the monitoring of the treatment and to make possible adjustments in lifestyle, for example in some cases not driving or operating machinery. One of the most dramatic – and tragic – examples of adverse side-effects was the deformities produced in unborn children resulting from the thalidomide drug discussed below.

The **dosing regime** for a drug refers to the amount of drug used for each dose and the frequency of administration. Determining this is usually quite difficult as there are so many variables involved – for example the age, sex and weight of the patient, as well as factors such as diet and environment. Interaction with other drugs must also be considered. Ideally the dosage should result in constant levels of the drug in the blood, but this is almost impossible to achieve other than by a continuous, intravenous drip. Drugs administered by the other methods described

The therapeutic window is the range of a drug's concentration in the blood between its therapeutic level and its toxic level.

will inevitably lead to fluctuations in the blood drug level between doses. The important thing is that the concentration in the bloodstream must remain within a certain range: above this range, unacceptable side-effects may occur, whilst below this range there may not be effective therapeutic outcomes. This target range is referred to as the **therapeutic window**.

Figure 15.2 The therapeutic window. ▶

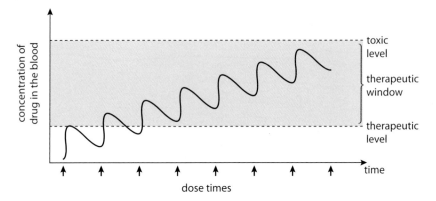

The range of concentrations that defines the therapeutic window varies greatly from one drug to the next.

Tolerance occurs when repeated doses of a drug result in smaller physiological effects.

When a person is given repeated doses of a drug, it sometimes happens that **tolerance** develops, that is a reduced response to the drug. So higher doses are needed to produce the same effect and this increases the chances of there being toxic side-effects. The mechanism by which tolerance to a drug develops is not always understood – it could be that the body has become able to metabolize and break down the drug more efficiently, or that the drug receptors in cells become less effective. For some drugs, tolerance develops to one effect of the drug and not to other effects.

It is possible to experience addiction even to one's own hormones and neurotransmitters (chemicals used for communication in the nervous system). For example, some people are addicted to exercise as this leads to the release of chemicals that can produce a 'high'. Susceptible people are driven to exercise increasingly and they suffer withdrawal symptoms such as depression if they cannot fulfil this need.

A related but different condition is **dependence** or **addiction**. This occurs when a patient becomes dependent on the drug in order to feel normal and suffers from **withdrawal symptoms** if the drug is not taken. Symptoms can be mild, such as headaches suffered on withdrawal from dependence on caffeine, or serious if the drug is toxic or shows tolerance, such as opiates, alcohol and barbiturates.

Research, development and testing of new pharmaceutical products is a long and costly process

Malaria is a disease that is both curable and preventable. But a child dies of malaria every 10 seconds; more than one million people die of malaria every year. Why do you think this is?

Pharmaceutical companies and research groups are constantly developing new drugs in response to demand. The goal is usually to develop drugs that are more effective and have fewer toxic side-effects than pre-existing drugs for the same condition, as well as drugs for new conditions such as SARS (severe acute respiratory syndrome). Every new drug developed represents a major investment of money, which makes the industry very selective in its focus. Hence a large amount of research goes into drugs to treat conditions such as obesity, depression, cancer, cardiovascular disease and ulcers, which are prevalent in the developed world where the market can support the cost. Much less attention and resources are given to researching drugs for conditions such as tropical diseases which are prevalent in the developing world.

Find out more about the spread of malaria, the problems of drug resistance in its treatment and the programmes aimed at ending the suffering caused by this disease.

Now go to www.heinemann.co.uk/hotlinks, insert the express code 4259P and click on these activities.

Most drugs have wide ranging, varied and potentially harmful effects, so it is clear that there must be stringent controls over the development and licensing of what is developed for the market. The details of this vary greatly from one country to another, so only general principles that are widely followed will be described here. The essential point is that as much information as possible about the full effect of the drug in an individual, including long-term effects, must be gathered before a drug can be approved and this is usually monitored at the governmental level. For every new drug that reaches the market, thousands of candidate molecules fail to meet the criteria and are rejected. This is one of the reasons why drug development is so costly. The average time for development of a drug from its first identification to its appearance on the market is about 10–12 years.

Discovery research

The first stage in drug development involves identifying and extracting compounds that have been shown to have biological activity and are known as **lead compounds** (pronounced to rhyme with 'need', not the element Pb!). Often these compounds have only low levels of activity, or possibly give negative side-effects, but they can still provide a start for the drug design and development process. Lead compounds are often derived from plants; for example, an anti-cancer agent extracted from yew trees led to the development of Taxol, and digitalis extracted from the foxglove flower led to heart medications. Microorganisms too have provided rich sources of lead compounds, particularly in the development of antibiotics, which we will study later.

Next the effectiveness of the lead compound is optimized by making and testing many chemically related compounds known as **analogues**. This process is often now fast-tracked by two relatively new techniques: **combinatorial chemistry** and **high-throughput screening**. These processes enable the production and testing of vast numbers of candidate medicines in a very short time. Following extensive laboratory tests, a potential medicine is then tested on animals, under strict legislative control. These tests help scientists to determine the dose to be administered in human trials.

Development research

There are usually three phases in the subsequent human trials, as shown in Figure 15.3, involving an increasing number of patients. The effectiveness of the drug is judged by the relative improvement in the patients who have received the real medication compared with those on a placebo in Phase III.

 The use of animals in drug trials is highly controversial and raises many questions for pharmaceutical researchers and legislators across the world. Supporters of the practice argue that almost every medical achievement over the last 100 years has involved the use of animals in some way. For example, the US and British governments both support the advancement of medical and scientific goals using animal testing, provided that the testing minimizes animal use and suffering. Opponents argue that the practice is intrinsically cruel and that animals have a right to freedom from such inflicted suffering. Many also consider it to be poor scientific practice since animal responses to drugs may not be a reliable predictor of human reactions. Concerns are also raised that the regulation of the use of animals in many countries is not well monitored.

 Find out more about the opposing sides in the debate on drug testing on animals.
Now go to
www.heinemann.co.uk/hotlinks, insert the express code 4259P and click on these activities.

Figure 15.3 Stages in the discovery and development of a new medicine.

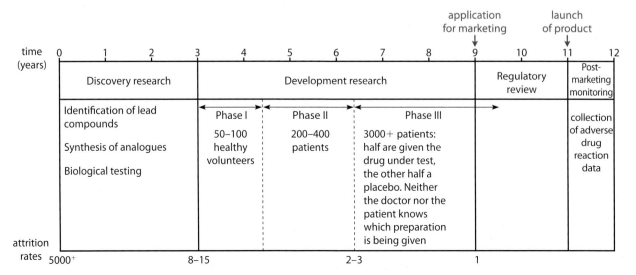

time (years)	0	1	2	3	4	5	6	7	8	9	10	11	12
									application for marketing			launch of product	

Discovery research	Development research			Regulatory review	Post-marketing monitoring
Identification of lead compounds Synthesis of analogues Biological testing	Phase I 50–100 healthy volunteers	Phase II 200–400 patients	Phase III 3000+ patients: half are given the drug under test, the other half a placebo. Neither the doctor nor the patient knows which preparation is being given		collection of adverse drug reaction data

attrition rates	5000+	8–15	2–3	1

335

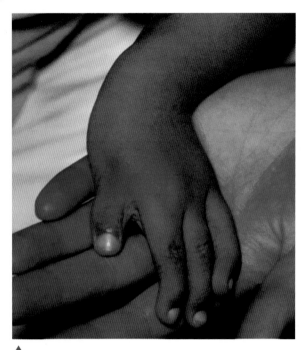

Close-up of the deformed hand and forearm of a 'thalidomide baby'. Thalidomide is a sedative drug that was administered to many pregnant women in the 1960s. It was withdrawn from the market after it was found to cause serious foetal abnormalities. This tragedy led to major changes in drug testing protocols.

Owing largely to the high rates of attrition (the fact that many trial drugs have to be rejected), the total cost of this process for every new drug that reaches the shelves is many hundreds of millions of dollars.

Over the last 50 years, many countries have adopted an additional regulatory step in this process, triggered by the disaster involving use of the drug **thalidomide**. During the late 1950s and early 1960s this drug was marketed initially in Germany as a sedative and anti-inflammatory medication and later prescribed to pregnant women in many countries to help reduce 'morning sickness' in their early months of pregnancy. Tragically, the drug had devastating effects on the development of the foetus and up to 12 000 children were born with severe birth defects, most notably missing or malformed limbs. In addition, many babies did not survive infancy. By the time the deformities in the newborns were linked with the thalidomide drug, it had been widely marketed in at least 46 countries.

Regulators realized then that it was not sufficient only to establish the safety and effectiveness of a drug *before* it went on the market. An additional system was needed to track medications once the population had access to them, when effects in different groups of people, including long-term effects, become known. Today, many countries maintain post-marketing safety surveillance programmes for all approved drugs and databases are available that give details of adverse drug reactions. This has sometimes led to the withdrawal of a drug from the market after years of usage. This happened, for example, in the USA with the Vioxx anti-inflammatory drug in 2004, following concerns that its long-term use caused an increased risk of heart attack and stroke. In November 2007, the pharmaceutical company Merck was forced to pay almost US$5 billion to settle lawsuits from people who claimed that the drug Vioxx had caused their heart attacks and strokes.

You can watch the documentary 'Cancer Warriors' with selective short chapters on developing and testing drugs and on thalidomide.
Now go to www.heinemann.co.uk/hotlinks, insert the express code 4259P and click on this activity.

You can watch a short documentary news clip about the issues surrounding the withdrawal of Vioxx from the market.
Now go to www.heinemann.co.uk/hotlinks, insert the express code 4259P and click on this activity.

The thalidomide drug was never marketed in the USA because of the intervention of Frances Kelsey, a pharmacologist working at the Food and Drug Administration (FDA). Despite pressure from thalidomide's manufacturer and the fact that it was already approved in over 20 European and African countries, she registered concerns about the drug's ability to cross the placenta into the foetal blood. Her insistence that further tests be carried out was dramatically vindicated when the effects of thalidomide became known. For her insightful work in averting a similar tragedy in the USA she was given a Distinguished Federal Service Award by President Kennedy.

All drugs carry risks as well as benefits. Who should ultimately be responsible for assessing the risk-to-benefit ratio of a drug in an individual – the pharmaceutical company, a government watch body, the doctor, or the patient?

Exercises

1 List the three different ways in which drugs can be injected into the body. Predict, giving a reason, which of the three methods will result in the drug having the most rapid effect.

2 State what is meant by tolerance towards a drug and explain why it is potentially dangerous.
© International Baccalaureate Organization [2003]

Quick reference for functional group identities and some important organic reactions

In the following sections on different classes of drugs, reference will be made to the functional groups of the molecules which are generally associated with their activity. It is important that you can recognize and identify these groups in different molecules. Some but not all of them were introduced in Chapter 10, so a brief summary of the important ones found in drugs is given here. (Note that R and R' refer to carbon-containing or alkyl groups.)

Structure of functional group	Name of functional group	Structure of functional group	Name of functional group
$C=C$	alkene; carbon–carbon double bond	$R-N{\overset{H}{\underset{H}{}}}$	primary amine
$-C-OH$	alcohol; hydroxyl	$R-N{\overset{H}{\underset{R'}{}}}$	secondary amine
$\overset{R}{\underset{R'}{}}C=O$	ketone	$R-N{\overset{R''}{\underset{R'}{}}}$	tertiary amine
(benzene ring)	benzene or phenyl ring	amide	amide
$-C{\overset{O}{\underset{OH}{}}}$	carboxylic acid	$-C{\overset{O}{\underset{O-R}{}}}$	ester
$R-O-R'$	ether	(pyridine ring)	a heterocyclic ring containing atoms other than C, usually N
$-Cl$	chloro	$-NO_2$	nitro

In addition, there are two common condensation reactions in organic chemistry that you should be able to recognize:

(i) Acid + alcohol → ester + water

$$R-C{\overset{O}{\underset{O-H}{}}} \quad + \quad R'-O-H \quad \longrightarrow \quad R-C{\overset{O}{\underset{O-R'}{}}} \quad + \quad H_2O$$

(ii) Acid + amine → amide + water

$$R-C{\overset{O}{\underset{O-H}{}}} \quad + \quad R'-N{\overset{H}{\underset{H}{}}} \quad \longrightarrow \quad R-C{\overset{O}{\underset{N{\overset{H}{\underset{R'}{}}}}{}}} \quad + \quad H_2O$$

● **Examiner's hint:** It is easy to confuse *amine* and *amide*. Amines are organic derivatives of ammonia, NH_3. In amides, the N is attached to a carbonyl carbon ($-C=O$), so these are derivatives of carboxylic acids. There is no $-C=O$ group in amines.

D.2   Antacids

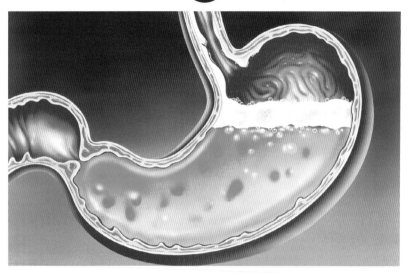

Acidity in the stomach is normal, but excess acidity is potentially harmful

The body keeps a tight control over the pH in cells and extra-cellular fluids, as changes in the H^+ concentration have significant effects on the activity of many molecules, especially catalysts known as enzymes. The gastro-intestinal tract, or gut, generates and maintains different pH environments along its length, which play an important role in controlling the activity of digestive enzymes.

The stomach is unusual in that it generates a pH as low as 1–2 by the production of hydrochloric acid from structures in the lining of the walls, known as gastric glands. The acid environment not only kills bacteria that may have been ingested with food, but also provides the optimum environment for the action of its digestive enzymes. However, some factors, such as excess alcohol, smoking, stress and some anti-inflammatory drugs, can cause excess production of this acidic secretion known as **gastric juice**. This can lead to the following problems:

- acid indigestion: a feeling of discomfort from too much acid in the stomach
- heartburn: acid from the stomach rising into the oesophagus – often called acid reflux
- ulcer: damage to the lining of the stomach wall, resulting in loss of tissue and inflammation.

Antacids are weak bases which neutralize excess acid

Drugs to help combat such excess acid are known as **antacids**. They work by neutralizing the hydrochloric acid, hence relieving the symptoms. Antacids are usually weakly basic compounds, often metal oxides or hydroxides, carbonates or hydrogencarbonates, which react with the acid to produce a salt and water. Note that these drugs do not directly coat ulcers or induce healing, but according to the dictum 'no acid, no ulcer', they do allow the stomach lining time to mend. For example:

Aluminium hydroxide $Al(OH)_3$

$$Al(OH)_3(s) + 3HCl(aq) \rightarrow AlCl_3(aq) + 3H_2O(l)$$

Magnesium hydroxide $Mg(OH)_2$

$$Mg(OH)_2(s) + 2HCl(aq) \rightarrow MgCl_2(aq) + 2H_2O(l)$$

Several antacid formulations contain both aluminium and magnesium compounds as they complement each other well. Magnesium salts tend to be faster acting, but because aluminium compounds dissolve more slowly they tend to provide longer lasting relief. In addition, magnesium salts tend to act as a laxative, whereas aluminium salts cause constipation. Aluminium has been linked with

Ulcers can occur in different regions of the gut and there are distinct differences in the relative frequency of occurrence of the different types of ulcer. For example, in the British population duodenal ulcers are more common, whereas in Japan gastric ulcers predominate. The reasons for the different occurrences are probably based on diet, but there are many other possible causes. Consider what some of these might be.

the development of Alzheimer's disease and although this is by no means proven, many people carefully limit its intake.

Other antacids contain metal carbonates and hydrogen carbonates which react with the acid to produce a salt, water and carbon dioxide. The latter can cause bloating of the stomach and flatulence. To avert this, **antifoaming agents** such as dimethicone are often added to the formulation.

Sodium hydrogen carbonate $NaHCO_3$

$$NaHCO_3(aq) + HCl(aq) \rightarrow NaCl(aq) + H_2O(l) + CO_2(g)$$

Calcium carbonate $CaCO_3$

$$CaCO_3(s) + 2HCl(aq) \rightarrow CaCl_2(aq) + H_2O(l) + CO_2(g)$$

Some antacids also contain **alginates** which float to the top of the stomach, forming a 'raft' which acts as a barrier preventing reflux into the oesophagus.

Note that because antacids change the pH of the stomach, they can alter other chemical reactions, including the absorption of other drugs. They should never therefore be taken for an extended period without medical supervision.

● **Examiner's hint:** In stoichiometry questions concerning antacids, remember that the molar ratio of antacid to acid will vary with different antacids. So make sure you are basing your answer on the correct balanced equation.

Exercise

3 Magnesium hydroxide and aluminium hydroxide can act as antacids.
   (a) Write an equation for the reaction of hydrochloric acid with each of these antacids.
   (b) Identify which antacid neutralizes the greater amount of acid if 0.1 mol of each antacid is used.
   (c) Suggest why potassium hydroxide is not used as an antacid.

D.3 Analgesics

Our body's ability to perceive pain is one of our very best defence mechanisms. We act immediately to try to eliminate the source of pain – and thus to reduce further damage to ourselves. Removing our hand from a hot plate, being aware that a sharp object has pierced our skin, or being virtually incapable of moving a broken limb are all examples of our innate abilities to protect ourselves.

But we all know that the sensation of pain is unpleasant – at best. At worst, it can dominate the senses and cause a debilitating effect, especially as many people have medical conditions that result in chronic pain. Therefore there is a need for painkillers, a class of drugs known as **analgesics**. Note though that pain is a symptom of a bigger problem – an injury or a disease – and therefore long-term relief is dependent on treating the underlying cause.

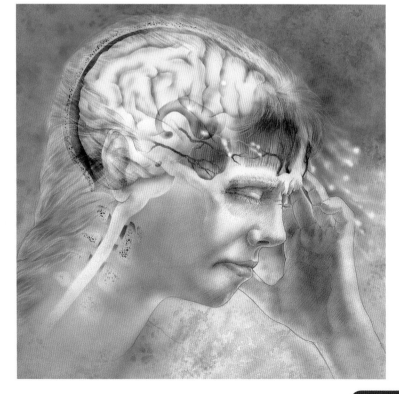

Conceptual artwork of a person suffering from a headache showing inflamed blood vessels and nerves around the brain. Analgesics work in different ways to block the pathway between the source of pain and perception by the brain.

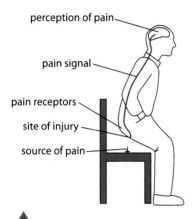

Figure 15.4 Pathways of pain in the body.

It could be argued that whereas mild analgesics seek to eliminate pain at source, strong analgesics only alter our ability to perceive pain. Consider the relative value of these two approaches to pain management.

Pain is detected as a sensation by the brain when nerve messages are sent from various **pain receptors** located around the body. These receptors are themselves stimulated by chemicals known as **prostaglandins**, which are released from cells damaged by thermal, mechanical or chemical energy. Once released, prostaglandins also mediate the **inflammatory response** by causing the dilation (widening) of blood vessels near the site of injury. In turn this can lead to swelling and increased pain. In addition, prostaglandins have an effect on the temperature regulation of the body which may result in increased temperature known as **fever**.

To be effective, a painkiller must somehow intercept or block this pathway somewhere between the source of pain and its perception in the brain.

Different analgesics work by blocking pain at different sites

Mild analgesics, including aspirin and non-steroidal anti-inflammatory drugs (NSAIDs) such as ibuprofen, act by preventing stimulation of the nerve endings at the site of pain. They inhibit the release of prostaglandins from the site of injury and so give relief to inflammation and fever as well as to pain. (Paracetamol is an exception as it inhibits prostaglandin release in the brain rather than at the site of injury.) Because these analgesics do not interfere with the functioning of the brain, they are also known as **non-narcotics**.

Strong analgesics include the drugs related to morphine, known as the opioids. This refers to their ability to bind to so-called opioid receptors in the brain, which then blocks the transmission of pain signals between brain cells and so alters the *perception* of pain. Because these analgesics act on the brain, they may cause drowsiness and possible changes in behaviour and mood, so are also known as **narcotics**. They are the most effective painkillers for severe pain, but owing to their side-effects and potential problems with dependence, their usage must be monitored through medical supervision.

In response to the fact that too often patients suffering with conditions such as advanced cancer were not receiving optimal pain control medication, the World Health Organization (WHO) developed a three-step 'analgesic ladder'. This simple guideline has had a great impact in achieving better standards of pain management.

1 use mild analgesics

2 add a weak opioid such as codeine or tramadol

3 in severe intractable pain, use strong opioids such as morphine, fentanyl or methadone.

Figure 15.5 The WHO three-step analgesic ladder.

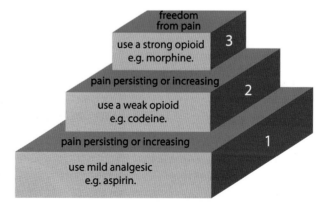

Despite the fact that cost-effective methods of pain control exist, they are not widely used everywhere. There are cultural, societal, political and economic factors that influence the availability of painkillers globally. Recognizing this as a deep problem, coalitions of doctors in many countries are pushing towards the goal of making access to pain management a universal human right. In 2004 a 'Global Day against Pain' was organized in Geneva, Switzerland, by several international organizations including the WHO.

Mild analgesics

Aspirin

From the time of Hippocrates in about 400 BC, it was known that chewing willow bark could give relief to pain and fever. But it was not until the early 1800s that it was demonstrated that the active ingredient in the bark is salicin which is converted to **salicylic acid** in the body (*salix* is the Latin name for willow). Although salicylic acid proved to be effective in treating pain, it tasted awful and caused the patient to vomit.

In 1890 the Bayer Company in Germany made an ester derivative of salicylic acid, which was more palatable and less irritable to the stomach, while still effective as an analgesic. It was named **aspirin**, in recognition of the plant spirea which produces a similar compound. Aspirin manufacture began that year and it became one of the first drugs to enter into common usage. Today it continues to hold its place as the most widely used drug in the world with an estimated production of over 100 billion standard tablets every year. It is widely used in the treatment of headaches, toothaches and sore throats. Also, because it is effective in reducing fever (known as an antipyretic) and inflammation, it is used to provide relief from rheumatic pain and arthritis.

In 1982 the British chemist John Vane won the Nobel Prize in Medicine for his discovery that aspirin works by blocking the synthesis of prostaglandins. This finding explains the analgesic effects of aspirin, as well as its effectiveness in reducing fever and inflammation and some of its significant side-effects. The latter can be both positive and negative as discussed below.

Aspirin reduces the ability of the blood to clot and this makes it useful in the treatment of patients at risk from heart attacks and strokes. Many people take a low daily dose of aspirin for this purpose. But this same side-effect means that aspirin is not suitable (and could be potentially dangerous) if taken by a person whose blood does not clot easily, or for use following surgery when blood clotting must be allowed to occur.

Recent research has also shown that regular intake of a low dose of aspirin may reduce the risk of colon cancer, although additional data are needed before aspirin is routinely recommended for this use.

Negative side-effects of aspirin include irritation and even ulceration of the stomach and duodenum, possibly leading to bleeding. This effect can be more acute when it is taken with ethanol in alcoholic drinks. A large number of people, especially those prone to asthma, are also allergic to aspirin, so it must be used with caution. It is not recommended for children under 12 because its use has been linked to Reye's syndrome, a rare and potentially fatal liver and brain disorder.

Aspirin is available in many formulations, which include various coatings and buffering components. These can delay the activity of the aspirin until it is in the small intestine to help alleviate some of its side-effects.

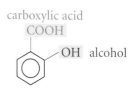

Figure 15.6 The structure of salicylic acid (2-hydroxybenzoic acid).

Figure 15.7 The structure of aspirin (2-ethanoyloxybenzenecarboxylic acid or acetyl salicylic acid, ASA).

The name 'Aspirin' was originally a trademark belonging to the pharmaceutical company Bayer. After Germany lost World War I, Bayer was forced to surrender this trademark (and also the one for 'Heroin') to Britain, France, Russia and the USA as part of the reparations of the Treaty of Versailles in 1919.

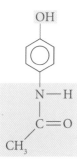

▲ **Figure 15.8** Structure of paracetamol (acetaminophen).

▲ Flower and seed head of *Papaver somniferum*, the opium poppy.

Paracetamol (also known as acetaminophen)

Paracetamol is a much younger drug than aspirin, having been marketed only since 1953.

Paracetamol is different from other mild analgesics as it is thought to act by reducing the production of prostaglandins in the *brain*, but does not affect prostaglandin production in the rest of the body. This means that it is not effective in reducing inflammation. It is one of the safest of all analgesics when taken correctly. It does not usually irritate the stomach and allergic reactions are rare. These are reasons why its use might make it favoured over aspirin, especially for children. However, an overdose or chronic use of paracetamol can cause severe and possibly fatal damage to kidneys, liver and brain. Also, when used in combination with ethanol by heavy drinkers, its toxic effect may be increased.

The table below summarizes and compares the relative advantages and disadvantages of aspirin and paracetamol.

	Aspirin	Paracetamol
analgesic properties (painkiller)	yes	yes
antipyretic properties (reduces fever)	yes	yes
reduces inflammation	yes	no
side-effects	stomach wall irritant, blood anti-coagulant	does not irritate stomach wall
severe side-effects (over-dosage)	Reye's syndrome in children	serious kidney, liver and brain damage
synergistic effect with alcohol	increased risk of stomach bleeding	toxic side-effects can be increased
allergic reactions	relatively common	rare
recommended use for children	no; can cause Reye's syndrome (although 'baby aspirin' is available)	yes

Strong analgesics

These drugs, the opioids, also known as narcotics, are all related to **opium** – an extract of poppy seeds. The first records of cultivation of the opium poppy go back to Mesopotamia more than 5000 years ago, the start of the long, complex and bloody history of this crop. It seems likely that no chemical product ever has been responsible for more wars, economic fortunes and legislative changes, and this continues to be true today.

 The so-called opium wars involving China, Britain, France and India in the late 19th century erupted from trade disputes involving opium. They ended in the imposition of several treaties by western countries on China, including the yielding of Hong Kong to Britain (which ended in 1997). Still today, opium production is a major, if illegal crop, particularly in South West Asia. It is estimated that Afghanistan produces 93% of the world's opiates and increasingly is processing more of the crop into heroin within the country. This market, estimated at US$4 billion a year, is approaching record levels. Most of the profits are, however, made outside the country by criminal gangs and networks. The government's eradication efforts have been largely ineffective and the USA plans to spray poppy plants with herbicides are highly controversial. The United Nations has called for an international effort to help address the problem of the Afghan opium trade.

The narcotic drugs derived from opium are primarily morphine and its derivatives. We will consider three of these here: **codeine**, **morphine** and diamorphine, known as **heroin**. These are powerful analgesics, acting on the central nervous system to block the perception of pain.

In addition, they have several other effects that can sometimes be used for therapeutic purposes, but sometimes are considered adverse side-effects. They include:

- causing constipation
- suppressing the cough reflex
- causing constriction of the pupil in the eye
- narcotic effects – to be discussed below.

The three drugs differ in their effectiveness as follows:

Codeine	increasing strength as analgesics
Morphine	increasing narcotic effects
Heroin	increasing side-effects

The table below compares the structure and effects of codeine, morphine and heroin.

	Codeine	Morphine	Diamorphine (heroin)
structure	codeine	morphine	heroin
functional groups	benzene ring ether (2) alkene alcohol (1) tertiary amine	benzene ring ether alkene alcohol (2) tertiary amine	benzene ring ether alkene ester – ethanoate (2) tertiary amine
obtained from	raw opium (0.5%)	raw opium (10%)	found in opium but usually obtained by reaction of morphine, so is known as a **semi-synthetic** drug
therapeutic uses	Sometimes used in a preparation with a non-narcotic drug such as aspirin or paracetamol in the second stage of the pain management ladder. Also used in cough medications and in the short-term treatment of diarrhoea.	Used in the management of severe pain, such as in advanced cancer. Can be habit forming and can lead to dependence, so use must be regulated by a medical professional.	Used medically only in a few countries legally (Britain and Belgium) for the relief of severe pain. The most rapidly acting and the most abused narcotic. Initially produces euphoric effects, but very high potential for causing addiction and increasing tolerance. Dependence leads to withdrawal symptoms and many associated problems.

Notice that these three drugs have a common basic structure that accounts for their similar properties, as well as some different functional groups.

Meet people deep in the throes of heroin addiction with no way out.

Now go to www.heinemann.co.uk/hotlinks, insert the express code 4259P and click on this activity.

The conversion of morphine into heroin involves an esterification reaction in which both its –OH groups are converted into ethanoate (ester) groups by reaction with ethanoic acid CH_3COOH. The loss of the two polar –OH groups means that heroin is less polar and so more lipid-soluble than morphine. This enables it to cross the blood–brain barrier quickly which is why it is faster acting than the other opioid drugs. In the brain it is hydrolysed to morphine by reversing the esterification reaction.

Heroin user slumped after injecting himself with heroin (diamorphine). The tourniquet around his arm is used to make the veins stand out to ease injection.

Heroin, a strong analgesic, is a highly addictive drug with powerful narcotic effects. Heroin abuse is associated with serious health conditions, including collapsed veins, spontaneous abortion, infectious diseases and can lead to fatal overdose.

The blood–brain barrier was first discovered by the German scientist Paul Ehrlich in the late 19th century, when he observed that a blue dye introduced into the blood of an animal coloured all its organs blue except the brain. Later experiments involved injecting the dye into the spinal fluid, when it was found that the brain became dyed but the rest of the body did not. This tight control over the movement of substances between fluids in the brain and blood vessels, the blood–brain barrier, is now known to be a membranic structure that helps to protect the brain. It is crossed more easily by small, lipid-soluble molecules than by larger and more polar molecules. One of the challenges in treating brain diseases such as tumours involves outwitting this natural defence of the brain so that it will allow therapeutic chemicals to enter.

Narcotic effects

The word *narcotic* is derived from a Greek word meaning numbness or stupor. It is used to describe the strong analgesics because of their effects on brain functioning. All three of the drugs described above produce narcotic effects, but heroin does so most acutely, so this will be discussed here.

In the short term, heroin induces a feeling of well-being and contentment, as it causes a dulling of pain and a lessening of fear and tension. There is often a feeling of euphoria in the initial stages after intake. Long-term regular use leads to constipation, reduced libido, loss of appetite and poor nutrition. Heroin users start to show dependence relatively quickly, so they cannot function properly without the drug and suffer from withdrawal symptoms such as cold sweats and anxiety when it is withheld. This is compounded by an increasing tolerance to the drug, so higher doses are needed to bring about relief. In most countries, access to the drug usually involves dealing in an illegal market and the cost of the supply often is beyond the individual's means. This in turn may lead to crime and other social problems. As the drug is taken by injection, the user commonly picks up infections such as HIV and hepatitis from unclean needles. In short, the life of the heroin addict is usually profoundly altered by the drug.

Visit this site for the research report 'Heroin abuse and addiction' from the Amercan National Institute on Drug Abuse.

Now go to www.heinemann.co.uk/hotlinks, insert the express code 4259P and click on this activity.

Helping heroin addicts to break their dependence is a slow and difficult process. Sometimes an alternative analgesic, **methadone**, is administered. It is taken orally and has a longer duration of action. This can reduce drug craving and prevent symptoms of withdrawal. Although its use is controversial in some countries, research has shown that methadone maintenance is the most effective treatment for opioid dependence, reducing the death rates of addicts receiving it to about one-tenth.

4 Aspirin and paracetamol (acetaminophen) are described as mild analgesics.
   (a) Explain the difference in the method of action of mild analgesics and strong analgesics.
   (b) Give one therapeutic effect of aspirin, other than reducing pain, which is common to paracetamol.
   (c) Give one therapeutic effect of aspirin which is not common to paracetamol.

5 Codeine, morphine and heroin are described as strong analgesics.
   (a) State two functional groups common to codeine, morphine and heroin.
   (b) A patient has been prescribed morphine following surgery. State the main effect and a major side-effect she will experience.

D.4 Depressants

Depressants are drugs that act on the brain and spinal cord (known as the central nervous system or CNS). The action of these drugs changes the communication between brain cells by altering the concentration or the activity of chemicals called **neurotransmitters**. As a result they cause a depression, or a *decrease* in brain activity that in turn influences the functioning of other parts of the body, such as the heart and the mechanisms determining breathing rate. (The analgesics discussed earlier are also examples of depressants.)

Be warned that the language here can be a little confusing. This is because the term 'depression' is also used to describe a clinical condition characterized by mood changes and loss of interest in normal activities. Individuals who suffer from this might have insomnia, fatigue, a feeling of despair and an inability to concentrate. Clinical depression is associated with a high proportion of all suicides. The drugs used to treat this are hence known as 'antidepressants'.

Depressants include drugs also classified as tranquilizers, sedatives and hypnotics and the differences between these is often a question of dosage as shown below.

Dosage effect	Low to moderate dose	High dose	Extremely high doses
	calmness	slurred speech	respiratory depression
	relief from anxiety	staggering gait	coma
	very relaxed muscles	altered perception	death
		sleep induced	
Description:	tranquilizer	sedative	hypnotic	lethal dose

increasing dosage →

We can see that in high doses these drugs can have very serious effects and so they must always be used with caution. In addition, many drugs of this type can elicit responses of tolerance and dependence and regular users can therefore suffer from withdrawal when a drug is not continued. As a specific example of a widely used depressant we will focus here on **ethanol**.

Ethanol

Ethanol, C_2H_5OH, is the alcohol present in beer, wine and hard liquor. Ingestion of fermented beverages containing ethanol was first recorded in the Egyptian Book of the Dead, dated approximately 5000 years ago. It was probably first discovered in the natural fermentation products from plants and microorganisms and then more systematically prepared from different natural substrates such as grapes and grains. The concentration of ethanol can be increased through distillation, yielding hard liquors such as vodka, whisky and gin. Today ethanol is the most widely used psychoactive drug and is legal in most countries, although often with age restrictions on its purchase.

Uses of ethanol

Ethanol has some antiseptic properties, so can be used on the skin before an injection or to clean a small wound. For this reason it is often carried in first aid kits. It also has the effect of hardening the skin, so it can be rubbed on to feet to prevent the formation of blisters, for example. Ethanol in alcoholic drinks is an important part of many diets and cultures, adding a sense of occasion to meals, rituals and festivities. In low doses it can help to create a mild excitement and users become more talkative, confident and relaxed. There is also some evidence that low doses of ethanol might have a beneficial effect on the circulation and diminish cardio-vascular diseases, perhaps owing to its mild anti-clotting effect.

Abuses of ethanol

As a CNS depressant, ethanol brings about changes in behaviour and these quickly become adverse as the dose increases. The effects of ethanol abuse are obviously multiplied by the duration over which it occurs and these are summarized here.

Short-term effects of ethanol abuse	Long-term effects of ethanol abuse
• loss of self-restraint; memory, concentration and insight are impaired • loss of balance and judgment • violent behaviour associated with domestic abuse and family breakdown • dangerous risk-taking behaviour leading to many accidents involving motor vehicles and machinery • dehydration caused by increased urine output leading to 'hangover' and loss of productivity • at high doses can cause vomiting, loss of consciousness, coma and death	• dependence known as alcoholism, associated with withdrawal symptoms • liver disease, e.g. cirrhosis, liver cancer • coronary heart disease • high blood pressure • fetal alcohol syndrome • permanent brain damage

In summary, chronic consumption of large amounts of ethanol is a major source of social and physiological problems. It has been said that if ethanol were to be discovered today it would probably not pass the regime of drug testing and would be a restricted drug.

◀ Alcohol is a depressant and long-term use of large quantities can have a radical impact on a person's health and lifestyle.

Metabolism of ethanol

Ethanol C_2H_5OH has the structure

The polar –OH group enables it to form hydrogen bonds with water, making it readily soluble in aqueous solution. As a small organic molecule it is also able to dissolve in lipids, which enables it to cross cell membranes with relative ease. Following ingestion, ethanol passes quickly from the gut into the blood, mostly through the stomach wall, and then circulates to all tissues of the body. This accounts for the short time interval between ingestion and the onset of ethanol-mediated effects. Approximately 90% of an ethanol load is broken down in the liver, with the remainder being eliminated by the kidneys and lungs. Ethanol also readily passes across the placenta to the fetus when consumed during pregnancy. In addition it passes readily into breast milk and is transmitted to the nursing infant.

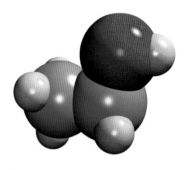

▲ Space-filled model of ethanol C_2H_5OH. The atoms are represented as colour-coded spheres: carbon (blue), hydrogen (yellow) and oxygen (red). Ethanol is the intoxicating component of all alcoholic beverages.

Synergistic effects of ethanol

Ethanol has the potential to increase the activity of other drugs when taken at the same time. This effect is known as **synergy**. It means that care must be taken when consuming alcoholic drinks alongside other medications, as the synergistic effects can lead to very serious, even fatal, results. One of the problems is that because ethanol is such a widely consumed and socially available drug, many people do not consider its interaction with other prescription and non-prescription drugs.

Here are some important examples:
- with aspirin, ethanol can cause increased bleeding of the stomach lining and increased risk of ulcers
- with other depressants such as barbiturates, including sleeping pills, ethanol can induce heavy sedation, possibly leading to coma
- with tobacco, ethanol appears to increase the incidence of cancers, particularly of the intestines and liver
- with many other drugs, ethanol can interfere with their metabolism by the liver, which can cause greater and more prolonged drug effects.

Visit the World Health Organization's site on substance abuse from where you can access the Global Alcohol Database which has comprehensive data, interactive maps and so on. You can also download the very interesting publication *Alcohol, Gender and Drinking Problems – Perspectives from Low and Middle Income Countries*.

Now go to www.heinemann.co.uk/hotlinks, insert the express code 4259P and click on this activity.

Techniques used for the detection of ethanol

Because of the potentially damaging effects that an individual's alcohol intake can have on other people, most countries have instituted processes to test for the presence of ethanol in the body. This is linked to legislation that sets limits for body ethanol concentration for the performance of certain activities. For example, an upper limit of 80 mg ethanol per 100 cm³ of blood is commonly set for driving a motor vehicle. Analysis of ethanol concentration is usually based on samples of the breath, blood or urine – or sometimes a combination of these. Recently, techniques have been developed which may make it possible to detect ethanol concentration in saliva or eye fluids.

Ethanol analysis of breath

Ethanol is a volatile compound and at body temperature in the lungs it establishes equilibrium between being dissolved in the blood and released into the air in the exhaled breath.

$$C_2H_5OH(aq) \rightleftharpoons C_2H_5OH(g)$$
in blood   in air spaces

The equilibrium constant K_c for this reaction has a fixed value at a particular temperature so measurement of the ethanol in the breath can be used to assess the blood alcohol concentration.

The simplest test involves a roadside **breathalyser** which contains crystals of potassium dichromate(VI) which are orange, but are changed to green chromium(III) Cr^{3+} as they oxidize the ethanol to ethanal and ethanoic acid (see oxidation of alcohols in Chapter 10).

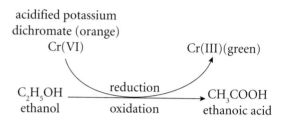

acidified potassium
dichromate (orange)
Cr(VI)   Cr(III)(green)

C_2H_5OH —— reduction ——→ CH_3COOH
ethanol   oxidation   ethanoic acid

The extent of the colour change can be measured using a photocell and so used to determine the ethanol concentration. However, this test is not very accurate and will usually lead to further, more accurate tests being carried out in a laboratory.

Alcohol breath test. The roadside breathalyser gives an immediate reading of whether the level of alcohol in the motorist's blood is over the legal limit.

A more accurate technique for breath analysis uses **infrared spectroscopy** in an apparatus called an **intoximeter**. The principle here (see Chapter 12) is that different molecules cause different absorption bands in the infrared part of the spectrum, as a result of vibrations of their particular bonds and functional groups. Hence ethanol has a characteristic absorption band at 2950 cm^{-1} owing to its C–H bonds. (Note that the O–H bond also gives a characteristic band but this bond is also present in water vapour, which will be a component of the breath sample.) The size of the peak can be used to measure ethanol concentration, when compared with a reference taken from the ambient air.

Figure 15.9 Infrared absorption spectrum of ethanol in the gas phase.

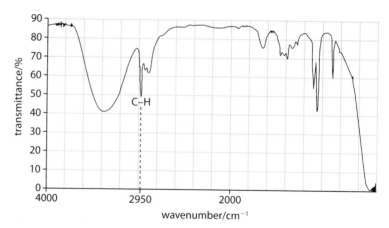

Worked example

People who suffer from diabetes often exhale propanone vapour in their breath. Explain why this can give a positive result in the infrared test for ethanol even if they have not consumed alcohol. Refer to the structure of propanone in your answer.

Solution

Propanone has the structure:

$$H-\overset{\overset{\displaystyle H}{|}}{\underset{\underset{\displaystyle H}{|}}{C}}-\overset{\overset{\displaystyle O}{\|}}{C}-\overset{\overset{\displaystyle H}{|}}{\underset{\underset{\displaystyle H}{|}}{C}}-H$$

and so contains C—H bonds which will give the same characteristic band at $2950\ cm^{-1}$ as ethanol.

Starting in 2008, the car manufacturer Volvo plans to incorporate the option of an 'alcolock' into their new cars. This is a fuel cell intoximeter which will automatically read the alcohol content of the driver's breath and accordingly determine whether the car will start or not. The feature aims to reduce the number of alcohol-related traffic accidents, which are responsible for millions of deaths worldwide every year.

A different version of the intoximeter uses a **fuel cell**. This works on the principle that in the presence of a catalyst, ethanol is oxidized in the air first to ethanoic acid and then to water and carbon dioxide. A fuel cell converts the energy released when oxidation occurs into a detectable electrical voltage that can be used to measure ethanol concentration very accurately.

Ethanol analysis in blood and urine

The most established method for ethanol analysis is **gas–liquid chromatography**, which must be carried out in a laboratory. In this technique, blood or urine is vaporized and injected into a stream of an inert gas (known as the mobile phase) over the surface of a non-volatile liquid (known as the stationary phase). The components of the vapour, including ethanol gas, move at different rates depending on their boiling points and relative solubility in the two phases. As a result, each leaves the column holding the liquid phase after a specific interval of time known as its **retention time**. So a peak at the retention time corresponding to ethanol can be used to confirm its presence in the vapour. The area under the peak is a measure of ethanol concentration relative to a known standard in the mixture such as propan-1-ol. The method allows for an accurate assessment of ethanol levels.

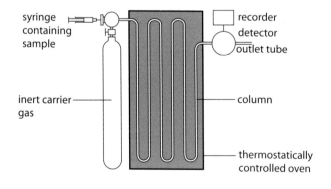
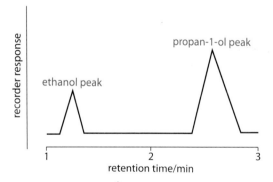

Figure 15.10 Gas–liquid chromatography apparatus and a gas–liquid chromatograph of an alcohol mixture.

Other depressants

The **benzodiazepines** are a major group of depressants. These drugs depress activity in the part of the brain that controls emotion and so are used as tranquilizers in the treatment of anxiety disorders and related insomnia. As well as being the most commonly used class of sleeping pill, they are also used as muscle relaxants. Although they are usually well tolerated by most people and cause relatively few side-effects, they can cause dependence. For this reason, they are used mostly in short-term treatments. Some widely used benzodiazepine drugs are diazepam, marketed as Valium® and nitrazepam, marketed as Mogadon®. Their structures are shown here.

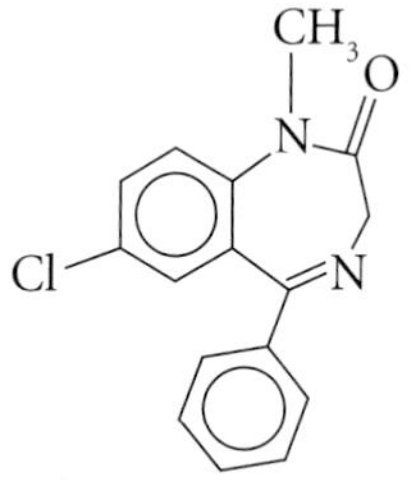

diazepam (Valium®) 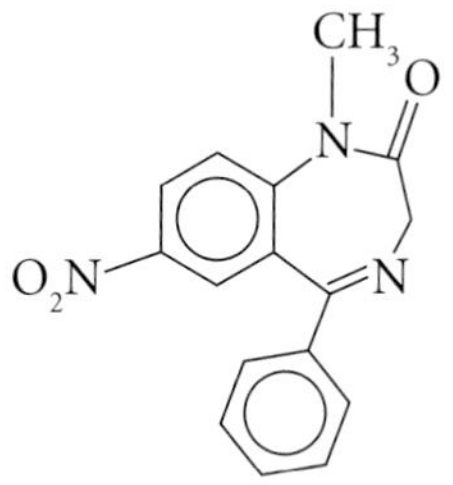   nitrazepam (Mogadon®)

You can see that, as the name benzodiazepine implies, they contain both benzene rings and the diazepine structure, which is a seven-membered heterocyclic ring containing carbon and two nitrogen atoms. As these molecules are largely non-polar, they have high lipid solubility and so are able to cross the brain–blood barrier.

Worked example

Name three structural features that these molecules of diazepam and nitrazepam have in common. Identify and name one different group in the two molecules.

Solution

Both molecules have two benzene rings, an amide group and a carbon–nitrogen double bond. The one difference is in the substitution in one of the benzene rings: chloro- in diazepam and nitro- in nitrazepam.

A widely used anti-depressant drug is fluoxetine hydrochloride, marketed as Prozac®. It functions by increasing the levels of serotonin – an important neurotransmitter in the brain. It is used in the treatment of depression, as well as eating and panic disorders. (Note that Prozac® does not depress the activity of the CNS so it is not a depressant.) Its structure is shown here.

● **Examiner's hint:** The structures of these drugs are given in the IB Data booklet so they do not have to be learned. However, you should be able to recognize different functional groups and compare structures.

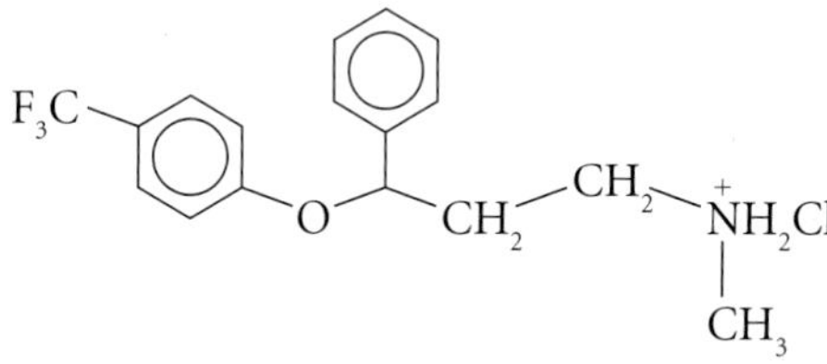

fluoxetine hydrochloride (Prozac®)

Exercises

6 Depressants include tranquilizers and sedatives.
   (a) State two effects on the body of taking:
      (i) a low dose of a tranquilizer
      (ii) a high dose of a sedative.
   (b) Explain why depressants are sometimes described as anti-depressants.
   © International Baccalaureate Organization [2004]

7 Ethanol is the most widely used depressant.
   (a) Discuss the harmful effects of a regular intake of large amounts of ethanol.
   (b) Ethanol can be detected using a breathalyser containing acidified potassium dichromate(VI). Explain what happens to both the ethanol and the dichromate(VI) ion in the reaction and the colour change that occurs.
   (c) Briefly describe two other methods that can be used for analysis of ethanol in the breath.

Stimulants

Stimulants are a different class of drugs that affect the central nervous system. Their function is largely opposite to that of depressants, as they *increase* the activity of the brain and hence the person's state of mental alertness. They are used to prevent excessive drowsiness through the day and so allow greater concentration and thought processes to be possible.

As with other nervous system drugs, stimulants have physiological effects on other parts of the body including the following:

- They can help to facilitate breathing by causing relaxation of the air passages and are used in the treatment of respiratory infections such as severe bronchitis.
- They may reduce appetite and so have been used as part of a treatment for obesity.
- They may cause palpitations or tremors to occur.
- When used in excess they can cause extreme restlessness, sleeplessness, fits, delusions and hallucinations.

Different stimulant drugs function in different ways but most commonly they alter the levels of **neurotransmitters**, chemicals that act as messengers in the nervous system. A few different examples will be discussed here.

Amphetamines: stimulants that mimic adrenaline

Adrenaline (also called epinephrine) is the hormone that is released in times of stress and enables the body to cope with sudden demands imposed by pain, shock, fear, cold and so on. If you have ever experienced a cold sweat when watching a scary movie, or had a racing pulse during a difficult exam, then you know the effects of adrenaline. The response, sometimes called the 'fight or flight' reaction, stimulates the pathways that:

- increase the heart rate and blood pressure
- increase the blood flow to the brain and muscles
- increase the air flow to the lungs
- increase mental awareness.

Adrenaline is very similar in both its structure and its physiological effects to a neurotransmitter called **noradrenaline** (or norepinephrine) which is responsible for communication in the part of the nervous system known as the **sympathetic nervous system**. Here its role is to stimulate the pathways described above.

One major group of stimulant drugs acts to mimic and enhance these effects of adrenaline and noradrenaline. They are known as the **amphetamines** and have a structure quite similar to that of adrenaline and noradrenaline.

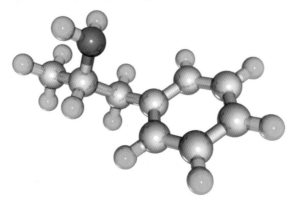

◀ Computer model of a molecule of the drug amphetamine. Carbon atoms are shown in grey, hydrogen atoms in light blue and the nitrogen atoms in dark blue.

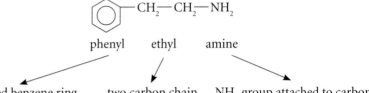

structure of adrenaline

structure of amphetamine

You can see that both molecules are derivatives of the phenyl ethyl amine structure.

$$\text{phenyl} \quad\quad CH_2 - CH_2 - NH_2$$

phenyl   ethyl   amine

substituted benzene ring   two carbon chain NH_2 group attached to carbon

Because of their role in stimulating the sympathetic nervous system, the amphetamines are called **sympathomimetic** drugs. In small doses, amphetamines increase mental alertness and physical energy. Side-effects include dilation of the pupils of the eyes and decreased appetite, as well as possible blurred vision and dizziness. Regular use of these drugs leads to the rapid development of both tolerance and dependence, coupled with serious long-term effects such as severe depression and reduced resistance to infection. Abuse of amphetamines through overuse is a serious problem.

Modifications to the amphetamine structure have produced some so-called **designer drugs** that are very powerful – and dangerously addictive stimulants. These include **methamphetamine**, known as 'speed' and 'crystal meth', and the drug 'ecstasy', which although illegal in most countries has markedly increased in distribution globally since the 1980s. It is believed that long-term use of these drugs causes serious brain damage and that in some people even smaller doses can be fatal.

Nicotine: stimulant and highly addictive drug

Watch the ABC News Special video 'Ecstasy rising'.

Now go to www.heinemann.co.uk/hotlinks, insert the express code 4259P and click on this activity.

Methamphetamine is dangerous not only to the user but to society at large. It is estimated that every kilogram of methamphetamine produced leaves behind about seven kilograms of toxic waste.

Drying tobacco leaves in Thailand.

The tobacco plant can grow in a wide variety of warm, moist climates and is farmed on most continents. China has the biggest production, followed by India, Brazil, the USA and Zimbabwe. It is estimated that tobacco is used to make the 5.5 trillion cigarettes that are smoked around the world every year.

Nicotine is one of the most widespread and abused stimulants. It is obtained from tobacco plants but is also found at low concentrations in tomato, potato, eggplant and green pepper plants. Usually it is taken in by inhalation of smoke from cigarettes, cigars and pipe tobacco, but it can also be taken by chewing. Its structure is

nicotine

As a lipid-soluble molecule, nicotine is able to cross the blood–brain barrier bringing about rapid effects on brain activity. Its action is to increase the levels of adrenaline as well as to alter the concentrations of certain neurotransmitters in the brain. As with other drugs, its effects change with increased consumption over time. These are summarized below.

Short-term effects of nicotine consumption	Long-term effects of nicotine consumption
<ul><li>increases concentration</li><li>relieves tension and boredom</li><li>helps to counter fatigue</li><li>increases heart rate and blood pressure</li><li>decreases urine output</li></ul>	<ul><li>high blood pressure</li><li>increases risk of heart disease including angina</li><li>coronary thrombosis</li><li>increases the level of fatty acids in the blood which can lead to atherosclerosis and stroke</li><li>over-stimulation of stomach acids which can lead to increased risk of peptic ulcers</li></ul>

Nicotine is a habit-forming drug, quickly leading to dependence or addiction. The addiction means that the person suffers withdrawal symptoms if they cease intake and these may include nausea, weight gain, drowsiness, inability to concentrate, depression and craving for cigarettes. One of the problems of nicotine addiction is that it is often linked to social factors such as peer pressure.

Tobacco is the second major cause of death in the world. It is currently responsible for about 5 million deaths each year (that is about 1 in 10 adult deaths worldwide). The World Health Organization states that if current smoking patterns continue this figure will rise to about 10 million deaths each year by 2020. Half the people who smoke today – that is about 650 million people – will eventually be killed by tobacco. In addition, the long-term inhalation of second-hand smoke (sometimes called passive smoking) is now known to have similarly harmful effects on health.

◀ Burning cigarettes release poisonous chemicals into the air, including nicotine, tar, soot and carbon monoxide. These are inhaled into the lungs of smokers and are also taken in by non-smokers breathing the same air.

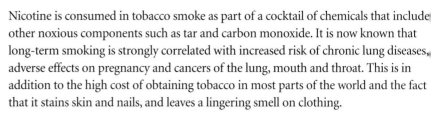

The World Health Organization Framework Convention on Tobacco Control was the world's first international public health treaty when it came into force in February 2005. It aims to help countries strengthen their tobacco control programmes, such as indoor smoking bans, and encourages comprehensive tobacco advertising bans and restrictions on distribution. Currently it has been ratified and is legally binding in 151 countries. Notable non-parties to the agreement are Russia, which has not signed it, and the USA, which has not ratified it.

Woman drying coffee beans in the sun in Laos. After picking, the beans are pulped, fermented, washed in water and finally dried in the sun, producing 'milled beans'.

In the last ten years or so, lawsuits in the USA against the tobacco industry have won some successes in claiming compensation for people affected by deaths attributable to tobacco use. The suits claimed that the industry knew of the carcinogenic effects of tobacco smoking but failed to make this information available. It is likely that similar law suits will follow. Now that more information about the effects of tobacco smoking is available, who should be responsible for the impact that it has on an individual's health?

For some light relief enjoy this humorous recording depicting how Sir Walter Raleigh, who introduced tobacco to Britain, may have explained the use of tobacco to his boss in London in the 16th century.

Now go to www.heinemann.co.uk/hotlinks, insert the express code 4259P and click on this activity.

Caffeine is found in the beans, leaves and fruit of over 60 plants where it acts as a natural pesticide, paralysing and killing certain insects that feed on the plants.

Nicotine is consumed in tobacco smoke as part of a cocktail of chemicals that include other noxious components such as tar and carbon monoxide. It is now known that long-term smoking is strongly correlated with increased risk of chronic lung diseases, adverse effects on pregnancy and cancers of the lung, mouth and throat. This is in addition to the high cost of obtaining tobacco in most parts of the world and the fact that it stains skin and nails, and leaves a lingering smell on clothing.

In short, tobacco smoking and nicotine intake can significantly compromise a person's health and well-being. This is perhaps best reflected in the fact that no serious athlete is a smoker and the safe pursuit of many activities such as diving and high altitude mountaineering preclude smokers.

Caffeine: the world's most widely used stimulant

Caffeine is present in coffee, tea, chocolate and colas. It is legal and unregulated almost everywhere; it is estimated that in North America 90% of adults consume caffeine daily. It acts to reduce physical fatigue and restore mental alertness, and is commonly used to help people work longer hours and cope with body clock changes. Its structure is shown here.

caffeine

Note that, like nicotine, caffeine contains heterocyclic rings (containing both carbon and nitrogen) and a tertiary amine group. In addition, caffeine contains two amide groups.

The main source of coffee beans is the Arabica plant which is grown in over 70 countries. The top coffee producers are Brazil, Colombia, India, Indonesia, Mexico, Puerto Rico and Vietnam. Although coffee has experienced a spike in popularity over the last 20 years, it has often been at the expense of the producers who have experienced a dramatic fall in price and often live in impoverished conditions. The 'fair trade coffee' movement has attempted to address the inequalities by assuring its customers that the coffee was purchased under fair conditions.

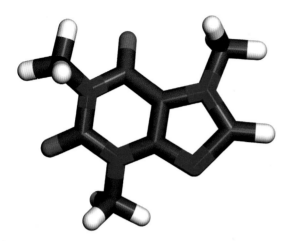

Model of a molecule of caffeine: nitrogen is shown in blue, oxygen in red and hydrogen in white. Notice the positions of the tertiary amine and amide groups.

Caffeine acts as a respiratory stimulant increasing the rate of energy release within cells. It also intensifies and prolongs the effects of adrenaline. Some of the main effects of caffeine, depending on the amount consumed, are summarized below.

Consumption of caffeine in small amounts	Consumption of caffeine in large amounts
• enhancement of mental energy, alertness and ability to concentrate • acts as a diuretic, increasing the volume of urine; can cause dehydration	• can cause anxiety, irritability and insomnia • can cause dependence; side-effects on withdrawal include headaches and nausea

In general, an intake of more than four cups of coffee per day may be considered non-beneficial. Pregnant women are advised to limit their caffeine intake.

Caffeine helps the body to absorb some analgesics and is often included in the formulation of headache pills and other medications.

There are many ways of preparing decaffeinated coffee but usually the beans are first soaked in hot water which dissolves out the caffeine. The water is then passed over activated charcoal which removes the caffeine by adsorption, but allows other components of the coffee, essential for its flavour, to remain. The water is then returned to the beans. Other processes use solvents to absorb caffeine selectively from the infused water. The extracted caffeine is used in soft drinks and in the preparation of caffeine tablets.

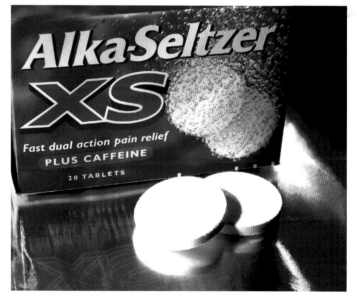

Alka-Seltzer tablets are used to treat indigestion, heartburn and associated aches and pains. They contain aspirin (analgesic), sodium hydrogen carbonate (antacid) and caffeine. The tablets effervesce in water, as seen on the packet.

Exercise

8 Look at the structures of caffeine and nicotine which are given in Table 20 of the IB Data booklet.
   (a) Describe two similarities in their structure, not including the presence of double bonds, methyl groups and nitrogen atoms.
   (b) Discuss the problems associated with nicotine consumption with reference to both short-term and long-term effects.

© International Baccalaureate Organization [2004]

D.6 Antibacterials

The first example of a chemical used to kill pathogens came from the observation that certain dyes used in the dyestuffs industry were able to kill some microorganisms. In 1891 this led to the treatment of malaria using methylene blue. Paul Ehrlich of Berlin (page 344) introduced the concept of a 'magic bullet', a chemical designed to target a specific disease but not touch the host cells, and successfully treated syphilis patients with an arsenical drug. Systematic screening for other potential antimicrobials led to the discovery of the **sulfonamide** drugs, such as Prontosil®, in 1933 with their seemingly miraculous ability to cure septicaemia. By 1940, the use of sulfonamides had dramatically reduced the number of deaths of mothers in childbirth.

However, it was the discovery of the chemicals known as **penicillins** that truly revolutionized modern medicine, as this gave birth to drugs now known as **antibiotics**. These are chemicals, usually produced by microorganisms, which act against other microorganisms. Their discovery is generally credited to Alexander Fleming, who was a Scottish microbiologist, working in 1928 on bacteria cultures. He noticed that a fungus (or mould) known as *Penicillium notatum* had contaminated some of his cultures and was therefore about to discard them as spoiled. However, his eye was drawn to the fact that the mould had generated a clear region around it where no bacterial colonies were growing. He concluded that something produced by the mould was specifically inhibiting the bacterial growth. Fleming published his findings, but as he and his collaborators were not chemists, they did not pursue the work of isolating and identifying the active ingredient.

Fleming's original culture plate contaminated by the fungus *Penicillium notatum*, photographed 25 years after the discovery in 1928. The clear region around the fungus where bacterial growth is inhibited can be clearly seen.

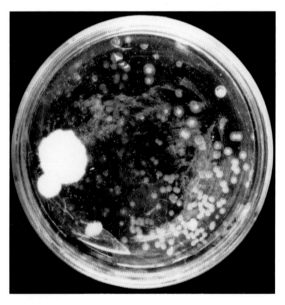

Fleming's discovery of penicillin is often described as serendipitous – a fortunate discovery made by chance or by accident. However, as Louis Pasteur once famously said 'Chance favours only the prepared mind'. Consider to what extent scientific discoveries are only possible by scientists who are trained in the principles of observation and interpretation.

In the early 1940s the Australian bacteriologist Howard Florey and German-born biochemist Ernst Chain, working in Oxford, England, picked up the research and successfully isolated penicillin as the antibacterial agent produced by the penicillium mould. It was used for the first time in human trials in 1941 – in the midst of World War II when there was an unprecedented demand for such a treatment for bacterial infections resulting from war wounds. Its rapid development and distribution is known to have saved thousands of lives in the later years of the war. For their work in discovering penicillin, Fleming, Florey and Chain shared the Nobel Prize in Medicine in 1945.

The main research and production of penicillin was moved to the USA in 1941 to protect it from the bombs pounding Britain during the war. Large-scale production methods were developed using deep fermentation tanks containing corn steep liquor through which sterile air was forced.

The isolation and development of penicillin occurred, however, before there was any understanding of its chemical structure or its mode of action. It was the work of British biochemist Dorothy Hodgkin in 1945 using X-ray crystallography, which determined the structure of **penicillin G**, the major constituent of the mould extract. Its structure is shown here.

Its core structure is a four-membered ring consisting of a nitrogen atom and three carbon atoms. Its antibacterial action lies in the fact that it inhibits the development of cross-links in bacterial cell walls, so weakening the walls and causing the bacteria to rupture and die during their reproductive phase. Its action is effective against a wide range of bacteria, many of which are responsible for infections of the ear, nose, throat and mouth, as well as at the sites of infection from wounds.

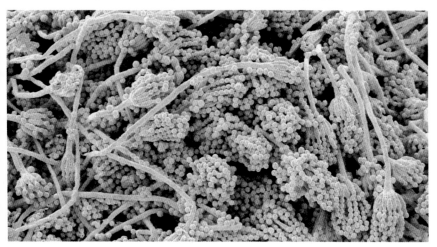

A disadvantage of penicillin G is that it is broken down by stomach acid and has to be injected directly into the blood. Different forms of penicillin have been developed by modifying the side chain (the part denoted as 'R' in the diagram above) and these enable the drug to retain its activity even when ingested in pill form.

Antibiotic resistance: are we killing the cures?

A major problem with the use of penicillin – and also other antibiotics – is that of **bacterial resistance**. This was observed as early as the 1940s when penicillin proved to be ineffective against some populations of bacteria. It is now known that these resistant bacteria produce an enzyme, **penicillinase**, which can open penicillin's four-membered ring and render it inactive.

During World War II, when the supply of penicillin could not meet demand, it became a practice to collect the urine from patients being treated to isolate and reuse the penicillin it contained. It was estimated that as much as 80% of early penicillin formulations was lost from the body in the urine.

▲ Dorothy Hodgkin (1910–1994), the British X-ray crystallographer who discovered the structures of penicillin, vitamin B$_{12}$ and insulin. She was awarded the Nobel Prize in Chemistry in 1964.

◄ Coloured scanning electron micrograph of *Penicillium* sp growing on bread. This is the mould that is used to produce the antibiotic penicillin.

Antibiotic resistance has become a major problem for some strains of tuberculosis (TB) and treatment may now require the use of several different antibiotics together. It is estimated today that one in seven new TB cases is resistant to the drugs most commonly used to treat it. In crowded conditions such as prisons in Russia, resistance rates are higher still, although the World Health Organization has had some success in introducing tough measures to stem a TB epidemic there. Antibiotic resistance must be faced on a global scale, as no country can protect itself from the importation of resistant pathogens through travel and trade.

Antibiotic resistance arises by genetic mutation in bacteria and would normally account for a very small proportion of the population. But the number of resistant organisms increases dramatically with increased exposure to the antibiotic. So the very success of antibiotics in fighting disease has led to this major challenge from widespread resistant strains, which today threatens their very usefulness. So-called **superbugs** are bacteria which carry several resistant genes and are a serious problem in many hospitals.

The problem of resistance has been compounded by the wide use of penicillins (and other antibiotics) in animal feeds to lower the incidence of disease in the stock. It is estimated that more than 55% of antibiotics produced in North America and Europe are given to food animals in the absence of disease. This has caused the antibiotics to enter the human food chain and hence increase the proportion of resistant bacteria.

Responses to the challenge of antibiotic resistance have included the following:

- developing different forms of penicillin, with modified side chains able to withstand the action of penicillinase
- controlling and restricting the use of antibiotics by legislation to make them prescription-only drugs; also encouraging doctors not to over-prescribe
- education and encouragement of patients in the importance of completing the full course of treatment with an antibiotic, referred to as 'patient compliance'. This is essential to prevent resistant bacteria prolonging the disease or spreading into the community.

Exercise

9 (a) State how penicillins prevent the growth of bacteria and explain why scientists continue to develop new penicillins.
(b) Explain the specific effects of modifying the side chain in penicillin.
(c) Discuss three ways in which human activities have caused an increase in the resistance to penicillin in bacteria populations.

D.7 Antivirals

Viruses: nature's most successful parasites

Figure 15.11 Examples of viruses.

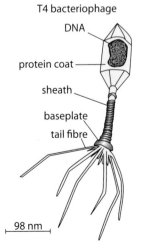

T4 bacteriophage

- DNA
- protein coat
- sheath
- baseplate
- tail fibre

98 nm

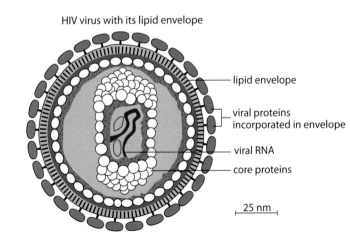

HIV virus with its lipid envelope

- lipid envelope
- viral proteins incorporated in envelope
- viral RNA
- core proteins

25 nm

Viruses are such small and simple structures that there is debate about whether they can be classified as living organisms in their own right. They contain only the two components protein and nucleic acid (either RNA or DNA), have no cellular structure and are only capable of reproducing inside another living cell. In all of these ways they are different from bacteria with their more complex cellular structure and ability to survive and reproduce independently from other living cells.

Viruses are in fact the original hijackers – they literally take over the functioning of another cell (the so-called 'host' cell) and use it to carry out their own reproduction. The host cell's components are used in the assembly of new viral particles and in the process the cell eventually dies, releasing thousands of viral particles into the body.

The war against viruses

Viral infections claim the lives of millions of people each year and are responsible for an even greater number of illnesses, many of them serious. Diseases such as measles, meningitis and polio are caused by viruses as well as relatively new diseases such as AIDS (acquired immune deficiency syndrome) and avian 'flu. Developing effective antivirals is therefore one of the most pressing challenges of modern medicine.

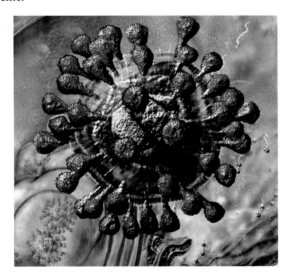

◄ Artwork of a SARS virus particle inside a cell. SARS (Severe Acute Respiratory Syndrome) is an often fatal lung disease that first appeared in China in late 2002 and spread rapidly through the world via air travel. The virus is related to the type that causes the common cold. Like all viruses it cannot replicate by itself but instead uses the machinery of the host cell to produce more copies of itself.

Treating viral infections is a challenge because the viruses live within cells and so cannot be easily targeted. Lacking the cell structure of bacteria, they are not attacked by antibiotics. Another problem is the speed at which they can multiply which means that they have often spread throughout the body by the time that symptoms appear. In addition, virus particles have a tendency to mutate rapidly (make small changes in their genetic material) and this changes their susceptibility to drugs. This is why, for example, different types of 'flu vaccine are developed each year according to the most abundant strain of virus around.

Polio was a common disease in the industrialized world until a successful vaccination was developed in the 1950s. It most commonly affected children under five years old, leaving many who survived crippled and paralysed. Immunization programmes have led to the eradication of the disease from most of the world, although some countries, notably India, Nigeria and Pakistan, remain polio-endemic. The Global Polio Eradication Initiative was launched in 1988 and tracks all new cases on a weekly basis.

Nonetheless there have been significant successes in the treatment of viral infections. Successful vaccination programmes, which generally enable the body to prepare specific **antibodies** against a virus, have reduced the incidence of diseases such as cholera, polio and measles. In 1980, the World Health Organization declared smallpox an eradicated disease.

Some antivirals work by altering the cell's genetic material (DNA) so that the virus cannot use it to multiply. Others block enzyme activity within the host cell, which prevents the virus from reproducing. In this case the progression of the disease will be halted and there will be relief from symptoms, but note that the virus is not completely eradicated from the body. This can cause a flare up on another occasion – this is what happens, for example, with some herpes infections that cause cold sores.

One reasonably effective antiviral drug is **amantadine**, which causes changes in the cell membrane that prevent the entry of the virus into the cells. It is therefore best used as a prophylactic (preventative) treatment or given before the infection has spread widely. It has been used in this way quite effectively in the treatment of influenza.

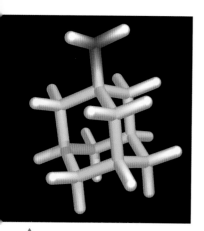

▲
Molecular model of amantadine antiviral drug. The drug is used to treat Influenza A infection in adults, as it prevents the ability of the virus to replicate its genetic material.

AIDS: a viral pandemic

The condition known as **AIDS**, caused by the virus **HIV** (human immunodeficiency virus), was first diagnosed in humans in 1981. It is characterized by a failure of the immune system, so that the body falls prey to life-threatening opportunistic infections such as pneumonia and forms of cancer. The infection has spread at an alarming rate through the global population and it is estimated that 40 million people are currently **HIV positive**, with a likelihood of developing AIDS. In some countries in sub-Saharan Africa it is believed that as many as one-third of the adult population may be affected.

HIV primarily infects vital white blood cells in the immune system called **CD4$^+$ T cells** by binding to specific receptor proteins on their surface and then penetrating the cell. As HIV is a **retrovirus** (having its genetic material in the form of RNA rather than DNA), it releases its RNA into the cell and the enzyme **reverse transcriptase** controls the synthesis of viral DNA from the RNA. The HIV DNA integrates into the cell's own DNA and replicates with it when the cell divides. Viral particles are produced within the host cell and are released in large numbers when the cell dies.

Computer artwork of HIV replication. The viral particles, shown in green, surround the white blood cell, shown in blue, and attach themselves to its surface using specific proteins for recognition. RNA, shown in pink, is then injected into the cell and, using reverse transcriptase, synthesizes DNA, which integrates into the host's chromosome. This can be seen to the right of the white cell nucleus. New viral particles are assembled within the cell and are shown at the bottom budding from the cell, taking part of the membrane as an envelope. ▶

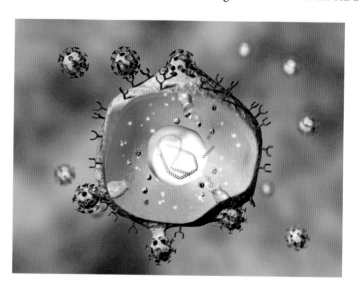

There are three main reasons why HIV is proving even more challenging than other viruses to defeat.

1　The virus destroys T helper cells, the very cells in the immune system that should be defending the body against it.

2　The virus tends to mutate very rapidly even within a patient. It is thought that there is more variation in HIV in a single patient than in influenza worldwide in a year! These variations mean that the virus 'escapes' the immune response, so the patient has to make a response to the new virus.

3　The virus often lies dormant within host cells, so the immune system has nothing to respond to.

Drugs to help in the fight against HIV, known as **antiretroviral drugs**, act at different stages in the HIV lifecycle. One target is to inhibit the enzyme reverse transcriptase, as this is specific to the virus and does not affect the host cell. The drug AZT, also known as zidovudine, works in this way and was the first antiretroviral drug approved for use in AIDS treatment. It does not destroy the HIV infection, but it has been effective in delaying the progression of the disease. It is also used as part of a regimen to prevent mother to child transmission of HIV during pregnancy. Other antiretrovirals act to block the binding of HIV to cell membranes or to inhibit the assembly of new viral particles within the cell. Although these drugs all produce side effects ranging from unpleasant to serious, they are proving successful in helping to prolong the length and quality of life of people infected with HIV.

Intense research into developing a vaccine for HIV/AIDS has so far failed to produce a fully effective result. This is mainly because of the problem of the variable nature of the virus within cells and the fact that the immune response seems to act too slowly in the case of HIV infection.

 Antiretroviral drugs usually need to be taken in combination with each other and over a long period of time to be effective. This is one of the reasons why they are generally expensive to administer and have been very poorly distributed in the countries where they are needed the most. However, in May 2007 the Clinton Foundation HIV/AIDS Initiative announced a commitment from major drug companies that reductions in price to US$1 per day would apply to the provision of antiretrovirals in 65 developing countries in Africa, Asia and Latin America.

Practice questions

1　Acidified potassium dichromate(VI) is commonly used in roadside tests for ethanol in the breath of persons operating motor vehicles. It reacts with the ethanol present to form ethanoic acid.

　(a) State the function of potassium dichromate(VI) and give the colour change that takes place in this reaction. (2)

　(b) Identify **two** other methods for the detection of ethanol in a person's breath or blood that are considered to be more accurate. (2)

　(c) State **one** harmful effect of aspirin that is more likely to occur if it is taken with ethanol. (1)

　(d) Diazepam and nitrazepam are two depressants that are very similar in their structures. State the name of **two** different functional groups present in both depressants. (2)

(Total 7 marks)
© International Baccalaureate Organization [2005]

2　(a) State the purpose of using an antacid. (1)

　(b) State and explain which would be more effective as an antacid, 1.0 mol of magnesium hydroxide or 1.0 mol of aluminium hydroxide. Support your answer with balanced equations. (3)

(Total 4 marks)
© International Baccalaureate Organization [2005]

3 Analgesics can be classified as mild or strong.

    (a) State and explain how each type of analgesic prevents pain. (4)

    (b) Aspirin is a common mild analgesic.

        (i) Outline **one** advantage and **one** disadvantage of using aspirin. (2)

        (ii) Acetaminophen (paracetamol) is often used as a substitute for aspirin. State **one** disadvantage of using acetaminophen. (1)

(Total 7 marks)

© International Baccalaureate Organization [2005]

4 The structures of some analgesics are shown in Table 20 of the IB Data booklet. Refer to this table when answering parts (a) and (b) of this question.

    (a) State the name of the nitrogen-containing functional group in each of the following molecules. (2)

        paracetamol   heroin

    (b) Naturally occurring morphine can be converted into synthetic heroin by reaction with ethanoic acid. Identify the group in the morphine molecule that reacts with ethanoic acid, the name of the type of reaction and the other product of the reaction. (3)

(Total 5 marks)

© International Baccalaureate Organization [2005]

5 Penicillins are molecules that can kill harmful microorganisms. Their general structure is shown in Table 20 of the IB Data booklet.

    (a) State the type of microorganism killed by penicillins and explain how they do this.(4)

    (b) Explain the effect of over-prescription of penicillins. (3)

(Total 7 marks)

© International Baccalaureate Organization [2005]

6 (a) Describe the differences between bacteria and viruses by referring to their structures and the way they multiply. (4)

    (b) Outline **two** ways in which antiviral drugs work. (2)

(Total 6 marks)

© International Baccalaureate Organization [2005]

7 Methylamphetamine (also known as methamphetamine or 'speed') and caffeine are stimulants with the following structures.

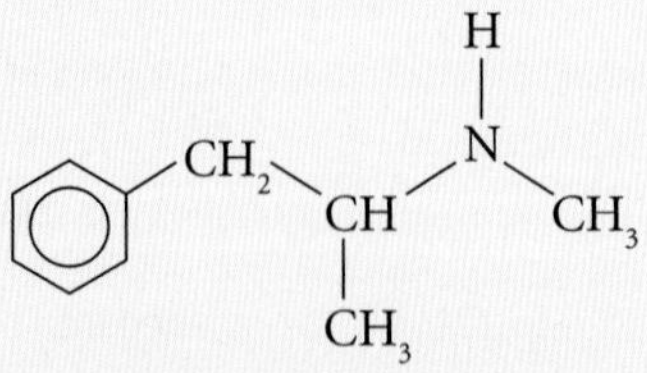

methylamphetamine 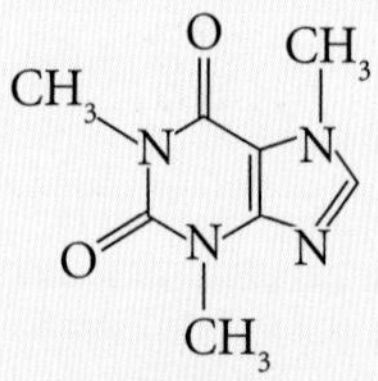   caffeine

    (a) (i) On the structure for methylamphetamine above, draw a ring around the amine group. (1)

        (ii) Determine whether both amine groups in caffeine are primary, secondary or tertiary. (1)

    (b) Caffeine contains the group

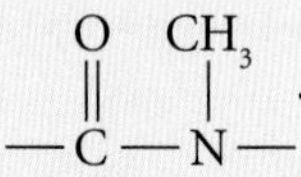

State the general name for this functional group. (1)

(c) A 'designer drug' with a structure related to methylamphetamine is ecstasy. Ecstasy tablets are sometimes contaminated with a substance called 4-MTA.

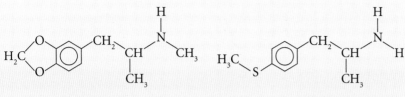

ecstasy   4-MTA

   (i) Methylamphetamine, ecstasy and 4-MTA are sympathomimetic drugs. Identify the structural similarity between the three drugs and adrenaline, the structure of which is given in the IB Data booklet. (1)

  (ii) Outline what is meant by the term *sympathomimetic drug* and state **one** example of a short-term effect sympathomimetic drugs have on the human body. (2)

 (iii) State **one** example of a long-term effect of taking stimulants. (1)

(Total 7 marks)

© International Baccalaureate Organization [2003]

8 (a) Many drugs are taken orally. State three other ways in which drugs may be taken by a patient. (2)

(b) State what is meant by the term *side-effect*. (1)

(c) One common type of drug taken orally is the antacid. Antacids such as sodium hydrogencarbonate are taken to reduce stomach acidity.

   (i) State the names of **two** metals, other than sodium, whose compounds are often used in antacids. (1)

  (ii) Give an equation for the neutralization of hydrochloric acid in the stomach by sodium hydrogencarbonate. (1)

 (iii) Explain how heartburn is caused. (1)

 (iv) Explain why dimethicone is added to some antacids. (1)

(Total 7 marks)

© International Baccalaureate Organization [2003]

9 (a) Aspirin is a widely used analgesic.

   (i) State the general names of the **two** functional groups attached to the benzene ring in a molecule of aspirin. (2)

  (ii) The use of aspirin can have beneficial effects for the user, but can also produce some unwanted side-effects. State **one** beneficial effect (other than its analgesic action) and **one** unwanted side-effect. (2)

(b) Morphine is a naturally occurring analgesic that can be converted into codeine.

   (i) Calculate the difference in relative formula mass between morphine and codeine. (1)

  (ii) Explain what is meant by developing tolerance towards codeine and state why this is dangerous. (2)

(Total 7 marks)

© International Baccalaureate Organization [2003]

16 Environmental chemistry: Option E

The effect of human activity on the environment is becoming increasingly global, spanning political and natural boundaries. An understanding of the impact of chemicals in air, water and soil is essential within and beyond the study of chemistry. The three areas of the environment are mutually interrelated systems: atmospheric pollutants such as nitrogen oxides fall to Earth in acid rain and pollute land and water, and discarded waste in landfill sites can be washed into groundwater and pollute our rivers. In this chapter we will discuss the sources and the effects of different pollutants and possible solutions to the problems they raise.

Some problems of pollution. Smoke and steam from power stations and factories contribute to atmospheric pollution, which causes acid rain and has been implicated in global warming. Water from power station cooling towers can cause thermal pollution. Water may also be contaminated by chemical spillages.

Assessment statements

E.1 Air pollution
E.1.1 Describe the main sources of carbon monoxide (CO), oxides of nitrogen (NO_x), oxides of sulfur (SO_x), particulates and volatile organic compounds (VOCs) in the atmosphere.
E.1.2 Evaluate current methods for the reduction of air pollution.

E.2 Acid deposition
E.2.1 State what is meant by the term *acid deposition* and outline its origins.
E.2.2 Discuss the environmental effects of acid deposition and possible methods to counteract them.

E.3 Greenhouse effect
E.3.1 Describe the *greenhouse effect*.
E.3.2 List the main greenhouse gases and their sources and discuss their relative effects.
E.3.3 Discuss the influence of increasing amounts of greenhouse gases on the atmosphere.

E.4 Ozone depletion
E.4.1 Describe the formation and depletion of ozone in the stratosphere by natural processes.
E.4.2 List the ozone-depleting pollutants and their sources.
E.4.3 Discuss the alternatives to CFCs in terms of their properties.

E.5 Dissolved oxygen in water
E.5.1 Outline biochemical oxygen demand (BOD) as a measure of oxygen-demanding wastes in water.
E.5.2 Distinguish between *aerobic* and *anaerobic* decomposition of organic material in water.
E.5.3 Describe the process of *eutrophication* and its effects.
E.5.4 Describe the source and effects of thermal pollution in water.

E.6 Water treatment
E.6.1 List the primary pollutants found in waste water and identify their sources.

E.6.2 Outline the primary, secondary and tertiary stages of waste water treatment and state the substance that is removed during each stage.

E.6.3 Evaluate the process to obtain fresh water from sea water using multi-stage distillation and reverse osmosis.

E.7 Soil

E.7.1 Discuss *salinization*, *nutrient depletion* and *soil pollution* as causes of soil degradation.

E.7.2 Describe the relevance of the *soil organic matter* (SOM) in preventing soil degradation and outline its physical and biological functions.

E.7.3 List common organic soil pollutants and their sources.

E.8 Waste

E.8.1 Outline and compare the various methods for waste disposal.

E.8.2 Describe the recycling of metal, glass, plastic and paper products and outline its benefits.

E.8.3 Describe the characteristics and sources of different types of radioactive waste.

E.8.4 Compare the storage and disposal methods for different types of radioactive waste.

Air pollution

Air is a mixture of gases with the composition shown.

Gas	Percentage composition
nitrogen (N_2)	78
oxygen (O_2)	21
argon (Ar)	1
water vapour	0–4
carbon dioxide (CO_2)	0.04 (= 400 ppm)

A pollutant is a substance which has a harmful effect on the environment and is present at concentrations greater than its natural levels as a result of human activity. The impact of human activity is illustrated by the increase in levels of carbon dioxide which have risen from levels of 275 ppm to 384 ppm since 1850 owing to the burning of fossil fuels.

'ppm' which stands for 'parts per million' is a unit of concentration.

The effect of air pollutants depends on their concentrations, their relative **toxicity** and the average length of time they remain in the environment before becoming harmless by natural processes. We can classify air pollutants as: **primary** pollutants which are emitted directly into the atmosphere and **secondary** pollutants which are produced when primary pollutants undergo chemical change in the atmosphere. Carbon dioxide produced from the combustion of fossil fuels is an example of a primary air pollutant. Other examples include carbon monoxide, sulfur dioxide (SO_2), nitrogen monoxide (NO) and volatile organic compounds (VOCs) such as the hydrocarbons. We will now discuss the natural and anthropogenic (human made) sources of each of these primary pollutants in turn, although their chemistry in the atmosphere is interrelated.

This household device is designed to detect excessive levels of carbon monoxide (CO) which can be produced by malfunctioning gas boilers or fires. After six hours of exposure, 35 ppm of CO produces headaches and dizziness. Within hours, 800 ppm of CO causes unconsciousness, with higher levels causing death.

Carbon monoxide

Carbon monoxide (CO) is toxic to humans as it affects oxygen uptake in the blood. It is absorbed by the lungs and binds to haemoglobin (Hb) in red blood cells more effectively than oxygen.

$$Hb + CO \rightleftharpoons COHb$$

haemoglobin   carboxyhaemoglobin

This prevents oxygen from being transported about the body. It can cause dizziness at low concentrations and be fatal at high levels. As it is a colourless odourless gas, it can rise to dangerous levels without being detected.

Sources

Anthropogenic sources include **incomplete combustion** of fossil fuels and forest fires, where there is a limited supply of oxygen. For example from the incomplete combination of coal:

$$2C(s) + O_2(g) \rightarrow 2CO(g)$$

Worked example

Give the balanced equation for the formation of carbon monoxide in the internal combustion engine caused by the incomplete combustion of octane, $C_8H_{18}(l)$.

Solution

First write the unbalanced equation:

$$C_8H_{18}(l) + \_O_2(g) \rightarrow \_CO(g) + \_H_2O(g)$$

Balance the carbon atoms and hydrogen atoms (from left to right):

$$C_8H_{18}(l) + \_O_2(g) \rightarrow \mathbf{8}CO(g) + \mathbf{9}H_2O(g)$$

Balance the oxygen atoms (from right to left):

$$C_8H_{18}(l) + \frac{17}{2} O_2(g) \rightarrow 8CO(g) + 9H_2O(g)$$

Multiply $\times 2$:

$$2C_8H_{18}(l) + 17O_2(g) \rightarrow 16CO(g) + 18H_2O(g)$$

Carbon monoxide pollution is a local pollution problem in urban areas as it is produced in heavy traffic. There are particularly high emission rates during rush hours.

Congested traffic during morning and evening rush hour can lead to high levels of carbon monoxide in the atmosphere.

Carbon monoxide is also formed from natural sources during the atmospheric oxidation of methane gas, CH_4. Methane is formed naturally by the decomposition of organic matter.

$$2CH_4(g) + 3O_2(g) \rightarrow 2CO(g) + 4H_2O(l)$$

This forest fire in Quebec, Canada is a source of carbon monoxide pollution.

Exercise

1 The levels of carbon monoxide were recorded in one location in the northern hemisphere during a 24-hour period. The results are shown in the figure.

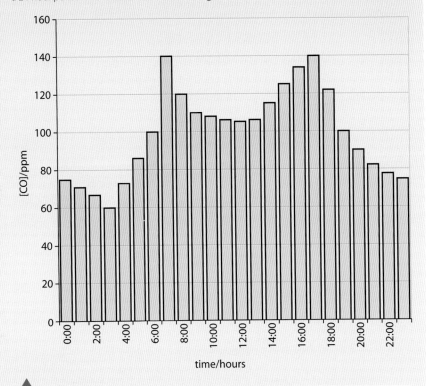

Figure 16.1 A 24-hour variation in carbon monoxide concentration over a localized area.

(a) The average concentration of carbon monoxide in the northern hemisphere is approximately 0.14 ppm. Comment on the high level of the concentrations recorded.

(b) Suggest why the concentrations reach two peaks during the 24-hour period.

Methods of control

The control of CO emission from the internal combustion engines is the best method of reducing CO levels. This can be done by controlling the air/fuel ratio to ensure that the air is in excess or using **catalytic converters** to oxidize carbon monoxide to carbon dioxide, or using a **thermal exhaust reactor**.

Lean burn engines

The equation for the complete combustion of octane is:

$$2C_8H_{18}(g) + 25O_2(g) \rightarrow 16CO_2(g) + 18H_2O(g)$$

It follows that an air/fuel ratio of between 14 to 15 by mass is needed for complete combustion (see Exercise 2). Maximum power is generally achieved using a mixture richer in the fuel with lower air:fuel ratios of approximately 12.5 but only at the cost of producing increased CO levels. Engines can misfire with leaner

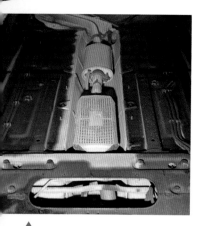

A catalytic converter on the underside of a car reduces the toxic emissions from an internal combustion engine by converting the harmful exhaust by-products into relatively harmless ones. A 90% reduction of pollution emission has been achieved without loss of engine performance or fuel economy. The addition of a catalytic converter to a car necessitates the use of unleaded fuel since the lead compounds added to regular petrol as anti-knocking agents contaminate the catalyst.

Figure 16.2 A thermal exhaust reactor. ▶

mixtures that have lower fuel content. Modern technology has produced **lean burn engines** with controlled fuel injections. These work effectively with mixtures with air/fuels ratios of 18 and produce low carbon monoxide emissions.

Catalytic converters

Exhaust emissions can be controlled by fitting **catalytic converters** to exhaust systems. The hot gases are mixed with air and passed over a platinum-based catalyst. There are two forms of catalyst.

- Oxidation catalysts are used in lean burn engines to convert carbon monoxide to carbon dioxide:

$$2CO(g) + O_2 \rightarrow 2CO_2(g)$$

- Three-way catalysts work in conventional engines. They not only oxidize carbon monoxide to carbon dioxide and hydrocarbons to water and carbon dioxide, but also reduce nitrogen monoxide (NO) to nitrogen gas:

$$2CO(g) + 2NO(g) \xrightarrow{\text{catalyst + moderate temp}} 2CO_2(g) + N_2(g)$$

Thermal converters

The **thermal exhaust reactor** takes advantage of the heat of the exhaust gases and makes the carbon monoxide react with more air to produce carbon dioxide. Any unburned volatile organic compounds such as hydrocarbon fuels are also oxidized to carbon dioxide and water.

$$2CO(g) + O_2(g) \rightarrow 2CO_2(g)$$

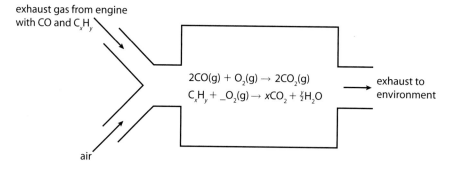

exhaust gas from engine with CO and C_xH_y

$$2CO(g) + O_2(g) \rightarrow 2CO_2(g)$$
$$C_xH_y + \_O_2(g) \rightarrow xCO_2 + \tfrac{y}{2}H_2O$$

exhaust to environment

air

Exercise

2 (a) The equation for the complete combustion of octane is:

$$2C_8H_{18}(g) + 25O_2(g) \rightarrow 16CO_2(g) + 18H_2O(g)$$

Calculate the mass of oxygen which reacts with 1.00 g of fuel.

(b) Assume that 20% of the air is made from oxygen by mass. Calculate the mass of air which reacts with 1.00 g of fuel.

(c) Explain why carbon monoxide is a dangerous pollutant.

(d) The complete combustion of a hydrocarbon C_xH_y can be expressed as:

$$C_xH_y + \_O_2(g) \rightarrow xCO_2(g) + \tfrac{y}{2}H_2O(l)$$

Deduce the coefficient of $O_2(g)$.

(e) Discuss the conditions that lead to the production of carbon monoxide in automobile engines.

(f) Describe two different methods of controlling carbon monoxide emissions from automobile engines.

(g) Catalytic converters convert carbon monoxide to carbon dioxide. State the environmental problem associated with CO_2 emissions.

Nitrogen oxides

Sources

There is no reaction between nitrogen and oxygen at room or moderately high temperature owing to the very high stability of the nitrogen–nitrogen triple bond. There are, however, many known nitrogen oxides which can be formed from natural or anthropogenic sources. The main pollutants are nitrogen monoxide, nitrogen dioxide, NO_2 and dinitrogen oxide, N_2O, which react with hydrocarbons to form photochemical smog and also form nitric acid (HNO_3) and so contribute to acid rain. Nitrogen dioxide is the most toxic and causes irritation of the eyes and nose, as well as breathing and respiratory problems.

All dinitrogen oxide and about 80% of nitrogen monoxide is produced naturally, from the decomposition of nitrogen-containing compounds by bacterial action in soil and from lightning storms:

$$N_2(g) + O_2(g) \xrightarrow{\text{lightning}} 2NO(g)$$

The anthropogenic sources of nitrogen oxides are shown in Figure 16.3.

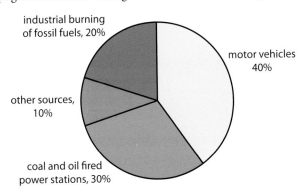

industrial burning of fossil fuels, 20%

motor vehicles 40%

other sources, 10%

coal and oil fired power stations, 30%

Figure 16.3 Anthropogenic sources of nitrogen oxides in the atmosphere.

Motor vehicles are the main source. Under conditions of high temperatures (around 1500 °C in automobile engines), nitrogen and oxygen in the air react to form nitrogen monoxide:

$$N_2(g) + O_2(g) \xrightarrow{\text{high temp}} 2NO(g)$$

The brown colour of photochemical smog is due to the presence of nitrogen dioxide, a secondary pollutant produced from the oxidation of NO.

$$2NO(g) + O_2(g) \rightarrow 2NO_2(g)$$

Methods of control

Lean burn engines

One of the problems of cleaning vehicle emissions is that conditions needed to oxidize carbon monoxide to carbon dioxide are the same conditions which promote the production of nitrogen oxides. A rich mixture with a high fuel content produces low NO_x but high CO emissions. Lean burn engines which use an air : fuel ratio of 18:1 can be used to reduce emission of both NO_x and CO.

Three-way catalytic converters

Nitrogen oxide emissions from car exhaust gases can be reduced by using three-way catalytic converters discussed earlier.

$$2CO(g) + 2NO(g) \xrightarrow{\text{catalyst + moderate temp}} 2CO_2(g) + N_2(g)$$

Smog over Los Angeles, California. The brown colour is due to the presence of nitrogen dioxide.

Exhaust gas recirculation

The amount of nitrogen oxide produced depends on the operating temperature of the engine. The **exhaust gas recirculation (EGR)** process recirculates the exhaust gases back into the engine. This lowers the operating temperature and reduces the nitrogen oxide emissions.

● **Examiner's hint:** Focus on the key chemistry when answering questions. The 'car exhaust' as a source of nitrogen oxides is not sufficiently detailed. They are formed from the combination of oxygen and nitrogen from the air at the high temperatures reached in the internal combustion engine.

Exercise

3 (a) Name a natural source of nitrogen monoxide in the atmosphere.
(b) Name an anthropogenic source of nitrogen monoxide.
(c) Identify the acid formed by the nitrogen oxides in the atmosphere which contributes to acid rain.

Sulfur oxides

There are two oxides: sulfur dioxide, SO_2 and sulfur trioxide, SO_3. Sulfur dioxide is a dangerous primary pollutant which can harm people, plants and materials. Natural sources of sulfur dioxide include volcanoes and rotting vegetables. It is also produced as a secondary pollutant by the oxidation of hydrogen sulfide:

$$2H_2S(g) + 3O_2(g) \rightarrow 2SO_2(g) + 2H_2O(l)$$

Anthropogenic sources include:

● Burning of sulfur-containing fossil fuels. Coal contains sulfur as elemental sulfur, as iron pyrites and as organic sulfides, since it was present in the proteins of the decayed organisms:

$$S(s) + O_2(g) \rightarrow SO_2(g)$$

● From smelting plants which oxidize sulfide ores to the metal oxides:

$$Cu_2S(s) + 2O_2(g) \rightarrow 2CuO(s) + SO_2(g)$$

● From sulfuric acid plants.

Burning coal in a power station releases sulfur dioxide and carbon dioxide into the atmosphere.

Sulfur trioxide is a secondary pollutant formed in the atmosphere by the reaction between the primary pollutant sulfur dioxide and oxygen. Sulfur trioxide can dissolve in water to form sulfuric acid:

$$2SO_2(g) + O_2(g) \rightarrow 2SO_3(g)$$
$$H_2O(l) + SO_3(g) \rightarrow H_2SO_4(aq)$$

The overall oxidation reaction can be summarized by the equation:

$$2H_2O(l) + 2SO_2(g) + O_2(g) \rightarrow 2H_2SO_4(aq)$$

Methods of control

Sulfur dioxide emissions can be reduced by removing the sulfur either before or after combustion.

Pre-combustion methods

The sulfur present in coal as a metal sulfide can be removed by crushing the coal and washing with water. The high density metal sulfide sinks to the bottom and so separates from the clean coal. Sulfur impurities in crude oil, mainly in the form of hydrogen sulfide, can be removed by mixing with basic potassium carbonate solution:

$$H_2S(g) + CO_3^{2-}(aq) \rightleftharpoons HS^-(aq) + HCO_3^-(aq)$$

The hydrogen sulfide can be recovered from solution by later reversing the reaction.

Post-combustion methods

The acidic sulfur dioxide can be removed from exhaust gases by two methods: **alkaline scrubbing** and **fluidized-bed combustion**.

In the alkaline scrubbing method an alkaline mixture is sprayed downwards into the exhaust gases.

Alkaline mixtures include:

- A slurry of calcium oxide (lime) or calcium carbonate (limestone) which reacts with sulfur dioxide to form calcium sulfate:

$$CaO(s) + SO_2(g) \rightarrow CaSO_3(s)$$

$$CaCO_3(s) + SO_2(g) \rightarrow CaSO_3(s) + CO_2(g)$$

$$2CaSO_3(s) + O_2(g) \rightarrow 2CaSO_4(s)$$

The calcium sulfate can be deposited in landfill or be used to make plasterboard.

- A slurry of magnesium oxide reacts in a similar way:

$$MgO(s) + SO_2(g) \rightarrow MgSO_3(s)$$

The magnesium oxide can be regenerated from the product:

$$MgSO_3(s) \xrightarrow{heat} MgO(s) + SO_2(g)$$

Sulfur dioxide is used in the manufacture of sulfuric acid.

In the **fluidized combustion** method, the coal is mixed with powdered limestone on a metal plate. A strong air flow passes through the mixture from below which makes the particles of limestone and coal float above the plate making the mixture behave like a *fluid*. The heat produced from combustion of the coal causes the calcium carbonate to break up to calcium oxide and carbon dioxide:

$$CaCO_3(s) \rightarrow CaO(s) + CO_2(g)$$

Figure 16.4 Alkaline scrubbing.

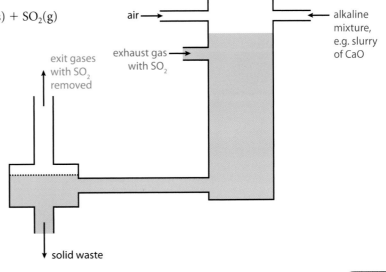

Sulfur dioxide is removed as it is formed by the combustion of coal. Calcium oxide reacts with sulfur dioxide in the presence of oxygen to form calcium sulfate:

$$CaO(s) + SO_2(g) \rightarrow CaSO_3(s)$$

$$2CaO(s) + 2SO_2(g) + O_2(g) \rightarrow 2CaSO_4(s)$$

Figure 16.5 Schematic diagram showing the workings of a fluidized combustion bed.

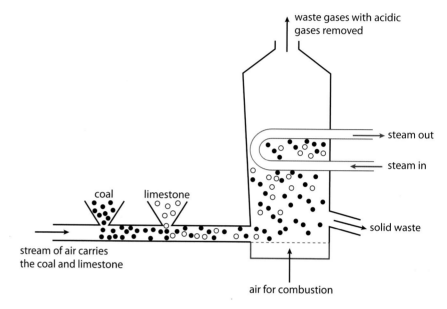

Sulfur dioxide emissions can also be reduced by using coal with a low sulfur content.

Exercise

4 (a) State the origins of the sulfur present in crude oil and coal.

(b) Describe one chemical method with balanced equations for removing sulfur dioxide from the emissions of power stations.

(c) Suggest a different type of approach, which does not involve a chemical reaction for reducing sulfur dioxide emissions from power stations.

Particulates

Particulates are solid particles of carbon or dust, or liquid droplets of mist or fog suspended or carried in the air. They generally have a diameter in the range 0.001–10 μm, which is just large enough to be seen. As many particulates are polar, they are attracted into water droplets and form **aerosols**. An aerosol is a gaseous suspension of very small particles of a liquid. Examples of particulates include soot from the incomplete combustion of hydrocarbons and coal in power stations, dust from the mechanical break-up of solid matter and sulfur from volcanic eruptions. Particulates enter the body during breathing and can affect the respiratory system and cause lung diseases such as emphysema, bronchitis and cancer. Although they are sometimes inert solids, they are dangerous pollutants because they can act as catalysts in the production of secondary pollutants and increase the harmful effects of gaseous pollutants. The particulates absorb other pollutants and hold them in the lungs for longer periods of time. Smaller particles are more dangerous than larger particles per unit mass because they have a larger surface area.

Sources

Natural sources of particulates include:
- dust from the mechanical break-up of solid matter
- sulfur from volcanic eruptions
- pollen, bacterial and fungal spores.

Anthropogenic sources include:
- soot from the incomplete combustion of hydrocarbons (e.g. diesel) and coal in power stations
- arsenic from insecticides
- asbestos from the construction industry. Asbestos is a material containing silicate crystals which is used to insulate buildings. Asbestos particles are released into the atmosphere when these buildings are demolished.
- fly ash from the combustion of fossil fuels in furnaces, which contains carbon and metal oxides. Mercury is present in fly ash and is also used in the manufacture of fungicides, pulp and paper.

Methods of control

Particulates and aerosols are removed naturally from the atmosphere by **gravitational settling** and by rain and snow. They can be prevented from entering the atmosphere by treating industrial emissions using physical methods such as **filtration, centrifugal separation, settling tanks, scrubbing** and **electrostatic precipitation**.

Settling tanks
Larger particulates can be removed using gravity settling tanks, which allow dust to settle out by gravity.

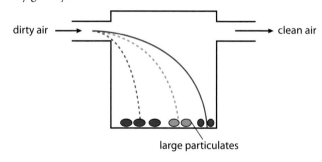

◀ **Figure 16.6** Gravity settling chambers.

Electrostatic precipitation

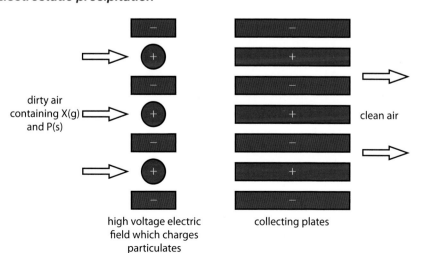

◀ **Figure 16.7** An electrostatic precipitator which removes particulates from the air.

As air passes through the strong electric field, the gas molecules X(g) are ionized:

$$X(g) \rightarrow X^+(g) + e^-$$

The electrons produced collect on the particulates P(s) and so they become strongly negatively charged:

$$P(s) + e^- \rightarrow P^-(s)$$

The P^-(s) ions are attracted to the positively charged collector plates. The collector plates have to be periodically shaken to remove the collected solid particles. This method can remove more than 98% of all particulate matter.

Wet scrubbers and cyclone separators

Particulates can be removed by **scrubbing** with clean water (see page 371). The water moves downwards as the gas move upwards and washes the particles out of the rising dirty air. In a cyclone separator the particulates are thrown outwards, where they can be collected as the exhaust gases are spun rapidly.

Volatile organic compounds

Organic air pollutants can have either a direct or indirect effect on the air quality. Extended exposure to chloroethene CH_3CH_2Cl, or aromatic hydrocarbons such as benzene, for example, can lead to cancer. Hydrocarbons can form secondary pollutants and **photochemical smog**.

Sources

Methane is released in large amounts by natural sources. It is produced by the bacterial anaerobic decomposition of organic matter in water and soil. Unsaturated hydrocarbons called **terpenes** are given out by plants. Anthropogenic sources include unburned petroleum products like gasoline emitted from car exhausts and other hydrocarbons released during the processing and use of petrol.

As particulate pollutants are solid particles, they are measured in different units (often micrograms per unit volume) from gaseous pollutants (ppm).

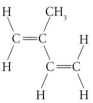

Terpenes are made from a number of 2-methylbuta-1,3-diene units.

Primary air pollutants

Pollutant	Anthropogenic source	Natural source	Methods of control
carbon monoxide, CO	incomplete combustion of carbon-containing fossil fuels; high concentrations build up locally: $2C_8H_{18}(l) + 17O_2(g) \rightarrow 16CO(g) + 18H_2O(l)$	from anaerobic decomposition of organic matter: $2CH_4(g) + 3O_2(g) \rightarrow 2CO(g) + 4H_2O(l)$	• thermal exhaust reactor • catalytic converter • use of lean burn engines
nitrogen oxides, NO_x	high temperatures in internal combustion engines produce mostly NO and small amount of NO_2: $N_2(g) + O_2(g) \rightarrow 2NO(g)$	bacterial decomposition of nitrogen containing compounds produces N_2O and NO; electrical storms: $N_2(g) + O_2(g) \rightarrow 2NO(g)$	• catalytic converter • use of lean burn engines • recirculation of exhaust gases
sulfur dioxide, SO_2	combustion of sulfur-containing coal; smelting and sulfuric acid plants: $S(s) + O_2(g) \rightarrow SO_2(g)$	no major sources of SO_2; oxidation of H_2S gas produced during the decay of organic matter and volcanic activity	• removal of sulfur from fossil fuels before burning • alkaline scrubbing • fluidized bed combustion
particulates	combustion of fossil fuels, break up of solid matter (asbestos), industrial plants	volcanic activity, forest fires, biological sources such as pollen and fungal spores	• gravity settling chambers • cyclone separators • electrostatic precipitators • wet scrubbers
volatile organic compounds	unburned petroleum, solvents	CH_4 from biological processes owing to bacterial decomposition of organic matter in bodies of water, trees; plants produce hydrocarbons called terpenes	• catalytic converters

Aromatic compounds are produced during the incomplete combustion of coal and wood. Volatile organic compounds are also released into the atmosphere from solvents and paints. The source of halogen organic compounds such as the chlorofluorocarbons (CFCs) is discussed later in the chapter.

Methods of control

Hydrocarbon emissions can be reduced by using an oxidation catalytic converter or thermal exhaust reactors as discussed earlier. The hydrocarbons are oxidized to carbon dioxide and water.

E.2 Acid deposition

All rain water is naturally acidic owing to the presence of dissolved carbon dioxide, which reacts with water to form carbonic acid:

$$CO_2(g) + H_2O(l) \rightleftharpoons H_2CO_3(aq)$$
carbonic acid

Carbonic acid is a weak acid:

$$H_2CO_3(aq) \rightleftharpoons H^+(aq) + HCO_3^-(aq)$$

The minimum pH of carbonic acid solutions is 5.6. Acid rain refers to solutions with a lower pH owing to the presence of sulfur and nitrogen oxides.

Acid deposition refers to the process by which acidic particles, gases and precipitation leave the atmosphere. It is a more general term than acid rain and extends to pollution in the absence of water. It is caused by the **sulfur** and **nitrogen oxides** discussed earlier. **Wet deposition** includes acid rain, fog and snow and **dry deposition** includes acidic gases and particles.

Acid rain is a secondary pollutant produced when acidic gases are oxidized and dissolve in water. Sulfur dioxide dissolves in water to form sulfurous acid $H_2SO_3(aq)$:

$$H_2O(l) + SO_2(g) \rightarrow H_2SO_3(aq)$$

Sulfuric acid $H_2SO_4(aq)$ is formed when the sulfur dioxide is oxidized to sulfur trioxide which then dissolves in water. The oxidation of sulfur dioxide can occur in the presence of sunlight or be catalysed by aerosols. There is some evidence that the atmosphere over urban areas is chemically more active owing to the presence of tiny particles of metals such as iron and manganese which can act as catalysts.

$$2SO_2(g) + O_2(g) \rightarrow 2SO_3(g)$$
$$H_2O(l) + SO_3(g) \rightarrow H_2SO_4(aq)$$

Exercise

5 Deduce the oxidation number of sulfur in the following:
   (a) SO_2
   (b) $H_2SO_3(aq)$
   (c) $H_2SO_4(aq)$

Sulfurous acid (H_2SO_3) is also called sulfuric(IV) acid. H_2SO_4 is more correctly known as sulfuric(VI) acid.

All rain water is naturally acidic owing to the presence of dissolved carbon dioxide, which reacts with water to form carbonic acid:

$$CO_2(g) + H_2O(l) \rightleftharpoons H_2CO_3(aq)$$
carbonic acid

Acid rain has a pH < 5.6.

Acid rain is not a recent discovery: the phrase was first coined to describe the rain in the English city of Manchester over a hundred years ago. It was not until the 1960s however that it began to be an important issue.

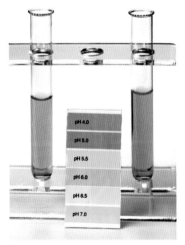

Test tubes of normal rain (left) and acid rain (right) with universal indicator added to show acidity. The normal rainwater has a pH of above 5.6, while the acid rain has a lower pH. In this example, the pH = 4.0.

The nitrogen oxides form nitrous acid ($HNO_2(aq)$) and nitric acid ($HNO_3(aq)$). Nitrogen monoxide produced from the combination of nitrogen and oxygen in the internal combustion engine is first oxidized in the air to nitrogen dioxide:

$$2NO(g) + O_2(g) \rightarrow 2NO_2(g)$$

Nitrogen dioxide dissolves in water to form a mixture of nitrous and nitric acid:

$$H_2O(l) + 2NO_2(g) \rightarrow HNO_2(aq) + HNO_3(aq)$$

Alternatively nitrogen dioxide can be oxidized to form nitric acid:

$$2H_2O(l) + 4NO_2(g) + O_2(g) \rightarrow 4HNO_3(aq)$$

Exercise

6 Deduce the oxidation number of nitrogen in the following:
(a) NO_2
(b) $HNO_2(aq)$
(c) $HNO_3(aq)$

Nitrous acid (HNO_2) is also called nitric(III) acid. HNO_3 is more correctly known as nitric(V) acid.

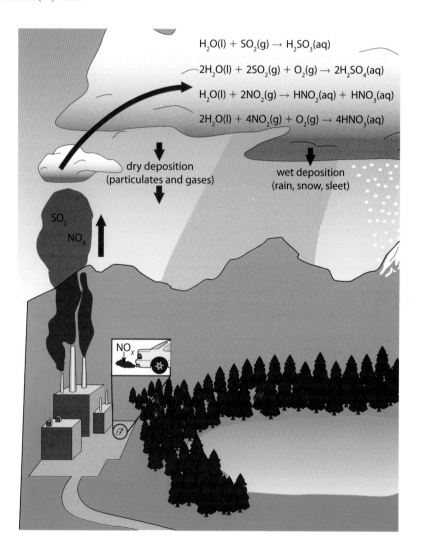

Figure 16.8 The formation of acid rain.

$$H_2O(l) + SO_2(g) \rightarrow H_2SO_3(aq)$$
$$2H_2O(l) + 2SO_2(g) + O_2(g) \rightarrow 2H_2SO_4(aq)$$
$$H_2O(l) + 2NO_2(g) \rightarrow HNO_2(aq) + HNO_3(aq)$$
$$2H_2O(l) + 4NO_2(g) + O_2(g) \rightarrow 4HNO_3(aq)$$

dry deposition (particulates and gases)

wet deposition (rain, snow, sleet)

SO_2
NO_x

NO_x

Effects of acid deposition

Effects on materials

The building materials marble and limestone are both forms of calcium carbonate. Both sulfur dioxide, in dry deposition, and sulfuric acid, in acid rain, react to form calcium sulfate.

$$2CaCO_3(s) + 2SO_2(g) + O_2(g) \rightarrow 2CaSO_4(aq) + 2CO_2(g)$$

$$CaCO_3(s) + H_2SO_4(aq) \rightarrow CaSO_4(s) + H_2O(l) + CO_2(g)$$

As calcium sulfate is more soluble than calcium carbonate it washes out of the limestone. Calcium sulfate has a greater molar volume than calcium carbonate so its formation causes expansion and stress in the stonework.

Sulfur dioxide, present in dry deposition, increases the rate of corrosion of metals:

$$Fe(s) + SO_2(g) + O_2(g) \rightarrow FeSO_4(s)$$

Acid rain corrodes metals. Metals such as iron dissolve in sulfuric acid to form salts:

$$Fe(s) + H_2SO_4(aq) \rightarrow FeSO_4(aq) + H_2(g)$$

The formation of iron(II) sulfate enables ionic conduction to occur which increases the rate of electrochemical corrosion reactions such as rusting.

The protective oxide layer is removed from other metals such as aluminium.

$$Al_2O_3(s) + 3H_2SO_4(aq) \rightarrow Al_2(SO_4)_3(aq) + 3H_2O(l)$$

▲ Statue eroded by acid rain in Venice, Italy.

Exercise

7 The equations for the corrosion of iron and limestone have been given for sulfuric acid present in acid rain. Give the corresponding equations for nitric acid present in acid rain.

Effects on plant life

Acid rain also damages plant life. It washes out important nutrients such as Mg^{2+}, Ca^{2+} and K^+ ions from the soil and releases the dangerous Al^{3+} ions from rocks into the soil. Without essential nutrients, plants starve to death: a reduction in Mg^{2+}, for example, causes a reduction in chlorophyll levels, which reduces the ability of plants to photosynthesize. This results in stunted growth and leaf loss. Aluminium minerals are generally insoluble – the Al^{3+} ions are generally 'trapped' in rock. They are, however, released in acid conditions, which damage the roots and so prevent the tree from taking up sufficient water and nutrients to survive. Sulfur dioxide, present in dry deposition, blocks the stomata (openings) in the leaves and prevents photosynthesis.

Dead trees resulting from the effects of acid rain and fumes from a nickel smelting plant in the background. ▶

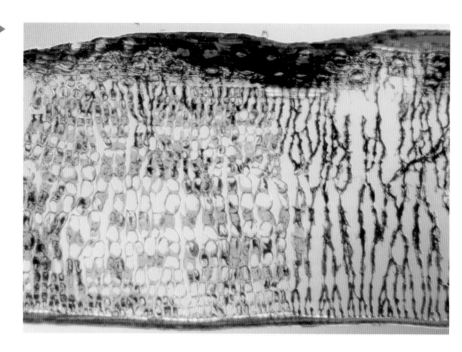

A spruce leaf damaged on the right by acid rain. The tissue most affected is known as the spongy mesophyll, which facilitates gaseous exchange with the atmosphere during photosynthesis.

Effects on water

Acidic rain has caused a number of lakes to become fishless or 'dead'. Trout and perch cannot survive at pH values below 5. Rivers are effectively dead at a pH of 4.0, as dangerous Al^{3+} ions 'trapped' in the rock dissolve under acid conditions.

$$Al(OH)_3(s) + 3H^+(aq) \rightarrow Al^{3+}(aq) + 3H_2O(l)$$

Aluminium ions interfere with the operation of the fish's gills and reduce their ability to take in oxygen.

The nitric acid present in acid rain poses a particular problem as the nitrates present can lead to **eutrophication** (see page 390). The nitrate ions promote excessive plant growth causing plants to need more oxygen to be available in the water supply, which can in turn lead to other plant deaths.

View of Lake Gardsjon, Sweden. Despite the idyllic scene, this lake has seen a hundred-fold increase in acidity over the last 40 years. Only the very hardiest plants and animals may now survive in the lake water.

Effects on human health

Breathing air containing acid gases irritates the respiratory tract from mucous membranes in the nose and throat to the lung tissue. This increases the risk of respiratory illnesses such as asthma, bronchitis and emphysema. It can also cause irritation to the eyes.

There is also a greater risk of poisonous metal ions such as Pb^{2+} and Cu^{2+} being released from pipes, or Al^{3+} ions being released from rocks. The presence of aluminium in water may be linked to Alzheimer's disease, a form of senile dementia.

One of the most controversial aspects of acid rain is that the polluter country and polluted countries are often not the same. Acid rain is a secondary pollutant and transported to other more remote areas. It is perhaps not surprising that the legislation to control acid rain has been the subject of intense political debate.

Control strategies

Acid deposition can be controlled by reducing the level of emissions of nitrogen and sulfur oxides. Possible methods were discussed earlier. Other solutions are to switch to alternative energy sources, such as wind, solar or tidal energy, or to reduce the demand for fossil fuels by using more public transport or more efficient energy transfer systems.

The damage caused by acid rain in lakes can be reduced by using lime (CaO) or calcium hydroxide $(Ca(OH)_2)$ to neutralize the acid:

$$CaO(s) + H_2SO_4(aq) \rightarrow CaSO_4(s) + H_2O(l)$$
$$Ca(OH)_2(s) + H_2SO_4(aq) \rightarrow CaSO_4(s) + 2H_2O(l)$$

Review the cause and effects of acid rain with this animation.

Now go to www.heinemann.co.uk/hotlinks, insert the express code 4259P and click on this activity.

Exercises

8 (a) Explain why natural rain has a pH of around 5.6. Give a chemical equation to support your answer.

(b) Acid rain may be 50 times more acidic that natural rain. One of the major acids present in acid rain originates mainly from burning coal. State the name of the acid and give equations to show how it is formed.

(c) The second major acid responsible for acid rain originates mainly from internal combustion engines. State the name of this acid and state two different ways in which its production can be reduced.

(d) Acid rain has caused considerable damage to buildings and statues made of marble $(CaCO_3)$. Write an equation to represent the reaction of acid rain with marble.

(e) State three consequences of acid rain.

(f) Suggest a method of controlling acid rain not involving a chemical reaction for reducing sulfur dioxide emissions from power stations.

9 The table gives some substances found in air.

Name	Formula
sulfur dioxide	SO_2
nitrogen monoxide	NO
particulates	–

(a) Identify the pollutant(s) which contribute(s) to acid rain.

(b) Identify the pollutant(s) which come(s) mainly from power stations.

(c) The presence of one of these pollutants makes the ill effects of the others worse. Identify the pollutant and explain why it has this effect.

(d) Emissions of one of these pollutants have been controlled by reaction with calcium oxide. Identify this pollutant and write an equation for the reaction with calcium oxide.

(e) Identify the pollutants that come primarily from motor vehicles and describe the basis for their production.

E.3 Greenhouse effect

The temperature of the Earth is maintained by a steady state balance between the energy received from the Sun and the energy leaving the Earth and going back into space. Incoming solar radiation is in the visible and ultraviolet region. Some of this radiation is reflected back into space and some is absorbed by gases in the atmosphere. Most passes through the atmosphere, however, and warms the surface of the Earth. The warm Earth surface then **radiates** some of this energy as **longer wavelength infrared** radiation which is **absorbed** by molecules such as carbon dioxide and water vapour in the lower atmosphere.

● **Examiner's hint:** Avoid using journalistic terms such as 'bounce off' or 'reflect' when talking about the greenhouse effect.

A covalent bond is like a spring in that it vibrates at a natural frequency. When infrared radiation has the same frequency as a covalent bond, the molecule absorbs the radiation and the bonds increase their vibrations. This makes the air warmer causing the air itself to radiate heat in turn. Some of this radiation is **re-radiated** back to the Earth's surface and some is re-radiated back into space. This natural process is called the **greenhouse effect** because the Sun's energy is trapped in a way that is similar to the way light energy is trapped by glass in a greenhouse. The glass lets light energy in but does not let heat energy out.

Figure 16.9 The greenhouse effect is a process by which the Earth warms up. The surface of the Earth absorbs some solar radiation (⟶), and re-radiates some at a longer (infrared, IR) wavelength (⟶), which can be absorbed and re-radiated by gases such as carbon dioxide in the atmosphere.

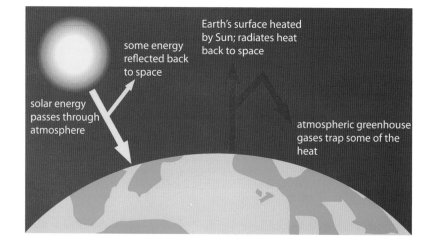

solar energy passes through atmosphere

some energy reflected back to space

Earth's surface heated by Sun; radiates heat back to space

atmospheric greenhouse gases trap some of the heat

The Mauna Loa Observatory monitors all atmospheric constituents that may contribute to climatic change, such as greenhouse gases and aerosols and those which cause depletion of the ozone layer.

Greenhouse gases and their sources

The greenhouse effect occurs naturally but there are concerns that human activities may be increasing its effect, leading to global warming. Water is the main greenhouse gas owing to its great abundance, but as it is produced from natural processes its contribution to global warming is generally not considered. The levels of carbon dioxide produced from burning fossil fuels has been increasing steadily over the last 150 years. Levels of carbon dioxide have been measured at Mauna Loa in Hawaii since the International Geophysical Year in 1957.

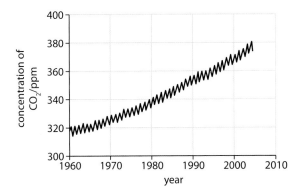

Figure 16.10 Graph showing the rising concentration of atmospheric CO_2 between 1958–2005 measured 4170 m up on Mauna Loa, Hawaii. The graph reveals the steady rise of CO_2 levels in the atmosphere each year owing to increasing fossil fuel consumption. The regular wobbles reflect seasonal plant growth in the spring and decay in the autumn in the northern hemisphere each year.

Exercise

10 (a) Suggest why the first measurements of CO_2 levels were taken at Mauna Loa in Hawaii and at the South pole.

(b) In 1959 the concentration of carbon dioxide was 316 ppm. In 2007 the reading was 384 ppm. Calculate the percentage increase in CO_2 levels between 1959 and 2007.

(c) Identify the major source of the increased CO_2 during this period.

(d) Explain the annual fluctuations in carbon dioxide levels.

(e) Identify two different means by which CO_2 can be removed from the atmosphere naturally and give a balanced equation for both of these.

(f) Suggest how the depletion of tropical forests can lead to an increase in carbon dioxide levels.

(g) Describe how CO_2 interacts with infrared radiation on the molecular level.

Investigate trends in carbon dioxide levels using data from Mauna Loa.
Now go to www.heinemann.co.uk/hotlinks, insert the express code 4259P and click on this activity.

The increase in levels of carbon dioxide can be compared to changes in average global temperatures during the same period. It is estimated that carbon dioxide contributes about 50% to global warming.

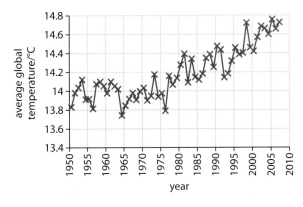

Figure 16.11 Global average temperatures from 1950 to 2007.

Not all gases are equally effective at absorbing infrared radiation. The ability to absorb infrared depends on the change in dipole moment that occurs as a molecule vibrates. Symmetric non-polar diatomic molecules such as N_2 and O_2 are not greenhouse gases as they do not absorb infrared radiation. The ability of a gas to absorb infrared is quantified by what is known as the **greenhouse factor**, which compares the ability of a substance to absorb infrared to carbon dioxide. Ten molecules of water, for example, have the same global warming effect as one molecule of carbon dioxide, and one molecule of methane has the same effect as 30 molecules of carbon dioxide. The chlorofluorocarbons have very high greenhouse factors, but are present in the atmosphere in relatively low amounts. They contribute about 14% to global warming.

Gas	Main source	Greenhouse factor	Relative abundance/%	Overall contribution to increased global warming/%
water (H_2O)	evaporation of oceans and lakes	0.1	0.10	–
carbon dioxide (CO_2)	increased levels owing to combustion of fossil fuels and biomass	1	0.036	50
methane (CH_4)	anaerobic decay of organic matter; increased levels caused by intensive farming	30	0.0017	18
CFCs (e.g. CCl_2F_2)	refrigerants, pollutants, foaming agents, solvents	≈20 000	≈0.000 01	14
ozone (O_3)	secondary pollutants in photochemical smog	2000	0.000 004	12
dinitrogen oxide (N_2O)	increased levels owing to artificial fertilizers and combustion of biomass	160	0.0003	6
sulfur hexafluoride (SF_6)	used as an insulator in the electrical industry	22 000	very low	0.05

How do greenhouse gases change the climate? See how the Earth's temperature changes with time.

Now go to www.heinemann.co.uk/hotlinks, insert the express code 4259P and click on this activity.

The rising levels of methane are linked to the world's population growth. More people need more food, which has increased the levels of intensive farming. Similarly the levels of dinitrogen oxides are increasing because of the use of nitrogen-based fertilizers.

Since 1850, glaciers have been in retreat worldwide. It is thought that global warming has accelerated this trend in recent years.

Influence of increasing amounts of greenhouse gases on the atmosphere

There is now little doubt that since the 19th century the amount of carbon dioxide and other anthropogenic greenhouse gases in the atmosphere have increased dramatically and the average temperature of the world has also increased, even if rather erratically. It has been suggested that the levels of carbon dioxide will double in about 100 years. Allowing for the effect of all the gases the temperature of the Earth could rise by 2 °C within 50 years. There are two likely effects of this:

- changes in agriculture and biodistribution as the climate changes
- rising sea-levels owing to thermal expansion and the melting of polar ice caps and glaciers.

Influence of particulates on the Earth's surface temperature

As we can see the pattern in global temperatures is complicated. The fall in temperatures during the 1960s, for example, has been linked to the increase in particulates produced by volcanic activity during this period. Particulates can lower the temperature by scattering light so that less radiation reaches the Earth.

Exercise

11 (a) Carbon dioxide contributes to the greenhouse effect. Give one natural source of this gas.

(b) Name a second carbon-containing greenhouse gas and state its source.

(c) Identify an air pollutant that counteracts the greenhouse effect and describe how it achieves this.

(d) Using carbon dioxide as an example, explain how greenhouse gases contribute to global warming.

(e) Describe the effects of global warming.

See an interview with the Nobel Laureate Professor Paul Crutzen. He talks about the greenhouse effect and his recent work on nuclear winter.

Now go to www.heinemann.co.uk/hotlinks, insert the express code 4259P and click on this activity.

The 2007 Nobel Peace prize was awarded to the Intergovernmental Panel on Climate Change and Al Gore. Hear a telephone interview with Rajendra Pachauri, Chairman of the IPCC following the announcement of the award.

Now go to www.heinemann.co.uk/hotlinks, insert the express code 4259P and click on this activity.

● **Examiner's hint:** When describing the greenhouse effect, do not base the whole of your answer only on rising sea levels and their causes. The effects on climate, agriculture and biodiversity and so on should also be included.

E.4 Ozone depletion

The layer of gas tens of kilometres above our heads is an essential part of the 'life support system' of our planet. The Earth is unique among the planets in having an atmosphere that is chemically active and rich in oxygen. Oxygen is present in two forms, normal oxygen O_2 and ozone O_3, and both forms play a key role in protecting life on the Earth's surface from harmful ultraviolet (UV) radiation. They form a protective screen which ensures that radiation that reaches the surface of the Earth is different from that emitted by the sun.

The structures of the different forms of oxygen are shown in the table.

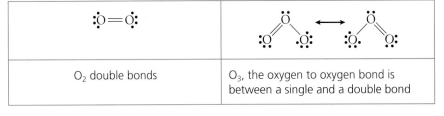

O_2 double bonds	O_3, the oxygen to oxygen bond is between a single and a double bond

Ozone is unusual in that it cannot be accurately represented by one Lewis structure. Experimental techniques for determining molecular structure show that the molecule is made up from two identical bonds, lying somewhere between a single and a double bond. The oxygen to oxygen bond in ozone is weaker than the double bond in O_2.

The natural formation and depletion of ozone

The temperature of the atmosphere generally decreases with height but at 12 km above the Earth's surface the temperature starts to rise because ultraviolet radiation is absorbed in a number of photochemical reactions. This part of the atmosphere is called the **stratosphere**.

Some people question the reality of climate change and question the motives of scientists who have 'exaggerated' the problem. How do we assess the evidence collected and the models used to predict the impact of human activities?

What effect does a highly sensitive political context have on objectivity? Can politicians exploit the ambiguity of conclusions coming from the scientific community for their own ends?

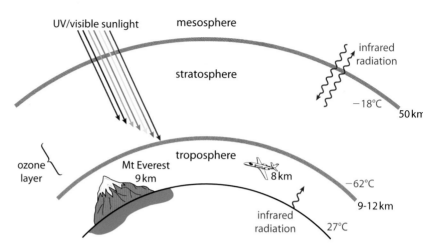

Regions of the atmosphere

In the stratosphere, the strong covalent double bond in normal oxygen O_2 is broken by high energy UV radiation to form two oxygen atoms:

$$O_2(g) \xrightarrow{\text{UV light}} O^{\bullet}(g) + O^{\bullet}(g)\,(\text{atomic oxygen})$$

The oxygen atoms have unpaired electrons. They are reactive **free radicals** and so react with another oxygen molecule to form ozone.

$$O^{\bullet}(g) + O_2(g) \rightarrow O_3(g)$$

This second step is *exothermic* and the energy given out raises the temperature of the stratosphere.

The bonds in ozone are weaker than the double bond in oxygen so ultraviolet light of lower energy is needed to break these bonds:

$$O_3(g) \xrightarrow{\text{UV light}} O^{\bullet}(g) + O_2(g)$$

The oxygen atoms then react with another ozone molecule to form two oxygen molecules.

$$O_3(g) + O^{\bullet}(g) \rightarrow 2O_2(g)$$

This is another exothermic reaction which produces heat and which maintains the relatively high temperature of the stratosphere. The level of ozone in the stratosphere – less than 10 ppm – stays at a constant level if the rate of formation of ozone is balanced by its rate of removal. This is known as a **steady state**. The whole process is described by the Chapman Cycle.

Step 1
$$O_2 \xrightarrow[\text{high energy UV}]{} 2O^{\bullet}$$

Step 2
$$O^{\bullet} + O_2 \underset{\substack{\text{Step 3} \\ \text{lower energy UV}}}{\overset{}{\rightleftarrows}} O_3$$

Step 4
$$O_3 + O^{\bullet} \xrightarrow{\text{(slow)}} 2O_2$$

This cycle of reactions is significant because dangerous ultraviolet light has been absorbed and the stratosphere has become warmer. Both these processes are essential for the survival of life on Earth.

Depletion of ozone by anthropogenic sources

Measurements of the concentration of ozone in the stratosphere have shown that the amount of ozone in the ozone layer has been decreasing, particularly over both the north and south poles.

Some pollutants, for example the **nitrogen oxides** and **chlorofluorocarbons (CFCs)**, act as catalysts for the decomposition of ozone to oxygen. For example, with nitrogen monoxide:

$$NO^{\bullet}(g) + O_3(g) \rightarrow NO_2^{\bullet}(g) + O_2(g)$$
$$NO_2^{\bullet}(g) + O(g) \rightarrow NO^{\bullet}(g) + O_2(g)$$

The nitrogen monoxide is acting as a catalyst because it is regenerated during the reaction. The sources of nitrogen monoxide were discussed earlier. Jet aircraft inject nitrogen oxides directly into the ozone layer owing to the direct combination of nitrogen and oxygen in the engine.

Since their discovery in the 1930s, there has been a build up of chlorofluorocarbons in the atmosphere and a mirror-image fall in high level altitudes of ozone concentrations. CFCs were used in aerosols, refrigerants, solvents, foaming agents and plastics as they have low reactivity, low flammability and low toxicity. Although they remain inert in the troposphere, they eventually diffuse into the stratosphere, where they are exposed to more high-energy UV radiation. Under such conditions, photochemical decomposition occurs producing reactive chlorine atoms. For example, with dichlorodifluoromethane CCl_2F_2 otherwise known as Freon:

$$CCl_2F_2(g) \rightarrow CClF_2^{\bullet}(g) + Cl^{\bullet}(g)$$

The weaker C–Cl bond breaks in preference to the C–F bond. The $Cl^{\bullet}$ atoms are free radicals and catalyse the decomposition of ozone in a similar way to nitrogen monoxide:

$$Cl^{\bullet}(g) + O_3(g) \rightarrow O_2(g) + ClO^{\bullet}(g)$$
$$ClO^{\bullet}(g) + O^{\bullet}(g) \rightarrow O_2(g) + Cl^{\bullet}(g)$$

The net effect of these steps is that one molecule of ozone reacts with one oxygen atom:

$$O_3(g) + O^{\bullet}(g) \rightarrow 2O_2(g)$$

As $Cl^{\bullet}$ atoms are regenerated, many thousands of ozone molecules can be destroyed by one $Cl^{\bullet}$ atom. CFCs, as discussed earlier, are also greenhouse gases.

Technician releasing a balloon to measure stratospheric ozone over the Arctic. This research was part of a joint project by NASA and the European Union to look at the amount and rate of stratospheric ozone depletion.

● **Examiner's hint:** CFCs cause the depletion of the ozone and they are greenhouse gases. Many students confuse the issues of global warming with those of ozone depletion.

Paul J. Crutzen (born 1933), Dutch chemist, holding a sheet showing the reaction of nitrogen oxides with ozone. Crutzen received the Nobel Prize in Chemistry in 1995 with Mario Molina and F. Sherwood Rowland for their work on atmospheric chemistry, particularly the formation and decomposition of ozone.

See an interview with the Nobel Laureate Professor F. Sherwood Rowland. He talks about his work on CFCs, his interest in environmental issues and the problem of global warming.

Now go to www.heinemann.co.uk/hotlinks, insert the express code 4259P and click on this activity.

Exercise

12 (a) Describe the molecular structure of ozone.

(b) Explain what is meant by the 'ozone layer'.

(c) Describe the formation and depletion of ozone in the ozone layer by natural processes using equations to describe all the reactions.

(d) Outline ways in which ozone levels are being decreased owing to human activities, using equations to support your answer.

(e) Explain how small amounts of human-produced substances can have major effects on the ozone layer.

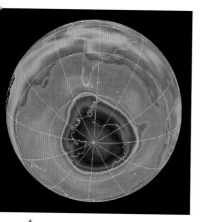

Satellite map showing a severe depletion or 'hole' in the ozone layer over Antarctica on October 3rd, 1990.

Phytoplankton bloom in the Bay of Biscay. The ozone layer protects marine life from harmful UV radiation.

Environmental impact of ozone depletion

The ozone layer protects the surface of the Earth from dangerous high-energy UV radiation, which can excite electrons and break bonds in biologically important molecules such as DNA and alter their properties. UV radiation induces skin cancer when genetic information is affected and can also cause eye problems such as cataracts and blindness. UV radiation can damage plant cells. This inhibits growth and photosynthesis and makes plants more susceptible to disease. UV radiation can also cause damage to life in the oceans: the larvae of fish, shrimp and crab and plankton near the surface are particularly affected, but the effects can be more far reaching. Zooplankton (tiny animals) and phytoplankton (tiny plants) are at the bottom of the marine food chain, and phytoplankton reduce levels of carbon dioxide and produce oxygen by photosynthesis. Any effects at this level can have a profound effect on the marine ecosystem. There is less food and oxygen available and the sea is less able to absorb carbon dioxide.

Alternatives to CFCs for the future

CFCs were used in aerosol cans, refrigerators, solvents and as blowing agents in plastics until the *Montreal Protocol* in 1987 decreed that the use of CFCs should be phased out. They are expected, however, to remain in the atmosphere during the next century because of their low reactivity. Fortunately, chemists have been able to use their knowledge of molecular structure to synthesize possible replacements. These must have similar properties, including low reactivity, but should not produce free radicals when exposed to UV light. The main problem with CFCs is the C–Cl bond, so replacements generally have fewer C–Cl bonds. Possible candidates include:

Three cans of (from left to right) car paint, furniture polish and an anti-oxidant are all free from CFCs. Various symbols conveying the CFC-free nature of these products are displayed.

- Hydrocarbons such as propane, C_3H_8 and 2-methylpropane ($CH_3CH(CH_3)CH_3$) are used as refrigerant coolants. The presence of a hydrogen atom in the place of a chlorine atom makes these compounds decompose less easily since the C–H bond is stronger than the C–Cl bond. They are, however, flammable.
- Fluorocarbons are not flammable and the very strong C–F bond makes them stable to ultraviolet radiation so they cannot catalyse ozone depletion.
- Hydrochlorofluorocarbons (HCFCs) contain hydrogen, chlorine, fluorine and carbon atoms in their molecules. Although they contain C–Cl bonds, most molecules are destroyed in the lower atmosphere before reaching the stratospheric ozone layer. They are 20 times less destructive than CFCs.
- Hydrofluorocarbons (HFCs), without any chlorine atoms, are considered the best alternative as they are not flammable. One such example is CF_3CH_2F, 1,1,1,2-tetrafluoroethane.

Unfortunately all these options are greenhouse gases and so may contribute to global warming.

Substance	Flammable	Toxicity
CCl_2F_2	no	moderate
$CH_3CH(CH_3)CH_3$	yes	high
CF_4	no	no known toxicological effects
$CHClF_2$	no	moderate
CF_3CH_2F	no	low

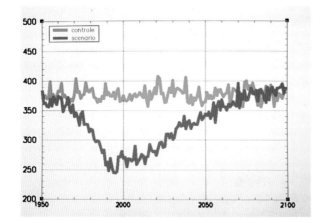

Forecast of the recovery in average ozone levels in the ozone layer above the Antarctic. The graph shows ozone levels (pink) returning to their 1950 level by 2100. The normal level is shown in green.

Exercise

13 (a) Discuss the environmental effects of rapid depletion of the ozone layer.
  (b) Discuss the relative advantages and disadvantages of using dichlorodifluoromethane (CHF_2Cl) and 2-methylpropane ($CH_3CH(CH_3)CH_3$) as alternatives to CFCs.

E.5 Dissolved oxygen in water

The survival of aquatic life depends on the dissolved gases such as carbon dioxide and oxygen. Most aquatic plants and animals require oxygen for aerobic respiration, and microorganisms consume oxygen when they decompose organic material. The **dissolved oxygen** content of water is one of the most important indicators of its quality. The lowest concentration of oxygen required for fish to survive is 0.003 g dm^{-3}, which compares with a maximum solubility of 0.009 g dm^{-3}. The non-polar oxygen molecule has a low solubility in the polar water solvent.

The level of organic pollution in water can be measured by the **biological oxygen demand (BOD)**. This is the amount of oxygen (in ppm) needed by bacteria to decompose the organic matter aerobically in a fixed volume of water over a set period of time, usually five days. The greater the quantity of degradable organic waste, the higher the BOD.

> The BOD is the quantity of oxygen needed to oxidize organic matter in a sample of water over a five-day period at a specified temperature.

Typical BOD values for samples of water of different quality are shown below.

BOD/ppm	Quality of water
<1	almost pure water
5	doubtful purity
10	unacceptable quality
100 to 400	waste from untreated sewage
100 to 10 000	waste water from meat-processing plant

> 1 ppm = 1 g of pollutant in 1 000 000 g of water.

Microorganisms such as bacteria need oxygen to metabolize the organic matter that constitutes their food. Organic carbon is oxidized to carbon dioxide, organic hydrogen to water and organic nitrogen to soluble nitrates. Phosphates and sulfates can also be produced by the oxidation of sulfur and phosphorus-containing compounds. Fish and other freshwater aquatic life cannot survive when the BOD is greater than the oxygen content. Fast flowing streams and rivers are generally less polluted because the oxygen levels are regenerated. The moving water allows oxygen from the atmosphere to dissolve in the water. Pollution is a particular problem in static bodies of water such as lakes which have only limited re-oxygenation.

The BOD can be measured by saturating the water sample with oxygen so that its concentration is known at 0.009 g dm^{-3}. The sample is then left at 25 °C for five days. This allows the bacteria time to use some of the dissolved oxygen to decompose any organic material in the water. The oxygen remaining is measured using a redox titration called the **Winkler method**.

Worked example

A 500 cm³ sample of water was saturated with oxygen and left for five days. The final oxygen content was measured using the following sequence of reactions:

$$2Mn^{2+}(aq) + 4OH^-(aq) + O_2(g) \rightarrow 2MnO_2(s) + 2H_2O(l) \quad (I)$$

$$MnO_2(s) + 2I^-(aq) + 4H^+(aq) \rightarrow Mn^{2+}(aq) + I_2(aq) + 2H_2O(l) \quad (II)$$

$$I_2(aq) + 2S_2O_3^{2-}(aq) \rightarrow S_4O_6^{2-}(aq) + 2I^-(aq) \quad (III)$$

It was found that 5.00 cm³ of a 0.0500 mol dm⁻³ solution of $Na_2S_2O_3(aq)$ was required to react with the iodine produced.

(a) Calculate how many moles of $Na_2S_2O_3(aq)$ reacted with the iodine in reaction (III).

(b) Deduce how many moles of iodine had been produced in reaction (II).

(c) Deduce how many moles of $MnO_2(s)$ had been produced in reaction (I).

(d) Deduce how many moles of $O_2(g)$ were present in the water.

(e) Calculate the solubility of oxygen in the water in g dm⁻³.

(f) Assume the maximum solubility of the water is 0.009 g dm⁻³ and deduce the BOD of the water sample.

Solution

(a) Amount of $Na_2S_2O_3(aq)$ = 5.00 × 0.0500/1000
    = 2.50 × 10⁻⁴ moles

(b) Amount of $I_2(aq)$ = ½(2.50 × 10⁻⁴ moles)
    = 1.25 × 10⁻⁴ moles

(c) Amount of $MnO_2(s)$ = 1.25 × 10⁻⁴ moles

(d) Amount of $O_2(g)$ = ½(1.25 × 10⁻⁴) moles
    = 0.0000625 moles

(e) Amount of $O_2(g)$ in 1 dm³ = 1.25 × 10⁻⁴ moles
    Mass in 1 dm³ = 0.004 g dm⁻³

(f) Oxygen used by bacteria (BOD) = 0.009 – 0.004 g dm⁻³
    = 0.005 g dm⁻³.

Aerobic and anaerobic decomposition

The production of foul smells is a symptom of water pollution, as it is a clear indication that anaerobic processes are occurring owing to an excess amount of oxygen-demanding waste. Under such conditions the elements in the organic compound are reduced rather than oxidized. Sulfur compounds, for example, are reduced to hydrogen sulfide which has a smell of rotten eggs. The table below contrasts the products of aerobic and anaerobic processes.

Element	Aerobic decay product	Anaerobic decay product
carbon	CO_2	CH_4
hydrogen	H_2O	CH_4, NH_3, H_2S and H_2O
oxygen	H_2O	H_2O
nitrogen	NO_3^-	NH_3 and amines
sulfur	SO_4^{2-}	H_2S
phosphorus	PO_4^{3-}	PH_3

Exercises

14 A stream contains 20 ppm by mass of an organic material which can be represented by $C_6H_{12}O_6$.
  (a) Calculate the mass of organic matter that is dissolved in 1 dm³ of the water.
  (b) Deduce the mass of oxygen needed to oxidize this organic matter.
  (c) Explain the presence of reduced products such as methane in the water.

15 The graph below represents the concentration of dissolved oxygen and the BOD level of a river at several distances from a meat processing plant.

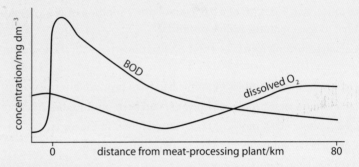

  (a) Identify the class of compounds from the meat-processing plant which could be responsible for the increase in BOD.
  (b) Explain the change in dissolved oxygen concentration from 0 to 30 km from the meat-processing plant.
  (c) Explain the change in oxygen concentration from 40 to 80 km.
  (d) Suggest the distances from the meat-processing plant where anaerobic decomposition will occur.

Fish killed owing to a lack of oxygen in water caused by river pollution. ▶

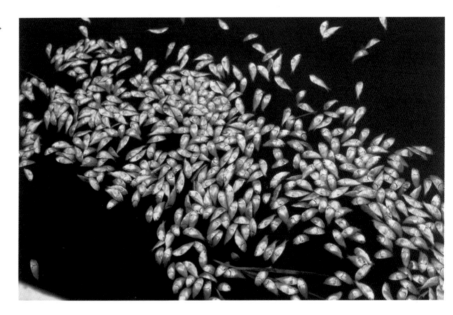

Eutrophication

The BOD of water can also increase as a result of the addition of extra nutrients such as nitrates and phosphates to the water. These ions promote excessive growth of plants and algae. The nitrate ion promotes plant growth through protein synthesis, as nitrogen is needed for amino acids and proteins and the phosphate ion is used in the storage and transfer of energy. This excessive addition of nutrients is known as **eutrophication**. When the algae die, owing to the limited oxygen available, the subsequent decay leads to a further increase in the amount of nutrients and the oxygen concentrations fall to levels which are insufficient for aerobic decomposition to take place. Anaerobic bacteria take over and produce gases such as ammonia and hydrogen sulfide which create unpleasant smells and poison the water. This will cause deaths and the process continues until there is no life remaining in the water.

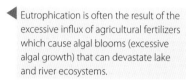 The word eutrophication derives from the Greek for 'well nourished'.

◀ Eutrophication is often the result of the excessive influx of agricultural fertilizers which cause algal blooms (excessive algal growth) that can devastate lake and river ecosystems.

The main contributors to eutrophication are artificial fertilizers used in intensive farming, which contain both the nitrate and phosphate ions, and detergents which contain phosphates. Nitrate ions can also enter water systems as nitric acid in acid rain. Phosphates can be removed from the water by reaction with Ca^{2+} or Al^{3+} ions to produce insoluble compounds:

$$3Ca^{2+}(aq) + 2PO_4^{3-}(aq) \rightarrow Ca_3(PO_4)_2(s)$$
$$Al^{3+}(aq) + PO_4^{3-}(aq) \rightarrow AlPO_4(s)$$

All nitrates are soluble and so they are more difficult to remove. Expensive **tertiary methods** such as **ion exchange** or **reverse osmosis**, which are discussed later in the chapter, must be used.

Thermal pollution

The discussion so far has focussed on the addition of unwanted substances to the environment. One important use of water is as a cooling agent, an application which results in the addition of heat to water systems. Water, removed from rivers in power stations, can be returned with a temperature increase of up to 20 °C. This is known as **thermal pollution**. The concentration of oxygen decreases with rising temperature and this has a number of harmful effects.

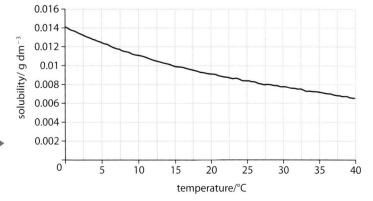

Figure 16.13 The solubility of oxygen at different temperatures. ▶

The oxygen concentration of the water may be insufficient for fish to survive. The metabolic rate of organisms increases with temperature and this places an additional demand on the oxygen in the water. If there is a large temperature change, biochemical processes may be so upset that organisms die.

The spawning, fertilization and hatching of eggs is very sensitive to temperature and unseasonable temperatures will upset life cycles.

Thermal pollution of water can be reduced by trickling water through a porous material and blowing air in the opposite direction. The heat is transferred to the air where its effects are less damaging.

Exercise

16 In order to survive, fish require water containing dissolved oxygen. Discuss briefly how an increase in each of the following factors affects the amount of dissolved oxygen in a lake:

(a) temperature

(b) organic pollutants

(c) nitrates and phosphates.

E.6 Water treatment

Primary pollutants in waste water and their sources

The source of organic nitrates and phosphates present in polluted water and some of their effects were discussed earlier. There is evidence that excessive nitrate levels can interact with haemoglobin and affect oxygen transport particularly in young babies. The low acidity of a young baby's stomach allows bacteria to exist, which reduce the nitrate(V) ion (NO_3^-) to the nitrate(III) ion (NO_2^-). This ion decreases the oxygen-carrying capacity of haemoglobin by oxidizing the Fe^{2+} to Fe^{3+} to form **methaemoglobin** which is not able to transport oxygen. In extreme and very rare cases, the baby turns blue owing to lack of oxygen, a condition known as **blue baby syndrome**. Nitrates are also a possible cause of stomach cancer in adults. Nitrates, NO_3^-, are converted to nitrites NO_2^-, which can then combine with amines from proteins to form other nitrogen compounds known as nitrosoamines which are carcinogenic.

$$HNO_2 + R_2NH \rightarrow R_2N\text{--}N{=}O + H_2O$$
$$\text{amine} \quad \text{nitrosamine}$$

Heavy metals

Heavy metals are serious water pollutants as they are poisonous. The heavy metal ions mercury, lead and cadmium interfere with the behaviour of other necessary ions in the body such as Ca^{2+}, Mg^{2+} or Zn^{2+}. Even very small traces of heavy metals can have very significant harmful effects.

The sources of each of these pollutants and their possible health and environmental hazards are summarized in the following table.

	Mercury	Lead	Cadmium
Source	paints, batteries and agriculture	lead paints, lead pipes and lead glazes on glasses and pottery and the use of tetraethyl lead in petrol	metal plating, rechargeable batteries, pigments; by-product of zinc refining
Health hazard	considered to be the most dangerous of the metal pollutants; causes serious damage to the nerves and the brain; symptoms of mercury poisoning are those resulting from damage to the nervous system: depression, irritability, blindness and insanity; Minamata disease	burning pains in the mouth and digestive system followed by constipation or diarrhoea; in severe cases there is a failure of the kidneys, liver and heart which can lead to coma and death; can cause brain damage, particularly in young children	as cadmium is in the same group as zinc it is able to replace zinc in the enzyme system, making them ineffective; Itai-Itai disease which makes bones brittle and easily broken; and kidney and lung cancer in humans
Environmental hazard	reproductive system failure in fish; inhibits growth and kills fish; biological magnification in the food chain	toxic to plants and domestic animals; biological magnification in the food chain	toxic to fish and produces birth defects in mice

Pesticides

Pesticides include insecticides, which kill insects, fungicides, which kill fungi, and herbicides, which kill weeds. As they are poisonous they can cause pollution problems when they are washed off land into water.

An example is DDT, derived from the old and imprecise name **d**ichloro-**d**iphenyl-**t**richloroethane. The structure of DDT is shown.

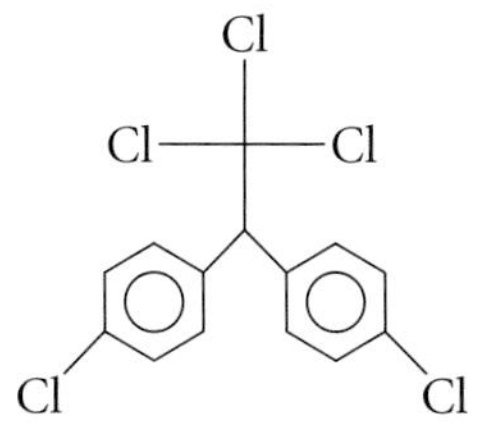

Although DDT is introduced into the environment at low levels which are harmless to birds and animals (including man), its use can have serious consequences. DDT is very stable and fat soluble and so remains in food chains allowing toxic levels to build up over a period of time in animals at the top of these food chains. This mechanism of accumulation is called **biological magnification**. DDT has been banned in many countries as it has had disastrous effects on bird life.

Dioxins

Dioxins is the general name for a range of compounds whose framework consists of two benzene rings connected via one or two oxygen atoms. Each benzene ring can have up to four chlorine atoms. The structure of dioxin is shown here. It is 10 000 times more poisonous than the cyanide ion.

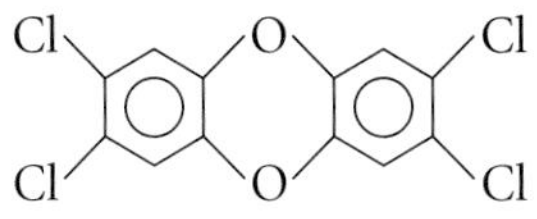

Dioxins are added to the environment when waste materials containing organochloro compounds are incinerated. There are also traces of dioxins in some weed killers (herbicides).

Dioxin persists in fat and liver cells. Symptoms are cirrhosis of the liver, damage to heart and memory, and concentration problems and depression. The skin disease **chloracne** is a result of the body attempting to remove the poison through the skin. Dioxin can cause malfunctions in fetuses. It was one of the herbicides present in Agent Orange during the Vietnam war.

Environmentalists investigating dioxin contamination of soil at Times Beach, Missouri.

Polychlorinated biphenyls (PCBs)

The polychlorinated biphenyls have a high electrical resistance and so are used in electrical transformers and capacitors. The structure is shown here. They contain a number of chlorine atoms attached to two connected benzene rings (biphenyl).

They persist in the environment and accumulate in fatty tissue. They reduce reproductive efficiency, impair learning in children and are thought to be carcinogenic.

Waste-water treatment

The purpose of waste-water treatment is to remove hazardous materials, reduce the BOD (biological oxygen demand) and kill microorganisms prior to discharge. Different types of treatment with different levels of effectiveness are carried out in the world, depending on the availability of resources, since the cost increases with more advanced treatment.

In some parts of the world, waste water can be discharged untreated into rivers or the sea, where it is eventually decomposed by microorganisms. Septic tanks or cess pits are used in some areas. The waste is broken down by bacteria and then the water is allowed to pass into the ground. Water treatment methods are classified as **primary, secondary** or **tertiary** methods. Each stage of treatment reduces the level of the pollution and thus the BOD.

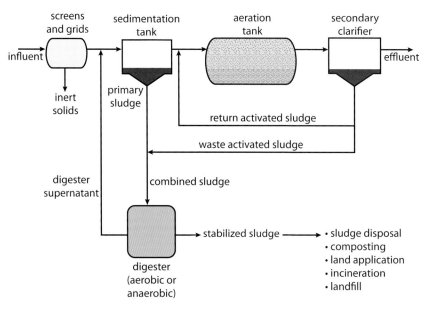

Figure 16.14 Primary and secondary treatment of water.

The purification of water includes both physical and chemical treatment.

Primary methods

In primary treatment, the waste water is first passed through screens and grids which filter out large **insoluble solid** objects and remove floating objects from the surface such as grease. The water is then passed into a sedimentation tank where it is allowed to settle. The resulting **sludge** is removed from the bottom. The mechanical process of sedimentation can be speeded up by adding chemicals which allow suspended particles to join together to form large clumps. This process is called **flocculation**.

Large clumps or **flocs** are formed by the addition of aluminium sulfate and calcium hydroxide into the water which form a precipitate of aluminium hydroxide:

$$Al_2(SO_4)_3(aq) + 3Ca(OH)_2(aq) \rightarrow 2Al(OH)_3(s) + 3CaSO_4(s)$$

Primary treatment is generally not sufficient to improve the quality of water to safe levels. A typical primary treatment domestic sewage plant can remove about 30–40% of the BOD waste. Secondary treatment is essential to reduce BOD levels further.

Secondary methods

Secondary sewage treatment involves bacterial activity and requires aeration in which large blowers are used to bubble air, or air enriched with oxygen, through waste water, mixed with bacteria-laden sludge. This allows aerobic bacteria to mix thoroughly with the sewage, to oxidize and break down most of the organic matter. The process is thus biological in nature and is called the **activated sludge process**. The water, containing decomposed suspended particles, is passed through a sedimentation tank where large quantities of biologically active sludge collect. Part of this is recycled and the rest has to be disposed of. Secondary sewage treatment can remove most (about 90%) of organic oxygen-demanding wastes and suspended particles.

Primary and secondary treatments cannot remove dissolved inorganic substances such as nitrates, phosphates and heavy metal ions, which require further tertiary treatment.

A rotary-sweeping 'trickling filter' skims lightweight solids from waste water over a bed of aerobic bacteria ('zoological slime') in a settling tank at a water treatment plant.

Tertiary sewage treatment

Precipitation

Tertiary sewage treatment involves specialized chemical, biological or physical processes which treat the water further after it has undergone primary and secondary treatments to remove the remaining organic materials and inorganic substances such as toxic metal ions and nitrate and phosphate ions. Heavy metal ions such as cadmium, lead and mercury can easily be removed by **precipitation** as sulfide salts, as their solubility in water is very low. Carefully controlled amounts of hydrogen sulfide gas are bubbled through a solution containing heavy metal ions, which are precipitated as sulfides which can then be removed by filtration. For example for cadmium ions:

$$Cd^{2+}(aq) + H_2S(g) \rightarrow CdS(s) + 2H^+(aq)$$

The excess hydrogen sulfide (being acidic) can then be easily removed.

The presence of phosphate ions can be decreased to very low levels by the addition of calcium or aluminium ions:

$$3Ca^{2+}(aq) + 2PO_4^{3-}(aq) \rightarrow Ca_3(PO_4)_2(s)$$

$$Al^{3+}(aq) + PO_4^{3-}(aq) \rightarrow AlPO_4(s)$$

Ion exchange

The nitrates are all soluble and so are more difficult to remove. Resins or zeolites can be used to exchange the nitrate ions in polluted water with hydroxide ions. Positive ions can also be exchanged with H^+ ions:

$$X-OH^-(\text{ion exchange}) + NO_3^-(aq) \rightarrow X-NO_3^-(\text{ion exchange}) + OH^-(aq)$$

$$Y-H^+(\text{ion exchange}) + M^+(aq) \rightarrow Y-M^+(\text{ion exchange}) + H^+(aq)$$

The H^+ and OH^- ions can then combine to form water:

$$H^+(aq) + OH^-(aq) \rightarrow H_2O(l)$$

The ion exchange resin can also be used to remove salt from sea water to make it fit to drink.

$$X–OH^-(\text{ion exchange}) + Cl^-(aq) \rightarrow X–Cl^-(\text{ion exchange}) + OH^-(aq)$$

$$Y–H^+(\text{ion exchange}) + Na^+(aq) \rightarrow Y–Na^+(\text{ion exchange}) + H^+(aq)$$

The method is very expensive for large volumes of water as the ion exchange resins and zeolites need to be regenerated.

Biological methods

Nitrate ions can also be removed by biological methods. Anaerobic organisms (denitrifying bacteria) turn the nitrogen in nitrates back to atmospheric nitrogen, N_2. Algae ponds can also be used to remove the nitrate ions which they use as nutrients, as discussed earlier.

Activated carbon bed method

Activated carbon consists of tiny carbon granules with a large surface area which have been treated and activated by high temperatures. They are able to adsorb organic chemicals readily from the waste water. Carbon beds are effective against many toxic organic materials and charcoal filters are often used to purify tap water for drinking purposes. The carbon can be reactivated by heating to a high temperature when the adsorbed organic matter is oxidized to carbon dioxide and water. The carbon surface is then available for reuse.

Distillation

Distillation can be used to obtain fresh water from sea water. The sea water is heated and then passed into an evacuated chamber where it boils, leaving dissolved compounds in solution. The steam is then passed through a condenser which is cooled by pipes containing more sea water The warm sea water is then heated and distilled in turn.

Reverse osmosis

Osmosis is the movement of water passing from a dilute to a concentrated solution through a **semi-permeable** membrane. A semi-permeable membrane allows the solvent but not the dissolved solutes to pass though it. This process can be reversed if a pressure of 70 atm (**the osmotic pressure**) is applied to the more concentrated salt solution. The water passes through the semi-permeable membrane and leaves the dissolved salts behind. The semi-permeable membrane must be able to withstand high pressures.

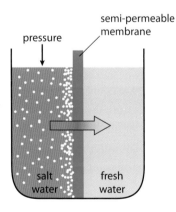

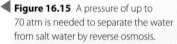
Figure 16.15 A pressure of up to 70 atm is needed to separate the water from salt water by reverse osmosis.

> **Osmosis is the movement of water from a dilute to a concentrated solution through a semi-permeable membrane. A semi-permeable membrane allows the solvent but not the dissolved solutes to pass though it.**

Chlorine and ozone treatment

The use of chlorine and ozone in water supplies has caused a dramatic fall in the number of deaths caused by bacteria. Chlorine is very effective in preventing the spread of waterborne infections such as typhoid fever. Chlorine remains in the water longer than ozone (has a higher retention time) and provides residual protection against pathogenic bacteria. It is not effective, however, against viruses. Chlorine can also chlorinate dissolved organic solvents to produce carcinogenic compounds. Ozone is more expensive than chlorine but it is more effective so less is needed. Unlike chlorine, however, ozone provides no residual protection against microorganisms. Ozone does, however, have the advantage that it kills viruses.

The advantages and disadvantages of treating water with chlorine and ozone are listed below:

Chlorine	Ozone
effective against bacteria but not against viruses	effective against both bacteria and viruses
cheaper to produce	more expensive
longer retention time	shorter retention time
can be easily liquefied and shipped	must be produced on the site because of high reactivity
can form toxic chloro-organic compounds	oxidized products are much less toxic
leaves a chemical taste behind	leaves no chemical taste behind
functions as a strong oxidizing agent	functions as a strong oxidizing agent

Exercise

17 (a) Name the type of substance removed by **filtration** and the equipment used to do this.
   (b) Many impurities in waste water are removed by secondary treatment. Describe how this is done.
   (c) State the name of the type of substance removed by **chemical precipitation** and a chemical used to do this.
   (d) List two different ways that ocean water could be converted into fresh water and outline on the molecular level how these methods work.

 Soil

All plants and land organisms depend on soil for their existence. It is formed by the biological, chemical and physical weathering of rock and is a mixture of inorganic and organic matter including air and water. Layers within the soil are called **horizons.** The top soil contains most of the living material and soil organic matter from the decomposition of dead organisms. The subsoil contains inorganic materials from the parent rock.

Different soils can be distinguished by their proportions of sand, silt and clay. These soil components have different particle sizes.

Soil component	Particle size/mm
gravel	2.000–60.000
sand	0.060–2.000
silt	0.006–0.060
clay	0.002–0.006

Soil provides plants with their only source of the macronutrients nitrogen, phosphorus, potassium, magnesium and sulfur. The elements carbon, hydrogen and oxygen are also available from the air. The dark colour of soil is due to the presence of **humus.** This decomposed organic matter is important to soil structure and acts as an important source of nutrients. The productivity of soil is affected by environmental conditions and pollution.

Soil degradation

Soil degradation occurs where human activity (either directly or indirectly) reduces the capacity of the soil to support life. Soil degradation can be caused by a variety of factors such as intensive farming, desertification, erosion and pollution. Acidification, salinity, nutrient depletion, chemical contamination and erosion are all forms of soil degradation. Soil degradation reduces crop production and there are considerable concerns about the current rate of soil degradation in some areas of the world.

Salinization

Salinization occurs when soils are irrigated continually. Irrigation waters contain dissolved salts, which are left behind in the soil after water evaporates. In poorly drained soils, the salts are not washed away and so begin to accumulate in the fertile topsoil. This can be observed as a whitish crust on the soil surface. Salinization is particularly acute in semi-arid areas where lots of irrigation water is used. Plants die in soil that is too salty, either directly when concentrations have reached toxic levels or indirectly by dehydration, as water cannot be taken up from the soil by the roots if the salt concentrations are too high. In some extreme cases, land is actually abandoned because it is too salty to farm profitably. The 'treatment' for salinization is to flush the soil with large volumes of water. This, however, can result in salinization of the rivers and groundwater.

Nutrient depletion

The nutrients and minerals needed for plants to grow are naturally returned to the soil when a plant dies and decomposes. This balance is upset when the crops are harvested and the nutrients removed from the soil with the plants. Primitive people raised crops until land lost its fertility, until it was realized that lost nutrients had to be replaced. In the past this was done by including legumes in crop rotations, adding manure or compost, or by ploughing the land to aerate the soil and then leaving it fallow to allow the soil time to renew itself. Legumes are host to nitrogen-fixing bacteria which use an enzyme, nitrogenase, to convert atmospheric nitrogen to ammonia. Nutrient depletion, however, can be a particular problem when land is farmed intensively. The nutrients can be replenished with the use of artificial fertilizers which provide plants with the missing nutrients, but their excessive use can have a serious environmental impact, as discussed earlier.

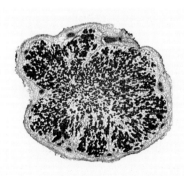
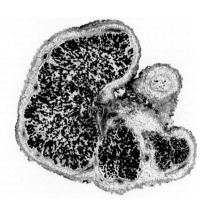

Light micrograph of sections through two root nodules from a broad bean plant. These root nodules are full of nitrogen-fixing bacteria.

This polluted soil is discoloured by chemical leachates from buried heavy metals and mine water.

Soil pollution

Soil pollution arises from a number of sources such as mining, the excessive use of agricultural chemicals and the improper disposal of toxic waste. A serious case of cadmium poisoning from mining, for example, occurred at Toyama in Japan in the 1950s. About 100 people died of Itai-Itai (Ouch-Ouch) disease which causes bones to become brittle and distorted.

Polluted soil contaminates plants, which in turn contaminate animals higher up in the food chain. Herbicides, insecticides and fungicides disrupt the food web, reduce the soil's biodiversity and ultimately ruin the soil. Frequently problems do not occur directly in the soil but in waterways where the pollutants are leached out of the soil. Acidic pollutants in the soil, for example from acid rain, can damage the growth of trees, as discussed earlier.

Soil organic matter

Soil organic matter, **SOM**, is the term generally used to represent the organic constituents of the soil. It includes plant and animal tissues, such as leaves, twigs and plant and animal parts, their partial decomposition products and the soil biomass. Although present as only about 5% of the mass, it plays a large role in determining the productivity of the soil. It is a source of food for microorganisms and plays an important role in maintaining soil structure. It is made up of high molecular mass organic materials, such as polysaccharides and proteins, and simpler substances, such as sugars, amino acids and other small molecules. The residue left after decomposition of organic material by bacteria is called **humus**. It takes about 400 years to make 1 cm of soil. Organic matter loosens the soil, which increases the amount of pore space. This has several important effects. The density of the soil is reduced and the soil structure improves. Soil particles stick together, forming aggregates or crumbs. As there is more pore space, the soil is able to hold more water and more air. Plants grown on healthy soils will not be as stressed by drought or excess water. Water also flows into the soil from the surface more quickly and it is also easier for plant roots to grow through the soil.

The lone pairs of electrons on the nitrogen atoms of protein molecules or the oxygen atoms of carboxyl of hydroxyl groups provide active sites which enable humus to bind to positive ions. Humic substances contain organic acids which can act as cation exchangers:

$$RCOOH(humus) + K^+(aq) \rightleftharpoons RCOOK(humus) + H^+(aq)$$

This exchange is reversible, the direction of reaction depending on the relative concentrations of the ions. This **cation exchange capacity (CEC)** allows humus to act as a time release capsule making nutrients available as they are needed. If potassium ions, for example, are taken out of solution by plants, the equilibrium will shift to the left and the humus will release more potassium ions back into the solution. Micronutrients are also prevented from being washed away by rain or during irrigation. This capacity to bind to metal ions allows humus to bind to toxic heavy metals, removing them from the wider ecosystem.

The presence of weak organic acids and their salts in humus allows it to act as a natural **buffer**:

$$RCOOH(humus) + H_2O(l) \rightleftharpoons RCOO^-(humus) + H_3O^+(aq)$$

A buffer resists changes in pH when small amounts of acid or alkali are added.

When the pH is low and the $H_3O^+(aq)$ concentration is high, the equilibrium moves from right to left. When the pH is high and the $H_3O^+(aq)$ concentration is low, the equilibrium moves from to left to right:

$$RCOOH(humus) + OH^-(aq) \rightleftharpoons RCOO^-(humus) + H_2O(aq)$$

Humus provides a source of energy and a source of the essential nutrient non-metal elements phosphorus, nitrogen and sulfur. As it has a dark colour, humus absorbs heat and this helps the soil to warm up during spring.

◀ Humus is a moist, rich organic substance formed from decaying plant matter. It provides an essential natural fertilizer for plants.

Exercise

18 The functions of SOM can be broadly classified into three groups: biological, physical and chemical. Give examples of the three different types of function.

The soil organic matter content depends on farming practices. Tillage reduces the organic matter in the soil, as oxygen is stirred into it, speeding up the action of soil microbes, which feed on organic matter. The more that the soil is tilled, the more organic matter is burned off. Plant residue is an important source of organic material. Crops that return little residue to the soil also lead to lower levels of organic matter. Historically, manure was present on most farms and used to keep up organic matter levels. As many farms no longer have livestock, this source of organic material is not available. Compost, manure or sewage sludge may add larger amounts of organic matter. Compost is very similar in composition to soil organic matter. It breaks down slowly in the soil and is very good at improving the physical condition of the soil. Manure and sludge may break down fairly quickly releasing nutrients for plant growth, but it may take longer to improve the soil using these materials. Conservation practices that protect the soil from erosion are important as they keep organic matter in place, although they will not add much organic matter to the soil.

Exercise

19 State two important functions of humus in the soil.

Organic soil pollutants

Humus has a strong affinity for organic compounds which have a low solubility in water. There are many different organic compounds which can pollute the soil and these tend to remain in the top layer of the soil as they are adsorbed by the humus. We have discussed petroleum hydrocarbons, agrichemicals, volatile organic compounds (VOCs), solvents, polyaromatic hydrocarbons (PAHs) and polychlorinated biphenyls (PCBs) in the sections on air and water pollutants. Other soil pollutants include organotin compounds and semi-volatile organic compounds (SVOCs).

E.8 Waste

An increase in the world population and consumption has led to a rapid growth in the quantity of solid waste which needs to be disposed of. Anti-air and anti-water pollution measures have also led to an increase in solid waste. The safe disposal of spent nuclear fuels poses particular problems. Treating and disposing of all this material, without harming the environment, is a serious global issue. In the western word it has been estimated that 3.5 tonnes of solid waste is thrown away for every man, woman and child each year.

The simplest way to deal with the waste is **open dumping**. It is inexpensive and convenient for the dumper, but is not generally suitable as it causes air and ground water pollution and encourages rodents and insects which can be a health hazard. Much of our waste has been used to **landfill** disused quarries, however, suitable sites are becoming harder to find and **incineration**, which greatly reduces the bulk, is also used. As both these methods create environmental damage, there is an increasing trend to recycle many materials.

Landfill sites are used to dispose of about 90% of the world's domestic waste. In time, the dump may be covered with soil, landscaped and sold to developers. The gas flare (centre) burns off gases produced by decomposition, preventing hazardous build up of pressure.

Waste disposal

Landfill

Landfill sites can be disused quarries or a natural pit. The purpose of a landfill is to bury the waste in such a way that it will be isolated from groundwater, will be kept dry and will not be in contact with air. The type of material dumped must be controlled to prevent chemical toxins leaching into local groundwater. Leaching may also be prevented by lining the site with synthetic materials or impermeable clay. Under these conditions, organic matter does not break down very rapidly. Forty-year-old newspapers have been recovered with easily readable print from old landfills.

Organic matter is decomposed by **anaerobic** bacteria to produce methane, which can be collected and used as a fuel, and hydrogen sulfide and organic acids. When a landfill closes, the site and the groundwater must be monitored for up to 30 years. The organic acids when leached out with rain water, for example, can transport heavy metal ions into the wider environment.

The use of non-biodegradable plastics poses additional problems as they are not broken down by bacteria. Some polyethene plastic bags, with added natural polymers such as starch, cellulose or protein, can be made to biodegrade. The bacteria decompose the natural polymer which breaks down the bag into smaller pieces. The synthetic polymer chains that remain have an increased surface area which speeds up the rate of decay further. The limited supply of oxygen, however, can prevent the bacteria from acting.

Incineration

Waste can be burned. This produces waste of a more uniform composition and reduces the bulk as most of the organic waste is converted into gases. The heat produced can be used to maintain the temperatures needed (800–1000 °C). There are problems, however, as the carbon dioxide produced is a greenhouse gas and carbon monoxide produced during incomplete combustion of plastics is poisonous. The combustion of PVC poses a particular problem as the hydrogen chloride produced causes acid rain. It must be removed from the fumes before they are released into the atmosphere. It is important to control the temperature to reduce the production of **dioxins**.

▲ Plastic waste is not biodegradable and persists for a long time, causing environmental problems.

Exercise

20 Which of the following is not achieved during incineration?
    A reduction in volume of solid waste
    B destruction of heavy metal ions
    C removal of organic matter
    D destruction of disease-causing bacteria.

Recycling

Ideally materials should be reused so that no waste is produced. If this is not possible the best alternative is recycling as it reduces:
- the use of raw materials
- energy costs
- the level of pollutants
- the need of land for waste disposal.

The main challenge is the separation and purification of the materials. Recycled materials tend to be a lower grade quality than new ones. As recycled material is sold to manufacturers it provides the local authorities who collect it with an extra source of income.

▲ Chemical waste incinerator, where toxic chemicals are broken down by high temperatures into harmless or non-toxic products.

Metals

Recycling metals saves the Earth's reserves of the ores and reduces energy costs. Aluminium from drink cans is worth recycling because of its resistance to corrosion and the high cost of the initial extraction process. The collecting, sorting and recycling of metals is an important industry. Disassembly lines exist in some countries to recover the metal from used cars. Steel can be easily separated from other metals by the use of magnets and other metals can be separated by their difference in density. Recycled metals are used as **alloys,** which reduces the need to purify the metal completely.

▲ Flattened car bodies in a scrap metal yard. Once stripped of useful spare parts, cars can be crushed and sent for recycling by the steel industry.

▲ Empty glass bottles and jars waiting to be recycled at a bottle bank.

▲ The recycling symbol on the bottom of a bleach bottle indicates that the plastic is high density polyethylene. Different plastics can be identified by different numbers. This assists in sorting plastics before they are recycled.

One aspect of 'caring' in the IB Learner profile is to show a personal commitment to service and act to make a positive difference to the environment. What impact do your actions make on your local environment?

Are there ethical obligations for humanity to treat the natural environment in a certain way?

Glass

The fragility of glass is an advantage in recycling because it can easily be broken into small pieces. As different colour glasses have different chemical compositions, they must first be separated. The glass is then crushed and melted so that it can be moulded into new products. Recycling of glass can reduce energy costs and the need for sandstone and limestone quarries. As glass is not degraded during the recycling process it can be recycled many times.

Plastics

This is a way of reducing the amount of new plastics made and so saves valuable crude oil reserves. The used plastics are heated in the absence of air when they split up into their monomers in a process known as **pyrolysis**. The products are separated by fractional distillation and used as chemical feedstock by the petrochemical industry to make other products including plastics. **Thermoplastics** can be melted down and remoulded. If recycling is to be successful and self-sustainable, the cost of recycling must be less than that needed to produce new materials. There are costs in sorting the different used plastics and melting them so that they can be reshaped. Mixtures of plastics are much weaker than the individual plastics so the recycled product is often of lower quality than the original and has a limited range of uses. Methods of mechanical separation have been developed but ideally the plastics should be collected separately.

Paper

Paper makes up a significant proportion of our domestic waste. It can be composted but does not generally decompose in landfill sites. Paper to be recycled must first be cleaned to have the ink and additives removed. It is then added to water where it disintegrates to form slurry. The cellulose fibres are separated in this mechanical process known as repulping. If white paper is needed, the paper is then bleached using peroxides. Recycled paper has a reduced strength as cellulose fibres are damaged during the repulping and so is used for low grade products such as cardboard and newspapers.

There are energy costs in transporting paper to the recycling plant.

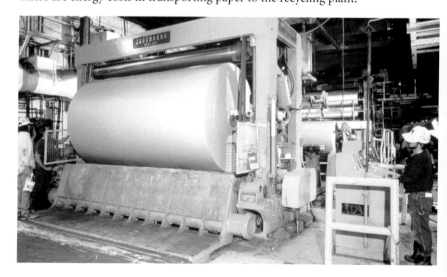

Recycled card on a printing press. Card such as this is used as a packaging material. ▶

Nuclear waste

An important aspect of the nuclear industry is the disposal of radioactive waste.

The radioisotopes which are used in research laboratories and for treating patients in hospitals are classified as **low level waste**. The spent fuel rods from nuclear power stations are **high level waste**. The method of disposal depends on the level of waste and the length of time it remains active. The time taken for the radioactivity to fall to half its initial value is called its **half life**. Low level wastes have low levels of activity and short half lives. High level wastes have high activity and long half lives.

Sources and characteristics of low and high level waste

Nature of waste	Source	Characteristics
low level	hospitals: items such as clothing, paper towels which are used where radioactive materials are handled; fuel containers	activity is low; short half life; high volume
high level	nuclear industry: spent fuel rods; military	activity is high; long half life; low volume

Storage and disposal of nuclear waste

Low level waste

As the decay process produces heat energy, low level waste is stored in cooling ponds of water until the activity has fallen to safe levels. The water is then passed through an ion exchange resin, which removes the isotopes responsible for the activity, and diluted before being released into the sea. Other methods of disposal include keeping the waste in steel containers inside concrete-lined vaults.

High level waste

Products formed from nuclear reactors can maintain dangerously high levels of radioactivity for thousands of years. There is no way to speed up the rate of the decay process. Waste disposal presents a formidable problem because daughter products from the decay process may themselves act as parents for other nuclear reactions. Remotely controlled machinery removes the spent rods from the reactor and transfers them to deep pools where they are cooled by water containing a neutron absorber. The fuel rods are often cased in ceramic or glass and then packed in metal containers before being buried deep in the Earth, either in impervious granite rock or in deep unused mines. The site selected for the disposal must safely contain the material for a very long period of time and prevent it from entering the underground water supply. Because there is always the problem that land masses (for example in an Earthquake) may move and the radioactive material escape, the waste is buried in remote places that are geologically stable.

Used fuel cooling and storage pond. Fuel rods are placed in the storage ponds awaiting reprocessing. The spent fuel is still highly radioactive and continues to generate heat. The water absorbs the heat and shields the operators from the radiation emitted by the fuel.

Drilling machinery being used to excavate underground bore holes into which nuclear waste may be placed. Before long-term nuclear waste is stored underground, the area must be examined for geological activity.

Practice questions

1 **(a)** Explain, with the help of an equation, why rain is naturally acidic. (2)
   (b) Catalytic converters are used in motor vehicles to reduce the emissions of acidic gases.
     (i) Give an equation to show the formation of nitrogen(II) oxide in a motor vehicle and identify the acid it forms in the atmosphere. (2)
     (ii) Nitrogen(II) oxide reacts with carbon monoxide in a catalytic converter to produce harmless substances. Deduce the equation for this reaction. (2)
       © International Baccalaureate Organization [2004]

2 For each of the primary pollutants below, state **one** chemical method used to reduce the amount entering the atmosphere and give **one** relevant equation relating to the chemistry behind the method.
   (a) carbon monoxide, CO   **(b)** nitrogen(II) oxide, NO
   (c) sulfur(IV) oxide, SO_2 **(d)** gasoline (petrol), C_8H_{18} (8)
       © International Baccalaureate Organization [2003]

3 Waste water (sewage) from homes and industries varies greatly in its content, but it is desirable to treat it before it is returned to the environment, especially to reduce the biological oxygen demand (BOD).
   (a) State what is meant by the term *biological oxygen demand*. (2)
   (b) Describe the main features of the activated sludge process used in secondary treatment and state the main impurities removed during this treatment. (5)
       © International Baccalaureate Organization [2003]

4 CFCs lower the concentration of ozone in the ozone layer. Following the 1987 *Montreal Protocol*, the use of CFCs is being phased out. Two alternatives to CFCs are HCFCs (e.g. chlorodifluoromethane, CHF_2Cl) and hydrocarbons (e.g. 2-methylpropane, C_4H_{10}).
   (a) Apart from being less harmful to the ozone layer, state **two** other properties that alternatives to CFCs must possess. (2)
   (b) Discuss the relative advantages and disadvantages of using chlorodifluoromethane and 2-methylpropane as alternatives to CFCs. (3)
       © International Baccalaureate Organization [2003]

5 The term *greenhouse effect* is used to describe a natural process for keeping the average temperature of the Earth's surface nearly constant.
   (a) Describe the greenhouse effect in terms of radiations of different wavelengths. (4)
   (b) Water vapour acts as a greenhouse gas. State the main natural and man-made sources of water vapour in the atmosphere. (2)
   (c) Two students disagreed about whether carbon dioxide or methane was more important as a greenhouse gas.
     (i) State **one** reason why carbon dioxide could be considered more important than methane as a greenhouse gas. (1)
     (ii) State **one** reason why methane could be considered more important than carbon dioxide as a greenhouse gas. (1)
   (d) Discuss the effects of global warming on the Earth. (4)
       © International Baccalaureate Organization [2004]

6 Nitrates in drinking water can cause health problems.
   (a) Identify **one** source of nitrates in drinking water and explain why nitrates can be a health problem. (2)
   (b) Identify the stage of waste water treatment in which nitrates can be removed and state **one** method for nitrate removal. (2)
       © International Baccalaureate Organization [2004]

7 Particulates are a type of primary air pollutant produced in several industries and by the burning of fuels.

   (a) The emission of particulates by some industries is reduced by an electrostatic method. Explain how this is done.   (3)

   (b) State **one** type of fuel that is very likely to produce particulates when burned.   (1)

   (c) Deduce the equation for a combustion reaction of methane in which particulates are formed.   (1)

© International Baccalaureate Organization [2004]

8 (a) Use equations to show how ozone undergoes natural depletion in the atmosphere.   (2)

   (b) Identify **one** pollutant that contributes to the lowering of the ozone concentration in the upper atmosphere. State a source of the pollutant identified.   (2)

   (c) Fluorocarbons and hydrofluorocarbons are now considered as alternatives to some ozone-depleting pollutants. Outline **one** advantage and **one** disadvantage of the use of these alternatives.   (2)

© International Baccalaureate Organization [2005]

9 Discuss the advantages and disadvantages of incineration as a method of disposal compared with landfill sites.   (4)

10 Describe the role of humus in retaining positive ions in the soil.   (2)

11 Radioactive waste from nuclear power stations is often divided into high level and low level wastes. Describe the materials present in these wastes and the methods used for storage and disposal.   (6)

© International Baccalaureate Organization [2003]

12 Identify four materials which are recycled and discuss the advantages and challenges of recycling.   (6)

13 Discuss *salinization* and *nutrient depletion* as causes of soil degradation.   (4)

14 Water that allows marine life to flourish needs a high concentration of dissolved oxygen. Several factors can alter the oxygen concentration.

   (a) State how an increase in temperature affects the oxygen concentration.   (1)

   (b) Eutrophication is a process that decreases the oxygen concentration of water. Explain how the accidental release of nitrates into a river can cause eutrophication.   (2)

© International Baccalaureate Organization [2003]

15 (a) Acid rain can affect plants and buildings.

     (i) Outline how acidic soil can damage the growth of trees.   (1)

     (ii) Give an equation for the reaction of acid rain on marble statues or limestone buildings.   (1)

   (b) Explain how the addition of calcium oxide to lakes could neutralize the effects of acid rain.   (1)

© International Baccalaureate Organization [2003]

16 Describe how pure water can be obtained from sea water by ion exchange. (You may assume that sea water is sodium chloride solution.)   (5)

© International Baccalaureate Organization [2004]

Practice questions 9, 10, 12, 13 © International Baccalaureate Organization

17 Food chemistry:

Option F

Food concerns us all, but our concerns vary depending on where we live in the world. In less industrially developed parts of the world, the production of adequate supplies of the nutrients needed for life is the priority and a large proportion of the population is involved in food production. In more developed countries, where food is produced by more industrial methods and is readily available, concerns are related to the quality, variety of food and the effects of food processing. Food chemistry is a study of the composition and properties of food, the chemical changes it undergoes during handling, processing and storage and the principles underlying the improvement of food. In this chapter we will discuss the chemistry of important molecules in food and the contribution that chemistry has made (and continues to make) towards maintaining and improving the quality of the food we eat.

Technician testing the suitability of food products for production.

Assessment statements

F.1 Food groups
F.1.1 Distinguish between a food and a nutrient.
F.1.2 Describe the chemical composition of lipids (fats and oils), carbohydrates and proteins.

F.2 Fats and oils
F.2.1 Describe the difference in structure between *saturated* and *unsaturated* (mono- and poly-unsaturated) fatty acids.
F.2.2 Predict the degree of crystallization (solidification) and melting point of fats and oils from their structure and explain the relevance of this property in the home and in industry.
F.2.3 Deduce the stability of fats and oils from their structure.
F.2.4 Describe the process of hydrogenation of unsaturated fats.
F.2.5 Discuss the advantages and disadvantages of hydrogenating fats and oils.

F.3 Shelf life
F.3.1 Explain the meaning of the term *shelf life*.
F.3.2 Discuss the factors that affect the shelf life and quality of food.
F.3.3 Describe the *rancidity* of fats.
F.3.4 Compare the processes of *hydrolytic* and *oxidative* rancidity in lipids.
F.3.5 Describe ways to minimize the rate of rancidity and prolong the shelf life of food.
F.3.6 Describe the traditional methods used by different cultures to extend the shelf life of foods.
F.3.7 Define the term *antioxidant.*
F.3.8 List examples of common, naturally occurring antioxidants and their sources.

F.3.9   Compare the structural features of the major synthetic antioxidants in food.

F.3.10 Discuss the advantages and disadvantages associated with natural and synthetic antioxidants.

F.3.11 List some antioxidants found in the traditional foods of different cultures that may have health benefits.

F.4 Colour

F.4.1   Distinguish between a *dye* and a *pigment*.

F.4.2   Explain the occurrence of colour in naturally occurring pigments.

F.4.3   Describe the range of colours and sources of the naturally occurring pigments anthocyanins, carotenoids, chlorophyll and haem.

F.4.4   Describe the factors that affect the colour stability of anthocyanins, carotenoids, chlorophyll and haem.

F.4.5   Discuss the safety issues associated with the use of synthetic colorants in food.

F.4.6   Compare the two processes of non-enzymatic browning (Maillard reaction) and caramelization that cause the browning of food.

F.5 Genetically modified foods

F.5.1   Define a *genetically modified* (GM) *food*.

F.5.2   Discuss the benefits and concerns of using GM foods.

F.6 Texture

F.6.1   Describe a dispersed system in food.

F.6.2   Distinguish between the following types of dispersed systems: *suspensions*, *emulsions* and *foams* in food.

F.6.3   Describe the action of emulsifiers.

F.1 Food groups

Foods and nutrients

Substances which are accepted as food by one community may be unacceptable in other parts of the world. What we are prepared to eat can depend on our social and religious background and psychological and other factors. The Codex Alimentarius Commission, which was set up by the World Health Organization (WHO) and the Food and Agriculture Organization (FAO) of the United Nations, defined food as: 'any substance, whether processed, semi-processed or raw, which is intended for human consumption, and includes drinks, chewing gum and any substance which has been used in the manufacture, preparation or treatment of "food" but does not include cosmetics or tobacco or substances used only as drugs'.

Food provides the **nutrients** that are essential for human beings to survive. A nutrient is any substance obtained from food and used by the body to provide energy, to regulate growth, and to maintain and repair the body's tissues. **Proteins, fats** and **oils**, **carbohydrates**, **vitamins**, **minerals** and **water** are considered to be nutrients. **Malnutrition** can occur when either too little or too much of the essential nutrients are eaten. The amount of the different components needed in a diet depends on age, mass, gender and occupation but a balanced diet should have the relative composition shown on the next page.

Nutrient	%
carbohydrate	60
protein	20–30
fats	10–20

The diet should also include the essential vitamins and minerals and a daily intake of 2 dm³ of water. A general deficiency of all six nutrients will lead to under-nutrition and eventually starvation.

A balanced diet

The human body requires chemicals to function and to grow. A good diet is essential for a healthy life. Many nutritionists are now suggesting a dietary pattern based on the food triangle opposite, which shows the proportion of different food groups in the diet.

Bread, cereal, grains and pasta provide carbohydrates; fruit and vegetables provide carbohydrates and vitamins; meat, fish, eggs and dairy products supply proteins and vitamins.

Food triangle showing a healthy diet. The pyramid shows what proportion of the diet should be made up by each of the major food groups. Carbohydrates should make up the largest part of the diet (60%), followed by proteins (20–30%). Fats (10–20%) and sugars should make up the smallest part of the diet.

Lipids (fats and oils)

Fats and oils belong to a group of compounds called **lipids**, which are insoluble in water and soluble in non-polar solvents. An average diet should contain about 10–20% fats. Fats, which are made from the elements carbon, hydrogen and oxygen, provide a more concentrated energy source than carbohydrates. The carbon atoms are less oxidized as the molecules have fewer oxygen atoms in their molecules and so more energy is released when the molecules are completely oxidized to carbon dioxide and water. The fat stored in adipose tissue provides **insulation**, which regulates the temperature of the body and **protective covering** for some parts of the body. Fats are also important components in cell structure and metabolism. Fats are **esters** of **propane-1,2,3-triol (glycerol)** and long chain carboxylic acids, called **fatty acids**. The structure of glycerol, propane-1,2,3-triol is:

$$CH_2OH$$
$$|$$
$$CHOH$$
$$|$$
$$CH_2OH$$

Compounds with three acids attached to the glycerol are known as **triglycerides**. They are formed by a condensation reaction:

If the three fatty acids in a triglyceride are the same it is called a **simple** glyceride; if they are different it is called a **mixed** glyceride. Most naturally occurring fats and oils are mixed glycerides. The chemical and physical properties of the fat depend on the nature of the fatty acid group R.

The R groups generally contain an even number of between 10 and 20 carbon atoms and are almost all straight-chain carboxylic acids as they are made from a series of ethanoic acid CH_3COOH molecules. Fats which are animal in origin are solid at room temperature and have **saturated** R chains with no carbon–carbon double bonds. Oils, which derive from plants and fish, have **unsaturated** R chains and are liquid at room temperature.

◄ Fats, which include butter and lard, and oils, which include castor oil and olive oil, are an essential part of the diet. Unsaturated fats, which are generally found in plant oils, are healthier than saturated fats, which are generally found in animal fats.

Carbohydrates

We generally obtain carbohydrates from plant foods such as cereals, fruit and vegetables. Carbohydrates have the empirical formula $C_m(H_2O)_n$. The main function of carbohydrates in our bodies is as an energy source. Plants are the main source of dietary carbohydrates, which are produced from carbon dioxide and water by **photosynthesis**:

$$6CO_2 + 6H_2O \rightarrow C_6H_{12}O_6 + 6O_2$$

Light supplies the energy needed for photosynthesis. Plants are able to synthesize a large number of different carbohydrates. **Sugars** are low molar mass carbohydrates, which are crystalline solids and dissolve in water to give sweet solutions.

Scanning electron micrograph (SEM) of crystals of granulated sugar. This sweetener is made from the chemical sucrose, extracted from sugar beet.

Monosaccharides

The simplest carbohydrates are called **monosaccharides**, with the empirical formula CH_2O. They are either **aldehydes** (alkanals) or **ketones** (alkanones), with one carbonyl group ($C=O$) and at least two hydroxyl ($-OH$) groups. Pentoses have five carbon atoms and hexoses have six carbon atoms. Examples of monosaccharides include glucose, fructose and ribose. They are soluble in water as the hydroxyl (OH) functional groups are able to form **hydrogen bonds** with the water molecules. Monosaccharides are the building blocks of disaccharides and polysaccharides.

An aldose is a monosaccharide containing one aldehyde group per molecule. A ketose is a monosaccharide containing one ketone group per molecule.

Exercise

1 Consider the following monosaccharides:

A
$$H$$
$$|$$
$$C=O$$
$$|$$
$$H-C-OH$$
$$|$$
$$H-C-OH$$
$$|$$
$$H-C-OH$$
$$|$$
$$CH_2OH$$

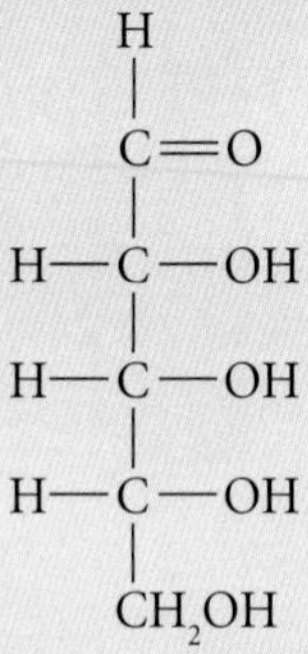

B
$$CH_2OH$$
$$|$$
$$C=O$$
$$|$$
$$HO-C-H$$
$$|$$
$$H-C-OH$$
$$|$$
$$H-C-OH$$
$$|$$
$$CH_2OH$$

C
$$CHO$$
$$|$$
$$H-C-OH$$
$$|$$
$$CH_2OH$$

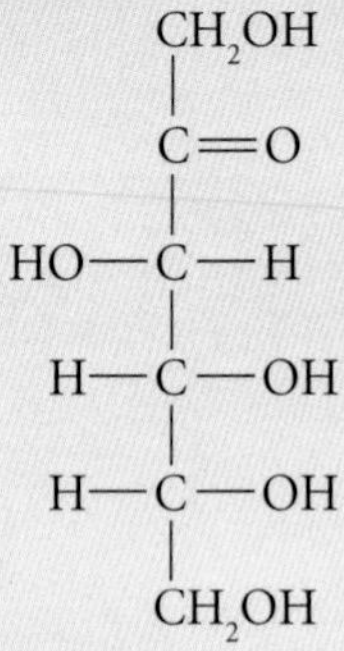

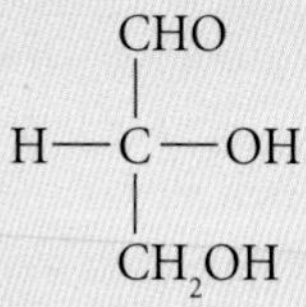

(a) Which of the molecules is an aldose?

(b) Which of the molecules is a triose?

(c) Which of the molecules is a ketose?

(d) Which of the molecules is a pentose?

(e) Which of the molecules is a hexose?

D-**glucose** is the most important monosaccharide as it is necessary for cellular respiration. It has the straight chain formula shown below. The carbon atoms are numbered, starting with 1 at the top in the carbonyl group and ending with 6 at the bottom.

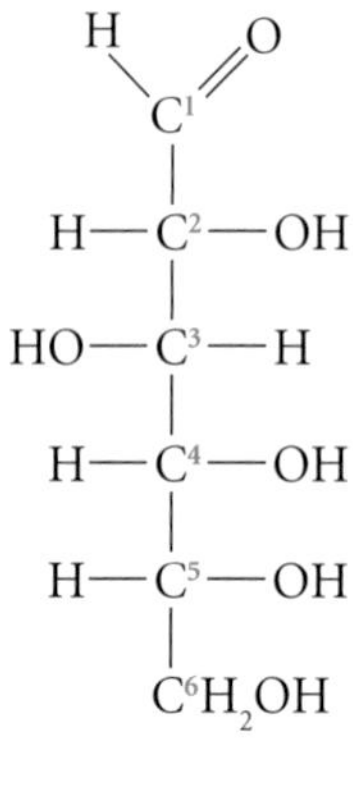

$$H \quad O$$
$$\diagdown \diagup$$
$$C^1$$
$$|$$
$$H-C^2-OH$$
$$|$$
$$HO-C^3-H$$
$$|$$
$$H-C^4-OH$$
$$|$$
$$H-C^5-OH$$
$$|$$
$$C^6H_2OH$$

Glucose is usually found in a ring or cyclic structure in aqueous solution with the OH group on C^5 attacking the carbonyl carbon atom.

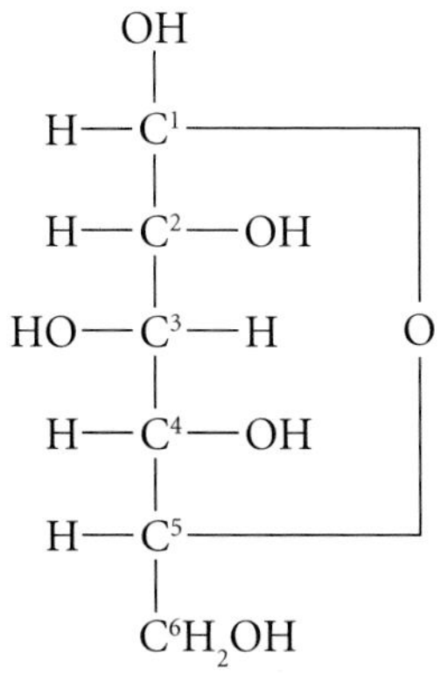

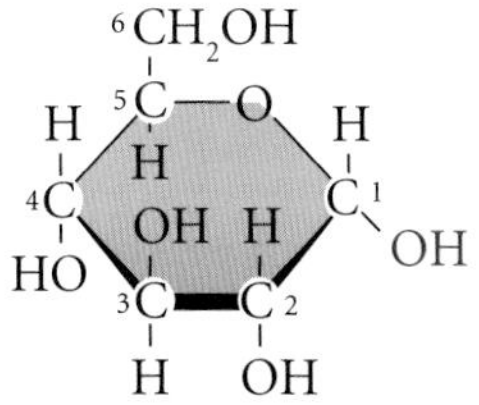

OH
|
H—C¹
|
H—C²—OH
|
HO—C³—H   O
|
H—C⁴—OH
|
H—C⁵
|
C⁶H₂OH

$^6CH_2OH$
^5C—O
H
^4C OH H C^1
HO
$_3C$—C_2
H OH
OH

The closing of the ring can result in two different isomers or **anomers** with the hydroxyl group on either side of the ring. The form shown is called α-D-glucose (see page 269 for more details).

Disaccharides

Disaccharides are formed in condensation reactions by the elimination of one water molecule from two monosaccharides. There are many disaccharides known, but those important to the food industry are maltose, lactose and sucrose.

Monosaccharides	Disaccharides
α-D-glucose + α-D-glucose	maltose
β-D-glucose + β-D-galactose	lactose
α-D-glucose + β-D-fructose	sucrose (table sugar)

Maltose, for example, is formed from the condensation reaction between two molecules of glucose. Two molecules of α-D-glucose are joined by a 1,4-glycosidic bond; the C¹ forms the linkage with the hydroxyl group on the C⁴ of the second α-D-glucose molecule.

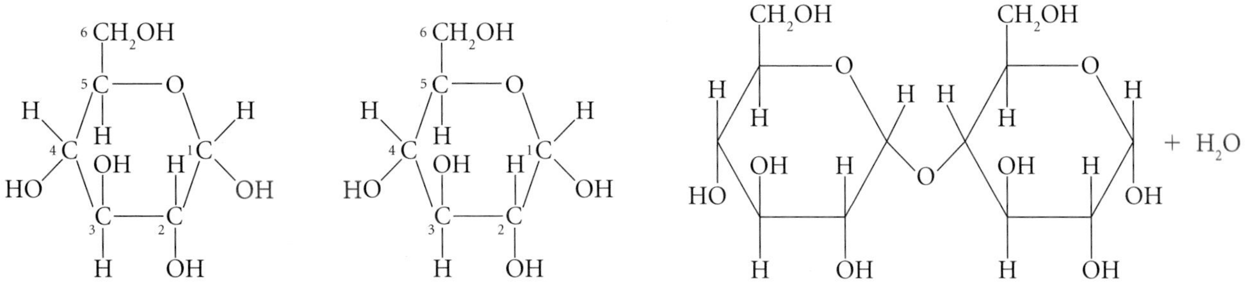

Maltose is used in brewing, soft drinks and foods.

Exercise

2 Lactose is found in milk. Its structure is shown here. Deduce the structural formulas of the two monosaccharides that react to form lactose.

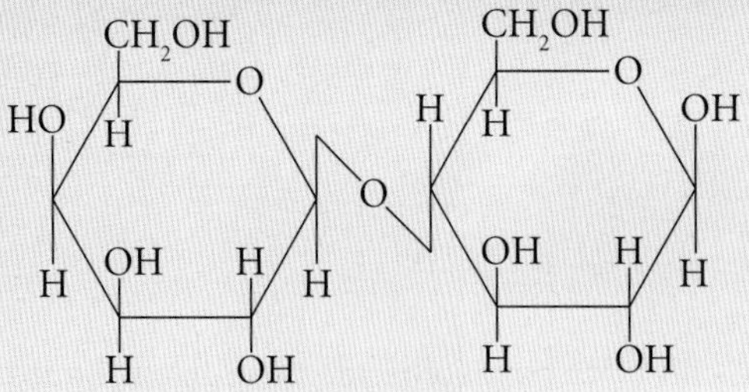

Polysaccharides

Polysaccharides are **condensation polymers** formed from monosaccharides with the elimination of water molecules. Glucose is the most important monomer of the naturally occurring polysaccharides.

Worked example

Deduce the empirical formula of the polysaccharide formed from glucose.

Solution

Formula of glucose = $C_6H_{12}O_6$

Polysaccharides are formed when one molecule of water is eliminated from each combination of glucose molecules.

General formula of polymer = $(C_6H_{10}O_5)_n$

Empirical formula = $C_6H_{10}O_5$

Polysaccharides act as energy stores. **Starch** is the polysaccharide in which glucose is stored in plants and **glycogen** is used as an energy store in animal cells. Polymers are ideal energy stores as their low solubility minimizes the amount of water entering the plant cells by osmosis. Starch is a polymer of α-D-glucose. It occurs in two forms: as an unbranched polymer (amylase) and a branched polymer (amylopectin).

part of an amylopectin molecule, which is highly branched

part of an amylose molecule, which consists of linear, unbranched chains of several hundred glucose molecules

Cellulose is a polysaccharide made from about 10 000 glucose molecules. As humans do not have the necessary enzymes to break the links between the glucose molecules it cannot be digested and so has no nutritional value. It is, however, valuable in the diet as fibre as it gives bulk to food which aids its passage through the alimentary canal. Cellulose is a major component of plant cell walls.

Exercises

3 (a) Describe how and where carbohydrates are produced.
(b) Outline the difference between monosaccharides and polysaccharides.
(c) Discuss the difference between starch and cellulose with regard to their:
   (i) simplest units and structures
   (ii) nutritional value of each for humans.

4 Cellulose is a carbohydrate made from approximately 10 000 glucose units. Explain why it is not classed as a nutrient, but is acknowledged as of value in the human diet.

Selection of foods rich in carbohydrates and dietary fibre. These include rice, bread, pasta, flour and oats. Carbohydrates are the main source of energy for the body. Dietary fibre is any carbohydrate that is not affected by digestion and thus makes up the bulk of faeces. Digestible carbohydrates are broken down in the gut to glucose, which is then distributed by the blood to cells which need energy.

Proteins

Proteins are vital components of all life. They are natural polymers made from combinations of 20 different 2-amino acids. As amino acids have both a carboxylic acid group and an amino group, they are able to undergo condensation reactions:

$$H_2N-\underset{\underset{R_1}{|}}{\overset{\overset{H}{|}}{C}}-\overset{\overset{O}{\|}}{C}-OH \;+\; HN-\underset{\underset{R_2}{|}}{\overset{\overset{H}{|}}{C}}-\overset{\overset{O}{\|}}{C}-OH \;\rightarrow\; H_2N-\underset{\underset{R_1}{|}}{\overset{\overset{H}{|}}{C}}-\overset{\overset{O}{\|}}{C}-\underset{\underset{H}{|}}{N}-\underset{\underset{R_2}{|}}{\overset{\overset{H}{|}}{C}}-\overset{\overset{O}{\|}}{C}-OH \;+\; H_2O$$

peptide bond

The product, a **dipeptide**, is an amide made up of two amino acids joined by a **peptide** bond or peptide linkage. One molecule of alanine and glycine, for example, can form two dipeptides:

$$H_2N-\underset{\underset{CH_3}{|}}{\overset{\overset{H}{|}}{C}}-\overset{\overset{O}{\|}}{C}-OH \;+\; HN-\underset{\underset{H}{|}}{\overset{\overset{H}{|}}{C}}-\overset{\overset{O}{\|}}{C}-OH \;\rightarrow\; H_2N-\underset{\underset{CH_3}{|}}{\overset{\overset{H}{|}}{C}}-\overset{\overset{O}{\|}}{C}-\underset{\underset{H}{|}}{N}-\underset{\underset{H}{|}}{\overset{\overset{H}{|}}{C}}-\overset{\overset{O}{\|}}{C}-OH \;+\; H_2O$$

$$H_2N-\underset{\underset{H}{|}}{\overset{\overset{H}{|}}{C}}-\overset{\overset{O}{\|}}{C}-OH \;+\; HN-\underset{\underset{CH_3}{|}}{\overset{\overset{H}{|}}{C}}-\overset{\overset{O}{\|}}{C}-OH \;\rightarrow\; H_2N-\underset{\underset{H}{|}}{\overset{\overset{H}{|}}{C}}-\overset{\overset{O}{\|}}{C}-\underset{\underset{H}{|}}{N}-\underset{\underset{CH_3}{|}}{\overset{\overset{H}{|}}{C}}-\overset{\overset{O}{\|}}{C}-OH \;+\; H_2O$$

Each amino acid can be identified by a three letter code (see Table 19 of the IB Data booklet). The two dipeptides can be represented as Ala–Gly and Gly–Ala.

A protein or polypeptide is formed when this process continues. The **primary structure** of a protein is the sequence of amino acids which form the protein.

Exercises

5 The structures of the amino acids threonine and valine are shown in Table 19 of the IB Data booklet. They can react with each other to form a dipeptide.

(a) Deduce the structures of the two possible dipeptides formed in the reaction between one molecule each of threonine and valine.

(b) How many different tripeptides can be formed using the three 2-amino acids, glycine, threonine and valine if each amino acid is used only once in each tripeptide?

6 The two ends of the primary structure of a ribonuclease molecule are shown below:

$$H_2N—Lys—Glu—Thr—Ala————Asp—Ala—Ser—Val—X$$

(a) Identify the functional group represented by X.

(b) Name the covalent bond formed between each pair of amino acids in the chain.

The **secondary** structure of a protein describes the way in which protein chains fold or align themselves by **intramolecular hydrogen bonding** between different groups at different positions along the protein chain. The **tertiary** structure describes the overall three-dimensional shape of the protein and is determined by a range of interactions such as:

- hydrogen bonding between polar groups on the side chain
- salt bridges (ionic bonds) formed between $—NH_2$ and $—COOH$ groups
- dipole–dipole interactions
- van der Waals' forces between non-polar groups
- disulfide bridges formed between two cystine molecules from different positions along the polymer chain.

Essential amino acids cannot be produced in the body and therefore must be supplied in the diet.

Animal protein is generally more valuable nutritionally than vegetable protein because animal protein contains the full complement of **essential amino acids**. Vegetable protein, in general, tends to lack one or more of the essential amino acids. Cereal protein, for example, lacks lysine, which is an essential amino acid.

Protein-rich foods including (from left) prawns, fish, meat, beans, eggs, nuts, mushrooms, milk, soya beans, tofu, cheese and yoghurt.

.2 Fats and oils

Most naturally occurring fats contain a mixture of saturated, mono-unsaturated and poly-unsaturated fatty acids with different chain lengths. They are classified according to the predominant type of unsaturation present.

Saturated and unsaturated fatty acids

The saturated fatty acids, which are often animal in origin, are all carboxylic acids with the general formula $C_nH_{2n+1}COOH$. The carbon chain is made from only single carbon–carbon bonds. The carbon atoms are bonded in a tetrahedral arrangement which allows the chains to pack closely together. The **van der Waals'** forces are sufficiently strong between the chains to make the compounds solid at room temperature.

Unsaturated fats contain the carbon–carbon double bond. This produces a 'kink' in the chain, which prevents the molecules from packing closely together and reduces the intermolecular forces. Unsaturated oils, which are often vegetable in origin, are liquids. The greater the number of C=C double bonds, the greater the separation between the chains and the lower the melting point.

> **Monounsaturated fatty acids contain one C=C double bond. Polyunsaturated oils contain more than one C=C double bond per fatty acid chain.**

Worked example

Consider the three fatty acids:
- stearic: $C_{17}H_{35}COOH$
- oleic: $C_{17}H_{33}COOH$
- linoleic: $C_{17}H_{31}COOH$

Deduce the number of carbon–carbon double bonds in each of the acids.

Solution

The general formula of a saturated fatty acid is $C_nH_{2n+1}COOH$. This gives $C_{17}H_{35}COOH$.
Stearic acid is a saturated acid.
To form a double bond, two H atoms need to be removed.
Oleic acid, $C_{17}H_{33}COOH$, has one carbon double bond.
Linoleic acid, $C_{17}H_{31}COOH$, has two carbon–carbon double bonds.

Exercise

7 The following table shows the melting point for a number of common fatty acids found in dietary fats and oils.

Name of acid	Formula	Structural formula	Melting point/°C
lauric	$C_{11}H_{23}COOH$	$CH_3(CH_2)_{10}COOH$	44
myristic	$C_{13}H_{27}COOH$	$CH_3(CH_2)_{12}COOH$	58
palmitic	$C_{15}H_{31}COOH$	$CH_3(CH_2)_{14}COOH$	63
stearic	$C_{17}H_{35}COOH$	$CH_3(CH_2)_{16}COOH$	70
oleic	$C_{17}H_{33}COOH$	$CH_3(CH_2)_7CH = CH(CH_2)_7COOH$	16
linoleic	$C_{17}H_{31}COOH$	$CH_3(CH_2)_4CH = CHCH_2CH = CH(CH_2)_7COOH$	−5

(a) Which of the fatty acids are solids at a room temperature of 25 °C?
(b) Describe and explain the trend in the melting points in the first four fatty acids listed.
(c) Describe and explain the pattern in the melting points of the last three acids mentioned.

> Linoleic acid is an essential fatty acid in our diet as our body is unable to synthesise it. The absence of the essential fatty acids in the diet may result in disorders such as eczema.

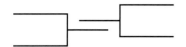

Figure 17.1 In a crystalline fat, the fatty acid chains align themselves so as to allow close packing between the fat molecules.

Triglyceride molecules can be thought of as having 'tuning fork' structures, with the three long limbs being the fatty acid chains. In a liquid oil, the triglyceride molecules are orientated randomly to one another and are constantly in motion. In a crystalline fat, they are tightly packed in a regular repeating pattern, with neighbouring triglycerides interacting through van der Waals' forces.

As fats consist of a mixture of triglycerides, they do not have sharp melting points and generally melt over a range of temperatures. Generally the more unsaturated the fat the lower its melting point and the less crystalline it will be. Mono-unsaturated (olive, canola and peanut) and poly-unsaturated fats (safflower, sunflower, corn, fish, linoleic, linolenic) are liquids and saturated fats (palm, coconut, lard, butter, shortening) are solids at room temperature.

Some examples of fats and oils. ▶

Mainly saturated fats (solids)	Mainly mono-unsaturated oils (liquids)	Mainly poly-unsaturated oils (liquids)
coconut, butterfat, beef fat, tallow	olive oil, canola oil, peanut oil	safflower, sunflower and soybean oils, corn oil, fish oil, linoleic and linolenic acids

Cis–trans or geometric isomerism arises as a result of the restricted rotation of the C=C bond. It occurs when two different groups are attached to each of the carbon atoms in a double bond. The **cis** isomer occurs when the same group (e.g. the H atom) has the same orientation relative to the double bond. The **trans** isomer occurs when the same group has the opposite orientation.

Cis and trans forms of unsaturated fats

As the carbon–carbon double bond does not allow free rotation, unsaturated fatty acids exist in two forms. The **trans** form has the hydrogen atoms on different sides of the carbon–carbon double bond.

The **cis** form has both hydrogen atoms on the same side of the double bond.

The *cis* and *trans* isomers are examples of **geometric** isomers.

As the molecules of the *cis* isomer cannot easily arrange themselves side by side to solidify, they tend to have lower melting points than the corresponding *trans* isomer. The *cis* isomer is the most common form of unsaturated fat, the *trans* form only occurs in animal fats and in processed unsaturated fats such as margarine.

The *trans* isomers are similar to saturated fats in that they lead to a greater risk of heart disease owing to the production of low-density (LDL) cholesterol. They are also harder to metabolize and excrete from the body than their *cis* isomers and so build up to dangerous levels in fatty tissue. The *trans* isomer is also less effective as an energy source.

The melting point of the fat is a key factor in determining which fat is used in a food. Fats used in confectionery, such as cocoa, melt at body temperature, whereas fats used in baking melt at higher temperatures. As fats are mixtures, they do not melt at a fixed temperature.

Cholesterol is a steroid and has the structural formula shown.

It is an essential component of cell membranes and is the starting material from which the human body synthesizes important compounds such as hormones and vitamin D. As cholesterol is insoluble in water, it cannot be transported in the bloodstream. It is made soluble by forming an association with **lipoproteins**, which are combinations of lipid and protein. **Low density lipoprotein** (LDL) transports cholesterol from the liver to the various synthesis sites in the body. Excessive LDL ('bad') cholesterol results in fatty material being deposited in the blood vessels. These deposits harden and constrict blood flow, resulting in increased risk of heart attacks and strokes. **High density lipoproteins** (HDL) 'good' cholesterol is thought to transport excess cholesterol back to the liver, where it is converted to bile acids and excreted. There is some evidence that eating large amounts of saturated or *trans*-unsaturated fats increases the tendency for cholesterol to be deposited in blood vessels, leading to a greater risk of heart disease. *Cis* isomers do not cause such deposits to form and reduce the chance of developing coronary heart disease.

Assorted cholesterol-rich foods including red meat and dairy products. Cholesterol is a fatty substance which is essential in moderation, but excess can be harmful. Foods such as brains (far left) have very high cholesterol levels. Too much cholesterol in the diet can lead to its deposition on the inside of the arteries, which can cause a stroke or a heart attack.

 Test your cholesterol IQ with this quiz.

Now go to www.heinemann.co.uk/hotlinks, insert the express code 4259P and click on this activity.

Stability of fats

Hydrolysis of fats

Oils and fats develop an unpleasant or **rancid** smell if they are kept too long. Rancid or 'off' food has a disagreeable smell, taste, texture or appearance. One cause of rancidity is the release of fatty acids produced during the **hydrolysis** of the fat by the water present in food. Free fatty acids are generally absent in the fats of living animal tissue, but can form by enzyme action after the animal has died.

 Hydrolysis is the splitting of a compound by reaction with water.

Fats are hydrolysed in the presence of heat and water to their fatty acids and propane-1,2,3-triol in the reverse of the **esterification** reaction.

$$CH_2O-\overset{\overset{\displaystyle O}{\|}}{C}-R_1$$
$$CH-O-\overset{\overset{\displaystyle O}{\|}}{C}-R_2 \ + \ 3H_2O \ \rightarrow$$
$$CH_2O-\overset{\overset{\displaystyle O}{\|}}{C}-R_3$$
fat

$$CH_2OH \qquad HO-\overset{\overset{\displaystyle O}{\|}}{C}-R_1$$
$$CHOH \ + \ HO-\overset{\overset{\displaystyle O}{\|}}{C}-R_2$$
$$CH_2OH \qquad HO-\overset{\overset{\displaystyle O}{\|}}{C}-R_3$$
glycerol   fatty acid

This hydrolysis reaction takes place more rapidly in the presence of certain microorganisms and is catalysed by the enzyme **lipase**. The fatty acids with four, six and eight carbon atoms, butanoic, hexanoic and octanoic, are released when the fats in milk and butter are hydrolysed and give their unpleasant 'off' smell and taste to butter and milk. Palmitic, stearic and oleic acids are produced during the hydrolysis of chocolate and give it an oily or fatty flavour. Lauric acid gives palm and coconut oil, in cocoa butter substitutes, a soapy flavour.

Hydrolysis also occurs during deep-fat frying owing to large amounts of water introduced from the food and the relatively high temperature used. **Hydrolytic rancidity** can also be substantially reduced by refrigeration.

Oxidation of fats

We saw in Chapter 10 that the alkenes are more reactive than the alkanes. Similarly, unsaturated fats are more reactive than saturated fats. The carbon–carbon double bonds in unsaturated fats react with oxygen (auto-oxidation), hydrogen (hydrogenation) and light (photo-oxidation).

The oxidation of unsaturated fats by molecular oxygen, which occurs in air in the absence of enzymes, is called **auto-oxidation**. When fat molecules break down to form volatile unpleasant tasting aldehydes and carboxylic acids, the process is known as **oxidative rancidity**. It is a **free radical** reaction which can also be initiated by light (**photo-oxidation**) or catalysed by enzymes or metal ions. In products like cheeses some rancid flavour is desirable but generally rancid flavours are unpleasant. As polyunsaturated oils contain a greater number of C=C double bonds, they generally become rancid more quickly. Oily fish such as mackerel and herring contain a high proportion of unsaturated fatty acids and are prone to oxidative rancidity. Extensive oxidation can lead to some polymerization with consequent increases in viscosity and browning.

Antioxidants, which are oxidized in preference to the fats or oils, can be used to reduce the rate of oxidation. Oxidation can also be substantially reduced by refrigeration.

Exercise

8 State the name of the food group which can become rancid and describe the two processes by which it can occur.

Hydrogenation of fats

Hydrogen can be added across the carbon–carbon double bond to decrease the level of unsaturation.

This is an important reaction as it increases the melting point, the hardness and chemical stability of the fat. It is used commercially to convert liquid oils into solid margarine and spreads. **Hydrogenation** is carried out at 140–225 °C, in the presence of a finely divided metal catalyst (Zn, Cu, Ni). The degree of saturation can be controlled by varying the pressure of the hydrogen and the nature of the catalyst. One of the disadvantages of the process, however, is that some unsaturated fats are produced in the less healthy *trans* form. The advantages and disadvantages of the hydrogenation process are compared below.

Vegetable spread containing omega-3 and -6 essential fatty acids. The terms omega-3 and omega-6 fatty acids refer to the position of the first double bond in the structure relative to the terminal $-CH_3$ group.

Advantages of hydrogenation	Disadvantages of hydrogenation
• changes a liquid oil to a semi-solid or solid, to make the melting point of an unsaturated fat more like that of a saturated fat • decreases the rate of oxidation (stability increases with increasing saturation) • increases hardness • controls the feel and plasticity (stiffness)	• mono- and poly-unsaturated fats are healthier for the heart than saturated fats • in partial hydrogenation, *trans* fatty acids can form • *trans* fatty acids are hard to metabolize, accumulate in fatty tissue, are difficult to excrete from the body, increase levels of LDL (bad) cholesterol and are a low-quality energy source

Shelf life

The quality of food changes owing to chemical reactions with the environment and the action of microorganisms. Some of these effects are beneficial: certain cheeses, for example, are deliberately produced by the actions of microorganisms. Controlled and selective hydrolysis is also used in the manufacture of yogurt and bread, but most changes brought about by microorganisms make food less acceptable.

A food reaches the end of its shelf life when it no longer maintains the expected quality desired by the consumer because of changes in flavour, smell, texture and appearance (colour, mass) or because of microbial spoilage. The shelf life is quantified in different ways in different parts of the world. A food that has reached the end of its shelf life may still be safe to consume but optimal quality is no longer guaranteed.

It has been argued that over-reliance on the authority of the *use by, best before* or *display until* dates has led us to ignore the evidence of our own senses and has led to unnecessary waste.

The demand for food is generally constant throughout the year, but most food production is seasonal. All food was once part of a living organism. Meat and fish are from organisms which had to be killed before the food becomes available. Fruits and vegetables are still living when they are harvested. Food contains enzymes and is therefore susceptible to change and spoilage. There are two types of food spoilage: **autolysis** and **microbial** spoilage. Autolysis is the breakdown of food by the enzymes present in the food and causes the release of nutrients from the cells. These nutrients then become available to microorganisms, which feed and multiply, eventually making the food unacceptable.

Most of the spoilage in food results from the activities of microorganisms.

The shelf life depends on the type of food, the temperature, the moisture content, the oxygen content and other factors such as the pH. Some examples are given below.

Type of food	Shelf life
green peas	4 to 6 hours
strawberries	1 to 2 days
raw meat	2 days
potatoes	6 to 9 months
wheat grain	several years

Salmonella bacterium dividing. The two new daughter cells are seen at the upper right and lower left, still joined by a thin connection (centre).

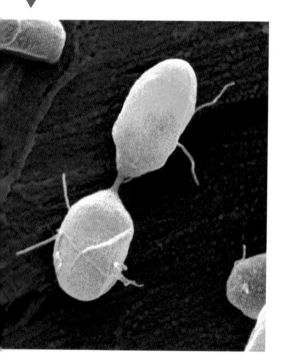

Some deterioration results from the action of enzymes naturally present in the food and from chemical reactions between the constituents in food and oxygen. We have already discussed rancidity which occurs when fats are broken down to give compounds with unpleasant smells and rancid flavours. Hydrolytic rancidity is caused by the breakdown of fats and oils into their component fatty acids and propane-1,2,3-triol (glycerol), and oxidative rancidity occurs when the unsaturated fatty acid chains are oxidized by the addition of oxygen across the carbon–carbon double bond.

When apples, bananas or potatoes are peeled and sliced, a relatively rapid change takes place depending on the time of year – the tissues brown in a process called enzymatic browning. This is due to the action of an enzyme which oxidizes phenols released in damaged cells with molecular oxygen at alkaline pH to give quininone.

$$\text{a phenol} \quad + \quad \tfrac{1}{2}O_2 \quad \rightarrow \quad \text{quinone} \quad + \quad H_2O$$

The quininone can undergo further reaction including polymerization to give brown products known as tannins. This browning reaction can be slowed down using reducing agents such as sulfur dioxide and ascorbic acid (vitamin C) or by reducing the activity of the enzyme by adding acid.

Factors that affect the shelf life and quality of food

There are a number of chemical factors that cause a decrease in the shelf life. Knowledge of the reactions which food undergoes is very important in food technology, as it can suggest ways of slowing down these changes.

Changes in the water content

Water is typically the most abundant constituent in food. It is bonded to the proteins and carbohydrates in the food by hydrogen bonding and plays a critical role in determining food quality, as it makes food juicy and tender. A reduction in water content can affect the texture, lead to the loss of nutrients and increase the rate of enzymatic browning and hydrolytic rancidity. Its presence in dried food can also produce undesirable chemical changes as it increases the rate of the degradation of the food by microorganisms. Water can be removed from food by either drying or smoking. Salting or adding sugars also reduce the water content by osmosis.

Oxygen and water from the air can be prevented from reacting with food if it is wrapped in an air-tight cover, or stored in a vacuum or unreactive gas such as nitrogen.

pH

The pH has a marked effect on the activity of most enzymes and the action of microorganisms. Bacteria require suitable nutrients and minerals and most prefer a neutral or slightly alkaline medium. Acid tolerance varies considerably among organisms, but most will grow at pH values ranging from 4.5 to 10. Reducing the pH inhibits microbial and enzymatic activity and has been widely practised for many years. Ethanoic acid is used to preserve food such as onions by pickling, and acids such as ascorbic, citric and malonic acids, which are naturally found in fruit and vegetables, are added to food to control enzymatic browning. A number of weak acids, such as sorbic and benzoic acids, are used as preservatives as they have little effect on flavour. Although a given concentration of a strong acid is more effective in lowering the pH than a weak acid, weakly dissociated acids are better preservatives. The concentration of the undissociated acid, rather than the hydrogen ion concentration, is the inhibitor.

Light

Light initiates the oxidation of fats and oils, which leads to rancidity, and of other nutrients such as vitamins. Exposure to light can also cause the natural colour of a food to fade.

Storing food in the dark or using packaging or coloured or opaque containers which prevent light from passing through to the food will stop photo-oxidation of fats and other photochemical free radical reactions.

Temperature

An increase in temperature can increase the rate of the chemical reactions which result in food spoilage. An increase in temperature can also affect the water content and thus the texture of the food. If the temperature is raised above 60 °C, the enzymes are denatured as the secondary and tertiary structure of the protein is disrupted. This can reduce the rate of the degradation reactions. Dairy products are often refrigerated as low temperatures slow down the rate of the lipase hydrolysis which produces rancidity.

Food preservation and processing

The aims of food preservation and processing are to prevent undesirable changes and bring about desirable ones. Food preservation techniques are designed to increase the food's shelf life beyond that of the raw material by reducing the deterioration in quality which inevitably occurs in unprocessed foods. Food processing can destroy or inactivate the microorganisms or enzymes involved in food spoilage, or it can create conditions which limit deterioration by reducing the rates of the degradation reactions.

Exercises

9 Suggest, giving a chemical explanation, why there should be no free space in a food container before it is sealed.

10 Explain how wrapping food in a coloured film can lead to an increase in its shelf life.

Traditional methods to extend shelf life

Some traditional methods of prolonging the shelf life of food were discussed earlier. Adding salt, sugar and smoking prolong the shelf life by reducing the water content. Pickling in ethanoic acid reduces the pH to levels which are too acidic for microorganisms to survive. Yoghurt keeps well because the lactic acid, formed by the action of microorganisms on lactose, decreases the pH to about 5.5, which is sufficiently acidic to slow down the growth of microorganisms. Wine keeps better than the grapes from which it is made because fermentation converts the sugars in the food to ethanol, which again limits bacterial growth:

$$C_6H_{12}O_6 \rightarrow 2C_2H_5OH + 2CO_2$$

Additives

More modern methods of preservation may involve the use of additives, which are chemical compounds which slow down the rate of deterioration of food. The addition of chemicals to prolong the shelf life of foods is strictly controlled by legislation. When correctly used, chemical preservatives are very effective.

A large number of acid preservatives are weak acids. Sorbic acid is used to reduce the mould and bacteria growth in cheese and breads. Benzoic acid and propanoic acid are added to fruit juices and carbonated drinks to reduce the growth of microorganisms. Meats are cured by adding salts such as sodium and potassium nitrite and nitrate, which fix the colour and inhibit the growth of microorganisms.

Reducing agents such as sulfur dioxide and sodium hydrogen sulfite delay the oxidative reaction involved in non-enzymic browning.

Sausages being removed from a smoke chamber. Smoking helps to cure or preserve them and also gives extra flavour.

Antioxidants

An antioxidant is a substance that delays the onset or slows the rate of oxidation. It is used to extend the shelf life of food. Antioxidants are added to foods such as oils, fats and butter as they react with oxygen-containing free radicals and so prevent oxidative rancidity.

Naturally occurring antioxidants

- Vitamin E, a fat-soluble vitamin, is a very effective natural antioxidant. It is found in foods such as wheat germ, nuts, seeds, whole grains, green leafy vegetables, and vegetable oils like canola and soya bean.

- Vitamin C (ascorbic acid) is found in citrus fruits, green peppers, broccoli, green leafy vegetables, strawberries, red currants and potatoes.
- β-carotene is found in carrots, squash, broccoli, sweet potatoes, tomatoes, kale, cantaloupe, melon, peaches and apricots.
- The element selenium is found in fish, shellfish, red meat, eggs, grains, chicken and garlic.

The action of antioxidants has been found to be improved by the use of synergists. Synergists (citric acid and ascorbic acid) function by forming complexes with metals such as copper, which otherwise catalyse oxidation.

Synthetic antioxidants

Unfortunately, for economic reasons, it is not always possible to use natural antioxidants. Many of the synthetic antioxidants can be distinguished from natural antioxidants by their molecular structures. They are often phenols, which have a hydroxyl group attached to the benzene ring.

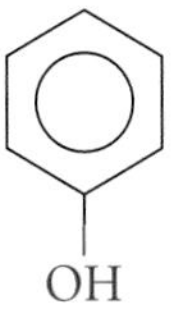

Another common structural unit found in many synthetic antioxidants is the **tertiary butyl group**, which has three methyl groups bonded to one carbon atom. These groups are free radical scavengers and react with the free radicals which would otherwise oxidize the food.

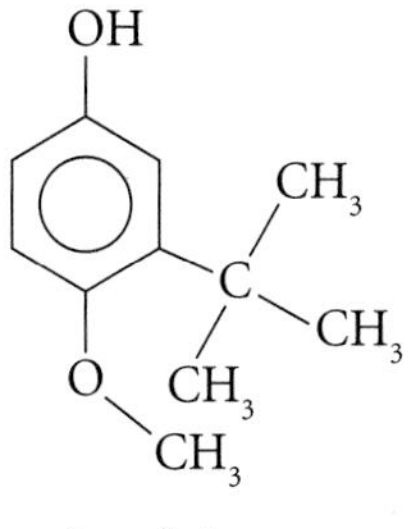

2-*tert*-butyl-4-hydroxyanisole (2-BHA)

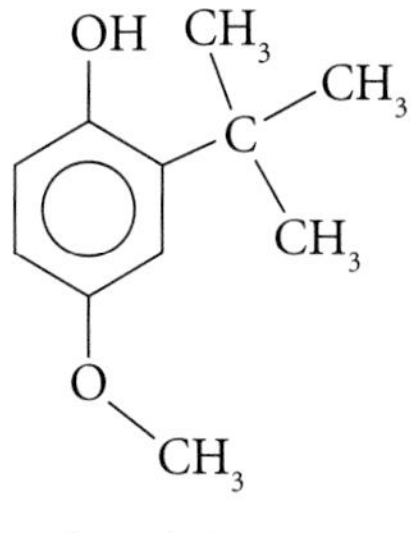

3-*tert*-butyl-4-hydroxyanisole (3-BHA)

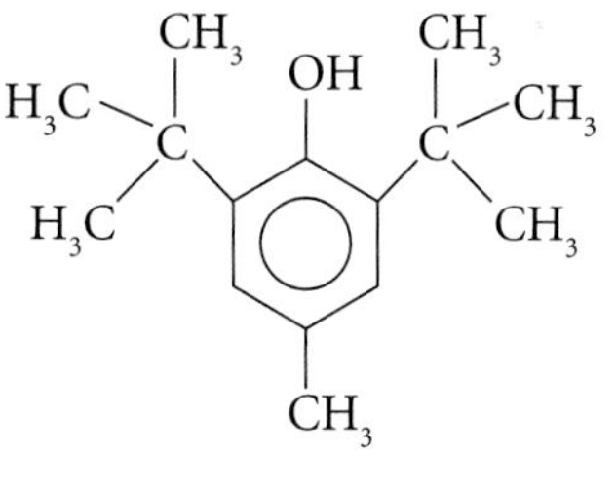

3,5-di-*tert*-butyl-4-hydroxytoluene (BHT)

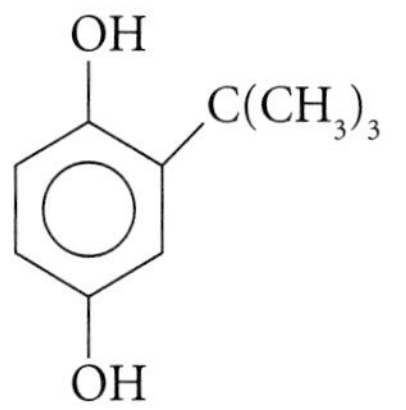

Figure 17.2 Some antioxidants.

tert-butylhydroquinone (TBHQ)

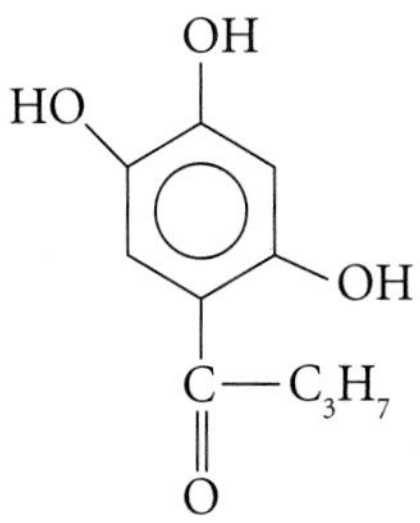

trihydroxybutyrophenone (THBP)

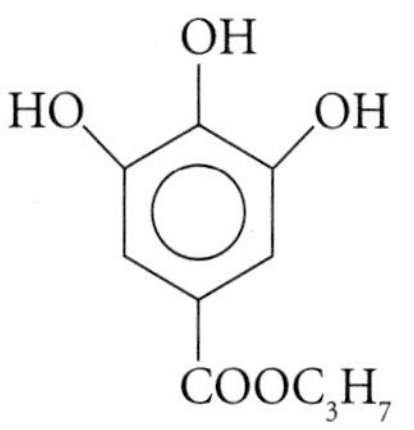

propyl gallate (PG)

Exercise

11 Identify the antioxidants in Figure 17.2 which have both a phenol group and a tertiary butyl group.

Antioxidants in traditional food

Many traditional foods used in different cultures are rich in antioxidants. Many vegetables and fruits contain the natural antioxidants vitamins C and E and the carotenoids. Carotenoids are compounds which have a distinctive structure with alternate single and double carbon–carbon (**conjugate**) bonds. They give foods like oranges, tomatoes and carrots their orange-red colours.

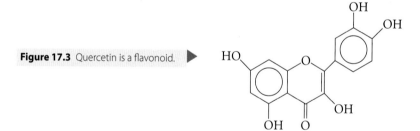

β-carotene

The role of carotenoids in food colour is discussed in Section F.4.

β-carotene can be used as an additive in margarine to provide it with a yellow colour and act as a precursor for vitamin A synthesis.

Another class of natural antioxidants are the **flavonoids**. These polyphenolic compounds are found in all citrus fruits, green tea, red wine, oregano and dark chocolate (containing at least 70% cocoa). It has been claimed that these natural antioxidants have positive health benefits such as preventing cancer and reducing blood pressure, by lowering LDL cholesterol and blood sugar levels.

Carrots contain large amounts of the yellow or orange pigment β-carotene, which is used by the body to make vitamin A.

Figure 17.3 Quercetin is a flavonoid.

Foods rich in quercetin. Quercetin is a flavonoid with antioxidant properties and is believed to be a powerful anticancer agent.

Green tea is a source of polyphenolic flavonoid compounds with powerful antioxidant properties.

Advantages and disadvantages of using natural antioxidants in food

Synthetic antioxidants are generally more effective at slowing down the rate of rancidity and less expensive than natural antioxidants. Natural antioxidants can also add unwanted colour and an aftertaste to food. The use of synthetic antioxidants is, however, an area of some concern as:

- Consumers perceive natural antioxidants to be safer than synthetic ones because they occur naturally in food.
- Naturally occurring vitamins C, E and carotenoids reduce the risk of cancer and heart disease by inhibiting the formation of free radicals.
- Vitamin C is vital for the production of hormones and collagen.
- β-carotene can be used as an additive in margarine to give colour (yellow) and act as a precursor for vitamin A.
- Natural oxidants can enhance the health benefits of existing foods and boost overall health and resilience.
- Consumers perceive synthetic antioxidants to be less safe because they are not naturally occurring in food.
- Policies regarding the labelling and safe use of food additives can be difficult to implement and monitor, especially in developing countries and internationally.

Exercises

12 State the names of two additives which are used to delay the growth of microorganisms and give examples of the food they are added to.

13 Explain how the traditional methods of pickling and fermentation preserve food.

F.4 Colour

Food, in addition to providing nutrients, must be attractive. Colour is an important property of foods that adds to our enjoyment of eating, and it is one of the first factors we evaluate when purchasing food. The yellow colour of the carotenoids or the red colour of anthocyanins, for example, gives us an indication of the ripeness of fruit. As we cannot taste food before we buy it, we rely on what our eyes tell us. Foods have colour because of their ability to reflect or emit different quantities of energy at wavelengths able to stimulate the retina in the eye. They absorb light in the visible region of the electromagnetic spectrum and transmit the remaining light in the visible spectrum which has not been absorbed. Red meat appears red as it absorbs green light and so reflects red which is the complementary colour.

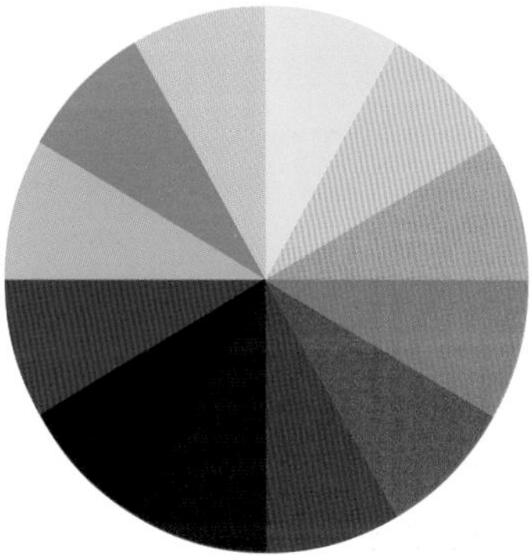

Figure 17.4 Complementary colours are opposite each other in the colour wheel and add together to make white.

Dyes and pigments

Food can be coloured naturally or artificially. A **pigment** is a naturally occurring colour found in the cells of plants and animals. The main pigments responsible for the colours of fruit, vegetables and meat are **porphyrins**, **carotenoids** and **anthocyanins**.

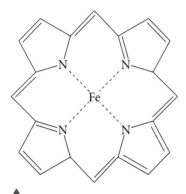

Figure 17.5 The structure of haem.

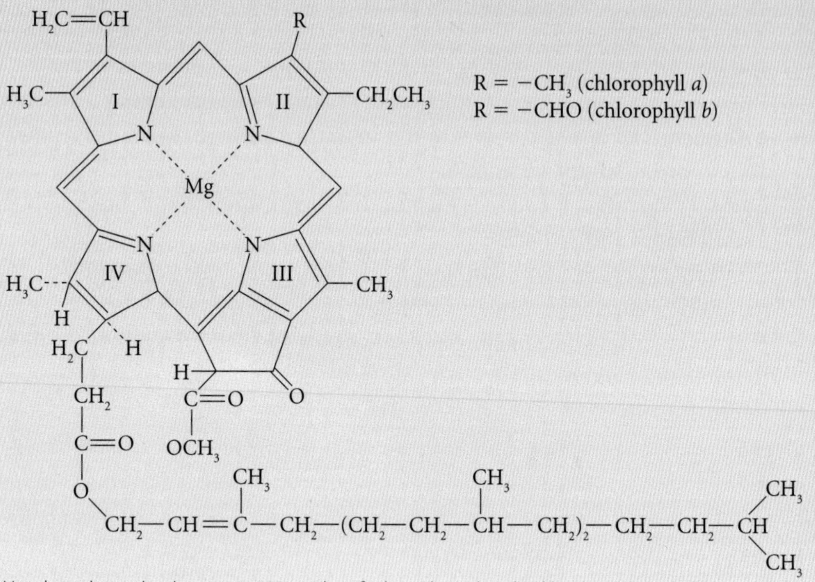

Figure 17.6 The structure of chlorophyll.

In a dative covalent or coordinate bond, the atoms share a pair of electrons which have both come from one of the bonding atoms.

Porphyrins

Porphyrins are complex ring-shaped molecules with a metal atom in the centre. **Haem** pigments are responsible for the colour of red meat and **chlorophyll** is the green pigment responsible for the colour of vegetables.

Exercise

14 The structure of chlorophyll which is present in green plants is shown.

R = −CH₃ (chlorophyll *a*)
R = −CHO (chlorophyll *b*)

Use the colour wheel on page 427 to identify the colour absorbed by the chlorophyll pigment.

There are two closely related forms of chlorophyll that have different R groups, as illustrated in the diagram. Chlorophyll *a* has a methyl group (CH_3) and chlorophyll *b* has an aldehyde CHO group. Both haem and chlorophyll have essentially the same structure with a metal ion at the centre. Four nitrogen atoms form a **dative covalent** bond with the metal ions at the centre.

Carotenoids

Carotenoids are fat-soluble, long-chain hydrocarbon molecules which range in colour from yellow to red. Carotenoids are the most common pigment in nature and are responsible for the pink colour of salmon and flamingos and the blue-green colour of lobsters and crabs. The low levels of carotenoids in grass are concentrated in dairy products and give butter its characteristic yellow colour. Carotenoids have nutritional value as they are antioxidants and can be converted to vitamin A.

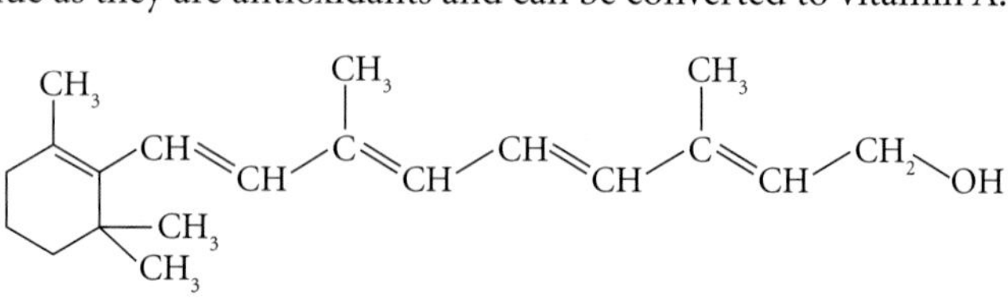

Figure 17.7 Carotenoids are structurally related to vitamin A. They contribute 30–100% of the vitamin A requirement in humans.

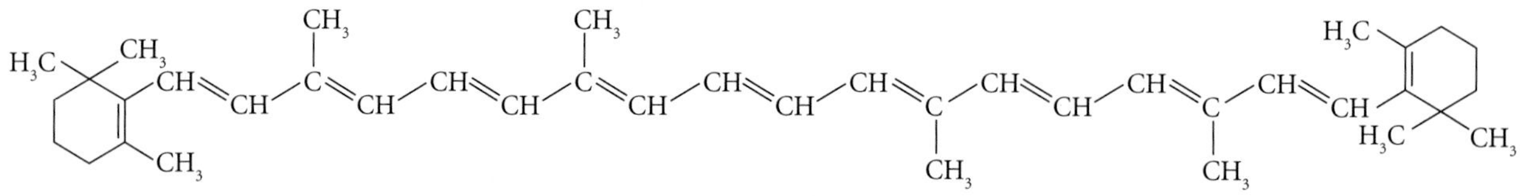

β-carotene

In addition to providing colour in fresh food, carotenoid pigments are also important in processed foods. However, processing and cooking, in particular, can affect the pigments.

Carotenoids are the most widespread pigment in nature. A large majority are produced by algae.

Anthocyanins

The anthocyanins are a sub-class of flavonoids responsible for a range of colours including yellow, red and blue. They are very water soluble and are the most widely distributed pigment in plants. They are present, for example, in strawberries and plums. Many anthocyanins are red in acidic conditions and turn blue at higher pH.

Over 500 different anthocyanins have been isolated from plants. They all have a similar three-ring $C6C3C6$ structure with conjugated carbon–carbon double bonds, which vary in the number of hydroxyl functional groups. The structure of the flavylium cation is shown.

R
OH
HO
O$^+$
R
O—glucose
OH

The word 'anthocyanin' is derived from two Greek words, *anthos* (flower) and *kyanos* (blue).

As sugars such as glucose can be coupled at different places and many different sugars are present in plants, a very large range of anthocyanins can be formed.

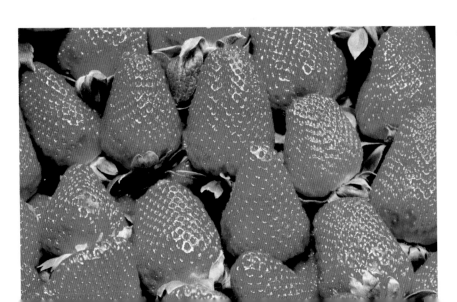

The red colour of strawberries is due to the presence of anthocyanins.

Cranberry fruit is rich in vitamins C and E, antioxidants and anthocyanins.

Find out about the chemistry of autumnal colours.

Now go to www.heinemann.co.uk/hotlinks, insert the express code 4259P and click on this activity.

Colours are added to foods in many parts of the world. The type of colorant permitted for use varies greatly between countries. Since international trade is becoming increasingly important, colour legislation is now of international concern. A worldwide list of permitted additives does not, however, exist. The Food and Agricultural Organisation (FAO) and the World Health Organization (WHO) have attempted to harmonize food regulations through their Codex Alimentarius.

Exercise

16 Explain the solubility in water of the anthocyanin below.

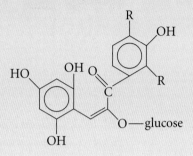

Synthetic dyes

Colour losses are unavoidable when food is processed. Many foods would appear to be very unappetizing without the addition of some artificial colouring. Synthetic compounds which are food-grade water-soluble substances and which are added to food to improve their colour are called **dyes**. The added dyes offset colour loss caused by exposure to light, changes of temperature or moisture, and compensate for natural or seasonal variations in food raw materials. As many artificial dyes that were used in the past are now known to be carcinogenic, they have to be thoroughly tested before use to ensure that they are safe for human consumption.

Synthetic dyes are sometimes found in imported foodstuffs even though they are illegal in the country where the food is sold. Sudan red is an industrial red dye used for colouring solvents, oils, shoe and floor polishes. It has been used by some companies to colour chilli powder, despite its carcinogenic properties.

Analysing spectra of food dyes

The visible spectrum of light ranges from 400 nm (violet) to about 700 nm (red orange).

Colour	Wavelength range/nm
red	630–700
orange	590–630
yellow	560–590
green	490–560
blue	450–490
violet	400–450

The amount of light absorbed at different wavelengths can be measured using a visible spectrometer. The visible spectrometer identifies which colours are absorbed. The wavelength which corresponds to maximum absorbance is λ_{max}.

Worked example

The absorbance of an artificial dye is shown. Identify λ_{max} and use the colour wheel plus the chart on page 430 to deduce the colour of the dye.

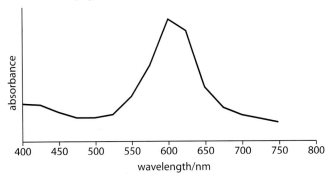

Solution

The wavelength which corresponds to the maximum absorbance is 600 nm.

Orange is absorbed.

The dye is blue (the complementary colour of orange).

Exercises

17 Identify the colour of the dye from its absorption spectrum.

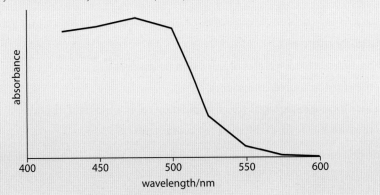

18 Lobsters change colour when they are cooked. The visible spectra of the carotenoid astaxanthin responsible for the colour is shown for live and cooked lobster.

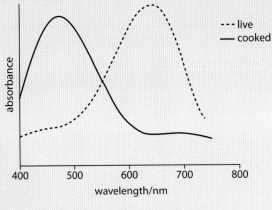

▲ Red astaxanthin when complexed with protein gives the blue or green hue found in live lobsters. When the lobster is cooked and the protein is denatured the lobster appears red.

Deduce the colour change that occurs when lobsters are cooked.

Colour stability of food pigments

As the previous exercise shows, any factor which changes the molecular structure will affect the wavelength of the light absorbed and thus result in a colour change. Food dyes are added to processed food because of the colour changes during processing. Colour stability depends on factors such as the presence or absence of light, oxygen, heavy metals and oxidizing or reducing agents, and variations in temperature and pH.

Stability of chlorophyll

Many pigments are thermally unstable and can also be affected by extremes of pH. The green colour of vegetables can fade to yellow and brown as they are cooked, owing to the thermal instability of chlorophyll. The thermal stability of chlorophyll depends on the pH.

In acidic solution, magnesium Mg^{2+} ions are removed and replaced by two H^+ ions. The $C_{20}H_{39}$ group is hydrolysed to leave a brown colour. Chlorophyll is more stable in alkaline solution and sodium hydrogen carbonate is sometimes added to water when vegetables are cooked as the alkaline conditions prevent the magnesium from leaving and an olive green colour is produced. We use the bright green colour of the chlorophyll as an indication of the freshness and vitamin content of the food.

Stability of haem

Three typical characteristics of transition metals are:

- they form coloured compounds
- they form complex ions (or co-ordination compounds with ligands)
- they are able to form different oxidation states.

Iron demonstrates all these properties in haem. In muscles, haem is associated with the purple–red protein myoglobin molecule, which binds to oxygen molecules to form the red oxymyoglobin molecule:

$$Mb-Fe^{2+} + O_2 \rightleftharpoons Mb-Fe^{2+}-O_2$$
purple-red   red

The Fe^{2+} is more stable than the Fe^{3+} ion in the non-polar environment provided by the side chains in the complex. The red oxymyoglobin does, however, undergo a slow auto-oxidation reaction to form the complex of the Fe^{3+} ion known as metamyglobin:

$$\underset{\text{purple-red}}{Mb-Fe^{2+}} \underset{\text{reduction}}{\overset{\text{oxidation}}{\rightleftharpoons}} \underset{\text{brown-red}}{Mb-Fe^{3+}}$$

This resulting complex has an undesirable brown colour.

To reduce the formation of the metamyglobin complex from auto-oxidation, meat needs to be stored in an oxygen-free atmosphere. Meats are packed in plastic films with low gas permeability and stored in an atmosphere of carbon dioxide.

Stability of anthocyanins

The structure of anthocyanins and their colour changes with pH. The flavylium cation discussed earlier found in acidic solution is bright red. In basic solution, a H^+ ion can be removed from the OH group on the left ring to form a quinoidal base which is blue.

| 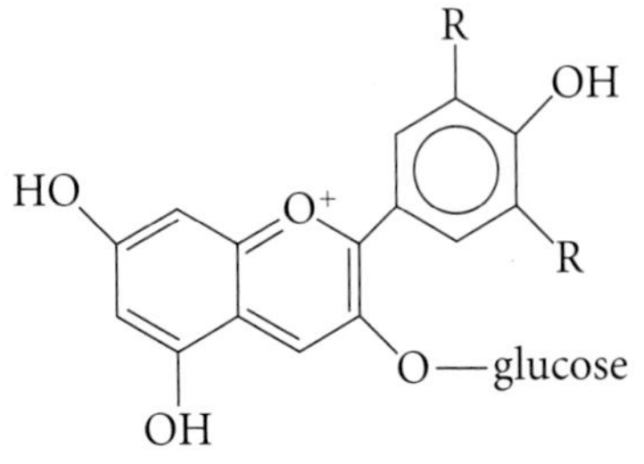 (AH⁺) flavylium red | ⇌ | 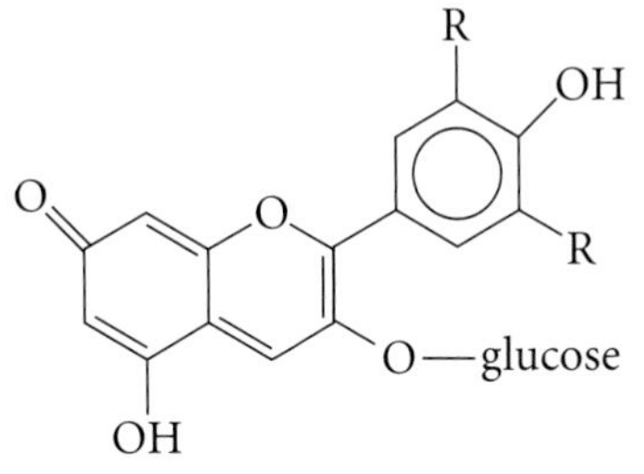 (A) quinonoid blue |

As the colour of anthocyanins is pH dependent, they can be used as acid–base indicators.

In aqueous solution anthocyanins can exists in four possible structural forms depending on the pH and temperature.

$$(A) \rightleftharpoons (AH^+) \rightleftharpoons (B) \rightleftharpoons (C)$$

| quinonoid | flavylium | carbinol base | chalcone |
| (blue) | (red) | (colourless) | (colourless) |

The species present at different pH values depends on the nature of the pigment. The colourless carbinol base is formed when hydroxide ions attack the carbon atom next to the oxygen atom in the middle hexagon. The species no longer has a carbon–oxygen double bond next to the benzene ring on the left and so loses its colour.

| 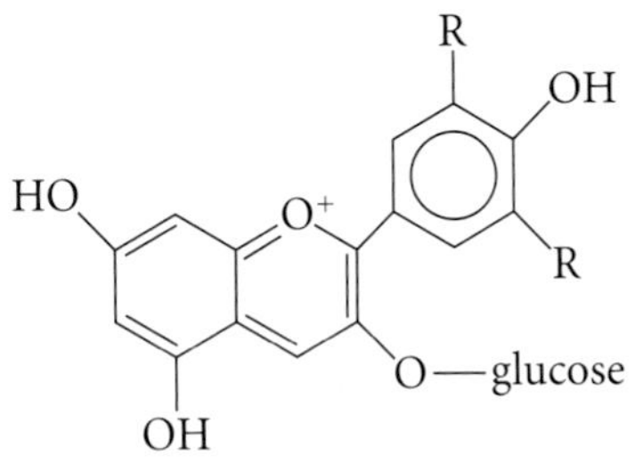 (AH⁺) flavylium red | ⇌ | 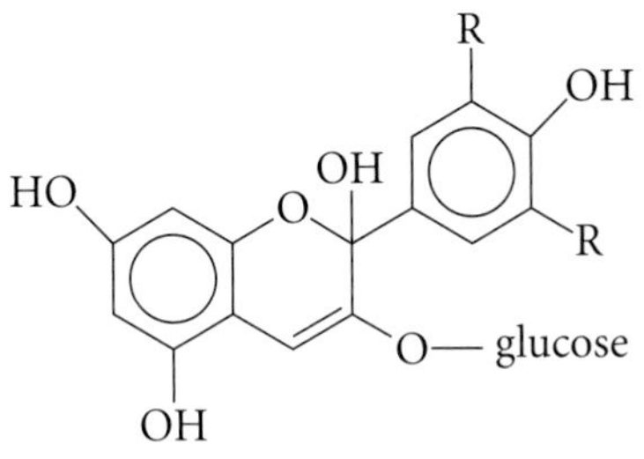 (B) carbinol pseudobase colourless |

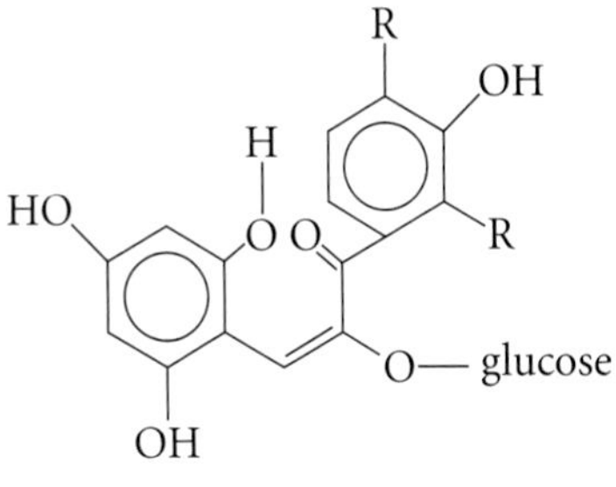

The colourless **chalcone**, which has a structure with only two hexagons, can also be produced in basic solution. As the stability of anthocyanin is also affected by the temperature, the colour of the anthocyanins can vary significantly during the cooking process. The anthocyanins are most stable and most highly coloured at low pH and low temperature. The equilibrium shown above moves to the right at higher temperatures. The less stable compounds thermally decompose at higher temperatures, which can result in a loss of colour and browning.

Exercises

19 The absorbance spectra of anthocyanins are very sensitive to changes in pH. Identify the wavelength λ_{max} which corresponds to maximum absorbance and suggest the colour of the pigment at the different pHs shown.

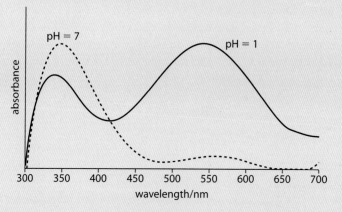

20 The anthocyanins can be used as acid–base indicators. Identify the wavelength λ_{max} which corresponds to maximum absorbance at the different pH values shown and suggest the colour of the pigment in acid and in basic conditions.

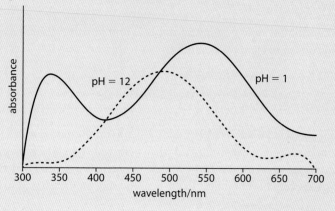

Red cabbage indicator being compared in acid and alkaline solutions.

The anthocyanins also form deeply coloured coordination complexes with Fe^{3+} and Al^{3+} ions that are present in metal cans. This produces a discoloration in canned fruit.

Stability of carotenoids

The multiple conjugated carbon–carbon double bonds which give the carotenoids their colour also makes them susceptible to oxidation catalysed by light, metals and hydroperoxides, which explains their role as antioxidants. The bread-making properties of flour improve with prolonged storage as the carotenoids in the flour are bleached to give the bread a more 'attractive' whiter crumb. Oxidation, however, can lead to a loss of vitamin A activity and produces 'off' odours. The carotenoids are stable up to 50 °C and at a pH in the range of 2−7 and, therefore, are not degraded by most forms of processing. With heating, the naturally occurring *trans* isomer rearranges to the *cis* isomer.

Non-enzymatic browning of food

Most enzymatic browning, which occurs when food is stored or when, for example, apples or potatoes are peeled and sliced, is undesirable. **Enzymatic browning** is a chemical process which occurs in fruits and vegetables containing the enzyme polyphenoloxidase. It produces brown pigments and is detrimental to quality. Enzymatic browning may be responsible for up to 50% of all losses during fruit and vegetable production. Under some conditions, however, sugars in the food can produce brown colours, which enhance the appearance and flavour of the food. There are two distinct processes which lead to this change: caramelization and Maillard browning.

Caramelization

Foods with high carbohydrate content and low nitrogen content can be **caramelized**. The process of caramelization starts with the melting of the sugar at temperatures above 120 °C. The compounds are dehydrated and double bonds are introduced into the structures. The small sugar molecules react together by condensation reactions to produce polymers with conjugated double bonds which absorb light and give brown colours. Smaller volatile molecules are also formed by a fragmentation reaction and these give the food unique flavours and fragrances. Caramelization produces desirable colour and flavour in bakery goods, coffee, soft drinks, beer and peanuts. Undesirable effects occur when the process is not controlled and all the water is removed and carbon is produced:

$$C_nH_{2m}O_m \rightarrow nC + mH_2O$$

Caramelization starts at relatively high temperatures compared to the other browning reactions and depends on the type of sugar. The table below shows the initial caramelization temperatures of some common pure carbohydrates.

Sugar	Initial caramelization temperature/°C
fructose	110
glucose	160
galactose	160
maltose	180
sucrose	160

The highest rate of colour development is caused by fructose as caramelization starts at a lower temperature.

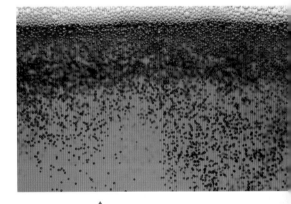

Caramelization occurs in the production of soft drinks such as cola.

Exercises

21 Explain why baked goods made from honey or fructose syrup are generally darker than those made with sugar.

22 Caramelization plays an important role in the roasting of coffee and the browning on the top of baked egg dishes.

Explain why caramelization occurs during the baking and roasting of foods, but not when they are boiled in water.

The rate and products of caramelization can be controlled by the use of catalysis. Acid catalysis operates at pH values below 3 and base catalysis at pH values greater than 9.

Maillard browning

The most common type of non-enzymatic browning is the **Maillard reaction** named after the French scientist Louis Camille Maillard (1878–1936), who studied the reactions of amino acids and carbohydrates. It is not a single reaction, but a complex series of reactions between amino acids and reducing sugars, usually at increased temperatures. The first step is the condensation reaction of a reducing sugar, such as glucose, with an amino acid which leads to the replacement of a $C{=}O$ in the aldehyde group of the sugar by a $C{=}N{-}R$ bond and the formation of water:

A series of dehydration, fragmentation and condensation reactions then follow to produce a complex mixture of products. Many different factors play a role in the Maillard reaction and thus in the final colour and aroma: the pH, type of amino acid and sugar, temperature, time, presence of oxygen, water activity and other food components are all important. The larger the sugar, for example, the slower it will react with amino acids. Five-carbon sugars (pentoses) react faster than six-carbon sugars (hexoses). As lysine has two amino groups, it is the amino acid which reacts the fastest and causes darker colours. This is why milk, which contains relatively large amounts of lysine, browns readily. Cystine, with only one amine group and a sulfur group, produces specific flavours, but produces the least colour of the amino acids.

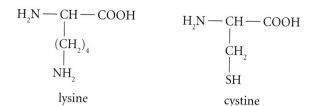

lysine   cystine

Although the Maillard reaction improves the colour and flavour of food and may have some beneficial anti-oxidant properties, it reduces the nutritional value of the food as amino acids and carbohydrates are lost.

Examples of Maillard browning include heating sugar and cream to make toffees, caramels, fudges and milk chocolate, and the flavours and colours produced during baking bread or frying and roasting meat.

See a video showing the chef Heston Blumenthal explaining how the Maillard reaction improves the flavours of roast meat.

Now go to www.heinemann.co.uk/hotlinks, insert the express code 4259P and click on this activity.

When cooking a casserole, the meat should be cooked in oil at high temperatures to allow Maillard reactions to brown the meat and add extra flavours.

Genetically modified foods

Genetic engineering is of major importance as it enables food scientists to alter the properties and processing conditions for foods. The DNA is the genetic material which determines the characteristics of an organism. Genetic engineering involves the alteration of the DNA of one or more of these genes to achieve improvements in the quality and the shelf life of foods. In the past this was done by cross breeding, but conventional plant breeding methods can be very time consuming and are often not very accurate. Genetic engineering can create plants with the exact desired trait very rapidly and with great accuracy.

It is also used to transfer DNA across species barriers that cannot be crossed by conventional techniques to produce foods which are not found in nature. One example of these **transgenic** organisms is corn into which bacterial DNA has been inserted. This allows the plant to produce a compound that is poisonous to certain caterpillars, which reduces the agricultural dependence on pesticides and herbicides. There are a number of possible benefits of genetically modified (GM) foods, but it is also an issue of public concern.

An example of a GM food is the Flavr Savr Tomato, which is genetically engineered chemically to 'turn off' the gene that produces a decay-promoting enzyme. The tomatoes can be left on the vine until ripe, picked and transported without rotting. This improves the flavour, appearance, nutritional value and shelf life of the food.

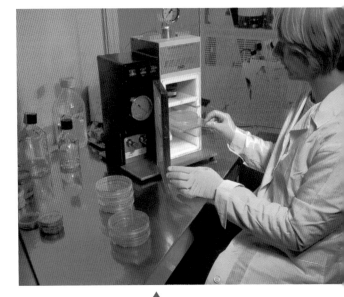

Plant biologist using a particle gun apparatus to introduce DNA into cultured plant cells. DNA-coated particles are fired into the plant cells and DNA enters the nuclei. This method is commonly used to create transgenic plants.

Tin of tomato puree whose label states that it has been made from genetically-engineered plants.

Benefits of GM foods

Genetic modification can add a gene to a cell to change cell behaviour, inactivate a gene in a cell to remove undesired behaviour, or modify a gene so that higher yields of products are obtained. This leads to a number of benefits:

 A genetically modified food is one derived or produced from a genetically modified organism.

Young genetically modified cotton plants being sprayed with herbicide. This transgenic cotton has been genetically engineered to be resistant to the herbicide. The cotton contains a bacterial gene which produces an enzyme that hydrolyses the herbicides into non-toxic compounds. This will theoretically increase crop yields.

- GM foods have improved flavour, texture and nutritional value.
- GM foods have longer shelf life.
- GM organisms are more resistant to disease and pests.
- Genetic modification provides increased crop yields in plants and feed efficiency in animals.
- GM plants are more resistant to herbicides and fungicides.
- Environmentally 'friendly' bio-herbicides and bio-insecticides can be produced.
- GM foods can lead to soil, water and energy conservation and improve natural waste management.
- Genetic modification can enable animals and plants to produce:
  - increased amounts of substances such as vitamins A and C which can improve human health. Anti-cancer substances and vaccines can also be incorporated into the food.
  - decreased amounts of substances which are detrimental to health such as unhealthy fats.
- GM plants can grow in a wider range of climatic conditions. Strains of rice, for example, have been developed with increased drought tolerance.

Transgenic rice research has developed strains of rice that have enhanced drought tolerance and fungal resistance and provided nutritional value with additional vitamin A.

Potential concerns

Many people are, however, concerned about the increased production of GM foods. Potential concerns include:

- uncertainties about the outcomes of genetic modifications given the relatively recent development of the technique
- links to increased allergies (for people involved in the processing of GM foods)
- the risk of changing the composition of a balanced diet by altering the natural nutritional quality of foods
- pollen from GM crops may escape to contaminate 'normal' crops or the wild population and so damage the natural ecosystem.

Exercises

23 Describe on a molecular level how a plant can be genetically modified to give a GM food.
24 State three benefits and three concerns of using genetically modified foods.

● **Examiner's hint:** Avoid sloppy language. The fact that anti-cancer substances can be incorporated into GM foods is an acceptable benefit, but 'cures cancer' is not.

GM foods raise issues of conflict of concepts and values. Examine the facts, language, statistics and images used in the debate over their use. How certain is the scientific community about the outcomes of genetic modifications? What is an acceptable risk and who should decide whether particular directions in research are pursued?

.6 Texture

Food, in addition to providing nutrients and colour, must have a pleasing texture. Whereas the taste, colour and smell of a food are chemical properties, the texture is a physical property. Many food ingredients are completely immiscible and so will form separate phases within the food. However, in some cases the size of these phases can be very small, so as to appear **homogeneous** to the naked eye. A **colloidal** particle is many times larger than an individual molecule but many times smaller than anything that can be seen with the naked eye. A colloid is a mixture of a dispersed phase and a continuous phase.

◀ **Figure 17.8** A dispersed system with a continuous and dispersed phase.

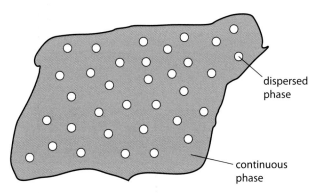

dispersed phase

continuous phase

A colloid is a mixture of a dispersed phase and a continuous phase (disperse medium). A colloid is not a solution, as although the colloid particles are not usually seen under a microscope, they are much larger than molecules and also bigger than the molecules of the continuous phase.

Milk is an example of such a dispersed system. It appears white because light is scattered by protein and fat droplets dispersed in water. Most foods are dispersed systems.

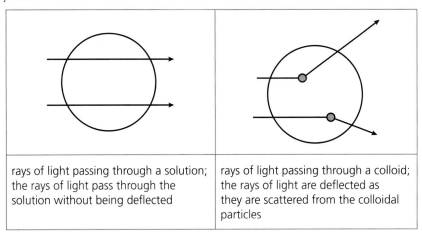

rays of light passing through a solution; the rays of light pass through the solution without being deflected	rays of light passing through a colloid; the rays of light are deflected as they are scattered from the colloidal particles

▲ Milk appears white because light is scattered by the fat particles dispersed in the continuous water phase.

Dispersed systems

A dispersed system is a **kinetically stable** mixture of one phase in another largely immiscible phase: it will separate into its components with different densities owing to action of gravity but this only happens very slowly.

Oil and vinegar are immiscible liquids. When shaken together they form an emulsion, a mixture of small droplets.	When left for a while, the two liquids separate into different layers.

There are eight different types of dispersed system classified according to the states of the components which make up the dispersed and continuous states. The most important ones in food generally contain a liquid phase as one of the components.

Continuous phase	Dispersed phase	Type	Example
gas	gas		none – all gases mix completely
gas	liquid	aerosol	mist, food smells
gas	solid	aerosol	smoke
liquid	gas	foam	whipped cream, egg whites, beer
liquid	liquid	emulsion	oil in water/milk, water in oil/butter
liquid	solid	solution/ suspension	molten chocolate
solid	gas	solid foam	bread, meringue
solid	liquid	gel	jam

Beer is an example of a foam.

A meringue is a solid foam; whipped cream is a foam.

25 Identify the type of dispersed system in each of the following foods.

Food type	Continuous phase	Dispersed phase	Type of dispersed system
ice cream			
bread			
jam			
salad cream			
beer			
whipped cream			
butter			

Emulsifiers

There are two important types of food emulsion, oil-in-water found in milk and salad dressing and water-in-oil emulsions such as butter. The non-polar oil molecules do not generally mix with the polar water molecules and so an **emulsifier** is often needed. These are substances which aid the mixing of the two phases and stabilize the dispersed state and prevent the mixture from separating into its two components. An emulsifier generally has a polar head which is **hydrophilic** and so attracted to the water and a non-polar tail which is **hydrophobic** and so dissolves in oil at the interface between the two phases.

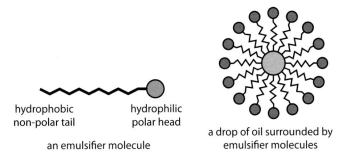

hydrophobic
non-polar tail

hydrophilic
polar head

an emulsifier molecule

a drop of oil surrounded by
emulsifier molecules

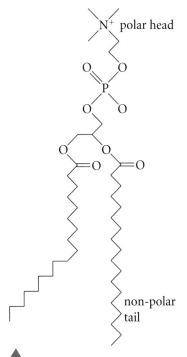

Figure 17.9 The polar head of lecithin mixes with water and its non-polar tail mixes with oil.

Lecithin is widely used as an emulsifier. It is present in egg yolk which is added to oil and water mixtures to make mayonnaise and other salad dressings. Mechanical energy is needed physically to make an emulsion, which is why beating, mixing and whisking are important culinary skills.

Whereas emulsifiers help the different phases to mix, **stabilizers** such as trisodium phosphate Na_3PO_4 are added to prevent the emulsions from separating out into the separate phases.

26 Describe and explain the characteristics of an emulsifier molecule.

27 Distinguish between the dispersed systems of suspensions, emulsions and foams.

Practice questions

1 Many nutritionists are now suggesting a dietary pattern based on the food triangle below. This gives the recommended percentage of each food group in a balanced diet.

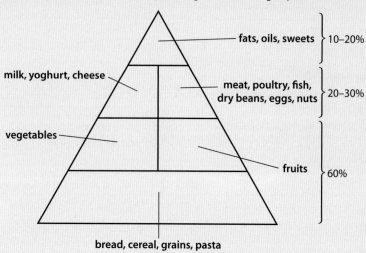

(a) Identify the major nutrient available from bread, cereal, grains and pasta and describe the principal role this nutrient plays in human nutrition. (2)

(b) Identify the major nutrients present in meat and fish. (2)

(c) Identify the class of nutrients available from fruits or vegetables but not generally available from the other food groups. (1)

(*Total 5 marks*)

2 Distinguish between a food and a nutrient. Give an example of a food that is not a nutrient. (3)

3 Ethanoic acid has the empirical formula $C_2H_4O_2$. Could the compound be classed as a carbohydrate? (2)

4 Polypeptides and proteins are formed by the condensation reactions of amino acids.

(a) Give the general structural formula of a 2-amino acid. (1)

(b) Give the structural formula of the dipeptide formed by the reaction of alanine and glycine. State the other substance formed during this reaction. (2)

(*Total 3 marks*)

© International Baccalaureate Organization [2003]

5 (a) State the empirical formula of all monosaccharides. (1)

(b) The structural formula of lactose is shown in Table 21 of the IB Data booklet.

(i) Deduce the structural formula of **one** of the monosaccharides that reacts to form lactose and state its name. (2)

(ii) State the name of the **other** monosaccharide. (1)

(*Total 4 marks*)

© International Baccalaureate Organization [2004]

6 Fats and oils can be described as esters of glycerol, $C_3H_8O_3$.

(a) Draw the structure of glycerol. (1)

(b) Glycerol can react with three molecules of stearic acid, $C_{17}H_{35}COOH$, to form a triglyceride. Deduce the number of carbon atoms in **one** molecule of this triglyceride. (1)

(c) A triglyceride is also formed in the reaction between glycerol and three molecules of oleic acid, $C_{17}H_{33}COOH$. State and explain which of the two triglycerides (the one formed from stearic acid or the one formed from oleic acid) has the higher melting point. (3)

(Total 5 marks)

© International Baccalaureate Organization [2003]

7 Most naturally occurring unsaturated fats are *cis* isomers, but hydrogenation of polyunsaturated fats can lead to the formation of *trans* isomers.
Distinguish between the types of isomers and state and explain which type of isomer generally has the higher melting point. (4)

8 (a) Explain the meaning of the term *shelf life*. (1)
   (b) State and explain two ways in which the packaging can increase the shelf life of food. (2)
   (c) Explain how antioxidants extend the shelf life of food. (2)
   (d) State the names of two antioxidants. (2)
   (e) The structure of the synthetic antioxidant BHA is given inTable 22 of the IB Data booklet. Explain its antioxidant properties with reference to its molecular structure. (2)

(Total 9 marks)

9 (a) Distinguish between a food pigment and a food dye. (1)
   (b) One group of chemicals responsible for the colour of some food has a structure closely related to vitamin A. Identify the class of compound and describe the structural feature responsible for their colours. (2)
   (c) Explain how changing the pH changes the colour of the anthocyanins. (2)

(Total 5 marks)

10 Compare the two processes of non-enzymatic browning (Maillard reaction) and caramelization in terms of the chemical composition of the food affected and the products formed. (4)

(Total 5 marks)

11 The structures of the amino acids are given in Table 19 of the IB Data booklet.
   (a) Identify an amino acid which can take part in a Maillard reaction when it is part of a protein chain and explain your answer. (3)
   (b) Suggest why it is unlikely that a polymer molecule could be responsible for a food's fragrance. (2)

(Total 6 marks)

12 (a) Distinguish between an emulsion and a foam and give one example of each. (4)
   (b) Lecithin is an example of a natural emulsifier found in egg yolk. Explain, with reference to its molecular structure, how it can act as an emulsifier for oil and water mixtures. (2)

13 (a) State how genetically modified food differs from unmodified food. (1)
   (b) List **two** benefits and **two** concerns of using genetically modified crops. (4)

(Total 5 marks)

© International Baccalaureate Organization [2003]

18 Further organic chemistry: Option G

If you look around the room you are in now you should be able to identify organic compounds everywhere: this book that you are reading, the clothes that you are wearing, probably the desk or table that you are working on (if it is made of wood or plastic) and definitely your own body – all of these are organic in nature. In fact it would be much easier to list the compounds around you that are *not* organic in nature! In Chapter 10 we learned some of the basics of organizing the study of this major branch of chemistry and explored the characteristic properties of a few homologous series.

A more in-depth study of organic chemistry involves a look at *how* reactions happen at the molecular level, the so-called **reaction mechanisms**. This study involves a breakdown of the reaction into a sequence of steps, each involving the making or breaking of bonds. As these steps can usually not be observed directly, evidence for their existence is derived indirectly from considerations of kinetic factors, that is, those which affect the rate of the reaction. Generally we are not able to prove that a particular mechanism is correct, only that it is consistent with the observed data. Modern laser technology, especially, is giving chemists a way to look at reactions that take place very fast, in 10^{-13} seconds for example, adding greatly to our knowledge. As we discuss the mechanisms of organic reactions in this chapter you are encouraged to assess the evidence given and ask yourself what further evidence would support – or refute – the proposed mechanism.

Understanding organic reactions at the molecular level makes it possible for research and industrial chemists to devise the most efficient conditions for synthetic reactions. Innovative products such as breathable fabrics, strong and biodegradable plastics and new superconducting materials are all the results of such research. Towards the end of this chapter you will have the chance to use your knowledge of organic reactions to work out possible routes for synthesis of some organic products.

Bottle of Taxol, a chemotherapy compound found in the bark of the Pacific yew tree which has proved highly effective in the treatment of breast and ovarian cancer. Organic chemists have been researching into synthetic pathways for producing the drug in order to provide a more sustainable supply to meet current demand. ▶

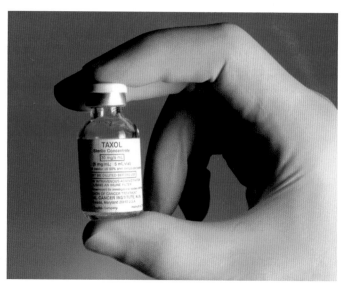

Assessment statements

G.1 Electrophilic addition reactions

G.1.1 Describe and explain the electrophilic addition mechanisms of the reactions of alkenes with halogens and hydrogen halides.

G.1.2 Predict and explain the formation of the major product in terms of the relative stabilities of carbocations.

G.2 Nucleophilic addition reactions

G.2.1 Describe, using equations, the addition of hydrogen cyanide to aldehydes and ketones.

G.2.2 Describe and explain the mechanism for the addition of hydrogen cyanide to aldehydes and ketones.

G.2.3 Describe, using equations, the hydrolysis of cyanohydrins to form carboxylic acids.

G.3 Elimination reactions

G.3.1 Describe, using equations, the dehydration reactions of alcohols with phosphoric acid to form alkenes.

G.3.2 Describe and explain the mechanism for the elimination of water from alcohols.

G.4 Addition–elimination reactions

G.4.1 Describe, using equations, the reactions of 2,4-dinitrophenylhydrazine with aldehydes and ketones.

G.5 Arenes

G.5.1 Describe and explain the structure of benzene using physical and chemical evidence.

G.5.2 Describe and explain the relative rates of hydrolysis of benzene compounds halogenated in the ring and in the side chain.

G.6 Organometallic chemistry

G.6.1 Outline the formation of Grignard reagents.

G.6.2 Describe, using equations, the reactions of Grignard reagents with water, carbon dioxide, aldehydes and ketones.

G.7 Reaction pathways

G.7.1 Deduce reaction pathways given the starting materials and the product.

G.8 Acid–base reactions

G.8.1 Describe and explain the acidic properties of phenol and substituted phenols in terms of bonding.

G.8.2 Describe and explain the acidic properties of substituted carboxylic acids in terms of bonding.

G.8.3 Compare and explain the relative basicities of ammonia and amines.

ⓘ Definitions and conventions used in organic chemistry

The study of organic chemistry involves recognizing several different types of reactant and reaction. Some of these were introduced in Chapter 10, others are new to this section, so you should find the following summary a useful reference as you work through the chapter.

Types of reactant

Saturated	Unsaturated
• compounds which contain only single bonds • for example: alkanes	• compounds which contain double or triple bonds • for example: alkenes, arenes

Aliphatics	Arenes
• compounds which do not contain a benzene ring; may be saturated or unsaturated • for example: alkanes, alkenes	• compounds which contain a benzene ring; they are all unsaturated compounds • for example: benzene, phenol

Electrophile (electron-seeking)	Nucleophile (nucleus-seeking)
• an electron-deficient species which is therefore attracted to parts of molecules which are electron rich • electrophiles are positive ions or have a partial positive charge • for example: NO_2^+, H^+, $Br^{\delta+}$	• an electron-rich species which is therefore attracted to parts of molecules which are electron deficient • nucleophiles have a lone pair of electrons and may also have a negative charge • for example: Cl^-, OH^-, NH_3 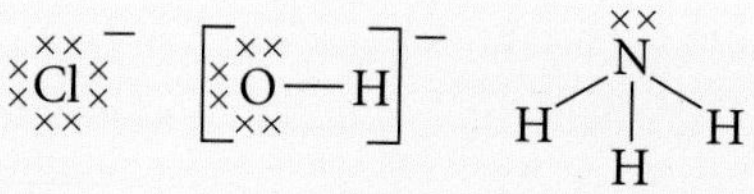

Types of reaction

Addition	• occurs when two reactants combine to form a single product • characteristic of unsaturated compounds • for example $C_2H_4 + Br_2 \rightarrow C_2H_4Br_2$ 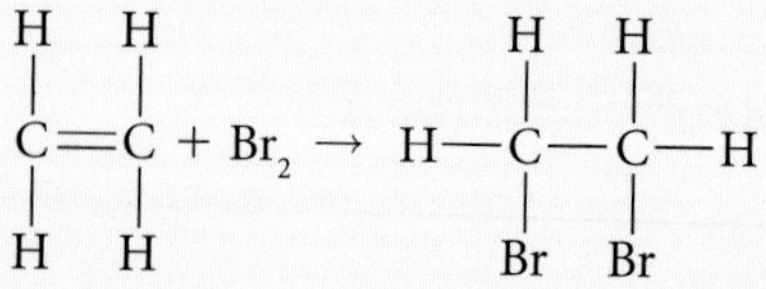
Substitution	• occurs when one atom or group of atoms in a compound is replaced by a different atom or group • characteristic of saturated compounds and aromatic compounds • for example $CH_4 + Cl_2 \rightarrow CH_3Cl + HCl$

Elimination	<ul><li>occurs when a small molecule is lost from a larger compound</li><li>usually results in the formation of a double or triple bond</li><li>when the molecule eliminated is H_2O, the reaction is **dehydration**</li><li>for example $C_2H_5OH \rightarrow C_2H_4 + H_2O$</li></ul>	$$H-\underset{\underset{H}{\mid}}{\overset{\overset{H}{\mid}}{C}}-\underset{\underset{H}{\mid}}{\overset{\overset{H}{\mid}}{C}}-O-H \; \rightarrow \; \underset{\underset{H}{\mid}}{\overset{\overset{H}{\mid}}{C}}=\underset{\underset{H}{\mid}}{\overset{\overset{H}{\mid}}{C}} + H_2O$$
Addition–elimination	<ul><li>occurs when two reactants join together (addition) and in the process a small molecule such as H_2O, HCl or NH_3 is lost (elimination)</li><li>reaction occurs between a functional group in each reactant</li><li>also called **condensation** reaction</li><li>for example $RNH_2 + R'COOH \rightarrow R'CONHR + H_2O$</li></ul>	$$R-N\underset{\underset{\text{amino}}{\overset{H}{\diagdown}}}{\overset{H}{\diagup}} + \underset{\underset{\text{acid}}{\overset{HO}{\diagup}}}{\overset{O}{\diagdown}}C-R' \rightarrow \underset{\text{amide}}{R-\underset{\underset{H}{\mid}}{N}-\overset{\overset{O}{\parallel}}{C}-R'} + H_2O$$

Types of bond breaking (bond fission)

Homolytic fission	Heterolytic fission
<ul><li>when a covalent bond breaks by splitting the shared pair of electrons between the two products</li><li>produces two free radicals each with an unpaired electron</li></ul>$$X\!:\!X \; \rightarrow \; X^{\bullet} + X^{\bullet}$$	<ul><li>when a covalent bond breaks with both the shared electrons going to one of the products</li><li>produces two oppositely charged ions</li></ul>$$X\!:\!X \; \rightarrow \; X\!:^{-} + X^{+}$$

Convention for depicting organic reaction mechanisms

Describing organic reaction mechanisms often involves showing the movement of electrons within bonds and between reactants. The convention adopted for this is a **curly arrow**, drawn from the site of electron availability, such as a pair of non-bonding electrons, to the site of electron deficiency, such as an atom with a partial positive charge.

For example:

$$X \overset{\frown}{} Y$$

represents e^- pair being pulled towards Y so Y becomes $\delta -$ and X becomes $\delta +$

$$X: \overset{\curvearrowright}{} \overset{\mid}{\underset{\mid}{C}}\!\!\overset{\delta +}{-}$$

nucleophile X attracted to e^- deficient C

The double-headed arrow represents the motion of an electron pair. Often the mechanism involves several steps in which electrons are transferred ultimately to an atom or group of atoms, which then detaches itself and is known as the **leaving group**. We will use blue throughout this chapter to show curly arrows and the pull of electrons.

▲ Tomatoes ripening on the vine. Ethene is produced in low levels by most parts of plants, regulating the ripening of fruit and the opening of flowers. Commercial suppliers take advantage of this by applying ethene to fruit to ensure that it is ripened at just the right time for sale.

G.1 **Electrophilic addition reactions**

Alkenes have a carbon–carbon double bond and readily undergo addition reactions

Alkenes are unsaturated molecules containing a carbon–carbon double bond C=C. They are able to undergo **addition** reactions in which one of the carbon–carbon bonds breaks and incoming atoms add to the new bonding positions available on the carbon atoms. This reactivity of alkenes makes them very versatile and important compounds in many synthesis pathways, as we described in Chapter 10.

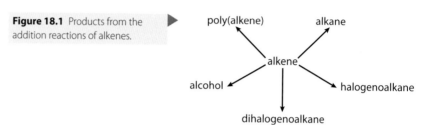

Figure 18.1 Products from the addition reactions of alkenes.

The double bond in alkenes actually consists of two different bonds, one sigma σ bond which forms along the bond axis (an imaginary line joining the nuclei of the two bonded atoms) and one pi π bond which is an area of electron density above and below the plane of the bond axis. Because electrons in the π bond are less closely associated with the nuclei, it is a weaker bond than the σ bond and so more easily breaks during the addition reactions.

> An addition reaction occurs when two reactants combine to form a single product. This type of reaction is characteristic of unsaturated compounds containing double or triple bonds.

The nature of the double bond in alkenes:

Note that the π bond is one bond, although it has two areas of electron density. When this bond breaks, reactants attach at each carbon atom:

$$\overset{120°}{\diagup}\text{C}=\text{C}\diagdown + \text{XY} \rightarrow -\overset{|}{\underset{|}{\text{C}}}-\overset{|}{\underset{|}{\text{C}}}-\\ \text{X} \quad \text{Y}$$

Alkenes have a planar triangular shape (120° bond angle) around the double-bonded carbons which is a fairly open structure that makes it easier for incoming groups to attack. As we will see, this is important in the mechanism of the reaction.

Halogens and hydrogen halides react as electrophiles in reactions with alkenes

Because it is an area of electron density, the π bond is attractive to **electrophiles**, species that either are electron deficient or that become electron deficient in the presence of the π bond.

Reactions between these reagents and alkenes are thus known as **electrophilic addition reactions**. Good examples include the addition of halogens and hydrogen halides. In these reactions the electrophile is produced through

▲ Molecular model of ethene, C_2H_4, showing the double bond between the two carbon atoms. This bond is the site of reactivity of alkenes and enables them to undergo addition reactions, producing a wide range of products.

heterolytic fission, as described in detail in the examples below. These addition reactions happen readily under mild conditions and are very important in several synthetic pathways.

(i) Ethene + bromine

When ethene gas is bubbled through bromine at room temperature, the brown colour of the bromine fades as it reacts to form the saturated product 1,2-dibromoethane:

$$
\underset{\text{ethene}}{\text{H}_2\text{C}=\text{CH}_2} \quad + \quad \underset{\substack{\text{bromine}\\\text{(brown/orange)}}}{\text{Br}-\text{Br}} \quad \rightarrow \quad \underset{\substack{\text{1, 2-dibromoethane}\\\text{(colourless)}}}{\text{H}-\text{CH}_2-\text{CH}_2-\text{H}}
$$

We learned in Chapter 10 that colour changes of this type are often used to show the presence of unsaturation. (Saturated hydrocarbons, the alkanes, will only react with halogens in the presence of UV light by a substitution reaction with a free radical mechanism so they do not decolourize bromine easily.)

The mechanism of the reaction is as follows:

• Bromine is a non-polar molecule, but as it approaches the electron-rich region of the alkene, it becomes polarized by electron repulsion.

Bromine molecule is polarized by an alkene

• The bromine atom nearest to the alkene's double bond (shown in red) gains a $\delta+$ charge and acts as the electrophile. Note the curly arrow is always drawn in the direction in which the electron pair moves. The bromine molecule splits **heterolytically** forming Br^+ and Br^- and the initial attack on the ethene in which the π bond breaks is carried out by the positive ion Br^+.

This step is slow, resulting in an unstable **carbocation** intermediate in which the carbon atom has a share in only six outer electrons and carries an overall positive charge.

• This unstable species then reacts rapidly with the negative bromide ion Br^- forming the product 1,2-dibromoethane.

1, 2-dibromoethane

Overall the equation for the reaction can be written as:

$$C_2H_4 + Br_2 \rightarrow CH_2BrCH_2Br$$

An electrophile is an electron-deficient species that is attracted to parts of molecules that are electron rich. Electrophiles are positive ions or have a partial positive charge.

The bromine test for an alkene. The tube on the right contains cyclohexene that has reacted with bromine water and decolourized it. This is because it contains a reactive double bond. The tube on the left contains benzene, showing that it has not decolourized the bromine water. We will learn in Section G.5 why, although it is unsaturated, benzene does not readily undergo addition reactions.

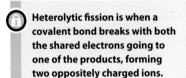

Heterolytic fission is when a covalent bond breaks with both the shared electrons going to one of the products, forming two oppositely charged ions.

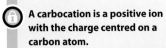

A carbocation is a positive ion with the charge centred on a carbon atom.

Similar reactions take place with other alkenes such as propene. For example:

$$CH_3CHCH_2 + Br_2 \rightarrow CH_3CHBrCH_2Br$$

propene   1,2-dibromopropane

Sometimes, when this reaction is carried out in the laboratory, bromine water is used in place of pure bromine and this can affect the product formed although the same decolourization change is seen. The first step shown earlier happens in the same way, but the carbocation can be attacked by water molecules in competition with Br^- because as they have lone pairs they too can donate electrons to the carbocation.

2-bromoethanol

As can be seen, this means that a bromoalcohol will be formed in place of the dibromo product and the relative concentrations of these products will depend on the strength of the bromine water used.

Chlorine reacts in a similar way to bromine in these reactions, forming the dichloro alkane or a chloroalcohol if chlorine water is used.

(ii) Ethene + hydrogen bromide

When ethene gas is bubbled through a concentrated aqueous solution of hydrogen bromide HBr, an addition reaction occurs fairly readily at room temperature, forming bromoethane:

bromoethane

The reaction occurs by a similar mechanism to that described above. HBr as a polar molecule undergoes heterolytic fission to form H^+ and Br^-, and the electrophile H^+ makes an initial attack on the alkene's double bond. The unstable carbocation intermediate that forms from this step then reacts quickly with Br^- to form the addition product.

The mechanism is as follows:

carbocation intermediate

carbocation intermediate   bromoethane

One piece of evidence that supports this mechanism is that the reaction is favoured by a polar solvent that facilitates the production of ions from heterolytic fission.

Evidence for this reaction mechanism can be gained by carrying out the same reaction, C_2H_4 and Br_2, with the additional presence of chloride ions Cl^-. It is found that the products are $BrH_2C–CH_2Br$ and $BrH_2C–CH_2Cl$. This is consistent with the mechanism described, as the carbocation formed in the first step is equally ready to combine with Br^- and Cl^-. The fact that no dichloro compound is ever formed in this reaction confirms that the initial attack was by the electrophile Br^+ formed from Br_2.

The other hydrogen halides react similarly with alkenes, HI more readily than HBr, owing to its weaker bond, and HCl less readily, owing to its stronger bond.

(iii) Propene + hydrogen bromide (unsymmetric addition)

When an unsymmetric alkene like propene is reacted with a hydrogen halide such as HBr, there are theoretically two different products that can be formed. These are isomers of each other resulting from two possible pathways of the electrophilic addition mechanism described above.

The compound 1,2-dichloroethane is synthesized by the addition of chlorine to ethene. Approximately 10 million tonnes of this are made per year in the USA and used both as a solvent and as a starting material for the manufacture of the plastic PVC (poly vinyl chloride).

$$H-\underset{\substack{1}}{C}=\underset{\substack{2}}{C}-C-H + HBr$$

(a) 1-bromopropane
(b) carbocation intermediates 2-bromopropane

Workers in a recycling facility in India with a pile of pens which will be recycled for their PVC content. PVC is the second largest commodity plastic in the world after polythene. PVC manufacture uses the addition reaction of chlorine to ethene.

The difference between these two depends on whether the attacking electrophile (H$^+$ formed from heterolytic fission of HBr) is more likely to bond to the carbon labelled 2 as in mechanism (a) above or to the carbon labelled 1 as in mechanism (b). So which is the more likely? The answer comes from considering which pathway will give the most stable carbocation during the addition process.

In Chapter 10 (page 209) we learned that alkyl groups around a carbocation stabilize it owing to their **positive inductive effects**, meaning that they push electron density away from themselves and so lessen the density of the positive charge. In (a) above the carbocation is a **primary carbocation** and is stabilized by *only one* such positive inductive effect, whereas in (b) a **secondary carbocation** forms in which there are *two* such effects and the stabilization is greater. Consequently the more stable carbocation in (b) will be more likely to persist and react with Br$^-$, leading to 2-bromopropane as the major product of the reaction.

primary carbocation
one positive inductive effect

secondary carbocation
two positive inductive effects:
more stable

You can listen to a tutorial explaining the electrophilic addition of halogens to alkenes.

Now go to www.heinemann.co.uk/hotlinks, insert the express code 4259P and click on this activity.

Thus the correct mechanism for the reaction is:

2-bromopropane

We can predict such an outcome for any reaction involving addition of a hydrogen halide to asymmetric alkenes by using what is known as **Markovnikov's rule**. This states: *the hydrogen will attach to the carbon that is already bonded to the greater numbers of hydrogens.* As we have seen this is based on the fact that the pathway that proceeds via the most stable carbocation will be favoured.

In more general terms Markovnikov's rule can be stated as *the more electropositive part of the reacting species bonds to the least highly substituted carbon atom in the alkene* (the one with the smaller number of carbons attached). Applying this rule enables us to predict the outcomes from any reactions involving unsymmetric reagents undergoing addition reactions with unsymmetric alkenes.

● **Examiner's hint:** Markovnikov's rule can be remembered as *'they that have are given more'.* The carbon with the most hydrogen atoms gets the incoming hydrogen; the carbon with the most substituents gets another substituent.

Markovnikov's rule: When an unsymmetrical reagent adds to an unsymmetrical alkene, the electrophilic portion of the reagent adds to the carbon that is bonded to the greater number of hydrogen atoms.

Worked example

Write names and structures for the two possible products of the addition of water to propene. Consider which is likely to be the major product and explain why.

Solution

The two possible reactions are:

Considering the carbocation that would be produced en route to each of these products by addition of the electrophile H^+:

We can see that the secondary carbocation in (ii) is more stable than the primary carbocation in (i) owing to the greater number of positive inductive effects available to spread the density of the positive charge. So this pathway is favoured, leading to the synthesis of propan-2-ol as the major product.

Vladimir Markovnikov (1838–1904) was a Russian chemist who also studied in Germany. He developed his famous rule in 1869 but as he refused to publish in a foreign language, these findings were unknown outside of Russia until 1899. It has been observed that his published work was not based on much of his own experimental work and may have been more of an inspired guess. 1869 was also the year that Mendeleyev, another Russian chemist, published his Periodic Table.

Exercises

1 Explain carefully why alkenes undergo electrophilic addition reactions. Outline the mechanism of the reaction between but-2-ene and bromine and name the product.

2 Predict the major product of the reaction between but-1-ene and hydrogen bromide. Explain the basis of your prediction.

3 By considering the polarity within the molecule ICl, determine how it would react with propene. Draw the structure and name the main product.

6.2 Nucleophilic addition reactions

Aldehydes and ketones have a carbon–oxygen double bond and undergo addition reactions

Aldehydes and ketones possess a carbon–oxygen double bond, known as a **carbonyl group** C=O. As in alkenes, this double bond consists of a σ bond and a weaker π bond that is the site of reactivity for addition reactions. Breakage of the π bond creates two new bonding positions leading to the formation of addition products. But, unlike in alkenes, the double bond in aldehydes and ketones is a **polar bond** resulting from the differing electronegativities of carbon and oxygen. Unequal electron sharing results in the carbon atom (known as the carbonyl carbon) being electron deficient ($\delta+$) while the oxygen atom is electron rich ($\delta-$). As we will see, this polarity leads to an entirely different mechanism for the addition reaction than that described for the alkenes.

$$\text{carbonyl group} \quad \overset{\delta+}{\underset{}{C}}=\overset{\delta-}{O}$$

Aldehydes and ketones both possess the carbonyl group C=O, but its position in the molecule differs. As described in Chapter 10, page 190, in aldehydes the carbonyl carbon is also bonded to at least one hydrogen atom (two in the case of methanal). In ketones, the carbonyl carbon is bonded to two alkyl (carbon-containing) groups. This means that the smallest ketone has three carbons (propanone, CH_3COCH_3):

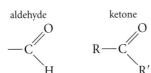

HCN reacts as a nucleophile in reactions with aldehydes and ketones

Aldehydes and ketones with their electron deficient ($\delta+$) carbonyl carbon atom are susceptible to attack by **nucleophiles**, species that are electron rich and so are attracted to a region of electron deficiency.

Aldehydes and ketones behave similarly in these reactions but aldehydes generally are more reactive as the electron deficiency ($\delta+$) on their carbonyl carbon is not reduced by two positive inductive effects as it is in ketones.

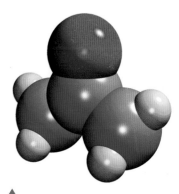

Computer model of a molecule of propanone $(CH_3)_2$ CO.

Reactions in which aldehydes and ketones react with nucleophiles are known as **nucleophilic addition reactions.** They include several reactions of biological and

Follow this interactive tutorial to help understand the relative reactivity of aldehydes and ketones – beware non-IUPAC names!

Now go to www.heinemann.co.uk/hotlinks, insert the express code 4259P and click on this activity.

Propanone, often referred to as acetone, is soluble in water and itself is a very important solvent. For example, it is used in thinning fibreglass resins and is a solvent for superglue. It is the active ingredient in nail polish remover and is used in the synthesis of plastics such as perspex. Small amounts of propanone are made in the human body and it is sometimes present in the exhaled breath of diabetics owing to their elevated glucose levels.

A nucleophile is an electron-rich species which is attracted to parts of a molecule that are electron deficient. Nucleophiles possess one or more lone pairs of electrons and may also carry a negative charge.

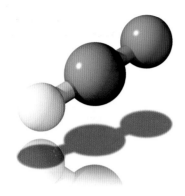

Molecular model of hydrogen cyanide, HCN, showing hydrogen in white, carbon in grey and nitrogen in blue. It is a colourless, poisonous gas which has a faint smell of almonds.

● **Examiner's hint:** When naming compounds containing the nitrile group —CN, remember to count the carbon of the functional group as part of the longest chain. For example, C_2H_5CN is *propane*nitrile as there is a total of three carbon atoms.

industrial significance such as the production of alcohols as solvents. We will study one example of this type of reaction here, the reaction with HCN.

The Lewis structure of HCN shows its bonding as follows:

$$H \overset{\bullet}{\underset{\times}{}} C \overset{\bullet\bullet}{\underset{\times\times}{}} N \overset{\times}{\underset{\times}{}}$$

$$H—C\equiv N \overset{\times}{\underset{\times}{}}$$

During the addition reaction, for example with ethanal, it adds across the $C{=}O$ double bond as follows:

$$CH_3—C\overset{O}{\underset{H}{}} + HCN \rightarrow CH_3—\overset{OH}{\underset{H}{C}}—CN$$

2-hydroxypropanenitrile

The $—C\equiv N$ group is a functional group known as nitrile (or cyano).

The mechanism of the reaction is as follows:

● HCN is usually generated during the reaction by the action of dilute HCl on KCN at 10–20°C.

$$HCl(aq) + KCN(aq) \xrightarrow{10-20°C} KCl(aq) + HCN(aq)$$

● As a weak acid, HCN dissociates in aqueous solution to form H^+ and CN^- ions.

$$HCN(aq) + H_2O(l) \rightleftharpoons H_3O^+(aq) + CN^-(aq)$$

$$\left[\overset{\times}{\underset{\times}{}} C \equiv N \overset{\times}{\underset{\times}{}} \right]^-$$

● CN^-, with its lone pair of electrons and negative charge, is a nucleophile and attacks the electron deficient carbonyl carbon breaking the π bond between C and O.

$$CH_3—\overset{\delta+}{C}\overset{\delta-}{\underset{H}{O}} + \overset{\times\times}{CN^-} \rightarrow CH_3—\overset{O^-}{\underset{H}{C}}—CN$$

● The intermediate ion with a negative charge then reacts rapidly with H^+ forming a hydroxyl group —OH bonded to the carbon. The resulting compound is thus known as a **hydroxynitrile** compound or a **cyanohydrin**:

$$CH_3—\overset{O^-}{\underset{H}{C}}—CN + H^+ \rightarrow CH_3—\overset{OH}{\underset{H}{C}}—CN$$

2-hydroxypropanenitrile

You can follow a description of the mechanism for the reaction between HCN and aldehydes and ketones.

Now go to www.heinemann.co.uk/hotlinks, insert the express code 4259P and click on this activity.

Worked example

Write equations for the reaction between butanone and HCN, showing all steps in the reaction and naming the product.

Solution

The product is 2-hydroxy-2-methylbutanenitrile.

The cyanide ion CN⁻ is highly toxic as it inhibits the enzyme cytochrome oxidase in the last reaction of aerobic respiration which passes electrons to oxygen. As a result, it prevents the release of energy in cells and quickly affects the heart and brain. A concentration of just 300 parts per million in the air can kill a person in a few minutes. It has been used as a poison many times in history including by the Nazis in gas chambers during the Holocaust. At the end of World War II, Adolf Hitler and his partner Eva Braun themselves committed suicide using cyanide. Cyanide compounds are used as insecticides and in rat poisons as well as illegally to capture fish from coral reefs. This practice has led to irreversible damage to the reefs and cases of cyanide poisoning in local fishermen. Many cyanide-containing compounds though are not toxic and are used in dyes such as Prussian blue.

The synthesis of nitrile compounds is an important step in reaction pathways

Addition of the –CN functional group to aldehydes and ketones results in a product with an additional carbon atom. So in the examples above *eth*anal becomes 2-hydroxy*prop*anenitrile (C2 → C3) and butanone becomes 2-hydroxy-2-*meth*ylbutanenitrile (C4 → C5). This is therefore a very important step in several industrial processes where the number of carbon atoms in a compound must be increased. This will be explored further in Section G.7.

The cyanohydrin product can be hydrolysed to yield the carboxylic acid. This is done by heating it using acid, for example HCl under reflux for several hours at 50 °C, which yields first the amide and then the carboxylic acid:

$$\text{CH}_3\text{CH(OH)CN} \xrightarrow{\text{H}_2\text{O}} \text{CH}_3\text{CH(OH)CONH}_2 \xrightarrow[\text{HCl}]{\text{H}_2\text{O}} \text{CH}_3\text{CH(OH)COOH} + \text{NH}_4\text{Cl}$$

2-hydroxypropanenitrile   amide intermediate   2-hydroxypropanoic acid (lactic acid)

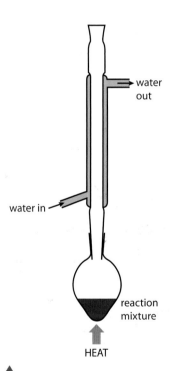

Figure 18.2 Reflux apparatus.

• **Examiner's hint:** Remember in Chapter 10 we introduced the idea of heating under reflux. It is often used in organic chemistry as a way of prolonging a reaction where the reactants are volatile and would otherwise escape as gases before reacting completely.

2-hydroxypropanoic acid is commonly known as lactic acid in biological systems. It is produced by many bacteria and also by animal muscle during anaerobic respiration when supplies of oxygen are insufficient to meet the energy demand. Its production in cells is linked to acidosis, a decrease in pH that can cause 'cramping'. The production of lactic acid by bacteria in the mouth is largely responsible for the tooth decay known as caries.

Worked example

Give the name and structure of the product for the hydrolysis reaction of 2-hydroxy-2-methylbutanenitrile. State the two functional groups in the organic product.

Solution

$$
\begin{array}{c}
\text{H} \quad \text{H} \quad \text{OH} \\
| \quad\ | \quad\ | \\
\text{H}-\text{C}-\text{C}-\text{C}-\text{C}\!\equiv\!\text{N} \\
| \quad\ | \quad\ | \\
\text{H} \quad \text{H} \quad \text{CH}_3
\end{array}
\xrightarrow[\text{hydrolysis}]{\text{acid}}
\begin{array}{c}
\text{H} \quad \text{H} \quad \text{OH} \quad\quad \text{O} \\
| \quad\ | \quad\ | \quad\ \diagup\!\!\parallel \\
\text{H}-\text{C}-\text{C}-\text{C}-\text{C} \\
| \quad\ | \quad\ | \quad\ \diagdown \\
\text{H} \quad \text{H} \quad \text{CH}_3 \quad \text{OH}
\end{array}
$$

2-hydroxy-2-methylbutanenitrile

2-hydroxy-2-methylbutanoic acid
functional groups: carboxylic acid, alcohol

Exercises

4 Give the structural formula of the organic product formed when propanone reacts with HCN in the presence of sodium cyanide and dilute hydrochloric acid.

5 Which would you expect to react more easily with HCN, propanone or propanal? Explain your answer.

> An elimination reaction occurs when a small molecule is lost from a larger compound. The reaction will produce an unsaturated product.

G.3 Elimination reactions

Dehydration is an elimination reaction in which water is released

Sometimes during an organic reaction, a compound rearranges its structure by the **elimination** of a small molecule. This creates a product that is unsaturated. When the small molecule removed in the reaction is water, it is known as a **dehydration** reaction.

Dehydration of alcohols produces alkenes

A good example of a dehydration reaction is the loss of water from alcohols, leading to the formation of alkenes.

$$
\begin{array}{c}
| \quad\ | \\
-\text{C}-\text{C}-\text{OH} \\
|
\end{array}
\rightarrow
\begin{array}{c}
| \quad\ | \\
-\text{C}\!=\!\text{C}- \\
\end{array}
+ \ \text{H}_2\text{O}
$$

It is the reverse of a reaction we discussed in Chapter 10 where alkenes undergo an addition reaction with water to produce alcohols (page 202). The nature of the reaction is determined by the specific reaction conditions used: the dehydration process is favoured by a temperature of about 180 °C.

The most familiar alcohol is ethanol, C_2H_5OH, which is produced by fermentation of yeast. It is readily soluble, owing to its ability to form hydrogen bonds with water and is present in wine and all other alcoholic drinks.

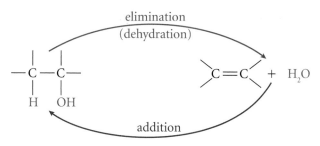

Figure 18.3 Interconversion of alkenes and alcohols through addition or elimination reactions.

There are two possible agents of dehydration that can be used in this reaction:

(i) concentrated sulfuric acid, H_2SO_4
   This is an effective agent of dehydration, but because it is also an oxidizing agent, it can cause other reactions to occur.

(ii) phosphoric acid, H_3PO_4
   This is a better reagent to use in the laboratory as it does not lead to as many side products.

The mechanism is as follows:

- Both H_2SO_4 and H_3PO_4 act as acid catalysts, donating a proton to the $-OH$ group in the alcohol. For example, with ethanol C_2H_5OH:
   (i) protonation

- Once protonated, the alcohol can readily lose H_2O, which is then known as the **leaving group**.
   (ii) loss of water

- This results in the formation of the unstable carbocation intermediate that rapidly loses H^+ to form the alkene.
   (iii) loss of H^+

ethene

In the laboratory, a convenient example of this reaction to study is the dehydration of cyclohexanol, $C_6H_{11}OH$, to form cyclohexene, C_6H_{10}. The cyclohexene can be collected by distillation.

W You can follow a tutorial of the mechanism of dehydration of an alcohol.

Now go to www.heinemann.co.uk/hotlinks, insert the express code 4259P and click on this activity.

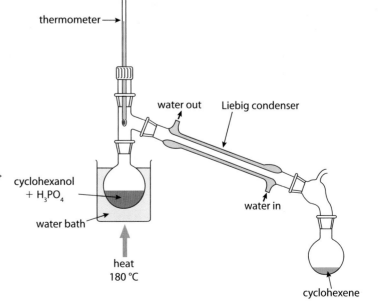

Figure 18.4 Apparatus to collect cyclohexene from the dehydration of cyclohexanol.

Different classes of alcohols differ in their tendency to undergo dehydration reactions

One piece of evidence that could be used to support the mechanism described above can be found by investigating the ease of dehydration of the three different classes of alcohols – primary, secondary and tertiary (see Chapter 10, page 196). Knowing that the mechanism proceeds via a carbocation intermediate, we would expect that the tertiary alcohol, in which the carbocation is stabilized by positive inductive effects from three alkyl groups, will be dehydrated more easily than the primary alcohol in which there is only one such inductive effect. Experimental evidence proves this to be the case and therefore supports the mechanism described. The ease of dehydration of the alcohols is in the order:

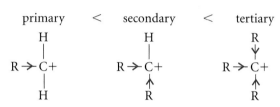

primary   <   secondary   <   tertiary

Exercises

6 There are two isomers of C_3H_7OH that can each be used in dehydration reactions to produce an alkene.
  (a) Draw and name the two isomers.
  (b) Name a suitable dehydrating agent for the reaction.
  (c) Show by diagrams whether you get the same or a different product in the reactions starting with each isomer.

7 Give the conditions and show the mechanism for the dehydration reaction starting with butan-1-ol.

G.4 Addition–elimination reactions

In some reactions, addition occurs in an early step in the mechanism, followed by elimination. Such reactions are therefore called **addition–elimination**, also known as **condensation**. They are important reactions in many synthetic processes, forming so-called **condensation polymers** including nylon, proteins and DNA.

A specific type of condensation reaction occurs when the nucleophilic addition to an aldehyde or ketone, as discussed in Section G.2, is followed by elimination of water. This most typically involves a nucleophile which contains the $-NH_2$ group. The water lost is from the oxygen of the carbonyl group and the two hydrogen atoms of the amino group of the nucleophile. The organic product involves the formation of a double bond between the carbonyl carbon and the nitrogen atom.

$$\diagdown C = O \; + \; \overset{H}{\underset{H}{\diagdown N -}}$$

$$\downarrow$$

$$\diagdown C = N \; + \; H_2O$$

DNP derivatives are used to identify aldehydes and ketones

The most common example of this type of addition–elimination reaction involves a reagent called **2,4-dinitrophenylhydrazine (2,4-DNP)**. It has the structure shown below. 'Phenyl' refers to a substituted benzene ring that we will discuss in the next section; the numbers 2 and 4 refer to the positions of the nitro groups, $-NO_2$, relative to the hydrazine group that is considered to be at position 1 in the ring.

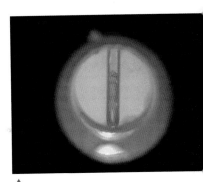

2, 4-dinitrophenylhydrazine

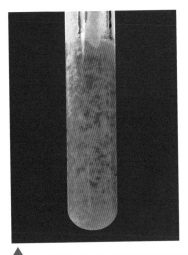

In reaction with aldehydes and ketones, it forms a condensation product known as a **2,4-dinitrophenylhydrazone** compound, which forms a yellow-orange precipitate which has a well-defined melting point. For example, with ethanal, CH_3CHO, the reaction is as follows:

2,4-DNP + ethanal → 2,4-dinitrophenylhydrazone derivative of ethanal + H_2O

Formation of the hydrazone derivative happens quickly with aldehydes and ketones and can be used for two purposes:
(i) to confirm the presence of a carbonyl group C=O in an unknown compound
(ii) to identify a particular aldehyde or ketone through melting point characterization.

Worked example

Write equations showing full structural formulas for the reactions between propanone and 2,4-dinitrophenylhydrazine.

Solution

(structure) + (propanone CH$_3$)$_2$C=O → (2,4-dinitrophenylhydrazone) + H_2O

● **Examiner's hint:** In writing out these equations it helps to mark in a different colour (red in the examples given here) the atoms that will take part in the reaction. Then it is easy to see how H_2O is eliminated and the new bond forms.

G.5 Arenes

Benzene and its derivatives are called **aromatic** compounds in reference to their fragrant smells.

Organic compounds that are derivatives of the hydrocarbon **benzene**, C_6H_6, are known as **arenes.** They form a special branch of organic chemistry and have properties that are distinct from all other organic compounds (which are known as **aliphatics**). The key to understanding these unique properties of arenes must come from an exploration of the structure of the parent arene molecule – benzene itself.

Benzene is a highly unsaturated molecule

Benzene was first isolated by Michael Faraday in 1825 and later shown by analysis to have the formula C_6H_6. It is a colourless and flammable liquid at room temperature with a sweet smell and a boiling point of 80 °C. It is immiscible in water, forming the upper of two layers, and is itself a useful solvent for organic compounds. It can be obtained from the fractional distillation of crude oil and from catalytic reforming of gasoline.

The 1:1 ratio of carbon to hydrogen in benzene indicates a high degree of unsaturation, greater than that of alkenes with their carbon–carbon double bond or alkynes with their carbon–carbon triple bond. This high unsaturation of benzene is demonstrated by the fact that it and all other arenes burn with a very smokey flame, the result of the presence of large amounts of unburned carbon.

Benzene is an important industrial solvent and is used in the synthesis of drugs, dyes and plastics such as polystyrene. Because of its frequent use, benzene has become widespread in the environment of developed countries. In the USA, petroleum contains up to 2% benzene by volume and it may be as high as 5% in other countries. But benzene is a toxic compound and a known carcinogen. Chronic exposure at low levels can lead to aplastic anaemia and leukaemia. Regulating bodies in many countries have set permissible exposure limits for benzene levels in drinking water, foods and air in the workplace. In 2005, the water supply to the city of Harbin in China was cut off because of a major benzene exposure resulting from an explosion in a petroleum factory.

Non-polar liquids like benzene can be separated from aqueous solutions using a separating funnel because they form a separate layer and the lower liquid can be drained away. Here the lower aqueous layer has been coloured purple to make the separation more visible.

Benzene does not behave like other unsaturated molecules

The higher the ratio of carbon to hydrogen in a hydrocarbon, the more smokey the flame.

Many early attempts to formulate the structure of benzene produced linear structures with multiple double and triple bonds such as:

Models like this were quickly found to be unacceptable as they did not fit observations of benzene's properties, including the fact that:

(i) benzene shows little tendency to undergo addition reactions of the type discussed in G.1 whereas these structures with double and triple bonds should be highly reactive in addition reactions.

(ii) benzene has no isomers but these molecules would be expected to have several isomeric forms resulting from different positions of the multiple bonds.

Instead, a cyclic arrangement of the carbon atoms was suggested and Kekulé proposed the first reasonably acceptable structure in 1865.

Friedrich August Kekulé von Stradonitz (1829–1896) was a German organic chemist who also spent parts of his working life in France, Switzerland and England. He was the principal founder of the theory of chemical structure, establishing the tetravalence of carbon and the ability of carbon atoms to link to each other. He provided the first molecular formulas using lines to represent bonds between atoms and most famously the ring structure of benzene. In addition, he was evidently an influential teacher, as three of the first five Nobel Prizes in Chemistry were won by his students: van't Hoff in 1901, Fischer in 1902 and Baeyer in 1905.

 It is claimed that Kekulé's model for benzene's structure came to him in a dream where he saw snakes biting each other's tails. Watch this short movie for a re-enactment.

Now go to www.heinemann.co.uk/hotlinks, insert the express code 4259P and click on this activity.

The Kekulé structure for benzene: 1,3,5-cyclohexatriene

Kekulé's structure for benzene proposed a six-membered ring of carbon atoms with alternating single and double bonds. Using IUPAC nomenclature this structure is 1,3,5-cyclohexatriene.

 which is usually drawn without the atoms marked as

The symmetry of this model explains many of the known properties of benzene, including the fact that benzene exists in only one form, that is with no isomers and that there are also no isomers of mono-substituted derivatives such as C_6H_5Br.

But when the Kekulé model is tested against other known properties of benzene, there are ways in which it does not offer a full explanation. These are summarized below.

Property	Prediction from Kekulé structure	Observation from studies on benzene
1 Number of isomers containing substituents on adjacent carbons (1,2 derivatives) e.g. 1,2-dibromobenzene	*Two* isomers would exist, depending on whether the substituents were on carbons attached by a single or a double bond. Br and Br	Only *one* form exists.
2 Bond lengths	Two different bond lengths would be found in the molecule, corresponding to: C—C, 0.154 nm and C=C, 0.134 nm.	• All carbon–carbon bonds are of equal length. • Carbon–carbon bond length in benzene is 0.139 nm, intermediate between single and double bonds.
3 Enthalpy of hydrogenation for the reaction $C_6H_6 + 3H_2 \rightarrow C_6H_{12}$	Would involve adding across three double bonds so should be equal to 3 times the hydrogenation of cyclohexene (C_6H_{10}) with one double bond; so theoretical value is: $3 \times -120 \text{ kJ mol}^{-1} = -360 \text{ kJ mol}^{-1}$	• The enthalpy change for the hydrogenation of benzene is -208 kJ mol^{-1}. • Reaction is much *less* exothermic than expected from the Kekulé structure, indicating that benzene is more stable.
4 Tendency to undergo addition reactions	Would have high tendency to undergo addition reactions due to three double bonds as sites of reactivity	Benzene does not readily undergo addition reactions.

Clearly the Kekulé structure must be developed to include a valid interpretation of *all* available data. X-ray diffraction studies which provide electron density maps have helped provide further insights into the structure.

 The study of the structure of benzene is a good example of how a model must change in the light of new evidence that is collected. But can scientists be free from bias when they are devising experiments to test their own theories?

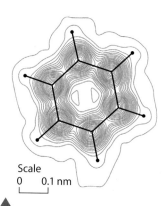

Scale
0   0.1 nm

Figure 18.5 Electron density map for benzene. The blue lines join parts of the molecule with equal electron density, showing that all bonds between carbon atoms are equal and of length 0.139 nm.

The special stability of the benzene ring is the result of delocalized electrons

The current model for the structure of benzene, like the Kekulé model, is a cyclic structure in which a framework of single bonds attaches each carbon to another on either side and to a hydrogen atom. So each carbon forms three single bonds with bond angles of 120° forming the planar shape.

This leaves one electron on each carbon atom. But instead of pairing up to form alternating double bonds, they spread themselves out evenly to be shared by all six carbon atoms. This is known as **delocalization** and the electrons are now effectively equally shared by all the bonded atoms. (We came across a similar situation of delocalization of electrons in our study of metallic bonding in Chapter 4, page 89). Delocalization of electrons in benzene produces a symmetrical 'cloud' of electron charge above and below the plane of the ring. This is a very stable arrangement and is associated with a lowering of the internal energy of benzene.

Figure 18.6 Structure of the benzene ring.

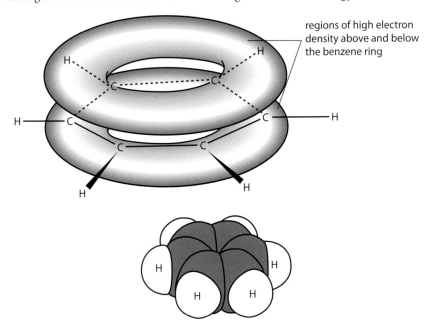

regions of high electron density above and below the benzene ring

◀ **Figure 18.7** Delocalized electrons form regions of high electron density above and below the planar benzene ring.

W Here is an applet that allows you to explore and rotate different models of benzene.

Now go to www.heinemann.co.uk/hotlinks, insert the express code 4259P and click on this activity.

◀ **Figure 18.8** A space-filling model of benzene, showing its planar shape.

The usual convention for depicting this structure of benzene uses a ring inside the hexagon to denote the delocalized electrons.

We can now use this model of the structure of benzene to interpret the observations made earlier that were not consistent with the Kekulé structure.

1. *Only one isomer of, for example, 1,2-dibromobenzene exists.*
   As benzene is a symmetrical molecule with no alternating single and double bonds, all adjacent positions in the ring are equal.
   For example, 1,2-dibromobenzene, $C_6H_4Br_2$

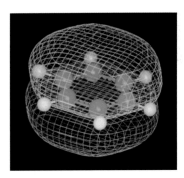

Computer graphics representation of the structure of benzene showing the delocalized electron clouds which confer great stability to the molecule. They appear as the blue and yellow cages above the flat plane of the molecule. Carbon atoms are shown in green and hydrogen atoms in white.

2. *All carbon–carbon bond lengths in benzene are equal and intermediate in length between single and double bonds.*
   This is because each bond contains a share of three electrons between the bonded atoms. Comparison of data from X-ray analysis shows the following:

Compound	Type of bond	Bond length (nm)
alkane	single bond C—C	0.154
alkene	double bond C=C	0.134
benzene		0.139

● **Examiner's hint:** Make sure that when you are writing the structure of benzene you do not forget to include the ring inside the hexagon. If you do and draw instead, this denotes an entirely different structure, cyclohexane, C_6H_{12}.

3. *Data for enthalpy of hydrogenation of benzene suggests an unusually stable compound.*

The special stability of benzene is the result of the spreading of the electrons by delocalization as this minimizes the repulsion between them. We can calculate the lowering of internal energy resulting from this by comparing the enthalpy of hydrogenation of benzene with that of other unsaturated cyclic 6-carbon molecules.

Figure 18.9 Enthalpy changes for the hydrogenation of cyclohexene, 1,3-cyclohexadiene, 1,3,5-cyclohexatriene and benzene.

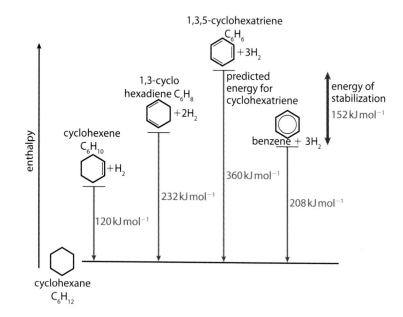

We can see that the enthalpy change for 1,3-cyclohexadiene when forming cyclohexane is almost twice that for cyclohexene – exactly what would be expected given that it has two double bonds. If benzene had three double bonds then its value should be three times this figure, the value shown above for the hypothetical 1,3,5-cyclohexatriene. The fact that its enthalpy of hydrogenation is 152 kJ mol^{-1} *lower* than this expected value is consistent with the fact that it does *not* have three discrete double bonds. This energy lowering as a result of the delocalized ring of electrons is called the **resonance energy** or the **stabilization energy** of benzene.

4. *Benzene is reluctant to undergo addition reactions and is more likely to undergo substitution reactions.*

Despite its unsaturation, addition reactions to benzene are energetically not favoured as they would involve disrupting the entire cloud of delocalized electrons. In other words the stabilization energy would have to be supplied and the product, lacking the delocalized ring of electrons, would be *less* stable. Instead benzene is more likely to undergo *substitution* reactions that preserve the arene ring. For example, benzene reacts with Br$_2$ in the presence of a suitable catalyst to form the substituted product bromobenzene, C$_6$H$_5$Br.

In the next section we will explore the chemistry of some of the substituted derivatives of benzene involving halogens.

Halogenated derivatives of benzene: reactivity depends on the position of the halogen

We learned in Chapter 10 (page 208) that halogenoalkanes undergo nucleophilic substitution reactions of the type:

$$C_2H_5Br \ + \ OH^- \ \rightarrow \ C_2H_5OH \ + \ Br^-$$

This is known as a hydrolysis reaction and produces an alcohol. It occurs as a result of the polar nature of the carbon–halogen bond causing the carbon atom to be electron deficient:

and so susceptible to attack by nucleophiles such as OH^-. You may find it useful to review that section before reading on, as we are going to be investigating to what extent a similar reaction will happen with halogenated arenes.

Arenes can be substituted with halogens in two quite distinct ways and as we will see this has a significant effect on their reactivity.

	Ring substituent	Side-chain substituent
Example	Chlorobenzene, C_6H_5Cl	Chloromethylbenzene, $C_6H_5CH_2Cl$
Position of halogen	Halogen is bonded directly to one of the carbons of the arene ring.	Halogen is bonded to a carbon of a side chain.

We will compare the tendency of these two types of halogenated arenes to undergo hydrolysis reactions.

Ring substituents

Compounds such as chlorobenzene are relatively inert and only undergo nucleophilic substitution of the halogen with extreme difficulty. This is largely due to the fact that the electronegative halogen draws the delocalized electron charge from the benzene ring onto the carbon of the carbon–halogen bond. This reduces the magnitude of the $\delta+$ on the carbon and hence decreases its susceptibility to nucleophilic attack.

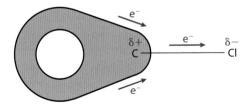

Figure 18.10 Strong pull of the electronegative halogen reduces the electron deficiency in the carbon of the carbon–halogen bond making it less susceptible to nucleophilic attack.

Interaction between non-bonding electrons in the halogen and the delocalized ring electrons also strengthens the carbon–halogen bond, further contributing to the lack of reactivity. Consequently chlorobenzene will only undergo hydrolysis with NaOH under conditions of high pressure and temperature.

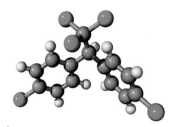

Molecular model of the pesticide DDT showing (in green) that it has two chlorine atoms directly attached to benzene rings and three other chlorine atoms in a side chain. The ring substituent chlorine atoms make it very resistant to reaction so it is highly persistent in the environment.

Side chain substituents

Compounds such as chloromethylbenzene undergo hydrolysis reactions with nucleophiles in much the same way as halogenoalkanes. So they react relatively easily when heated with aqueous NaOH, forming the alcohol as follows.

$$\text{C}_6\text{H}_5{-}\text{CH}_2\text{Cl} + \text{NaOH} \rightarrow \text{C}_6\text{H}_5{-}\text{CH}_2\text{OH} + \text{NaCl}$$

This is because the environment of the carbon–halogen bond is similar here to that in halogenoalkanes and the electron deficient ($\delta+$) carbon is susceptible to nucleophilic attack in a similar way.

DDT (dichlorodiphenyltrichloroethane)

is a complex halogenoarene and one of the best known and most controversial pesticides. It was used to great effect starting from World War II to control the mosquitoes that are responsible for the spread of diseases such as malaria and typhus. The World Health Organization suggests that 5 million human lives were saved in the early years of its use. But in 1962 the publication of *Silent Spring* by American biologist Rachel Carson put the spotlight on the major negative environmental impacts of indiscriminate spraying of DDT in the USA. Because the compound has chlorine atoms attached directly to benzene rings, it does not undergo reactions that would break it down and so it passes unchanged through food chains. Birds and large fish that feed high in the chain therefore accumulate high concentrations of DDT and suffer toxic effects. In addition, many insects have developed resistance to its effects. The agricultural use of DDT in most parts of the world has now been banned, although its use in vector control continues in some places and remains controversial.

Who should determine the balance between the individual's right to freedom from disease and society's right to freedom from environmental degradation?

Exercises

9 Benzene is a hydrocarbon. Write the equation for its complete combustion and say what type of flame you would expect to see when it burns.

10 Describe the bonding in a benzene molecule and use it to explain benzene's energetic stability.

11 Ethene contains a carbon–carbon double bond and can undergo an addition reaction with hydrogen. Would you expect benzene to react with hydrogen more or less readily than ethene? Explain your answer.

G.6 Organometallic chemistry

As the name implies, organometallic compounds contain a metal covalently bonded within an organic compound. Many of these compounds exist in biological systems, such as **haemoglobin** in blood, which contains Fe bonded to a nitrogen–carbon ring structure, and **chlorophyll** in green plants, which contains Mg similarly bonded.

Synthetic organometallic compounds are also quite widespread including $Pb(C_2H_5)_4$, tetraethyl lead, which was used as a petroleum additive (see page 195) and $Al(C_2H_5)_3$, triethyl aluminium, which is an important catalyst in polymerization reactions.

Grignard reagents: organic compounds containing magnesium

Of particular interest to organic chemists involved in synthesis reactions is a group of organometallic compounds known as **Grignard reagents**. These are characterized by the presence of magnesium Mg and a halogen, giving the general formula R–Mg–X, where X is the halogen, for example C_2H_5–Mg–Br. As we will see, they are a convenient tool for extending the length of the carbon chain in reaction pathways.

The presentation address for the award of Grignard's Nobel Prize neatly summarizes the significance of these compounds:

> '*Investigations … which revealed that metallic magnesium in the presence of ether reacts on organic derivatives of chlorine, bromine and iodine by forming ether-soluble organic compounds of magnesium. These latter compounds in turn react extremely readily with a large number of other organic substances, so that carbon combines with carbon i.e. forming a true organic synthesis.*'

Synthesis of Grignard reagents

The reagents are usually prepared *in situ* as they are not very stable. Turnings or granules of magnesium are treated with a solution of a halogenoalkane dissolved in *dry* ether and left to stand. A small crystal of iodine is sometimes added to initiate the reaction.

$$CH_3CH_2I + Mg \xrightarrow[\text{dry ether}]{(C_2H_5)_2O} \underset{\text{ethyl magnesium iodide}}{CH_3CH_2MgI}$$

The reaction is vigorous and exothermic, so it boils of its own accord forming a cloudy solution. It is essential that the ether solvent used is dry as the product would react with water.

The nature of the bonding in the Grignard reagent is complex but it is known that the magnesium–carbon bond is largely covalent and highly polar, with Mg being the more electropositive element and the magnesium–halogen bond being predominantly ionic.

For example:

$$\overset{\delta-}{CH_3CH_2}\!\!-\!\!\overset{\delta+}{Mg}Br$$

So the carbon attached to the Mg has a partial negative charge $(\delta-)$. This can therefore act as a nucleophile, attacking electron deficient $(\delta+)$ carbons in other molecules and leading to products with an increased number of carbon atoms.

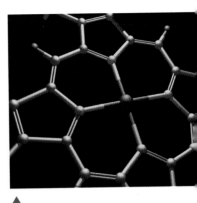

Computer graphic of the molecular structure of a haem group in the blood protein haemoglobin showing Fe (red) bonded to nitrogen (yellow) and carbon (grey). The flat ring structure around the Fe enables it to bind to oxygen and carry it through the body.

Victor Grignard (1871–1935) was a French chemist who spent a period fighting for his country in World War I. But he was soon demobilized and commissioned to study chemical warfare in Paris. It is interesting to note that at the same time, and in a neighbouring country, Fritz Haber was developing poison gases for the German army. Grignard's most famous work on developing and using organic magnesium compounds in synthesis reactions earned him the Nobel Prize in Chemistry in 1912.

● **Examiner's hint:** Note that *ethers*, such as C_2H_5—O—C_2H_5 diethyl ether, contain an oxygen 'bridge' between two carbon atoms. They have low solubility in water and are useful laboratory solvents. Do not confuse them with *esters* which are derivatives of carboxylic acids.

Grignard reagent $\xrightarrow[\text{acid hydrolysis}]{\text{addition of Grignard reagent}}$ product has increased number of carbon atoms

You can follow some of the reactions of Grignard reagents in this tutorial.

Now go to www.heinemann.co.uk/hotlinks, insert the express code 4259P and click on this activity.

Reactions of these reagents with a variety of different organic compounds are known as **Grignard reactions.**

Grignard reactions: reactions which increase the length of the carbon chain

Some of the typical reactions of Grignard reagents are given below showing the diversity of products which can be synthesized. Iodides react more readily than the other halides and so are used in these examples. Usually these reactions occur in two steps:

- addition of the Grignard reagent
- hydrolysis in acid solution

but for clarity the overall reaction as one step is shown here.

In all these examples, the Grignard reagent, methyl magnesium iodide, is used and the methyl group CH_3 is coloured red throughout. This should enable you to keep track of the carbon atoms during the reaction and observe how the product results from addition of carbon to the starting molecule.

1 Preparation of alkanes; reaction of Grignard reagent with water:

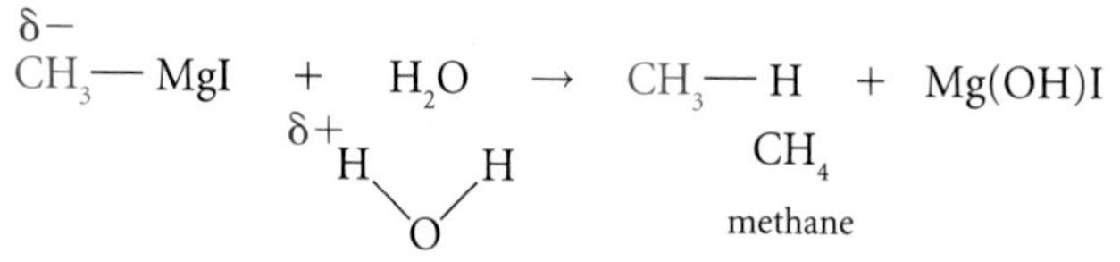
δ−
CH3—MgI + H2O → CH3—H + Mg(OH)I
δ+
H H
O
CH4
methane

2 Preparation of primary alcohols: reaction of Grignard reagent with methanal:

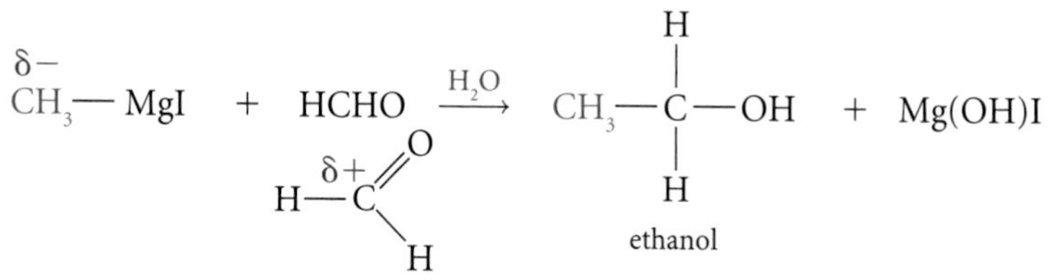
δ−
CH3—MgI + HCHO
H2O
CH3—C—OH + Mg(OH)I
H
H
δ+
H—C
O
H
ethanol

3 Preparation of secondary alcohols: reaction of Grignard reagent with other aldehydes:

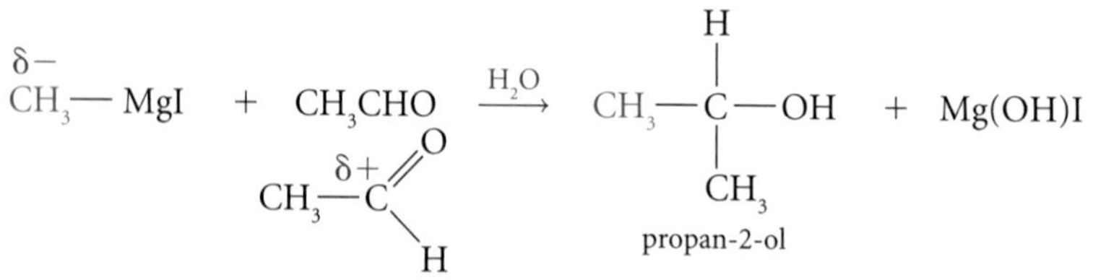
δ−
CH3—MgI + CH3CHO
H2O
CH3—C—OH + Mg(OH)I
H
CH3
δ+
CH3—C
O
H
propan-2-ol

4 Preparation of tertiary alcohols: reaction of Grignard reagents with ketones:

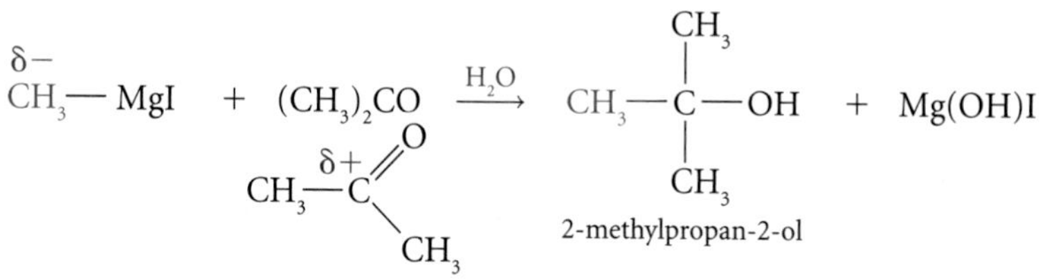
δ−
CH3—MgI + (CH3)2CO
H2O
CH3—C—OH + Mg(OH)I
CH3
CH3
δ+
CH3—C
O
CH3
2-methylpropan-2-ol

5   Preparation of carboxylic acid; reaction of Grignard reagents with CO_2:

$$\overset{\delta-}{CH_3} — MgI \quad + \quad CO_2 \quad \xrightarrow{H_2O} \quad CH_3 — C \overset{\displaystyle O}{\underset{\displaystyle OH}{\Big\langle}} \quad + \quad Mg(OH)I$$
$$\underset{O=C=O}{\overset{\delta+}{}}$$

ethanoic acid

● **Examiner's hint:** Remember that the addition of HCN to aldehydes and ketones (Section G.2) can also increase the length of the carbon chain, but always by just one carbon. By contrast, Grignard reagents provide the ability to increase the length of the chain by different amounts depending on the particular reagent used, for example use of *ethyl* magnesium iodide in these reactions would increase the chain length by *two* carbons in each case.

Worked example

Describe how you could convert bromoethane into butan-2-ol using a Grignard reagent.

Solution

React the bromoethane with magnesium turnings in dry ether. This will make the Grignard reagent C_2H_5—Mg—Br, a *two*-carbon species. As the desired product is a secondary alcohol and has *four* carbon atoms, you will need to react this reagent with a *two*-carbon aldehyde, that is ethanal, and hydrolyse it in acid.

$$C_2H_5Br \quad + \quad Mg \quad \rightarrow \quad C_2H_5 — MgBr$$

$$C_2H_5 — MgBr \quad + \quad CH_3CHO \quad \rightarrow \quad C_2H_5 — \overset{\displaystyle H}{\underset{\displaystyle OH}{\overset{|}{\underset{|}{C}}}} — CH_3 \quad + \quad Mg(OH)Br$$

ethanal · butan-2-ol

Using Grignard reagents, the **following reactants can be converted into the following products:**

water → **alkanes**
methanal → **primary alcohols**
other aldehydes → **secondary alcohols**
ketones → **tertiary alcohols**
CO_2 → **carboxylic acid**
The product in all these reactions has more carbon atoms than the reactant.

Exercises

12 Give the names and structures of the compounds that result from the complete reaction of ethylmagnesium bromide with:
   (a) propanal
   (b) carbon dioxide
   (c) butanone
   (d) water.

13 Describe how you could convert iodomethane into pentan-2-ol using a Grignard reagent.

Organic chemist synthesizing a chemotherapy agent, a drug used in the treatment of cancer. Reactions in synthetic organic chemistry often proceed in steps through the production of intermediate compounds.

G.7 Reaction pathways

The use of Grignard reagents has shown us one way in which organic compounds can be synthesized from different starting molecules. In fact, this is only one example of the many conversions possible in organic chemistry. Sequences of organic reactions where one substance can be converted through several steps into another quite different organic compound are known as **reaction pathways** and play an essential part in modern industrial chemistry. Now that we have studied some reactions in addition to those in Chapter 10, we can start to put them together and build up pathways of organic synthesis.

Working out a pathway between a stated reactant and product is a bit of a puzzle and it helps to consider starting at either end. So think about the typical reactions of the given starting molecule and also work backwards by thinking of typical reactions that yield the given product.

We can summarize some of the main reactions that we have studied in this chapter in the following scheme.

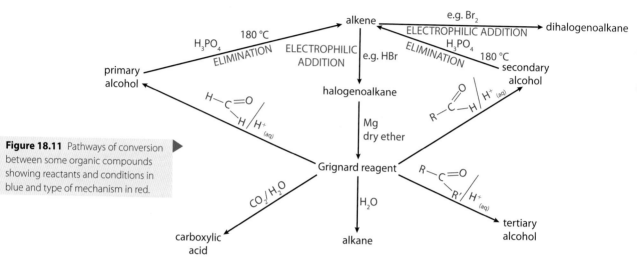

Figure 18.11 Pathways of conversion between some organic compounds showing reactants and conditions in blue and type of mechanism in red.

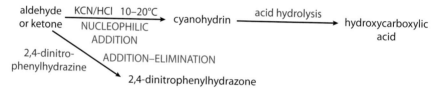

Remember, if the product has more carbon atoms than the reactant, you will have to use either:

● CN^- ions in reaction with a halogenoalkane (adds one carbon atom)
   or
● a Grignard reagent (adds different numbers of carbon atoms).

Worked example

Starting with propan-1-ol, write equations for the steps you would use to convert it into 2-bromopropane. Show all reagents and conditions for the reactions.

Solution

$$H-\overset{\overset{\displaystyle H}{|}}{\underset{\underset{\displaystyle H}{|}}{C}}-\overset{\overset{\displaystyle H}{|}}{\underset{\underset{\displaystyle H}{|}}{C}}-\overset{\overset{\displaystyle H}{|}}{\underset{\underset{\displaystyle H}{|}}{C}}-OH \xrightarrow[\text{dehydration}]{180\ ^\circ C} H-\overset{\overset{\displaystyle H}{|}}{C}=\overset{\overset{\displaystyle H}{|}}{C}-\overset{\overset{\displaystyle H}{|}}{\underset{\underset{\displaystyle H}{|}}{C}}-H \ +\ H_2O$$

$$H-\overset{\overset{\displaystyle H}{|}}{C}=\overset{\overset{\displaystyle H}{|}}{C}-\overset{\overset{\displaystyle H}{|}}{\underset{\underset{\displaystyle H}{|}}{C}}-H \ +\ HBr \xrightarrow{\text{addition}} H-\overset{\overset{\displaystyle H}{|}}{\underset{\underset{\displaystyle H}{|}}{C}}-\overset{\overset{\displaystyle H}{|}}{\underset{\underset{\displaystyle Br}{|}}{C}}-\overset{\overset{\displaystyle H}{|}}{\underset{\underset{\displaystyle H}{|}}{C}}-H$$

2-bromopropane

Exercises

14 Describe how you would make butane in two steps starting with a halogenoalkane. Show all reagents and conditions in the reactions.

15 Explain how butanone can be converted into a hydroxy-substituted acid in two steps. Give the name and structure of the product.

6.8 Acid–base reactions

Carboxylic acids

We are familiar with the fact that carboxylic acids, such as methanoic acid, HCOOH, show acidic properties. For example, they react with a carbonate to release CO_2 and with a base to form a salt and water (Chapter 8, page 151). The basis of their acidic nature can be understood by looking at the structure and bonding in the $-$COOH functional group.

The carbonyl (C$=$O) group has an electron-deficient ($\delta+$) carbon due to electron withdrawal by the more electronegative oxygen across the double bond (electrons in the π bond are more loosely held and so more easily polarized than those in the σ bond). This $\delta+$ carbon draws electrons from the $-$OH group, increasing the positive charge on the hydrogen and thus facilitating the release of H^+. So the acid is a **proton donor**, showing Brønsted–Lowry acid behaviour.

$$HCOOH(aq) + H_2O(l) \rightleftharpoons HCOO^-(aq) + H_3O^+(aq)$$

The carboxylate ion $HCOO^-$ (the conjugate base of HCOOH) produced in this reaction has a **delocalized structure** in which its electron charge is spread equally between its two oxygen atoms. This results in the two carbon–oxygen bonds being equal, which stabilizes the ion, favouring its formation in the equilibrium above.

But how can we explain the fact that not all acids that contain this same $-$COOH group are of equal strength?

- What is the effect of substituted groups, for example Cl, on acid strength?
- What is the influence of carbon chain length on acid strength?

To answer these questions we must consider the effects of the substituted and/or extra alkyl groups on the stability of the carboxylate anion described above. Groups that increase its stability will cause it to be a weaker base and hence increase the strength of the acid, pulling the equilibrium above further to the right; conversely groups which decrease the stability of the anion will cause it to be a stronger base and hence decrease the strength of the acid as the equilibrium will lie further to the left.

There are two main types of substituent according to whether they have a tendency to withdraw electrons (electronegative) or to donate electrons (positive inductive effect). These opposite influences are described in the table below.

Electron withdrawing groups (electronegative atoms)	Electron donating groups (positive inductive effect)
e.g. —Cl 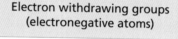	e.g. —CH$_3$
• the withdrawal of electrons by Cl helps to delocalize the negative charge on the anion, increasing its stability and causing it to be a weaker base • acid strength increased	• the pushing of electrons from the alkyl group makes the negative charge more concentrated in the anion, decreasing its stability and causing it to be a stronger base • acid strength decreased

The strength of carboxylic acids decreases with increasing carbon chain length. Substitution of halogens into the carbon skeleton increases the acid strength.

Phenol has antiseptic properties and was used by Joseph Lister in his pioneering work on antiseptic surgery. But intake can be toxic and phenol injections were used as a means of execution in Nazi concentration camps during World War II. Phenol derivatives are found widely in nature such as in the female hormone estradiol, the amino acid tyrosine and the neurotransmitters serotonin and noradrenaline. In the laboratory, the widely used pH indicator phenolphthalein contains two phenol groups.

So we can now predict the relative strengths of different acids.
- Chloro-substituted forms of an acid are all stronger acids than the parent acid and increase in strength with increasing substitution. For example:

ethanoic acid < chloroethanoic acid < dichloroethanoic acid < trichloroethanoic acid

increasing acid strength →

- Increasing carbon chain length (larger alkyl groups) decreases the strength of the acid owing to a stronger positive inductive effect.

methanoic acid > ethanoic acid > propanoic acid > butanoic acid

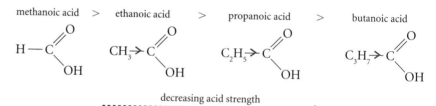

decreasing acid strength →

Alcohols and phenols

Alcohols (R—OH) and phenol (C$_6$H$_5$OH) both contain the —OH group, but in alcohols it is attached to a carbon chain whereas in phenol it is attached directly to a carbon of the benzene ring. Substituted phenols have additional substituted groups in the benzene ring.

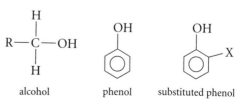

alcohol   phenol   substituted phenol

In order to compare the acidic properties of these molecules, we need to consider the chemical environment of the —OH group.

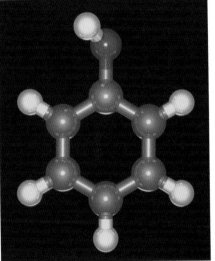

In alcohols, the —OH group is attached directly to an alkyl group which has a positive inductive effect, pushing electrons onto the oxygen atom. This strengthens the O–H bond relative to water, making release of H^+ more difficult. In addition, the alkoxide ion $R—O^-$ has the negative charge centred on the oxygen atom (with no delocalization) which makes it unstable and increases its tendency to accept protons, driving the equilibrium below to the left.

$$CH_3OH(aq) + H_2O(l) \rightleftharpoons CH_3O^-(aq) + H_3O^+(aq)$$

So alcohols are *less* acidic than water.

In phenol, the –OH group is not attached to an alkyl group but instead to the benzene ring itself. So there is no positive inductive effect to strengthen the O—H bond here. Also in the phenoxide ion, $C_6H_5O^-$, the negative charge on the oxygen atom can to some extent be delocalized around the ring, causing its charge density to be decreased. As a result, it will have less of a tendency to accept protons, so is a weaker base.

$$C_6H_5OH(aq) + H_2O(l) \rightleftharpoons C_6H_5O^-(aq) + H_3O^+(aq)$$

Molecular model of phenol, C_6H_5OH, showing the –OH group bonded directly to the benzene ring.

So phenol is a *stronger* acid than aliphatic alcohols. An aqueous solution of phenol has a pH of less than 7 at 25 °C but it is a much weaker acid than carboxylic acids.

Worked example

How would you expect the acidic properties of hydroxymethyl benzene, $C_6H_5CH_2OH$, to compare with those of phenol C_6H_5OH?

Solution

In hydroxymethyl benzene:

the —OH is attached to an alkyl group and so will behave more like an alcohol than like phenol. The negative charge on the anion will not be delocalized so it will be a weaker acid than phenol. (This is similar to the situation we discussed in Section G.5 where halogens substituted in a side chain of an arene have properties that resemble those of halogenoalkanes.)

Bisphenol A, a molecule containing two phenol groups, is widely used in making polymers, such as the polycarbonate plastics that are used in reuseable water bottles, food containers and water pipes. Bisphenol A has become controversial because it may mimic hormones, especially estradiol (estrogen) and so give rise to a range of health problems. Studies in 2008 showed that the risk of the chemical leaching from the plastic is increased when it is heated and so particular concern has been expressed about its use in babies' bottles that are routinely used for warm liquids and heated during sterilization. While debate continues about safe levels, some retailers have withdrawn these products and several governments have legislation pending that would affect their use.

In substituted phenols there are other groups attached to the benzene ring in addition to the —OH group. We can consider their effects on the acid strength of the —OH group by determining whether they have a tendency to withdraw or to donate electrons to the ring and how this will affect the stability of the anion.

Substituent groups that withdraw electrons, for example —Cl and —NO_2, will increase its acidity through further delocalization of the negative charge of the conjugate base. On the other hand, substituent groups which donate electrons, for example —CH_3, will decrease acidity through increasing the charge density on the ring and hence make the anion less stable.

Computer model of a molecule of 2,4,6-trinitrophenol (picric acid). The —OH group is shown at the bottom of the ring and the three NO_2 groups are shown in red and light blue at the 2, 4 and 6 positions. It is a highly explosive chemical.

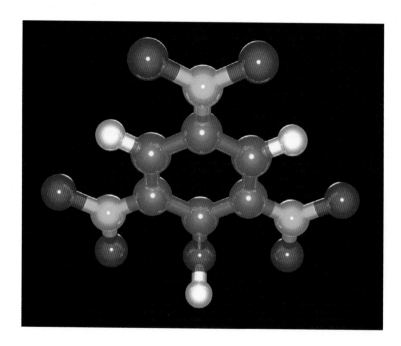

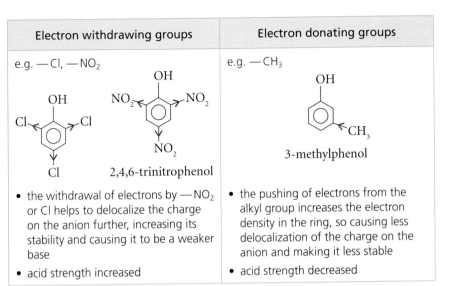

Electron withdrawing groups	Electron donating groups
e.g. — Cl, —NO$_2$ **2,4,6-trinitrophenol**	e.g. —CH$_3$ 3-methylphenol
• the withdrawal of electrons by —NO$_2$ or Cl helps to delocalize the charge on the anion further, increasing its stability and causing it to be a weaker base • acid strength increased	• the pushing of electrons from the alkyl group increases the electron density in the ring, so causing less delocalization of the charge on the anion and making it less stable • acid strength decreased

So the relative acidic strength of phenol and some substituted phenols is:

3-methylphenol $<$ phenol $<$ 2,4,6-trinitrophenol and 2, 4, 6-trichlorophenol

→

acid strength increasing

The differing acidic strengths of alcohols, such as ethanol and phenol, can be illustrated by comparing their reactions with aqueous solutions of sodium hydroxide. Phenol reacts to produce a colourless solution containing sodium phenoxide:

$$C_6H_5OH(aq) + NaOH(aq) \rightarrow C_6H_5O^- Na^+(aq) + H_2O(l)$$

whereas there is no reaction with ethanol. Note that although phenol is a stronger acid than aliphatic alcohols, it is still a very weak acid and is unable to react with sodium carbonate to liberate CO_2.

 Alcohols are weaker acids than water. Phenols are stronger acids than alcohols but weaker than carboxylic acids. alcohols<water<phenols< carboxylic acids

2,4,6-trinitrophenol (TNP) is closely related to the well-known explosive TNT – trinitrotoluene. TNT has a —CH$_3$ group in place of the —OH group in the benzene ring.

TNP (known as picric acid) is also an explosive and was used by most military powers in the 19th century. In December 1917, a French cargo ship fully loaded with wartime explosives, including over 2000 tonnes of picric acid and over 200 tonnes of TNT, entered the harbour of Halifax on the east coast of Canada. It was not flying warning flags for its dangerous cargo to avoid being targeted by the German Navy. A collision with another vessel occurred which caused the boat to catch fire and explode with more force than any previous man-made explosion. Over 2000 people lost their lives, over 9000 were injured and the city of Halifax was devastated. Picric acid has largely been replaced by TNT for use as an explosive over the last 100 years as its acidic nature causes corroding of metal bomb castings

Exercise

16 (a) Explain why ethanol is less acidic than water.
(b) Use your knowledge of the reaction of sodium with water (Chapter 3) and your answer to (a) to predict how sodium would react with ethanol.
(c) For each of the following pairs, state which is the stronger acid. Explain your choice by referring to the substituents:
  • methanoic and ethanoic acid
  • chloroethanoic acid and bromoethanoic acid.

 You can learn more about the Halifax explosion and the power of TNT and picric acid.

Now go to www.heinemann.co.uk/hotlinks, insert the express code 4259P and click on this activity.

Ammonia and amines

Amines can be considered to be organic derivatives of ammonia in which one or more hydrogen atoms is replaced by an alkyl group.

	Ammonia	Primary amine	Secondary amine	Tertiary amine
Example		ethylamine	dimethylamine	trimethylamine
Structure	NH_3	$C_2H_5NH_2$	$(CH_3)_2 NH$	$(CH_3)_3 N$
Description	• three H atoms attached to N • no R groups	• two H atoms attached to N • one R group	• one H atom attached to N • two R groups	• no H atoms attached to N • three R groups

The —NH_2 group (amino) is ubiquitous in biological systems as amino acids are the building blocks of proteins. Many amines have a fishy smell that is sometimes noticeable when proteins in meats decompose. Amines are also of great importance in the dyestuffs industry especially the arenes such as phenylamine, $C_6H_5NH_2$, which were used in the first synthetic dyes – the azo compounds. Methyl orange, a widely used pH indicator is a derivative of phenylamine and many drugs including amphetamines are amine derivatives (Chapter 15).

Ammonia is a weak base owing to the lone pair of electrons on the nitrogen atom. This basic behaviour can be described by both of the definitions of bases discussed in Chapter 8:

- Brønsted–Lowry base: NH_3 accepts a proton
- Lewis base: NH_3 donates a lone pair of electrons.

$$NH_3(aq) + H_2O(l) \rightleftharpoons NH_4^+(aq) + OH^-(aq)$$

Methyl orange indicator is commonly used in titrations because it gives a distinct colour change with pH. It is an aromatic amine derivative.

Looking at the structures of amines, we would expect them to show similar basic properties as they too have a lone pair on the nitrogen atom. For example:

$$C_2H_5NH_2(aq) + H_2O(l) \rightleftharpoons C_2H_5NH_3^+ (aq) + OH^-(aq)$$

In addition, the alkyl groups, by pushing electrons onto the nitrogen through their positive inductive effects, increase the electron density of the lone pair and hence its ability to accept a proton. The amines are therefore *stronger* bases than ammonia. Secondary amines with two alkyl groups are stronger bases than primary amines having only one alkyl group.

ammonia   primary amines   secondary amines

increasing basic strength

Tertiary amines present an anomaly. By virtue of their three alkyl groups and greater inductive effects we would expect them to be more basic than secondary amines, but this is not the case. The explanation comes from a consideration of another factor that influences basic strength – the ability of the protonated amine (the positive ion) to stabilize itself in water. This depends largely on the extent to which it can form hydrogen bonds with water. Tertiary amines, having only one hydrogen atom attached to nitrogen in the protonated form, are less able to stabilize themselves in this way and are thus ionized less readily. This is why they are weaker bases than secondary amines.

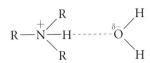

A tertiary amine ion has very limited ability to stabilize itself by hydrogen bonding.

Overall the basic strength of amines increases in the following order:

ammonia < tertiary amine < primary amine < secondary amine

Worked example

How would you expect the basic strength of methylamine and ethylamine to compare?

Solution

They are both primary amines, but the larger alkyl group in ethylamine has a stronger positive inductive effect, increasing the electron density on the lone pair of the nitrogen, making it a stronger base.

Reactions of amines as bases

As typical bases, amines and ammonia react with dilute acids to produce salts. Amine salts are soluble white crystalline solids.

Amines are stronger bases than ammonia. Secondary amines are stronger bases than primary amines and tertiary amines.

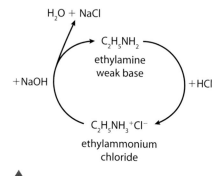

$$NH_3(aq) + HCl(aq) \rightarrow NH_4Cl(aq)$$
ammonium chloride

$$C_2H_5NH_2(aq) + HCl(aq) \rightarrow C_2H_5NH_3^+Cl^-(aq)$$
ethylammonium chloride

Because these are salts of weak bases, they will react with a strong base such as NaOH to form the salt of the strong base and release the free amine.

$$C_2H_5NH_3^+Cl^-(aq) + NaOH(aq) \rightarrow C_2H_5NH_2(aq) + NaCl(aq) + H_2O(l)$$

Figure 18.12 Interconversions of amines and their salts.

Summary of main types of organic reaction mechanisms with examples from this chapter

Electrophilic addition	Electrophilic substitution	Nucleophilic addition	Nucleophilic substitution
addition of Br_2 to alkenes	substitution of Br_2 in benzene (not described in this chapter)	addition of HCN to aldehydes and ketones Grignard reactions	substitution of OH^- in halogenoalkanes

Practice questions

1 On being reacted separately with HBr, 2-methylbut-1-ene and 2-methylbut-2-ene produce the same major product but different minor products.

 (a) Draw the structural formula of the major product and explain why it is formed in terms of the stability and structure of the organic intermediate. (4)

 (b) Draw the structural formulas of the two minor products. (2)

 (Total 6 marks)
 © International Baccalaureate Organization [2005]

2 (a) Name and outline the mechanism for the reaction of ethanal with hydrogen cyanide. (5)

 (b) Give the structure of the compound formed when the product from reaction (a) is hydrolysed. (1)

 (Total 6 marks)
 © International Baccalaureate Organization [2005]

3 Propene contains a $C=C$ double bond whereas propanal contains a $C=O$ double bond.

 (a) State and explain **two** similarities and **two** differences in the way in which the atoms are bonded in the covalent double bond in the two compounds. (4)

 (b) Both propene and propanal typically undergo addition reactions. State the type of addition reaction that takes place with each compound. (2)

(c) Hydrogen cyanide reacts with ethanal to form 2-hydroxypropanenitrile. Describe the mechanism of this reaction using 'curly arrows' to show the movement of pairs of electrons. (4)

(Total 10 marks)

© International Baccalaureate Organization [2003]

4 Cyclohexanone can react with 2,4-dinitrophenylhydrazine in aqueous solution.
   (a) State the type of reaction that takes place. (1)
   (b) Write a balanced equation for this reaction using structural formulas for the reactants and products. (2)
   (c) Explain how the product from this particular reaction can be used to confirm that the reactant was cyclohexanone and not any other carbonyl compound. (1)

(Total 4 marks)

© International Baccalaureate Organization [2003]

5 (a) Write an equation for the reaction of ethylamine with water. (2)
   (b) Explain why aminoethane (ethylamine) is more basic than ammonia. (2)
   (c) Explain why 2,4,6-trinitrophenol is more acidic than phenol. (2)

(Total 6 marks)

6 This question is based on the following reaction scheme.

$$W \longrightarrow X \longrightarrow Y$$
$$C_5H_{10} \qquad C_5H_{11}Br \qquad C_5H_{11}MgBr$$

   (a) W has the structure:

$$\underset{H}{\overset{H}{>}}C=C\underset{C_3H_7}{\overset{H}{<}}$$

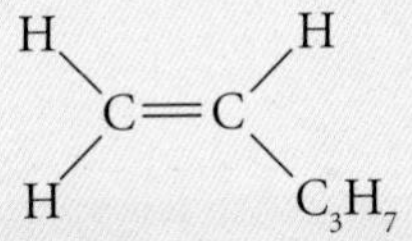

   (i) State the full name of W. (2)
   (ii) Name the reactant and state the reaction mechanism by which W is converted to X. (2)
   (iii) Explain how Markovnikov's rule is applied to determine the structure of X. Give the name and full structural formula of X. (4)
   (iv) Write equations (using 'curly arrows' to represent the movement of electron pairs) to show the mechanism of the reaction in which X is formed. (4)

   (b) The reaction for converting X to Y is used in many organic synthesis pathways.
   (i) State the conditions used for carrying out this reaction. (2)
   (ii) Explain why Y is so useful in synthesis reactions. Your answer should make reference to the bonding and structure of Y and give an example of a synthesis reaction in which it is used. (4)

(Total 18 marks)

7 Separate samples of $C_6H_5CHClCH_3$ and chlorobenzene are warmed with aqueous sodium hydroxide. State, with a reason, which compound would react more slowly. (2)

© International Baccalaureate Organization [2003]

Theory of knowledge

Introduction

In Theory of Knowledge you are encouraged to reflect on your own experience as a knower. Which ways of knowing do you use to justify your chemical knowledge? Does chemistry give you a 'true' picture of reality? How does the knowledge you gain in your chemistry class differ from that gained in other subjects? What are the ethical implications of technological developments in the subject? Chemistry has been hugely successful in giving us explanations of the material world and has also made a significant contribution to improving our quality of life, but does it offer certainty?

Ways of knowing: perception

What does the figure right represent?

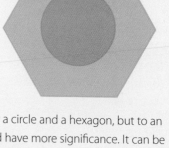

To many people this is simply a circle and a hexagon, but to an IB chemistry student it should have more significance. It can be interpreted as a benzene ring, or perhaps a representation of the IB Diploma programme. How you choose to interpret the picture will depend on the context in which it is presented. This illustrates an important point. Perception is an active process which includes an element of personal interpretation.

Chemistry and technology

Chemistry deals with **empirical knowledge**. This is knowledge acquired by the senses, enhanced, if necessary, by technology. We are now able to see things which are beyond the direct limits of our senses. Is this what a metal surface really looks like?

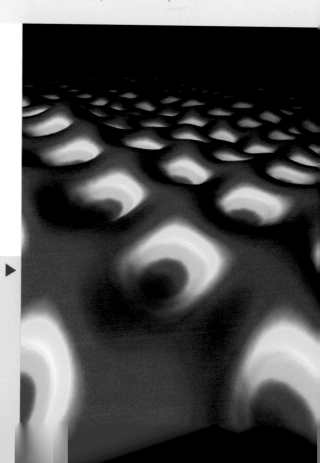

This picture is obtained by firing a beam of polarized ^{3}He atoms towards a metal surface. The metal can be seen as a lattice of positive metal ions (blue) in a sea of electrons (red).

The scientific method

Should the natural sciences be regarded more as a method or more as a system of knowledge? When you do experimental work in the IB programme, you are assessed against the criteria of Design, Data collection and processing, and Conclusion and evaluation, which suggests that scientists work in a particular way. Is this an accurate picture of how real science is done?

Richard Feynman (1918–1988), one of the great physicists of the 20th century, gave the following description of the scientific method:

'In general we look for a new law by the following process. First we guess it. Then we compute the consequences of the guesses to see what would be implied if the law was right. If it disagrees with experiment, it is wrong. In that simple statement is the key to science.... It does not make any difference how smart you are, or what is your name – if it disagrees with experiment it is wrong.... It is true that one has to check a little to check that one is wrong'.

Ways of knowing: induction

How do individual observations lead to theories and scientific laws of nature? Imagine an experiment in which you test the pH of some aqueous solutions of the different oxides.

Oxide	Acid/alkali
$Na_2O(s)$	alkali
$MgO(s)$	alkali
$CO_2(g)$	acid
$SO_2(g)$	acid
$CaO(s)$	alkali
$N_2O_5(g)$	acid

Two possible explanations which fit the pattern are:
- All solid oxides are alkalis. All gaseous oxides are acidic.
- All metal oxides are alkalis. All non-metal oxides are acidic.

We have used **induction** to draw the two general conclusions. Inductive logic allows us to move from specific instances to a general conclusion. Although it appeals to common sense, it is logically flawed. Both conclusions are equally valid based on the evidence but both conclusions could be wrong. Just because something has happened many times in the past does not prove that it will happen in the future. This is the **problem of induction**. The philosopher Bertrand Russell illustrated the danger of generalization by considering the case of the philosophical turkey. The bird reasoned that since he had been fed by the farmer every morning, he always would be. Sadly this turkey discovered the problem with induction on Thanksgiving Day! Are you acting in the same way as the turkey when you draw conclusions in your experimental work?

How do we justify the use of induction? Consider the following form of reasoning:

- On Monday I used induction and it worked.
- On Tuesday I used induction and it worked.
- On Wednesday I used induction and it worked.
- On Thursday I used induction and it worked.
- On Friday I used induction and it worked.
- Therefore I know that induction works.

What form of reasoning is used here to justify induction?

Karl Popper (1902–1994) realized that scientific verification doesn't actually prove anything and decided that science finds theories, not by verifying statements, but by **falsifying** them. Popper believed that even when a scientific theory had been successfully and repeatedly tested, it was not necessarily true. Instead it had simply not been proved false, yet! Observing a million white swans does not prove that all swans are white, but the first time we see a black swan we can firmly disprove our theory.

No matter how many times we record in our notebooks the observation of a white swan, we get no closer to proving the universal statement that all swans are white. This black swan inhabits lakes, rivers and coastal areas in Australia.

Ways of knowing: deduction

Deductive logic allows us to move from general statements to specific examples.

The conclusions of deductive logic must be true if the general statements on which it is based are correct. Deductive reasoning is the foundation of mathematics. We can use this reasoning to test our scientific hypotheses. Consider again the pH of the oxides tabulated earlier. The two competing hypotheses could be distinguished by considering the pH of a non-metal oxide such as phosphorus oxide, which is a solid at room temperature. The two hypotheses, when used as starting points (**premises**), lead to two different conclusions using deductive reasoning.

• All solid oxides are alkalis.	• All non-metal oxides are acidic.
• Phosphorus oxide is solid.	• Phosphorus oxide is a non-metal oxide.
• **Phosphorus oxide is an alkali**.	• **Phosphorus oxide is an acid**.

 How have scientists and philosophers made use of Karl Popper's ideas? Are we any closer to proving scientific principles are 'true'? Now go to www.heinemann.co.uk/hotlinks, insert the express code 4259P and click on this activity.

When the pH of phosphorus oxide is tested and shown to be an acid we can be certain that the first hypothesis is false, but we cannot be sure that the second is definitely true.

If it survives repeated tests, it may, however, become accepted as scientific truth, but it is not certain. No matter how many tests a hypothesis survives, we will never prove that it is true in the same way as mathematical proof is true. All scientific knowledge is provisional.

There are still problems, however, with this view of science. When your results don't match up with the expected values in a chemistry investigation, do you abandon the accepted theories or do you explain the differences as being due to experimental error, faulty instruments or contaminated chemicals?

The curve and straight line in the graph both fit the experimental data.

Same data, different hypothesis

It is always possible to think of other hypotheses that are consistent with the given set of data. The hypothesis: 'Oxides with one oxygen in the formula are alkalis, oxides with more than one oxygen are acids' also fits the data presented. For the same reason, an infinite number of patterns can be found to fit the same experimental data.

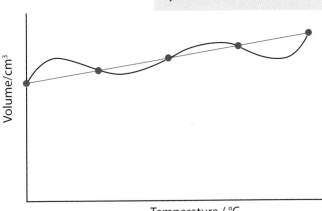

You may argue that the straight line in the graph above is more suitable as it is simpler, but on what grounds do we base the assumption that simplicity is a criterion for truth? The idea that the simplest explanations are the best is inspired by the principle – named after the medieval philosopher William of Occam – known as Occam's razor.

Albert Einstein said 'Explanations must be as simple as possible – and no simpler'.

Rejecting anomalous results: confirmation bias

We often dismiss results which don't fit the expected pattern because of experimental error. In the example on the next page is it reasonable to reject the point not on the line?

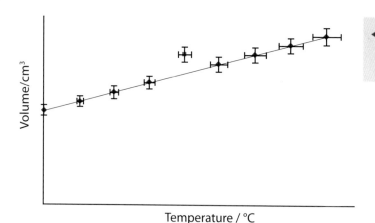

Volume/cm³

Temperature / °C

◄ When are you justified in dismissing a data point which does not fit the general pattern?

Are the models and theories that scientists use merely pragmatic instruments or do they actually describe the natural world?

Scientists use models to clarify certain features and relationships. They can become more and more sophisticated but they can never become the real thing. Models are just a representation of reality. The methane molecule, for example, can be represented in a number of forms. All these models of methane are based on the model of the atom discussed in Chapter 2. Although this is one of the most successful scientific models, it is not complete as it fails to explain the electron arrangement of atoms after calcium in the Periodic Table. To explain the chemistry of all the elements, a more sophisticated model that involves considering an electron as a wave is needed.

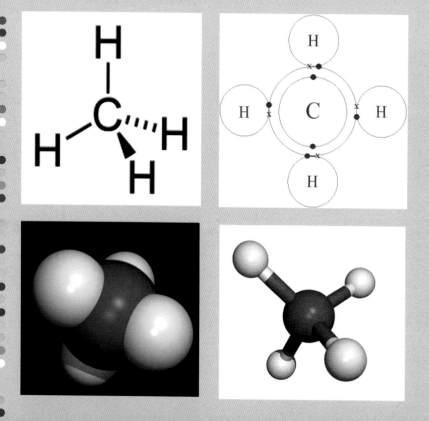

The evidence for the wave nature of electrons comes from the diffraction pattern observed when a beam of electrons is passed through a metal structure, which is similar to that observed when light is passed through a diffraction grating (see below). We now recognise that the 'true' nature of the electron, or indeed anything, cannot be completely described by a single model. Both the wave model and the particle model are needed. This should not surprise us as models are often based on our everyday experience which does not apply to the small scale of the atom. To understand nature at this level, scientists must go beyond their experience and use their imagination.

The wave particle duality of the electron illustrates a general knowledge issue. Two sources of knowledge can often give conflicting results and it is for us, as knowers, to see if the conflict is real or a limitation of our ways of knowing.

This is a diffraction grating pattern formed by laser light (red), which has passed through an array of crossed gratings. Light is generally considered as a wave.

▲

This is an electron diffraction pattern of a binary alloy of 90% titanium and 10% nickel. The pattern can be explained by considering an electron as a wave.

J.J. Thomson won the Nobel Prize in 1906 for measuring the mass of an electron, that is for showing it to be a 'particle'. His son G.P. Thomson won the Nobel Prize in 1937 for showing the electron to be a 'wave'. This is not necessarily a contradiction. It is a question of particles sometimes behaving as waves. Our everyday classification of phenomena into 'wave' and 'particle' breaks down at the sub-atomic scale. This limitation of our experience should not, however, shackle our understanding of the sub-atomic world.

Science and pseudoscience: alchemy and homeopathy

If you have ever dropped sugar into a glass of a carbonated water you will have noticed that it fizzes. Can you offer an explanation for this?

If someone suggested that it was because there was an 'evil demon' present in the drink who was responding angrily to being assaulted by sugar granules you would probably reject this as a non-scientific explanation, but what makes this non-scientific? A scientific theory must be testable. It is difficult to imagine an experiment which could be designed to prove the 'evil demon' theory *false*. A theory that can be used to explain everything explains nothing.

It is worth reflecting, however, that many of the experimental techniques of chemistry have their origins in the pseudo-science of alchemy.

▲ Add sugar to any of these drinks and awake an evil demon!

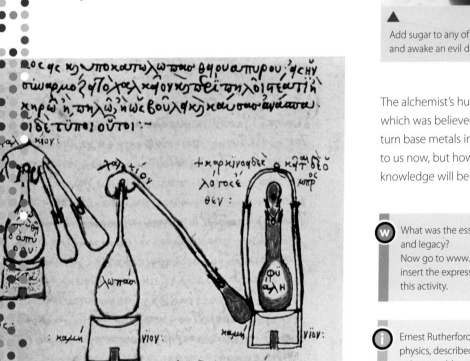

▲ A page from a treatise on alchemy written by Zosimus of Panapolitus (4th century). Some of the equipment drawn is found in a modern chemistry laboratory.

The alchemist's hunt for the Philosopher's Stone, which was believed to give eternal life and could turn base metals into gold, seems very naïve to us now, but how do you think our chemical knowledge will be viewed 500 years from now?

W What was the essence of alchemy, its history and legacy?
Now go to www.heinemann.co.uk/hotlinks, insert the express code 4259P and click on this activity.

i Ernest Rutherford, the father of nuclear physics, described himself as an alchemist as he was able to change one element into another by nuclear reactions.

In 1661, with the publication of *The Sceptical Chemist*, Robert Boyle established chemistry as a separate science. He is famous for *Boyle's law*, which states the relationship between pressure and volume for a fixed mass of gas.

The natural sciences of chemistry, physics and biology are classed as experimental sciences in the IB Diploma hexagon. What counts as an experiment and must a subject involve experiments if it is to be scientific? There are number of activities that are claimed by those who practise them to be scientific, such as astrology, homeopathy and crystology. The label 'science' adds authority to the claims, but how do we distinguish a genuine science from a fake or **pseudo-science**?

A hierarchy of disciplines

Is it possible to place the different scientific disciplines in a hierarchy and which criteria would you use for your choice? Chemical theories can help our understanding of biology: hydrogen bonding explains the double helix structure of DNA, and much of chemistry relies on physics; hydrogen bonding in turn is explained in terms of electrostatic attraction. Is this direction of explanation ever reversed? The view that one subject can be explained by terms of the components of another is called **reductionism**. Is physics in some way 'better' than the other sciences and where would you place mathematics, which has been described as both the queen and servant of the sciences in this hierarchy? Our knowledge of the Periodic Table and atomic structure suggests that there are limits to the number of elements in nature. Is chemistry in some way the most complete science? Which of the natural sciences, physics, chemistry or biology is most directly based on direct observation?

Homeopathy is an alternative medicine that aims to treat diseases by giving extremely dilute doses of compounds that cause the same symptoms as the disease. The more dilute the dosage, the more powerful the remedy. Some of the most powerful doses are so dilute that it is likely they do not contain a single molecule of the active substance. Practitioners attribute this to the 'memory' of the water in which they have been diluted. Conventional science has subjected these claims to intense scrutiny, but firm evidence of anything other than the placebo effect has not yet been found.

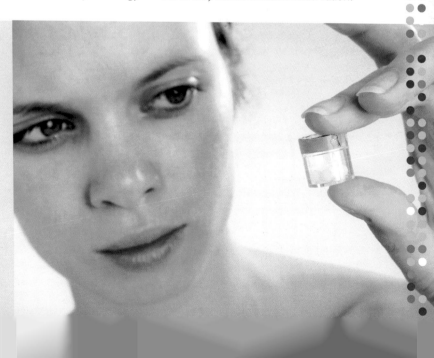

How does chemical knowledge change with time?

We have seen that the inductive and falsification theories of science give an incomplete description of how science progresses. An alternative view was offered by Thomas Kuhn (1922–1996). Kuhn suggested that science does not develop by the orderly accumulation of facts and theories, but by dramatic revolutions which he called **paradigm shifts**.

A paradigm can be thought of as a model or world view accepted by the scientific community. Kuhn distinguished between periods of **normal science** in which new discoveries are placed within the current paradigm and **extraordinary science** which produces results which do not fit the current paradigm. Isaac Newton, John Dalton, Charles Darwin and Albert Einstein are all revolutionary scientists who changed the way we look at the world by proposing new paradigms.

The idea of a paradigm shift can be illustrated by considering the picture on the right.

As Kuhn says 'What were ducks in the scientists' world before the revolution, are rabbits afterwards…'.

Atomic theory is one of the most important paradigms of chemistry. Dalton's model of the atom as being indivisible collapsed when the proton, neutron and electrons were discovered.

▲ In one paradigm, the picture can be interpreted as a duck; in another paradigm, it can be interpreted as a rabbit. Turn the page through 90° and experience a paradigm shift.

Paradigm shifts: phlogiston theory and the discovery of oxygen

When a solid such as magnesium burns, it crumbles into an ash. It seems quite natural to assume that the metal is giving something off as it burns. It was originally believed that all flammable materials contain phlogiston, derived from the Greek for flame, which was absorbed by the air as substances burn. In this theory, substances stop burning when all the phlogiston has been released or when the air is saturated with the phlogiston released. The crisis in the paradigm occurred when careful measurements showed that a mass increase occurred during combustion. Some explained this result within the phlogiston paradigm by suggesting that phlogiston could have a negative mass but it was rejected in favour

Ⓦ Although Priestley (1733–1804) almost certainly isolated oxygen, Lavoisier (1743–1794) understood it first. Find out more about what happens when two great minds collide and a paradigm collapses.
Now go to www.heinemann.co.uk/hotlinks, insert the express code 4259P and click on this activity.

of the modern oxygen theory of combustion. As substances burn more brightly in oxygen, the gas was originally called 'dephlogisticated air' by Joseph Priestly, who is one of the scientists credited with its discovery. The discovery of oxygen, however, made the term 'phlogiston' meaningless.

A widely held stereotype of scientific progress is that of an idealistic young innovator challenging the ideas of the establishment. This is rationalized in Kuhn's model of science as individual scientists are often reluctant to make such leaps. This highlights the role of creative thinking in scientific progress. The need to be a risk taker and think out of the box is emphasized by Richard Feynman: 'One of the ways of stopping science would be to only experiment in the region where you know the law'.

Max Planck said 'A new scientific theory does not triumph by convincing its opponents and making them see the light, but rather because its opponents eventually die out and a new generation grows up that is familiar with it'.

Ways of knowing: language

The language of alchemy was cryptic and secretive as the knowledge it communicated was thought to be too powerful to share with the general public. The names of many chemicals were derived from their natural origin and were not related to their composition.

The language of modern chemistry, by contrast, is precise and an effective tool for thought. When asked to draw the different isomers of C_7H_{16} it is very easy to draw the same structure twice. The IUPAC nomenclature, however, allows you to distinguish the different isomers.

According to the phlogiston paradigm, a substance is released into the air when a candle burns. We now know that the carbon and hydrogen in the candle combine with oxygen in the air to form carbon dioxide and water.

heptane	2-methylhexane	3-methylhexane
2,2-dimethylpentane	2,3-dimethylpentane	2,4-dimethylpentane
3,3-dimethylpentane	3-ethylpentane	2,2,3-trimethylbutane

◄ The nine isomers of C_7H_{16}. The names help you to distinguish the different structures.

The use of oxidation numbers has also allowed us to develop a systematic nomenclature for naming inorganic substances.

Chemistry, of course, also has its own universal language. Balanced equations allow us to use mathematics to solve chemical problems. The ability to attach numbers to substances allows the chemist to use mathematics as a precise tool to investigate the material world. Language should be a tool and not an obstacle to knowledge.

Measurement: the observer effect

Measurement has allowed the chemist to attach numbers to the properties of materials, but the act of measurement can change the property being measured. Adding a thermometer to a hot beaker of water, for example, will cause the temperature to decrease slightly and adding an acid–base indicator, which is itself a weak acid, will change the pH of the solution.

Generally such effects can be ignored, as measures are taken to minimize these effects. Only a few drops of indicator are used, for example, and thermometers are deigned to have a low heat capacity. The **observer effect** can cause significant problems at the atomic scale, however, which led the physicist Werner Heisenberg (1901–1976) to comment: 'What we observe is not nature itself but nature exposed to our mode of questioning'. The observer effect is also significant in the human sciences. Can your school director observe a 'normal' chemistry class?

Methyl orange is a weak acid. The addition of the indicator will change the pH of the solution it is measuring.

Knowledge and belief

It should be clear from the previous discussion that science does not offer complete certainty and absolute truth. Do you know that sodium chloride is made up from Na^+ and Cl^- ions or do you simply believe this to be the case? What is needed to change a belief into knowledge?

Chemistry and ethics

Progress in science and technology has an impact on our lives. Often these effects are positive – drugs and medicines have made our lives safer and the development of new materials has made our lives more comfortable, but technological developments can also bring suffering and injustice. Industry and technology have had a negative impact on the environment. How do we decide what is the right and wrong use of science? These are ethical questions. There is often disagreement about what is 'right' and what is considered acceptable change over time. Ethical issues raise difficult questions about risk versus benefits. In many cases the science is so new that judging long-term benefits and risks is difficult. Developments in chemistry can create new ethical issues. There are also more direct concerns about how scientists should conduct their work. Scientists generally work in communities, not in isolation, and are expected to report their results honestly and openly in an atmosphere of trust. Science is, however, a human endeavour and scientists, like the rest of humanity, can be motivated by envy, vanity and ambition.

Is science, or ought it to be, value-free? Some would argue that it is the aim of science to describe the world as it is and not as it should be. The natural sciences and ethics are different areas of knowledge which use different ways of knowing to answer different questions. It is for society to decide what to do with scientific issues – that is the moral question.

Some people do, however, fear the consequence of scientists interfering with nature. The arguments for and against the use of genetically modified foods, for example, were discussed in Chapter 17. Who decides what is and what is not a legitimate area of scientific research? The scientific community or society at large? The fear of scientific discoveries is, of course, understandable. As discussed in Chapter 15, scientists believed that thalidomide was so safe that it was prescribed to pregnant women to control morning sickness, with tragic consequences. Who is responsible when things go wrong?

"But do I have the RIGHT...?"

▲ Does the scientist have the right to bring two wires together? The chemist is faced with similar ethical dilemmas and must balance potential benefits against potential risks.

Chemistry and TOK assessment

In your TOK essays you are expected to make connections between the knowledge issues raised and your own experiences as a learner. It is helpful to support your argument with examples drawn from your IB diploma courses as well as from other sources. In your TOK presentations, you are asked to apply your TOK thinking skills to a contemporary issue. This can be an opportunity, for example, to reflect on the moral and ethical implications of scientific developments. Your chemistry course offers a wide range of experiences for reflection.

 Richard Feynman is one of the most original thinkers of the 20th century. In this interview he discusses the nature of science and its relation to other areas of knowledge.
Now go to www.heinemann.co.uk/hotlinks, insert the express code 4259P and click on this activity.

Some examples of prescribed essay titles for you to consider

- Is it a simple matter to distinguish a scientific argument from a pseudo-scientific argument? (May 2003)
- In what ways has technology expanded or limited the acquisition of knowledge? (May 2002)
- For some people, science is the supreme form of all knowledge. Is this view reasonable or does it involve a misunderstanding of science or of knowledge? (May 2005)
- 'The whole of science is nothing more than a refinement of everyday thinking.'
  Could this be said of all areas of knowledge? (May 2002)
- Do we have to learn to think scientifically in order to find the truth? (May 2001)
- In science, one tries to tell people, in a way that can be understood by everyone, something that no-one ever knew before. But in poetry, it's the exact opposite. (Paul Dirac).
  Do both these approaches enjoy equal success in explaining human knowledge? (May 2003)
- Art upsets, science reassures. Analyse and evaluate this claim. (May 2002)
- To what extent may the subjective nature of perception be regarded as an advantage for artists but an obstacle to be overcome for scientists? (May 2005)

Internal assessment

Your final result in IB chemistry is determined by:

- your performance in the three examination papers – **external assessment** contributing 76% of the final mark
- your laboratory work – **internal assessment** contributing 24% of the final mark.

The laboratory component is assessed primarily by your teacher (although the marks are standardized by the IB in a process known as **moderation**, to ensure that the same standards are being applied fairly across all IB schools).

The mark you achieve for internal assessment is based on the application of specific **assessment criteria** to your laboratory work. Each criterion is divided into subheadings known as **aspects** and each of these has a separate descriptor for assessment. You must fulfil the expectations of all the aspects when a particular criterion is being addressed.

Three of the assessment criteria (Design, Data collection and processing, Conclusion and evaluation) are based on some of the written work that you submit as part of your laboratory programme. Each of these is assessed at least twice during your course. The details of the criteria are given below with notes to guide you about how to achieve the best possible result and avoid some of the common pitfalls. It is a good idea to focus only on the descriptor under 'Complete/2' for each aspect so that you are aiming for the top score in each case.

Design

Levels/marks	Aspect 1	Aspect 2	Aspect 3
	Defining the problem and selecting variables	Controlling variables	Developing a method for collection of data
Complete/2	Formulates a focused problem/research question and identifies the relevant variables	Designs a method for the effective control of the variables	Develops a method that allows for the collection of sufficient relevant data
Partial/1	Formulates a problem/research question that is incomplete **or** identifies only some relevant data	Designs a method that makes some attempt to control the variables	Develops a method that allows for the collection of insufficient relevant data
Not at all/0	Does not identify a problem/research question **and** does not identify any relevant variables	Designs a method that does not control the variables	Develops a method that does not allow for any relevant data to be collected

Aspect 1: defining the problem and selecting variables

You must give a research question or aim which is a clear statement of what you are going to investigate. It must be much more focused and specific than the general theme provided by your teacher. It will probably say something like 'To find out how … is affected by a change in …'

Here you must identify the variables:
Independent variable (also known as the manipulated variable) refers to the factor that you control and for which you set the values; the **dependent variable** (also known as the responding or measured variable) is the factor that you measure as the experiment proceeds. **Control variables** are factors which must be kept as constant as possible during the experiment so that they do not interfere with the interpretation of the results. (Often an analysis of the control variables may lead to identification of some systematic errors.)

Aspect 2: controlling variables

Here you must clearly state *how* each variable that you identified above will be controlled. If it is not possible to keep a particular variable constant (for example the temperature rise in the laboratory during the course of the experiment), then you should try to monitor the fluctuation during the experiment.

You should record full details of all the apparatus selected. This includes, for example, the size of glassware used, how the reactants are measured, and so on. Similarly, you should include full details of reactant concentrations, mass or volume, the time taken for each step, and so on. For example, instead of saying '25.00 cm³ of solution X was put in the beaker and heated', it is much better to say '25 cm³ of solution X was measured with a 25.00 ± 0.06 cm³ pipette, transferred to a 200 cm³ beaker and heated on a hot plate until …' A clear, labelled diagram is often an effective way of describing the experimental set-up.

Remember the guideline that there should be sufficient detail in your written report to enable someone else to reproduce your work exactly.

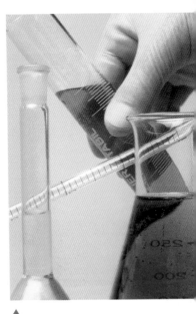

Selecting the most appropriate piece of glassware for each stage in the experiment is very important.

Aspect 3: developing a method for collection of data

The definition of 'sufficient relevant data' depends on the particular experiment, but you should devise an experiment to collect enough data so that you can answer the aim and evaluate the results. Often this will involve plotting a graph of the effect of changes in the independent variable on the dependent variable, and you will need at least *five* data points to do this. For some experiments, it may be necessary to take repeated measurements to calculate a mean; in others (e.g. titration) it may involve a trial run and then repeats until consistent results are obtained.

Data collection and processing

Levels/marks	Aspect 1	Aspect 2	Aspect 3
	Recording raw data	Processing raw data	Presenting processed data
Complete/2	Records appropriate quantitative and associated qualitative raw data, including units and uncertainties where relevant	Processes the quantitative raw data correctly	Presents processed data appropriately and, where relevant, includes errors and uncertainties
Partial/1	Records appropriate quantitative and qualitative raw data, but with some mistakes or omissions	Processes quantitative raw data, but with some mistakes and/or omissions	Presents processed data appropriately, but with some mistakes and/or omissions
Not at all/0	Does not record any appropriate quantitative raw data **or** raw data are incomprehensible	No processing of raw data is carried out or major mistakes are made in the processing	Presents processed data inappropriately **or** incomprehensibly

Aspect 1: recording raw data

Raw data includes:

- numerical measurements of the variables – quantitative data
- relevant observations – qualitative data.

It is acceptable to convert handwritten data into word-processed form after you have finished the experiment, but raw data must be the actual numbers recorded before any processing occurs. So, for example, in an experiment involving titration, it would be the actual readings on the burette, not just the final titre. The best way to record your data is in a table that must have clear headings showing units and uncertainties. The number of significant digits must be consistent in every reading and in the uncertainty stated.

Aspect 2: processing raw data

This should involve some mathematical manipulation of the raw data to determine an experimental value. It may involve taking the average of several readings, doing a calculation of a physical quantity from experimental data, or transforming data into a form suitable for graphical representation such as taking logs or reciprocal values of data.

Note that simply taking tabulated data and presenting it in graphical form does not count as data processing, but if you can calculate the best-fit line through the points and determine the gradient, then you have addressed this aspect of the criterion.

Aspect 3: presenting processed data

Your processed data must be presented in a format that leads to easy interpretation such as a table, graph, spreadsheet, and so on. Graphs must be clearly titled, with appropriate scales, labelled axes with units and accurately plotted data points with a suitable best-fit line or curve. Avoid the common mistake of graphs that are too small. The final result must have clear SI units and the correct number of significant figures.

Remember to include both quantitative and qualitative data in your results.

When the data are processed, the uncertainties collected at the same time must also be considered by propagating the random errors through the calculation. This is explained fully in Chapter 11.

Conclusion and evaluation

Levels/marks	Aspect 1	Aspect 2	Aspect 3
	Concluding	Evaluating procedure(s)	Improving the investigation
Complete/2	States a conclusion with justification based on a reasonable interpretation of the data	Evaluates weaknesses and limitations	Suggests realistic improvements with respect to identified weaknesses and limitations
Partial/1	States a conclusion based on a reasonable interpretation of the data	Identifies some weaknesses and limitations, but the evaluation is weak or missing	Suggests only superficial improvements
Not at all/0	States no conclusion or the conclusion is based on an unreasonable interpretation of the data	Identifies irrelevant weaknesses and limitations	Suggests unrealistic improvements

Aspect 1: concluding

Make a clear statement of conclusion by using your results to answer the original aim. Where possible compare the results with data values and calculate a percentage error between your results and the literature value. You can compare this value with the total estimated random error determined by the propagation of uncertainties. If the experimental error is much greater than the random error, then systematic errors are probably responsible. Consider the direction in which systematic errors might have influenced the results.

Aspect 2: evaluating procedure(s)

Here consider the design of the experiment and method of the investigation, including the precision and accuracy of the measurements. Consider what assumptions you have made in the design.

Aspect 3: improving the investigation

Use the weaknesses identified above to guide you in suggesting improvements. These should aim to address reducing random error, removing systematic error and obtaining greater control of variables. 'More time' and 'use more accurate equipment' are not very helpful.

Manipulative skills

Levels/marks	Aspect 1	Aspect 2	Aspect 3
	Following instructions	Carrying out techniques	Working safely
Complete/2	Follows instructions accurately, adapting to new circumstances (seeking assistance when required)	Competent and methodical in the use of a range of techniques and equipment	Pays attention to safety issues
Partial/1	Follows instructions but requires assistance	Usually competent and methodical in the use of a range of techniques and equipment	Usually pays attention to safety issues
Not at all/0	Rarely follows instructions **or** requires constant supervision	Rarely competent and methodical in the use of a range of techniques and equipment	Rarely pays attention to safety issues

This criterion is assessed over the duration of the course rather than in any specific investigation. You can help yourself to do well here by coming to the classes well prepared, having read any information you were given beforehand and showing an awareness of the investigation. Being alert to health and safety considerations at all times is also essential here.

Personal skills

Levels/marks	Aspect 1	Aspect 2	Aspect 3
	Self-motivation and perseverance	Working within a team	Self-reflection
Complete/2	Approaches the project with self-motivation and follows it through to completion	Collaborates and communicates in a group situation and integrates the views of others	Shows a thorough awareness of their own strengths and weaknesses and gives thoughtful consideration to their learning experience
Partial/1	Completes the project but sometimes lacks self-motivation	Exchanges some views but requires guidance to collaborate with others	Shows limited awareness of their own strengths and weaknesses and gives some consideration to their learning experience
Not at all/0	Lacks perseverance and motivation	Makes little or no attempt to collaborate in a group situation	Shows no awareness of their own strengths and weaknesses and gives no consideration to their learning experience

This criterion is assessed during the group 4 project. Your teacher may suggest that you produce a written form of self-evaluation and you may also take part in peer evaluation within your group. If you are enthusiastic about the project and communicate well with your group, you are likely to be successful here.

Advice on the Extended Essay

The Extended Essay is a compulsory part of the IB Diploma. It is an independent 40-hour research project in an IB subject of your choice. The final essay, of up to 4000 words of formally presented, structured writing, is the longest assignment of the two-year programme. Although this may sound daunting, it is a great opportunity to investigate a topic of particular interest and produce knowledge that is new to you. It shares with the theory of knowledge (TOK) course a concern with interpreting and evaluating evidence and constructing reasoned arguments. The marks awarded for the Extended Essay and TOK are combined to give a maximum of three bonus points.

An Extended Essay in chemistry must have a clear chemical emphasis and not be more closely related to another subject. For example, a chemistry Extended Essay in an area such as biochemistry will be assessed on its chemical and not its biological content. It should include chemical principles and theory. Although it is not a requirement, the best chemistry Extended Essays tend to be those based on experiments performed in a school laboratory, as this allows the most personal input. It is easier for you to plan and modify your experimental procedures when you are familiar with the equipment.

The best chemistry Extended Essays are often based on experiments carried out in a school laboratory.

Some advice

Before you start

- Read a copy of the subject-specific details of an Extended Essay in chemistry including the assessment criteria.
- Read some previous essays and try to identify their strengths and weaknesses.
- Draw up a list of possible research questions including the techniques you would use to address these questions. Many of the best essays are written by students investigating relatively simple phenomena using apparatus and materials that can be found in most school laboratories. The table below lists some possible approaches, which involve techniques that are generally available. Some Extended Essays may involve a combination of two of these approaches.
- acid–base titration
- chromatography
- data logging probes
- electrochemistry
- extension of a standard investigation
- field work
- heat changes
- literature based
- measuring mass changes using an analytical balance
- measuring volume changes of gases using a gas syringe
- redox titration
- spectrophotometry

The research question

- Spend time working out the research question. This is the key to a successful Extended Essay. You should choose a topic that interests you as you will be spending 40 hours on this. As initiative and personal involvement are assessed, higher grades are generally given to essays when students have chosen their own research question. Don't choose anything that is too complicated or difficult. Your question must be sharply focused and capable of being addressed in 40 hours and 4000 words. For example, *The ratio of oxygen and chlorine produced at the anode during the electrolysis of different concentrated solutions of aqueous sodium chloride solution*, is better than *The electrolysis of salt*.
- If you realise there is a problem with your research question change it to something that can be answered!

Use a range of resources including the internet and any libraries available.

During the research process

- Safety is a priority. Don't do anything in the laboratory without checking with your supervisor.
- Use a range of resources to find out what others have done in the area. Textbooks should never be the only source of information. Don't spend all your time online. Use the school and other local libraries if possible.
- Keep written records of everything that you do and make a note of all references, including the date when internet sites were accessed so that you can build up your footnotes and bibliography as you go along.

- Record all experimental data, including the dates when the experiments were performed and any uncertainties in your measurements. In your preliminary investigations, write down any problems and challenges you encountered and record any modifications. Use your imagination to design new equipment if necessary.

While writing the essay

Make sure that you address the stated research question and the Extended Essay assessment criteria. The criteria are different to those used in your class experimental work, which is assessed by the internal assessment criteria discussed on page 492.
- Include explanations of any theory not covered in the IB subject guide, including the chemistry of any specialized techniques you have used.
- Use the appropriate chemical language and make sure that all chemical equations are balanced.
- Include sufficient details of any experimental procedure to allow others to repeat the work.
- Check any calculations and make sure that all experimental data are presented correctly.
- Discuss the limitations of the experimental method and any systematic errors. Consider any questions which are unresolved at the end of your research and suggest new questions and areas for possible further investigation.
- Let your enthusiasm and interest for the topic show and emphasize clearly your own personal contribution.
- Although 4000 words may seem a lot, many students find that they have to cut out words in the final draft as they have written too much!

After completing the essay

- Write the abstract.
- Check and proof-read the final version carefully.
- Use the assessment criteria to grade your essay. Are you satisfied with the grade you award yourself?

The assessment criteria

	Maximum Achievement Levels	Mark
A: Research question	The research question is clearly stated in the introduction and sharply focused, making effective treatment possible within the word limit. *It is perfectly reasonable to formulate the research question as a statement or as a hypothesis.*	2
B: Introduction	The context of the research question is clearly demonstrated. The introduction clearly explains the significance of the topic and why it is worthy of investigation. *The research question should be related to existing knowledge in chemistry, including the underlying chemical theory. Some research questions may require some essential background knowledge that is not related to chemistry.*	2
C: Investigation	An imaginative range of appropriate sources has been consulted, or data have been gathered and relevant material has been carefully selected. The investigation has been well planned. *For non-experimental essays include details of how you selected your data. Primary sources (original scientific publications, personal communications, interviews) and secondary sources (textbooks, newspaper articles, reviews) should be distinguished and you should comment on their reliability. You should provide sufficient information for any experimental work to be repeated. It should be clear which experiments you have designed and which you have altered, adapted or improved from existing methods.*	4

D: Knowledge and understanding	The essay demonstrates a very good knowledge and understanding of the topic studied.	4
	Where appropriate, the essay clearly and precisely locates the investigation in an academic context.	
	The underlying chemistry should be explained. You are not expected to explain basic chemistry included in the Diploma Programme chemistry course, but you are expected to show that you fully understand the relevant principles and ideas and can apply them correctly. You should also demonstrate that you understand the theory behind any techniques or apparatus used.	
E: Reasoned argument	Ideas are presented clearly and in a logical and coherent manner.	4
	The essay succeeds in developing a reasoned and convincing argument in relation to the research question.	
	A good argument in chemistry will almost certainly include consideration and comparison of different approaches and methods directly relevant to the research question. Straightforward descriptive or narrative accounts that lack analysis do not usually advance an argument and should be avoided.	
F: Application of analytical and evaluative skills	The essay shows effective and sophisticated application of appropriate analytical and evaluative skills.	4
	A thorough understanding of the reliability of all data used to support the argument should be shown. Inadequate experimental design or any systematic errors should be exposed. The magnitude of uncertainties in physical data should be evaluated and discussed. Approximations in models should be accounted for and all assumptions examined thoroughly. Where possible, the quality of sources accessed or data generated should be verified by secondary sources or by direct calculations.	
G: Use of language	The language used communicates clearly and precisely. Terminology appropriate to the subject is used accurately, with skill and understanding.	4
	Correct chemical terminology and nomenclature should be used consistently and effectively throughout the Extended Essay. Relevant chemical formulas (including structural formulas), balanced equations (including state symbols) and mechanisms should be included. The correct units for physical quantities must always be given and the proper use of significant figures is expected.	
H: Conclusion	An effective conclusion is clearly stated; it is relevant to the research question and consistent with the evidence presented in the essay.	2
	It should include unresolved questions where appropriate to the subject concerned.	
	The conclusion must be consistent with the argument presented and should not merely repeat material in the introduction or introduce new or extraneous points to the argument. It is a good idea to consider unresolved questions and to suggest areas for further investigation.	
I: Formal presentation	The formal presentation is excellent. This criterion assesses the extent to which the layout, organization, appearance and formal elements of the essay consistently follow a standard format. The formal elements are: title page, table of contents, page numbers, illustrative material, quotations, documentation (including references, citations and bibliography) and appendices (if used).	4
	The essay must not exceed 4000 words of narrative. Graphs, figures, calculations, diagrams, formulas and equations are not included in the word count. For experiments where numerical results are calculated from data obtained by changing one of the variables, it is generally good practice to show one example of the calculation. The remainder can be displayed in tabular or graphical form.	
J: Abstract	The abstract clearly states the research question that was investigated, how the investigation was undertaken and the conclusion(s) of the essay.	2
	The abstract is judged on the clarity with which it presents an overview of the research and the essay, not on the quality of the research question itself, nor on the quality of the argument or the conclusions.	
K: Holistic judgement	The essay shows considerable evidence of qualities such as intellectual initiative, depth of understanding and insight.	4
	• *Intellectual initiative: Ways of demonstrating this include the choice of topic and research question and the use of novel or innovative approaches to address the research question.*	
	• *Insight and depth of understanding: These are most likely to be demonstrated as a consequence of detailed research, reflection that is thorough and by well-informed and reasoned argument that consistently and effectively addresses the research question.*	
	• *Originality and creativity: This will be apparent by clear evidence of a personal approach backed up by solid research and reasoning.*	

Bibliography and references

It is **required** that you acknowledge all sources of information and ideas in an approved academic manner. Essays that omit a bibliography or that do not give references are unacceptable. Your supervisor or school librarian will be able to give you advice on which format to follow. One method gives the author followed by the publication (in italics), the publisher and then the date of publication, for example:

C. Brown and M. Ford, *Standard Level Chemistry*, Heinemann Baccalaureate, 1st edition, 2008.

Internet references should include the title of the extract used as well as the website address, the date it was accessed and, if possible, the author. You should always exercise caution when using information from websites that do not give references or that cannot be cross-checked against other sources. The more important a particular point is to the essay, the more the quality of its source needs to be evaluated.

Viva voce

After you have handed in the final version you may be given a short interview or *viva voce* by your supervisor, who is required to write a report on your project. This is an opportunity to discuss the successes and challenges of the project and for you to reflect on what you have learned from the experience.

Strategies for success in IB chemistry

During the course

Take responsibility for your own learning. When you finish your study of a topic in class, it is a really good time to check back through the assessment statements at the start of each chapter and make sure that you are comfortable with each expectation. Spend extra time on parts where you are less confident of your knowledge and understanding. Using additional sources of information such as other books, journals and the web links in this book will help to spark your curiosity, deepen your understanding and give you a grasp of the wider contexts of the topic. The more you do, the more you will enjoy the course and the more successful you will be.

The practice questions at the end of each chapter are IB questions from previous years' papers, so they are a very good way of testing yourself at the end of each topic. (The answers used by examiners in marking the papers are also given at the end of the book).

Preparing for the examination

Organize your time for review well ahead of the examination date on a topic by topic basis. While you are studying, make sure that you test yourself as you go – being able to recognize the content on the page is very different from being able to produce it yourself on blank paper. Effective revision generally involves using lots of scrap paper to test your knowledge and understanding. Practise writing balanced equations, drawing diagrams, structural formulas, and so on.

Remember that you need to cover the work from the entire course so try to make your study cumulative, which involves seeing how the topics are inter-related and how they reinforce the same concepts. There is not much choice of questions in the examination so make sure that you do not miss anything out. When you have finished your review of a particular topic, it is a good idea to test yourself with IB questions and time yourself according to how much time you are given for each type of question.

In the examination

The external assessment of Standard Level chemistry consists of three examination papers as follows.

	% of total mark	Duration/hours	Description of examination
Paper 1	20	$\frac{3}{4}$	30 multiple-choice questions
Paper 2	32	$1\frac{1}{4}$	Section A: one data-handling question and several compulsory short-answer questions Section B: one extended-response question from a choice of three
Paper 3	24	1	several short-answer questions in each of the two options studied

Paper 1: Multiple choice questions on the core (Chapters 1–11)

You are not allowed to use your calculator or the IB Data booklet in this paper, but you will be given a copy of the Periodic Table. The questions will give you any other data that you need and any calculations will be straightforward.

There is no penalty for wrong answers so make sure that you do not leave any blanks. Read *all* the given options A–D for each question – it is likely that more than one answer is close to being correct but you must choose the best answer available.

Paper 2: Written answers on the core (Chapters 1–11)

You are given five minutes' reading time for this paper. It is a good idea to spend this time looking at the questions in Section B as you have to make a choice here.

Note the number of marks given in brackets for each part of a question and use this to guide you in the amount of detail required. In general, one mark represents one specific fact or answer. Take note of the command terms used in the questions as these also guide you about exactly what is required. It is a good idea to underline these terms on the question paper to help you focus your answer. Sometimes questions include several different instructions, for example 'Write the equation for the reaction between X and Y, identify the conjugate acid and base pair and describe what will be observed during this reaction'. In these cases it is easy to miss a part of the question; avoid this by crossing off the parts of the question on the paper as you go (much as you cross items off a shopping list so you can see what you might have missed).

It is essential to show all your workings in calculations very clearly. Also pay attention to significant figures and include units in your answers. When a question has several parts which all follow on from each other, you will not be penalized more than once for the same mistake. So, for example, if you make a mistake in part (a) of a question, but then use that wrong answer in a correct method in part (b), you will still get full marks for part (b) – *provided that your method was clear.* So never give up!

Paper 3: Written answers on the options

You have five minutes' reading time for this paper also. Make sure that you turn to the two options you have studied and do not be distracted by the other sections of the paper.

Divide your time equally between the two options (half an hour each) and answer the questions as fully as you can. Remember these questions are testing your knowledge and understanding of *chemistry*, so be sure to give as much relevant detail as you can, giving equations and specific examples wherever possible. The examiner can only give you credit for what you write down so do not assume anything. Show off!

Answers

The answers to the practice questions below are as given to the IB examiners. The following notes may help you to interpret these and make full use of the guidance given.

- There are no half marks awarded. Each mark is shown by the number in brackets (1)
- Points worth single marks are separated from each other by a semicolon (;)
- Alternate possible answers are separated from each other by a forward slash (/)
- Any answer given in **bold** or underlined *must* be present to score the mark
- Information in brackets (....) is not needed to score the mark
- Notes given in italics are to guide the examiner on what to accept / reject in their marking
- OWTTE means 'or words to that effect' – so alternate wording which conveys the same meaning can be equally rewarded
- ECF means 'error carried forward' - so examiners must award a mark for an incorrect answer from an earlier part of a question used correctly in a subsequent step
- −1 (U) means lose 1 mark for incorrect or absent units
- −1 (SF) means lose 1 mark for incorrect significant figures

Chapter 1: Answers to exercises

1. $n(H) = 6 \times 0.04 = 0.24$ moles
   $N(H) = 0.24 \times 6.02 \times 10^{23} = 1.5 \times 10^{23}$
   (calculator value $= 1.4448 \times 10^{23}$)

2. $M_r(Mg(NO_3)_2) = 24.31 + (14.01 \times 2) + (6 \times 16.00)$
   $= 148.33$

3. $n(C_2H_5OH) = 2.3/46 = 0.050$ moles
   $n(H) = 6 \times 0.050$ moles $= 0.30$ moles
   $N(H) = 0.30 \times 6.02 \times 10^{23} = 1.8 \times 10^{23}$

4. $n = 4.90/98 = 0.050$ moles
   $N = 0.0500 \times 6.02 \times 10^{23} = 3.01 \times 10^{22}$

5.

	S	O
mass / g	40	60
moles	$= 40/32.06$ $= 1.247\,66$	$= 60/16.00$ $= 3.75$
simplest ratio	$= 1.247\,66/1.247\,66$ $= 1$	$= 3.75/1.247\,66$ $= 3.0$ (calculator value: 3.005 63)

empirical formula: SO_3

6.

	Ni	S	O
mass / g	37.9	20.7	41.4
moles	$= 37.9/58.71$ $= 0.645\,55$	$= 20.7/32.00$ $= 0.646\,875$	$= 41/16.00$ $= 2.5625$
simplest ratio	$= 0.645\,55/0.645\,55$ $= 1$	$= 0.646\,875/0.645\,55$ $= 1.00$ (calculator value: 1.002 058 87)	$= 2.5625/0.645\,55$ $= 3.97$ ≈ 4 (calculator value: 3.969 508 58)

empirical formula: $NiSO_4$

7. B

8.

	Carbon	Hydrogen
mass / g	17.8	1.5
moles	$= 17.8/12.01$ $= 1.482\,0983$	$= 1.5/1.01$ $= 1.485\,148\,51$
simplest ratio	$= 1.482\,0983/1.478\,95$ $= 1.00$ (calculator value: 1.002 1305)	$= 1.485\,148\,51/1.478\,95$ $= 1.00$ (calculator value: 1.004 192 95)

	Chlorine	Fluorine
mass / g	52.6	28.1
moles	$= 52.6/35.45$ $= 1.483\,779\,972$	$= 28.1/19.00$ $= 1.478\,95$
simplest ratio	$= 1.483\,779\,972/1.478\,95$ $= 1.00$ (calculator value: 1.003 267 597)	$= 1.478\,95/1.478\,95$ $= 1$

empirical formula: CHClF
molecular formula: $C_2H_2Cl_2F_2$

9. Molecules of perfume are in rapid / random motion; and will diffuse / spread out.

10. B

11. (a) $N_2(g) + O_2(g) \rightarrow 2NO(g)$
    (b) $2NO(g) + O_2(g) \rightarrow 2NO_2(g)$
    (c) $2H_2O(l) + 4NO_2(g) + O_2(g) \rightarrow 4HNO_3(aq)$

12. $n(C_3H_8(g)) = 2.267\,059\,624$
    $n(CO_2(g)) = 6.801\,178\,871$
    $m(CO_2(g)) = 299$ g $=$ (calculator value: 299.3199)

13. $m(Fe_2O_3) = 1144$ g (calculator value: 1143.777 977)

14. N_2 is the limiting reagent.
    mass of $NH_3 = 487$ kg (calculator value: 486.509 636)
    % yield $= 220/487 \times 100\% = 45.2\%$

15. (a) $50\,cm^3$ (b) $260\,cm^3$ O_2 needed; $160\,cm^3$ CO_2 produced

16. $2.24\,dm^3$ (calculator value: 2.239 491 025)

17. $112\,cm^3$ (calculator value: 111.776 4471)

18. $3.0\,dm^3$

19. $P_1V_1/T_1 = P_2V_2/T_2$
    $V_2 = 22.4 \times 298/273 = 24.45 \approx 24\,dm^3$

20. $M = 86.2\,g\,mol^{-1}$ (calculator value: 86.237 230 69)
    molecular formula: C_6H_{14}

21. $m = 2.81$ g (calculator value: 2.8055)

22. (a) $n(H_2SO_4) = 0.00125$
    $[H_2SO_4] = 0.0822\,mol\,dm^{-3}$
    (calculator value: 0.082 236 8421)
    (b) $V(CO_2)(g) = 56\,cm^3$

Chapter 1: Answer for TOK

It is almost certain that the glass would contain at least one of the original molecules. There are more molecules in a glass of water then there are glasses of water in the oceans.

Chapter 1: Answers to practice questions

1. B   2. D   3. C   4. D

5. Al $\frac{20.3}{26.98}$ Cl $\frac{79.70}{35.45}$ or similar working (*no penalty for use of 27 or 35.5*);
   empirical formula $AlCl_3$;
   molecular formula: $n = 267/133.5 = 2$;
   Al_2Cl_6;
   Full credit can be obtained if the calculations are carried out by another valid method.
   Two correct formulas but no valid method scores. (2 max)
   (*Total 4 marks*)

6. (a) $Na_2CO_3 + 2HCl \rightarrow 2NaCl + H_2O + CO_2$; (2)
   Award (1) for correct products, (1) for correct balancing. State symbols are not required. Accept correct equation with hydrated salt. Accept ionic equation and partial neutralization.

   (b) $n(Na_2CO_3) = \frac{1}{2}n(HCl)$
   $n(HCl) = (48.80/1000) \times 0.1000 = 0.00488$ moles
   concentration of $Na_2CO_3 = 0.00244 \times (1000/25)$
   $= 0.0976 \, mol \, dm^{-3}$ (3)
   Award (3) for correct answer.
   Award (3) for correct answer based on equation in (a), i.e. allow ECF from (a). Note −1(SF) is possible.

   (c) $M_r \, Na_2CO_3 = 2(22.99) + 12.01 + 3(16.00) = 105.99$
   Accept 106.
   mass of Na_2CO_3 reacting with $HCl(aq)$
   $= 0.00244 \times 105.99 = 0.259 \, g$
   Allow ECF from (b) and M.
   mass of Na_2CO_3 in $1.000 \, dm^3 = 0.259 \times (1000/25)$
   $= 10.36 \, g$ (3)
   Note −1(U) is possible.

   (d) mass of water in crystals $= (27.82 − 10.36) = 17.46 \, g$
   Allow ECF from (b) and (c).
   number of moles of water $= 17.46/18.02 = 0.9689$
   Accept 0.97.
   mole ratio $Na_2CO_3 : H_2O = 0.0976 : 0.9689$
   $x = 10$ (4)
   (*Total 12 marks*)

7. (a) molecules move from ice to water and water to ice / $H_2O(s) \rightleftharpoons H_2O(l)$ / *OWTTE* mentioning particles / molecules; at the same rate; (2)
   (b) molecules leave skin surface / evaporate / intermolecular forces are overcome on evaporation; causing cooling effect / heat taken from skin / endothermic process; (2)
   (*Total 4 marks*)

8. (a) mole ratio $C:H = \frac{85.6}{12.01} : \frac{14.4}{1.01} = 7.13 : 14.3$;
   No penalty for using integer atomic masses.
   empirical formula: CH_2 (2)

   (b) (i) number of moles of gas $n = \frac{PV}{RT} = \frac{mass}{molar \, mass}$;
   $\dfrac{1.01 \times 10^2 \, kPa \, (0.399 \, dm^3);}{8.314 \, \dfrac{J}{mol \, K} \, (273 \, K)}$
   $\dfrac{1.00 \, g}{0.017 \, mol} = 56.3 \, (g \, mol^{-1})$ (2)

OR

molar mass is the $\dfrac{\text{mass of the molar volume}}{22.4 \, dm^3}$ at STP;

$\dfrac{1.00 \times 22.4}{0.399} = 56.1 \, (g \, mol^{-1})$
Accept answers in range 56.0 to 56.3.
Accept two, three or four significant figures.

   (ii) C_4H_8; (1)
   No ECF

9. (a) the particles/molecules of ammonia gas are in rapid/random/constant motion; and will diffuse/spread out/ *OWTTE*; (2)
   (b) less time;
   (the particles/molecules of ammonia gas will have) greater velocity/greater kinetic energy/greater rate of diffusion/move faster; (2)
   Do not accept 'greater energy'.

Chapter 2: Answers to exercises

1.

Species	No. of protons	No. of neutrons	No. of electrons
^7Li	3	4	3
^1H	1	0	1
^{14}C	6	8	6
$^{19}F^-$	9	10	10
$^{56}Fe^{3+}$	26	30	23

2.

Species	No. of protons	No. of neutrons	No. of electrons
$^{40}_{20}Ca^{2+}$	20	20	18
$^{40}_{18}Ar$	18	22	18
$^{39}_{19}K^+$	19	20	18
$^{35}_{17}Cl^-$	17	18	18

3.

Species	No. of protons	No. of neutrons	No. of electrons
^2_1H	1	1	1
$^{11}_5B$	5	6	5
$^{16}_8O^{2-}$	8	8	10
$^{19}_9F^-$	9	10	10

Answer = C

4. for example: mass / density / for gases: rate of diffusion

5. The deflection in a mass spectrometer is proportional to the charge / mass ratio.
   Answer = C

6. Both atoms have the same atomic number. They have the same number of protons and electrons.
   They have a different mass number and a different number of neutrons.
   Answer = B

7. Let x atoms be ^{20}Ne atoms.
   The remaining atoms are ^{22}Ne: no. of ^{22}Ne atoms $= 100 − x$
   Total mass $= 20x + (100 − x)22 = 2200 − 2x$
   Average mass $= (2200 − 2x)/100$

From the Periodic Table we see that the relative atomic mass of neon = 20.18

$20.18 = (2200 − 2x)/100$

$2018 = 2200 − 2x$

$2x = 2200 − 2018 = 182$

$x = 91$; abundance $^{20}Ne = 91\%$

8. B, the electron arrangement for silicon is 2,8,4. Three energy levels are occupied.

Chapter 2: Answers to practice questions

1. C   2. A   3. D   4. A

5. (a) continuous spectrum has all colours / wavelengths / frequencies whereas line spectrum has only (lines of) sharp / discrete / specific colours / wavelengths / frequencies;   (1)
   (b) lines get closer together towards high energy;   (1)
   (c) line represents electron transitions between energy levels / *OWTTE*;   (1)
                             (*Total 3 marks*)

6. (a) line starting at $n = 1$;
   line finishing at $n = ∞$ (*not above* ∞)
   arrow pointing upward;   (2 max)
   3 correct(2), 2 correct (1).
   (b) line from $n = 3$ to $n = 2$;
   arrow pointing downward (*in any transition*);   (2)

7. (a) atoms of the same element / same number of protons / same atomic number;
   having different numbers of neutrons / different (mass number);   (2)
   Award only (1) max if reference made to elements but not atoms.
   (b) relative atomic mass
   $$= \frac{36 × 0.337 + 38 × 0.0630 + 40 × 99.6}{100};$$ (2)
   (c) 23 electrons; 26 protons; 30 neutrons;   (2)
   Award (2) for three correct, (1) for two correct.

8. (a) mass / density / for gases: rate of effusion or diffusion / melting point / boiling point;   (1)
   Do not accept mass number.
   (b) if $^{35}Cl = x$, then $(x = 35.00) + (1 − x) 37.00 = 35.45$
   Award (1) for set up.
   therefore, $x = 0.775$;   (2)
   $^{35}Cl = 77.5\%$ and $^{37}Cl = 22.5\%$;
   Need both for mark.

9. (a) 2, 8, 8
   (b) K^+ / Ca^{2+} / Sc^{3+} / Ti^{4+};
   $Cl^−$ / $S^{−2}$ / $P^{3−}$;   (2)
   Accept other suitable pairs of ions.

Chapter 3: Answers to exercises

1.

Element	Period	Group
helium	1	2
chlorine	3	7
barium	6	2
francium	7	1

2. (a) A period is a horizontal row in the Periodic Table and a group is a vertical column.
   (b) 2, 8, 5; electrons are in three energy levels; there are five outer electrons.

3. 5

4. Phosphorus exists as molecules with four atoms: P_4. Sulfur exists as molecules with eight atoms: S_8. There are stronger van de Waal's forces between the larger S_8 molecules.

5. D   6. C   7. $Cl^−>Cl>Cl^+$ 8. B

9. sodium floats on the surface; it melts into a sphere; there is fizzing / effervescence / bubbles (*accept sound is produced*); solution gets hot; white smoke is produced
   $2Na + 2H_2O → 2Na^+ + 2OH^− + H_2$

10. The reactivities of the alkali metals increase but those of the halogens decrease.

11. C   12. A   13. B

Chapter 3: Answers to practice questions

1. B   2. B   3. D   4. A

5. (a) (i) Na has lower nuclear charge / number of protons; electrons removed are from same energy level / shell; Na has larger radius / electron further from the nucleus;   (2 max)
   (ii) Na electron closer to nucleus / in lower energy level / Na has less shielding effect;   (1)
   (b) chlorine has a higher nuclear charge; attracts the electron pair / electrons in bond more strongly;   (2)
                             (*Total 5 marks*)

6. oxides of:
   Na, Mg: basic;
   Al: amphoteric;
   Si to Cl: acidic;
   Ar: no oxide;
   $Na_2O + H_2O → 2NaOH$;
   $SO_3 + H_2O → H_2SO_4$;   (4)

7. (a) loss of 2 electrons / outer electrons; 3 shells to 2; net attractive force increases;   (2 max)
   (b) $P^{3−}$ has one more shell than Si^{4+}; some justification in terms of electron loss / gain; net attractive forces;   (2 max)
   (c) same electron arrangement / both have two complete shells; extra protons in Na^+ (attract the electrons more strongly);   (2)
                             (*Total 6 marks*)

8. (a) (i) *aluminium oxide:* amphoteric;
   (ii) *sodium oxide:* basic;
   (iii) *sulfur dioxide:* acidic;   (3)
   (b) (i) $Na_2O + H_2O → 2Na^+ + 2OH^−$;
   (ii) $SO_2 + H_2O → H_2SO_3$;   (2)
   Accept NaOH; and $H^+ + HSO_3^− / 2H^+ + SO_3^{2−}$.

9. (a) *Li to Cs:* atomic radius increases;
   because more full energy levels are <u>used</u> or <u>occupied</u> / <u>outer</u> electrons further from nucleus / outer electrons in a higher shell; ionization energy decreases;
   because the electron removed is further from the nucleus / increased repulsion by inner-shell electrons; (4)
   Accept <u>increased</u> shielding effect.
   (b) *Na to Cl:* atomic radius decreases;
   because nuclear charge increases and electrons are added

to same main (outer) energy level;
ionization energy increases;
because nuclear charge increases and the electron
removed is closer to the nucleus / is the same energy
level; (4)
Accept 'core charge' for 'nuclear charge'.
In (a) and (b) explanation mark is dependent on correct trend.

10. (a) atomic radius of N > O because O has greater nuclear charge;
greater attraction for the outer electrons / *OWTTE*; (2)
 (b) atomic radius of P > N because P has outer electrons in an energy level further from the nucleus / *OWTTE*; (1)
 (c) N^{3-} > N / ionic radius > atomic radius because N^{3-} has more electrons than protons; so the electrons are held less tightly / *OWTTE*; (2)
 Award (1) for greater repulsion in N^{3-} due to more electrons (no reference to protons).

(*Total 5 marks*)

Chapter 4: Answers to exercises

1. (a) KBr
 (b) $Pb(NO_3)_2$
 (c) Na_2SO_4
 (d) $(NH_4)_3PO_4$

2. B   3. D

4. (a) H $\overset{\times\times}{\underset{\times\times}{\times}}$ F $\times$

 (b)

 (c)

 (d)

 (e)

 (f)

 (g) H $\overset{\times}{\times}$ C $\times\times\times$ C $\overset{\times}{\times}$ H

5. (a) $\overset{\delta+}{H} — \overset{\delta-}{Br}$

 (b) $\overset{\delta-}{O}=\overset{\delta+}{C}=\overset{\delta-}{O}$

 (c) $\overset{\delta+}{Cl} — \overset{\delta-}{F}$

 (d) $O=O$ no polar bonds

 (e)

6. (a) 105° bond angle, shape is bent

 (b) 109.5° bond angle, shape is tetrahedral

 (c) H — C ≡ N 180° bond angle, shape is linear

 (d) 107° bond angle, shape is pyramidal

 (e) 120° bond angle, shape is planar triangular

7. (a) molecule is a pyramidal polar molecule

 (b) molecule is a tetrahedral non-polar molecule

 (c) molecule is a linear polar molecule

Chapter 4: Answers to practice questions

1. B   2. B   3. B   4. D
5. C   6. A   7. D   8. D
9. A   10. C   11. B   12. C
13. B

14. (a) (i) ; (2)

 ;

 Accept dots, crosses, a combination of dots and crosses or a line to represent a pair of electrons.

 (ii) CO_2 is linear; two charge centres or bonds and no lone pairs (around C);
 H_2S is bent / V-shaped / angular;
 two bond pairs, two lone pairs (around S); (4)
 (iii) CO_2 is non-polar, H_2S is polar;
 bond polarities cancel CO_2 but not in H_2S; (2)
 (b) CH_3Cl – dipole–dipole attractions;
 CH_4 – van der Waals' / dispersion / London forces;
 CH_3OH – hydrogen bond; (3)

(*Total 11 marks*)

15. (a) (1)

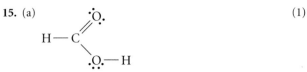

No mark without lone electron pairs.
Correct shape not necessary.
Do not award mark if dots / crosses and bond lines are shown.
Accept lone pairs represented as straight lines.

(b) (i) $O-C-O = 120° / H-C-O = 120°$;
(ii) $C-O-H \simeq 109° / < 109°$; (2)
No mark for 109.5°
Accept answer in range $100-109°$

(c) length: $C=O < C-O$;
strength: $C=O > C-O$;
greater number of electrons between nuclei pull atoms together and require greater energy to break; (3)
or
double bonds are shorter / single bonds are longer;
double bonds are stronger / single bonds are weaker;
Accept stronger attraction between nuclei and (bonding) electrons.

(*Total 6 marks*)

16. (a) (i) $W^{3+}Y^{3-}$;
Award (1) for formula (WY) and (1) for charges $(W^{3+} Y^{3-})$ (2)
Accept WY, charges W: 3+ Y: 3− for
Answers must be in terms of W and Y.

(ii) XZ_2; (1)
Accept XZ.
Answers must be in terms of X and Z.

(b) 7 protons, 8 neutrons, 10 electrons; (2)
Award (2) for three correct and (1) for two correct.

(c) $Si-Cl$ bonds are covalent;

$$:\overset{..}{\underset{..}{Cl}}:$$
$$:\overset{..}{\underset{..}{Cl}}:\overset{..}{\underset{..}{Si}}:\overset{..}{\underset{..}{Cl}}:$$
$$:\overset{..}{\underset{..}{Cl}}:$$
(3)

Accept lines for electron pairs.
Award (1) for covalent bonds and (1) for lone pairs.

(d) find number of electron pairs / charge centres in (valence shell of) <u>central atom</u>;
electron pairs / charge centres (in valence shell) of central atom repel each other;
to positions of minimum energy / repulsion / maximum stability;
pairs forming a double or triple bond act as a single bond;
non-bonding pairs repel more than bonding pairs / OWTTE; (3 max)
Do not accept repulsion between bonds and atoms.
Award (1) each for any three points.

(e) (i) SCl_2 two bonding pairs, two non-bonding pairs;
angular / bent / non-linear / V-shaped;
Both these marks can be scored from a diagram.
$90° <$ angle $< 107°$;
C_2Cl_2 two charge centres around each C;
linear;
Both these marks can be scored from a diagram.
angle = 180°; (6)

(ii) SCl_2 is polar;
C_2Cl_2 is non-polar;
no net dipole movement for C_2Cl_2 but angular SCl_2 has a resultant dipole *OWTTE*; (3)
Mark can be scored from a diagram.
Allow ECF based on the answers given to (i).

(*Total 20 marks*)

17. (a) (i) as molecules become larger / heavier / have higher M_r values / number of electrons increases;
van der Waals' / London / dispersion forces increase; (2)

(ii) hydrogen bonding **between molecules** in H_2O;
this bonding is stronger (than van der Waals' forces); (2)
Must be an implied comparison with (a)(i).

(b) (i) tetrahedral (*accept correct 3-D diagram*);
bent / V-shape / angular (*accept suitable diagram*); (2)

(ii) $105°$ (*accept $103-106°$*);
lone pairs **repel** each other more than bonding pairs; (2)
Do not accept repulsion of atoms.

(c) bonds are polar as Cl more electronegative than Si;
Allow 'electronegativities are different'.
molecule is symmetrical, hence polar effects cancel out / OWTTE; (2)

(d) (i) A − sodium iodide, B − sodium, C − iodine (*three correct (1)*); (1)
Accept correct formulas.

(ii) A − ionic bonding;
B − metallic bonding;
C − van der Waals' forces (and covalent bonding); (3)

(e) (i) (for Na) (lattice of) positive ions / atoms;
delocalized / free electrons / sea of electrons;
(for NaI) oppositely charged ions / positive and negative ions;
free to move (only) in molten state; (4)

(ii) forces between I_2 molecules are weak;
ionic / metallic bonding strong(er); (2)

(*Total 20 marks*)

Chapter 5: Answers to exercises

1. B
2. B
3. $\Delta T =$ heat/mc
$\Delta T = 500/100c = 5/c$
The substance with the smallest specific heat capacity has the largest temperature increase: A.
4. heat $= mc\Delta T$
$\Delta T = 100/100c$
$\Delta T = 1/c = 7.25°C$
$T = 25.0 + 7.25 = 32.3°C$
5. A
6. heat produced $= 150.00 \times 4.18 \times (31.5-25.0)/(0.05 / 30.97)$ J
$= 2500$ kJ (*precision of answer limited by precision of temperature difference*)
The value is lower than the literature value owing to heat losses and incomplete combustion.

7. $\Delta H = -c_{H_2O} \times \Delta T_{H_2O} / ([CuSO_4]) \, kJ$
$= -4.18 \times (70.0-20)/1.00$
$= -209 \, kJ \, mol^{-1}$

8. C
9. $-114.1 \, kJ$
10. $+330 \, kJ \, mol^{-1}$
11. $-57.2 \, kJ \, mol^{-1}$
12. I and III
13. B
14. $-124 \, kJ \, mol^{-1}$
15. $-484 \, kJ \, mol^{-1}$

Chapter 5: Answers to practice questions

1. D   2. C   3. B   4. D   5. A
6. enthalpy change associated with the formation of one mole of a compound / substance from its elements; in their standard states / under standard conditions;
$2C(s) + 3H_2(g) + \frac{1}{2}O_2(g) \rightarrow C_2H_5OH(l);$ (5)
Award (1) for formulas and coefficients, (1) for state symbols.
7. (a) $\Delta H^{\ominus} = \Delta H^{\ominus}_f(products) - \Delta H^{\ominus}_f(reactants)$
$= (-1669) - (-822) = -847 \, kJ$
Ignore units; exothermic (ECF from sign of $\Delta H^{\ominus}$).   (3)
(b)

For the diagram   (1)
ECF from sign of ΔH in (a).
298 K/25°C and 1 atm/101(.3) kPa;
Both needed for the mark.   (2)
(Total 6 marks)

Chapter 6: Answers to exercises

1. Reaction gives off a gas: change in volume could be measured.
Reaction involves purple MnO_4^- ions, being reduced to colourless Mn^{2+} ions: colorimetry could be used.
Reaction involves a change in the concentration of ions (23 on the reactants side and 2 on the products side): conductivity could be used.
All techniques enable continuous measurements to be made from which graphs could be plotted of the measured variable against time.
2. C; none of the other answers are correct statements.
3. A will not affect the rate of the reaction, B and C will both increase the rate; the answer is D as this is the only change of condition which will *decrease* the rate.
4. (a) $2CO(g) + 2NO(g) \rightarrow 2CO_2(g) + N_2(g)$
(b) CO is a toxic gas which when inhaled combines with haemoglobin in the blood and prevents it from carrying oxygen. NO is a primary air pollutant which is oxidized in the air to form acidic oxides that contribute to acid rain. It also reacts with other pollutants in the atmosphere to form smog.

(c) This arrangement will increase the surface area of the catalyst in contact with the exhaust gases and so will increase the efficiency.
(d) Catalytic behaviour depends on the catalyst interacting with the gases, leading to reaction on its surface. With increasing temperature, the increased kinetic energy of the exhaust gases allows them to collide and bond with the catalyst more quickly.
(e) Although catalytic converters have helped to reduce pollution from cars considerably, they by no means remove it completely. They are not effective when the engine is cold and it is estimated that 80% of pollution occurs in the first 3 minutes after starting. There are other pollutants in car exhausts which are not removed by the catalyst, for example ozone, sulfur oxides and many particulates. In addition the catalytic converter itself increases the output of carbon dioxide which is a serious pollutant because of its 'greenhouse gas' properties.

Chapter 6: Answers to practice questions

1. D   2. A   3. D   4. B
5. C   6. B   7. C
8. (a) (i) it is decreasing; less frequent collisions / fewer collisions per second or (unit) time;   (2)
(ii) reactant(s) used up / reaction is complete;   (1)
Do not accept reaction reached equilibrium.
(b) (i) it would increase;   (1)
Accept a quantitative answer such as 'doubles'.
(ii) more frequent collisions; collisions or molecules have more energy (*OWTTE*); more molecules with energy $\geqslant E_a$;   (3)
(iii) rate would be lower; smaller surface area;   (2)
(Total 9 marks)

9. (a) increase in product concentration per unit time / decrease in reactant concentration per unit time;   (1)
Accept change instead of increase or decrease.
(b) (i) high activation energy / not enough molecules have E_a / *OWTTE*;
incorrect collision geometry / *OWTTE*;
infrequent collisions;   (2 max)
Award (1) for any two reasons.
(ii) more energetic collisions / more molecules have (energy $\geqslant$) E_a;
more <u>frequent</u> collisions / collide more often;   (2)
(iii) add a catalyst;
increase the (total) pressure / decrease the volume of the container;
increase the concentration of C (or D);   (2 max)
Do not accept surface area.
Award (1) for any two.
(Total 7 marks)

10. (a) molecules must have sufficient / minimum energy / energy $\geqslant$ activation energy;
appropriate collision geometry / correct orientation;   (2)

(b) increased frequency of collisions / collisions more likely;
Not just 'more collisions', there must be a reference to time.
increased proportion of molecules with sufficient energy to react / $E \geqslant E_a$;
Not 'activation energy is reduced'.
proportion of molecules with $E \geqslant E_a$ is more important;
Dependent on correct second marking point. (3)
(Total 5 marks)

11. (a) measure volume of carbon dioxide / CO_2 / gas produced / measure pH;

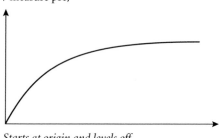

Starts at origin and levels off.
measure mass of chemicals / apparatus;

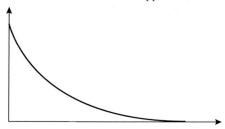

Starts high and decreases.
Graph should show increase as reaction progresses (as HCl is consumed). (4)

(b) Method 1: use powdered $MgCO_3$ / OWTTE; particles collide more frequently / increased surface area / OWTTE;
Method 2: increase (reaction) temperature / heat / warm; more of the collisions are successful / more particles with $E \geqslant E_a$ / OWTTE;
Method 3: increase acid concentration; more frequent (reactant) collisions;
Method 4: add catalyst; lowers activation energy / E_a / OWTTE;
Award (2) each for any three methods. (6 max)

(c) (i) stays the same; $MgCO_3$ was already in excess; (2)
(ii) stays the same; same quantities of reactants used; (2)
(Total 14 marks)

Chapter 7: Answers to exercises

1. (a) $K_c = \dfrac{[NO_2]^2}{[NO]^2[O_2]}$

(b) $K_c = \dfrac{[CH_3COOC_3H_7]\,[H_2O]}{[CH_3COOH]\,[C_3H_7OH]}$

(c) $K_c = \dfrac{[NO_2]^4[H_2O]^6}{[NH_3]^4\,[O_2]^7}$

2. (a) $N_2O_4(g) \rightleftharpoons 2NO_2(g)$
(b) $CH_4(g) + H_2O(g) \rightleftharpoons CO(g) + 3H_2(g)$

Chapter 7: Answers to practice questions

1. A   2. C   3. D
4. B   5. D   6. C
7. B   8. C   9. B

10. (a) (position of) equilibrium shifts to the left / towards reactants;
(forward) reaction is exothermic / ΔH is negative / the reverse reaction is endothermic / OWTTE; (2)
Do not accept 'Le Chatelier's principle' without some additional explanation.

(b) (position of) equilibrium shifts to the right / towards products;
fewer gas molecules on the right hand side / volume decreases in forward reaction / OWTTE; (2)
Do not accept 'Le Chatelier's principle' without some additional explanation.
(Total 4 marks)

11. (a) $200°C$, 600 atm (*both for (1), units not needed*); (1)
Allow the 'highest pressure and the lowest temperature'.

(b) (i) yield increases / equilibrium moves to the right / more ammonia;
4 (gas) molecules → 2 / decrease in volume / fewer molecules on the right-hand side; (2)
(ii) yield decreases / equilibrium moves to the left / less ammonia;
exothermic reaction / OWTTE; (2)

(c) high pressure expensive / greater cost of operating at high pressure / reinforced pipes etc. needed;
lower temperature − greater yield, but **lowers** rate; (2)
Do not award a mark just for the word 'compromise'.

(d) $K_c = \dfrac{[NH_3]^2}{[N_2]\,[H_2]^3}$ (*ignore units*); (1)
(Total 8 marks)

12. (a) $(K_c=)\dfrac{[NO_2]^2}{[N_2O_4]}$
(horizontal line) concentration of reactant and product remains constant / equilibrium reached;
(magnitude of) K_c greater than 1;
Accept 1.6
product concentration greater than reactant concentration; (4)

(b) increased temperature shifts equilibrium position to right;
(forward) reaction is endothermic / absorbs heat; (2)

(c) increased pressure shifts equilibrium to left;
fewer (gas) moles / molecules on left; (2)

(d) both / forward and reverse rates increased / increase in forward reverse rates are equal;
activation energy reduced;
position of equilibrium unchanged;
concentration / amount of reactants and products remain constant;
value of K_c unchanged;
K_c only affected by changes in temperature; (6)
(Total 14 marks)

Chapter 8: Answers to exercises

1. (a) HSO_3^-
   (b) $CH_3NH_3^+$
   (c) C_2H_5COOH
   (d) HNO_3
   (e) HF
   (f) H_2SO_4
2. (a) $H_2PO_4^-$
   (b) CH_3COO^-
   (c) HSO_3^-
   (d) SO_4^{2-}
   (e) O^{2-}
   (f) Br^-
3. (a) CH_3COOH / CH_3COO^- NH_3 / NH_4^+
        acid / base   base / acid
   (b) CO_3^{2-} / HCO_3^- H_3O^+ / H_2O
        base / acid   acid / base
   (c) NH_4^+ / NH_3 NO_2^- / HNO_2
        acid / base   base / acid
4. (a) Lewis acid Zn^{2+}
   Lewis base NH_3
   (b) Lewis acid $BeCl_2$
   Lewis base Cl^-
   (c) Lewis acid Mg^{2+}
   Lewis base H_2O
5. D, CH_4 because it does not possess a lone pair.
6. C, there is no exchange of H^+.
7. (a) $H_2SO_4(aq) + CuO(s) \rightarrow CuSO_4(aq) + H_2O(l)$
   (b) $HNO_3(aq) + NaHCO_3(s)$
                    $\rightarrow NaNO_3(aq) + H_2O(l) + CO_2(g)$
   (c) $H_3PO_4(aq) + 3KOH(aq) \rightarrow K_3PO_4(aq) + 3H_2O(l)$
   (d) $6CH_3COOH(aq) + 2Al(s) \rightarrow 2Al(CH_3COO)_3(aq) + 3H_2(g)$
8. B, CH_3COOH because it will have the lowest concentration of ions.
9. This is a dilution of $10\times$ so its $[H^+]$ will decrease $10\times$. pH will increase by 1 unit.
10. HCl, CH_3COOH, NaCl, $C_2H_5NH_2$, NaOH

Chapter 8: Answers to practice questions

1. A   2. D   3. B   4. B   5. B
6. B   7. D   8. D   9. A   10. D
11. (a) (pH =) 1; a tenfold increase in the <u>hydrogen ion</u> / H^+ concentration; (2)
   Accept calculation / strong acid / completely ionized (for reason).
   (b) (pH)>2 and <7;
   (ethanoic acid is a) weak acid / partially ionized in solution; (2)
   Accept pH>1 (ignore reference to <7) / calculation.
   (*Total 4 marks*)
12. (a) strong acid completely dissociated / ionized;
   weak acid only partially dissociated / ionized;
   $HCl(aq) \rightarrow H^+(aq) + Cl^-(aq)$;
   $CH_3COOH(aq) \rightleftharpoons CH_3COO^-(aq) + H^+(aq)$; (4)
   Insist on both arrows as shown, state symbols not needed.
   Also accept $H_2O(l)$ and $H_3O^+(aq)$ in equations.

(b) (i) bubbling / effervescence / dissolving of $CaCO_3$ / gas given off (*do not accept CO_2 produced*);
   more vigorous reaction with HCl / *OWTTE*; (2)
   (ii) $2HCl(aq) + CaCO_3(s) \rightarrow CaCl_2(aq) + CO_2(g)$
   $+ H_2O(l)$; (2)
   (1) for correct formulas, (1) for balanced equations, state symbols not essential.
   (iii) amount of $CaCO_3 = \dfrac{1.25}{100.09} = 0.0125$ mol (*no penalty for use of 100*);
   amount of $HCl = 2 \times 0.0125 = 0.0250$ mol (*allow ECF*);
   volume of $HCl = 0.0167$ dm^3 / 16.7 cm^3 (*allow ECF*); (3)
   (iv) 1:1 ratio of $CaCO_3$ to CO_2 / use 0.0125 moles CO_2 (*allow ECF*);
   $(0.0125 \times 22.4) = 0.28$ dm^3 / 280 cm^3 / 2.8×10^{-4} m^3 (*allow ECF*); (2)
   Accept calculation using $pV = nRT$.
   (*Total 13 marks*)

Chapter 9: Answers to exercises

1. (a) $NH_4^+ = N -3, H +1$
   (b) $CuCl_2 = Cu +2, Cl -1$
   (c) $H_2O = H +1, O -2$
   (d) $SO_2 = S +4, O -2$
   (e) $Fe_2O_3 = Fe +3, O -2$
   (f) $NO_3^- = N +5, O -2$
   (g) $MnO_2 = Mn +4, O -2$
   (h) $PO_4^{3-} = P +5, O -2$
   (i) $K_2Cr_2O_7 = K +1, Cr +6, O -2$
   (j) $MnO_4^- = Mn +7, O -2$

2. (a)
$$\overset{\displaystyle \overbrace{}^{\text{reduction}}}{Sn^{2+}(aq) + 2Fe^{3+}(aq) \rightarrow Sn^{4+}(aq) + 2Fe^{2+}(aq)}$$
    $+2$ $+3$ $+4$ $+2$
      oxidation

(b)
reduction
$$Cl_2(aq) + 2NaBr(aq) \rightarrow Br_2(aq) + 2NaCl(aq)$$
   0 $+1-1$ 0 $+1-1$
      oxidation

(c)
reduction
$$2FeCl_2(aq) + Cl_2(aq) \rightarrow 2FeCl_3(aq)$$
   $+2-1$ 0 $+3-1$
      oxidation

(d)
reduction
$$2H_2O(l) + 2F_2(aq) \rightarrow 4HF(aq) + O_2(g)$$
   $+1-2$ 0 $+1-1$ 0
      oxidation

(e)
reduction
$$I_2(aq) + SO_3^{2-}(aq) + H_2O(l) \rightarrow 2I^-(aq) + SO_4^{2-}(aq) + 2H^+(aq)$$
0 $+4-2$ $+1-2$ -1 $+6-2$ $+1$
      oxidation

3. (a) $Ca(s) + 2H^+(aq) \rightarrow Ca^{2+}(aq) + H_2(g)$
  $\quad\;\; 0 \qquad\;\; +1 \qquad\qquad +2 \qquad\qquad 0$
  oxidation: $Ca(s) \rightarrow Ca^{2+}(aq) + 2e^-$
  reduction: $2H^+(aq) + 2e^- \rightarrow H_2(g)$

(b) $2Fe^{2+}(aq) + Cl_2(aq) \rightarrow 2Fe^{3+}(aq) + 2Cl^-(aq)$
  $\quad\;\; +2 \qquad\quad 0 \qquad\qquad +3 \qquad\quad -1$
  oxidation: $2Fe^{2+}(aq) \rightarrow 2Fe^{3+}(aq) + 2e^-$
  reduction: $Cl_2(g) + 2e^- \rightarrow 2Cl^-(aq)$

(c) $Sn^{2+}(aq) + 2Fe^{3+}(aq) \rightarrow Sn^{4+}(aq) + 2Fe^{2+}(aq)$
  $\quad\;\; +2 \qquad\quad +3 \qquad\qquad +4 \qquad\quad +2$
  oxidation: $Sn^{2+}(aq) \rightarrow Sn^{4+}(aq) + 2e^-$
  reduction: $2Fe^{3+}(aq) + 2e^- \rightarrow 2Fe^{2+}(aq)$

(d) $Cl_2(aq) + 2Br^-(aq) \rightarrow 2Cl^-(aq) + Br_2(aq)$
  $\quad\;\; 0 \qquad\quad -1 \qquad\qquad -1 \qquad\quad 0$
  oxidation: $2Br^-(aq) \rightarrow Br_2(aq) + 2e^-$
  reduction: $Cl_2(aq) + 2e^- \rightarrow 2Cl^-(aq)$

4. (a) $Zn(s) + SO_4^{2-}(aq) + 4H^+(aq)$
  $\qquad\qquad\qquad \rightarrow Zn^{2+}(aq) + SO_2(g) + 2H_2O(l)$

(b) $2I^-(aq) + HSO_4^-(aq) + 3H^+(aq)$
  $\qquad\qquad\qquad \rightarrow I_2(aq) + SO_2(g) + 2H_2O(l)$

(c) $NO_3^-(aq) + 4Zn(s) + 10H^+(aq)$
  $\qquad\qquad\qquad \rightarrow NH_4^+(aq) + 4Zn^{2+}(aq) + 3H_2O(l)$

(d) $I_2(aq) + 5OCl^-(aq) + H_2O(l)$
  $\qquad\qquad\qquad \rightarrow 2IO_3^-(aq) + 5Cl^-(aq) + 2H^+(aq)$

(e) $2MnO_4^-(aq) + 5H_2SO_3(aq)$
  $\qquad \rightarrow 2Mn^{2+}(aq) + 3H_2O(l) + 5SO_4^{2-}(aq) + 4H^+(aq)$

5. (a) $H_2(g) + Cl_2(g) \rightarrow 2HCl(g)$
  $\quad\;\; 0 \qquad\;\; 0 \qquad\quad +1\;-1$
  oxidizing agent: Cl_2
  reducing agent: H_2

(b) $2Al(s) + 3PbCl_2(s) \rightarrow 2AlCl_3(s) + 3Pb(s)$
  $\quad\;\; 0 \qquad\;\; +2\;-1 \qquad\;\; +1\;-1 \qquad 0$
  oxidizing agent: Pb^{2+}
  reducing agent: Al

(c) $Cl_2(aq) + 2KI(aq) \rightarrow 2KCl(aq) + I_2(aq)$
  $\quad\;\; 0 \qquad\;\; +1\;-1 \qquad\; +1\;-1 \qquad 0$
  oxidizing agent: Cl_2
  reducing agent: I^-

(d) $CH_4(g) + 2O_2(g) \rightarrow CO_2(g) + 2H_2O(l)$
  $\quad\; -4\;+1 \qquad\; 0 \qquad\quad +4\;-2 \qquad +1\;-2$
  oxidizing agent: O_2
  reducing agent: CH_4

6. (a) $CuCl_2(aq) + Ag(s)$
  No reaction, Cu is a more reactive metal than Ag.

(b) $Fe(NO_3)_2(aq) + 2Al(s) \rightarrow 2Al(NO_3)_3(aq) + Fe(s)$
  Al is a more reactive metal than Fe, so is able to reduce Fe^{3+}.

(c) $2NaI(aq) + Br_2(aq) \rightarrow 2NaBr(aq) + I_2(aq)$
  Br is a more reactive non-metal than I, so is able to oxidize I^-.

(d) $KCl(aq) + I_2(aq)$
  No reaction, Cl is a more reactive non-metal than I.

7. (a) $w > x > y > z$
(b) (i) will not occur
  (ii) will not occur

8. (a) Zn / Zn^{2+} $\qquad$ Fe / Fe^{2+}
  anode $\qquad\qquad$ cathode
  $Zn(s) \rightarrow Zn^{2+}(aq) + 2e^-$
  $Fe^{2+}(aq) + 2e^- \rightarrow Fe(s)$

(b) Fe / Fe^{2+} $\qquad\qquad$ Mg / Mg^{2+}
  cathode $\qquad\qquad\quad$ anode
  $Fe^{2+}(aq) + 2e^- \rightarrow Fe(s)$
  $Mg(s) \rightarrow Mg^{2+}(aq) + 2e^-$

(c) Mg / Mg^{2+} $\qquad\qquad$ Cu / Cu^{2+}
  anode $\qquad\qquad\qquad$ cathode
  $Mg(s) \rightarrow Mg^{2+}(aq) + 2e^-$
  $Cu^{2+}(aq) + 2e^- \rightarrow Cu(s)$

9.

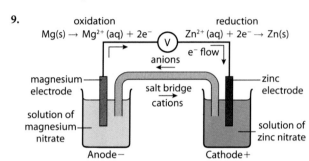

10. The iron spatula would slowly dissolve as it is oxidized to Fe^{2+} ions. Copper metal would precipitate as Cu^{2+} ions are reduced. The blue colour of the solution would fade, as Cu^{2+} ions are removed.

11. (a) KBr
  At anode: $2Br^-(l) \rightarrow Br_2(l) + 2e^-$
  At cathode: $2K^+(l) + 2e^- \rightarrow 2K(l)$

(b) MgF_2
  At anode: $2F^-(l) \rightarrow F_2(g) + 2e^-$
  At cathode: $Mg^{2+}(l) + 2e^- \rightarrow Mg(l)$

(c) ZnS
  At anode: $S^{2-}(l) \rightarrow S(l) + 2e^-$
  At cathode: $Zn^{2+}(l) + 2e^- \rightarrow Zn(l)$

Chapter 9: Answers to practice questions

1. D	**2.** A	**3.** A	**4.** B	**5.** B
6. D	**7.** D	**8.** B	**9.** D	**10.** B
11. D	**12.** D	**13.** B		

14. (a) (i) Fe reactant +2 AND Fe product +3
  Mn product +2 AND Mn reactant +7; $\qquad$ (2)
  Do not accept Roman numerals.
  (ii) Fe^{2+} / iron(II) ions / ferrous ions; $\qquad$ (1)
  Do not accept 'iron'.
  (iii) CH_3OH oxidation state −2;
  CH_2O oxidation state 0;
  (change is) oxidation / dehydrogenation; $\qquad$ (3)

(b) (i) silver nitrate; $\qquad$ (1)
  (ii) oxidation;
  $Cu \rightarrow Cu^{2+} + 2e^-$ $\qquad$ (2)
  (iii) (silver nitrate) solution turns blue / grey or black or silver solid forms;
  copper ions form / Cu^{2+} ions form / silver deposited; $\qquad$ (2)

(c) (i) sodium chloride crystals consist of ions in a rigid lattice / ions cannot move about;
   when melted the ions are free to move or ions move when a voltage is applied;
   in electrolysis positive sodium ions or Na^+ ions move to the negative electrode or cathode;
   and negative chloride ions or Cl^- move to the positive electrode or anode; (4)

(ii) sodium formed at cathode or negative electrode;
   $Na^+ + e^- \rightarrow Na$;
   chlorine formed at anode or positive electrode;
   $2Cl^- \rightarrow Cl_2 + 2e^-$; (4)
   1st and 3rd marks can be scored in (c) (i).

(iii) manufacture of sodium and chlorine / one stated use of chlorine or sodium; (1)

(*Total 20 marks*)

Chapter 10: Answers to exercises

1. (a) Chloroethene

(b) 2-aminoethanoic acid

2. (a)

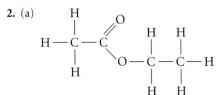

(ii)

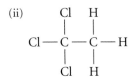

3. primary chloroalkane

H—C—Cl chloromethane

secondary choroalkane

2-chloropropane

tertiary chloroalkane

2-chloro-2-methylpropane

Chapter 10: Answers to practice questions

1. B	**2.** B	**3.** D	**4.** B	**5.** B
6. D	**7.** D	**8.** C	**9.** D	**10.** C

11. (a) (i) a series of (organic) chemicals with the same general formula (C_nH_{2n+2}) / neighbouring members differing by CH_2 / similar chemical properties / gradation of physical properties / same functional group / *OWTTE*; (2 max)
   Award (1) each for any two.

(ii) a compound containing carbon and hydrogen <u>only</u>; (1)

(iii) containing only single (carbon to carbon) bonds / no multiple (carbon to carbon) bonds / *OWTTE*; (1)
   Accept hydrocarbon containing maximum number of hydrogens.

(b) (i) boiling point increases as number of carbons increases / *OWTTE*;
   increased surface area / greater van der Waals' forces / increased M_r / increased intermolecular forces / *OWTTE*; (2)

(ii) exothermic / energy released / products have less energy than reactants (1)

(c) carbon dioxide;
   water; (2)
   Accept formulas.

(*Total 9 marks*)

12.

Structural formula	Name
$CH_3CH_2CH_2CH_3$	butane / n-butane
$CH_3CH(CH_3)CH_3$	(2)-methylpropane

(4)

Accept more detailed formulas, penalizing missing H atoms once only.
If more than these two formulas are given, subtract (1) for each extra formula.
Mark names separately. Accept these two names only.

(*Total 4 marks*)

13. (a) same general formula / C_nH_{2n};
   formulas of successive members differ by CH_2;
   similar chemical properties / same functional group;
   gradation / gradual change in physical properties; (3 max)
   Award (1) each for any three.

---

4. Bromine + ethane
initiation
$Br_2 \xrightarrow{UV\ light} 2Br^{\bullet}$ bromine radicals
propagation
$Br^{\bullet} + C_2H_6 \rightarrow C_2H_5^{\bullet} + HBr$
$C_2H_5^{\bullet} + Br_2 \rightarrow C_2H_5Br + Br^{\bullet}$
$C_2H_5Br + Br^{\bullet} \rightarrow C_2H_4Br^{\bullet} + HBr$
$C_2H_4Br^{\bullet} + Br_2 \rightarrow C_2H_4Br_2 + Br^{\bullet}$
termination
$Br^{\bullet} + Br^{\bullet} \rightarrow Br_2$
$C_2H_5^{\bullet} + Br^{\bullet} \rightarrow C_2H_5Br$
$C_2H_5^{\bullet} + C_2H_5^{\bullet} \rightarrow C_4H_{10}$
Overall, these reactions show how a mixture of products is formed.

(b) but-2-ene;
Accept 2-butene.
strongest intermolecular / van der Waals' forces;
largest (molecular) mass / size / surface area / area of
contact; (3)
(c) $CH_2CHCH_2CH_2CH_3$ / $CH_3CHCHCH_2CH_3$ / any correct
branched structure;
Accept more detailed formula.
pent-1-ene / pent-2-ene; (2)
Name must match formula.
Accept 1-pentene, 2-pentene.
(d) $C_4H_8 + HBr \rightarrow CH_3CH_2CHBrCH_3$;
*Award (1) for all molecular formulas correct and (1) for
correct product structure.*
*Award (1) for completely correct equation starting with
but-1-ene.*
addition; (3)
(e) oxidation / redox;
(potassium) dichromate (VI) / $Cr_2O_7^{2-}$;
(sulfuric) acid;
distilling off propanal as it is formed;
heating under reflux (to obtain propanoic acid); (5)
(f) (propan-1-ol) hydrogen bonding;
(propanal) dipole−dipole attractions;
(propanoic acid) hydrogen bonding;
propanoic acid > propan-1-ol > propanal; (4)
(Total 20 marks)

14. (a) mole ratio $C:H = \dfrac{85.6}{12.01} : \dfrac{14.4}{1.01} = 7.13 : 14.3$;
No penalty for using integer atomic masses.
empirical formula is CH_2; (2)
(b) (i) number of moles of gas $n = \dfrac{PV}{RT} = \dfrac{mass}{molar\ mass}$;
$\dfrac{1.01 \times 10^2\,kPa\,(0.399\,dm^3)}{8.314\,\dfrac{J}{mol\,K}(273\,K)}$;
$\dfrac{1.00\,g}{0.017\,mol} = 56.3\,(g\,mol^{-1})$
OR
molar mass is the $\dfrac{mass\ of\ the\ molar\ volume}{22.4\,dm^3}$ at STP
$= \dfrac{1.00 \times 22.4}{0.399} = 56.1\,(g\,mol^{-1})$;
Accept answers in range 56.0 to 56.3.
Accept two, three or four significant figures. (2)
(ii) C_4H_8; (1)
No ECF
(c) carbon monoxide / carbon is produced;
CO is toxic / poisonous / forms carboxyhemoglobin /
interferes with oxygen transport in the body;
carbon (soot) is harmful to the respiratory system;
(2 max)
Award (1) each for any two.
(Total 7 marks)

15. (a) one general formula / same general formula;
differ by CH_2;
similar chemical properties;
gradual change in physical properties;
Award (1) for any two from last three.
functional group: atom or group of atoms responsible
for the characteristic
reactions of the molecule / homologous series; (3)

(b) ethanol lower / ethanoic acid higher;
due to larger mass of ethanoic acid / stronger
intermolecular forces / stronger van der Waals' forces /
stronger hydrogen bonding; (2)
No mark for H bonding.
(Total 5 marks)

Chapter 11: Answers to exercises

1. The smallest division is 0.1 so the uncertainty is ± 0.05.

2. The missing diamond has a mass between 9.87 and 9.97 g.
The found diamond has a mass between 9.9 and 10.3 g.
As the ranges overlap, it **could** be the missing diamond.

3. (a) $4 \times 10^{-2}\,g$
(b) $2.22 \times 10^2\,cm^3$
(c) $3.0 \times 10^{-2}\,g$
(d) $3 \times 10^{\circ}C$

4. (a) 4
(b) unspecified
(c) 3
(d) 4

5. A

6. number of moles $=$ concentration $\times$ volume / 1000
$= 1.00 \times 10.0 / 1000 = 0.0100\,mol\,dm^{-3}$
% uncertainty in concentration $= 0.05/1.00 = 5\%$
% uncertainty in volume $= 0.1/10.0 = 1\%$
% uncertainty in number of moles $= 5 + 1\% = 6\%$
absolute uncertainty in number of moles $= 6/100 \times 0.0100$
$= 0.0006$
number of moles $= 0.0100 \pm 0.0006\,mol\,dm^{-3}$

7. B

Chapter 11: Answers to practice questions

1. B   2. B   3. C   4. B
5. A   6. C   7. A   8. B

9. (a) $\Delta T = 43.2 - 21.2°C = 22.0°C$
absolute uncertainty $= \pm 0.2°C$
(b) % uncertainty $= 0.2/22.0 \times 100\% = 1\%$
(c) $\Delta H = -4.18 \times 22.0/0.500 = -184\,mol^{-1}$
(d) 1%
(e) absolute uncertainty $= 1/100 \times 184 \pm 20\,kJ\,mol^{-1}$
(f) experimental value for $\Delta H = -184 \pm 20\,kJ\,mol^{-1}$
The literature value is outside this range.
The random errors involved in reading the thermometer
do not account for these differences.
There are systematic errors. The assumptions on which
the calculation is based are not stictly valid. Some of
the heat of reaction passes into the surroundings and
the other uncertainties in the measurements cannot be
ignored. It should also be noted that the standard value
for ΔH refers to standard conditions of 298K and 1 atm.

10. percentage error

$$= \left(\frac{(\text{accepted value} - \text{experimental value})}{\text{accepted value}} \right) \times 100\%$$

$$= \left(\frac{(-217 - -210)}{-217} \right) \times 100\%$$

$$= \left(\frac{-7}{-217} \right) \times 100\%$$

$$= 3\%$$

Reasons for discrepancies bwtween experimental and literature enthalpy change are discussed in Chapter 5.

Chapter 12: Answers to exercises

1. $E = 6.63 \times 10^{-34}$ J s $\times 1.0 \times 10^5$ s^{-1} = 6.63×10^{-29} J
   $E_{\text{mole}} = 6.63 \times 10^{-29} \times 6.02 \times 10^{23} = 3.99 \times 10^{-5}$ J mol^{-1}

2. $f = 4.00 \times 10^{-20} / 6.63 \times 10^{-34} = 6.03 \times 10^{13}$ s^{-1}

3. ^{1}H NMR absorptions are due to transitions between different energy states in the nucleus;
   IR absorptions are due to bond vibrations;
   nuclear transitions are at a much lower energy than bond vibrations;

4. A

5. I and II

6. $1/\lambda = 2100$ cm^{-1} = 210 000 m^{-1}
   $\lambda = 1/210\,000$ m $= 4.76 \times 10^{-6}$ m
   $f = 3.00 \times 10^8 \times 210\,000 = 6.30 \times 10^{13}$ s^{-1}

7. The polarity (of bond or molecule) changes as the bonds are bent or stretched.

8. Hex-1-ene shows an absorption in the range 1610−1680 cm^{-1} due to the presence of the C=C bond.

9. C−H

10. CH_3OCH_3

11. Empirical formula CH_2O. Molecular formula $C_2H_4O_2$.

    Molecular structure $CH_3 \overset{\overset{\textstyle O}{\|}}{-} C - OH$.

12. A (The spectrum on the left) corresponds to $CH_3CH_2CHO^+$.
    B (The spectrum on the right) corresponds to $CH_3COCH_3{}^+$.
    Similarities
    Both have molecular ion corresponding to 58.
    Differences
    A has peak corresponding to 29 ($C_2H_5{}^+$) and 28 (loss of C_2H_5).
    B has peak corresponding to 43 corresponding to loss of loss of $CH_3{}^+$.

13. (a)

mass / charge		mass / charge	
15	$CH_3{}^+$	43	loss of CH_3
29	$C_2H_5{}^+$	58	$C_4H_{10}{}^+$

    (b) $CH_3CH_2CH_2CH_3$

14. (a) 2
    (b) 1
    (c) 1
    (d) 2

15. 14 H atoms: C_6H_{14} (hexane)

Chemical shift/ppm	No. of H	Type of proton
0.9−1.0	6	$2 \times CH_3$
1.3−1.4	8	$4 \times CH_2$

    $CH_3CH_2CH_2CH_2CH_2CH_3$
    The H atoms in the CH_2 groups are in two different environments but these are not distinguished at the level of resolution of the spectrum.

16. The H atoms are in 3 different environments. There are 3 peaks in the ^{1}H NMR spectrum.

17. Magnetic resonance imaging (NMR). The radio waves are not harmful and the technique is non-invasive. It can be used to distinguish between different types of soft tissue.

18.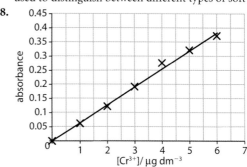

    $[Cr^{3+}]$ (from graph for absorbance 0.215) = 3.34 µg dm^{-3}

19.

	Stationary phase	Mobile phase
Adsorption	solid	liquid
Partition	liquid	liquid / gas

20. (a) Components more soluble in ethanol.
    (b) Green colour is made up from a mixture of at least four different components.
    (c) Component not soluble in ethanol.
    (d) Graphite (from pencil) is not soluble in ethanol.
    (e) Components which are not soluble in ethanol could be soluble in different solvent.
    (f) Mobile phase is the ethanol solvent / stationary phase: water in the fibres of the paper.

21. R_f values: A 0.17, B 0.50, C 0.67
    Polar molecules interact fairly strongly with the polar Si−O bonds of the stationary phase and so have smaller R_f values.

Chapter 12: Answers to practice questions

1. (a) (H−O−H) bond angle changes / bending;
       (H−O) bond length changes / stretching;
       polarity (of bond or molecule) changes;   (3)
   (b) A has O−H group / is an alcohol;
       B has C=O is a carbonyl compound / aldehyde or ketone;   (2)
   (c) CH_3CH_2CHO;
       CH_3COCH_3;   (2)

(d) B is CH_3COCH_3;
no 14 or 29 means no CH_2 or C_2H_5 / 15 and 28 indicates CH_3 and CO; (2)

(e) CH_3COCH_3 would have one line; (2)
CH_3CH_2CHO would have three lines / *accept splitting pattern*;

(Total 11 marks)

2. (a) (stationary phase) − water in the fibres of the paper (*do not accept just paper as the stationary phase*);
(mobile phase) − the solvent;
(partition) − distribution between the two phases;
(solvent front) − how far the solvent moves up the paper;
(R_f value) − the distance travelled by one component divided by the distance travelledby the solvent;
Above five points essential.
dyes spotted near bottom of paper;
bottom of paper placed in solvent;
solvent front below base line at beginning;
use of container with lid;
left until solvent near top of paper; (8)
Any three of these, (1) each.

(b) (i) 0.16 (*accept answer in range 0.14−0.20*); (2)
Allow (1) for = 0.3

(ii) mixture as more than one spot; (1)
(Total 11 marks)

3. the bond in both molecules vibrates / stretches; only the stretching in H−I causes a change in dipole moment; (2)

4. determine λ_{max};
make up different solutions of known concentrations from the standard;
measure the absorbance for each concentration at λ_{max};
plot a calibration curve and read off value of unknown concentration from its absorbance; at a fixed wavelength the absorption is directly proportional to the concentration provided the same pathlength is used / Beer−Lambert law only works for dilute solutions; (5)

5. (a) (C / D) − $(CH_3)_3COH$;
(C / D) − $(CH_3)_2CHCH_2OH$; (2)
C and D can be either way round.

(b) they have same functional groups / they all have an absorption in the range 2840−3095 / 1000−1300 / 3230−3550 cm^{-1}; (1)

(c) (i) the number of different chemical environments of the hydrogen atoms / protons / OWTTE; (1)

(ii) 5; (1)
Accept 6 (if TMS has been included).

(iii) *A*
3:2:2:2:1; (2)
Order not important.
B
3:3:2:1:1; (2)
Order not important.

(d) (i) (this is due to) the molecular ion / $C_4H_{10}O^+$ / $C_4H_9OH^+$; (1)

(ii) peak at 45 due to CH_3CHOH^+ / loss of C_2H_5;
peak at 31 due to CH_2OH^+ / loss of C_3H_7; (2)
(Total 12 marks)

6. (a) A is the ultraviolet / UV;
electronic transitions;
B is the infrared / IR;
molecular vibrations;
A is higher energy than B; (5)

(b) (i) A (because) electron transitions occur; (1)
(ii) B from vibration frequencies; (1)
(Total 7 marks)

Chapter 13: Answers to exercises

1. $q = mc\Delta T$
temperature rise = $27.96 − 18.50 = 9.46°C$ (K)
therefore heat evolved = 225.00 (g) $\times 4.18$ (J g^{-1} K^{-1})
$\times 9.46$ (K) = 8897.13 J
M_r (glucose) = 180 g mol^{-1}
therefore, energy value of glucose
$$= \frac{8897.13 \text{ (J)}}{1.50 \text{ (g)}} \times 180 \text{ g mol}^{-1}$$
$$= 1067\,655.6 \text{ J mol}^{-1}$$
$$= 1070 \text{ kJ mol}^{-1}$$

2. Isoleucine has an isoelectric point = 6.0
Therefore, at pH < 6.0 it will be positively charged and so attracted to the cathode;
at pH > 6.0 it will be negatively charged and so attracted to the anode.

3. Glutamic acid has an isoelectric point = 3.2
Histidine has an isoelectric point = 7.6
Therefore, pH between 3.2 and 7.6 would achieve separation, e.g. pH 5.0
Glutamic acid will be negatively charged and attracted to the anode.
Histidine will be positively charged and attracted to the cathode.

4. (a) CH_2O

(b) (i)

β-galactose or α-glucose

(ii) α-glucose or β-galactose

(c) energy sources; energy storage; precursors for formation of other biologically important molecules.

5. 10.16 g $I_2 = \frac{10.16}{254}$ moles I_2
$= 0.04$ moles I_2
therefore, 0.02 moles fat : 0.04 moles I_2.
so, 2 double bonds in the fat.

6. Vitamin C is water soluble.
Vitamin A or D is fat soluble.
Vitamin C has several OH groups, whereas vitamin A or D has fewer OH groups.
Vitamin A or D has large non-polar / hydrocarbon part / chain / ring.
Vitamin C has hydrogen bonding and vitamin A or D has van der Waals' forces.

7. (a) hormone or steroid
(b) alcohol or hydroxyl (*not hydroxide*)
alkene or carbon−carbon double bond
(c) 6

Chapter 13: Answers to practice questions

(1) (a)

$$HOH_2C-\overset{\overset{\displaystyle H}{|}}{C}-\overset{\overset{\displaystyle H}{|}}{C}-\overset{\overset{\displaystyle OH}{|}}{C}-\overset{\overset{\displaystyle H}{|}}{C}-CHO$$
$$\quad\quad\ \ \ \underset{OH}{|}\ \ \underset{OH}{|}\ \ \underset{H}{|}\ \ \ \underset{OH}{|}$$
(1)

No penalty for 'sticks' or for OH groups written back-to-front, e.g. OH− instead of HO−.

(b) the −OH group on the first carbon atom is inverted in β-glucose; (1)

(c) one (amylose) is a straight chain polymer whereas the other (amylopectin) is branched;
one (amylose) has only 1,4 bonds (between the monomers) whereas the other (amylopectin) has 1,4 and 1,6 bonds; (2)

(d) M_r for sucrose = 342;
heat evolved = 0.631 (kg) × 4.18 (kJ kg⁻¹ K⁻¹) × 6.22 (K) = 16.4 kJ;
calorific value = $\dfrac{16.4 \times 342}{1.00}$ = 5.61 × 10³ kJ mol⁻¹; (3)

Allow answers in range 5610 to 5620.
Penalize for more than 5 significant figures.
ECF from incorrect M_r.

(*Total 7 marks*)

2. (a) RCH(NH₂)COOH; (1)
(b) H₂NCH(CH₃)CONHCH₂COOH /
H₂NCH₂CONHCH(CH₃)COOH;
water / H₂O; (2)

(c) structure / catalysis or enzymes / energy source / oxygen transport; (2)
Any two, (1) each. Accept specific structures, e.g. hair, muscle.

(d) (i) acid / hydrochloric acid / HCl (*accept H₂SO₄*);
Accept base / NaOH.
concentrated / heat or high temperature or boil / time (*any two, (1) each*); (4)

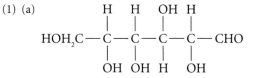

C—N / C—N / peptide / amide;

(ii) mixture / amino acids spotted on paper / gel;
apply voltage;
develop / ninhydrin / organic dye;
measure distances moved / compare with known samples / measure isoelectric points and compare with data; (4)
Marks may be given for a suitable diagram.

(*Total 13 marks*)

3. (a) condensation;
water / H₂O; (2)

(b)
$$H_2N-CH-CO-NH-CH-COOH$$
$$\quad\quad\ \ |\quad\quad\quad\quad\quad\quad\ \ |$$
$$\quad\quad CH_2-SH\quad\quad\quad CH_2-OH$$

$$H_2N-CH-CO-NH-CH-COOH$$
$$\quad\quad\ \ |\quad\quad\quad\quad\quad\quad\ \ |$$
$$\quad\quad CH_2-OH\quad\quad\quad CH_2-SH$$
(2)

(c) Arg–His–Leu;
Arg–Leu–His;
His–Arg–Leu;
His–Leu–Arg;
Leu–Arg–His;
Leu–His–Arg; (3 max)
Award (3) for all six correct, (2) for five or four, (1) for three.

(d) (i) hydrogen bonding; (1)
(ii) van der Waals' forces / hydrophobic interactions / dispersion forces;
ionic bonding / (formation of) salt bridges / electrostatic attractions;
covalent bonding / (formation of) disulfide bridges;
(2 max)
Award (1) each for any two.
Do not accept sulfur bridges on hydrogen bonding.

(*Total 10 marks*)

4. (a) (i)
$$H-\overset{\overset{\displaystyle H}{|}}{C}-O-H$$
$$H-\overset{|}{C}-O-H$$
$$H-\underset{\underset{\displaystyle H}{|}}{\overset{|}{C}}-O-H$$
(1)

(ii) 57; (1)
(iii) (the one from) stearic acid;
saturated / no (C to C) double bonds;
chains pack close together / stronger intermolecular forces / van der Waals' forces etc; (3)
Ignore hydrogen bonding. If wrong choice made, only third mark can be scored.

(b) $\dfrac{7.61}{253.8}$ = 0.03 (mol);
3 (double bonds) (*ECF*); (2)
Correct answer scores (2). If 6 is given, with no working, award (1).

(*Total 7 marks*)

5. (a) saturated fats have only single C−C bonds / unsaturated fats have C=C bonds; (1)
Do not accept references to double or single bonds without mention of carbon.

(b) palmitic acid is saturated / linoleic acid is unsaturated / *OWTTE*;
palmitic acid chains are straighter / linoleic acid chains are more kinked / *OWTTE*;
palmitic acid chains can pack more closely / linoleic acid chains can pack less closely / *OWTTE*;
palmitic acid has stronger van der Waals' forces / linoleic acid has weaker van der Waals' forces; (3 max)

(c) heat released by oil = mass of water × specific heat of water × change in temperature / q
= $mc\Delta t = 1000 \times 4.18 \times 47.3$;
calorific value = $\dfrac{1000 \times 4.18 \times 47.3}{5.00\,\text{g}}$;
= 39.5 to 40 (kJ g^{-1}); (4)

(d) energy source / energy storage;
thermal insulation;
provide protection to parts of the body;
required for the cell membrane; (2 max)
Award (1) each for any two.
(*Total 10 marks*)

6. (a) stearic acid is saturated, linoleic acid is unsaturated / contains C=C double bonds;
stearic acid molecules can pack closer together than linoleic acid molecules / *OWTTE*;
van der Waals' forces are weaker / *OWTTE*; (3)

(b) (i) zero (it is saturated so iodine cannot add); (1)

(ii) amount $\dfrac{100}{280} = 0.357$mol;
mass of I$_2$ = $2 \times 0.357 \times 254 = 181$ g; (2)

(c) H$_2$C—O—CO—C$_{17}$H$_{31}$
 HC—O—CO—C$_{17}$H$_{35}$
 H$_2$C—O—CO—C$_{17}$H$_{31}$ (1)
Accept acid residues in a different order.
(*Total 7 marks*)

7. (a) carbonyl / ketone;
Accept alkanone but not aldehyde.
alkene; (2)

(b) progesterone;
ovaries; (2)

(c) change release of hormones / FHS / LH (from hypothalamus / pituitary gland);
prevent ovulation / egg release;
prevent attachment of egg to uterus;
prevent sperm from reaching egg; (3)
Award (1) each for any three.
Do not accept 'mimic pregnancy'.
(*Total 7 marks*)

8. (a) *vitamin A*
night blindness / xerophthalmia;
vitamin C
scurvy / scorbutus;
vitamin D
rickets; (2)
Award (2) for 3 correct, (1) for 2 correct.

(b) vitamin A is stored (in the body) because it is fat soluble;
vitamin C is excreted because it is water soluble; (2)
(*Total 4 marks*)

9. (a) *vitamin A*
retinol is fat soluble;
vitamin C
ascorbic acid is water soluble;
vitamin D
calciferol is fat soluble;
fat soluble because mainly composed of hydrocarbon chain / non polar groups;
water soluble because of presence of several / many hydroxyl / OH / polar groups (5)
Last (2) can be scored even if classification wrong or not attempted.

(b) Ca^{2+} / calcium;
Do not accept Ca.
vitamin D / calciferol; (2)

(c) vitamin A / retinol;
alkene; (2)

(d) helps to form collagen / connective tissue / acts as antioxidant;
scurvy / scorbutus; (2)

(e) dissolves in water;
oxidized / destroyed by heating / boiling; (2)
(*Total 13 marks*)

10. (a) Tyr–Val–His; Tyr–His–Val; His–Tyr–Val;
His–Val–Tyr; Val–
His–Tyr; Val–Tyr–His;
There are a total of 6 different peptides possible from 3 amino acids: $3 \times 2 \times 1$; (3)

(b) There are a total of 24 different peptides that can be synthesized from 4 amino acids: $4 \times 3 \times 2 \times 1$; (2)
(*Total 5 marks*)

11. (a) The tertiary structure is the result of interactions between the R groups of the polypeptide chain. These include hydrophobic interactions (van der Waals' forces) between non-polar side-chains; hydrogen bonds between polar side chains; disulfide bridges between cystine residues; ionic bonds between chardged side chains. (4)

(b) The tertiary structure can be disrupted by temperature change; pH change. (4)
Temperature affects the tertiary structure because the increasing kinetic energy causes some intramolecular forces such as van der Waals' forces and hydrogen bonds to be broken.
pH affects the tertiary structure because the change in [H$^+$] changes the state of ionization of the R groups and so alters their attraction to and repulsion from each other. (4)
(*Total 12 marks*)

12. (a) Micronutrients are needed in the diet in extremely small amounts, generally less than 0.005% of the body mass. They include vitamins such as vitamin A, B, C and D as well as minerals such as Fe, Zn, I, Mo and Cu.
Macronutrients are needed in the diet in relatively large amounts, they include carbohydrates, lipids, proteins, Na, Ca, P, S and Cl. (5)

(b)
Deficiency of	Deficiency disease
vitamin A	xerophthalmia
vitamin C	scurvy
vitamin D	rickets
Fe	anaemia
I	goitre, mental retardation
Se	Kashin–Beck disease
(3)

(c) Fortification of certain staple foods such as rice and flour with micronutrients; supply of nutritional supplements particularly in places where certain deficiencies are known (e.g. iodine); possible changes and improvements in nutrient content through genetic modification. (3)
(*Total 11 marks*)

Chapter 14: Answers to exercises

1. (a) carbon
   (b) oxygen and powdered lime (calcium oxide / calcium carbonate)
   (c) The impurities are oxidized and the oxidized impurities combine with the lime to form slag.

2. (a) bauxite
   (b) silicon dioxide and iron(III) oxide
   (c) Aluminium is more reactive than carbon.
   (d) Aluminium ions are attracted towards the negative electrode where they are reduced to aluminium atoms:
   $Al^{3+} + 3e^- \rightarrow Al$
   (e) Aluminum is more reactive than hydrogen. Hydrogen gas would be produced as the hydrogen from the water is reduced in preference to the aluminium.
   (f) The oxygen produced at the anode from the oxide ions:
   $2O^{2-} \rightarrow O_2 + 4e^-$
   Reacts with the carbon to produce carbon dioxide:
   $C + O_2 \rightarrow CO_2$
   (g) The alloy is stronger than the pure metal.

3. (a) $C_{11}H_{24} \rightarrow C_5H_{12} + 3C_2H_4$
   (b) Increases the yield of the more useful lower fractions used as fuels for cars.
   Produces the more reactive alkenes, which can be used as chemical feedstock, to make useful products such as plastics.
   (c) Lower temperatures needed. Catalysts act selectively increasing the yield of the desired product.
   (d) Alumina / silica / zeolite.

4. (a)

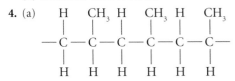

   (b)

   isotactic polypropene
   (c) Isotactic polypropene has a regular structure with the methyl groups pointing in the same direction and so is crystalline and tough.
   (d) $M_r = (3 \times 12.01) + (6 \times 1.01) = 42.09$
   $n = 2.1 \times 10^6 / 42.09 = 50\ 000$
   (e) The chains in a polymer are not all the same length.

5. (a) Plastics are easily moulded; non biodegradable and have low density.
   (b)

Method	Advantages	Disadvantages
land fill	simple method to deal with large volumes	plastics are not biodegradable; limited sites
incineration	reduces volume; plastics are concentrated energy source	CO_2 is a greenhouse gas; CO is poisonous; HCl produced from combustion of PVC causes acid rain
recycling	conserves natural resources	plastics need to be sorted

   (c) Bacteria do not have the enzymes needed to break C−C bonds in plastics.
   (d) Natural polymers (e.g. starch, cellulose or protein) can be added. The bacteria break down the natural polymer in the soil and so the bag is broken down into smaller pieces.

6. (a) Lower temperatures needed − reduced energy costs. Catalysts act selectively increasing the yield of the desired product. They are not used up and so can be reused over a long periods of time.
   (b) Sulfur impurities block the active sites of the catalyst; they are adsorbed on the surface more strongly than reactant molecules.

7. (a) Oxidation number increased from 0 to +2. Pb(s) is oxidised.
   (b) $Pb(s) + SO_4^{2-}(aq) \rightarrow PbSO_4(s) + 2e^-$
   (c) $PbSO_4$ is insoluble: the Pb^{2+} ions do not disperse into solution.
   (d) Advantage: delivers large amounts of energy over short periods.
   Disadvantage: heavy mass. lead and sulfuric acid could cause pollution.

8. (a) Low reactivity of C−H bond due to high bond energy and low polarity.
   (b) Increases polarity. Molecule can change orientation when electric field applied.
   (c) Additional benzene ring makes molecule more rod-shaped and rigid.

9. (a) No. of diameters = 10×10^{-6} m / 1×10^{-9}m
   = $10^{-5} / 1 \times 10^{-9} = 10^4 = 10\ 000$
   (b) Strong covalent C−C bonds must be broken.
   (c) Range of tube lengths with different structures lead to less regular structure in solid which reduces strength. As properties sensitive to tube length − difficult to produce tubes with required properties.
   (d) Size of nano particles similar to wavelength of harmful UV radiation. UV is scattered not absorbed.

Chapter 14: Answers to practice questions

1. (a) $Fe_2O_3 + 3CO \rightarrow 2Fe + 3CO_2$;   (1)
   (b) $Fe_3O_4 + 4H_2 \rightarrow 3Fe + 4H_2O$;   (1)
   (c) oxygen passed in;
   at high temperature / pressure / with high degree of purity;
   impurities / one named impurity oxidized;
   one equation from those listed;
   but including $2C + O_2 \rightarrow 2CO$;
   lime / limestone / CaO / $CaCO_3$ added;
   which react with / removes some oxides; one equation such as
   $CaO + SiO_2 \rightarrow CaSiO_3$;
   scrap iron / steel added; to lower temperature / because other reactions are exothermic   (6 max)
   Award (1) each for any 6.
   (d) chromium / nickel;   (1)
   (*Total 9 marks*)

2. (a) (i) $CH_2 = CHCH_3$; (1)

(ii)

harder / more rigid / higher melting point / stronger / denser;
crystalline / chains closer together; (3)

(b) polystyrene beads contain pentane / volatile hydrocarbon;
heating causes pentane to evaporate;
white / opaque / lower density / better insulator / (better) shock absorber; (4)
Any two properties, (1) each.

(c) carbon dioxide is a greenhouse gas / CO_2 causes global warming, climate change etc.;
produces toxic chlorine compounds / causes acid rain due to HCl; (2)
(Total 10 marks)

3. (a) addition of plasticizers;
more flexible / flexibility; (2)

(b)

Polymer disadvantages	PVC disadvantages
difficult to dispose of polymer properly; fills up landfill sites; litter; lack of biodegradability; use of natural resources;	burning produces toxic gases / HCl;

Award (1) each for any two. (3)
(Total 5 marks)

4. (a) $H_2 + 2OH^- \rightarrow 2H_2O + 2e^-$;
$O_2 + 2H_2O + 4e^- \rightarrow 4OH^-$; (2)

(b) less waste heat produced / more chemical energy converted to useful energy / less polluting / uses renewable energy source / more efficient; (1)
(Total 3 marks)

5. (a)

	Liquid	Liquid crystal
Molecular arrangement	disordered	disordered
Molecular orientation	disordered	ordered

(2)

(b) the phase transitions of thermotropic liquid crystals depend on temperature;
the phase transitions of lyotropic liquid crystals depend on both temperature and concentration; (2)

(c) the molecules / ions group together to form a spherical arrangement;
the hydrophilic heads are exposed to water shielding the non-polar tails; (2)
(Total 6 marks)

6. (a) heterogeneous catalysts are in different phase to the reactants;
they can be easily removed by filtration; (2)

(b) large surface area for reactants to be adsorbed;
the shape and size of the tubes makes them shape selective catalysts, only reactants of the appropriate geometry can interact effectively with the active sites; (2)

(c) properties / toxicity of the nanoparticles is size dependent;
need to regulate for type of material and size of particles; (2)
(Total 6 marks)

7. ability of molecule to transmit liquid depends on its relative orientation;
as molecule is polar, the orientation can be controlled by the application of a small voltage;
no applied voltage, light can be transmitted and the display appears light;
when voltage applied, the orientation of the molecules changes and display appears dark;
areas of the display that are light and dark controlled, to display different shapes; (5)

8. (a) research and technology development in the 1 nm to 100 nm range; (1)

(b) possible applications will be broad including healthcare, medicine security, electronics, communications and computing;
toxicity regulations are difficult as properties depend on size of particle;
unknown health effects, because new materials have new health risks;
concern that the human immune system will be defenceless against particles on nanoscale;
responsibilities of the industries;
political issues, such as need for public education for informed debate and for public involvement in policy discussions; (4)
(Total 5 marks)

9. (a) Al_2O_3; (1)

(b) it acts as a solvent;
it lowers the operating temperature / melting point;
it saves heat / energy; (3)
Award (1) each for any two.

(c) $Al^{3+} + 3e^- \rightarrow Al$;
$2O^{2-} \rightarrow O_2 + 4e^-$; (2)

(d) carbon / graphite / C;
burns / oxidizes / reacts with oxygen;
$C + O_2 \rightarrow CO_2$; (3)

(e) (aluminium is) more valuable / more expensive to produce / electricity needed to produce it; (1)
(Total 10 marks)

10. (a) (i) one electrode is made of Pb;
the other electrode is made of PbO_2;
electrolyte is H_2SO_4;
$Pb + SO_4^{2-} \rightarrow PbSO_4 + 2e^-$;
$PbO_2 + 4H^+ + SO_4^{2-} + 2e^- \rightarrow PbSO_4 + 2H_2O$; (5)

(ii) oxidation;
electrons are released / oxidation number of Pb increases; (2)
If reduction given, second mark cannot be scored.
(Total 7 marks)

11. (a) LDPE has (more) branching / HDPE has less / no branching;
van der Waals' forces (between chains);
weaker forces in LDPE / stronger forces in HDPE;
LDPE has lower melting point / HDPE has higher melting point;

LDPE is more flexible / softer / weaker / HDPE is more rigid / harder / stronger;
LDPE has low tensile strength / HDPE has high tensile strength; (4 max)
Award (1) each for any four.
(b) melts / softens / changes shape when heated / *OWTTE*; (1)
(*Total 5 marks*)

Chapter 15: Answers to exercises

1. intramuscular / into muscles
intravenous / into veins
subcutaneous / into fat
The fastest will be intravenous as the drug can be transported quickly all over the body in the bloodstream.

2. Tolerance occurs when repeated doses of a drug result in smaller physiological effects. It is potentially dangerous because increasing doses of the drug are used in response and this might get close to or exceed the toxic level.

3. (a) $Mg(OH)_2 + 2HCl \rightarrow MgCl_2 + 2H_2O$
$Al(OH)_3 + 3HCl \rightarrow AlCl_3 + 3H_2O$
(b) $Al(OH)_3$ reacts with H^+ in a mole ratio of 1:3;
$Mg(OH)_2$ reacts with H^+ in a mole ratio of 1:2;
So 0.1 mol $Al(OH)_3$ will neutralize the greater amount.
(c) KOH is a strong alkali so would be dangerous for body cells; it is corrosive and would upset the pH.

4. (a) Mild analgesics intercept pain at the source; they interfere with the production of substances that cause pain.
Strong analgesics bond to receptor sites in the brain; they prevent the transmission of pain impulses; they alter the perception of pain.
(b) reducing fever / antipyretic
(c) anti-inflammatory; anti-clotting of blood so can help to prevent heart attacks and strokes

5. (a) ether; alkene (carbon−carbon double bond)
(b) main effect: pain relief;
side-effect: constipation;

6. (a) (i) interference with nerve impulse transmissions; calming, relief from anxiety and tension;
(ii) sleep induced; decreases heart rate and breathing rate; can cause loss of consciousness, coma and even death;
(b) because they relieve the symptoms of clinical depression;

7. (a) dependence can develop;
reduction of concentration, judgement and balance;
increased risk of accidents, e.g. when driving;
increased probability of violence and crime;
adverse effects on pregnant women;
can cause stomach problems and ulcers;
can cause cirrhosis of liver and heart disease;
(b) Ethanol is oxidized to ethanoic acid; the potassium dichromate (VI) is reduced to chromium (III). The colour changes from orange to green.
(c) Ethanol can also be detected using infrared spectroscopy and by use of a fuel cell to generate a voltage.

8. (a) both contain a six-membered ring, a five-membered ring, a tertiary amine group;
(b) short-term effects: increased heart rate and blood pressure;

antidiuretic so decreases urine output;
long-term effects: increased risk of heart disease; risk of addiction; increased risk of lung, mouth and throat cancer; reduction in capacity of blood to carry oxygen;

9. (a) Penicillin prevents bacteria from manufacturing cell walls during their reproductive cycle.
New penicillins are constantly being developed to overcome the fact that many bacteria have become resistant to existing antibiotics.
(b) Modification of the side chain in penicillin enables it to pass through the digestive system without being broken down by stomach acid. As a result, it can be ingested in pill form rather than having to be injected directly into the blood.
(c) Over-use of antibiotics has increased the proportion of resistant bacteria;
people not completing their course of antibiotics has increased the spread of resistant bacteria;
use of antibiotics in animal feeds has introduced antibiotics into human food chain and so increased proportion of resistant bacteria.

Chapter 15: Answers to practice questions

1. (a) oxidizing agent / accepts electrons;
orange to green; (2)
(b) (gas-liquid) chromatography;
infrared spectroscopy; (2)
(c) stomach bleeding / 'corrodes lining' of stomach; (1)
(d) amide / ketone / carbonyl;
(tertiary) amine; (2)
(*Total 7 marks*)

2. (a) used to overcome / neutralize (excess) acidity in the stomach; (1)
(b) aluminium hydroxide neutralizes more acid / more HCl / more H^+ ions / contains more OH^- ions;
$Al(OH)_3 + 3H^+ \rightarrow Al^{3+} + 3H_2O$;
$Mg(OH)_2 + 2H^+ \rightarrow Mg^{2+} + 2H_2O$; (3)
Accept equations with HCl.
(*Total 4 marks*)

3. (a) *mild analgesic*
intercepts pain at the source / *OWTTE*;
by interfering with the production of substances / (enzymes) that cause pain / prostaglandins / *OWTTE*;
strong analgesic
binds to pain receptors in the brain;
preventing the transmission of nerve impulses; (4)
(b) (i) *advantage*
prevents inflammation / thins blood / effective against blood clots / prevents strokes / quick acting / prevents the recurrence of heart attacks / relieves symptoms of arthritis / rheumatism / reduces fever;
disadvantage
irritates the stomach lining / produces allergic reactions / Reye's syndrome / causes stomach bleeding / causes stomach ulcers; (2)
(ii) may cause kidney / liver damage; (1)
(*Total 7 marks*)

4. (a) amide;
   (tertiary) amine; (2)
   Do not accept primary or secondary amine.
   (b) OH / alcohol / phenol / hydroxyl;
   esterification / condensation;
   water / H_2O; (3)
   (*Total 5 marks*)

5. (a) bacteria;
   interfere with cell wall formation;
   prevent formation of cross-links (within wall);
   size / shape of cell cannot be maintained;
   water enters the cell / osmosis occurs;
   cell bursts / disintegrates; (4 max)
   Award (1) each for any three of the last five points.
   (b) (overprescription) makes penicillins less effective;
   they destroy useful bacteria;
   allow a resistant population to build up / *OWTTE*; (3)
   (*Total 7 marks*)

6. (a) bacteria are larger / viruses are smaller;
   bacteria are cellular / viruses are non-cellular;
   bacteria have / nucleus / cytoplasm / cell membrane /
   organelles / opposite for viruses;
   bacteria can feed / excrete / respire / grow outside cells /
   opposite for viruses;
   Accept 'bacteria are living whereas viruses are non-living'.
   viruses insert DNA/RNA into cells / rely on a host cell to
   reproduce;
   bacteria multiply by cell division / binary fision / mitosis
   / meiosis; (4 max)
   Award (1) each for any four.
   (b) they alter the host cell's genetic material;
   they prevent the virus from multiplying;
   they alter the virus's binding site on the cell wall / they
   alter the structure of the cell wall to prevent the virus
   entering;
   they prevent viruses from leaving the cell; (2 max)
   Award (1) each for any two.
   (*Total 6 marks*)

7. (a) (i)

   The ring must circle the N atom to gain the mark.
   (ii) tertiary; (1)
   (b) amide / N-methylamide (*accept peptide*); (1)
   (c) (i) they all contain the phenylethylamine structure /
   contain a benzene ring linked to two carbon atoms
   attached to an amine group; (1)
   (ii) sympathomimetic drugs mimic the effect of
   adrenaline / stimulate the sympathetic nervous
   system;
   speed up the heart / increase sweat production /
   increase rate of breathing; (2)
   (iii) weight loss / constipation / emotional instability; (1)
   (*Total 7 marks*)

8. (a) rectally / by suppository, by inhalation, by injection
   (parenterally), by applying to skin / topically; (2)

*(2) for three, (1) for two. Award (1 max) if intravenous,
subcutaneous and intramuscular are given.*
   (b) an effect produced as well as the one intended /
   unwanted or undesired effect; (1)
   (c) (i) magnesium / Mg, aluminium / Al, calcium / Ca; (1)
   Any two for (1).
   (ii) $NaHCO_3 + HCl \rightarrow NaCl + H_2O + CO_2$; (1)
   (iii) acid from the stomach rises into the oesophagus;(1)
   (iv) as an anti-foaming agent / to prevent problem in
   (iii) / to prevent flatulence; (1)
   (*Total 5 marks*)

9. (a) (i) carboxylic (acid) / alkanoic (acid); ester; (2)
   Accept only these names.
   (ii) *Any one of the following (1).*
   beneficial effects
   used to treat mini-strokes;
   prevents heart attacks / reduces risk of heart attack
   / thins the blood / anti-coagulant;
   relieves symptoms of rheumatological diseases /
   anti-inflammatory;
   reduces fever; (1)
   Any one of the following (1).
   side-effects
   stomach bleeding;
   allergic reaction;
   Reye's syndrome;
   hearing loss;
   tinnitus (ringing in the ears);
   gastrointestinal irritation (e.g. heartburn, nausea); (1)
   (b) (i) 14 / 14.03 (*ignore units*); (1)
   (ii) increasing amounts needed to produce same effect;
   increasing amounts cause damage / death; (2)
   (*Total 7 marks*)

Chapter 16: Answers to exercises

1. (a) CO is a local pollution problem produced by the
   combustion of hydrocarbon in a limited air supply.
   (b) Peaks correspond to morning and evening rush hour
   traffic.
2. (a) 1 mole of C_8H_{18} reacts with 25/2 moles of O_2
   114.26 g of C_8H_{18} reacts with 400 g of O_2
   1.00 g of C_8H_{18} reacts with 3.50 g of O_2
   (b) mass of air = 5 × 3.50 g = 17.5 g
   (c) CO affects oxygen uptake in the blood. It is absorbed by
   the lungs and binds to haemoglobin in red blood cells
   more effectively than oxygen. This prevents oxygen from
   being transported around the body.
   (d) number of O on right = $2x + y/2$
   number of O_2 on left = $x + y/4$
   (e) Carbon monoxide is a local pollution problem in
   urban areas as it is produced in heavy traffic. There are
   particularly high emission rates during rush hours. It is
   produced when the air/fuel ratio is low.
   (f) lean burn engines, catalytic converters, thermal exhaust
   reactor (see text for details);
   (g) CO_2 is a greenhouse gas;
3. (a) electrical storms and biological processes;
   (b) high temperature combination of nitrogen and oxygen
   in internal combustion engine;
   (c) nitric acid;

4. (a) Sulfur is present in the amino acid cysteine which is a component of proteins.
   (b) A slurry of calcium oxide (lime) or calcium carbonate (limestone) reacts with sulfur dioxide to form calcium sulfate:
   $$CaO(s) + SO_2(g) \rightarrow CaSO_3(s)$$
   $$CaCO_3(s) + SO_2(g) \rightarrow CaSO_3(s) + CO_2(g)$$
   $$2CaSO_3(s) + O_2(g) \rightarrow 2CaSO_4(s)$$
   (c) Use alternative energy source to fossil fuels or use coal with a low sulfur content.

5. (a) +4   (b) +4   (c) +6
6. (a) +4   (b) +3   (c) +5

7. $Fe(s) + 2HNO_3(aq) \rightarrow Fe(NO_3)_2(aq) + H_2(g)$
   $CaCO_3(s) + 2HNO_3(aq) \rightarrow Ca(NO_3)_2(aq) + H_2O(l) + CO_2(g)$

8. (a) Contains dissolved carbon dioxide which reacts with water to form carbonic acid:
   $$CO_2(g) + H_2O(l) \rightleftharpoons H_2CO_3(aq)$$
   (b) sulfuric acid:
   $$S(s) + O_2(g) \rightarrow SO_2(g) / 2SO_2(g) + O_2(g) \rightarrow 2SO_3(g)$$
   $$H_2O(l) + SO_3(g) \rightarrow H_2SO_4(aq)$$
   (c) nitric acid:
   reduced by use of lean burn engines, catalytic converters, recirculation of exhaust gases;
   (d) $CaCO_3(s) + H_2SO_4(aq) \rightarrow$
   $$CaSO_4(aq) + H_2O(l) + CO_2(g)$$
   (e) effects on materials, plant life and human health (see text for details);
   (f) Use alternative energy source to fossil fuels or use coal with a low sulfur content.

9. (a) SO_2 and NO
   (b) SO_2 and particulates
   (c) Particulates act as catalysts in the production of secondary pollutants. They absorb other pollutants and hold them in the lungs for longer periods of time.
   (d) $SO_2(g)$: $CaO(s) + SO_2(g) \rightarrow CaSO_3(g)$
   (e) NO: formed from the combination of nitrogen and oxygen at the high temp of the internal combustion engine.

10. (a) distant from localized areas of pollution; figures present an accurate measure of global levels of CO_2.
    (b) % increase = (increase/ initial value) $\times$ 100%
    $$= \frac{(384 - 316)}{316} \times 100\% = 21.5\%$$
    (c) combustion of fossil fuels
    (d) The annual variation is due to CO_2 uptake by growing plants. The uptake is highest in the northern hemisphere springtime.
    (e) photosynthesis: $6CO_2 + 6H_2O \rightarrow C_6H_{12}O_6 + 6O_2$
    CO_2 dissolves in water: $CO_2 + H_2O \rightleftharpoons H_2CO_3(aq)$
    (f) decreased level of photosynthesis: less CO_2 taken in by plants
    (g) CO_2 absorbs infrared which leads to increased vibrations and bending of the bonds.

11. (a) respiration, volcanic eruption, complete aerobic decomposition of organic matter, forest fires;
    (b) methane produced from anaerobic decomposition;
    (c) smoke particulates: block out the sunlight;
    (d) high energy short wavelength radiation passes through the atmosphere;

lower energy / longer wavelength radiated from the earth's surface is absorbed by vibrating bonds in CO_2 molecules;
   (e) melting of polar ice caps, thermal expansion of oceans will lead to rise in sea levels which can cause coastal flooding; crop yields reduced, changes in flora and fauna distribution, drought, increased rainfall, desertification;

12. (a) The oxygen to oxygen bond is between a single and a double bond. The molecule is angular with a bond angle of 120°. It can be represented as two resonance hybrids:

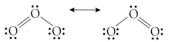

   (b) The ozone layer occurs in the stratosphere. In this region ultraviolet light causes the formation of ozone from oxygen.
   (c) UV light
   $$O_2(g) \rightarrow O^\bullet(g) + O^\bullet(g) \text{(atomic oxygen)}$$
   $$O^\bullet(g) + O_2(g) \rightarrow O_3(g)$$
   UV light
   $$O_3(g) \rightarrow O^\bullet(g) + O_2(g)$$
   $$O_3(g) + O(g) \rightarrow 2O_2(g)$$
   (d) NO_x and CFCs act as catalysts for the decomposition of ozone to oxygen.
   e.g. $CCl_2F_2(g) \rightarrow CClF_2^\bullet(g) + Cl^\bullet(g)$
   $Cl^\bullet(g) + O_3(g) \rightarrow O_2(g) + ClO^\bullet(g)$
   $ClO^\bullet(g) + O^\bullet(g) \rightarrow O_2(g) + Cl^\bullet(g)$
   (e) The $Cl^\bullet$ atoms are regenerated.

13. (a) effects on humans, plants, marine ecosystems and weather (see text for details);
    (b) 2-methylpropane more flammable than CHF_2Cl; CHF_2Cl contains a C—Cl bond so can form $Cl^\bullet$ free radicals with UV radiation.
    Both gases can both absorb IR radiation and are greenhouse gases.

14. (a) $1 \, dm^3$ of $H_2O = 1000 \, g$
    $1 \, ppm = 1 \, g$ in $10^6 \, g$ of water $= 0.001 \, g \, dm^{-3}$
    $20 \, ppm = 0.020 \, g \, dm^{-3}$
    (b) $M_{C_6H_{12}O_6} = (6 \times 12.01) + (12 \times 1.01) + (6 \times 16.00)$
    $= 180.18$
    $n_{C_6H_{12}O_6} = 0.0200/180.18$
    $n_{O_2} = (0.02/180.18) \times 6$
    $m_{O_2} = (0.02/180.18) \times 6 \times 32 = 0.0213 \, g$
    (c) The BOD is greater than the maximum solubility. Anaerobic decomposition occurs.

15. (a) dissolved organic waste from the meat processing plant;
    (b) The levels of oxygen decrease as it is used by bacteria to oxidise the organic waste.
    (c) Moving water allows oxygen from the atmosphere to dissolve in the water.
    (d) When the BOD is greater than the dissolved O_2: at distances up to 60 km.

16. (a) Solubility decreases with temperature, and rate of metabolism increases. The levels of dissolved O_2 decrease.
    (b) Oxygen is used by bacteria to decompose organic matter. Levels of oxygen decrease.
    (c) increase in algae growth; more oxygen needed for respiration; insufficient O_2: plants die and O_2 needed for decomposition.

17. (a) Insoluble solid objects are removed by passing water though a grid or sand bed.
    (b) activated sludge process; air passed through the sewage and the organic mater is oxidized by bacteria; some sludge is recycled.
    (c) Metal ions are removed by adding alkali or hydrogen sulfide.
    Phosphate ions are removed by adding calcium ions: Ca^{2+}.
    (d) distillation, ion exchange, reverse osmosis (see text for details).

18. Biological: provides source of energy and nutrients (P, N, S), contributes to the resilience of the soil/plant system.
    Physical: improves structural stability, influences water-retention properties, alters thermal properties.
    Chemical: contributes to the cation exchange capacity (CEC), enhances buffering ability, complexes cations (enhanced P availability), reduces concentrations of toxic cations, promotes the binding of SOM to soil minerals.

19. For example: source of energy and nutrients (P, N, S), adds to cation exchange capacity.

20. B

Chapter 16: Answers to practice questions

1. (a) carbon dioxide (dissolves, reacts) / carbonic acid formed;
    $CO_2 + H_2O \rightleftharpoons H^+ + HCO_3^-$;   (2)
    Ignore state symbols.
    Accept H_2CO_3 or $2H^+ + CO_3^{2-}$ as products.
    Do not accept oxides of nitrogen or sulfur as contributing to naturally acidic rain.
    (b) (i) $N_2 + O_2 \rightarrow 2NO$;
        Ignore state symbols.
        nitric acid / nitrous acid;   (2)
        Name or formula
    (ii) $2NO + 2CO \rightarrow N_2 + 2CO_2$;   (2)
        Ignore state symbols.
        Award (1) for correct products, (2) if equation correct.
        (*Total 6 marks*)

2. (a) catalytic converter / lean burn engine / thermal exhaust reactor;
    $2CO + O_2 \rightarrow 2CO_2$;   (2)
    For catalytic converter also accept $2CO + 2NO \rightarrow CO_2 + N_2$
    (b) catalytic converter;
    $2CO + 2NO \rightarrow 2CO_2 + N_2$;   (2)
    (c) (alkaline) scrubbing / fluidized bed combustion;
    $CaCO_3 + SO_2 \rightarrow CaSO_3 + CO_2 / CaO + SO_2 \rightarrow CaSO_3$;   (2)
    (d) catalytic converter;
    $2C_8H_{18} + 25O_2 \rightarrow 16CO_2 + 18H_2O$;   (2)
    Accept thermal exhaust reactor but not lean burn.
        (*Total 8 marks*)

3. (a) amount of oxygen needed to decompose organic matter (in water sample);
    in a specified time / five days / at a specified temperature / $20°C$;   (2)
    (b) aeration / use of oxygen;
    use of bacteria / microorganisms;

organic matter;
broken down / oxidized;
sedimentation tank / settling process;   (5)
All marks can be scored from a suitably labelled diagram.
        (*Total 7 marks*)

4. (a) *Any two from*
    low boiling point / volatile / non-reactive / non-toxic / non flammable / inflammable / does not act as a greenhouse gas;   (2)
    (b) C_4H_{10} more flammable than CHF_2Cl;
    CHF_2Cl still contains a $C-Cl$ bond (so can form radicals with UV radiation);
    C_4H_{10} and CHF_2Cl can both absorb IR radiation / cause global warming / are greenhouse gases;   (3)
    Award marks for any other correct advantages / disadvantages.
    Award (1) for '2-methylpropane flammable'.
        (*Total 5 marks*)

5. (a) incoming radiation / energy / heat / light (from Sun) is short wavelength / ultraviolet (radiation);
    long wavelength / infrared radiation leaves Earth's surface;
    (some of this radiation) is absorbed / trapped by gases in the atmosphere;
    by (vibration in) bonds in molecules / re-radiates heat back to the Earth;   (4)
    (b) *natural*
    (evaporation from) oceans / seas / rivers / lakes;
    man-made
    burning (any specified) fossil fuel;   (2)
    Do not accept objects such as 'cars' or 'car exhausts' or 'aeroplanes' without a reference to combustion.
    (c) (i) more abundant / *OWTTE*;   (1)
        (ii) more effective (at absorbing energy) / *OWTTE*;   (1)
    (d) melting of polar ice caps;
    thermal expansion of oceans / rise in sea levels / coastal flooding;
    stated effect on agriculture (e.g. crop yields reduced);
    changes in flora and fauna distribution;
    stated effect on climate (e.g. drought / increased rainfall / desertification);   (4 max)
    Do not accept 'climate change' alone.
    Award (1) each for any four.
        (*Total 12 marks*)

6. (a) fertilizer runoff / animal or human waste;
    carcinogenic / lowers oxygen levels in the body / blue baby syndrome / infantile methaemoglobinaemia;   (2)
    (b) tertiary; ion exchange / microorganisms / algal ponds;   (2)
        (*Total 4 marks*)

7. (a) precipitation;
    high voltage / (voltage between) oppositely charged electrodes;
    particulates collect on / are attracted to / electrodes / plates / wire;
    solids shaken off / fall to bottom of container;   (3 max)
    Award (1) each for any three.
    (b) coal / diesel (fuel) / wood;   (1)
    (c) $CH_4 + O_2 \rightarrow C + 2H_2O$;   (1)
    Ignore state symbols.
        (*Total 5 marks*)

8. (a) $O_3 \rightarrow O_2 + O^{\bullet}$;
   $O_3 + O^{\bullet} \rightarrow 2O_2$; (2)
   Accept O instead of $O^{\bullet}$ in both equations.

(b) chlorofluorocarbons / CFCs;
   from refrigerants / propellants for aerosols / fire
   extinguishers / foaming agents / cleaning solvents /
   coolant / air-conditioning systems;
   or
   oxides of nitrogen / NO_x;
   (from) internal combustion engine / power stations / jet
   aeroplanes; (2)

(c) *advantage*
   does not produce $Cl^{\bullet}$ / no weak $C-Cl$ bonds/stable /
   has same properties as CFCs / no (free) radicals formed /
   hydrofluorocarbons have shorter (atmospheric) lifetime;
   disadvantage
   greenhouse gas / global warming / hydrofluorocarbons
   are flammable; (2)
   (*Total 6 marks*)

9.

Method	Advantages	Disadvantages
landfill	efficient method to deal with large volume;	not popular with locals; needs to be maintained and monitored after use; (1 max)
incineration	reduces volume; energy source; (1 max)	cans cause pollutants: such as greenhouse gases and dioxins;

(4)

10. humic substances contain organic acids which to bind to
   metal ion;
   this allows humus to bind to toxic heavy metals removing
   them from the wider ecosystem;
   cation exchange capacity (CEC) allows humus to release
   metal ions as they are needed; (2)
   Award (1) each for any two.

11. (high level) − contains fission products;
   (low level) − clothing / fuel cans / other;
   stored under water;
   buried underground;
   encased in steel / concrete;
   vitrified / made into glass; (6 max)
   The last four marks can be scored without reference to either
   type of waste.

12. metals; paper; glass; plastics;
   Award (1) each for any two.
   advantages
   saves natural resources; saves energy; reduces pollution;
   disadvantages
   metals/plastics/paper needs to be sorted; (6)

13. *salinization*
   irrigation waters contain dissolved salts, which are left
   behind after water evaporates;
   plants cannot grow in soil that is too salty;
   nutrient depletion
   agriculture disrupts the normal cycling of nutrients through
   the soil food web when crops are harvested;
   this removes all the nutrients and minerals that they
   absorbed from the soil while growing; (4)

14. (a) decreased; (1)
   (b) plant life / algae increases (then dies);
   decay consumes dissolved oxygen; (2)
   (*Total 3 marks*)

15. (a) (i) it leaches nutrients (Ca^{2+}, Mg^{2+}, K^+) from the soil;
   or it lowers the concentration of Mg^{2+} so reduces
   the amount of chlorophyll / photosynthesis;
   or it increases the concentration of Al^{3+} (from
   rocks) which damages roots; (1 max)
   (ii) $CaCO_3 + 2H^+ \rightarrow Ca^{2+} + CO_2 + H_2O$; (1)
   Accept full equations with HNO_3, H_2SO_3 or H_2SO_4.

(b) CaO is a basic oxide / CaO neutralizes the acid in the
   lake / equation to represent this; (1)
   (*Total 3 marks*)

16. zeolites / silicates / resins;
   sodium ions / Na^+ removed;
   Do not accept Na.
   replaced by hydrogen ions / H^+;
   chloride ions / Cl^- removed;
   Do not accept Cl or chlorine.
   replaced by hydroxide or hydroxyl ions / OH^-;
   H^+ and OH^- react together; (5 max)
   Any five, (1) each.
   Penalise missing 'ions' once only.

Chapter 17: Answers to exercises

1. (a) A, C
   (b) C
   (c) B
   (d) A
   (e) B

2.

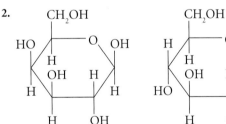

3. (a) Carbohydrates are produced in green plants from CO_2
   and H_2O using sunlight energy.
   (b) monosaccharides: small molecules (eg. $C_6H_{12}O_6$).
   polysaccharides: much larger molecules formed by
   condensation reactions of the monosachharides.
   (c) (i) Starch and cellulose have the same smallest unit:
   glucose e.g. ($C_6H_{10}O_5$). They differ in the way these
   units are connected.
   (ii) Starch provides energy per gram but cellulose offers
   no energy.
   (iii) Starch is a source of energy as it can be broken
   down into glucose for respiration. Cellulose cannot
   be digested and so has no nutritional values. It
   is, however, valuable in the diet as fibre as it gives
   bulk to food which aids its passage through the
   alimentary canal.

4. Cellulose is not absorbed by the human body so it does not provide nutritional value; i.e. it does not provide energy, regulate growth, or repair of the body's tissues. It adds bulk to the faeces because of its water-binding capacity and assists the passage of waste through the intestine.

5. (a) H$_2$N—CH—CO—NH—CH—COOH

        CH$_3$—CH—OH   CH$_3$—CH—CH$_3$

    H$_2$N—CH—CO—NH—CH—COOH

        CH$_3$—CH—CH$_3$ CH$_3$—CH—OH

(b) 6

6. (a) COOH carboxylic acid
   (b) peptide

7. (a) Melting point above 25°C; lauric, myristic, palmitic, and stearic acid are solids at room temperature.
   (b) Melting point increases as van der Waals' forces increase with size of the R group, due to an increase in number of electrons.
   (c) An increase in the number of the C=C double bonds adds kinks to the structure which reduces the ability of the molecules to pack together. The intermolecular forces are weaker and the melting points decrease.

8. fats and oils; hydrolytic and oxidative rancidity;

9. Removal of air reduces the rate of oxidation reactions.

10. Reduced light levels decreases rate of photo oxidation reactions.

11. 2-*tert*-butyl-4-hydroxyanisole, 3-*tert*-butyl-4-hydroxyanisole, 3, 5-di-*tert*-butyl-4-hydroxytoluene, *tert*-butylhydroquinone have both groups.

12. Sorbic acid is used in cheese and breads. Benzoic acid and propanoic acid are added to fruit juices and carbonated drinks. Sodium and potassium nitrite and nitrate are added to meat to inhibit the growth of microorganisms.

13. Pickling in ethanoic acid reduces the pH to levels which are too acidic for micro-organisms to survive. Fermentation produces ethanol which limits bacterial growth.

14. The complementary colours to green are violet and red.

15. The molecule is fat soluble as it is non-polar due to the long hydrocarbon chain. It has only one hydroxyl group.

16. It is very soluble in water because of the presence of four hydroxyl groups and a polar carbonyl group. It can form hydrogen bonds with water molecules.

17. λ_{max} = 475 nm. Blue light is absorbed. The dye is yellow/orange.

18. Cooked lobster: $\lambda_{max} \approx 480-490$ nm. Blue / green light is absorbed. The lobster is red.
    Live lobster: $\lambda_{max} \approx 650$ nm. Red / orange light is absorbed. The lobster is blue.

19.

pH	λ_{max}	Colour absorbed	Colour of pigment
1	550	green	red
7	350	no visible	colourless

20.

pH	λ_{max}	Colour absorbed	Colour of pigment
1	550	green	red
12	475	blue	orange/yellow

21. Caramelization of fructose starts at lower temperature: highest rate of browning.

22. The process of caramelization starts with the melting of the sugar at temperatures above the boiling point of water (starts at 120°C).

23. The DNA of the genes is altered. DNA-coated particles are fired into the plant cell and enter the nuclei.

24. For example: (see text).

Benefits	Concerns
Improved flavour, texture and the nutritional value Longer shelf-life Increased crop yields in plants and feed efficiency in animals	Uncertainties about the outcomes Links to increased allergies (for people involved in their processing) Pollen from GM crops may escape to contaminate 'normal' crops

25.

Food type	Continuous phase	Dispersed phase	Type of dispersed system
ice cream	liquid	solid	sol
bread	solid	gas	solid foam
jam	solid	liquid	gel
salad cream	liquid	liquid	emulsion
beer	liquid	gas	foam
whipped cream	liquid	gas	foam
butter	solid	liquid	gel

26. Has a polar hydrophilic head which is attracted to water and a non-polar hydrophobic tail which dissolves in oil at the phase interface.

27. They are all colloidal mixtures and be distinguished by the phases present:

Type	Continuous phase	Disperse phase	Examples
foam foam solid	liquid/solid	gas	whipped cream, egg whites, beer, bread, meringue
emulsion	liquid	liquid	oil in water/milk water in oil/butter
suspension	liquid	solid	molten chocolate.

Chapter 17: Answers to practice questions

1. (a) carbohydrates;
       energy (sources);   (2)
   (b) protein;
       fats and oils;   (2)
   (c) vitamins   (1)
   (Total 5 marks)

2. food: any substance, whether processed, semi-processed or raw that is intended for human consumption;
nutrient: a substance obtained from food and used by the body to provide energy, regulate growth, maintenance and repair of the body's tissues;
food not nutrient: pepper (2)

3. no: it is not an aldehyde (alkanals) or ketone (alkanones) with one carbonyl group ($C=O$);
and at least two hydroxyl ($-OH$) groups; (2)

4. (a) $RCH(NH_2)COOH$; (1)
   (b) $H_2NCH(CH_3)CONHCH_2COOH$ / $H_2NCHCO_2HCH(CH_3)COOH$;
   water / H_2O; (2)
   (*Total 5 marks*)

5. (a) CH_2O; (1)
   (b) (i)

   (β-)galactose

   (β-)glucose (2)
   (ii) (β-)glucose / (β-)galactose; *Whichever not given in (b)(i)* (1)
   (*Total ? marks*)

6. (a)

   (1)
   (b) 57; (1)
   (c) (the one from) stearic acid;
   saturated / no C to C double bonds;
   chains pack close together / stronger intermolecular forces / van der Waals' forces etc; (3)
   (*Total 5 marks*)

7. *cis* isomer has carbon atoms on same side of double bond, *trans* isomer has carbon atoms on opposite sides;
the *cis* isomer has lower melting point;
as the molecules of the *cis* isomer cannot easily arrange themselves side by side;
which reduces the van der Waal's forces; (4)

8. (a) a food reaches the end of its shelf life when it no longer maintains the expected quality desired by the consumer because of changes in flavour, smell, texture and appearance (colour, mass) or because of microbial spoilage; (1)
   (b) using an inert gas, which minimizes contact with oxygen;
   by covering food using low-gas-permeability packaging film or hermetic sealing;
   minimizing the amount of air in the headspace above oil and canning;
   Any two, (1) each. (2)
   (c) antioxidants delay the onset or slow the rate of oxidation;
   they are oxidized instead of the food and so remove oxygen / they interrupt the formation of free radicals; (2)
   (d) for example: vitamin C / vitamin E / β-carotene / selenium;
   BHA / BHT / PG / THBP / TBHQ; (2)
   (e) phenolic group / hydroxyl group attached to the benzene ring;
   tertiary butyl group / carbon bonded to three methyl groups; (2)
   (*Total 9 marks*)

9. (a) a dye is a food-grade synthetic water-soluble colorant;
   a pigment is a naturally occurring colorant found in the cells of plants and animals; (2)
   (b) carotenes;
   presence of multiple unsaturated carbon$-$carbon double bonds / conjugated double bonds; (2)
   (c) changing the pH changes the structure/ the degree of conjugation of the double bond;
   the molecules will absorb/reflect different regions in the visible spectrum; (2)
   (*Total 6 marks*)

10. caramelization: foods with high carbohydrate content, and low nitrogen content;
compounds are dehydrated;
sugar molecules react together by condensation reactions to produce polymers;
with conjugated double bonds which absorb light and give brown colours;
Any two, (1) each. (2)
Maillard reaction: reactions of amino acid and carbohydrate;
condensation reaction which replaces $C=O$ with $C=N-R$;
a series of dehydration/fragmentation/condensation reactions then follow to produce a complex mixture of products;
Any two, (1) each. (2)
(*Total 4 marks*)

11. (a) Maillard reaction: reaction between primary amine/NH_2 and carbohydrate/$C=O$ group;
   amino acid has two primary amino groups;
   arginine / lysine; (3)
   (b) polymers have large intermolecular forces between molecule;
   molecules not volatile; (2)
   (*Total 5 marks*)

12. (a) an emulsion is a stable mixture of one liquid in another liquid;
e.g. salad dressing / milk / butter;
a foam is a stable mixture of a gas in a liquid;
e.g. whipped cream / egg whites / beer; (4)

(b) the polar head of lecithin allows it to mix with water; non-polar hydrocarbon tail allows it to mix with oil; (2)
(Total 6 marks)

13. (a) GM food contains a single gene / DNA that has been (artificially) incorporated from another organism / *OWTTE*; (1)

(b) *Any two benefits from:*
improve flavour / improve texture / improve nutritional value / increase shelf-life / make plants more resistant to disease / more resistant to insect attack / more resistant to herbicides / increases (crop) yield etc;
Any two concerns from:
outcome of alterations uncertain / may cause disease / may escape to contaminate normal crops / may alter ecosystem etc; (4)
(Total 5 marks)

Chapter 18: Answers to exercises

1. Alkenes have a double bond which is an electron dense region and so is susceptible to attack by electrophiles which are themselves electron deficient. They undergo addition reactions because they are unsaturated; one of the bonds in the double bond breaks and incoming groups can add to the two carbon atoms.
When bromine approaches but-2-ene, it is polarized by the electron density in the double bond. Electrons in the bromine−bromine bond are repelled away from the double bond, leading to the heterolytic fission of the bromine molecule. The Br^+ product now attaches itself to one of the carbon atoms as the carbon−carbon bond breaks. This produces an unstable carbocation which then rapidly reacts with the Br^- ion. The product is 2,3-dibromobutane.

2. But-1-ene + HBr → 2-bromobutane
Application of Markovnikov's rule enables us to predict that the electrophile H^+ will add to the terminal carbon forming a secondary carbocation, as this is stabilized by the positive inductive effect of the alkyl groups. Br^- will then add to carbon 2 forming 2-bromobutane.

3. ICl is polarized: $I^{\delta+} Cl^{\delta-}$ owing to the greater electronegativity of Cl than I. So when it undergoes heterolytic fission it will form I^+ and Cl^-. By application of Markovnikov's rule, the I^+ will attach to the terminal carbon, while Cl^- will add to carbon 2. The product is therefore 1-iodo-2-chloropropane.

4.

2-hydroxy-2-methylpropanenitrile

5. Propanal will react more easily than propanone with HCN. The reaction mechanism is nucleophilic attack; propanal has a higher magnitude $\delta+$ on its carbonyl carbon than propanone because it only has one positive inductive effect, so it is more susceptible to nucleophilic attack.

6. (a)

propan-1-ol

propan-2-ol

(b) phosphoric acid
(c) Both reactions yield propene.

7. Butan-1-ol is dehydrated by heating with phosphoric acid to 180°C. The mechanism involves protonation by the acid catalyst, followed by loss of water and loss of a proton, regenerating the acid.

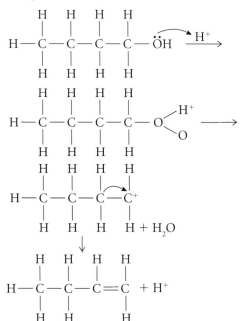

8. Addition of 2,4 DNP to the carbonyl compound will yield an orange precipitate of crystals of 2,4-dinitrophenylhydrazone. These can be purified using recrystallization and then used in a melting point determination. Comparing the melting point value obtained with data tables will enable the identity of the hydrazone compound to be characterized from which the initial carbonyl compound can be deduced.

9. $2C_6H_6 + 15O_2 \rightarrow 12CO_2 + 6H_2O$
Benzene burns with a very smokey flame.

10. Benzene is a cyclic molecule with a planar framework of single bonds between the six carbon atoms and six hydrogen atoms. The carbon atoms are also bonded to each other by a delocalized cloud of electrons which forms a symmetrical region of electron density above and below the plane of the ring. This is a very stable arrangement, so benzene has much lower energy than would be expected.

11. Benzene will react with hydrogen less readily than ethene, as it does not have discrete carbon–carbon double bonds. Instead it has a delocalized ring of electrons, which is energetically stable and therefore difficult to break.

12. (a) pentan-3-ol:

$$C_2H_5Mg\,Br + C_2H_5 \!-\! C \overset{O}{\underset{H}{\diagdown}} \rightarrow C_2H_5 \!-\! \overset{OH}{\underset{H}{C}} \!-\! C_2H_5$$

(b) propanoic acid: $C_2H_5MgBr + CO_2 \rightarrow C_2H_5COOH$

(c) 3-methylpentan-3-ol:

$$C_2H_5Mg\,Br + C_2H_5\,COCH_3 \rightarrow C_2H_5 \!-\! \overset{OH}{\underset{CH_3}{C}} \!-\! C_2H_5$$

(d) ethane: $C_2H_5MgBr + H_2O \rightarrow C_2H_6$

13. This involves converting a one-carbon molecule CH_3I into a five-carbon secondary alcohol. So the Grignard reagent must react with a four-carbon aldehyde.
Therefore, first make a Grignard reagent by reacting CH_3I with Mg turnings in dry ether, then react the reagent with butanal and hydrolyse the product in acid.

$$CH_3I + Mg \xrightarrow{(C_2H_5)_2O} CH_3Mg\,I$$

$$CH_3Mg\,I + C_3H_7\,CHO \rightarrow C_3H_7 \!-\! \overset{OH}{\underset{H}{C}} \!-\! CH_3$$

pentan-2-ol

14. Start with a four-carbon halogenoalkane such as C_4H_9I. React it with Mg turnings in dry ether to make the Grignard reagent C_4H_9MgI. Hydrolyse this reagent with water to form butane.

$$C_4H_9I + Mg\,I \xrightarrow{(C_2H_5)_2O} C_4H_9MgI$$

$$C_4H_9Mg\,I + H_2O \rightarrow C_4H_{10} + Mg(OH)\,I$$

15. React butanone with HCN, using HCl and KCN. This will yield 2-hydroxy-2-methylbutanenitrile. Hydrolyse this with acid under reflux to yield 2-hydroxy-2-methylbutanoic acid.

$$CH_3 \!-\! C \overset{O}{\underset{C_2H_5}{\diagdown}} \xrightarrow{HCN} CH_3 \!-\! \overset{OH}{\underset{CN}{C}} \!-\! C_2H_5$$

$$\xrightarrow{H^+} CH_3 \!-\! \overset{OH}{\underset{C_2H_5}{C}} \!-\! COOH$$

16. (a) The C_2H_5 group in ethanol has a positive inductive effect which pushes electrons onto the O of the O–H bond. This strengthens it, making it more difficult for it to break and release H^+. Water has no such inductive effect and therefore a weaker O–H bond, so it releases H^+ more readily.

(b) Sodium reacts very vigorously with water, releasing hydrogen gas as water ionizes. Sodium reacts much less vigorously with ethanol, releasing hydrogen gas fairly slowly. This is because of the lower tendency for ethanol to break its O–H bond than water.

(c) Methanoic acid is a stronger acid than ethanoic acid. This is because the inductive effect of the $-CH_3$ group in ethanoic acid makes the ethanoate ion CH_3COO^- less stable.
Chloroethanoic acid is a stronger acid than bromoethanoic acid because Cl is more electronegative than Br and so has a greater effect in withdrawing electrons from the ethanoate ion which helps to stabilize it through delocalization.

Chapter 18: Answers to practice questions

1. (a)

$$CH_3-\underset{\underset{Br}{|}}{\overset{\overset{CH_3}{|}}{C}}-CH_2-CH_3$$

tertiary carbocation;
more stable;
due to 3 electron releasing alkyl groups / positive
inductive effect; (4)

(b)

$$\underset{\underset{Br}{|}}{CH_2}-\underset{\overset{CH_3}{|}}{CH}-CH_2-CH_3$$

$$CH_3-\underset{\underset{Br}{|}}{CH}-\underset{\overset{CH_3}{|}}{CH}-CH_3$$

(2)

(Total 6 marks)

2. (a) nucleophilic addition reaction; (5)

$$\underset{\substack{or \\ :CN^-}}{H-CN} \overset{H_3C}{\underset{H}{\overset{\delta+}{\diagup}}}\overset{\delta-}{C{=}O}\ (1) \longrightarrow NC-\underset{\underset{H}{|}}{\overset{\overset{CH_3}{|}}{C}}-O^-$$

(1) (1)
intermediate

$$\overset{H^+}{\longrightarrow} NC-\underset{\underset{H}{|}}{\overset{\overset{CH_3}{|}}{C}}-OH$$

(1)
product

(b)

$$H-\underset{\underset{COOH}{|}}{\overset{\overset{CH_3}{|}}{C}}-OH$$

(1)

(Total 6 marks)

3. (a) *similarities*
both double bonds are made up of one σ bond and one
π bond;
the electrons are at 120° to the two other bonds attached
to the C atom(s) / the carbon atom is sp² hybridized in
both bonds;
*Do not award a mark for simply stating that both are
covalent.*
differences
the (shared) electrons are closer to the O atom in
propanal / the bond in propanal is polar / *OWTTE*;
the C=O bond is shorter / stronger than the C=C bond
(*this data is available from the Data Booklet*); (4)

(b) propene: electrophilic (addition);
propanal: nucleophilic (addition); (2)

(c)

$$\underset{\substack{or \\ CN^-}}{H-CN} \overset{H_3C}{\underset{H}{\overset{\delta+}{\diagup}}}\overset{\delta-}{C{=}O}\ (1) \longrightarrow NC-\underset{\underset{H}{|}}{\overset{\overset{CH_3}{|}}{C}}-O^- \overset{H^+}{\diagup}$$

(1) (1)
Mark for intermediate

$$\longrightarrow NC-\underset{\underset{H}{|}}{\overset{\overset{CH_3}{|}}{C}}-OH$$

(1)
*Do not penalize if NC
is the wrong way round*
(4)

(Total 10 marks)

4. (a) addition – elimination / condensation; (1)

(b)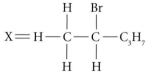

*Award (1) for correct structural formula of the organic
product and (1) for including water in the equation.* (2)

(c) The (crystalline) solid has a characteristic melting
point; (1)

(Total 4 marks)

5. (a) $C_2H_5NH_2 + H_2O \rightleftharpoons C_2H_5NH_3^+ + OH^-$; (2)

(b) alkyl group is electron releasing / positive inductive effect;
electron density on N atom greater; (2)

(c) NO_2 group is electron withdrawing / negative inductive
effect;
negative charge delocalized on the ring; (2)

(Total 6 marks)

6. (a) (i) pent-1-ene; (2)

(ii) HBr;
electrophilic addition; (2)

(iii)

$$X{=}H-\underset{\underset{H}{|}}{\overset{\overset{H}{|}}{C}}-\underset{\underset{H}{|}}{\overset{\overset{Br}{|}}{C}}-C_3H_7$$

2-bromopentone

(Markovnikov's rule states that) H adds to
whichever C already has more H; (3)
Allow both formed via secondary carbocations.

(iv)

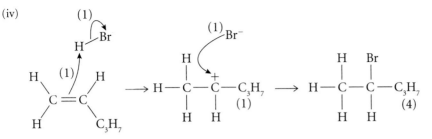

suitable diagram with
curly arrow from C=C to H of HBr;
curly arrow from H−Br bond to Br;
structure of carbocation $CH_3CH_2CH^+CH_2CH_3$;
attack by Br^- on carbocation;   (4)

(b) (i) react the halogenoalkane with Mg turnings in dry
ether, $(C_2H_5)_2O$;   (2)

(ii) $C_5H_{11}MgBr$ contains a bond between carbon and
magnesium which is very polarized, resulting in an
e^- rich carbon atom: $\overset{\delta-}{C}-\overset{\delta+}{Mg}$;
this is able to act as a nucleophile on e^- deficient
carbon atoms in other organic molecules, leading
to synthesis reactions in which the product has a
larger number of carbon atoms than the reactant,
e.g.
$C_5H_{11}MgBr + HCHO \rightarrow C_5H_{11}CH_2OH$;   (4)
$\quad\quad\quad\quad$ methanal $\quad\quad$ hexan-1-ol
$\quad\quad\quad\quad\quad\quad\quad\quad\quad$ (*Total 17 marks*)

7. chlorobenzene;
nucleophile / OH^- repelled by delocalized electrons /
carbon atom being attacked is less electron-deficient /
carbon−chlorine bond is stronger;   (2)

Index

in calculated results 218–21
degrees of 215
in digital instruments 216
experimental errors 217–18
graphs 223
in measurement 214, 215–18
multiplication and division 220–1
percentage uncertainty and error 219
propagation of 220–1
sources of 215–16
systematic errors 221
universal indicator 151, 158
unsaturated compounds 446
unsaturated fats 275, 411, 417–21
addition reactions 276, 277
trans form 418–19
uranium 38

V

vaccination programmes 359, 360
valence electrons 47
Valence Shell Electron Pair Repulsion
(VSEPR) theory 78
van der Waals' forces 56–7, 84–5, 91, 186, 197
vanadium oxide 311, 312
Velcro 183
viruses 358–61
visible light 43–4, 230

vitamins 279, 280–1
antioxidants 424, 425, 426, 427
deficiencies 281–2
volatile organic compounds (VOC) 365,
374–5, 402
volatility of compounds 197
voltaic cells 172–6, 178
connected half cells 174–6
volumetric analysis 27–9

W

waste 402–5
incineration 402, 403
landfill sites 364, 402–3
nuclear 405–6
recycling 403–4
waste water treatment 394–8
active carbon bed method 397
biological methods 397
chlorine and ozone 397–9
distillation 397
ion exchange 396–7
precipitation 396
primary and secondary 395
reverse osmosis 397
tertiary methods 396–7
water
acid-base reactions 147–8

dissolved oxygen in water 388–92
greenhouse factor 382
hydrogen bonding 87
reaction with alkenes 202
thermal pollution 391–2
treatment 392–8
water pollution
dioxins 393–4
heavy metals 392–3
pesticides 393
wave-particle duality 485
white blood cells 330
white light 43
Winkler method 388
Wohler, Friedrich 185

X

X rays 230
xerophthalmia 282

Z

zeolites 302, 312, 396–7
Ziegler-Natta catalyst 305
zinc
half cell 173–4
as reducing agent 170, 171, 172–3
zwitterions 258